HOMELAND SECURITY AND TERRORISM

Readings and Interpretations

Second Edition

JAMES J.F. FOREST
University of Massachusetts – Lowell

RUSSELL D. HOWARD
Monterey Institute of International Studies

JOANNE C. MOORE
United States Army

The McGraw·Hill Companies

HOMELAND SECURITY AND TERRORISM: READINGS AND INTERPRETATIONS, SECOND EDITION

Published by McGraw-Hill, a business unit of The McGraw-Hill Companies, Inc., 1221 Avenue of the Americas, New York, NY 10020.

Some ancillaries, including electronic and print components, may not be available to customers outside the United States.

This book is printed on acid-free paper.

This text is published by the **Contemporary Learning Series** group within the McGraw-Hill Higher Education division.

2 3 4 5 6 7 QVS/QVS 21 20 19 18 17

MHID: 0-07-802629-6
ISBN: 978-0-07-802629-4

Acquisitions Editor: *Joan L. McNamara*
Senior Developmental Editor: *Jill Meloy*
Marketing Director: *Adam Kloza*
Marketing Manager: *Nathan Edwards*
Content Licensing Specialist: *DeAnna Dausener*
Project Manager: *Erin Melloy*
Cover Designer: *Studio Montage, St. Louis, MO*
Cover Image: *Photo by Andrea Booher/ FEMA News Photo*
Buyer: *Jennifer Pickel*
Media Project Manager: *Sridevi Palani*
Compositor: *Laserwords Private Limited*

Library of Congress Cataloging-in-Publication Data

Forest, James J. F.

Homeland security and terrorism: readings and interpretations/James J. F. Forest, University of Massachusetts, Lowell, Russell D. Howard, Monterey Institute of International Studies, Joanne C. Moore, United States Army.—Second Edition.

pages cm

Includes bibliographical references and index.

ISBN 978-0-07-802629-4 (alk. paper)—ISBN 0-07-802629-6 (alk. paper) 1. Terrorism—United States—Prevention. 2. Civil defense—United States. 3. National security—United States. 4. Civil rights—United States. I. Howard, Russell D. II. Moore, Joanne C., Major. III. Howard, Russell D. Homeland security and terrorism. IV. Title.

HV6432.H72 2014
363.325'170973—dc23

2012048219

www.mhhe.com

Contents

Topic Guide

This topic guide suggests how the selections in this book relate to the subjects covered in your course. You may want to use the topics listed on these pages to search the Web more easily. **All sections and their articles that relate to each topic are listed below the bold-faced term.**

Foreword

It was perhaps inevitable. With the killing of Osama bin Laden and the absence of any major, new terrorist attack in the United States since September 11, 2001, the first calls to declare victory in the war on the terrorism are increasingly heard. The last significant international attack by al-Qaeda, after all, took place in London years ago. And today, more pressing domestic issues, such as the economy and jobs, or international challenges like the rogue regimes of Iran and North Korea as well as a rising China, it is argued, require our attention to an extent that terrorism and homeland security no longer do.[1]

The elation that followed the 2011 U.S. Navy SEAL raid on bin Laden's hideout in Abbottabad, Pakistan, however, only partially explains this development. Equally as consequential for al-Qaeda's waning fortunes, many believe, has been the "Arab Spring," which since February 2011 has completely transformed the political landscape of the Middle East and North Africa. These two separate and unrelated developments have been widely heralded as signaling the demise, or at least the beginning of the end, of al-Qaeda.[2]

But, although bin Laden's death has inflicted a crushing blow on al-Qaeda, it is not yet clear that has necessarily been a lethal one. Similarly, while the mostly nonviolent, mass protests of the "Arab Spring" in 2011 were successful in overturning hated despots, thus appearing to discredit al-Qaeda's longstanding message that only violence and jihad could achieve the same ends, since then serious terrorist threats and challenges have surfaced across the region. Accordingly, however, much of the core al-Qaeda organization has been weakened by bin Laden's killing and the effectiveness of the U.S. drone attacks, the strength of key al-Qaeda allies such as al-Qaeda in the Arabian Peninsula (AQAP)

[1] See, for example, Peter Bergen, "Time to declare victory: al Qaeda is defeated," Security Clearance 27 June 2012, at: http://security.blogs.cnn.com/2012/06/27/time-to-declare-victory-al-qaeda-is-defeated-opinion/.

[2] See Lee Ferran, "Al Qaeda 'Shadow of Former Self', US Counter-Terror Official Says," *abc news Investigative*, 30 April 2012 at http://abcnews.go.com/blogs/headlines/2012/04/al-qaeda-shadow-of-former-self/; Phil Stewart, "Strikes on al Qaeda leave only "handful" of targets," *Reuters* (U.S. Edition), 11 June 2012 at: http://www.reuters.com/article/2012/06/22/us-usa-panetta-saudi-idUSBRE85L05320120622; "Pannetta says al-Qaeda defeat 'within reach,'" *Al Jazeera*, 9 July 2011 accessed at: http://english.aljazeera.net/news/asia/2011/07/201179211045505379.html; Greg Miller, "U.S. Officials believe al-Qaeda on the brink of collapse," *Washington Post*, 26 July 2011; and, Bergen, "Time to declare victory: al Qaeda is defeated."

is arguably increasing while al-Qaeda's ideology also gains new adherents across North and West Africa and in the Levant. Continued instability in Pakistan and the rise in violence from various internal militant groups (often affiliated with al-Qaeda) coupled with the deterioration of relations with the United States have also undermined the progress achieved in recent years against terrorism in South Asia.

In addition, in the time since the heady, early days of the "Arab Spring," continued instability and disorders in some of the countries most directly affected by those politically seismic events have also created new opportunities for al-Qaeda and its allies to regroup, reorganize, and exploit. The fact that the intelligence and security services of those countries affected most profoundly by the months of protest and upheaval are also less focused on al-Qaeda and other transnational threats and more concerned with rebuilding and adapting both to new, hopefully, more democratic regimes as well as to governments where religious extremists exercise greater influence than ever before have in some instances created new space in which militant organizations have begun to establish themselves. Cooperation by these services and agencies with their counterparts in the West and elsewhere, accordingly, may no longer be as popular or even tolerated by domestic opinion. Indeed, the number of failed or failing states in the aftermath of the changes witnessed across North Africa and the Middle East has grown alarmingly since 2011, thus further exacerbating existing dangers.

As the distinguished editors of this second edition of *Homeland Security and Terrorism*—Dr. James J. Forest, Brigadier General (retired) Russell D. Howard, and Lieutenant Colonel Joanne Moore—well know, terrorism is an inherently cyclical phenomenon, which ebbs and flows but also often crests to unleash powerfully destabilizing and tragic forces, whose repercussions affect countries and peoples far removed from the immediate locus of the original conflict. Hence, in a still uncertain and anxious world, where the ability to communicate widely, instantly, and inexpensively is able to transform parochial acts of violence into global security concerns, the words of that great American patriot and president Thomas Jefferson have never been more relevant. "Eternal vigilance," he wrote, "is the price of liberty." The need for "eternal vigilance" is the message at the heart of this impressive collection, which builds on the acclaimed, seminal, first edition of *Homeland Security and Terrorism.*

The editors bring to this updated volume the same "Combating Terrorism Center" (CTC) ethos of scholarly gravitas, policy relevance, and practical, real-world application that informed and endowed its predecessor. Readers will doubtless recall that General Howard was the founding Director of the CTC. LTC Moore was his executive secretary throughout the CTC's formative years, and Dr. Forest was the first Director of Education at the CTC. *Homeland Security and Terrorism* thus provides a comprehensive overview of the principal threats still facing the American homeland along with the means with which those threats can best be countered within a framework of the fundamental constitutional rights and civil liberties accorded to every U.S. citizen.

The collection is divided into four units. UNIT ONE addresses the "Definitions and Frameworks" of homeland security: covering the range of homeland security threats—past, present, and future—facing the United States, its citizens, and those sworn to protect them. This section effectively challenges the reader to consider the various dimensions of what constitutes homeland security and how the country can best be protected given a highly fluid, continuously evolving, threat environment.

In UNIT TWO, "Response and Resilience," the editors have collected a series of insightful articles that depict how the United States is either responding to, or laying the foundation upon which to respond to, the threats and challenges described in UNIT ONE. The chapters in this section cover the responsibilities, policies, and policy implementation roles of the various federal, state, and local organizations and homeland security agencies involved in securing the United States from terrorist attack. The interaction and interoperability of government agencies at all levels alongside cooperation and interaction with the private and nonprofit sectors in all matters pertaining to homeland security forms the basis of a discussion that is designed to stimulate debate and deeper examination of these issues. As such, readers are themselves encouraged to develop their own thoughts and approaches to the most important homeland security challenges of today and tomorrow.

UNIT THREE is devoted to an examination of the legal and ethical challenges inherent in protecting the homeland and developing effective countermeasures to threats within the framework of federal, state, and local laws and regulations. Several chapters in this unit also appeared in the first edition of *Homeland Security and Terrorism* and after careful review were retained because of their continued relevance and perspicacity. UNIT THREE thus offers multiple perspectives on the legal and ethical parameters intrinsic to maintaining the balance between freedom and security, while providing those charged with the country's defense and protection of its citizens, infrastructure, and institutions the tools that they require: while still upholding America's core constitutional values and freedoms. Accordingly, this section challenges the reader to determine how best to maintain this balance given the competing considerations of the nature and extent of the threat; the provisions of the Constitution and especially of the Bill of Rights; more recent legislation such as the USA PATRIOT Act; and, indeed, America's citizen expectations for both security and the inalienable personal freedoms that have defined our country for more than 200 years.

The final unit, titled "Alternatives to Explore," is a deliberately eclectic mix of opinion and analysis that considers the future of homeland security and attendant policy options from a number of different viewpoints. Of special interest in this section are the perspectives offered about other countries' approaches to homeland issues, the policies that they have adopted, and implementation issues that they have faced. UNIT FOUR is thus distinguished by its rich detailing of "best practices" options from outside the United States that readers can evaluate and perhaps apply to similar needs and situations in this country. Like the entire volume, the chapters in this section were selected not just for the expert content, but also for their ability to provide compelling "theory to practice" narratives and thus stimulate lively debate and discussion in classes and among practitioners seeking new information and a wider perspective on many of the key issues that confront them on a daily basis.

As a contributor myself to the second edition of *Homeland Security and Terrorism*, it is impossible for me to be completely objective in my opinion of the book. However, as Director of the Center for Security and the Security Studies Masters degree program at Georgetown University, I am familiar with much of the scholarly literature pertaining to homeland security and terrorism. No other work to my knowledge so effectively and cogently combines as eclectic a group of homeland security experts in one easily accessible volume. Indeed, none relates homeland security theory to practice better than this second edition of *Homeland Security and Terrorism.*

Professor Bruce Hoffman
Georgetown University,
Washington, DC

Preface

Homeland Security and Terrorism is a collective effort, with chapters written and edited by noted terrorism experts, homeland security practitioners, government officials, police and fire officials, military officers, educators, business executives, medical personnel, lawyers, and other citizens with relevant expertise. The first edition of this textbook was published in 2005, and while a great deal has changed in the world of homeland security over the past seven years, much has remained surprisingly the same. For example, modest improvements have been made to security at our nation's borders and maritime ports of entry. Airport security has changed as well—in 2005, we could still bring water bottles and other drinks through security checkpoints, but that ended following the attempt by al-Qaeda operatives in August 2006 to attack up to ten transatlantic flights from the UK using liquid explosives disguised as energy drinks. We have also seen a significant number of other attempted terrorist attacks inspired by al-Qaeda's ideology, but involving U.S. citizens or permanent residents with no direct ties with any known al-Qaeda associate other then online communications. Indeed, the increasing threat of so-called "homegrown terrorism" is perhaps the most dramatic change we have seen over the last seven years.

Meanwhile, it is also important to note that several things have not changed at all since the first edition was published. For example, most of the political, legal, and ethical debates surrounding homeland security from 2005—such as illegal immigration, surveillance, and civil rights protections—remain largely the same in 2012. And of course, just as it has for decades, the homeland remains under threat of a terrorist attack from groups that have nothing to do with Islamist extremism, including anti-abortionists, right-wing extremists, and violent environmentalists.

Today, our intelligence and law enforcement professionals at the federal, state, and local levels face a constant challenge of monitoring and thwarting potential threats to innocent lives. The continually evolving nature of this threat has led to significant growth in academic courses, degree programs, and professional development seminars in homeland security throughout the United States over the past seven years. Our textbook has become one of the most popular resources for these programs, and we are confident that this newly revised edition will be equally well received.

We begin the book with selections on the challenges of defining what is—and is not—considered to be under the purview of homeland security. This section is followed by examinations of various aspects of the terrorist threat to the U.S. homeland, with particular attention to "homegrown" and "lone wolf" terrorism. And the final part of Unit One provides analyses on specific areas of potential vulnerability and concern to homeland security and law enforcement agencies, including public transportation, cybersecurity, and our nation's borders. Together, these chapters are useful for framing the challenges faced by homeland security and law enforcement professionals today and in the future.

In Unit Two, we turn our focus toward understanding how the United States is responding to the threats and challenges identified in the first part of this book. Much has been written in recent years about what various federal, state, and local agencies do to support the homeland security mission, so the selections provided here are meant to amplify and expand—rather than duplicate—that knowledge. In the first section, authors examine national dimensions of our nation's homeland security efforts, with a particular focus on organizational structures, financial challenges, and the need to maintain a critical balance between preparation and overreaction to the WMD threat. This is followed by a section on state and local dimensions, and the final section explores the critically important topic of resilience. Overall, the readings in Unit Two illustrate how securing the homeland is one of the most complex missions, requiring a coordinated and integrated effort from all levels of society—the federal government, state and local governments, and the private and nonprofit sectors.

Unit Three provides a diverse collection of perspectives on the legal and ethical controversies surrounding contemporary efforts to secure the homeland. Amid the flurry of activity meant to protect America from future terrorist attacks, we face an additional challenge of maintaining a balance between freedom and security. Clearly, in reacting to global terrorism we cannot allow our freedoms to be diminished. As Benjamin Franklin so aptly put it, "They that can give up essential liberty to obtain a little temporary safety deserve neither liberty nor safety." Readings on homeland security intelligence, illegal immigration, law enforcement, and USA PATRIOT Act reflect some of the most important dimensions of the debate over how to effectively maintain a balance between freedom and security. And finally, the chapters in Unit Four offer a diverse set of opinions and assessments about the present and future prospects of homeland security.

Throughout the volume, our intention has to provide point–counterpoint materials that instructors will find useful for promoting lively classroom discussions and debates on the enduring challenges of homeland security. Instructors and students will also find that these chapters provoke thoughtful questions for research papers and final exam questions. In the introductions to each Unit, we have also assembled a short list of learning objectives, discussion questions, and recommended resources for further study. Overall, this volume will be a useful tool for learning about the many contemporary challenges of homeland security, and how we can respond to them with increasing sophistication and success.

Acknowledgments

This Second Edition of *Homeland Security and Terrorism* is the culmination of extensive collaboration between a retired U.S. special forces general officer, a senior active duty U.S. Army officer, and a civilian university professor—each whom has been committed for over a decade to making a long-term contribution to the education of current and future generations of security professionals throughout the United States. We are inspired to do so every day by the many men and women who serve their country, state, and city in a wide range of security-related efforts. The sacrifices these people make every day on our behalf often go unrecognized, but it is through their combined efforts that we remain the greatest country in the world.

Without the assistance of Margaret Nencheck, we would still be struggling to find our way through the complex and contested terrain of homeland security topics and issues to address in a textbook of this sort, and we offer her our deepest thanks. We also greatly appreciate all the contributors to this volume. Throughout this project, we have been blessed with an abundance of authors dedicated to our shared goal of understanding and improving homeland security, and we are sincerely grateful for their hard work and commitment to excellence. The insights and suggestions they have provided in these pages will undoubtedly inform discussions and debate in a variety of academic, professional and policymaking arenas for the foreseeable future. And of course, we also thank Bruce Hoffman for his generous time providing a Foreword for this book.

This book is part of a series published by McGraw-Hill, which includes *Terrorism and Counterterrorism* (4th edition, 2011), *Weapons of Mass Destruction and Terrorism* (2nd edition, 2012), and *Defeating Terrorism* (2005). Each of these books has become a popular resource for college and university courses worldwide, as well as professional development seminars and generally curious readers at large. Our collaboration with Jill Meloy at McGraw-Hill throughout this series continues to be truly enjoyable, and we thank her and her staff for their hard work and professionalism.

And finally, to our families and our partners, we offer our sincere appreciation for their patience and support throughout this project.

Editors

James J.F. Forest, Ph.D., is associate professor at the University of Massachusetts Lowell and senior fellow at the U.S. Joint Special Operations University. He previously served nine years on the faculty of the U.S. Military Academy, six of those years as Director of Terrorism Studies. Dr. Forest has published fourteen books and dozens of articles on terrorism, weapons of mass destruction, and homeland security. His degrees are from Boston College, Stanford University, and Georgetown University.

Brigadier General Russell D. Howard (Retired) was a career Special Forces officer and founding director of the Combating Terrorism Center at the U.S. Military Academy, West Point. He is also the former Director of the Jebsen Center for Counter-terrorism Studies at the Fletcher School at Tufts University. Presently, General Howard is the Director of the Terrorism Research and Education Program at the Monterey Institute of International Studies. His recent publications include *Weapons of Mass Destruction and Terrorism*, 2nd Edition (2012), *Terrorism and Counterterrorism: Understanding the New Security Environment*, 3rd Edition (2012), and *Defeating Terrorism: Shaping the New Security Environment* (2004), all published by McGraw-Hill.

Lieutenant Colonel Joanne Moore is a senior advisor within the office of the Secretary of Defense for Policy. She has served in a variety of positions within the Army as a Strategist and a Military Police Officer. She has been deployed throughout the world and taught at the U.S. Military Academy.

James J.F. Forest
Russell D. Howard
Joanne C. Moore

Unit One

Definitions and Frameworks

We begin the book with two different perspectives on the challenge of defining what is—and is not—considered to be in the purview of homeland security. First, Chris Bellavita of the Naval Postgraduate School explores in detail a variety of definitions of homeland security used by organizations and professionals. He then describes how these definitions reflect a broader homeland security ecosystem in which various entities seek resources that will help them obtain organizational or political survival and growth. His analysis concludes that homeland security is a continuously evolving social construction, a reality shaped by social and political processes.

Next, Shawn Reese of the Congressional Research Service discusses the evolution of homeland security strategic documents, definitions, and missions. He then analyzes the policy question of how this diversity of homeland security definitions and missions may impede the development of a coherent national homeland security strategy. Policymakers develop strategy by identifying national interests, prioritizing goals to achieve those national interests, and arraying instruments of national power to achieve the national interests. However, he concludes that developing an effective homeland security strategy may be complicated if the key concept of homeland security is not defined and its missions are not aligned and synchronized among different federal entities with homeland security responsibilities.

The readings in the second part of UNIT ONE describe various aspects of the terrorist threat to the U.S. homeland. First, in a rather provocative piece, Ohio State University Professor John Mueller and Mark Stewart (University of Newcastle, Australia) argue that America's reaction to the terrorist attacks of September 11, 2001, was very likely disproportionate to the real threat Al Qaeda has ever presented either as an international menace or as an inspiration to homegrown amateurs. Yet, they note that fear of Al Qaeda terrorism continues to dominate public discourse, resulting in massive amounts of funding being spent and people being harmed or killed in the name of our nation's counterterrorism agenda. Finally, when examining the amount of funds spent on the nation's response to the perceived terrorist threat, they conclude that a great deal of money (over $1 trillion by some estimates) has been spent on "homeland security" without deriving any real benefit.

Then Peter Bergen and Katherine Tiedemann of the New America Foundation and Professor Bruce Hoffman of Georgetown University provide a scholarly analysis on the evolving nature of the Al Qaeda terrorist threat to U.S. targets at home and abroad, based on a variety of sources. They note that the threat is less severe than the catastrophic proportions of a 9/11-like attack, but is also more complex and more diverse than at any time since 2001.

According to their analysis, Al Qaeda or its allies continue to have the capacity to kill dozens, or even hundreds, of Americans in a single attack. A key shift in the past couple of years is the increasingly prominent role in planning and operations that U.S. citizens and residents have played in the leadership of Al Qaeda and aligned groups, and the higher numbers of Americans attaching themselves to these groups. Another development is the increasing diversification of the types of U.S.-based jihadist militants, and the groups with which those militants have affiliated. Indeed, these jihadists do not fit any particular ethnic, economic, educational, or social profile. Meanwhile, Al Qaeda's ideological influence on other jihadist groups is on the rise in South Asia and has continued to extend into countries like Yemen and Somalia; Al Qaeda's top leaders are still at large, and American overreactions to even unsuccessful terrorist attacks arguably have played into the hands of the jihadists. However, they also note that things have not gone entirely well for Al Qaeda. For example, the ramped-up campaign of drone attacks in Pakistan has proven quite effective. Increasingly negative Pakistani attitudes and actions against militants based on their territory are mirrored by increasingly hostile attitudes toward Al Qaeda and allied groups in the Muslim world in general. And erstwhile militant allies have now also turned against Al Qaeda. Overall, their analysis offers a balanced perspective on the contemporary threat posed by this global terror network.

Terrorism scholar Joshua Sinai follows with a case study of a particular terrorist plot linked to Al Qaeda, which illustrates the network's strategy and ability to motivate U.S. citizens and residents with an ideology of political violence. In this instance, Najibullah Zazi and two of his high school friends planned to strap explosives to their bodies and head for the Grand Central and Times Square subway stations in New York City, where they would board packed trains at rush hour and blow themselves up to inflict maximum fatalities. Their plot was timed to coincide with the eighth anniversary of 9/11 in mid-September 2009, and had they succeeded, estimated casualties could have been in the thousands. In addition to demonstrating the threat of "homegrown extremists," Sinai's case study also explores the federal, state, and local efforts to prevent this attack and highlights the critical role of working in close coordination with allied government counterparts, including the British, Canadian, Pakistani, and Scandinavian intelligence and security services. Overall, his analysis concludes that responding to this type of threat requires information and intelligence sharing across domestic agency levels as well as transnationally.

Next, James Carafano of the Heritage Foundation draws lessons and implications to consider from the terrorist attacks in Mumbai, India, in November 2008. He begins by noting that armed terrorist assaults against populated areas are neither an unprecedented nor a remote threat. The best defense against organized armed assaults is to stop them before they occur by developing and maintaining effective counterterrorism, intelligence, and information-sharing programs. Further, if a terrorist group is successful in carrying out such an attack, prior preparation is essential for dealing with the aftermath. This preparation must include an effective and integrated national homeland security system that brings together law enforcement, emergency responders, and federal assets.

Finally, the threat of lone-wolf terrorism—exemplified by Nidal Hasan or Anders Breivick—is examined by Edwin Bakker and Beatrice de Graff of Leiden University (the Netherlands). After a brief discussion of the conceptual difficulties associated with the term "lone-wolf terrorism," the authors argue that these acts are almost impossible to categorize or systematize, let alone forecast. Thus, it is not the profile of the perpetrator, but the modus operandi that offers clues for a better response to this particular threat. Furthermore, almost all lone operators have displayed a degree of commitment to, and identification with, extremist movements—providing leads for preventing new rounds of radicalization within this potential group of sympathizers or followers. They conclude their analysis with some observations about Islamist lone-wolf terrorism and right-wing extremists, and the role of virtual communities with which lone operators identify themselves.

And in the third and final part of UNIT ONE, authors address specific areas of potential vulnerability and concern to homeland security and law enforcement agencies. First, Jack Riley of the Rand Corporation explores the security of commercial passenger aviation. He notes that three changes over the last ten years—reinforced cockpit doors, changes to the visa approval process, and perhaps most importantly vigilant passengers and crew—have made it much harder for any terrorist to succeed in replicating the kind of suicide plane attacks that took place on 9/11. Major changes have also taken place at airport screening checkpoints, but there is growing public discontent with some of these changes. Riley argues that the United States has pursued policies with very little regard to the costs they impose on travelers or the net reduction in risk that they generate and concludes that we should use the next decade to develop smarter, more sustainable, and more practical solutions to air passenger security.

Then James Robbins of the American Foreign Policy Council examines the ways in which many terrorists have sought to attack so-called "soft targets." He notes that Chechens have been particularly prone to attack targets like hospitals, theaters, schools, apartment complexes, subway stations, and so forth. Adequately protecting these kinds of targets, however, can be costly and can negatively impact civil liberties. Thus, there is a need for risk balancing and prioritization in spending resources for hardening targets. Government agencies must seek to find the greatest security for the greatest number of people among a predetermined set of targets based on terrorist targeting priorities (potential number of casualties, symbolism, disruption potential, etc.). At the same time, decision makers and the general population should understand that a degree of risk must inevitably be accepted because it is impossible to protect everyone everywhere from every type of threat.

In the next selection, George Washington University Professor Frank Cilluffo and private consultant Paul Byron Pattak explore the overlapping threats of information warfare, cybercrime, and cyberterrorism, arguing that the United States must come to a new understanding of conflict and the rules of engagement in cyberspace. The involvement of non-state actors, public opinion, and the media in this new form of conflict underscores the role of individuals in the national security arena and suggests that the nation's security focus is strategically misplaced. Their analysis concludes that federal, state, and local government agencies must establish a genuine partnership with private industry and the general public in order to adequately secure the United States from the cyberthreat.

And finally, John Sullivan of the Los Angeles Sheriff's Department examines the homeland security challenges associated with the nearly 2,000-mile border between the United States and Mexico. In addition to the well-publicized violence caused by Mexican drug cartels in recent years, Sullivan notes that many U.S. gangs have strong working links with Central American and Mexican gangs, making this transnational threat a very real challenge to the complex web of federal, state, local, and tribal law enforcement agencies responsible for our security. Responding to this challenge involves a range of operations including *interdiction* (disrupting illegal movements across borders), aimed at *deterrence* of cross-border crime (dissuading would-be smugglers, criminals, and terrorists from making illegal border crossings), and supported by *intelligence* (increasingly networked in nature) to collect, fuse, analyze, and disseminate operational warning. His analysis concludes that communications, cooperation, and intelligence sharing along the border involving the range of enforcement and security agencies and responders must be enhanced.

As a whole, this collection of essays and research articles in UNIT ONE will be useful for lectures, discussions, and research papers on the challenges faced by homeland security and law enforcement professionals today and in the future.

Learning Objectives

After reading and discussing the materials provided in UNIT ONE, students will be able to articulate the challenges of defining "homeland security" and the importance of such a definition to organizational strategies. Students will also develop a solid understanding of several kinds of terrorist threats to the U.S. homeland and vulnerabilities that could be exploited by those who seek to harm our citizens.

Recommended Resources

Ackerman, Gary, Jeffrey M. Bale, and Kevin S. Moran. "Assessing the Threat to Critical Infrastructure." In James Forest and Russell Howard (eds.), *Weapons of Mass Destruction and Terrorism* (New York: McGraw-Hill, 2012).

Department of Homeland Security, *Bottom Up Review Report* (July 2010). Online at: www.dhs.gov/xlibrary/assets/bur_bottom_up_review.pdf

Department of Homeland Security, *Department of Homeland Security Strategic Plan: Fiscal Years 2012–2016* (February 2012). Online at: www.dhs.gov/strategic-plan-fiscal-years-fy-2012-2016

Department of Homeland Security, *National Strategy for Homeland Security* (October 2007). Online at: www.dhs.gov/national-strategy-homeland-security-october-2007

Department of Homeland Security, *Quadrennial Homeland Security Review Report to Congress* (February 2010). Online at: www.dhs.gov/quadrennial-homeland-security-review-qhsr

DiRenzo, Joe and Christopher W. Doane. "America's Maritime Homeland Security Challenge: Ports, Waterways and Coastal Borders," in James Forest (ed.), *Homeland Security: Protecting America's Targets* (Westport, CT: Praeger, 2006).

Homeland Security Act (HSA) of 2002, Public Law 107-296 (November 2002). Online at: www.gpo.gov/fdsys/pkg/PLAW-107publ296/content-detail.html

Kolb, Lawrence, Sean Duggan, and Laura Conley. *Integrating Security: Preparing for the National Security Threats of the 21st Century.* Center for American Progress (November 16, 2009). Online at www.americanprogress.org/issues/2009/11/pdf/integrating_security.pdf.

Ranum, Marcus J. *The Myth of Homeland Security* (Wiley: Indianapolis, 2004).

Spagnolo, Peter. "The Threat of Terrorism to America's Mid-Sized Cities," in James Forest (ed.), *Homeland Security: Protecting America's Targets* (Westport, CT: Praeger, 2006).

The United States Commission on National Security in the 21st Century, *Road Map for National Security: Imperative for Change*, (February 15, 2001). Online at http://govinfo.library.unt.edu/nssg/PhaseIIIFR.pdf.

Tomashot, Shane and Matthew H. Wahlert. "Protecting the Superbowl: The Terrorist Threat to Sporting Events," in James Forest (ed.), *Homeland Security: Protecting America's Targets* (Westport, CT: Praeger, 2006).

Section 1.1

Defining Homeland Security

Changing Homeland Security

What is Homeland Security?

Christopher Bellavita

> *The United States, through a concerted national effort that galvanizes the strengths and capabilities of Federal, State, local, and Tribal governments; the private and non-profit sectors; and regions, communities, and individual citizens—along with our partners in the international community—will work to achieve a secure Homeland that sustains our way of life as a free, prosperous, and welcoming America.*
>
> —Homeland Security Vision, *2007 National Strategy*[1]

The vision announced six years after the September 11, 2001 attacks is another effort to clarify why the nation engages in the activity called homeland security. It draws a picture of everyone working together to ensure the United States remains a free, wealthy, and friendly nation. The vision suggests both the nobility of our hopes and the innocence of an America untainted by globalism's *realpolitik.*

One still hears the question asked, "What is homeland security?" Is it a program, an objective, a discipline, an agency, an administrative activity, another word for emergency management? Is it about terrorism? All hazards? Something completely different?[2]

Even though there is no explicit agreement about the definition, this does not prevent people from having long and occasionally contentious conversations about the details of homeland security. It is as if we (the people who care about homeland security) carry around a preferred definition in whatever part of the brain holds definitions. We talk about homeland security and only rarely mention what that word means. If words do matter, if we are ever to reach the state envisioned in the *Strategy,* do we need to know what homeland security is?

There are at least seven defensible definitions of homeland security.[3] These definitions—and there may be more than seven—are "ideal types" (as that phrase was used by Max Weber)[4] and are based on assertions about what homeland security emphasizes or ought to emphasize. In a metaphorical sense, each definition represents a set of interests that claims a niche in the homeland security ecosystem. As in a biological system, these semantic entities struggle for resources to sustain themselves, to grow, and to reproduce their point of view within the rest of the ecosystem. As the homeland security ecosystem continues to evolve and interact with its environment, one can expect *variation* on particular aspects of the definitions, *selection* by others of the pieces of the definition that confer the most survival value, and *reproduction* elsewhere in the ecosystem of particular homeland security definitions.[5]

The definitions discussed in this paper draw attention to:

1. *Terrorism.* Homeland security is a concerted national effort by federal, state and local governments, by the private sector, and by individuals to prevent

terrorist attacks within the United States, reduce America's vulnerability to terrorism, and minimize the damage and recover from attacks that do occur.

2. *All Hazards.* Homeland security is a concerted national effort to prevent and disrupt terrorist attacks, protect against man-made and natural hazards, and respond to and recover from incidents that do occur.
3. *Terrorism and Catastrophes.* Homeland security is what the Department of Homeland Security—supported by other federal agencies—does to prevent, respond to, and recover from terrorist and catastrophic events that affect the security of the United States.
4. *Jurisdictional Hazards.* Homeland security means something different in each jurisdiction. It is a locally directed effort to prevent and prepare for incidents most likely to threaten the safety and security of its citizens.
5. *Meta Hazards.* Homeland security is a national effort to prevent or mitigate any social trend or threat that can disrupt the long-term stability of the American way of life.
6. *National Security.* Homeland security is an element of national security that works with the other instruments of national power to protect the sovereignty, territory, domestic population, and critical infrastructure of the United States against threats and aggression.
7. *Security Über Alles.* Homeland security is a symbol used to justify government efforts to curtail civil liberties.

Why so many definitions? If we had the focus provided by a common definition, we could determine what had to be done to make the homeland secure, provide resources for the appropriate programs, measure our progress, and improve things where needed.

In that construction, homeland security is a type of machine. It consists of parts combined in a particular way to accomplish a function. A common definition of homeland security would guide the behaviors of people who want to make the machine work effectively and efficiently.

Is agreeing on one definition the only way to promote this unity of effort?

One argument says "yes." This is the "If you don't know where you're going, how are you going to get there?" theory. Absent a clear vision, goal or objective—for our purposes, different ways of saying the same thing—we will not have an effective way to know whether tax money spent in the name of homeland security is doing any good.

A contrary view claims, "If you don't know where you're going, you may end up someplace interesting." In the days following September 11, 2001, the nation stumbled along the edge of chaos. The magnitude of the terrorist threat was unclear. Vulnerable targets were everywhere. The potential consequences of more attacks were unthinkable.

In response, the nation acted. Money was spent for policies, equipment, services, and facilities that had little apparent relationship to any carefully crafted definition of homeland security.[6]

The strategy in the early days was "ready, fire, aim." Aiming happens after one tries a lot of things: Build on what works. Get rid of what does not. The process may not be elegant, but it is an acceptable way to discover what to do in an uncertain and complex environment.[7]

Seven years later—almost—is the homeland security environment any less uncertain? Are we any clearer than we were on September 12, 2001 about what homeland security is? Why is there still disagreement, even if only semantic, about what homeland security means?

Homeland Security Is about Terrorism

From a correspondence view of truth, the last question could be rephrased as "What objective reality does the term homeland security refer to?" This view asks if there is (or there ought to be) something concrete in the world that accurately corresponds to "homeland security." The question asks about the ontology of homeland security.

The events of September 11, 2001 provide a visceral answer to that question. Four planes were hijacked. Three were flown into buildings. One was flown into the earth. Thousands of people died.

No one disputes that homeland security as a national focus resulted directly from that attack.[8] A foundational truth of homeland security is to make sure such an attack does not happen again. That commitment is enshrined both in the original *National Strategy For Homeland Security* definition and repeated in the *Strategy's* October 2007 update:

> Homeland security is a concerted national effort to prevent terrorist attacks within the United States, reduce America's vulnerability to terrorism, and minimize the damage and recover from attacks that do occur.[9]

The definition is straightforward. It can be adjusted by making it clear that "national effort" includes federal, state, and local governments, the private sector, international partners, and individuals. However, at its core, homeland security is about preventing terrorism and responding appropriately when we are attacked. If we are attacked again in a significant way, discussions about alternative definitions of homeland security will vanish. At least for a while.

Homeland Security Is about All Hazards

There are practical difficulties with the *Terrorism* definition of homeland security. It does not fully correspond to the behavior taking place under the name of homeland security. There just is not that much terrorism in the United States to warrant spending the billions of dollars we have spent.[10] Many of the same state and local public safety professionals who are expected to prevent and respond to terrorist attacks have other work to do. As one police chief of a major American city said at a 2007 conference, "I had 169 murders in my city last year; Osama bin Laden did not commit one of them."

Attention given to terrorism issues can be attention taken away from other work—like gangs, drugs, earthquake preparedness, public health services, and getting ready for wildfire or hurricane season.

Another form of this position maintains that the skills, equipment, and knowledge needed to respond to most emergencies (often symbolized by the phrase "all hazards") will also come into play when people are needed to *respond* to a terrorist attack. States and communities do not have the resources to focus attention solely on terrorism.

Hurricane Katrina fed the narrative that the attention to terrorism since September 11, 2001 undermined the U.S. emergency preparedness system.[11] Empirically, disasters in their various natural and human-caused guises are much more prevalent than terrorist attacks.[12] If we focus on the actual threats, and on the skills needed to prepare for those threats, homeland security ought to be about all hazards.

One popular textbook echoes this view. "The U.S. government defines homeland security as the domestic effort . . . to defend America from terrorists. In practice, homeland security efforts have also come to comprise general preparedness under the all-hazards doctrine. . . ."[13]

The national government contemplated changing the definition of homeland security for its updated *National Strategy.* A September 2007 "pre-decisional slide"[14] offered language that captured the all hazards perspective:

> Homeland security is a concerted national effort to prevent *and disrupt* terrorist attacks, *protect against man-made and natural hazards, and respond to and recover from incidents* that do occur. [Emphasis in original]

A DHS employee told me this was the definition the Homeland Security Council wanted, but there were a "few minor bureaucratic and legislative" issues that had to be ironed out first. I was told, in September of 2007, that it would be straightened out within a few weeks. That does not seem to have happened yet.

Authorized or not, a definition of homeland security that includes "all hazards" is probably the de facto definition for many people.

All Hazards Is Not All Hazards

If one looks more closely at the concept of "all hazards" it does not include every imaginable hazard.

> All hazards does not literally mean being prepared for any and all hazards that might manifest themselves in a particular community, state or nation. What it does mean is that *there are things that commonly occur in many kinds of disasters,* such as the need for emergency warning or mass evacuation, *that can be addressed in a general plan* and that that plan can provide the basis for responding to unexpected events.[15] [Emphasis added]

Therefore, "building capacity to deal with the most probable events will increase capacity to deal with less probable events."[16]

Some advocates of the all hazards view of homeland security maintain that terrorism fits appropriately within the conceptual frames of emergency management.[17] This argument suggests that preparing to respond—or responding—to a chemical incident, for example, will be roughly the same if the incident is accidental or intentional. The argument assumes that while terrorism may be somewhat different from other emergencies, it may not be that much different.

Experience suggests terrorism can be substantially different from other emergencies. For example, on January 17, 1997 a bomb went off outside a family planning clinic near Atlanta, Georgia. One hour later, a second bomb exploded at the same location, in the area where first responders staged. A similar incident, again involving a primary and a secondary device, happened a month later.[18] The same tactic is commonly used in Iraq.[19] The Department of Homeland Security grant guidance for 2008, perhaps anticipating a probable future, emphasizes planning for improvised explosive devices in the United States.[20] Terrorists are intelligently adaptive in a way other hazards are not.[21]

Mutual aid is a core element in state and city all hazards response plans. One can easily envision mayors and governors not releasing certain emergency assets in the event of widespread and coordinated terrorist attacks on schools, malls, or other targets.

Perhaps more perniciously, a dominant focus on all hazards runs the risk of unintentionally neglecting prevention efforts. Already it is not unusual in discussions of prevention to hear "no one knows what prevention is, anyway; let alone how to measure it." Or "we're not going to be able to stop everything."[22] If we get comfortable saying we cannot stop everything, then assuredly we will be right.

The sensibly intentioned focus on high frequency events (wildfires, floods, and so on) erodes over time the initial motivation for even having something called homeland security. Attention to terrorism risks becoming just another annex in a comprehensive emergency management plan. We can easily return to the days when "we lacked a unifying vision, a cohesive strategic approach, and the necessary institutions within government to secure the Homeland against terrorism."[23]

If the nation is not attacked again in any significant way, "all hazards" is likely to dominate the homeland security ecosystem.

Homeland Security Is about Terrorism and Catastrophes

The *National Strategy* that defines homeland security as primarily an effort to prevent terrorist attacks also acknowledges that:

> Certain non-terrorist events that reach catastrophic levels can have significant implications for homeland security. The resulting national consequences and possible cascading effects from these events might present potential or perceived vulnerabilities that could be exploited, possibly eroding citizens' confidence in our Nation's government and ultimately increasing our vulnerability to attack. This Strategy therefore recognizes that effective preparation for catastrophic natural disasters and man-made disasters, *while not homeland security per se,* can nevertheless increase the security of the Homeland.[24] [Emphasis added]

With one hand, the federal government removes catastrophes from the official definition of homeland security. With the other hand, catastrophes are added back in as a friendly amendment to an informal definition. This action draws attention to homeland security as something that is largely an activity of the federal government. It fits a philosophy that sees the federal government having the primary responsibility to "insure domestic Tranquility and provide for the common defence."[25]

If formalized, such a definition might read as follows: *Homeland security is what the Department of Homeland Security—supported by other federal agencies—does to prevent, respond to and recover from terrorist and catastrophic events that affect the security of the United States.*

Homeland security is not the same thing as the Department of Homeland Security.[26] Occasionally this has to be mentioned. Even in 2008 it is not unusual to be at a conference of state, local, and federal officials involved in homeland security and have the phrase "homeland security" quickly morph into a synonym for "DHS." If public safety officials think that way, what must the American people believe?

Allegedly, Secretary Chertoff has to remind people sometimes that he is the Secretary of the *Department* of Homeland Security, not the Secretary *of* homeland security. In public presentations, he has cautioned against a "'Soviet-style' management, where there's that heavy hand of government on everything" related to homeland security; some matters, he has said, ought to be state and local concerns.[27]

But the earlier discussion about homeland security as *All Hazards* and the infrequency of domestic terrorism, suggests local governments eventually may be less willing to carry their end of the *Homeland Security as Terrorism* banner, leaving the bulk of the work to the federal government. This is not because homeland security is unimportant, but because other priorities require more attention and resources.

With some waning exceptions, state and local governments complain that the federal government is paying more attention to terrorism than to other domestic security matters.[28] As one police chief said, "I have a healthy respect for the federal government and the importance of keeping this nation safe. . . . But I also live every day as a police chief in an American city where violence every day is not foreign and is not anonymous but is right out there in the neighborhoods."[29] Emergency management specialists have made similar arguments about the dangers to emergency preparedness of attending too much to terrorism.[30]

It is not difficult to envision that as more time passes without a terrorist attack, and as other issues make claims on public budgets, homeland security for most locales will be understood, in fact, as what the federal government does.

DHS seems positioned to accept, very reluctantly, this perspective. After reiterating the importance of sharing homeland security responsibilities among levels of government and the private sector, Secretary Chertoff noted,

> There are some matters that are national [i.e., federal] responsibilities. . . . [In] the area of national priorities, we [DHS] actually have to be operators, and we have to focus and make sure we can do those operational incidents. . . . [This] includes securing our borders. . . . It includes looking at high-consequence terrorists attacks that could have a national or at least a regional impact. . . . It involves really catastrophic responses that overwhelm local and state government; and that's why we're doing planning with the National Guard and the military for the first time in a way we've never done before, so that in that kind of emergency, we really could step in and play a national role.[31]

A 2007 report of an exercise simulating a nuclear explosion in an American city made a similar, if not more direct, observation:

> The federal government should stop pretending that state and local officials will be able to control the situation on the Day After [a nuclear explosion]. The pretense persists in Washington planning for the Day After that its role is to "support" governors and mayors, who will retain authority and responsibility in the affected area. While this is a reasonable application of our federal system to small and medium-sized emergencies, it is not appropriate for large disasters like a nuclear detonation. As the fiasco after Hurricane Katrina suggests, most cities and states will quickly be overwhelmed by the magnitude of the humanitarian, law and order, and logistical challenges of responding to a nuclear detonation. Yet this fiction persists stubbornly in the nation's

> preparedness bureaucracies at all levels: state and local governments guard their supposed "authorities" under the federal system, and Washington seeks to evade responsibility. The result is a failure to plan realistically. Instead, the federal government should plan on the basis that in the event of a nuclear detonation, it will shoulder principal responsibility for all aspects of response. On the first day after the event, of course, federal assets will not yet have made it to the scene. But shortly thereafter they should plan to outnumber and supercede the state and local responders.[32]

In some grim but plausible future, the federal government may become the only player on the homeland security stage.

Homeland Security Is about Jurisdictional Hazards

C. Wright Mills wrote, "Let every man be his own methodologist."[33] The jurisdiction-based view of homeland security analogously argues, "Let everyone come up with his or her own definition."

Jurisdictions do not all face the same threats or risks. Florida has hurricanes. Montana has wildfires. Ohio has floods. Arkansas has tornadoes. The northwest has earthquakes. The Great Lake states have severe winter storms. New York City, Washington DC, and other major urban areas risk more terrorist attacks. Each county in the United States has unique experiences with particular hazards.

If we suspend the need for a single national definition, homeland security can be different things to different jurisdictions. This construction can justify using resources provided under the homeland security umbrella for local preparedness priorities. "When we get an announcement about a homeland security grant," one state emergency management official told me, "we look at what we need across the state for our emergency management priorities. Then we look at what the grant guidelines say we need to do. We try to write the grant so it satisfies the guidelines, but still lets us do what's important to us, whether or not DHS would agree it's homeland security. We call that dual use."[34] In this view, "homeland security" is whatever it needs to be to justify receiving grants.

The "it all depends" perspective may be the most accurate description of how jurisdictions *treat*—as opposed to *define*—homeland security. Homeland security thus refers to how jurisdictions actually behave rather than how a policy or strategy says they should behave. It is the homeland security equivalent of "theory in use."[35]

From a public choice perspective, one would expect that officials and citizens in local jurisdictions have the greatest incentive to prepare for incidents that have frequently happened to them and are likely to happen again, whether terrorism, natural or man-made disaster.[36] Homeland security derives its foundation from local experience, not federal decree. A definition that expresses this view might read: *Homeland security means something different in each jurisdiction. It is a locally directed effort to prevent and prepare for incidents most likely to threaten the safety and security of its citizens.*

This perspective seems also to mirror emergency management. One author describes the importance of tailoring emergency planning to the uniqueness of each jurisdiction:

> Emergency planning normally begins with the identification of the disasters that have occurred in a community in the recent past. These are the known and,

> generally, the most probable hazards. Planners may then focus on the disasters that have occurred in the distant past by going through newspaper archives, history books, and other documents and by interviewing long-time residents.[37]

What are the likely incidents that threaten the safety and security of local jurisdictions? One illustrative way to answer the question is to look at major incidents that have occurred in states. A Federal Emergency Management Agency database categorizes four types of disasters.[38] Figure 1 and Table 1 show the types of disasters FEMA recorded between September 11, 2001 and December 31, 2007.

The disasters listed seem clearly within the purview of emergency management—"the discipline dealing with risk and risk avoidance," according to one definition.[39]

One of the Principles of Emergency Management proposed in 2007 by a FEMA working group is, "All hazards within a jurisdiction must be considered as part of a thorough risk assessment and prioritized on the basis of impact and likelihood of occurrence."[40] Terrorism appears but once in the previously referenced FEMA data: on September 11, 2001. If homeland security is a part of a doctrine that plans for the most probable incidents, most of the country can safely ignore terrorism as a threat.

The Hazards and Vulnerability Research Institute aids efforts to look at jurisdiction-specific vulnerabilities in the United States by identifying county differences in "social vulnerability." Their work examines "where there is uneven capacity for preparedness and response and where resources might be used most effectively to reduce the pre-existing

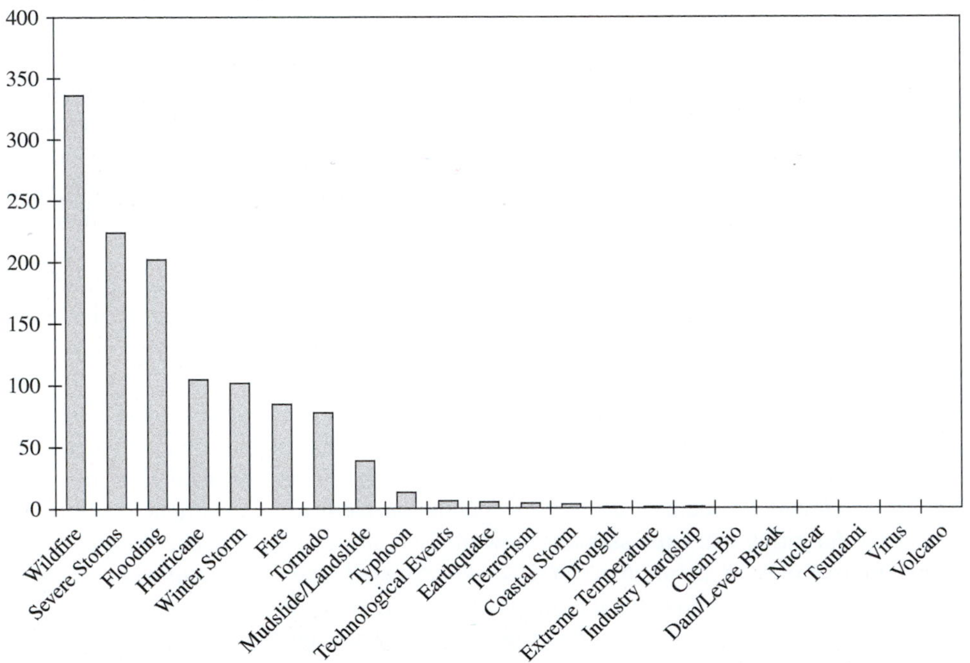

FIGURE 1 Types of Disasters Recorded by FEMA from September 11, 2001 through December 31, 2007.

TABLE 1 Frequency of Disaster Types: September 11, 2001 through December 31, 2007

Wildfire	336
Severe Storms	224
Flooding	202
Hurricane	105
Winter Storm	102
Fire	85
Tornado	78
Mudslide/Landslide	39
Typhoon	13
Technological Events	6
Earthquake	5
Terrorism	4
Coastal Storm	3
Drought	1
Extreme Temperature	1
Industry Hardship	1
Chem-Bio	0
Dam/Levee Break	0
Nuclear	0
Tsunami	0
Virus	0
Volcano	0

vulnerability."[41] The Institute also offers a database (called SHIELDUS) that allows one to identify county-level hazards for eighteen types of incidents that occurred from 1960 through 2005.[42]

"Security" is derived from Latin. Its lexical roots describe a condition "without care." Homeland security, however it is defined, seeks to create conditions so citizens can live without having to care about certain hazards.

At one level, discussed earlier, "all hazards" means planning for what all emergencies have in common. That focus draws attention to the possibility, if not desirability, of doctrine. At another level, all hazards means planning for the emergencies each community has actually experienced or is likely to experience. This focus draws attention to the uniqueness of disasters to individual communities. All disasters may have some things in common. But for the citizens who go through a disaster, each disaster is unique. In that respect, the security of their most specific and significant homeland—their community—will also be unique.

Homeland Security Is about Meta Hazards

Ecosystems have outliers, entities struggling to find a niche and survive. Tailoring the definition of homeland security for an individual jurisdiction is one end of a continuum. At the other end is a definition that focuses on hazards that affect everyone in the nation.

As noted, "all hazards" does not literally mean all. Some significant perils are neglected. Patrick Massey has written about what he calls generational hazards—hazards "created by present generations . . . [that] take many decades to metastasize before finally reaching a disastrous end-state that impacts future generations."[43] Others have written about "slowly moving disasters," such as famine and droughts.[44] Massey contrasts events "done to us"—terrorism, wildfire, storms, etc.—with what we as a nation do to ourselves. His threat list includes the impact on future generations of:

1. Growing federal fiscal debt
2. Global warming
3. Inferior math, science, and engineering education
4. Decaying physical infrastructure
5. The privatization of government services
6. Dependence on foreign energy
7. Aging population

To this could be added concerns about inadequate health care, drug-resistant disease, food security, open borders, mass immigration, cyber security, pandemics, foreign ownership of U.S. debt, or other trends that threaten the nation's long-term survival—including obesity.[45]

A definition from this perspective says homeland security could be about practically anything. One might respond, "If homeland security is about everything, it is about nothing." The nation has finite resources that can effectively be used only to address the most probable and most immediate threats.

But can we risk ignoring generational, slow moving, or very low probability non-terrorist hazards because they are not already in an organization's portfolio, or they do not occur within an election cycle?

What is the worst that could happen to our national security if the planet actually is warming, if nondiscretionary parts of the federal budget continue to increase, if infrastructure continues to deteriorate, it energy costs continue to rise? What happens to the nation's security if a disease like SARS "attacks the public health infrastructure and the people who take care of the sick."[46] Who is responsible for preventing or mitigating hazards like these?

If one extends the *National Strategy's* definition of homeland security beyond terrorism to include "all hazards"—as has been proposed—why not keep going and include every important hazard that threatens the nation's physical, social, and political security? *Homeland security is a national effort to prevent or mitigate any social trend or threat that can disrupt the long-term stability of the American way of life.*

This definition would position "routine disasters" (such as emergencies, disasters, and perhaps even many catastrophes)[47] as emergency management issues, domestic terrorism primarily as a law enforcement concern, health threats as public health and medical care issues, and so on. Homeland security as a national activity, and the Department of Homeland Security as the central coordinating element for all potential hazards, would transform itself into an endeavor that addresses the significant "meta issues" that fall in the cracks and that otherwise are the responsibility of no single level of government or organization.[48]

It is unreasonable to expect homeland security or the Department of Homeland Security to make a shift like this anytime soon. But environments change. One could envision FEMA leaving DHS and regaining its status as a "cabinet-level agency."[49] Preventing domestic terrorist incidents could return to being primarily a law enforcement responsibility.[50] Airport security might revert back to the private sector, supported by new smart technology. Immigration, border and port security could be integrated into other organizations. In theory, the nation could see a once behemoth DHS outlive its initial purpose. A fanciful idea, doubtlessly; but what if? Can the nation's understanding of homeland security transcend a comparatively short-term focus on terrorism and disasters?

Homeland Security Is about National Security

The term "national security," as it is currently understood, reportedly was rarely used before the late 1940s. When President Truman asked Congress in 1945 to establish what initially was called a "national *defense* council," the term "defense" was soon replaced by the word "security." "Defense" seemed too narrow an idea. Security was selected "to emphasize the need for a broad and comprehensive front" to protect the nation. Truman's effort subsequently led to the creation of the National *Security* Act and the National *Security* Council.[51]

Sixty years after the National Security Act we again have a distinction between defense and security. Some people believe the divide creates problems. They suggest it is "a distinction without a difference" to differentiate homeland security (protecting against internal threats) and homeland defense (protecting against external threats), one that "impedes the unity of effort between" the Departments of Defense and Homeland Security.[52]

Sixty years after the National Security Act, why maintain a separation between defense and security? Why not combine homeland security and homeland defense and call the entire project "national security?" If that were done, a homeland security definition might look something like this: *Homeland security is an element of national security that works with the other instruments of national power to protect the sovereignty, territory, domestic population, and critical infrastructure of the United States against threats and aggression.*

Fusing security and defense has deep roots in U.S. history. Rader describes homeland defense before the Revolution.

> [Early] settlers of the Thirteen colonies faced a variety of threats including Indians, Spaniards, Frenchmen, Hollanders and pirates. Lacking the resources to support fulltime soldiers, they met their defense needs with less costly militia. Twelve of thirteen colonies passed legislation requiring each adult male from 16 to 60 ". . . to own a modern weapon, train regularly with his neighbors, and stand ready to repel any attack on his colony."[53]

Garamone describes how defending the American homeland from external and internal threats has been the first priority of the military since the Republic began. "When George Washington became president in 1789, 'common defense' primarily meant two things: defeating a foreign invasion and defending against Indians."[54]

Lowenberg reviews the evolution of these early efforts to protect the homeland from perceived threats. He describes "how the right of the states to raise, maintain and employ their own military forces (known since 1824 as the 'National Guard') is guaranteed by the U.S. Constitution and by the constitutions and statutes of the several states and territories."[55]

One could argue that from an historical perspective, homeland security and homeland defense have, until this century, been essentially the same activity. Larsen and David, writing presciently in October 2000, argue "In the 21st century, the term 'homeland defense' is nearly synonymous with how we used the term 'national security' in the latter half of the 20th century."[56] It does not seem strained to incorporate homeland security in their observation.

William Safire, author of what stands as the best description of the origins and uses of the term homeland security, suggests why the formal split between homeland defense and homeland security happened.

> [In 1997], the U.S. government got into the homeland act. In the Quadrennial Defense Review mandated by Congress, a defense panel was set up to rethink military strategy up to 2020. The panel foresaw a need to counter potential terrorism and other "transnational threats to the sovereign territory of the nation." Its recommendation of an "increased emphasis on homeland defense" did not get much attention.
>
> Almost one month after the Sept. 11, 2001, attack on the U.S., the Bush administration established an Office of Homeland Security. Why was security substituted for defense? A rationale was set forward that security was the umbrella term, incorporating local and national public-health preparedness for attack, the defense of the nation offered by the armed services, plus the intelligence and internal security activities of the C.I.A., F.B.I. and local police. (In fact, I'm told by secret nomenclature sources, security was chosen because the Defense Department did not want any jurisdictional confusion with the new White House organization.)[57]

Potential jurisdictional confusion is one explanation. Another reason is to avoid pressure to share some of the Department of Defense budget (an estimated 500 billion dollars in 2008) with the Department of Homeland Security (whose 2008 budget was less than one-tenth the DoD budget).[58]

For some purposes, the Department of Homeland Security is already part of the national security structure. The National Security Act of 1947 (designed primarily to reform the post World War II military and intelligence apparatus) notes that "it is the intent of Congress to *provide a comprehensive program for the future security of the United States.*"[59] [Emphasis added] Homeland security arguably is part of a comprehensive program. In SEC.3. (50 U.S.C. 401a), the National Security Act directs that "the term 'intelligence community' includes . . . (J) *the elements of the Department of Homeland Security* concerned with the analyses of foreign intelligence information." [Emphasis added]

It is a stretch to say this means Congress wants homeland defense and security to be merged. But it does present a picture of the camel's nose under the tent.

There is more.

The National Security Act says the National Security Council should advise the president about the "integration of domestic, foreign, and military policies relating to the national security so as to enable the military services and the other departments and agencies of the Government to cooperate more effectively in matters involving the national security."[60] Some observers have suggested combining the Homeland Security Council "with the National Security Council to form a single, integrated advisory body" would improve the integration contemplated by the Act.[61]

Viewing homeland security as part of the national security apparatus does not imply eliminating state and local public safety involvement, at least for the less-than-catastrophic concerns. But after Hurricane Katrina some elected officials argued that the military should play a much more aggressive role in homeland security, particularly in response activities.[62] Others counseled caution.[63]

The Department of Defense however seems unambiguous about the strategic role it wants to assume in homeland security. According to its homeland security doctrine, there is a clear difference between homeland defense and homeland security:

> To preserve the freedoms guaranteed by the Constitution of the United States, *the Nation must have a homeland that is secure from threats and violence, including terrorism.* Homeland security (HS) is the Nation's first priority, and it requires a national effort. The Department of Defense (DOD) has a key role in that effort. . . . Critical to understanding the overall relationship is an understanding of the distinction between the role that DOD plays with respect to securing the Nation and HS, and the policy in the NSHS [National Homeland Security Strategy], which has the Department of Homeland Security (DHS) as the lead. *HS at the national level has a specific focus on terrorist threats. The DOD focus in supporting HS is broader.*[64] [Emphasis in original document]

Attempts to alter this doctrine will likely meet resistance from defense interests. But future attacks inside the United States or other catastrophes like Katrina may give more impetus to efforts to formally integrate homeland security and defense.

One might claim that in a time of need, homeland security and defense already are integrated. The same military doctrine that separates the two activities allows also for the military to assume a domestic homeland security role:

> DOD recognizes that threats planned or inspired by "external" actors may materialize internally. The reference to "external threats" does not limit where or how attacks could be planned and executed. DOD is prepared to conduct homeland defense missions whenever the President, exercising his constitutional authority as Commander in Chief, authorizes military actions.[65]

From the perspective sketched in this section, homeland security means preventing and responding to anything that threatens national security. The president of the United States gets to say what that is.

Homeland Security Über Alles

Shortly after 5:00 a.m., a man and woman were awakened by a banging noise downstairs. In a few moments, police surrounded them. The man was arrested, taken to a facility, held for five days, questioned nonstop without access to an attorney, and then released without any action taken against him.[66]

This incident happened over twenty years ago, in Northern Ireland. One might have briefly thought this happened in the United States. Some people believe this describes what homeland security could be. For other people, this *is* homeland security.[67]

William Crowe, a former chairman of the Joint Chiefs of Staff said, "The real danger lies not with what the terrorists can do to us, but what we can do to ourselves when we are spooked."[68] There is a view that homeland security is a dangerously dysfunctional reaction to being spooked by September 11, 2001. Some people believe homeland security may be a greater threat to the country than terrorism.

For this part of the ecosystem: *Homeland security is a symbol used to justify government efforts to curtail civil liberties.*

Homeland security in this construction has the status of a meme—"a replicator in human culture that acts in ways similar to the way a gene acts under evolutionary biology principles."[69] The significance of a meme is not whether the idea it covers is true, but whether the idea is replicated in the culture.[70]

Homeland security as a meme stands for more than what DHS or related agencies do programmatically. Homeland Security represents instead an admixture of facts, interpretations, half-truths, emotions, misunderstandings, rumors, and lies about what government does to protect the nation. For example:

Thousands of Arabs in the United States disappeared after 9/11/01. People can be detained indefinitely and incommunicado whether they are American citizens or not. Air travelers—including babies and frail old men in wheelchairs—have to remove parts of their clothing to prove to the government they are not terrorists. Border agents persecute economic refugees. Corporations freely open their customer files to government agents. Secret watch lists are filled with errors that cannot or will not be corrected. Immigration officials separate hard-working parents from their children because the adults do not have the correct "papers." Racial profiling is increasingly more acceptable. The homeland security alert levels are used only when they have political value.[71] Americans who have done nothing wrong have their telephone calls, e-mail, Internet activity and other communications monitored by secret government agencies. Animal rights and environmental activists are considered terrorists. Video cameras are everywhere. The government is aiming for total awareness of all information. Although he may be twenty years delayed, Big Brother has arrived.[72]

The amalgam of fact, anecdote, and myth supports a narrative that "the government" and its corporate masters—one definition of fascism—ignore the Constitution's guarantee of fundamental liberties to serve specific political and economic interests. And it is all justified in the name of a more secure America.

Corroborating arguments for this view come not just from websites that proclaim the U.S. government covers up the truth about the September 11th attacks.[73] The Constitution is *Not A Suicide Pact,* proclaims the title of a book written by an intellectually renowned federal judge. Civil liberties and putative inalienable rights can be adjusted to serve public safety needs.[74]

"Be careful what you say. Be careful what you do," the United States Attorney General cautions Americans after September 11, 2001.[75] The Senate majority leader warns "When you're in this type of conflict, when you're at war, civil liberties are treated differently."[76] The opposition leader of the House adds his thoughts: "We're not going to have all the openness and freedom we have had. We need to find a new balance between freedom and security."[77] The president vows "we must not let foreign enemies use the forums of liberty to destroy liberty, itself. Foreign terrorists and agents must never again be allowed to use our freedoms against us."[78] Citizens agree. A poll taken shortly after

September 11, 2001 found that two-thirds of Americans would be willing to give up "some civil liberties" to fight terrorism.[79]

Factoids like these are used to support a claim that government-induced fear increasingly rules the nation, and homeland security is its agent.

Judith K. Boyd used memetics to describe the post 9/11 homeland security zeitgeist. She writes how fear has emerged in popular culture as one of four dominant themes surrounding homeland security.

> Immediately after the attacks on September 11, 2001, President Bush gave notice to the American public that they were no longer safe: "The American people need to know that we're facing a different enemy than we have ever faced. This enemy hides in shadows, and has no regard for human life. This is an enemy who preys on innocent and unsuspecting people, runs for cover." This sense of an enemy lurking in the shadows or living amongst American neighborhoods as part of a sleeper cell waiting to be activated resonated through television, books, and images. . . . But there is also a sense of fear regarding our own government—what is it doing in secret places with secret things. When the government is not forthcoming about its methodology . . . the result is that people go to the darkest places of their minds and imagine what could be going on. The result is an image of Homeland Security as an Orwellian Big Brother with the motto "See All, Know All," taking innocent people "down the rabbit hole as a suspected terrorist," perhaps even to torture them.[80]

The world has seen this strategy of fear and secrecy used before. One author, describing Germany in the 1930s, writes:

> What happened . . . was the gradual habituation of the people, little by little, to being governed by surprise; to receiving decisions deliberated in secret; to believing that the situation was so complicated that the government had to act on information which the people could not understand, or so dangerous that, even if the people could understand it, it could not be released because of national security. And their sense of identification with Hitler, their trust in him, made it easier to widen this gap and reassured those who would otherwise have worried about it.[81]

Fast-forward eight decades to a February 2008 exchange between a magazine writer and an FBI agent:

> "The public is never going to see the evidence we have," [the FBI agent] says. "We don't want to reveal our hand or tip our sources. You cannot judge the nature of the terrorist threat to the United States based on the public record."
>
> "But with such strictures," I ask, "how does a citizen become informed about the threat?"
>
> "I have access to the information," [the FBI agent] says. "I have a lot of faith in the judgment of the common citizen. A lot of people understand the nature of the threat."[82]

Contemporary writers talk about how the country is *Trapped in the War on Terror,* and describe how the threat is *Overblown: How Politicians and the Terrorism Industry Inflate National Security Threats and Why We Believe Them.*[83] They describe how, because of *Bush's Law: The Remaking of American Justice,*[84] and the *Terror Presidency,*[85] the nation is *Less Safe; Less Free.*[86] *The Lucifer Effect*[87] explains how manipulating situational and group forces can make good people act like Americans did at Abu Ghraib and elsewhere. Another writer describes how the fear generated by terrorism and other catastrophes gives rise to "disaster capitalism," and new markets for the private sector.[88]

As happened to Germany in the 1930s, government is becoming the people's master rather than their servant:

> This separation of government from people, this widening of the gap, took place so gradually and so insensibly, each step disguised (perhaps not even intentionally) as a temporary emergency measure or associated with true patriotic allegiance or with real social purposes. And all the crises and reforms (real reforms, too) so occupied the people that they did not see the slow motion underneath, of the whole process of government growing remoter and remoter.[89]

One author warns about the potential for "The End of America."[90] She identifies ten steps required to transform an open society into a dictatorship; the steps are based, she argues, on how this has been done in the past:

1. Invoke an external and internal threat
2. Establish secret prisons
3. Develop a paramilitary force
4. Surveil ordinary citizens
5. Infiltrate citizens' groups
6. Arbitrarily detain and release citizens
7. Target key individuals
8. Restrict the press
9. Cast criticism as "espionage" and dissent as "treason"
10. Subvert the rule of law

The author believes each of the steps has already been initiated, helped directly by homeland security. At present, she says, "only a handful of patriots are trying to hold back the tide of tyranny for the rest of us. . . . Americans turn away quite leisurely, keeping tuned to Internet shopping and *American Idol.*" Her concern is not confined to one president's administration.

> What if . . . there is another attack—say, God forbid, a dirty bomb? The executive can declare a state of emergency. History shows that any leader, of any party, will be tempted to maintain emergency powers after the crisis has passed. With the gutting of traditional checks and balances, we are no less endangered [whomever the president is]—because any executive will be tempted to enforce his or her will through edict rather than the arduous, uncertain process of democratic negotiation and compromise.[91]

The Ecological Battlefield of Homeland Security

In ancient Rome, major wars were often fought simultaneously on many smaller battlefields. Generals fighting in the middle of a battle frequently operated in the blind because there was "great confusion . . . rumors and misinformation pouring in on both sides from many directions." Commanders who were able to gain the high ground could see what was going on in the fight and shape their strategic moves.[92] Seeing homeland security from another dimension—in this case observing an ecosystem—might also confer strategic advantage to scholars and practitioners who want to help homeland security evolve.

The intent of this essay was to look for plausible answers to the question, "What is homeland security." I proposed seven potential definitions, some more tenable than others. I argued that metaphorically, the definitions help describe a homeland security ecosystem.[93] The definitions represent interests seeking to claim resources that give advantage for organizational or political survival and growth. The resources include space on the public policy agenda, money, semantic dominance, and doctrinal preeminence.

The argument has been made that a single definition would be desirable and beneficial for a number of reasons, mostly having to do with efficiency and effectiveness criteria. But there is no one authority that can command everyone to use language the same way. Other important and often used terms—like terrorism, justice, disaster, or emergency management—also do not have single definitions. Yet we make progress in understanding and using each of those ideas. The absence of agreement can be seen as grist for the continued evolution of homeland security as a practice and as an idea.

Even if people did agree to define homeland security with a single voice, there would still be the matter of behavior. What people, organizations, and jurisdictions do is as instructive as what they say.

I am unaware of research that comprehensively describes what jurisdictions do behaviorally under the homeland security rubric. But in my experience, the emergency management "community of interest" and the fire services tend to constellate around the *All Hazards* definition, law enforcement tends to cohere around *Homeland Security as Preventing Terrorism,* people who work for a federal agency tend toward *Terrorism and Major Catastrophes,* and the Department of Defense sees homeland security as what civilians do.[94] No doubt there are exceptions to these generalizations.

I have found comparatively few proponents of the *Meta, Jurisdictional,* or fear-based *Security-Over-Everything* views. The community that sees *Homeland Security as National Security* is also small, but in my view it is growing.

Independently of the work done for this paper, a colleague gathered information from fifty homeland security practitioners who were graduates of the Naval Postgraduate School's homeland security master's degree program.[95] One question asked was "What does homeland security mean to you?" As shown in Figure 2, almost 40 percent—the largest group—gave a definition that either blended elements of the definitions discussed here, or did not define the term. *All Hazards, Terrorism* and *National Security* were the next most frequently mentioned.

So what is the "truth" about all of this? What is homeland security?

A *pragmatic* view of truth can be represented by something a fire chief told me. "There are lots of definitions, and they will be activated at different times and we each have different roles to play in different scenarios."[96] A productive research task would be

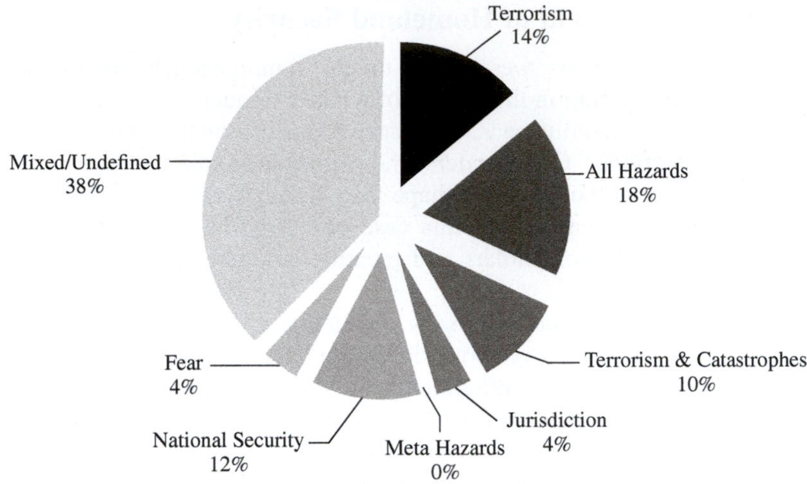

FIGURE 2 What is homeland security? Definitions from 50 Practitioners

to identify the different times, the different roles, and the different scenarios that trigger the variety of definitions.

One could also derive a *correspondence* view of the truth—the "objective reality"—by discovering what it is people actually do when they claim to be doing homeland security. That research may have already been done. I am unaware of it.

From a *coherence* perspective, truth is defined not so much by its correspondence to an objective reality, but rather by how well it adheres to the beliefs and practices of particular communities of interest.[97] Most of the definitions discussed in this paper are based on a coherence view of truth.

Richard Rorty reportedly said, "Truth is what your colleagues let you get away with."[98] And if your colleagues believe homeland security is about terrorism, about all hazards, or other potential definitions, then that is the truth.

In an ecosystem shaped by Rorty's image of truth, homeland security is a continuously evolving social construction, a reality shaped by social processes.[99] Those processes can be constrained by semantic stovepipes that insist on one worldview. Expanding one's network of colleagues who talk and write about these issues can help dissolve stovepipes. Such conversations will contribute to the continued evolution of the homeland security ecosystem.

Critical Thinking Questions

1. What are the most basic elements of any definition of homeland security?
2. Does a person's view toward the definition of homeland security depend on what his or her professional occupation is (e.g., military, intelligence, law enforcement, border patrol, emergency management)? Why or why not?
3. What individuals within a particular organization have the final say in determining what is and is not considered a homeland security issue?

Notes

1. Homeland Security Council, *National Strategy for Homeland Security* (Washington, DC: Department of Homeland Security, October 2007), 13.
2. The July 2002 version of the *National Strategy for Homeland Security* defines homeland security as "a concerted national effort to prevent terrorist attacks within the United States, reduce America's vulnerability to terrorism, and minimize the damage and recover from attacks that do occur." Office of Homeland Security, *National Strategy for Homeland Security* (Washington, DC: Office of Homeland Security, 2002), 2. The Homeland Security Act of 2002 does not define homeland security. Section 101(b)(1) of the Act, however, takes the *National Strategy's* definition of homeland security and makes it the primary mission of the Department of Homeland Security. The Department of Defense, in its *Joint Publication 1-02* (as Amended Through 04 March 2008), also known as "Department of Defense Dictionary of Military and Associated Terms," defines homeland security a slightly different way: "A concerted national effort to prevent terrorist attacks within the United States; reduce America's vulnerability to terrorism, major disasters, and other emergencies; and minimize the damage and recover from attacks, major disasters, and other emergencies that occur" (243). The idea of homeland security as a program, an objective, a discipline, an agency, an administrative activity, comes from "Homeland Security—The States' Focused Efforts for Victory in the War on Terror;" *Policy Options Document for the National Governors Association,* edited by Glen Woodbury (Unpublished Draft, December 24, 2004), 3. Available from the author.
3. Defensible in this context means a plausible, if not sometimes compelling case can be made that homeland security is or ought to be considered in a particular way. The "is" case is based on behaviors that are going on under the name homeland security. The "ought" case is based on a desire on the part of some stakeholders to shape how other people view homeland security.
4. Weberian ideal types are not meant to represent what is normatively "the best," nor every element that could be included in the definition sets presented in this paper. They are intended to characterize the central features of a particular type. Gerth and Mills in their introduction to Max Weber, *From Max Weber: Essays in Sociology* (New York: Oxford University Press, 1946) explain ideal types this way: "The term 'ideal' has nothing to do with evaluations of any sort. For analytical purposes, one may construct ideal types of prostitution as well as religious leaders. The term does not mean that either prophets or harlots are exemplary or should be imitated as representatives of an ideal way of life." (59)
5. For an extended treatment of the application of the Darwinian model to security, see Raphael D. Sagarin and Terence Taylor, eds., *Natural Security: A Darwinian Approach to a Dangerous World* (Berkeley: University of California Press, 2008). For an evolutionary approach to organizations and systems, see P.R. Lawrence and N. Nohria, *Driven: How Human Nature Shapes Our Choices,* Warren Bennis signature series (San Francisco: Jossey-Bass, 2002).
6. For examples with respect to one homeland security domain, aviation security, see "Airport security technology under scrutiny," *CNET News.com*, http://news.cnet .com/2100-1001-272938.html; "Let Computers Screen Air Baggage," *Wired.com*, http://www.wired.com/politics/security/commentary/securitymatters/2006/03/70470;

"TSA puts security technology to the test," *USATODAY.com,* http://www.usatoday.com/money/industries/travel/2007-10-01-security-tech_N.htm. "Airport Security Technology Stuck In the Pipeline," *Washingtonpost.com*, http://www.washingtonpost.com/wp-dyn/content/article/2008/02/07/AR2008020704067_pf.html. "Can someone explain why there are so many different lines to a checkpoint?" *Evolution of Security,* http://www.tsa.gov/blog/. The argument about the relationship to desired outcome and behavior persists: "TSA will receive $7.1 billion this year, most of which it will spend on screeners at all U.S. airports. However, the probability of attacks in the style of 9/11 dropped close to zero in the few months after the attacks when airlines installed—at relatively low cost—simple cockpit barricades. In theory then, another 9/11 type of attack cannot happen. Since September 2001, however, screening every bag of every airline passenger to prevent another 9/11 type of attack will cost taxpayers over $34 billion by the end of FY2009. Furthermore, screening checked bags does not necessarily reduce the probability of the destruction of airplanes since screeners do not systematically check carry-on bags, air freight, or people for explosives." Veronique De Rugy, "Facts and Figures about Seven Years of Homeland Security Spending" (Mercatus Center, George Mason University, Working paper No. 08-02, March 2008), 7, http://www.mercatus.org/Publications/pubID.4475,cfilter.0/pub_detail.asp (Internal citations in the quoted material are omitted.)

7. Larsen argues that this approach—which he terms Ready! Shoot! Aim!—"is a common error in the practice of homeland security" because people have not "taken the time to understand the fundamentals." R.J. Larsen, *Our Own Worst Enemy: Asking the Right Questions About Security to Protect You, Your Family and America* (New York: Warner Books, 2007), 136. Others have argued that in times of chaos and complexity, doing something—anything—can be a valid method of discovering the right something to do. See, for example, David J. Snowden and Mary E. Boone, "A Leader's Framework for Decision Making," *Harvard Business Review* (November 2007).
8. There was some attention to homeland security prior to the September 11, 2001 attacks, but the concept had little public visibility. As noted in the 2007 *National Strategy* "Homeland security before September 11 existed as a patchwork of efforts undertaken by disparate departments and agencies across all levels of government." (3) The U.S. Commission on National Security/21st Century (known as the Hart-Rudman Commission) detailed much of those pre-September 11, 2001 patchwork efforts. For example, see The United States Commission on National Security/21st Century, *Road Map for National Security: Imperative for Change* (February 15, 2001), 10–29. See also Note 58, below, for information about the origin of the phrase "homeland security."
9. Homeland Security Council, *National Strategy for Homeland Security* (October 2007), 3. United States, Office of Homeland Security, *National Strategy for Homeland Security* (July 2002), 2.
10. De Rugy, "Facts and Figures," 2.
11. See for examples, Eric Holdeman, "Destroying FEMA," August 30, 2005, http://www.washingtonpost.com/wp-dyn/content/article/2005/08/29/AR2005082901445.html; Department of Homeland Security, "A Performance Review of FEMA's Disaster Management Activities in Response to Hurricane Katrina" (Washington, DC: Department of Homeland Security, March 2006), 2–3. Eric Klinenberg and Thomas

Frank, "Looting Homeland Security," *Rolling Stone,* December 15, 2005, http://www.rollingstone.com/politics/story/8952492/looting_homeland_security. G. Haddow, J. Bullock, and D.P. Coppola, *Introduction to Emergency Management,* 3rd Ed. (Butterworth-Heinemann, 2007), 1.

12. For data on this point, see http://www.terrorisminfo.mipt.org/Terrorism-in-the-United-States.asp (for terrorist incident information), and http://www.fema.gov/femaNews/disasterSearch.do?action=Main (for significant disasters). Wikipedia has a list of terrorist incidents in the United States covering the 1830s to 2008, available at http://en.wikipedia.org/wiki/Terrorism_in_the_United_States. I have not verified the accuracy of that list.
13. Mark A. Sauter and James Jay Carafano, *Homeland Security: A Complete Guide to Understanding, Preventing, and Surviving Terrorism* (New York: McGraw-Hill, 2005), xiv.
14. See Slide 6 in Anon., "Revising the National Strategy for Homeland Security," Draft/Pre-Decisional Information, September 2007. (Available from author.)
15. William Waugh, "Terrorism and the All-Hazards Model" revised version of paper presented on the IDS Emergency Management On-Line Conference (June 28-July 16, 2004), 1, http://training.fema.gov/emiweb/downloads/Waugh%20-%20Terrorism%20and%20Planning.doc. The author also indicates "All-hazards planning . . . is based upon the most likely disasters and the most 'popular.'" Using *all hazards* to mean focusing on likely and popular disasters and not *all* disasters is confusing to someone outside the emergency management community. It is perhaps as confusing as Homeland Security Presidential Directive 8's definition of *prevention* is to someone outside the homeland security community: "activities undertaken . . . *during the early stages* of an incident to reduce the likelihood . . . of . . . terrorist attacks." [Emphasis added]
16. Waugh, "Terrorism and the All-Hazards Model," 2.
17. Bullock, et al, *Introduction to Emergency Management,* 1st Ed., 91. See also Carol Cwiak, Emergency Management Program Faculty, North Dakota State University "Commentary on Year in Review article" in February 1, 2008 *FEMA Emergency Management Higher Education Program Report.* (Available from author.)
18. "2 Bomb Blasts Rock Abortion Clinic at Atlanta; 6 Are Injured," *New York Times,* June 14, 2008, http://query.nytimes.com/gst/fullpage.html?res=9D0DE4DC173BF934A25752C0A961958260. "In Latest Atlanta Bombing, 5 Are Injured at a Gay Bar," *New York Times,* February 23, 1997, http://query.nytimes.com/gst/fullpage.html?res=950CE3D7103EF930A15751C0A961958260.
19. AOL Video, "Secondary IED detonates near VBIED aftermath," *video.aol.com,* http://video.aol.com/video-detail/secondary-ied-detonates-near-vbied-aftermath/2019894776. On the likelihood of simultaneous attacks, even in the event of a nuclear attack, see Belfer Center for Science and International Affairs, Harvard, "The Day After: Action in the 24 Hours Following a Nuclear Blast in an American City," 14–15, http://belfercenter.ksg.harvard.edu/publication/2140/day_after.html.
20. "States Chafing at U.S. Focus on Terrorism," *NYTimes.com,* May 26, 2008, http://www.nytimes.com/2008/05/26/us/26terror.html?_r=1&hp&oref=slogin.
21. Waugh notes, "Terrorism is not like natural or even other man-made hazards. But, then again, a tornado is not like a hurricane and certainly not like an earthquake." Bullock, et al. (2005) observe that "No hurricane or earthquake has ever advanced a

human agenda," 92. The view expressed in the "all hazards" section of my paper is that an attack by an intelligent enemy places terrorist events in a category substantially different from non-terrorist incidents. It remains an open question, as Waugh writes, "whether terrorism is so different from other threats that the "all-hazards" approach is inappropriate or ineffective," 1–2. The details in the after-action descriptions of the response to the September 11, 2001 attacks in New York and Arlington, Virginia—combined with the rarity of such attacks—suggests terrorism *is* different. National Commission on Terrorist Attacks upon the United States, *The 9/11 Commission Report: Final Report of the National Commission on Terrorist Attacks Upon the United States* (New York: Norton, 2004), 285, 314–315; and *Arlington County After-Action Report On The Response To The September 11 Terrorist Attack On The Pentagon* (Annex D, no date).

22. For example, the *National Strategy for Homeland Security* defines prevention as the nation's primary homeland security strategic objective. Wayne Blanchard et al., "Principles of Emergency Management," www.training.fema.gov/EMIWeb/edu/docs/emprinciples/Principles%20of%20Emergency%20Management%20Brochure.doc, write "Emergency management must give greater attention to *prevention* and mitigation activities." Elsewhere in the Principles, prevention is defined as a *subset* of mitigation. Obviously the emergency management community thinks preventing terrorism is important. But it could be argued that incorporating prevention within mitigation is starting out on a path metaphorically analogous to the preeminence FEMA lost when it became a subset of the Department of Homeland Security.
23. *National Homeland Security Strategy* (2007), 3.
24. Ibid.
25. The words are from the Preamble to the United States Constitution. However, Bullock et al. (2005) argue "The Constitution entrusts the states with responsibility for public health and safety . . . and assigns the federal government to a secondary role," 2.
26. De Rugy points out that the Department of Homeland Security accounts for only slightly more than 50 percent of total federal spending for homeland security.
27. DHS, "Remarks by Homeland Security Secretary Michael Chertoff to the National Congress for Secure Communities," December 17, 20007, http://www.dhs.gov/xnews/speeches/sp_1197986846840.shtm.
28. "States Chafing at U.S. Focus on Terrorism," *NYTimes.com*, May 26, 2008, http://www.nytimes.com/2008/05/26/us/26terror.html?_r=1&hp&oref=slogin.
29. Ibid.
30. Holdeman, "Destroying FEMA." For a pre-Katrina example, see George Haddow, "The Challenges of Emergency Management Planning in 2005," *Disaster Resource,* http://www.disaster-resource.com/articles/05p_056.shtml and William M. Arkin, "Natural Disasters Perfunctory Concerns—Early Warning," *Washingtonpost.com*, September 15, 2005, http://blog.washingtonpost.com/earlywarning/2005/09/natural_disasters_perfunctory.html.
31. DHS, "Michael Chertoff to National Congress."
32. Belfer Center, "The Day After," 10.
33. C.W. Mills, *The Sociological Imagination* (New York: Oxford University Press, 1959), 224.
34. May 2008 personal conversation with a senior state emergency management official who wished, for obvious reasons, to remain anonymous. His comment is supported

by De Rugy: "Unfortunately, many studies have shown that the government is using a substantial portion of new homeland security spending for politically motivated items that are unlikely to have any effect on terrorism." DeRugy, "Facts and Figures," 7.

35. Chris Argyris, "Teaching Smart People How To Learn," *Harvard Business Review* (May-June 1991); Reprinted in Harvard Business Review, *Business Classics: Fifteen Key Concepts for Managerial Success* (Cambridge, MA: Harvard Business Review, 1991), 152.
36. For a discussion of the role public choice theory can play in homeland security, see Samuel H. Clovis, Jr., "Federalism, Homeland Security and National Preparedness: A Case Study in the Development of Public Policy," *Homeland Security Affairs* II, no. 3 (October 2006), http://www.hsaj.org/?article=2.3.4
37. Waugh, "Terrorism and the All-Hazards Model." He also adds, "Other hazards may be added to the list if it is determined that there may be some probability of them causing risk to life and/or property or to the environment. . . . The media, political leaders, influential residents, or influential participants in the planning process or the larger community may encourage attention to hazards of very low probability or even of no discernible possibility. . . . The point is that these less probable or even improbable hazards may be included in the planning. That's politics and the planning process is, after all, political as well as technical. It is also human nature. If the community is lucky, the planners give greatest attention to the biggest risks. All-hazards planning, then, is based upon the most likely disasters and the most 'popular.'" 1.
38. Federal Emergency Management Agency (FEMA), http://www.fema.gov/femaNews/disasterSearch.do?action=Main. The four types of disasters included major disaster declarations, emergency declarations, fire management assistance declarations, and fire suppression authorizations.
39. Bullock, et al., "Introduction to Emergency Management," 1st ed., 1. Like "homeland security," there are different definitions of emergency management. Blanchard, et al., "Principles of Emergency Management" define it as *"the managerial function charged with creating the framework within which communities reduce vulnerability to hazards and cope with disasters."* Brenda Phillips, in a 2003 paper (available from the author) reviews a number of emergency management definitions and synthesizes what she finds as "*the management of risk in order to protect life and property through a comprehensive effort that involves non-linear activities tied to mitigation, preparedness, response and recovery.*" Brenda D. Phillips, "Disasters by Discipline: necessary dialogue for emergency management education" (October 2003), 8–9. I would like to thanks Carol Cwiak for making me aware of the Phillips' paper.
40. Blanchard, et al., "Principles of Emergency Management."
41. See http://www.cas.sc.edu/geog/hrl/sovi.html. "Generally defined, vulnerability is the potential for loss of life or property due to hazards. The hazards-of-place model combines the biophysical vulnerability (physical characteristics of hazards and environment) and social vulnerability to determine an overall place vulnerability. Social vulnerability is represented as the social, economic, demographic, and housing characteristics that influence a community's ability to respond to, cope with, recover from, and adapt to environmental hazards."
42. http://www.cas.sc.edu/geog/hrl/SHELDUS.html.
43. Patrick J. Massey,"Generational Hazards," *Homeland Security Affairs* III, no. 3 (September 2007), http://www.hsaj.org/?article=3.3.3, 2.

44. Worldwatch Institute, "Disasters and Peacemaking: Helping Communities Heal," (n.d.), http://www.worldwatch.org/node/3916.
45. Science Blog, "Too Fat to Fight: Obesity Becomes National Security Issue," http://www.scienceblog.com/cms/too_fat_to_fight_obesity_becomes_national_security_issue. J. Enriquez, *The United States of America: Polarization, Fracturing, and Our Future* (Crown: 2005). On "food security" as opposed to "food safety," see http://www.foodsecurityresearch.ca/index.php?s=downturns.
46. The SARS quote is from a personal correspondence with Mary Jones, Deputy Director, Iowa Department of Public Health, May 2008. For a comprehensive review of other domestic and global trends that could affect the nation's security see Project on National Security Reform, "Vision Working Group Primer," Draft, February 25, 2008. (Available from the author.)
47. For definitions of the three terms, see E.L. Quarantelli, "Emergencies, Disasters and Catastrophes Are Different Phenomena" (2000), www.udel.edu/DRC/preliminary/pp304.pdf.
48. "Meta" is used in this construction to mean something outside the normal conceptual boundaries. In this case it refers to issues that are not typically perceived as threats to the nation's security, but arguments could be—and have been—developed to identify the issues as potential threats.
49. There is some question whether FEMA was ever an official cabinet agency, as opposed to a more informal designation as a "cabinet-level" agency. A knowledgeable emergency management colleague sent me the following information on this point: "The President may include anyone in Cabinet meetings as he/she chooses and that is how they did it with FEMA in the Clinton Administration. No legislation or executive order, so it was pro forma."
50. Mike German, *Thinking Like a Terrorist: Insights of a Former FBI Undercover Agent,* 1st ed (Washington, DC: Potomac Books, 2007). "U.S. Cites Big Gains Against Al Qaeda," *washingtonpost.com*, May 29, 2008, http://www.washingtonpost.com/wp-dyn/content/article/2008/05/29/AR2008052904116.html. For another argument about the possible decline of Al Qaeda, see Marc Sageman, *Leaderless Jihad: Terror Networks in the Twenty-First Century* (Philadelphia: University of Pennsylvania Press, 2008).
51. Mark Neocleous, "From Social to National Security: On the Fabrication of Economic Order," *Security Dialogue* 37 (2006): 363–364.
52. Paul N. Stockton and Patrick S. Roberts. "Findings from the Forum on 'Homeland Security After the Bush Administration: Next Steps in Building Unity of Effort,'" *Homeland Security Affairs* IV, no. 2 (June 2008): 11, www.hsaj.org. For a different perspective, and a comment on the flexibility of definitions, see "An Interview With Assistant Secretary Of Defense For Homeland Defense," *Joint Forces Quarterly* (January 2006): 10–11. "Although those [official] definitions [of homeland defense and homeland security] are helpful, at the end of the day, Secretary [Donald] Rumsfeld is the warfighter, and Secretary [Michael] Chertoff is one of our nation's senior law enforcement officials, and, in combination, these two cabinet officers use their authorities to achieve the common purpose of protecting the American people."
53. Neil E. Rader, "Homeland Defense: The Evolution, The Threat, and the Air Force Role," *USAWC Strategic Research Project* (U.S. Army War College, March 11, 2002), 1–2.
54. Jim Garamone, "A Short History of Homeland Defense," (Armed Forces Press Service, October 25, 2001), http://www.defenselink.mil/news/newsarticle.aspx?id=44614.

55. Timothy J. Lowenberg, "The Future Role of the National Guard in National Defense and Homeland Security," Chapter VI in Woodbury, *Policy Options Document,* 14.
56. Randall J. Larsen, USAF and Ruth A. David, "Homeland Defense: Assumptions First, Strategy Second," *Strategic Review* (Fall 2000), http://www.homelandsecurity.org/journal/articles/article1.htm, 2.
57. William Safire, "The Way We Live Now: On Language; Homeland" *New York Times,* January 20, 2002. http://query.nytimes.com/gst/fullpage.html?res=9401E3DC1238F933A15752C0A9649C8B63&sec=&spon=&pagewanted=all.
58. De Rugy notes that DHS does not spend its entire budget for homeland security. She shows only $35 billion of the DHS' 2009 budget of $50.5 billion goes directly to homeland security-related activities. Her analysis appears to rely primarily on the "homeland security as terrorism" definition. De Rugy, "Facts and Figures," 2.
59. The National Security Act of 1947 (as amended) SEC. 2. [50 U.S.C. 401].
60. National Security Act, Sec. 101. [U.S.C. 402] (a)
61. Stockton and Roberts, "CISAC Forum," 11. The authors also note, "Other participants argued that homeland security issues would inevitably be given short shrift in any such unified arrangement." For an analysis of the Homeland Security Council, see also Harold C. Relyea, "Organizing for Homeland Security: The Homeland Security Council Reconsidered" (Washington, DC: Congressional Research Service, March 19, 2008), especially pages 5–6.
62. See, for example, recommendations from the U.S. Conference of Mayors, which included such suggestions as, "The federal government should allow for greater military involvement in the immediate response to such overwhelming disasters, at the very least during the first days and weeks of response and when requested by local or state governments. Cities need a mechanism to request direct assistance in [the] form of military assets during a major natural disaster or terrorist attack. It is too cumbersome for cities to have to go through the state apparatus. The federal government should identify a lead military agency to work directly with local governments on the deployment of federal resources needed immediately prior to and after a disaster." Ed Somers, "O'Neill Presides at First Chertoff/USCM Meeting, New Homeland Security Action Plan Released," October 31, 2005, http://www.usmayors.org/uscm/us_mayor_newspaper/documents/10_31_05/chertoff.asp.
63. Thomas Goss, "'Who's in Charge?' New Challenges in Homeland Defense and Homeland Security," *Homeland Security Affairs* II, no. 1 (April 2006), http://www.hsaj.org/?article=2.1.2
64. Department of Defense, *Homeland Security, Joint Publication 3–26* (Washington, DC: Department of Defense, August 2, 2005), v.
65. Ibid, vi.
66. P. Hillyard, *Suspect Community: People's Experience of the Prevention of Terrorism Acts in Britain* (London: Pluto Press in association with Liberty, 1993). 1.
67. For example, a review of Eric Lichtblau's *Bush's Law: The Remaking of American Justice* (2008) reports the story of an Oregon attorney who was suspected of being involved with the Madrid train bombings. "You feel the growing apprehension, then fear, as [Brandon] Mayfield, his wife and children detect that someone has been secretly breaking into their house for many weeks. One day one of the children is at home as the door handle jiggles. He scurries to the attic, terrified. This is Cujo, not homeland security. Mayfield was detained and, according to his lawyers, threatened

with the death penalty. Only the Spaniards' eventual arrest of the fingerprint's real owner, an Algerian, saved him. What if it hadn't?" Eric Lichtblau, "Bush's Law," Review, *NYTimes.com*, June 6, 2008, http://www.nytimes.com/2008/06/08/books/review/Stein-t.html?_r=1&8bu&emc=bua2&oref=slogin.

68. Cited in Stephen Flynn, *The Edge of Disaster: Rebuilding a Resilient Nation* (New York: Random House, 2007), 93.
69. Judith K. Boyd, "Introducing The Future Now: Using Memetics And Popular Culture To Identify The Post 9/11 Homeland Security Zeitgeist" (master's thesis, Naval Postgraduate School, March 2008), 27. Boyd notes the concept of a meme originated with Richard Dawkins, *The Selfish Gene* (New York: Oxford University Press, 1976).
70. Boyd, "Introducing the Future Now," 29, citing Steven Johnson, *Everything Bad is Good for You: How Today's Popular Culture is Actually Making Us Smarter* (New York: Riverhead Books, 2005), 205.
71. Tim Dickinson, "Truth or Terrorism? The Real Story Behind Five Years of High Alerts," *Rolling Stone,* February 7, 2008, http://www.rollingstone.com/politics/story/18056504/truth_or_terrorism_the_real_story_behind_five_years_of_high_alerts.
72. For some video examples of the point made in this paragraph, see "9–11 The Greatest Lie Ever Sold," http://www.youtube.com/watch?v=i_nKpHYLpeA; "The Big Brother State" (about the trend as it applies to the western liberal democracies), http://www.youtube.com/watch?v=jJTLL1UjvfU; "Be Careful What You Say 2," http://www.youtube.com/watch?v=MvRX-PQmLMQ; "Get Naked ! For a Safe and Secure America" http://www.youtube.com/watch?v=iMMXO_GmWw0. Satires of the point can be seen at http://www.aclu.org/pizza/images/screen.swf and http://www.safenow.org/.
73. http://www.911truth.org/ and "The Empire Of "The City" (World Superstate), Part 1," http://video.google.com/videoplay?docid=4675077383139148549 (Primarily the first thirty minutes.)
74. R.A. Posner, *Not a Suicide Pact: The Constitution in a Time of National Emergency* (Oxford University Press, USA, 2006).
75. Olivia Crawford, "War in the Locker Room—God, Iraq Split Americans," *Pacific News Service,* March 31, 2003, http://news.pacificnews.org/news/view_article.html?article_id=53f096e159193465bb0f22029864bde9.
76. Richard Lacayo, "Terrorizing Ourselves," *TIME,* September 24, 2001, from http://www.time.com/time/magazine/article/0,9171,1000878,00.html.
77. Cited by Janis Besler Heaphy, "Commencement Address," *Common Dreams,* December 17, 2001, http://www.commondreams.org/views01/1217-08.htm.
78. White House, "President Says U.S. Attorneys on Front Line in War," November 2001, http://www.whitehouse.gov/news/releases/2001/11/20011129-12.html.
79. Cited in "The coming loss of liberties. On its way to the USA," *Issues & Views,* September 17, 2001, http://www.issues-views.com/index.php/sect/24000/article/24010
80. Boyd, "Introducing the Future Now," 127. The quote from President Bush is from U.S. Executive Office of the President, "Remarks by President Bush at Photo Op," September 12, 2001, http://www.whitehouse.gov/news/releases/2001/09/20010912-4.html.
81. M. Mayer, *They Thought They Were Free: The Germans, 1933–45,* 2nd ed. (University Of Chicago Press, 1966). Quoted selection available at http://www.thirdreich.net/Thought_They_Were_Free.html.

82. Guy Lawson, "The Fear Factory," *Rolling Stone,* February 7, 2008, http://www.rollingstone.com/politics/story/18137343/the_fear_factory/print.
83. Ian Lustick, *Trapped in the War on Terror* (Philadelphia: University of Pennsylvania Press, 2006); John E. Mueller, *Overblown: How Politicians and the Terrorism Industry Inflate National Security Threats, and Why We Believe Them* (New York: Free Press, 2006).
84. Eric Lichtblau, *Bush's Law: The Remaking of American Justice,* 1st ed. (New York: Pantheon Books, 2008).
85. Jack L. Goldsmith, *The Terror Presidency: Law and Judgment Inside the Bush Administration* (New York: W.W. Norton & Co., 2007).
86. David Cole, *Less Safe, Less Free: Why America Is Losing the War on Terror* (New York: New Press, 2007).
87. Philip G. Zimbardo, *The Lucifer Effect: Understanding How Good People Turn Evil* (New York: Random House Trade Paperbacks, 2008).
88. Naomi Klein, *The Shock Doctrine: The Rise of Disaster Capitalism,* 1st ed. (New York: Metropolitan Books/Henry Holt, 2007), Part V.
89. Mayer, *They Thought They Were Free.*
90. Naomi Wolf, *The End of America: Letter of Warning to a Young Patriot* (White River Junction, Vt. Chelsea Green Publications, 2007). A summary of her argument can be found at Naomi Wolf, "Fascist America, in 10 easy steps," *The Guardian,* 24 April 2008, http://www.guardian.co.uk/world/2007/apr/24/usa.comment.
91. Wolf, "Fascist America."
92. M. Kaku, *Hyperspace: A Scientific Odyssey Through Parallel Universes, Time Warps, and the Tenth Dimension* (New York: Anchor Books, 1995), 13.
93. Elizabeth M. Prescott, "Corporations and Bureaucracies Under a Biological Lens," in Sagarin and Taylor, *Natural Security,* 80. The author thanks Lindsay Estes for creating Figure 3.
94. For a May 2008 view of law enforcement's perspective on homeland security, see Major Cities Chiefs Association, *Twelve Tenets To Prevent Crime And Terrorism: "A White Paper by the Homeland Security Committee*" (May 2008), http://www.majorcitieschiefs.org/press.shtml
95. Professor Joseph Ryan, Pace University, is conducting the study. I thank him for sharing his data.
96. Author's personal communication with William H Austin Fire Chief West Hartford Fire Department, May 2008.
97. P. Thagard, *Coherence in Thought and Action* (Cambridge, MA: MIT Press, 2000), 20.
98. W. Desmond, *Art, Origins, Otherness: Between Philosophy and Art* (Albany, NY: State University of New York Press, 2003), 280.
99. P.L. Berger and T. Luckmann, *The Social Construction of Reality: A Treatise in the Sociology of Knowledge* (New York: Anchor, 1967).

Defining Homeland Security

Analysis and Congressional Considerations

Shawn Reese

Summary

Ten years after the September 11, 2001, terrorist attacks, the U.S. government does not have a single definition for "homeland security." Currently, different strategic documents and mission statements offer varying missions that are derived from different homeland security definitions. Historically, the strategic documents framing national homeland security policy have included national strategies produced by the White House and documents developed by the Department of Homeland Security (DHS). Prior to the 2010 *National Security Strategy,* the 2002 and 2007 *National Strategies for Homeland Security* were the guiding documents produced by the White House. In 2011, the White House issued the *National Strategy for Counterterrorism.*

In conjunction with these White House strategies, DHS has developed a series of evolving strategic documents based on the two national homeland security strategies and include the 2008 *Strategic Plan—One Team, One Mission, Securing the Homeland;* the 2010 *Quadrennial Homeland Security Review* and *Bottom-Up Review;* and the 2012 *Department of Homeland Security Strategic Plan.* The 2012 DHS strategic plan is the latest evolution in DHS's process of defining its mission, goals, and responsibilities. This plan, however, only addresses the department's homeland security purview and is not a document that addresses homeland security missions and responsibilities that are shared across the federal government.

Varied homeland security definitions and missions may impede the development of a coherent national homeland security strategy, and may hamper the effectiveness of congressional oversight. Definitions and missions are part of strategy development. Policymakers develop strategy by identifying national interests, prioritizing goals to achieve those national interests, and arraying instruments of national power to achieve the national interests. Developing an effective homeland security strategy, however, may be complicated if the key concept of homeland security is not defined and its missions are not aligned and synchronized among different federal entities with homeland security responsibilities.

This report discusses the evolution of national and DHS-specific homeland security strategic documents and their homeland security definitions and missions, and analyzes the policy question of how varied homeland security definitions and missions may affect the development of national homeland security strategy. This report, however, does not examine DHS implementation of strategy.

Introduction and Issue

Ten years after the 9/11 terrorist attacks, policymakers continue to grapple with the definition of homeland security. Prior to 9/11, the United States addressed crises through the separate prisms of national defense, law enforcement, and emergency management. 9/11 prompted a strategic process that included a debate over and the development of homeland security policy. Today, this debate and development has resulted in numerous federal entities with homeland security responsibilities. For example, there are 30 federal entities that receive annual homeland security funding excluding the Department of Homeland Security (DHS). The Office of Management and Budget (OMB) estimates that 48% of annual homeland security funding is appropriated to these federal entities, with the Department of Defense (DOD) receiving approximately 26% of total federal homeland security funding. DHS receives approximately 52%.[1]

Congress and policymakers are responsible for funding homeland security priorities. These priorities need to exist, to be clear and cogent, in order for funding to be most effective. Presently, homeland security is not funded on clearly defined priorities. In an ideal scenario, there would be a clear definition of homeland security, and a consensus about it; as well as prioritized missions, goals, and activities. Policymakers could then use a process to incorporate feedback and respond to new facts and situations as they develop. This report examines how varied, and evolving, homeland security definitions and strategic missions may affect the prioritization of national homeland security policy and how it may affect the funding of homeland security. To address this issue, this report first discusses and analyzes examples of strategic documents, their differing homeland security definitions, and their varying homeland security missions.

Evolution of the Homeland Security Concept

The concept of homeland security has evolved over the last decade. Homeland security as a concept was precipitated by the terrorist attacks of 9/11. However, prior to 9/11 such entities as the Gilmore Commission[2] and the United States Commission on National Security[3] discussed the need to evolve the way national security policy was conceptualized due to the end of the Cold War and the rise of radicalized terrorism. After 9/11, policymakers concluded that a new approach was needed to address the large-scale terrorist attacks. A presidential council and department were established, and a series of presidential directives were issued in the name of "homeland security." These developments established that homeland security was a distinct, but undefined concept.[4] Later, the federal, state, and local government responses to disasters such as Hurricane Katrina expanded the concept of homeland security to include significant disasters, major public health emergencies, and other events that threaten the United States, its economy, the rule of law, and government operations.[5] This later expansion of the concept of homeland security solidified it as something distinct from other federal government security operations such as homeland defense.

Homeland security as a concept suggested a different approach to security, and differed from homeland defense. Homeland defense is primarily a Department of Defense (DOD) activity and is defined as ". . . the protection of U.S. sovereignty, territory, domestic population, and critical defense infrastructure against external threats and aggression, or other threats as directed by the President."[6] Homeland security, regardless of the definition or strategic document, is a combination of law enforcement, disaster, immigration, and terrorism issues. It is primarily the responsibility of civilian agencies at all levels. It is a coordination of efforts at all levels of government. The differences between homeland security and homeland defense, however, are not completely distinct. A international terrorist organization attack on and within the United States would result in a combined homeland security and homeland defense response, such as on 9/11 when civilian agencies were responding to the attacks while the U.S. military established a combat air patrol over New York and Washington, DC. This distinction between homeland security and homeland defense, and the evolution of homeland security as a concept, was reflected in the strategic documents developed and issued following 9/11.

Evolution of Homeland Security Strategic Documents

The evolution of this new and distinct homeland security concept has been communicated in several strategic documents. Today, strategic documents provide guidance to all involved federal entities and include the 2010 *National Security Strategy* and the *2011 National Strategy for Counterterrorism.* There are also strategic documents that provide specific guidance to DHS entities and include the 2010 *Quadrennial Homeland Security Review,* the *Bottom-Up Review,* and the 2012 *Department of Homeland Security Strategic Plan.* Prior to issuance of these documents, national and DHS homeland security strategic documents included the 2002 and 2007 *National Strategies for Homeland Security* and the 2008 *Department of Homeland Security Strategic Plan.* All of these documents have varying definitions for "homeland security" and varying missions derived from these definitions.

While the definitions and missions embodied in these strategic documents have commonalities, there are significant differences. Natural disasters are specifically identified as an integral part of homeland security in five of the seven documents, and only three documents—2008 and 2012 DHS *Strategic Plans* and the *Bottom-Up Review*—specifically include border and maritime security, and immigration in their homeland security definition. All of these mentioned issues are important and require significant funding. However, the lack of consensus about the inclusion of these policy areas in a definition of homeland security may have a negative or unproductive consequences for national homeland security operations. A consensus definition would be useful, but not sufficient. A clear prioritization of strategic missions would help focus and direct federal entities' homeland security activities. Additionally, prioritization affects Congress' authorization, appropriation, and oversight activities.

Effects on Congressional Responsibilities

As deficit reduction causes demand for reduced federal spending, Congress may pay more critical attention to homeland security funding. With reduced funding comes the need for higher degrees of organization, focus, and clarity about the purpose and objectives of national homeland security policy. Limited resources heighten the importance of prioritization and need for efficient and effective federal spending. If homeland security policy priorities are unclear, Congress' ability to provide effective authorization, appropriation, and oversight may be hampered.

Definitions and Missions as Part of Strategy Development

Definitions and missions are part of strategy development. Policymakers develop strategy by identifying national interests, prioritizing missions to achieve those national interests, and arraying instruments of national power to achieve national interests.[7] Strategy is not developed within a vacuum. President Barack Obama administration's 2010 *National Security Strategy* states that strategy is meant to recognize "the world as it is" and mold it into "the world we seek."[8] Developing strategy, however, may be complicated if the key concept of homeland security is not succinctly defined, and strategic missions are not aligned and synchronized among different strategic documents and federal entities.

Evolution of the Homeland Security Definitions and Missions

Prior to 9/11, federal, state, and local governments responded to domestic terrorist attacks in an ad hoc manner. These terrorist attacks, and the governments' responses, however, did not significantly affect how policymakers perceived, defined, and prioritized security as related to the homeland. Two examples of these domestic terrorist attacks are the 1993 World Trade Center (WTC) and the 1995 Alfred Murrah Federal Building bombings.

On February 26, 1993, radicalized Islamic terrorists[9] detonated a bomb beneath the WTC. In response, President Clinton ordered his National Security Council to coordinate the bombings' response and investigation. The CIA's Counterterrorist Center and the National Security Agency, along with the FBI, were among the numerous federal agencies that participated in the investigation.[10] This use of the National Security Council was an ad-hoc response specifically to this event, and it did not result in the development of strategic documents. On April 19, 1995, Timothy McVeigh exploded a bomb-laden truck in front of the Alfred P. Murrah Federal Building in Oklahoma City. Following this bombing, President Clinton directed the Department of Justice (DOJ) to assess the vulnerability of federal facilities to terrorist attacks or violence and to develop recommendations for minimum security standards.[11] These standards, however, were not a wide-ranging strategy for U.S. homeland security strategy. It was the 9/11 terrorist attacks that initiated the debate and development of a broader homeland security strategy.

The 9/11 terrorist attacks on New York City, Pennsylvania, and Washington, DC, were a watershed event. As with the 1993 WTC and 1995 Oklahoma City bombings, the federal, state, and local government's response to the 9/11 terrorists attacks was ad hoc. In New York City, first responders included such entities as the New York police and fire departments, and Port Authority and WTC employees.[12] Following the attack, federal entities such as the FBI, DOD, and elements of the intelligence community (IC) coordinated their efforts in investigating and tracking down the responsible terrorists. However, following the 9/11 initial response and subsequent investigations, it was determined that there was a need to reorganize the government to prepare for, mitigate against, respond to, and recover from future attacks.[13] This decision to reorganize the government resulted in an evolution of homeland security definitions and missions.

The debate over and development of homeland security definitions persists as the federal government continues to issue and implement homeland security strategy. All of the strategic documents in this report define homeland security as security efforts, however, each one defines these efforts in different terms.

2002–2009 Strategic Document Evolution

The first homeland security strategy document issued by the Bush Administration was the 2003 *National Strategy for Homeland Security,* which was revised in 2007.[14] In 2008, DHS issued *Strategic Plan—One Team, One Mission, Securing Our Homeland.* The 2007 *National Strategy for Homeland Security* primarily focused on terrorism, whereas the 2008 *Strategic Plan* included references to all-hazards and border security. Arguably, the 2003 and 2007 *National Strategies for Homeland Security* addressed terrorism due to such incidents as the 9/11 terrorist attacks; and the attempted bombing[15] of American Airlines Flight 93 on December 22, 2001. Whereas the 2008 *Strategic Plan* addressed terrorism and all-hazards due to natural disasters such Hurricane Katrina which occurred in 2005. These documents were superseded by several documents which are now considered the principle homeland security strategies.

2010–Present Document Evolution

The White House and DHS are the principal source of homeland security strategies. The primary national homeland security strategic document developed by the White House is the *2010 National Security Strategy,* which unlike the 2007 *National Strategy for Homeland Security* addresses all-hazards and is not primarily terrorism focused.[16] DHS's strategic documents are the 2010 *Quadrennial Homeland Security Review;* the 2010 *Bottom-Up Review;* and the 2012 *Strategic Plan.* DHS states that these documents are nested in the 2010 *National Security Strategy.*[17] At the national level, the 2010 *National Security Strategy* guides not just DHS's homeland security activities, but it also guides all federal government entity mission activities. One way to understand the breadth of these activities is to examine federal homeland security funding.

Federal Homeland Security Mission Activities and Funding

The strategic homeland security documents provide federal entities information on the national approach to homeland security. These documents are intended to identify federal entity responsibilities in the area of homeland security and assist federal entities in determining how to allocate federal funding for that purpose.

In an effort to measure federal homeland security funding, Congress required OMB to include a homeland security funding analysis in each presidential budget.[18] OMB requires federal departments, agencies, and entities to provide budget request amounts based on the following six 2003 *National Strategy for Homeland Security* mission areas:

- Intelligence and Warning;
- Border and Transportation Security;
- Domestic Counterterrorism;
- Protecting Critical Infrastructure and Key Assets;
- Defending against Catastrophic Threats; and
- Emergency Preparedness and Response.[19]

OMB, however, notes that the *National Strategy for Homeland Security* was revised in 2007, and that revision consolidated these six mission areas into three: (1) prevent and disrupt terrorist attacks; (2) protect the American people, critical infrastructure, and key resources; and (3) respond to and recover from incidents that do occur. The strategy also states that these original 2003 mission areas are still used to ensure "continuity and granularity."[20] OMB does not address President Obama Administration's issuance of the 2010 *National Security Strategy* which supersedes the 2007 *National Strategy for Homeland Security*.

In FY2012 appropriations and the FY2013 budget requests, thirty federal departments, agencies, and entities receive annual homeland security funding excluding DHS. OMB estimates that 48% of annual homeland security funding is appropriated to these federal entities, with DOD receiving approximately 26% of total federal homeland security funding. DHS receives approximately 52%. The following table provides FY2012 appropriations and FY2013 budget request homeland security mission amounts for all federal entities.

This allocation of federal homeland security funding reveals that approximately 50% is *not* appropriated for DHS missions or activities. Additionally, it could mean that relying on detailed DHS strategies is insufficient and that a coordinating and encompassing national homeland security definition may be important to prioritizing homeland security activities and funding.

The 2010 *National Security Strategy* states that homeland security is "a seamless coordination among federal, state, and local governments to prevent, protect against, and respond to threats and natural disasters."[21] Homeland security requires coordination because numerous federal, state, and local entities have responsibility for various homeland security activities. The proliferation of responsibilities entitled "homeland security activities" is due to a couple of factors. One factor is that homeland security developed from the pre-9/11 concept of law enforcement and emergency management. Another factor is the continuously evolving definition of "homeland security." Some degree of evolution of the homeland security concept is expected. Policymakers respond to events and crises like terrorist attacks and natural disasters by using and adjusting strategies, plans, and operations. These strategies, plans, and operations also evolve to reflect changing priorities. The definition of homeland security evolves in accordance with the evolution of these strategies, plans, and operations.

Definitions

The following table provides examples of strategic documents and their specific homeland security definitions.

Some common themes among these definitions are:

- the homeland security enterprise encompasses a federal, state, local, and tribal government and private sector approach that requires coordination;
- homeland security can involve securing against and responding to both hazardspecific and all-hazards threats; and
- homeland security activities do not imply total protection or complete threat reduction.

Each of these documents highlight the importance of coordinating homeland security missions and activities. However, individual federal, state, local, and tribal government efforts

TABLE 1 FY2012 Appropriations and FY2013 Request for Homeland Security Mission Funding by Agency

(budget authority in millions of dollars)

Department	FY2012 Enacted	FY2013 Request	FY2013 Request as % of Total
Agriculture	570.1	551.4	0.80
Commerce	289.6	304.1	0.44
Defense	17,358.4	17,955.1	26.05
Education	30.9	35.5	0.05
Energy	1,923.3	1,874.7	2.72
Health and Human Services	4,146.8	4,112.2	5.97
Homeland Security	35,214.7	35,533.7	51.57
Housing and Urban Development	3.0	3.0	–[a]
Interior	57.6	56.7	0.08
Justice	4,055.4	3,992.8	5.79
Labor	46.3	36.6	0.05
State	2,283.4	2,353.8	3.42
Transportation	246.6	243.3	0.35
Treasury	123.0	121.1	0.18
Veterans Affairs	394.5	383.7	0.56
Corps of Engineers	35.5	35.5	0.05
Environmental Protection Agency	101.8	102.6	0.15
Executive Office of the President	10.4	11.0	0.02
General Services Administration	38.0	59.0	0.09
National Aeronautics and Space Administration	228.9	216.1	0.31
National Science Foundation	443.9	425.9	0.62
Office of Personnel Management	1.3	0.6	–[b]
Social Security Administration	234.3	252.1	0.37
District of Columbia	15.0	25.0	0.04
Federal Communications Commission	-	1.7	–[c]
Intelligence Community Management Account	8.8	-	-
National Archives and Records Administration	22.6	22.5	0.03
Nuclear Regulatory Commission	78.4	76.6	0.11
Securities and Exchange Commission	8.0	8.0	0.01
Smithsonian Institution	97.0	100.1	0.15
U.S. Holocaust Memorial Museum	11.0	11.0	0.02
Total	**67,988.0**	**68,905.2**[d]	**100%**[e]

Source: U.S. Office of Management and Budget, *Budget of the United States Government, Fiscal Year 2013: Analytical Perspectives*, February 2012, "Appendix – Homeland Security Mission Funding by Agency and Budget Account," http://www.whitehouse.gov/sites/default/files/omb/budget/fy2013/assets/homeland_supp.pdf.

a. This amount is less than 0.01%.

b. This amount is less than 0.01%.

c. This amount is less than 0.01%.

d. The majority of this funding is categorized as protecting critical infrastructure and key assets.

e. Percentages in column may not equal 100 due to rounding.

TABLE 2 Summary of Homeland Security Definitions

Document	Definition
2007 *National Strategy for Homeland Security* (White House)	A concerted national effort to prevent terrorist attacks within the United States, reduce America's vulnerability to terrorism, and minimize the damage and recover from attacks that do occur.[a]
2008 *U.S. Department of Homeland Security Strategic Plan, Fiscal Years 2008–2013* (DHS)	A unified national effort to prevent and deter terrorist attacks, protect and respond to hazards, and to secure the national borders.[b]
2010 *National Security Strategy* (White House)	A seamless coordination among federal, state, and local governments to prevent, protect against and respond to threats and natural disasters.[c]
2010 *Quadrennial Homeland Security Review* (DHS)	A concerted national effort to ensure a homeland that is safe, secure, and resilient against terrorism and other hazards where American interests, aspirations, and ways of life can thrive.[d]
2010 *Bottom-Up Review* (DHS)	Preventing terrorism, responding to and recovering from natural disasters, customs enforcement and collection of customs revenue, administration of legal immigration services, safety and stewardship of the Nation's waterways and marine transportation system, as well as other legacy missions of the various components of DHS.[e]
2011 *National Strategy For Counterterrorism* (White House)	Defensive efforts to counter terrorist threats.[f]
2012 *Strategic Plan* (DHS)	Efforts to ensure a homeland that is safe, secure, and resilient against terrorism and other hazards.[g]

a. Office of the President, Homeland Security Council, *The National Homeland Security Strategy,* Washington, DC, October 2007, p. 1.

b. U.S. Department of Homeland Security, *One Team, One Mission, Securing the Homeland: U.S. Homeland Security Strategic Plan, Fiscal Years 2008–2013,* Washington, DC, 2008, p. 3.

c. Office of the President, *National Security Strategy,* Washington, DC, May 2010, p. 2.

d. U.S. Department of Homeland Security, *Quadrennial Homeland Security Review,* Washington, DC, February 2010, p. 13.

e. U.S. Department of Homeland Security, *Bottom-Up Review,* Washington, DC, July 2010, p. 3.

f. Office of the President, National Strategy for Counterterrorism, Washington, DC, June 2011, p. 11.

g. U.S. Department of Homeland Security, Department of Homeland Security Strategic Plan: Fiscal Years 2012–2016, Washington, DC, February 2012, p. 2. This document does not explicitly state a definition for "homeland security" but it does define DHS's "vision."

are not identified in the documents. Homeland security—according to these documents—is preventing, responding to, and recovering from terrorist attacks, which is consistent with evolving homeland security policy after 9/11.

The focus of the definition of homeland security communicated in these strategy documents differs in regard to two areas that may be considered substantive. Natural disasters are specifically identified as an integral part of homeland security in only four of the six documents, but are not mentioned in the 2007 *National Strategy for Homeland*

Security and the 2011 *National Strategy for Counterterrorism.*[22] Only one document—the *Bottom-Up Review*—specifically includes border and maritime security, and immigration in their homeland security definition. The 2012 *Strategic Plan* uses the encompassing terms "other hazards" to define any threat other than terrorism. These issues are significant and call for substantial funding. An absence of consensus about the inclusion of these policy areas may result in unintended consequences for national homeland security operations. For example, not including maritime security in the homeland security definition may result in policymakers, Congress, and stakeholders not adequately addressing maritime homeland security threats, or more specifically being able to prioritize federal investments in border versus intelligence activities.

The competing and varied definitions in these documents may indicate that there is no succinct homeland security concept. Without a succinct homeland security concept, policymakers and entities with homeland security responsibilities may not successfully coordinate or focus on the highest prioritized or most necessary activities. Coordination is especially essential to homeland security because of the multiple federal agencies and the state and local partners with whom they interact. Coordination may be difficult if these entities do not operate with the same understanding of the homeland security concept. For example, definitions that don't specifically include immigration or natural disaster response and recovery may result in homeland security stakeholders and federal entities not adequately resourcing and focusing on these activities. Additionally, an absence of a consensus definition may result in Congress funding a homeland security activity that DHS does not consider a priority. For example, Congress may appropriate funding for a counterterrorism program such as the State Homeland Security Grant Program when DHS may have identified an all-hazards grant program, such as Emergency Management Performance Grant Program, as a priority.

It is, however, possible that a consensus definition and overall concept exists among policymakers and federal entities, but that it isn't communicated in the strategic documents.[23]

Finally, DHS Deputy Secretary Jane Lute recently stated that homeland security ". . . is operation, it's transactional, it's decentralized, it's bottom-driven," and influenced by law enforcement, emergency management, and the political environment. Conversely, DHS Deputy Secretary Lute stated that national security ". . . is strategic, it's centralized, it's top-driven," and influenced by the military and the intelligence community.[24] Some see in these comments as a reflection of a DHS attempt to establish a homeland security definition that is more operational than strategic and an illustration of the complexity of a common understanding of homeland security and its associated missions.

Missions

Varied homeland security definitions, in numerous documents, result in all the homeland security stakeholders identifying and executing varied strategic missions. Homeland security stakeholders include federal departments and agencies, state and local governments, and non-profit and non-governmental organizations. The strategic documents in this report identify numerous homeland security missions such as terrorism prevention; response and recovery; critical infrastructure protection and resilience; federal, state, and local emergency management and preparedness; and border security. As noted earlier, none of these

TABLE 3 Summary of Homeland Security Missions and Goals

Document	Missions and Goals
2007 *National Strategy for Homeland Security* (White House)	- Prevent and disrupt terrorist attacks. - Protect the American people, critical infrastructure and key resources. - Respond to and recover from incidents that do occur. - Strengthen the foundation to ensure long term success.[a]
2008 *U.S. Department of Homeland Security Strategic Plan, Fiscal Years 2008–2013* (DHS)	- Protect the nation from dangerous people. - Protect the nation from dangerous goods. - Protect critical infrastructure. - Strengthen the nation's preparedness and emergency response capabilities. - Strengthen and unify the department's operations and management.[b]
2010 *National Security Strategy* (White House)	- Strengthen national capacity. - Ensure security and prosperity at home. - Secure cyberspace. - Ensure American economic prosperity.[c]
2010 *Quadrennial Homeland Security Review* (DHS)	- Prevent terrorism and enhance security. - Secure and manage our borders. - Enforce and administer our immigration laws. - Safeguard and secure cyberspace. - Ensure resilience to disasters.[d] - Provide essential support to national and economic security.[e]
2010 *Bottom-Up Review* (DHS)	- Prevent terrorism and enhance security. - Secure and manage borders. - Enforce and manage immigration laws. - Safeguard and secure cyberspace. - Ensure resilience to disasters. - Improve departmental management and accountability.[f]
2011 *National Strategy for Counterterrorism* (White House)	- Protect the American people, homeland, and American interests. - Eliminate threats to the American people's, homeland's, and interests' physical safety. - Counter threats to global peace and security. - Promote and protect U.S. interests around the globe.[g]
2012 *Strategic Plan* (DHS)	- Preventing terrorism and enhancing security. - Securing and managing our borders. - Enforcing and administering our immigration laws. - Safeguarding and securing cyberspace. - Ensuring resilience to disasters.[h] - Providing essential support to national and economic security.[i]

a. Office of the President, Homeland Security Council, *National Strategy for Homeland Security,* Washington, DC, October 2007, p. 1.

b. U.S. Department of Homeland Security, *One Team, One Mission, Securing the Homeland: U.S. Homeland Security Strategic Plan, Fiscal Years 2008–2013,* Washington, DC, 2008, p. 6–25.

c. Office of the President, *National Security Strategy,* Washington, DC, May 2010, p. 14.

d. U.S. Department of Homeland Security, *Quadrennial Homeland Security Review,* Washington, DC, February 2010, p. 2.

f. U.S. Department of Homeland Security, *Bottom-Up Review,* Washington, DC, July 2010, pp. i–ii.

g. Office of the President, *National Strategy for Counterterrorism,* Washington, DC, June 2011, p. 8.

h. U.S. Department of Homeland Security, *Department of Homeland Security Strategic Goal: Fiscal Years 2012–2016,* Washington, DC, February 2012, pp. 3–18.

i. The 2012 Strategic Plan does not designate this as a specific mission, but it does state that "DHS contributes in many ways to these elements to broader U.S. national and economic security while fulfilling its homeland security missions." U.S. Department of Homeland Security, *Department of Homeland Security Strategic Goal: Fiscal Years 2012–2016,* Washington, DC, February 2012, p. 19.

documents specifically task a federal entity with the overall homeland security responsibilities. The table above summarizes the varied missions in these strategic documents.

These documents all identify specific missions as essential to securing the nation. All of the documents state that the nation's populace, critical infrastructure, and key resources need protection from terrorism and disasters. This protection from both terrorism and disasters is a key strategic homeland security mission. Some, but not all, of the documents include missions related to border security, immigration, the economy, and general resilience. Members of Congress and congressional committees, however, have sometimes criticized these documents.

Senator Susan Collins—current Ranking Member, Committee on Homeland Security and Governmental Affairs—expressed disappointment in the *Quadrennial Homeland Security Review* and *Bottom-Up Review* because it does not communicate priorities and stated that it does not compare favorably to the most recent *Quadrennial Defense Review.*[25] The *Quadrennial Defense Review* identifies national security and U.S. military priorities and these priorities through a process ". . . from objectives to capabilities and activities to resources."[26] Furthermore, the *Quadrennial Homeland Security Review* missions are different from the *2007 National Strategy for Homeland Security*[27] missions, and neither identifies priorities, or resources, for DHS, or other federal agencies. Since the *National Strategy for Homeland Security* and the *Quadrennial Homeland Security Review* missions are differing and varied, and because the *Quadrennial Homeland Security Review* does not specifically identify a strategic process to achieve the missions, one may assume that this document is solely operational guidance. Additionally, some critics found the *Bottom-Up Review* lacking in detail and failing to meet its intended purpose.[28]

Further congressional criticism includes an observation on the absence of a single DHS strategy. At a recent House Homeland Security Committee's Subcommittee on Oversight, Investigations and Management hearing, Chairman Michael McCaul stated that ". . . DHS needs a single strategic document which subordinate agencies can follow and make sure the strategy is effectively and efficiently implemented. This single document should conform to the National Security Strategy of the United States of America. If the agencies do not have clearly established list of priorities, it will be difficult to complete assigned missions."[29]

Other criticism includes the Council on Foreign Relations' (CFR) discussion of 2010 *National Security Strategy* (NSS). CFR states that the ". . . one thing that the NSS discussion of resilience omits, but which the Deputy National Security Adviser John Brennan has emphasized, is that despite all the homeland security precautions, there is likely to be a successful attack. When that happens, real resilience will entail a calm, deliberate response and confidence in the durability of the country's institutions."[30] Multiple definitions, missions, and an absence of prioritization results in consequences to the nation's security.

Analysis and Considerations

Policymakers are faced with a complex and detailed list of risks, or threats to security, for which they then attempt to plan. However, managing those risks 99% of the time with even a single failure may lead to significant human and financial costs.[31] Homeland security is essentially about managing risks. The purpose of a strategic process is to develop missions to achieve that end. Before risk management can be accurate and adequate, policymakers must ideally coordinate and communicate. That work to some degree depends on developing a foundation of common definitions of key terms and concepts. It is also necessary, in order to coordinate and communicate, to ensure stakeholders are aware of, trained for, and prepared to meet assigned missions. At the national level, there does not appear to be an attempt to align definitions and missions among disparate federal entities. DHS is, however, attempting to align its definition and missions, but does not prioritize its missions; there is no clarity in the national strategies of federal, state, and local roles and responsibilities; and, potentially, funding is driving priorities rather than priorities driving the funding.

DHS is aligning its definition and missions in the *Quadrennial Homeland Security Review,* the *Bottom-Up Review,* and the 2012 *Strategic Plan;* however, DHS does not prioritize the missions. DHS prioritizes specific goals, objectives, activities, and specific initiatives within the missions, and prioritizes initiatives across the missions. There is still no single national homeland security definition, nor is there a prioritization of national homeland security or DHS missions.

There is no evidence in the existing homeland security strategic documents that supports the aligning and prioritization of the varied missions, nor do any of the documents convey how national, state, or local resources are to be allocated to achieve these missions. Without prioritized resource allocation to align missions, proponents of prioritization of the nation's homeland security activities and operations maintain that plans and responses may be haphazard and inconsistent. Another potential consequence of the absence of clear missions is that available funding then tends to govern the priorities.

Congress may decide to address the issues associated with homeland security strategy, definitions, and missions, in light of the potential for significant events to occur similar to the 9/11 terrorist attacks and Hurricane Katrina. Many observers assert that these outstanding policy issues result from the varied definitions and missions identified in numerous national strategic documents. Additionally, they note that these documents do not consistently address risk mitigation associated with the full range of homeland security threats. From this perspective one piece missing from these documents, and their guidance, is a discussion of the resources and fiscal costs associated with preparing for low risk, but high consequence threats.

Specifically, Congress may choose to consider a number of options addressing the apparent lack of a consensus homeland security definition that prioritizes missions by requiring the development of a more succinct, and distinct, national homeland security strategy. One of these options might be a total rewrite of a national homeland security strategy. This option would be similar to the Bush Administration's issuance of national homeland security strategies in 2002 and 2007. Such a strategy could include a definitive listing of mission priorities based on an encompassing definition that not only includes DHS specific responsibilities, but all federal department and agency responsibilities. A strategy that includes priorities could improve Congress's and other policymakers' ability to make choices between competing homeland security missions. This option would also be a departure from the current Administration's practice of including national homeland security guidance in the *National Security Strategy.*

Another option would be to build upon the current approach by requiring the Administration to develop the *National Security Strategy* that succinctly identifies homeland security missions and priorities. Alternatively, Congress may determine that the present course of including national homeland security guidance in the *National Security Strategy* is adequate, and may focus strictly on DHS activities. This option would entail DHS further refining its *Quadrennial Homeland Security Review* which it has begun to do with its 2012 *Strategic Plan.*

It has been argued that homeland security, at its core, is about coordination because of the disparate stakeholders and risks.[32] Many observers assert that homeland security is not only about coordination of resources and actions to counter risks; it is also about the coordination of the strategic process policymakers use in determining the risks, the stakeholders and their missions, and the prioritization of those missions.

Without a general consensus on the physical and philosophical definition and missions of homeland security, achieved through a strategic process, some believe that there will continue to be the potential for disjointed and disparate approaches to securing the nation. From this perspective general consensus on the homeland security concept necessarily starts with a consensus definition and an accepted list of prioritized missions that are constantly reevaluated to meet risks of the new paradigm that is homeland security in the 21st century. These varied definitions and missions, however, may be the result of a strategic process that has attempted to adjust federal homeland security policy to emerging threats and risks.

Critical Thinking Questions

1. What are the implications of there being so many definitions of homeland security?
2. Do these implications differ according to whether you work in a local, state, or federal organization? Explain.
3. Does the lack of a universally defined concept of homeland security undermine our nation's ability to protect its infrastructure and citizens? Why, or why not?

Notes

1. U.S. Office of Management and Budget, *Budget of the United States Government, Fiscal Year 2013: Analytical Perspectives,* February 2012, "Appendix—Homeland Security Mission Funding by Agency and Budget Account," http://www.whitehouse.gov/sites/default/files/omb/budget/fy2013/assets/homeland_supp.pdf.
2. For information on the Gilmore Commission, see http://www.rand.org/nsrd/terrpanel.html. The Gilmore Commission was established prior to 9/11; however, it released its fifth and final report in December 2003.
3. For information on the U.S. Commission on National Security, see http://www.fas.org/irp/threat/nssg.pdf. The U.S. Commission on National Security was established in 1998 and issued its final report in February 2001. The commission did reference the idea of "homeland security" in early 2001.
4. Harold C. Relyea, "Homeland Security and Information," *Government Information Quarterly,* vol. 19, 2002, p. 219.
5. Nadav Morag, "Does Homeland Security Exist Outside the United States?," *Homeland Security Affairs,* vol. 7, September 2011, p. 1.
6. U.S. Department of Defense, *Homeland Defense,* Joint Publications 3–27, Washington, DC, 2007, p. vii.

7. Terry L. Deibel, *Foreign Affairs Strategy: Logic for American Statecraft* (New York: Cambridge University Press, 2007), p. 5.
8. Executive Office of the President, *National Security Strategy,* Washington, DC, May 2010, p. 9.
9. An FBI investigation identified the following individuals as the culprits: Mohammed Salameh, Ahmad Ajaj, Ramzi Yousef, Mahmoud Abouhalima, and Sheikh Omar Abdel Rahman (often called the "Blind Sheikh"). All of these individuals were prosecuted and convicted.
10. National Commission on Terrorist Attacks Upon the United States, *The 9/11 Commission Report,* Washington, DC, July 22, 2004, p. 71.
11. U.S. Government Accountability Office, *Building Security: Interagency Security Committee Has Had Limited Success in Fulfilling Its Responsibilities,* GAO-02-1004, September 2002, p. 5.
12. National Commission on Terrorist Attacks Upon the United States, *The 9/11 Commission Report,* Washington, DC, July 22, 2004, p. 315.
13. National Commission on Terrorist Attacks Upon the United States, *The 9/11 Commission Report,* Washington, DC, July 22, 2004, p. 399. The 9/11 Commission determined that there needed to be a unity of effort across the foreign domestic divide, in the IC, in sharing information, and in Congress.
14. This report does not provide the 2003 *National Strategy for Homeland Security* definitions and missions due to it being revised in 2007.
15. Richard Reid was dubbed the "Shoe Bomber" because of his disguising of the bomb within his shoe.
16. President Obama's Administration addresses the terrorism issue specifically in the 2011 *National Strategy for Counterterrorism.*
17. U.S. Department of Homeland Security, 2012 Department of Homeland Security Strategic Plan: Fiscal Years 2012–2016, Washington, DC, February 2012, p. A-3.
18. P.L. 107–296 (Homeland Security Act of 2002), sec. 889.
19. Office of Management and Budget, *Circular No. A-11: Preparation, Submission, and Execution of the Budget,* Instructions for Homeland Security Data Collection, Washington, DC, August 2011, http://www.whitehouse.gov/sites/default/files/omb/assets/a11_current_year/homeland.pdf.
20. Ibid.
21. Office of the President, *National Security Strategy,* Washington, DC, May 2010, p. 2.
22. The *National Strategy For Counterterrorism* would not mention any hazard or threat other than terrorism.
23. Examination of such a possibility is beyond the scope of this report.
24. Christopher Bellavita, "A new perspective on homeland security?" Homeland Security Watch, December 20, 2011, http://www.hlswatch.com/2011/12/20/a-new-perspective-on-homeland-security/.
25. U.S. Congress, Senate Committee on Homeland Security and Governmental Affairs, *Charting a Path Forward: The Homeland Security Department's Quadrennial Review and Bottom-Up Review,* 111th Cong., 2nd sess., July 21, 2010.
26. U.S. Department of Defense, *Quadrennial Defense Review,* Washington, DC, February 2010, p. iii.
27. The 2007 *National Strategy for Homeland Security* is the most recent national strategy specifically on homeland security.

28. Katherine McIntire Peters, "DHS Bottom-Up Review is long on ambition, short on detail," *GovernmentExecutive.com*, July 2010.
29. U.S. Congress, House Committee on Homeland Security, Subcommittee on Oversight, Investigations, and Management, *Is DHS Effectively Implementing a Strategy to Counter Emerging Threats?,* 112th Cong., 2nd sess., February 3, 2011.
30. Stephen Biddle, Laurie Garrett, and James M. Lindsay, et al., "Obama's NSS: Promise and Pitfalls," *Council on Foreign Relations,* May 28, 2010, http://www.cfr.org/defensehomeland-security/obamas-nss-promise-pitfalls/p22240.
31. Donald F. Kettl, *System Under Stress: Homeland Security and American Politics,* 2nd ed., Washington, DC, *CQPress,* 2007, p. 82.
32. Ibid.

Section 1.2

Defining the Threat

The Terrorism Delusion

America's Overwrought Response to September 11

John Mueller and Mark G. Stewart

On November 22, 1963, Lee Harvey Oswald, a deluded little man with grandiose visions of his own importance, managed, largely because of luck, to assassinate President John F. Kennedy. Since then, many people have contended that such a monumental event could not have been accomplished by such a trivial person. Some of these disbelievers have undertaken elaborate efforts to uncover a bigger conspiracy behind the deed.

On September 11, 2001, a tiny group of deluded men—members of al-Qaida, a fringe group of a fringe group with grandiose visions of its own importance—managed, again largely because of luck, to pull off a risky, if clever and carefully planned, terrorist act that became by far the most destructive in history. As with the assassination of President Kennedy, there has been great reluctance to maintain that such a monumental event—however counterproductive to al-Qaida's purpose—could have been carried out by a fundamentally trivial group, and there has been a consequent tendency to inflate al-Qaida's importance and effectiveness. At the extreme, the remnants of this tiny group have even been held to present an "existential" threat to the very survival of the United States.[1]

In the wake of September 11, recalls Rudy Giuliani, mayor of New York at the time of the attacks, "[a]nybody, any one of these security experts, including myself, would have told you on September 11, 2001, we're looking at dozens and dozens and multiyears of attacks like this." Journalist Jane Mayer observes that "the only certainty shared by virtually the entire American intelligence community" in the months after September 11 "was that a second wave of even more devastating terrorist attacks on America was imminent."[2] Under the prevailing circumstances, this sort of alarm was understandable, but it does not excuse the experts from dismissing an alternative hypothesis—that the attacks that occurred on that day were an aberration.[3]

Finally, on May 1, 2012, nearly ten years after the September 2001 terrorist attacks, the most costly and determined manhunt in history culminated in Pakistan when a team of U.S. Navy Seals killed Osama bin Laden, a chief author of the attacks and one of history's most storied and cartooned villains. Taken away with bin Laden's bullet-shattered body were written documents and masses of information stored on five computers, ten hard drives, and one hundred or more thumb drives, DVDs, and CD-ROMs. This, it was promised, represented a "treasure trove" of information about al-Qaida—"the mother lode," said one U.S. official eagerly—that might contain plans for pending attacks.[4] Poring through the material with great dispatch, however, a task force soon discovered that al-Qaida's members were primarily occupied with dodging drone missile attacks, complaining about the lack of funds, and watching a lot of pornography.[5]

Although bin Laden has been exposed mostly as a thing of smoke and mirrors, and although there has been no terrorist destruction that remotely rivals that inflicted on September 11, the terrorism/counterterrorism saga persists determinedly, doggedly, and anticlimactically onward, and the initial alarmed perspective has been internalized. In the process, suggests Glenn Carle, a twenty-three-year veteran of the Central Intelligence

Agency where he was deputy national intelligence officer for transnational threats, Americans have become "victims of delusion," displaying a quality defined as "a persistent false belief in the face of strong contradictory evidence."[6] This condition shows no sign of abating as trillions of dollars have been expended and tens of thousands of lives have been snuffed out in distant wars in a frantic, ill-conceived effort to react to an event that, however tragic and dramatic in the first instance, should have been seen, at least after a few years had passed, to be of limited significance.

This article is a set of ruminations on the post–September 11 years of delusion. It reflects, first, on the exaggerations of the threat presented by terrorism and then on the distortions of perspective these exaggerations have inspired—distortions that have in turn inspired a determined and expensive quest to ferret out, and even to create, the nearly nonexistent. It also supplies a quantitative assessment of the costs of the terrorism delusion and concludes with a discussion of how anxieties about terrorism persist despite exceedingly limited evidence that much fear is justified.

Delusions about the Terrorist "Adversary"

People such as Giuliani and a whole raft of "security experts" have massively exaggerated the capacities and the dangers presented by what they have often called "the universal adversary" both in its domestic and in its international form.

The Domestic Adversary

To assess the danger presented by terrorists seeking to attack the United States, we examined the fifty cases of Islamist extremist terrorism that have come to light since the September 11 attacks, whether based in the United States or abroad, in which the United States was, or apparently was, targeted. These cases make up (or generate) the chief terrorism fear for Americans. Table 1 presents a capsule summary of each case, and the case numbers given throughout this article refer to this table and to the free web book from which it derives.[7]

In 2009, the U.S. Department of Homeland Security (DHS) issued a lengthy report on protecting the homeland. Key to achieving such an objective should be a careful assessment of the character, capacities, and desires of potential terrorists targeting that homeland. Although the report contains a section dealing with what its authors call "the nature of the terrorist adversary," the section devotes only two sentences to assessing that nature: "The number and high profile of international and domestic terrorist attacks and disrupted plots during the last two decades underscore the determination and persistence of terrorist organizations. Terrorists have proven to be relentless, patient, opportunistic, and flexible, learning from experience and modifying tactics and targets to exploit perceived vulnerabilities and avoid observed strengths."[8]

This description may apply to some terrorists somewhere, including at least a few of those involved in the September 11 attacks. Yet, it scarcely describes the vast majority of those individuals picked up on terrorism charges in the United States since those attacks. The inability of the DHS to consider this fact even parenthetically in its fleeting discussion is not only amazing but perhaps delusional in its single-minded preoccupation with the extreme.

TABLE 1 The American Cases (by number, title, type, year of arrest, and description)

This table contains cases of Islamist extremist terrorism that have come to light since the terrorist attacks of September 11, 2001, whether based in the United States or abroad, in which the United States was, or apparently was, targeted.

1 The shoe bomber *4* 2001 British man tries to blow up a U.S.-bound airliner with explosives in his shoes but is subdued by passengers and crew

2 Padilla *1* 2002 American connected to al-Qaida who had discussed a dirty bomb attack returns to the United States and is arrested

3 Mount Rushmore *3* 2002 Crucially aided by an informant, two men in Florida, one of them possibly connected to an al-Qaida operative, plot to bomb local targets as well as Mount Rushmore before September 11, and are arrested and tried the next year

4 El Al at LAX *4* 2002 His business and marriage failing dismally, a depressed anti-Israel Egyptian national shoots and kills two at the El Al ticket counter at Los Angeles airport before being killed himself in an act later considered to be one of terrorism

5 Lackawanna *1* 2002 Seven Americans in Lackawanna, New York, are induced to travel to an al-Qaida training camp, but six return disillusioned—all before the terrorist attacks of September 11—and are arrested the next year

6 Paracha *2* 2003 A young Pakistani seeks to help an al-Qaida operative enter the country to attack underground storage tanks and gas stations

7 Ali *2* 2003 A U.S. citizen joins a terrorist cell in Saudi Arabia and plots to hijack a plane in the United States and to assassinate President George W. Bush when he is arrested by the Saudis and extradited to the United States for trial

8 Columbus and the Brooklyn Bridge *2* 2003 American connected to al-Qaida discusses shooting up a shopping mall in Columbus, Ohio, with two friends, then scouts taking down the Brooklyn Bridge for al-Qaida but decides it is too difficult

9 Barot and the financial buildings *2* 2004 Group in London tied to al-Qaida scouts out financial buildings in the United States with an eye to bombing them, but never gets to the issue of explosives

10 Albany *3* 2004 Two men in Albany, New York, effectively help fund an informant's terror plot

11 Nettles *3* 2004 Under the nickname of "Ben Laden," an American with a long history of criminal and mental problems plots to blow up a federal courthouse in Chicago and reaches out for help to a Middle Eastern terrorist group, but gets the FBI

12 Herald Square *3* 2004 Loud-mouthed jihadist in New York and a schizophrenic friend attract informant who helps them lay plans to bomb Herald Square subway station

13 Grecula *3* 2005 An American with visions of being an modern-day Spartacus agrees to build a bomb to be exploded in the United States for undercover agents claiming to be al-Qaida

14 Lodi *1* 2005 American in Lodi, California, who may have attended a training camp in Pakistan but with no apparent plan to commit violence is arrested with the aid of an informant

15 JIS *2* 2005 American in jail masterminds a plot by three others to shoot up military recruitment centers, synagogues, and a nonexistent military base in the Los Angeles area but, although close to their first attack, the plot is disrupted when they leave a cellphone behind at a funds-raising robbery

16 The pipeline bomber and the terrorism hunter *3* 2005 An American offers on the internet to blow up pipelines in Canada as an aid to al-Qaida and attracts the attention of a freelance informant

17 University of North Carolina *4* 2006 To punish the U.S. government for actions around the world, a former student, after failing to go abroad to fight or to join the air force so he could drop a nuclear bomb on Washington, D.C., drives a rented SUV onto campus to run over as many Americans as possible and manages to injure nine

18 Hudson River tunnels *2* 2006 Angered by the U.S. invasion of Iraq, several men based in Lebanon plot to flood railway tunnels under the Hudson River, but are arrested overseas before acquiring bomb materials or setting foot in the United States

19 Sears Tower *3* 2006 Seven men in Miami plot with an informant, whom they claim they were trying to con, to take down the Sears Tower in Chicago, then focus on closer buildings

20 Transatlantic airliner bombings *2* 2006 Small group in London, under intense police surveillance from the beginning, plots to explode liquid bombs on U.S.-bound airliners

21 Rockford *3* 2006 Loud-mouthed jihadist attracts attention of an informant and together they plot to explode grenades at a shopping mall in Rockford, Illinois

22 Fort Dix *3* 2007 Small group target practices, buys guns, and plots to attack Fort Dix, New Jersey, with the aid of an informant who joins the group when the FBI is told they took a jihadist video into a shop to be duplicated

23 JFK airport *3* 2007 Small group, with informant, plots to blow up fuel lines serving John F. Kennedy International Airport in New York

24 Vinas *2* 2008 New York man travels to Pakistan, is accepted into al-Qaida, and plots to plant a bomb in the United States, but is being watched and talks after being arrested

25 Bronx synagogues *3* 2009 Four men, with crucial aid from an informant, plot to bomb synagogues in Bronx, New York, and shoot down a plane at a military base

26 Little Rock *4* 2009 American man travels to Middle East to get training, but fails, and on return, working as a lone wolf, eventually shoots and kills one soldier at a military recruitment center in Little Rock, Arkansas

27 Boyd and Quantico *2* 2009 Complicated conspiracy in North Carolina, including an informant, gathers weapons and may have targeted Quantico Marine Base

28 Zazi *2* 2009 Afghan-American and two friends travel to Pakistan to join the Taliban, but are recruited by al-Qaida to plant bombs on New York subways instead, and are under surveillance throughout

29 Springfield *3* 2009 Loud-mouthed jihadist plots, with informants, to set off a bomb in Springfield, Illinois

30 Dallas skyscraper *3* 2009 Jordanian on a student visa rouses interest from the FBI in internet postings and, together with three agents, tries to detonate a fake bomb in the basement of a Dallas skyscraper

31 Mehanna *2* 2009 Well-educated Muslim jihadist may have plotted briefly to shoot up a shopping center in the Boston area and tried to join insurgency in the Middle East, but is arrested for spreading jihadist propaganda

32 Fort Hood *4* 2009 Military psychiatrist, acting as a lone wolf, shoots up a military deployment center in Fort Hood, Texas, killing twelve soldiers and one civilian, shortly before he is supposed to be deployed to the war in Afghanistan

33 The underwear bomber *4* 2009 Nigerian man tries to blow up a U.S.-bound airliner with explosives in his underwear but is subdued by passengers and crew

34 Times Square *4* 2010 Pakistani-American gets training in Pakistan and on his own tries, but fails, to set off a car bomb in Times Square in New York

35 Alaska *3* 2010 Muslim convert in a remote Alaskan town plots the assassination of twenty with the aid of an undercover agent

36 Parcel bombs on cargo planes *2* 2010 An effort by al-Qaida in the Arabian Peninsula to set off parcel bombs implanted in printer cartridges on cargo planes bound for the United States is disrupted

37 DC Metro bomb plot *3* 2010 Pakistani-American aids FBI operatives posing as al-Qaida in a plot to bomb the Metro in Washington, D.C.

38 Oregon *3* 2010 Teenaged Somali-American jihadist, unable to go abroad to fight, works with FBI operatives, who were apparently alerted by his father, to set off a van bomb at a Christmas tree lighting ceremony in Portland, Oregon

39 DC Metro–Facebook *2* 2010 Virginia man brags without substance to a female Facebook correspondent that he will soon bomb the Washington Metro and is quickly arrested for making interstate threats, receiving a light sentence

40 Baltimore *3* 2010 Baltimore man seeks allies on Facebook for violent jihad, and the FBI supplies him with an informant and a fake SUV bomb with which he tries to blow up a military recruitment center

41 Texas *2* 2011 Saudi student in Texas, flunking out and displaying intense new discontent on his blog and Facebook profile, is arrested after buying bomb-making materials and considering potential targets, including crowded streets in distant New York and a local residence of former President George W. Bush

(*continued*)

TABLE 1 *(Continued)*

42 Manhattan's pair of lone wolves *3* 2011 Upset with how the United States treats Muslims around the world, a mentally ill American citizen, with accomplice and undercover officer, purchases weapons as the first step in a plot to blow up synagogues, the Empire State Building, and other targets in New York and New Jersey

43 Pentagon shooter *2* 2011 A U.S. Marine reservist with jihadist literature shoots at military buildings in the Washington, D.C., area and is arrested as he seeks to desecrate the graves of veterans of the wars in Iraq and Afghanistan

44 Seattle *3* 2011 Two financially destitute men, angry over U.S. foreign policy, are arrested in Seattle after they purchase an FBI-supplied machine gun that they plan to use to attack a military recruiting center after they save up enough money to purchase bullets and other material

45 Abdo *2* 2011 A U.S. Army private, unwilling to wage war on Muslims, is arrested after he buys ammunition and bomb materials to explode in a restaurant popular with soldiers

46 Model planes *3* 2011 Seeking to "decapitate" the U.S. "military center," a mentally ill hobbyist plots with police operatives to attack the Pentagon and Capitol with remote-controlled model planes bearing explosives and then to assault the buildings

47 Iran and Scarface *3* 2011 An Iranian-American used-car salesman from Texas, nicknamed "Scarface" from the results of an earlier street brawl, is arrested for engaging in a movie-like plot with another man (still at large), with members of the Iranian government, and with a police operative to hire a Mexican drug cartel to blow up Saudi Arabia's ambassador in a Washington restaurant for $1.5 million (wiring the operative $100,000 as a down payment) and to bomb the Israeli embassy in that city

48 Pimentel *3* 2011 A naturalized U.S. citizen and Muslim convert, hostile to U.S. military ventures in the Middle East, seeks to make pipe bombs using match heads to attack various targets

49 Tampa *3* 2012 Under suspicion after he walked into a store seeking to purchase an al-Qaida flag, an Albanian-American loner in Tampa, Florida, plots with a police operative to detonate a car bomb, fire an assault rifle, wear an explosive belt, and take hostages, in addition to bombing nightclubs, a police center, a bridge, and a Starbuck's coffee shop, to avenge wrongs against Muslims and to bring terror into the hearts of his victims

50 Capitol bomber *3* 2012 A Moroccan man, who had overstayed his visa for years and had been thrown out of his apartment for nonpayment of rent, concludes that the war on terror is a war on Muslims, plots with FBI undercover operatives, and is arrested as he seeks to carry out a suicide bombing at the Capitol

Case Types

1 An Islamist extremist conspiracy or connection that, in the view of the authorities, might have eventually developed into a plot to commit violence in the United States

2 An Islamist extremist terrorist plot to commit violence in the United States, no matter how embryonic, that was disrupted

3 An Islamist extremist plot to commit violence in the United States that was essentially created or facilitated in a major way by the authorities and then rolled up with arrests when enough evidence was accumulated

4 An Islamist extremist terrorist or terrorist group that actually reached the stage of committing, or trying to commit, violence in the United States

Source: Drawn from John Mueller, ed., *Terrorism since 9/11: The American Cases* (Columbus: Mershon Center, Ohio State University, 2012), http://www.polisci.osu.edu/faculty/jmueller/since.html.

In sharp contrast, the authors of the case studies, with remarkably few exceptions, describe their subjects with such words as incompetent, ineffective, unintelligent, idiotic, ignorant, inadequate, unorganized, misguided, muddled, amateurish, dopey, unrealistic, moronic, irrational, and foolish.[9] And in nearly all of the cases where an operative from the police or from the Federal Bureau of Investigation was at work (almost half of the total), the most appropriate descriptor would be "gullible."

In all, as Shikha Dalmia has put it, would-be terrorists need to be "radicalized enough to die for their cause; Westernized enough to move around without raising red flags; ingenious enough to exploit loopholes in the security apparatus; meticulous enough to attend to the myriad logistical details that could torpedo the operation; self-sufficient enough to make all the preparations without enlisting outsiders who might give them away; disciplined enough to maintain complete secrecy; and—above all—psychologically tough enough to keep functioning at a high level without cracking in the face of their own impending death."[10] The case studies examined in this article certainly do not abound with people with such characteristics.

In the eleven years since the September 11 attacks, no terrorist has been able to detonate even a primitive bomb in the United States, and except for the four explosions in the London transportation system in 2005, neither has any in the United Kingdom. Indeed, the only method by which Islamist terrorists have managed to kill anyone in the United States since September 11 has been with gunfire—inflicting a total of perhaps sixteen deaths over the period (cases 4, 26, 32).[11] This limited capacity is impressive because, at one time, small-scale terrorists in the United States were quite successful in setting off bombs. Noting that the scale of the September 11 attacks has "tended to obliterate America's memory of pre-9/11 terrorism," Brian Jenkins reminds us (and we clearly do need reminding) that the 1970s witnessed sixty to seventy terrorist incidents, mostly bombings, on U.S. soil every year.[12]

The situation seems scarcely different in Europe and other Western locales. Michael Kenney, who has interviewed dozens of government officials and intelligence agents and analyzed court documents, has found that, in sharp contrast with the boilerplate characterizations favored by the DHS and with the imperatives listed by Dalmia, Islamist militants in those locations are operationally unsophisticated, short on know-how, prone to making mistakes, poor at planning, and limited in their capacity to learn.[13] Another study documents the difficulties of network coordination that continually threaten the terrorists' operational unity, trust, cohesion, and ability to act collectively.[14]

In addition, although some of the plotters in the cases targeting the United States harbored visions of toppling large buildings, destroying airports, setting off dirty bombs, or bringing down the Brooklyn Bridge (cases 2, 8, 12, 19, 23, 30, 42), all were nothing more than wild fantasies, far beyond the plotters' capacities however much they may have been encouraged in some instances by FBI operatives. Indeed, in many of the cases, target selection is effectively a random process, lacking guile and careful planning. Often, it seems, targets have been chosen almost capriciously and simply for their convenience. For example, a would-be bomber targeted a mall in Rockford, Illinois, because it was nearby (case 21). Terrorist plotters in Los Angeles in 2005 drew up a list of targets that were all within a 20-mile radius of their shared apartment, some of which did not even exist (case 15). In Norway, a neo-Nazi terrorist on his way to bomb a synagogue took a tram going the wrong way and dynamited a mosque instead.[15]

Although the efforts of would-be terrorists have often seemed pathetic, even comical or absurd, the comedy remains a dark one. Left to their own devices, at least a few of these often inept and almost always self-deluded individuals could eventually have committed some serious, if small-scale, damage.[16]

The Foreign Adversary

As noted, the September 11 terrorist attacks were by far the most destructive in history—no terrorist act before or since has killed more than a few hundred people—and the tragic event seems increasingly to stand as an aberration, not as a harbinger. Accordingly, it is surely time to consider that, as Russell Seitz put it in 2004, "9/11 could join the Trojan Horse and Pearl Harbor among stratagems so uniquely surprising that their very success precludes their repetition," and, accordingly, that "Al Qaeda's best shot may have been exactly that."[17]

In fact, it is unclear whether al-Qaida central, now holed up in Pakistan and under sustained attack, has done much of anything since September 11 except issue videos filled with empty, self-infatuated, and essentially delusional threats. For example, it was in October 2002 that Osama bin Laden proclaimed, "Understand the lesson of New York and Washington raids, which came in response to some of your previous crimes. . . . God is my witness, the youth of Islam are preparing things that will fill your hearts with fear. They will target key sectors of your economy until you stop your injustice and aggression or until the more short-lived of us die." And in January 2006, he insisted that the "delay" in carrying out operations in the United States "was not due to failure to breach your security measures," and that "operations are under preparation, and you will see them on your own ground once they are finished, God willing."[18]

Bin Laden's tiny group of 100 or so followers does appear to have served as something of an inspiration to some Muslim extremists, may have done some training, has contributed a bit to the Taliban's far larger insurgency in Afghanistan, and may have participated in a few terrorist acts in Pakistan.[19] In his examination of the major terrorist plots against the West since September 11, Mitchell Silber finds only two (cases 1 and 20) that could be said to be under the "command and control" of al-Qaida central (as opposed to ones suggested, endorsed, or inspired by the organization), and there are questions about how full its control was even in these two instances.[20]

This highly limited record suggests that Carle was right in 2008 when he warned, "We must not take fright at the specter our leaders have exaggerated. In fact, we must see jihadists for the small, lethal, disjointed and miserable opponents that they are." Al-Qaida "has only a handful of individuals capable of planning, organizing and leading a terrorist organization," and although it has threatened attacks, "its capabilities are far inferior to its desires."[21] Impressively, bin Laden appears to have remained in a state of self-delusion even to his brutal and abrupt end. He continued to cling to the belief that another attack such as September 11 might force the United States out of the Middle East, and he was unfazed that the first such effort had proven to be spectacularly counterproductive in this respect by triggering a deadly invasion of his base in Afghanistan and an equally deadly pursuit of his operatives.[22]

Other terrorist groups around the world affiliated or aligned or otherwise connected to al-Qaida may be able to do intermittent damage to people and infrastructure, but nothing that is very sustained or focused. In all, extremist Islamist terrorism—whether associated with al-Qaida or not—has claimed 200 to 400 lives yearly worldwide outside war zones. That is 200 to 400 too many, of course, but it is about the same number as bathtub drownings every year in the United States.[23]

In addition to its delusional tendencies, al-Qaida has, as Patrick Porter notes, a "talent at self-destruction."[24] With the September 11 attacks and subsequent activity, bin Laden and his followers mainly succeeded in uniting the world, including its huge Muslim population, against their violent global jihad.[25] These activities also turned many radical Islamists against them, including some of the most prominent and respected.[26]

No matter how much states around the world might disagree with the United States on other issues (most notably on its war in Iraq), there is a compelling incentive for them to cooperate to confront any international terrorist problem emanating from groups and individuals connected to, or sympathetic with, al-Qaida. Although these multilateral efforts, particularly by such Muslim states as Libya, Pakistan, Sudan, Syria, and even Iran, may not have received sufficient publicity, these countries have felt directly threatened by the militant network, and their diligent and aggressive efforts have led to important breakthroughs against the group.[27] Thus a terrorist bombing in Bali in 2002 galvanized the Indonesian government into action and into making extensive arrests and obtaining convictions. When terrorists attacked Saudis in Saudi Arabia in 2003, the government became considerably more serious about dealing with internal terrorism, including a clampdown on radical clerics and preachers. The main result of al-Qaida-linked suicide terrorism in Jordan in 2005 was to outrage Jordanians and other Arabs against the perpetrators. In polls conducted in thirty-five predominantly Muslim countries by 2008, more than 90 percent condemned bin Laden's terrorism on religious grounds.[28]

In addition, the mindless brutalities of al-Qaida-affiliated combatants in Iraq—staging beheadings at mosques, bombing playgrounds, taking over hospitals, executing ordinary citizens, performing forced marriages—eventually turned the Iraqis against them, including many of those who had previously been fighting the U.S. occupation either on their own or in connection with the group.[29] In fact, they seem to have managed to alienate the entire population: data from polls in Iraq in 2007 indicate that 97 percent of those surveyed opposed efforts to recruit foreigners to fight in Iraq; 98 percent opposed the militants' efforts to gain control of territory; and 100 percent considered attacks against Iraqi civilians "unacceptable."[30]

In Iraq as in other places, "Al Qaeda is its own worst enemy," notes Robert Grenier, a former top CIA counterterrorism official. "Where they have succeeded initially, they very quickly discredit themselves."[31] Grenier's improbable company in this observation is Osama bin Laden, who was so concerned about al-Qaida's alienation of most Muslims that he argued from his hideout that the organization should take on a new name.[32]

Al-Qaida has also had great difficulty recruiting Americans. The group's most important, and perhaps only, effort at this is the Lackawanna experience, when a smooth-talking operative returned to the upstate New York town in early 2000 and tried to convert young Yemini-American men to join the cause (case 5). In the summer of 2001, seven agreed to accompany him to an al-Qaida training camp, and several more were apparently planning to go later. Appalled at what they found there, however, six of the seven returned home and helped to dissuade those in the next contingent.

The Undisclosed Adversary

The discussion thus far has dealt with an assessment of Islamist extremist terrorism since September 11 as disclosed in the public record. In general, any terrorist threat, whether domestic or foreign, appears limited. On occasion, however, intelligence officials claim to have thwarted additional terrorist plots but cannot disclose information about them for various reasons.

In working on an extensive report about how U.S. intelligence efforts (and budgets) were massively increased after September 11, the *Washington Post*'s Dana Priest says that she frequently heard this claim. In response, she "asked them to share with us anything they could, plots that were foiled that we could put in the paper because we didn't have many examples. We said give us things, just in generalities." But "we didn't receive anything back."[33]

That such claims may be exaggerated is further suggested by the fact that when a terrorist plot has been uncovered, policing agencies have generally been anything but tight-lipped about their accomplishment, instead parading their deed and often exaggerating the direness of the threat presented by those detained.[34] Examples include two instances in 2011 in which the New York Police Department prominently announced terrorism arrests of people even the FBI did not think worth pursuing (cases 42 and 48). Relatedly, the huge dump of classified information released by WikiLeaks in 2010 contained no really significant new disclosures—almost all of the information was already essentially public, though in many cases less textured and nuanced.[35]

Arrests are made, of course, only when prosecutors think they have enough evidence to obtain a conviction. In addition, however, authorities may have encountered a number of loud-mouthed aspirational terrorists and, lacking enough evidence to convict on terrorism charges, have levied lesser ones, such as immigration violations, to put them away.[36] These untrumpeted plots, however, are probably even less likely than the disclosed ones to lead to notable violence.

Also, if undisclosed plotters have been so able and so determined to commit violence, and if there are so many of them, why have they committed so little of it before being waylaid? And why were there so few plots in the months and years following the September 11 attacks before "enhanced" security measures were effectively deployed? Given the massively increased policing efforts after September 11, any sensible terrorist would want to act as quickly as possible before being detected. (This same conclusion holds for the argument that there are many more would-be terrorists whom U.S. authorities have not yet discovered.)

It is also useful to consider an earlier example in which U.S. officials targeted a particular conspiratorial group. For decades, they exaggerated the degree to which domestic communists—"masters of deceit" and the "enemies from within"—presented a threat to the republic. In a 1958 book, for example, FBI Director J. Edgar Hoover insisted that the American Communist Party was working "day and night to further the communist plot in America" with "deadly seriousness"; that a "Bolshevik transmission" was in progress that was "virtually invisible to the non-communist eye, unhampered by time, distance, and legality"; that it was "creating communist puppets throughout the country"; and that it had for "its objective the ultimate seizure of power in America."[37] Thus impelled, his agency spent a prodigious amount of time and public money pursuing the harmless and the nearly so.[38]

Finally, the vast majority of even the craftiest terrorist conspirators fail to carry out their plots. Therefore, any policing effort that disrupts them is likely to waylay impotent scheming far more than it does consummated violence. Thus, in his book, *Mastermind,* about a central plotter of the September 11 attacks, Khalid Sheikh Mohammed, Richard Miniter lists his subject's admitted (or claimed) involvement with other terrorist efforts. These include the 1993 World Trade Center and the 2002 Bali bombings; plots on

Heathrow airport, Big Ben, the Empire State Building, the Panama Canal, and buildings in Los Angeles, Seattle, and Chicago; plans to assassinate President Bill Clinton, the Pope, and several Pakistani prime ministers; and two efforts to infiltrate agents into the United States. Whatever the validity of these claims, many of which may be inflated, all of the ventures (except for the Bali bombings), either failed or did not even begin to approach fruition. In addition, the role of the "mastermind" in the Bali case, according to Miniter, was simply to supply some money.[39]

The Delusions of Counterterrorism

It seems increasingly likely that the official and popular reaction to the terrorist attacks of September 11, 2001, has been substantially deluded—massively disproportionate to the threat that al-Qaida has ever actually presented either as an international menace or as an inspiration or model to homegrown amateurs.

Applying the extensive datasets on terrorism that have been generated over the last decades, we conclude that the chances of an American perishing at the hands of a terrorist at present rates is one in 3.5 million per year—well within the range of what risk analysts hold to be "acceptable risk."[40] Yet, despite the importance of responsibly communicating risk and despite the costs of irresponsible fearmongering, just about the only official who has ever openly put the threat presented by terrorism in some sort of context is New York's Mayor Michael Bloomberg, who in 2007 pointed out that people should "get a life" and that they have a greater chance of being hit by lightning than of being a victim of terrorism—an observation that may be a bit off the mark but is roughly accurate.[41] (It might be noted that, despite this unorthodox outburst, Bloomberg still managed to be re-elected two years later.)

Indeed, much of the reaction to the September 11 attacks calls to mind Hans Christian Andersen's fable of delusion, "The Emperor's New Clothes," in which con artists convince the emperor's court that they can weave stuffs of the most beautiful colors and elaborate patterns from the delicate silk and purest gold thread they are given. These stuffs, they further convincingly explain, have the property of remaining invisible to anyone who is unusually stupid or unfit for office. The emperor finds this quite appealing because not only will he have splendid new clothes, but he will be able to discover which of his officials are unfit for their posts—or in today's terms, have lost their effectiveness. His courtiers, then, have great professional incentive to proclaim the stuffs on the loom to be absolutely magnificent even while mentally justifying this conclusion with the equivalent of "absence of evidence is not evidence of absence."

Unlike the emperor's new clothes, terrorism does of course exist. Much of the reaction to the threat, however, has a distinctly delusionary quality. In Carle's view, for example, the CIA has been "spinning in self-referential circles" in which "our premises were flawed, our facts used to fit our premises, our premises determined, and our fears justified our operational actions, in a self-contained process that arrived at a conclusion dramatically at odds with the facts." The process "projected evil actions where there was, more often, muddled indirect and unavoidable complicity, or not much at all." These "delusional ratiocinations," he further observes, "were all sincerely, ardently held to have constituted a rigorous, rational process to identify terrorist threats" in which "the avalanche of reporting confirms its validity by its quantity," in which there is a tendency to "reject incongruous or contradictory facts as erroneous, because they do not conform to accepted reality," and in which potential dissenters are not-so-subtly reminded of career dangers: "Say what you want at meetings. It's your decision. But you are doing yourself no favors."[42]

Consider in this context the alarming and profoundly imaginary estimates of U.S. intelligence agencies in the year after the September 11 attacks that the number of trained al-Qaida operatives in the United States was between 2,000 and 5,000.[43] Terrorist cells, they told reporters, were "embedded in most U.S. cities with sizable Islamic communities," usually in the "run-down sections," and were "up and active" because electronic intercepts had found some of them to be "talking to each other."[44] Another account relayed the view of "experts" that Osama bin Laden was ready to unleash an "11,000 strong terrorist army" operating in more than sixty countries "controlled by a Mr. Big who is based in Europe," but that intelligence had "no idea where thousands of these men are."[45] Similarly, FBI Director Robert Mueller assured the Senate Intelligence Committee on February 11, 2003, that, although his agency had yet to identify even one al-Qaida cell in the United States, "I remain very concerned about what we are not seeing," a sentence rendered in bold lettering in his prepared text. Moreover, he claimed that such unidentified entities presented "the greatest threat," had "developed a support infrastructure" in the country, and had achieved both the "ability" and the "intent" to inflict "significant casualties in the U.S. with little warning."[46]

Over the course of time, such essentially delusionary thinking has been internalized and institutionalized in a great many ways. For example, an extrapolation of delusionary proportions is evident in the common observation that, because terrorists were able, mostly by thuggish means, to crash airplanes into buildings, they might therefore be able to construct a nuclear bomb. Brian Jenkins has run an internet search to discover how often variants of the term "al-Qaida" appeared within ten words of "nuclear." There were only seven hits in 1999 and eleven in 2000, but the number soared to 1,742 in 2001 and to 2,931 in 2002.[47] By 2008, Defense Secretary Robert Gates was assuring a congressional committee that what keeps every senior government leader awake at night is "the thought of a terrorist ending up with a weapon of mass destruction, especially nuclear."[48]

Few of the sleepless, it seems, found much solace in the fact that an al-Qaida computer seized in Afghanistan in 2001 indicated that the group's budget for research on weapons of mass destruction (almost all of it focused on primitive chemical weapons work) was $2,000 to $4,000.[49] In the wake of the killing of Osama bin Laden, officials now have many more al-Qaida computers, and nothing in their content appears to suggest that the group had the time or inclination, let alone the money, to set up and staff a uranium-seizing operation, as well as a fancy, super-high-technology facility to fabricate a bomb. This is a process that requires trusting corrupted foreign collaborators and other criminals, obtaining and transporting highly guarded material, setting up a machine shop staffed with top scientists and technicians, and rolling the heavy, cumbersome, and untested finished product into position to be detonated by a skilled crew—all while attracting no attention from outsiders.[50]

If the miscreants in the American cases have been unable to create and set off even the simplest conventional bombs, it stands to reason that none of them were very close to creating, or having anything to do with, nuclear weapons—or for that matter biological, radiological, or chemical ones. In fact, with perhaps one exception, none seems to have even dreamed of the prospect; and the exception is José Padilla (case 2), who apparently mused at one point about creating a dirty bomb—a device that would disperse radiation—or even possibly an atomic one. His idea about isotope separation was to put uranium into a pail and then to make himself into a human centrifuge by swinging the pail around in great arcs.[51]

Even if a weapon were made abroad and then brought into the United States, its detonation would require individuals in-country with the capacity to receive and handle the complicated weapons and then to set them off. Thus far, the talent pool appears, to put mildly, very thin.

There is delusion, as well, in the legal expansion of the concept of "weapons of mass destruction." The concept had once been taken as a synonym for nuclear weapons or was meant to include nuclear weapons as well as weapons yet to be developed that might have similar destructive capacity. After the Cold War, it was expanded to embrace chemical, biological, and radiological weapons even though those weapons for the most part are incapable of committing destruction that could reasonably be considered "massive," particularly in comparison with nuclear ones.[52] And as explicitly rendered into U.S. law, the term was extended even further to include bombs of any kind, grenades, and mines; rockets having a propellant charge of more than four ounces; missiles having an explosive or incendiary charge of more than one quarter ounce; and projectile-spewing weapons that have a barrel with a bore more than a half inch in diameter.[53] It turns out then that the "shot heard round the world" by revolutionary war muskets was the firing of a WMD, that Francis Scott Key was exultantly, if innocently, witnessing a WMD attack in 1814; and that Iraq was full of WMD when the United States invaded in 2003—and still is, just like virtually every other country in the world.

After September 11, the delusional—or at least preposterous—expanded definition of WMD has been routinely applied in the United States. Many of those arrested for terrorism have been charged with planning to use "weapons of mass destruction" even though they were working, at most, on small explosives or contemplating planting a hand grenade in a trash bin.

Delusion is also present in the commonly held belief that terrorists target the United States because they oppose its values. Almost none of the actual or would-be terrorists in the cases in Table 1, however, had any problem with American society even though many (but certainly not all) were misfits, suffered from personal identity crises, were friendless, came from broken homes, were often desperate for money, had difficulty holding jobs, were on drugs, were petty criminals, experienced various forms of discrimination, and were, to use a word that pops up in quite a few of the case studies and fits even more of them, "losers."

A common feature in the literature is to assess the process by which potential terrorists become "radicalized." This may not be a particularly good way to look at the phenomenon, however, because the concept tends to imply an ideological motivation to the violence.[54] In almost all of the cases in Table 1, the overwhelming driving force did not stem particularly from ideology, but rather from a simmering, and more commonly boiling, outrage at U.S. foreign policy—the wars in Iraq and Afghanistan, in particular, and the country's support for Israel in the Palestinian conflict. Religion was a key part of the consideration for most, but not because they wished to spread sharia law or to establish caliphates. Rather they wanted to protect their religion against what was commonly seen to be a concentrated war upon it in the Middle East by the U.S. government and military.[55] (None seems to remember, or perhaps in many cases ever knew, that the United States strongly favored the Muslim side in Bosnia and in Kosovo in the 1990s, as well as, of course, in the Afghan war against the Soviet Union in the 1980s.) As a result, military installations within the United States were fairly common targets—though not very good ones if one is seeking to do maximum damage and inflict maximum shock. It is at military bases and recruitment centers that 14 of the 16 deaths caused by Islamist extremists since September 11 were inflicted—and only one of the victims was a civilian (cases 26 and 32).[56]

In addition to the would-be terrorists in Table 1 who focused on targets within the United States, others have sought to fight against U.S. interests abroad—to join the insurgencies in Iraq and Afghanistan or to defend Somalia against Ethiopian invaders. Hostility to U.S. foreign policy is obviously the primary motivator for these individuals.

Although the thousands upon thousands of al-Qaida operatives once thought to be flourishing in the United States were never found, there have been efforts to make that delusion more fully fit reality. The quest has impelled an expansion of the policing and domestic intelligence apparatus so massive that no one really has a full grasp of its extent.[57] As part of the process, the public has been asked to send in terrorism tips to the point where, within a few years after 2001, the New York Police Department was receiving tens of thousands each year on its trademarked "If You See Something, Say Something" hotline. None, however, had led to terrorism arrest.[58] This experience could be taken to suggest that the tipster campaign has been something of a failure. Or it could suggest that there might not be all that much to be found. By definition, however, delusion cannot be undermined by repeated inadequacy or disconfirmation. Thus, although the government receives more than 5,000 "threats" a day, the admonition from FBI Director Mueller has remained: "No counterterrorism lead goes uncovered." Under that strict order, huge amounts of money are being expended on what some in the FBI call "ghost chasing."[59] Meanwhile, New York continues to spend $2 million to $3 million annually (much of it coming from grants from the federal government) to publicize its hotline.[60] And, in one of her early public announcements after becoming secretary of homeland security in 2009, Janet Napolitano indicated that she wanted to inspire even more participation by the public in the quest to ferret out terrorists.[61]

Another approach to the problem of the near dearth of domestic terrorists is to create them—to make, in a sense, the invisible visible—and the police seem increasingly to be getting better at this enterprise.[62] In the last few years, police operatives embedded in terrorist plots in the United States have considerably outnumbered actual would-be terrorists, and, at least in some cases, there seems to be a condition of dueling delusions: a Muslim hothead has delusions about changing the world by blowing something up, and the authorities have delusions that he might actually be able to overcome his patent inadequacies to do so.

The process involves linking the hothead up with a police or an FBI operative who stokes delusions and eventually supplies the hothead with bogus weapons. When the hothead takes possession of weaponry he would never have been able to put together on his own, or, more commonly of late, plants it near his target and then presses a phony detonator button, he is arrested (see, in particular, cases 21, 22, 25, 29, 30, 38, 40, 42, 44, 46, 49, 50).

The self-interested efforts of the police operatives clearly have had a seductive effect in some cases, and often the process seems to be one in which an able con man is set among the gullible—not unlike the situation in the emperor's court.[63] Interestingly, the operative often seems to have been considerably older than the informed-upon, and there is frequently a pattern in which a police operative becomes something of a father-like figure to young, insecure men, many of whom grew up mostly without one.[64] Operatives and informants have been crucial to the development and detection of twenty-four of the fifty plots—those identified as case type 3 in Table 1.

Left to their own devices, some of the gulled would-be terrorists—often hate-filled but generally pretty lost and incompetent—might eventually have done something violent on their own. It seems likely, however, that most (as in cases 3, 10, 11, 12, 14, 16, 19, 21, 22, 23, 25, 29, 30, 35, 37, 38, 39, 40, 41, 42, 44, 46, 48, 49, 50) would never have become operationally engaged in plotting terrorist Att(a)cks without the creative, elaborate, and costly sting efforts of the police.[65] And, given their natural incapacities, even those who did attempt to inflict violence on their own were likely either to fail in their efforts or to commit destruction of quite limited scope.

Calculating the Costs of the Counterterrorism Delusion

Delusion is a quality that is difficult to quantify. Nevertheless, there may be a way to get a sense of its dimensions—or at least of its cost consequences.

We have argued that terrorism is a limited problem with limited consequences and that the reaction to it has been excessive, and even delusional. Some degree of effort to deal with the terrorism hazard is, however, certainly appropriate—and is decidedly not delusional. The issue then is a quantitative one: At what point does a reaction to a threat that is real become excessive or even delusional?

At present rates, as noted earlier, an American's chance of being killed by terrorism is one in 3.5 million in a given year. This calculation is based on history (but one that includes the September 11 attacks in the count), and things could, of course, become worse in the future. The analysis here, however, suggests that terrorists are not really all that capable, that terrorism tends to be a counterproductive exercise, and that September 11 is increasingly standing out as an aberration, not a harbinger. Moreover, it has essentially become officially accepted that the likelihood of a large-scale organized attack such as September 11 has declined and that the terrorist attacks to fear most are ones that are small scale and disorganized.[66] Attacks such as these can inflict painful losses, of course, but they are quite limited in their effect and, even if they do occur, they would not change the fatality risk for the American population very much.

The key question, then, is not "Are we safer?" but rather one posed shortly after September 11 by risk analyst Howard Kunreuther, "How much should we be willing to pay for a small reduction in probabilities that are already extremely low?"[67] That such questions are not asked, and that standard considerations of acceptable risk are never broached, suggests denial at best and delusion at worst.

Since September 11, expenditures in the United States on domestic homeland security alone—that is, excluding overseas expenditures such as those on the wars in Iraq and Afghanistan—have expanded by more than $1 trillion.[68] According to a careful assessment by a committee of the National Academy of Sciences in a 2010 report, these massive funds have been expended without any serious analysis of the sort routinely carried out by DHS for natural hazards such as floods and hurricanes. The committee could not find "any DHS risk analysis capabilities and methods" adequate for supporting the decisions made, noted that "little effective attention" was paid to "fundamental" issues, was (with one exception) never shown "any document" that could explain "exactly how the risk analyses are conducted," and looked over reports in which it was not clear "what problem is being addressed."[69]

Similar conclusions emerged from a study focusing on intelligence spending by Dana Priest and William Arkin. They calculate that it has increased by 250 percent since September 11 "without anyone in government seriously trying to figure out where the overlaps and waste were"—an apt description of a delusionary process. After receiving a "steady diet of vague but terrifying information from national security officials," they continue, American taxpayers "have shelled out hundreds of billions of dollars to turn the machine of government over to defeating terrorism without ever really questioning what they were getting for their money. And even if they did want an answer to that question, they would not be given one, both because those same officials have decided it would gravely harm national security to share such classified information—and because the officials themselves don't actually know."[70]

The extent of the overspending on domestic homeland security can be assessed, and the cost consequences of the counterterrorism delusion can be measured, by applying standard cost-benefit and risk-analytic procedures of the sort called for by the National Academy of Sciences committee, procedures that have been codified in international conventions.[71] Under this approach, the benefit of a security measure tallies the gains—the improvement in the security situation—generated by a security measure. It is a function of three elements:

(probability of a successful attack) × (losses sustained in the successful attack) × (reduction in risk generated by the security measure).

The probability of a successful attack is the likelihood that a successful terrorist attack will take place if the security measure were not in place. The losses sustained in the successful attack include the fatalities and other damage—both direct and indirect—that will accrue as a result of a successful terrorist attack, taking into account the value and vulnerability of potential targets, as well as any psychological and political effects. The reduction in risk generated by the security measure is the degree to which the security measure foils, deters, disrupts, or protects against the attack.

This benefit, a multiplicative composite of three considerations, is then compared to the costs of providing the risk-reducing security necessary to attain the benefit. If the benefit of a security measure outweighs its costs, it is deemed to be cost effective.

The interaction of these variables can be seen in an example. Suppose there is a dangerous curve on a road that results in an accident once every five years, as cars occasionally overshoot the curve and plummet down a hill. The probability of an accident each year under present conditions would be 20 percent (or 0.20). Suppose further that the accident results in one death, several injuries, and the totaling of a car, as well as some property damage. If the value of the life is taken to be, say, $4.5 million, the total losses from the accident might sum to $5 million.

Measures are then taken to reduce this risk. These could be ones that lower the probability of an accident by, for example, erecting warning signs, or they could be ones that reduce the losses sustained in the accident by, for example, installing a barrier so that cars that overshoot the curve are prevented from toppling down the hill. Suppose further that such measures result in a yearly reduction of risk of 50 percent (or 0.50). The benefit of the safety measures, applying the previous equation to this example, would then be

$$0.20 \times \$5 \text{ million} \times 0.50, \text{ or } \$500{,}000.$$

One would then need to compare this with the cost of the risk reduction measures. If their cost, all things considered, is less than $500,000 per year, the benefits would outweigh the costs, and the measures would be deemed cost effective.

This same approach can be used in a "break-even analysis" to calculate, in the case of terrorism, how many otherwise successful attacks would have to take place to justify the increase since September 11 in domestic expenditures on risk-reducing security measures. To do this, we think of the "benefit" as the cost of the security measure. The equation then becomes

$$\text{(cost of the security measure)} = \text{(probability of a successful attack)} \times \text{(losses sustained in the successful attack)} \times \text{(reduction in risk generated by the security measures)},$$

which is then manipulated for break-even purposes to be

$$\text{(probability of a successful attack)} = \text{(cost of the security measure)} / [\text{(losses sustained in the successful attack)} \times \text{(reduction in risk generated by the security measures)}].$$

We apply several estimates and assumptions. First, we include in our cost measure only enhanced local, state, and federal security expenditures and enhanced intelligence costs since September 11 (totaling $75 billion per year), leaving out many other expenditures including those incurred by the private sector, opportunity costs, and costs abroad such as those attending the terror-related wars in Iraq and Afghanistan. Second, we deal with the consequences of a rather large attack something similar to, or probably somewhat larger than, the car bomb attempt in Times Square in 2010, one exacting $500 million in damage (the vast majority of terrorist attacks inflict far less damage). Third, we assume that security measures in place before September 11 continue and that these, combined with the extra public vigilance induced by September 11, reduce the likelihood of a successful terrorist attack or reduce the losses sustained in such an attack by 50 percent.[72] And fourth, we assume that the enhanced security expenditures since September 11 have successfully reduced the likelihood of a successful terrorist attack or have reduced the losses sustained in such an attack by a further 45 percent, leading to an overall risk reduction of 95 percent.

For an enhanced security cost of $75 billion, losses sustained set at $500 million, with a reduction in risk of 0.45, the yearly probability of a successful attack for the enhanced expenditures to justify their cost would need to be at least

$$\$75 \text{ billion} / [\$500 \text{ million} \times 0.45] = 333.$$

That is, for enhanced U.S. domestic expenditures on homeland security to be deemed cost effective under a set of assumptions that substantially biases the consideration toward finding them cost effective, they would have had to deter, prevent, foil, or protect against 333 very large attacks that would otherwise have been successful every year. That would be about one a day. This calculation offers something of an illustrative estimate of the cost consequences of the counterterrorism delusion.[73]

Perpetual Anxiety

If September 11 is an aberration, as it increasingly seems to be, then the experience should gradually be considered a tragic irrelevance, not one that fundamentally determines consequent activities, perceptions, planning, and expenditures. Therefore, anxieties about terrorism should be receding. Yet, as documented in Figure 1, 35 to 40 percent of the American people continue since late 2001 to profess worry—even in the aftermath of the death of Osama bin Laden—that they or a family member might become a victim of terrorism. This is a startling phenomenon, and one that has a distinctly delusionary quality, given that no terrorist since 2001 has been able to detonate even the simplest of bombs in the United States, there has been no really sizable terrorist attack in the country (and the largest one that has occurred, the killing of thirteen at Fort Hood in 2009, scarcely stoked wide alarm), and an American's chance of being killed by a terrorist is, as noted earlier, about one in 3.5 million per year.

The American public has come to pay less attention to terrorism, as other concerns—the wars in the Middle East and, more lately, the economy—have dominated its responses to questions about the most important problem facing the country. However, polling trends on questions specifically about terrorism generally conform to the pattern found in Figure 1. Worries about flying because of the risk of terrorism registered at the same level in 2010 as in 2002. If anything, respondents felt that the country was less safe from terrorism in 2010 than it was in 2003 or 2004. Confidence that the government could protect them from terrorism was the same in 2012 as in 2002. Moreover, estimates of the likelihood of "another terrorist attack causing large numbers of Americans to be lost" stood a few months after bin Laden's death in 2011 at essentially the same level as in

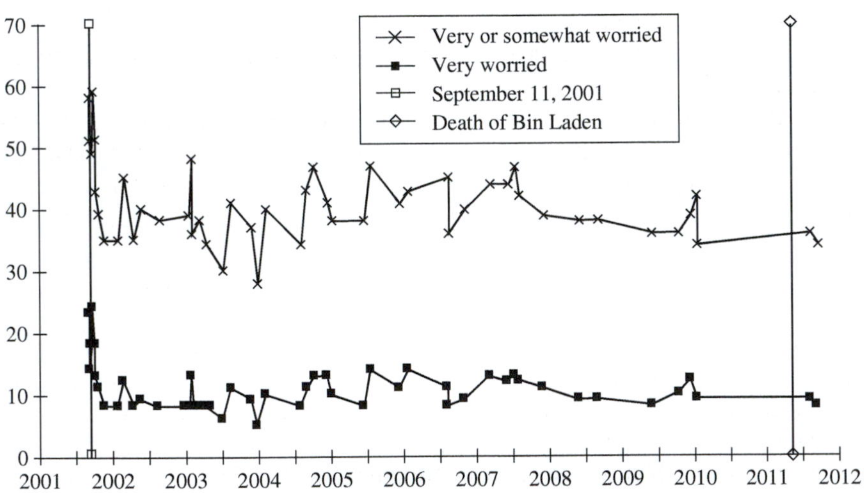

FIGURE 1 Worry about Becoming a Victim of Terrorism since the September 11 Attacks

Sources: "Terrorism in the United States," *gallup.com*, May 5, 2012; and *pollingreport.com*.

2001, with more than 70 percent of respondents deeming such a dire event to be very or somewhat likely, and the same held for a question about which side was winning the war against terrorism.[74]

These persistent anxieties stem in part from the peculiar trauma of the September 11 attacks themselves and, similar to those generated by Pearl Harbor, they have proven to have had a lasting impact on perceptions.[75] Reinforcing the unease may be the anthrax letter attacks that followed shortly after September 11and perhaps also an airliner crash (unrelated to terrorism) in New York on November 12 and the failed effort of the shoe bomber (case 1) on December 22. Anxiety may also derive from the perception that, unlike terrorists who seem mainly out to draw attention to their cause (in Brian Jenkins's assessments, only 72 people perished in the hundreds of bombings of the 1970s, Muslim extremist terrorists seem to be out to kill as many people as possible. Fear has been notably maintained as well by the popularity and the often knee-jerk acceptance of the highly questionable, if not precisely delusional, notion that terrorists will eventually (or even soon) acquire weapons that can kill in massive numbers and then detonate them in an American city.

In addition, U.S. government officials have maintained their ability to stoke fear. Even as it was announced by counterterrorism officials in 2010 that the "likelihood of a large-scale organized attack" has been reduced, DHS Secretary Napolitano was explaining that this means that al-Qaida franchises are now able "to innovate on their own" (presumably developing small-scale disorganized attacks), with the result that the threat "in some ways" is now the highest it has been since September 11. A senior Obama administration analyst implies that the situation is as bad as ever: "[Al-Qaida] lacks the ability to plan, organize and execute complex, catastrophic attacks, but the threat persists."[76] In addition, officials have also shifted their focus to "homegrown" terrorism with some success, even though this reflects not so much the rise of local would-be terrorists as the abandonment, or the discrediting, of the notion that large numbers of non-homegrown terrorists are abroad in the land.

Moreover, foiled plots can seem, or be made to seem, scarier than successful ones because the emphasis is on what the terrorist plotters hoped to do or might have been able to do, not with what they were likely to do.[77] Thus, when terrorists in 2009 were foiled in their plot to detonate four suicide bombs on the New York subway, various experts (including the attorney general of the United States) opined that the attack, if successful, might have killed between 200 and 500 people (case 28).[78] This ignored the experience in July 2005 when two sets of terrorists each attempted to set off four bombs on the crowded transit system in London. The first set killed 52, while the second killed none because the bombs were ill constructed. Presumably, the London bombers could have killed more if, in the first case, the bombs had been placed differently or, in the second, if they had been constructed properly. But because the number of dead is known, it is that number, not an imagined one, that ought to be the basis of comparison.[79] There were also extravagant death tallies imagined for the foiled transatlantic airliner plot of 2006 (case 20) and for the amazingly inept would-be Times Square bomber of 2010 (case 34).[80]

Official alarmism has actually tapered off in recent years, however, and predictions that the country must brace itself for a large imminent attack, so common in the first several years after September 11, are rarely heard.[81] Anxiety about terrorism, then, seems substantially to be a bottom-up phenomenon rather than one inspired by policymakers, risk entrepreneurs, politicians, and members of the media, who seem more nearly to be responding to the fears (and exacerbating them) than creating them.

Whatever the genesis, Americans seem to have internalized their anxiety about terrorism, and politicians and policymakers have come to believe that they can defy it only at their own peril. Concern about appearing to be soft on terrorism has replaced concern about seeming to be soft on communism, a phenomenon that lasted far longer than the dramatic episodes that generated it.[82] In his assessment of the reaction to the September 11 attacks, anthropologist Scott Atran muses, "Perhaps never in the history of human conflict have so few people with so few actual means and capabilities frightened so many."[83] Figure 1 suggests that this extraordinarily exaggerated and essentially delusional response may prove to be perpetual.

Critical Thinking Questions

1. Do you agree with the assertion that a great deal of money has been spent on homeland security with little or no real benefit? Why or why not?
2. How can we assess whether the U.S. reaction to Al Qaeda was disproportionate?
3. If another attack of the same scale as 9/11 were to take place tomorrow, would we deem our nation's homeland security efforts a failure? Why or why not?

Notes

1. For example, Bruce Riedel, an adviser in Barack Obama's administration, held the al-Qaida threat to the country to be "existential" in 2009. Riedel, interview by Margaret Warner, *NewsHour with Jim Lehrer,* October 16, 2009. Department of Homeland Security Secretary Michael Chertoff had previously pushed the discussion to a new level when he designated the threat from terrorism to be "a significant existential" one. Quoted in Shane Harris and Stuart Taylor Jr., "Homeland Security Chief Looks Back, and Forward," *govexec.com*, March 17, 2008, http://www.govexec.com/defense/2008/03/homeland-security-chief-looks-back-and-forward/26507. For the "survival" concern, see, in particular, Michael Scheuer, *Imperial Hubris: Why the West Is Losing the War on Terror* (Dulles, Va.: Brassey's, 2004), pp. 160, 177, 226, 241, 242, 250, 252, 263. On this issue, see also Glenn L. Carle, *The Interrogator: An Education* (New York: Nation Books, 2011), p. 293; and John Mueller and Mark G. Stewart, "Hardly Existential: Thinking Rationally about Terrorism," *foreignaffairs.com*, April 2, 2010, http://www.foreignaffairs.com/articles/66186/john-mueller-and-mark-g-stewart/hardly-existential/.
2. Miles O'Brien and Carol Costello, interview with New York Mayor Rudy Giuliani, "Giuliani: 'Have to Be Relentlessly Prepared,'" CNN, July 22, 2005; and Jane Mayer, *The Dark Side: The Inside Story on How the War on Terror Turned into a War on American Ideals* (New York: Doubleday, 2008), p. 3.
3. On this issue, see John Mueller, "Harbinger or Aberration? A 9/11 Provocation," *National Interest,* Fall 2002, pp. 45–50.
4. Alison Gendar and Helen Kennedy, "U.S. Commandos Find 'Mother Lode' of Material on Al Qaeda inside Osama Bin Laden's Compound," *New York Daily News,* May 4, 2011.
5. Greg Miller, "Bin Laden Documents Reveal Strain, Struggle in al-Qaida," *Washington Post,* July 1, 2011; and Scott Shane, "Pornography Is Found in bin Laden Compound Files, U.S. Officials Say," *New York Times,* May 13, 2011. See also David Ignatius, "The bin Laden Plot to Kill President Obama," *Washington Post,* March 16, 2012.

6. Carle, *The Interrogator,* pp. 269, 293, 298–299.
7. John Mueller, ed., *Terrorism since 9/11: The American Cases* (Columbus: Mershon Center, Ohio State University, 2012), http://polisci.osu.edu/faculty/jmueller/since.html.
8. Department of Homeland Security, *National Infrastructure Protection Plan: Partnering to Enhance Protection and Resiliency* (Washington, D.C.: Department of Homeland Security, 2009), p. 11. This contrasts with the evaluation of Michael Sheehan, New York's deputy director for counterterrorism, who concluded in 2003 that "Al Qaeda was simply not very good. . . . [W]e underestimated Al Qaeda's capabilities before 9/11 and we overestimated them after." Sheehan, *Crush the Cell: How to Defeat Terrorism without Terrorizing Ourselves* (New York: Crown, 2008), p. 14. According to journalist Christopher Dickey, when Sheehan told his bosses Raymond Kelly and David Cohen of this conclusion, they "were taken aback." It was "not so much that they disagreed," but rather that they worried that support for counterterrorism might crumble if Sheehan's conclusion were made public. All agreed that "it would be better if Sheehan kept his estimate to himself for a while." Dickey, *Securing the City: Inside America's Best Counterterror Force—the NYPD* (New York: Simon and Schuster, 2009), pp. 118–119.
9. See also Bruce Schneier, "Portrait of the Modern Terrorist as an Idiot," *Schneier on Security* blog, June 14, 2007, http://www.schneier.com; and Daniel Byman and Christine Fair, "The Case for Calling Them Nitwits," *Atlantic,* July/August 2010.
10. Shikha Dalmia, "What Islamist Terrorist Threat? Al Qaeda Doesn't Have What It Takes to Hurt America," *reason.com*, February 15, 2011, http://www.reason.com/archives/2011/02/15/ what-islamist-terrorist-threat/.
11. See also Risa A. Brooks, "Muslim 'Homegrown' Terrorism in the United States: How Serious Is the Threat?" *International Security,* Vol. 36, No. 2 (Fall 2011), p. 39.
12. Brian Michael Jenkins, *Would-Be Warriors: Incidents of Jihadist Terrorist Radicalization in the United States since September 11, 2001* (Santa Monica, Calif.: RAND, 2010), pp. 8–9.
13. Michael Kenney, "'Dumb' Yet Deadly: Local Knowledge and Poor Tradecraft among Islamist Militants in Britain and Spain," *Studies in Conflict & Terrorism,* Vol. 33, No. 10 (October 2010), pp. 911–932.
14. Mette Eilstrup-Sangiovanni and Calvert Jones, "Assessing the Dangers of Illicit Networks: Why al-Qaida May Be Less Dangerous Than Many Think," *International Security,* Vol. 33, No. 2 (Fall 2008), pp. 7–44.
15. John Horgan, *Walking Away from Terrorism: Accounts of Disengagement from Radical and Extremist Movements* (New York: Routledge, 2009), p. 44.
16. John J. Miller, "FBI Response to *Rolling Stone* Magazine Article," *Rolling Stone,* February 22, 2008.
17. Russell Seitz, "Weaker Than We Think," *American Conservative,* December 6, 2004. See also Gene Healy, "The Manufacture of Terror," *Liberty,* November 2002, pp. 59–60; and Mueller, "Harbinger or Aberration?"
18. For sources of these threats and of additional threats, see John Mueller and Mark G. Stewart, *Terror, Security, and Money: Balancing the Risks, Benefits, and Costs of Homeland Security* (New York: Oxford University Press, 2011), p. 36.
19. See Marc Sageman, *Leaderless Jihad: Terror Networks in the Twenty-first Century* (Philadelphia: University of Pennsylvania Press, 2008); and David Ignatius, "The Fading Jihadists," *Washington Post,* February 28, 2008.
20. Mitchell Silber, *The Al Qaeda Factor: Plots against the West* (Philadelphia: University of Pennsylvania Press, 2012).

21. Glenn L. Carle, "Overstating Our Fears," *Washington Post,* July 13, 2008.
22. Michael Hirsh, "Bin Laden Journal Reveals Future Planning, Possible Targets," *National Journal,* May 11, 2011. On this belief in 2001, see Fawaz A. Gerges, *The Rise and Fall of Al Qaeda* (New York: Oxford University Press, 2011), pp. 90–91; and Peter Bergen, "Al Qaeda at 20: Dead or Alive?" *washingtonpost.com,* August 17, 2008. For other evidence of bin Laden's delusional ramblings, see Ignatius, "The bin Laden Plot to Kill President Obama"; and David Ignatius, "A Lion in Winter," *Washington Post,* March 18, 2012.
23. Anthony H. Cordesman tallies "major attacks by Islamists" outside Iraq: 830 fatalities from April 2002 through July 2005. Cordesman, *The Challenge of Biological Terrorism* (Washington, D.C.: Center for Strategic and International Studies, 2005), pp. 29–31. Brian Michael Jenkins tallies "major terrorist attacks worldwide" by "jihadist extremists" outside Afghanistan, Iraq, Israel, Palestine, Algeria, Russia, and Kashmir: 1,129 fatalities from October 2001 through April 2006. Jenkins, *Unconquerable Nation: Knowing Our Enemy, Strengthening Ourselves* (Santa Monica, Calif.: RAND, 2006), pp. 179–184. IntelCenter tallies "most significant attacks executed by core Al Qaeda, regional arms and affiliate groups excluding operations in insurgency theaters": 1,632 fatalities from January 2002 through July 2007. IntelCenter, "Jihadi Attack Kill Statistics," August 17, 2007, p. 11, http://www.intelcenter.com/JAKS-PUB-v1-8.pdf. On the yearly bathtub drownings in the United States, see Mueller and Stewart, *Terror, Security, and Money,* p. 52 and chap. 2.
24. Patrick Porter, "Long Wars and Long Telegrams: Containing Al Qaeda," *International Affairs,* Vol. 85, No. 2 (March 2009), p. 300.
25. Joby Warrick, "U.S. Cites Big Gains against Al Qaeda," *Washington Post,* May 30, 2008. See also Fawaz A. Gerges, *The Far Enemy: Why Jihad Went Global* (New York: Cambridge University Press, 2005), chap. 5.
26. Peter Bergen and Paul Cruickshank, "The Unraveling: The Jihadist Revolt against bin Laden," *New Republic,* June 11, 2008; Lawrence Wright, "The Rebellion Within," *New Yorker,* June 2, 2008; and Gerges, *The Rise and Fall of Al Qaeda.*
27. Gerges, *The Far Enemy,* p. 232, and, for a tally of policing activity, pp. 318–319. See also Paul R. Pillar, *Terrorism and U.S. Foreign Policy* (Washington, D.C.: Brookings Institution Press, 2003), pp. xxviii–xxix; Marc Lynch, "Al Qaeda's Media Strategies," *National Interest,* Spring 2006, pp. 54–55; Sageman, *Leaderless Jihad,* p. 149; Juan Cole, *Engaging the Muslim World* (New York: Palgrave Macmillan, 2009), p. 163; and Max Abrahms, "Does Terrorism Really Work? Evolution in the Conventional Wisdom since 9/11," *Defence and Peace Economics,* Vol. 22, No. 6 (2011), pp. 583–594.
28. For Indonesia, see Marc Sageman, *Understanding Terror Networks* (Philadelphia: University of Pennsylvania Press, 2004), pp. 53, 142, 173. For Saudi Arabia, see Gerges, *The Far Enemy,* p. 249; and Sageman, *Understanding Terror Networks,* pp. 53, 144. For Jordan, see Pew Global Attitudes Project, "The Great Divide: How Westerners and Muslims View Each Other," June 22, 2006, Pew Research Center, http://www.pewglobal.org/2006/06/22/the-great-divide-how-westerners-and-muslims-view-each-other/; and Lynch, "Al Qaeda's Media Strategies," pp. 54–55. For the 2008 polls, see Fawaz Gerges, "Word on the Street: What Osama bin Laden and George W. Bush Get Wrong about Muslims," *Democracy,* Summer 2008, p. 75, http://www.democracyjournal.org/pdf/9/Gerges.pdf. See also Pillar, *Terrorism and U.S. Foreign Policy,*

p. xxiv; and Fareed Zakaria, "Post-9/11, We're Safer Than We Think," *Washington Post,* September 13, 2010.

29. Bob Woodward, "Why Did Violence Plummet? It Wasn't Just the Surge," *Washington Post,* September 8, 2008; and Frederic Wehrey, "The Iraq War: Strategic Overreach by America—and also by al Qaeda," in Brian Michael Jenkins and John Paul Godges, eds., *The Long Shadow of 9/11: America's Response to Terrorism* (Santa Monica, Calif.: RAND, 2011), pp. 47–55.
30. Andrew Mack, "Dying to Lose: Explaining the Decline in Global Terrorism," in Mack, ed., *Human Security Brief 2007* (Vancouver, British Columbia: Human Security Report Project, School for International Studies, Simon Fraser University, 2008), pp. 15–17.
31. Quoted in Warrick, "U.S. Cites Big Gains against Al Qaeda." See also Peter Bergen and Paul Cruickshank, "Al Qaeda: Self-Fulfilling Prophecy," *Mother Jones,* November/December 2007; Brian Michael Jenkins, *Will Terrorists Go Nuclear?* (Amherst, N.Y.: Prometheus, 2008), p. 191; and Gerges, *The Rise and Fall of Al Qaeda.*
32. Ignatius, "The bin Laden Plot to Kill President Obama." See also Ignatius, "Lion in Winter."
33. *Talk of the Nation,* NPR, July 19, 2010, transcript.
34. As David Johnston and Scott Shane write, "Since the terrorist attacks of Sept. 11, 2001 senior government officials have announced dozens of terrorism cases that on close examination seemed to diminish as legitimate threats." Johnston and Shane, "Terror Case Is Called One of the Most Serious in Years," *New York Times,* September 25, 2009. See also Erik J. Dahl, "The Plots That Failed: Intelligence Lessons Learned from Unsuccessful Terrorist Attacks against the United States," *Studies in Conflict and Terrorism,* Vol. 34, No. 8 (August 2011), p. 624.
35. Bill Keller, executive editor of the *New York Times,* interview by John Mueller, Berkeley, California, April 9, 2011.
36. One FBI estimate is that only one terrorism case in four leads to terrorism charges. Simpler criminal charges are used to deal with other cases. Garrett M. Graff, *The Threat Matrix: The FBI at War in the Age of Terror* (New York: Little, Brown, 2011), p. 557.
37. J. Edgar Hoover, *Masters of Deceit: The Story of Communism in America and How to Fight It* (New York: Holt, Rinehart, and Winston, 1958), p. 81. See also Joseph McCarthy, "Enemies from Within," speech to the Women's Club, Wheeling, West Virginia, February 9, 1950. On the parallels between domestic terrorism and domestic communism, see Mueller and Stewart, *Terror, Security, and Money,* pp. 185–188.
38. On this issue, see, in particular, Alexander Stephan, *"Communazis": FBI Surveillance of German Émigré Writers* (New Haven, Conn.: Yale University Press, 2000).
39. Richard Miniter, *Mastermind: The Many Faces of the 9/11 Architect, Khalid Shaikh Mohammed* (New York: Sentinel, 2011), pp. 2, 157.
40. Mueller and Stewart, *Terror, Security, and Money,* chap. 2 and, especially, p. 52. To put this number in context, an American's yearly chance of becoming a victim of homicide is 1 in 22,000; of being killed in an automobile accident, 1 in 8,000; of dying from cancer, 1 in 500.
41. Sewell Chan, "Buzz over Mayor's 'Get a Life' Remark," *Empire Zone Blog, New York Times,* June 6, 2007, http://empirezone.blogs.nytimes.com/. On this issue, see also John Mueller, *Overblown: How Politicians and the Terrorism Industry inflate National Security Threats* (New York: Free Press, 2006), pp. 151–152.

42. Carle, *The Interrogator,* pp. 249, 274, 275, 288. See also Robert Jervis, *Why Intelligence Fails: Lessons from the Iranian Revolution and the Iraq War* (Ithaca, N.Y.: Cornell University Press, 2010), pp. 23–24, 49, 51–52, 191–192.
43. Bill Gertz, "5,000 in U.S. Suspected of Ties to al Qaeda; Groups Nationwide Under Surveillance," *Washington Times,* July 11, 2002; and Richard Sale, "U.S. al Qaida Cells Attacked," UPI, October 31, 2002.
44. Sale, "U.S. al Qaida Cells Attacked."
45. Andy Lines, "War on Terror: Bin Laden Army: 11,000 Terror Agents Set to Strike," *Mirror* (London), September 24, 2001.
46. Director Mueller's testimony can be found at http://www.fbi.gov/congress/congress.htm. In 2005 an FBI report found that, despite years of well-funded sleuthing, the Bureau had yet to uncover a single true al-Qaida sleeper cell in the United States. The report was secret but managed to be leaked. Brian Ross, "Secret FBI Report Questions Al Qaeda Capabilities: No 'True' Al Qaeda Sleeper Agents Have Been Found in U.S.," *ABC News,* March 9, 2005. Fox News reported that the FBI, however, observed that "just because there's no concrete evidence of sleeper cells now, doesn't mean they don't exist." "FBI Can't Find Sleeper Cells," Fox News, March 10, 2005.
47. Jenkins, *Will Terrorists Go Nuclear?* pp. 250–251.
48. Quoted in Bob Graham, *World at Risk: The Report of the Commission on the Prevention of WMD Proliferation and Terrorism* (New York: Vintage, 2008), p. 43.
49. Anne Stenersen, *Al-Qaida's Quest for Weapons of Mass Destruction: The History behind the Hype* (Saarbrücken, Germany: VDM Verlag Dr. Müller, 2008), pp. 35–36.
50. For the extended argument that the likelihood of atomic terrorism is vanishingly small, see John Mueller, *Atomic Obsession: Nuclear Alarmism from Hiroshima to Al Qaeda* (New York: Oxford University Press, 2010), chaps. 12–15. See also John Mueller, "The Truth about al Qaeda: Bin Laden's Files Revealed the Terrorists in Dramatic Decline," *foreignaffairs.com,* August 2, 2011, http://www.foreignaffairs.com/articles/68012/john-mueller/the-truth-about-al-qaeda/; and Jenkins, *Will Terrorists Go Nuclear?*
51. Graff, *The Threat Matrix,* p. 366.
52. On this issue, see Mueller, *Atomic Obsession,* pp. 11–13.
53. On the history of WMD and for data on use of the term, see W. Seth Carus, "Defining 'Weapons of Mass Destruction,'" Occasional Paper, No. 42006 (Washington, D.C.: National Defense University Press, Center for the Study of Weapons of Mass Destruction, 2006). See also John Mueller and Karl Mueller, "The Rockets' Red Glare: Just What Are 'Weapons of Mass Destruction,' Anyway?" *foreignpolicy.com,* July 7, 2009, http://www.foreignpolicy.com/articles/2009/07/07/the_rockets_red_glare/; David C. Rapoport, "Terrorists and Weapons of the Apocalypse," *National Security Studies Quarterly,* Vol. 5, No. 1 (Summer 1999), pp. 49–67; Peter Bergen, "WMD Terrorism Fears Are Overblown," CNN, December 5, 2008, http://articles.cnn.com/2008-12-05/politics/Bergen.wmd_1_nuclear-weapons-chemical-weapons-mass-destruction?_S_PM:Politics/; and Mueller, *Atomic Obsession,* pp. 11–15.
54. See also Mark Sedgwick, "The Concept of Radicalization as a Source of Confusion," *Terrorism and Political Violence,* Vol. 22, No. 4 (2010), pp. 479–494; and Brooks, "Muslim 'Homegrown' Terrorism in the United States," pp. 12–14.
55. See also Robert A. Pape and James K. Feldman, *Cutting the Fuse: The Explosion of Global Suicide Terrorism and How to Stop It* (Chicago: University of Chicago Press,

2010), pp. 76–79; Stephen M. Walt, "Why They Hate Us (II): How Many Muslims Has the U.S. Killed in the Past 30 Years?" *Stephen M. Walt: A Realist in an Ideological Age, Foreign Policy,* blog, November 30, 2009, http://walt.foreignpolicy.com; Peter Bergen, "Five Myths about Osama bin Laden," *Washington Post,* May 6, 2011, http://www.washingtonpost.com/opinions/five-myths-about-osama-bin-laden/2011/05/05/AFkG1rAG_story.html; James Fallows, *Blind into Baghdad: America's War in Iraq* (New York: Vintage, 2006), p. 142; Daniel L. Byman, "Al Qaeda as an Adversary: Do We Understand Our Enemy?" *World Politics,* Vol. 56, No. 1 (October 2003), pp. 143–148; and John J. Mearsheimer, "Imperial by Design," *National Interest,* January/February 2011, p. 24. Although the tiny number of people plotting terrorist attacks in the United States display passionate hostility to U.S. foreign policy, there is, of course, a far greater number of people who share much of the same hostility, but are in no sense inspired to commit terrorism to express their deeply held views. On this issue, see also Brooks, "Muslim 'Homegrown' Terrorism in the United States," p. 14. Marc Sageman has provided an arresting comparison with Jewish youths who felt called upon to go abroad to fight for besieged Israel in wars in 1948, 1967, and 1973. Sageman, *Leaderless Jihad,* pp. 74–75.

56. See Brooks, "Muslim 'Homegrown' Terrorism in the United States," p. 38.
57. See, in particular, Dana Priest and William M. Arkin, *Top Secret America: The Rise of the New American Security State* (New York: Little, Brown, 2011).
58. William Neuman, "In Response to M.T.A.'s 'Say Something' Ads, a Glimpse of Modern Fears," *New York Times,* January 7, 2008.
59. Graff, *The Threat Matrix,* 398–399, 579.
60. Manny Fernandez, "A Phrase for Safety after 9/11 Goes Global," *New York Times,* May 10, 2010. See also John Mueller, "Terror Tipsters," *Skeptics* blog, *National Interest,* January 24, 2012, http://www.nationalinterest.org/blog/the-skeptics/.
61. Spencer S. Hsu, "Security Chief Urges 'Collective Fight' against Terrorism," *Washington Post,* July 29, 2009.
62. See also Brooks, "Muslim 'Homegrown' Terrorism in the United States," pp. 18–20; Schneier, "Portrait of the Modern Terrorist as an Idiot"; and Trevor Aaronson, "The Informants," *Mother Jones,* October 2011, pp. 30–43.
63. On the easing of restrictions on domestic intelligence-gathering that occurred in late 2008 and made such operations easier and more frequent, see Brooks, "Muslim 'Homegrown' Terrorism in the United States," p. 17; and Charlie Savage, "F.B.I. Casts Wide Net under Relaxed Rules for Terror Inquiries, Data Show," *New York Times,* March 26, 2011.
64. On this process in a different context, see Sageman, *Leaderless Jihad,* p. 79.
65. In imposing the minimum sentence allowed by law (twenty-five years) on those convicted in the Bronx synagogues plot (case 25), the judge, while acknowledging that the men were "prepared to do real violence," also noted that they were "utterly inept" and on a "fantasy terror operation" and that "only the government could have made a 'terrorist'" out of the plot's leader, "whose buffoonery is positively Shakespearean in its scope." Quoted in Benjamin Weiser, "3 Men Draw 25-Year Terms in Synagogue Bomb Plot," *New York Times,* June 29, 2011. She also said, "I believe beyond a shadow of a doubt that there would have been no crime here except the government instigated it, planned it and brought it to fruition," adding, however, "that does not mean there is no

crime." Quoted in Peter Finn, "Documents Provide Rare Insight into FBI's Terrorism Stings," *Washington Post,* April 13, 2012.

66. Richard A. Serrano, "U.S. Faces 'Heightened' Threat Level," *Los Angeles Times,* February 10, 2011.
67. Howard Kunreuther, "Risk Analysis and Risk Management in an Uncertain World," *Risk Analysis,* Vol. 22, No. 4 (August 2002), pp. 662–663. See also John Mueller, "Some Reflections on What, If Anything, 'Are We Safer?' Might Mean," *Cato Unbound,* September 11, 2006, http://www.catounbound.org; and Brooks, "Muslim 'Homegrown' Terrorism in the United States," p. 43.
68. Mueller and Stewart, *Terror, Security, and Money,* pp. 1–3.
69. National Research Council of the National Academies, *Review of the Department of Homeland Security's Approach to Risk Analysis* (Washington, D.C.: National Academies Press, 2010). The report also notes that DHS risk assessment for natural hazards is "near state of the art," is "based on extensive data," has been "validated empirically," and appears "well suited to near-term decision needs." As far as we can determine, this report received no media attention whatever when it was released.
70. Priest and Arkin, *Top Secret America,* pp. xviii–xix, 103.
71. For a much more extensive application and discussion of this approach, see Mueller and Stewart, *Terror, Security, and Money.*
72. This may substantially understate the risk reduction by pre–September 11 measures. Notes Michael Sheehan, "The most important work in protecting our country since 9/11 has been accomplished with the capacity that was in place when the event happened, not with any of the new capability bought since 9/11. I firmly believe that those huge budget increases have not significantly contributed to our post-9/11 security. . . . The big wins had little to do with the new programs." Sheehan, *Crush the Cell,* p. 263.
73. These considerations focus, as noted, on the costs of domestic homeland security spending, not on those abroad. The costs may sometimes intersect, however. Because of the vagueness of the concept of "material support for terrorism," many Somali-Americans were reluctant to aid in the catastrophic famine taking place in their home country in areas partly occupied by a people officially designated as a terrorist group, resulting in a considerable human toll. Mary Beth Sheridan, "U.S. May Ease Anti-Terror Rules to Help Starving Somalis," *Washington Post,* August 2, 2011.
74. Poll trends are posted at http://polisci.osu.edu/faculty/jmueller/terrorpolls.pdf.
75. There may also be parallels with Pearl Harbor in that the attack proved to be an aberration. As H.P. Willmott notes, "[N]ot a single operation planned after the start of the war [by the Japanese] met with success."Willmott, *Empires in the Balance: Japanese and Pacific Allied Strategies to April 1942* (Annapolis: Naval Institute Press, 1982), p. 91. See also John Mueller, "Pearl Harbor: Military Inconvenience, Political Disaster," *International Security,* Vol. 16, No. 3 (Winter 1991/92), pp. 172–203.
76. On Napolitano, see Serrano, "U.S. Faces 'Heightened' Threat Level"; on the senior official, see Ignatius, "The bin Laden Plot to Kill President Obama." See also Mitchell D. Silber, "The Mutating al Qaeda Threat: Terrorists Are Adapting and Expending," *Washington Times,* December 30, 2011. For commentary on the phenomenon, see Heather Mac Donald, "The Ever-Renewing Terror Threat," *Secular Right,* February 13, 2011, http://secularright.org; Brooks, "Muslim 'Homegrown' Terrorism in the United States," pp. 43–44; and John Mueller, "Why al Qaeda May Never Die," *Skeptics* blog, May 1, 2012, http://nationalinterest.org.

77. See Schneier, "Portrait of the Modern Terrorist as an Idiot."
78. Tom Hays, "Feds: Terror Suspects' Mingling Fed NYC threat," *KIDK.com*, September 26, 2009; and "Justice Department Oversight—Part 1—Newsflash," Associated Press, April 14, 2010.
79. The train bombings in Madrid in 2004 killed 191, but were accomplished by detonating ten bombs, not four. Even this death toll is lower than the attorney general's lowest estimate for the New York subway case.
80. Interestingly, however, the plot dreamed up since September 11 that could potentially have caused the most damage was the one that aspired to topple the Sears Tower in Chicago (case 19). Even if the toppling failed to create the planners' hoped-for tsunami, thousands would have died—perhaps even tens of thousands—and the damage to the neighborhood would have been as monumental as that to the building. The plotters, however, had no capacity to carry out this colossal deed, so their expressed desire is not taken seriously even though the case is generally known as the Sears Tower plot. Analysts should apply this kind of reasonable reticence more broadly for aborted or foiled plots.
81. For an array of such predictions, see http://polisci.osu.edu/faculty/jmueller/PREDICT.PDF.
82. Mueller and Stewart, *Terror, Security, and Money,* pp. 185–188.
83. Scott Atran, *Talking to the Enemy: Faith, Brotherhood, and the (Un)making of Terrorists* (New York: Ecco, 2010), p. xiv.

Assessing the Jihadist Terrorist Threat to America and American Interests

Peter Bergen, Bruce Hoffman, and Katherine Tiedemann

Al Qaeda and allied groups continue to pose a threat to the United States. Although it is less severe than the catastrophic proportions of a 9/11-like attack, the threat today is more complex and more diverse than at any time over the past nine years. Al Qaeda or its allies continue to have the capacity to kill dozens, or even hundreds, of Americans in a single attack. A key shift in the past couple ofyears is the increasingly prominent role in planning and operations that U.S. citizens and residents have played in the leadership of Al Qaeda and aligned groups, and the higher numbers of Americans attaching themselves to these groups. Another development is the increasing diversification of the types of U.S.-based jihadist militants, and the groups with which those militants have affiliated. Indeed, these jihadists do not fit any particular ethnic, economic, educational, or social profile. Al Qaeda's ideological influence on other jihadist groups is on the rise in South Asia and has continued to extend into countries like Yemen and Somalia; Al Qaeda's top leaders are still at large, and American overreactions to even unsuccessful terrorist attacks arguably have played, however inadvertently, into the hands of the jihadists. Working against Al Qaeda and allied groups are the ramped-up campaign of drone attacks in Pakistan, increasingly negative Pakistani attitudes and actions against the militants based on their territory, which are mirrored by increasingly hostile attitudes toward Al Qaeda and allied groups in the Muslim world in general, and the fact that erstwhile militant allies have now also turned against Al Qaeda. This article is based on interviews with a wide range of senior U.S. counterterrorism officials at both the federal and local levels, and embracing the policy, intelligence, and law enforcement communities, supplemented by the authors' own research.

The New Threat

"Mom, I'm in Somalia! Don't worry about me; I'm okay," was how 17-year-old Burhan Hassan's worried mother discovered where her son had gone weeks after he and six other Somali-American youths disappeared from their homes in the Minneapolis–St. Paul area shortly after Election Day 2008. Almost without exception, the youths who slipped away were described as good boys[1] who were "good students [who] had no problems with the law."[2] But what especially troubled their relatives and others in the tight-knit émigré community was that no one could explain how the impoverished young men were able to pay for the $2,000 airline tickets they used to travel to Somalia.[3] "My nephew, he doesn't have money for a ticket," the uncle of one lamented. "None of these kids do."[4] According to Abdisalem Adam, a teacher and head of the local Dar al-Hijrah Islamic Center, "Up to now, no one knows who recruited them. But they obviously did not wake up one morning and decide to go [to Somalia]."[5]

The youths were radicalized and recruited in the United States and trained in Somalia by al-Shabab ("the Youth"),[6] an Al Qaeda ally that deliberately emulates its mentor organization—down to its reliance on training camps, a safe haven, the use of the Internet for propaganda purposes, and suicide attacks. Indeed, it is believed that their trainer in Somalia was Saleh Ali Nabhan, the longtime Al Qaeda commander implicated in both the 1998 bombing of the American embassy in Nairobi and the 2002 attack on Israeli tourists at a hotel in Mombasa, who was killed last year. Two of these youths have become the first known Americans to have carried out suicide terrorist attacks.[7]

Nor are these the only persons to have left the United States to train in terrorist camps abroad. They in fact are part of a disquieting trend that has emerged in recent years that includes five young men from Alexandria, Virginia, who sought to fight alongside the Taliban and Al Qaeda and were arrested in Pakistan; Bryant Neal Vinas and Abu Yahya Mujahdeen al-Adam, two American citizens arrested in Pakistan for their links to Al Qaeda; Najibullah Zazi, the Afghan-born, Queens-educated Al Qaeda terrorist convicted of plotting simultaneous suicide attacks on the New York City subway; and most recently Faisal Shahzad, the Pakistani Taliban-trained, naturalized American citizen who tried to bomb New York City's Times Square in May 2010.

Threat Assessment: Al Qaeda and Allied Groups and Those Inspired by Its Ideas Continue to Pose a Threat to the United States

Although it is less severe than the catastrophic proportions of a 9/11-like attack, the threat today is more complex and more diverse than at any time over the past nine years.

Threats are measured by intent and capabilities. Al Qaeda continues to hope to inflict mass-casualty attacks in the United States. Indeed, Al Qaeda leaders have said since 9/11 that the United States is owed millions of deaths because of its supposed crimes against Islam. However, the group's capabilities to implement such a large-scale attack are currently far less formidable than they were nine years ago or indeed at any time since.

Al Qaeda or one of its allies might, however, successfully carry out bombings against symbolic American targets that would kill dozens, such as the subways of Manhattan, as was the plan in September 2009 of Najibullah Zazi; or they might blow up an American passenger jet, as was the intention three months later of the Nigerian Umar Farouq Abdulmutallab, who had been recruited by Al Qaeda in the Arabian Peninsula. Had that bombing attempt succeeded, it could have killed hundreds.

This level of threat is likely to persist for years to come; however, Al Qaeda is believed to lack the capability to launch a 9/11-level attack sufficiently deadly in scope to completely reorient American foreign policy, as those attacks did. And it is worth recalling that only 14 Americans have been killed in *jihadist* terrorist attacks in the United States since 9/11, something that was hardly predictable in the immediate wake of the attacks on Washington and New York.[8]

Despite Al Qaeda's long interest in acquiring chemical, biological, radiological, and nuclear (CBRN) weapons, on the infrequent occasions that it or its affiliates have tried to deploy crude versions of these weapons their efforts have fizzled, as was evident in the largely ineffectual campaign of chlorine bomb attacks by "Al Qaeda in Iraq" in 2007.

Militant *jihadist* groups will be able to deploy only crude chemical, biological, or radiological weapons for the foreseeable future, and these will not be true "weapons of mass destruction," but rather weapons of mass disruption, whose principal effect will be panic but likely few deaths.

Indeed, a survey of the 172 individuals indicted or convicted in Islamist terrorism cases in the United States between 11 September 2001 and 11 September 2010 by the Maxwell School at Syracuse University and the New America Foundation found that *none* of the cases involved the use of CBRN. (In the one case where a radiological plot was initially alleged—that of the Hispanic-American Al Qaeda recruit Jose Padilla—that allegation was dropped when the case went to trial.)

The Diversification of the Threat

Al Qaeda and its allies arguably have been able to establish at least an embryonic terrorist recruitment, radicalization, and operational infrastructure in the United States with effects both at home and abroad.

The year 2009 was a watershed in terrorist attacks and plots in the United States, with a record total of 11 *jihadist* attacks, *jihadist*-inspired plots, or efforts by Americans to travel overseas to obtain terrorist training.[i] They included two actual attacks (at Fort Hood, Texas, which claimed the lives of 13 people, and the shooting of two U.S. military recruiters in Little Rock, Arkansas), five serious but disrupted plots, and four incidents involving groups of Americans conspiring to travel abroad to receive terrorist training. According to the authors' count, in 2009 at least 43 American citizens or residents aligned with Sunni militant groups or their ideology were charged or convicted of terrorism crimes in the U.S. or elsewhere, the highest number in any year since 9/11. In the first nine months of 2010, 20 were similarly charged or convicted.[ii] See Figure 1 for a worldwide map of significant events since 2008 by Al Qaeda, its affiliates, or those inspired by its ideas.

There is a spectrum of adversaries today arrayed against the United States. At the low end are individuals simply inspired to engage in terrorist attacks completely on their own—such as the Jordanian national who overstayed his visa in an attempt to bomb a Dallas office building,[9] or the Muslim convert with a similarly far-fetched plan to bomb a federal courthouse in Springfield, Illinois.[10] But in other instances, terrorist groups either actively recruited individuals in the United States, deliberately motivated others to carry out terrorist attacks on U.S. soil, or directed trained operatives in the execution of coordinated strikes against American targets within its borders.

Al Qaeda and its Pakistani, Somali, and Yemeni allies arguably have been able to accomplish the unthinkable—establishing at least an embryonic terrorist recruitment, radicalization, and operational infrastructure in the United States with effects both at home and abroad. And, by working through its local allies, the group has now allowed them to co-opt American citizens in the broader global Al Qaeda battlefield. Considering individual *jihadist* groups will help illuminate trends about the changing threat faced by the Obama administration.

[i] A more detailed description of those attacks and plots can be found in Appendix A.

[ii] See Appendix B for the names and ethnicities of those indicted or convicted from 2003 to September 2010.

Zarein Ahmedzay and Adis Medunjanin.[21] While in Pakistan, Zazi, Ahmedzay, and Medunjanin received instruction from Al Qaeda trainers in the fabrication of improvised explosive devices using such commercially available materials as hydrogen peroxide (e.g., hair bleach), acetone, flour, and oil to carry out the suicide bomb attacks planned for the New York City subway in September 2009. Zazi pleaded guilty to his role in the plot in February 2010; Ahmedzay similarly pleaded guilty on 23 April 2010.[22]

Zazi and his co-conspirators were part of a continuing effort by Al Qaeda and its allies to target the United States. This was made clear in the superseding indictment filed by the U.S. Department of Justice on 7 July 2010, in connection with the plot to attack the New York City subway. That indictment details a plot directed by "leaders of Al Qaeda's external operations program dedicated to terrorist attacks in the United States and other Western countries" and involving an "American-based Al Qaeda cell." It further describes how the plot was organized by three long-standing and senior Al Qaeda operatives—Saleh al-Somali, Adnan El Shukrijumah, and Rashid Rauf.[23]

Al-Somali was among Al Qaeda's earliest recruits from outside the inner circle of Saudis, Yemenis, and Egyptians who had either served or fought in Afghanistan during the 1980s and 1990s and formed the movement's original hardcore. He is believed to have joined Al Qaeda at least as far back as the early 1990s and may have recently been killed in a U.S. drone strike in Pakistan.[24]

Shukrijumah is similarly well known to authorities. A 34-year-old native of Saudi Arabia, Shukrijumah lived in Brooklyn during the 1990s, where his father worked for Sheikh Omar Abdel Rahman, the so-called "Blind Sheikh," an Egyptian-born cleric who was implicated in a follow-on plot to the 1993 World Trade Center bombing that involved attacks on New York City bridges and tunnels, and the United Nations headquarters building. The younger Shukrijumah later moved to Florida and in 2003 was placed on the FBI's "Most Wanted" list as a result of his growing role in Al Qaeda attack planning. The subject of a $5 million reward, Shukrijumah was described by American law enforcement at the time as an "imminent threat to U.S. citizens and interests."[25] That assessment remains highly relevant, if not prescient, today.

Finally, British-born Rashid Rauf has long been involved with Al Qaeda plots both in Pakistan and abroad. He played a key role in the two assassination attempts against Pakistani President Pervez Musharraf in December 2003 and was regarded as a protégé of Abu Faraj al-Libi, then Al Qaeda's number three commander.[26] Rauf was also pivotal to the planning and orchestration of the 2006 plot to blow up seven U.S. and Canadian passenger airliners en route from London to North America. Like al-Somali, he is now believed to have been killed in a U.S. drone strike in Pakistan.[iii]

It is significant that both Zazi and Faisal Shahzad, the would-be Times Square bomber, had tribal and family ties in Pakistan that they used to make contact with either Al Qaeda or the Pakistani Taliban. These links greatly facilitated their recruitment. British authorities have always regarded the high volume of traffic between Britain and Pakistan, involving upwards of 400,000 persons annually, as providing prime opportunities for the radicalization and recruitment of British citizens and residents.[27] These same concerns

[iii] It is worth emphasizing that the U.S. counterterrorism measures targeting Al Qaeda's senior leadership do not appear to have impacted the intentions of the group's leaders: bin Laden and al-Zawahiri have long been opposed to the United States and its allies, and killing the long line of "Al Qaeda number threes" has not changed this appreciably.

now exist among U.S. authorities, given the ease with which Zazi and Shahzad readily made contact with the Pakistan-based terrorist movements.[28]

Bryant Neal Vinas and Abu Yahya Mujahdeen al-Adam, both American citizens, have been arrested during the past two years in Pakistan for their links to Al Qaeda. While it is easier to dismiss the threat posed by wannabes who are often snared without difficulty by the authorities, or to discount as aberrations the homicides inflicted by lone gunmen, these incidents show the activities of trained U.S. terrorist operatives who are part of an identifiable organizational command-and-control structure and are acting on orders from terrorist leaders abroad.

In addition to Zazi and Shahzad, five Muslim-Americans from Northern Virginia volunteered for *jihad* in the Afghanistan/Pakistan theater in 2009. As of early October 2010, they were in custody in Pakistan, charged with planning terrorist attacks. Similarly, a group of seven American citizens and residents of the town of Willow Creek, North Carolina, led by Daniel Boyd, a convert to Islam who had fought in the Afghan *jihad* against the Soviets, conceived of themselves as potential participants in overseas holy wars from Israel to Pakistan, and some traveled abroad to scope out their opportunities, according to federal prosecutors. Boyd purchased eight rifles and a revolver, and members of his group allegedly did paramilitary training on two occasions in the summer of 2009.[29]

The Threat from Al Qaeda in the Arabian Peninsula

Al Qaeda in the Arabian Peninsula has been looking to expand its terrorist attacks beyond Yemen and Saudi Arabia, as demonstrated by the failed attempt to explode a bomb on a flight over Detroit on Christmas Day 2009.

Al Qaeda in the Arabian Peninsula (AQAP) was the group responsible for Umar Jrouq Abdulmutallab's botched attempt to explode a bomb on Northwest Airlines Flight 253 over Detroit on Christmas Day 2009. Abdulmutallab boarded the flight in Amsterdam, bound for Detroit with some 300 passengers and crew on board. Secreted in his underwear was a bomb made with 80 grams of PETN, a plastic explosive that was not detected by airport security in Amsterdam or the Nigerian city of Lagos, from where he had originally flown. He also carried a syringe with a chemical initiator to set off the bomb.[30] As the plane neared Detroit, the young man tried to initiate his bomb with the chemical, setting himself on fire and suffering severe burns. Some combination of his own ineptitude, faulty bomb construction, and the quick actions of the passengers and crew who subdued him and extinguished the fire prevented an explosion that might have brought down the plane near Detroit, killing all on board and also likely killing additional Americans on the ground. Immediately after he was arrested, Abdulmutallab told investigators that the explosive device "was acquired in Yemen along with instructions as to when it should be used."[31]

The Northwest Airlines plot had been presaged in virtually every detail a few months earlier, several thousand miles to the east of Detroit. On 28 August 2009, the Saudi deputy minister of interior, Prince Mohammed bin Nayef, survived a bomb attack launched by AQAP. Because he leads Saudi Arabia's counterterrorism efforts against Al Qaeda, the prince is a key target for the terrorist group. Prince Nayef was responsible for overseeing the kingdom's terrorist rehabilitation program, and some two dozen important members of Al Qaeda had previously surrendered to him in person. Abdullah Hassan al-Asiri, the would-be assassin, was a Saudi who had fled to Yemen, and posed as a militant willing to surrender personally to Prince Nayef.[32] During the month of Ramadan, traditionally a time of repentance in the Muslim world, Asiri gained an audience with the prince at his private residence in Jeddah, presenting himself as someone who could persuade other militants to surrender. Pretending that he was reaching out to those militants, Asiri briefly called some members of Al Qaeda to tell them that he was standing by Prince Nayef. After he finished the call, the bomb blew up, killing Asiri but only slightly injuring the prince, who was a few feet away. A Saudi government official characterized the prince's narrow escape as a "miracle."[33]

According to the official Saudi investigation, Asirihad concealed in his underwear a bomb made of PETN, the same plastic explosive that would be used in the Detroit case, and he exploded the 100-gram device using a detonator with a chemical fuse, as Abdulmutallab would attempt to do on the Northwest flight. Prince Nayef's attacker also had had to pass through metal detectors before he was able to secure an audience with the prince. Shortly after both of the failed attacks, AQAP asserted responsibility for the operations and released photographs of the bombers taken while they were in Yemen.

If Umar Farouq Abdulmutallab had succeeded in bringing down Northwest Airlines Flight 253, the bombing not only would have killed hundreds but also would have had a large effect on the U.S. economy, already reeling from the worst recession since the Great Depression, and would have devastated the critical aviation and tourism businesses. It also would have likely dealt a crippling blow to Barack Obama's presidency. According to the White House's own review of the Christmas Day plot, there was sufficient information known to the U.S. government to determine that Abdulmutallab was likely working for Al Qaeda's affiliate in Yemen and that the group was looking to expand its terrorist attacks beyond the Arabian Peninsula.[34] As a senior Obama administration official responsible for counterterrorism explained shortly afterward, "AQAP was looked upon as a lethal organization, but one focused [only] on the Arabian Peninsula. We thought they would attack our embassy in Yemen or Saudi Arabia"—not a plane in the skies over America.[35] Yet the intelligence community "did not increase analytic resources working" on that threat, while information about the possible use of a PETN bomb by the Yemeni group was well known within the national security establishment, including to John Brennan, Obama's top counterterrorism adviser, who was personally briefed by Prince Nayef about the assassination attempt against him.[36] As Obama admitted in a meeting of his national security team a couple of weeks after the Christmas Day plot, "We dodged a bullet."[37]

Several other recent incidents have been linked with AQAP. A shooting last June by a self-professed AQAP operative outside a military recruiting station in Little Rock, Arkansas, killed one recruiter and wounded another; a November 2009 massacre at Fort Hood, Texas, claimed the lives of 13 people. Both shooters—Abdulhakim Mujahid Muhammad (nee Carlos Bledsoe) and Army Maj. Nidal Hasan—were connected with this same local Al Qaeda franchise. And the American-born firebrand cleric Anwar al-Awlaki, now a key AQAP operative, was involved in the radicalization of Abdulmutallab, Hasan, Shahzad, and several other persons arrested in locales as diverse as England, the United States, and most recently Singapore.[38]

The Threat from al-Shabab

Today, Shabab and its allies control about half of south-central Somalia. The group has managed to plant Al Qaeda-like ideas into the heads of even its American recruits, and has shown that it is capable ofcarrying out operations outside of Somalia.[39]

In September 2009, the Somali Islamist insurgent group al-Shabab formally pledged allegiance to Al Qaeda leader Osama bin Laden,[40] following a two-year period in which it had recruited Somali-Americans and other U.S. Muslims to fight in the war in Somalia. Six months earlier, bin Laden had given his imprimatur to the Somali *jihad* in an audiotape titled "Fight On, Champions of Somalia."[41] After it announced its fealty to bin Laden, Shabab was able to recruit larger numbers of foreign fighters; by one estimate, up to 1,200 were working with the group by 2010.[42] Today, Shabab and its allies control about half of south-central Somalia.[43]

Shabab managed to plant Al Qaeda-like ideas into the heads of even its American recruits. Shirwa Ahmed, an ethnic Somali, graduated from high school in Minneapolis in 2003, then worked pushing passengers in wheelchairs at the Minneapolis airport. During this period Ahmed was radicalized; the exact mechanisms of that radicalization are still murky, but in late 2007 he traveled to Somalia. About a year later, on 29 October 2008, Ahmed drove a truck loaded with explosives toward a government compound in Punt-land, northern Somalia, blowing himself up and killing about 20 people, including United Nations peacekeeping troops and international humanitarian assistance workers. The FBI matched Ahmed's finger, recovered at the scene, to fingerprints already on file for him.[44] Ahmed was the first American terrorist suicide attacker anywhere. It's possible that 18-year-old Omar Mohamud of Seattle was the second. On 17 September 2009, two stolen UN vehicles loaded with bombs blew up at the Mogadishu airport, killing more than a dozen peacekeepers of the African Union. The FBI suspects that Mohamud was one of the bombers.[45]

The chances of getting killed in Somalia were quite high for the couple of dozen or so Americans who had volunteered to fight there. In addition to the two young men who conducted suicide operations, six other Somali-Americans ages 18 to 30 were killed in Somalia between 2007 and 2009, as was Ruben Shumpert, an African-American convert to Islam from Seattle.[46] Given the high death rate of the Americans fighting in Somalia, as well as the considerable attention this group has received from the FBI, it is unlikely that American veterans of the Somali war pose much of a threat to the United States itself. It is plausible, however, now that Shabab has declared itself to be an Al Qaeda affiliate, that U.S. citizens in the group might be recruited to engage in anti-American operations overseas.

Indeed, Shabab has shown that it is capable of carrying out operations outside of Somalia, bombing two groups of fans watching the World Cup on television in Kampala, Uganda, on 11 July 2010, killing more than 70.[47] Eight months earlier, a 28-year-old Somali man armed with a knife and an ax had forced himself into the home of Kurt Westergaard—a Danish cartoonist who had depicted the Prophet Mohammed with a bomb in his turban—and tried unsuccessfully to break into the panic room where Westergaard was hiding. Danish intelligence officials say the suspect has links with Shabab and Al Qaeda leaders in eastern Africa.[48]

The Threat from Al Qaeda in Iraq

Al Qaeda in Iraq (AQI) has lost the ability to control large swaths of the country and a good chunk of the Sunni population as it did in 2006, but the group has proven surprisingly resilient.

In 2008 there was a sense that Al Qaeda in Iraq (AQI), Al Qaeda's Iraq-focused affiliate, was on the verge of defeat. The American ambassador to Iraq, Ryan Crocker, said, "You are not going to hear me say that Al Qaeda is defeated, but they've never been closer to defeat than they are now."[49] Certainly AQI has lost the ability to control large swaths of the country and a good chunk of the Sunni population as it did in 2006, but the group has proven surprisingly resilient, as demonstrated by the fact that it conducted large-scale bombings in central Baghdad in 2009 and 2010. AQI can also play the nationalist card quite effectively in the north, especially over the disputed city of Kirkuk, which is claimed by both Iraq's Arabs and Kurds, and Iraqi officials believe that AQI is entering into new marriages of convenience with Sunni nationalist groups that only three years ago it was at war with. It is worth noting that in the first three months of 2010, the National Counterterrorism Center found that there were more terrorist incidents in Iraq—566—than in any other country in the world; these attacks killed 667 people.[50] AQI proves that even a weakened and numerically reduced terrorist group, which has suffered successive losses of key top leaders, is still capable of inflicting severe pain on a targeted society, thus undermining public trust in the ability of the authorities to maintain order and protect its citizens.

The Threat from Al Qaeda in the Islamic Maghreb

Al Qaeda in the Islamic Maghreb (AQIM) has so far not been able to carry out attacks in the West and is one of the weakest of Al Qaeda's affiliates, only having the capacity for infrequent attacks in North Africa.

In September 2006, the leader of the Algerian Salafist Group for Call and Combat, Abu Musab Abdul Wadud, explained that Al Qaeda "is the only organization qualified to gather together the mujahideen." Subsequently taking the name "Al Qaeda in the Islamic Maghreb," the group, which had traditionally focused only on Algerian targets, conducted a range of operations: bombing the United Nations building in Algiers, attacking the Israeli embassy in Mauritania, and murdering French and British hostages.[51] AQIM has so far not been able to carry out attacks in the West and is one of the weakest of Al Qaeda's affiliates, only having the capacity for infrequent attacks in North Africa. But through kidnappings of Western tourists, aid workers, and others, it has demonstrated a stubborn capacity to raise operational funds through ransoms, which it reportedly has shared with like-minded *jihadist* groups elsewhere.[52]

The Threat from Other Al Qaeda Allies

The Threat from the Taliban in Pakistan[iv]

The Taliban in Pakistan has begun to reach beyond Pakistan's borders to plot attacks in Europe and the United States.

In 2008, for the first time,[53] the Taliban as a movement began planning seriously to attack targets in the West. According to Spanish prosecutors, Baitullah Mehsud, then the Pakistani Taliban's leader, sent a team of would-be suicide bombers to Barcelona to attack the subway system in January 2008.[54] Pakistani Taliban spokesman Maulvi Omar

[iv] The Taliban in Pakistan is distinct from the Taliban in Afghanistan, a locally focused insurgency that has not attempted to attack the American homeland.

confirmed this later in a videotaped interview, in which he said that those suicide bombers "were under pledge to Baitullah Mehsud" and were sent because of the Spanish military presence in Afghanistan.

In March 2009, Baitullah Mehsud threatened an attack in America, telling the Associated Press by phone, "Soon we will launch an attack in Washington that will amaze everyone in the world." This was largely discounted at the time as bloviating, but by the end of the year the Pakistani Taliban were training an American recruit for just such an attack. Faisal Shahzad, who had once worked as a financial analyst in the accounting department at the Elizabeth Arden cosmetics company in Stamford, Connecticut, traveled to Pakistan, where he received five days of bomb-making training from the Pakistani Taliban in the tribal region of Waziristan.[55] During his time there, Shahzad also met with Hakimullah Mehsud, the new leader of the Pakistani Taliban following Baitullah's death, and a video of that meeting released by the Taliban's propaganda division shows the two shaking hands and hugging.[56]

Armed with his training from the Pakistani Taliban and $12,000 in cash, Shahzad returned to Connecticut, where he purchased a Nissan Pathfinder. He spent a fast four months from training to building his bomb, which he placed in the SUV and attempted to detonate in Times Square on 1 May 2010, around 6 p.m., when the sidewalks were thick with tourists and theatergoers. The bomb, which was designed to act as a fuel-air explosive, was a dud. Shahzad was arrested two days later as he tried to leave JFK Airport if for Pakistan.[57]

Media accounts have largely painted Shahzad as a feckless terrorist, but though his attack may have been rushed and therefore botched, that does not mean it was not deadly serious. The training he received was arguably too cursory and too compressed in terms of instruction to provide Shahzad with the requisite skills needed to succeed in Times Square last May. But in fact, Shahzad did a number of things indicating that he had received some at least rudimentary countersurveillance techniques: He eliminated one of the Vehicle Identification Numbers on his SUV; he purchased the type of fertilizer that would not trigger suspicions that he was building a fertilizer-based bomb; and he avoided building a hydrogen peroxide-based bomb, as large-scale purchases of hydrogen peroxide that do not appear to have a legitimate purpose are now likely to draw law enforcement attention in the United States. "A successful Faisal Shahzad," a senior local law enforcement official said, "is our worst case scenario."[58]

The Threat from Lashkar-e-Taiba

The Mumbai attacks of 2008 showed that Al Qaeda's ideas about attacking Western and Jewish targets had also spread to Pakistani militant groups like Lashkar-e-Taiba, which had previously focused only on Indian targets.

Over a three-day period in late November 2008, Lashkar-e-Taiba (LeT) carried out multiple attacks in Mumbai targeting five-star hotels housing Westerners, as well as a Jewish-American community center. Additional incidents involved the Pakistan-born U.S. citizen David Headley (who had changed his name from Daood Sayed Gilani). Headley's reconnaissance efforts on behalf of Lashkar-e-Taiba were pivotal to the attacks in Mumbai. Last year he also planned an operation to kill those responsible for the 2005 publication in a Danish newspaper of cartoons of the Prophet Mohammed, which many Muslims had deemed to be offensive.[59]

One of the more predictable foreign policy challenges of the next years is a "Mumbai II": a large-scale attack on a major Indian city by a Pakistani militant group that kills hundreds. The Indian government showed considerable restraint in its reaction to the provocation of the Mumbai attacks in 2008. Another such attack, however, would likely produce considerable political pressure on the Indian government to "do something." That something would likely involve incursions over the border to eliminate the training camps of Pakistani militant groups with histories of attacking India. That could lead in turn to a full-blown war for the fourth time since 1947 between India and Pakistan. Such a war involves the possibility of a nuclear exchange and the certainty that Pakistan would move substantial resources to its eastern border and away from fighting the Taliban on its western border, so relieving pressure on all the militant groups based there, including Al Qaeda.

The Threat from Uzbek Militant Groups[60]

Among Al Qaeda's affiliates in Pakistan's tribal areas, the Islamic Movement of Uzbekistan (IMU) and its spinoff, the Islamic Jihad Union (IJU), seem to have attracted the most Westerners recently—several dozen in the last three years, the majority from Germany, including at least 30 Germans in 2009.[61]

Unlike its parent organization, the IMU, whose primary goal is to establish an Islamic state in Uzbekistan and has not explicitly threatened the German homeland in its propaganda, the IJU has thrown its weight behind Al Qaeda's global *jihad,* as demonstrated by the "Sauerland cell." Two Germans and two Turks who received training in weapons, poisons, martial arts, and bomb-making from the IJU in North Waziristan in the summer of 2006 were arrested in September 2007 and accused of plotting to attack American facilities in Germany, including Ramstein Air Base, and clubs and bars popular with U.S. troops. German officials said the Sauerland cell had stockpiled 730 kg of hydrogen peroxide that, when mixed with other materials, could have made explosives equivalent to 550 kg of dynamite.[62] In March 2010, three of the men were convicted of membership in a terrorist organization, and the fourth of supporting a terrorist organization; all four were convicted of conspiracy to commit murder and of preparing explosive devices. They received sentences of up to 12 years in prison.[63]

The Sauerland cell set up a recruitment and facilitation network that has continued to serve as a pipeline to Pakistan's Federally Administered Tribal Areas for German would-be militants; there may also be similar networks for the IMU. Both groups regularly feature their German members in German-language recruitment videos, and one September 2009 tape showed an entire village of German *jihadists* and their families living in the mountains of Waziristan.[64] As of October 2010, German antiterrorism police officials said that some 220 people traveled from Germany to Pakistan and Afghanistan to seek militant training, and at least 70 received it.[65]

Trends in the Changing Threat Environment

1. *Who are these* jihadists? *A key shift in the threat to the homeland since around the time President Barack Obama took office is the increasing "Americanization" of the leadership of Al Qaeda and aligned groups, and the larger numbers of Americans attaching themselves to these groups.*

Anwar al-Awlaki, the Yemeni-American cleric who grew up in New Mexico, is today playing an important operational role in Al Qaeda in the Arabian Peninsula,[66] while Adnan Shukrijumah, the Saudi-American who grew up in Brooklyn and Florida, is now effectively Al Qaeda's director of external operations. In 2009, Shukrijumah tasked Najibullah Zazi and two other Americans to attack targets in the United States. Omar Hammami, a Baptist convert to Islam from Alabama, is both a key propagandist and a military commander for al-Shabab, the Somali Al Qaeda affiliate,[67] while Chicagoan David Headley played a role in scoping the targets for the Lashkar-e-Taiba attacks on Mumbai in late 2008 that killed more than 160 people.

There is little precedent for the high-level operational roles that Americans are currently playing in Al Qaeda and affiliated groups other than the case of Ali Mohamed, an Egyptian-American former U.S. Army sergeant, who was a key military trainer for Al Qaeda during the 1990s until his arrest after the bombings of the two American embassies in Africa in 1998.

Al Qaeda and like-minded groups have also successfully attracted into their ranks dozens of American citizens and residents as foot soldiers since January 2009. Most prominent among them are Najibullah Zazi and Faisal Shahzad.

2. *These would-be* jihadists *do not fit any particular ethnic, economic, educational, or social profile.*

Comforting theories about poverty, lack of education, and lack of opportunity have long figured prominently in explanations for the eruption of terrorism.[68] Indeed, in the aftermath of the attacks of 11 September 2001, this debate over the "root causes" of terrorism acquired new relevance and greater urgency. A succession of global leaders seemed to fasten on poverty, illiteracy, and lack of education as the sources of worldwide terrorism and insurgency.[69] "We fight against poverty because hope is an answer to terror," President George W. Bush, for example, declared before the United Nations Financing for Development Conference in March 2002."We will challenge the poverty and hopelessness and lack of education and failed governments that too often allow conditions that terrorists can seize and try to turn to their advantage."[70] His statement was but one of a plethora of similar panaceas repeatedly provided in the wake of 9/11.[v]

Nearly a decade later, such arguments are still heard. In February 2009, for example, Pakistani Prime Minister Yusuf Raza Gilani attempted to rally support for his government's controversial truce with Taliban fighters in the Swat Valley by claiming that, since illiteracy is the source of terrorism and insurgency, greater peace and stability in the region would now enable leaders in Islamabad to improve education in Swat and thereby eliminate political violence.[71] Following the attempted Christmas Day bombing, President Barack Obama implied such a causal connection with respect to AQAP's resurgence in Yemen.[72]

But the historical and contemporary empirical evidence fails to support such sweeping claims—with Faisal Shahzad himself the latest example. Shahzad had a degree in computing and an MBA. Until he quit his job, he was gainfully employed. He had a wife and

[v] World figures as diverse as British Prime Minister Tony Blair, Pope John Paul II, Malaysian Prime Minister Mahathir Mohamad, Jordanian Prime Minister Ali Abul Ragheb, and Phillippine President Gloria Macapagal-Arroyo, as well as Nobel Peace Prize laureates Elie Wiesel, Desmond Tutu, the Dalai Lama, Kim Dae-jung, and Oscar Arias Sanchez, similarly identified these same "root causes."

two children and, for all intents and purposes, seemed to be living the suburban American dream with a single-family home in Shelton, Connecticut.

Umar Farouq Abdulmuttalab—the Christmas Day would-be bomber—similarly defied the conventional wisdom about the stereotypical suicide terrorist. He was a graduate of University College, London, one of Britain's best universities, and is the son of a wealthy Nigerian banker and former government official. Not only did he hold a degree in engineering from a very good university, but he was cosmopolitan: Having lived abroad, he was at ease traversing the globe without arousing suspicion.[73] As the terrorism expert Walter Laqueur explained seven years ago, for terrorists to survive, much less thrive, in today's globalized, technologically savvy and interconnected world, they have to be

> educated, have some technical competence and be able to move without attracting attention in alien societies. In brief, such a person will have to have an education that cannot be found among the poor in Pakistani or Egyptian villages or Palestinian refugee camps, only among relatively well-off town folk.[74]

Nor do the would-be *jihadists* fit any particular ethnic profile. According to the authors' analysis of the 57 Americans whose ethnicities are known who were charged or convicted of Islamist terrorism crimes in the United States or elsewhere between January 2009 and September 2010, 21 percent (12) were Caucasian-Americans, 18 percent (10) Arab-Americans, 14 percent (8) South Asian-Americans, 9 percent (5) African-Americans, 4 percent (2) Hispanic-Americans, and 2 percent (1) Caribbean-American. The single largest bloc was Somali-Americans at 31 percent, a number that reflects the recent crackdown by federal authorities on support networks for Americans traveling to Somalia to fight with Shabab.[75]

The American "melting pot" has not provided a firewall against the radicalization and recruitment of American citizens and residents, although it has arguably lulled the United States into a sense of complacency that homegrown terrorism could not happen here. Before the 7 July 2005 suicide attacks on the London transportation system, the British believed that there was perhaps a problem with the Muslim communities in Europe but certainly not with British Muslims in the United Kingdom, who were better integrated, better educated, and wealthier than their counterparts on the Continent.

By stubbornly wrapping itself in this same false security blanket, the United States lost five years to learn from the British experience. Well over a year ago, federal authorities became aware of radicalization and recruitment occurring in the United States when Somali-Americans started disappearing from the Minneapolis–St. Paul area and turning up in Somalia with Shabab. Administration officials and others believed it was an isolated, one-off phenomenon. But it was not—as grand juries in Minnesota and San Diego can attest, along with ongoing FBI investigations in Boston, two locations in Ohio, and Portland, Maine. The number of Somali-Americans who left the United States to train in Somalia turned out to be far higher than initially believed, and once they were in Somalia some were indeed being trained by Al Qaeda.

In sum, the case of the Somali-Americans turned out to be a Pandora's Box. By not taking more urgently and seriously the radicalization and recruitment that was actually occurring in the United States, authorities failed to comprehend that this was not an isolated phenomenon, specific to Minnesota and this particular immigrant community. Rather, it indicated the possibility that even an embryonic terrorist radicalization and recruitment infrastructure had been established in the U.S. homeland. Shahzad is the latest person to jump out of this box.

3. *Where are the* jihadists *operating? The United States used to be generally the target of Sunni militant terrorists, but now the country is also increasingly exporting American militants to conduct* jihad *overseas.*

Not only was David Headley responsible for much of the surveillance of the targets for the 2008 Mumbai attacks, he also traveled in 2009 to the Danish capital, Copenhagen, where he reconnoitered the *Jyllands-Posten* newspaper for an attack. A year earlier Osama bin Laden had denounced the publication of cartoons of the Prophet Mohammed in the *Jyllands-Posten* as a "catastrophe" for which retribution would be meted out. Following his trip to Denmark, Headley traveled to Pakistan to meet with Ilyas Kashmiri, who runs Harakat-ul-Jihad Islami, a terrorist organization tied to Al Qaeda.[76] Headley was arrested in Chicago in October 2009 as he was preparing to travel to Pakistan again. He told investigators that he was planning to kill the *Jyllands-Posten's* editor who had commissioned the cartoons, as well as Kurt Westergaard, who had drawn the cartoon he found most offensive, the Prophet Mohammed with a bomb concealed in his turban.

Similarly, Colleen R. LaRose, a 46-year-old Caucasian-American high school dropout known in *jihadist* circles by her Internet handle "Jihad Jane," traveled to Europe in the summer of 2009 to scope out an alleged attack on Lars Vilks, a Swedish artist who had drawn a cartoon of the Prophet Mohammed s head on the body of a dog.[77]

By the end of 2009, 14 American citizens and residents (all but one of Somali descent) had been indicted for recruiting at least 20 others to fight in Somalia, or for fundraising for Shabab. Zazi, Shahzad, the "Northern Virginia Five," and allegedly Daniel Boyd are other examples of American citizens or residents who at one point sought to join *jihadist* groups abroad.

Al Qaeda's Strategy

In assessing the proliferation of terrorist threats to the American homeland, senior U.S. counterterrorism officials now repeatedly call attention to Al Qaeda's strategy of "diversification"—mounting attacks involving a wide variety of perpetrators of different nationalities and ethnic heritages to defeat any attempt to "profile" actual and would-be perpetrators and to overwhelm already information-overloaded law enforcement and intelligence agencies. "Diversity," one senior local law enforcement official explained, "is definitely the word."[78] Similarly, in a 30 June 2010, interview at the Aspen Security Forum, Michael Leiter, director of the National Counterterrorism Center, also identified this trend. "What we have seen, which is I think most problematic to me and most difficult for the counterterrorism community," he explained,

> is a diversification of that threat. We not only face Al Qaeda senior leadership, we do face a troubling alignment of Al Qaeda and some more traditional Pakistani militant groups in Pakistan, and, is as well known to this group and most Americans, the threat of Abdulmutallab that has highlighted the threat we see from Al Qaeda in Yemen, the ongoing threat we see from Al Qaeda elements in East Africa.[79]

The variety of the perpetrators and nature of their U.S. plots is remarkable. As discussed above, these have included: trained Al Qaeda operatives like Najibullah Zazi, the Afghan-born U.S. resident who sought to replicate the 7 July 2005 suicide attacks on London transport in Manhattan; motivated but less competent recruits like the five youths from a Washington, D.C., suburb who in December 2009 sought training in Pakistan; dedicated sleeper agents like the U.S. citizen and Drug Enforcement Administration informant[80] David Headley, whose reconnaissance efforts on behalf of Lashkar-e-Taiba were pivotal to the 2008 attacks in Mumbai; bona fide "lone wolves" like Nidal Hasan, the U.S. Army major responsible for murdering 13 persons at Fort Hood, Texas; and other individuals with murkier terrorist connections like Abdulhakim Muhammad (nee Carlos Bledsoe), an African-American convert to Islam who returned from Yemen last year and killed a U.S. military recruiter in Little Rock, Arkansas, and has now claimed in court to have done so on behalf of AQAP; and, finally, the clueless incompetents who are easily apprehended by the authorities, such as the Jordanian national who overstayed his U.S. tourist visa and plotted to bomb a downtown Dallas office tower last September, and the convert to Islam who wanted to blow up a federal building in Springfield, Illinois, that same month.

This is part and parcel of a strategy that Al Qaeda has also pushed on other groups. The strategy is deliberately designed to overwhelm, distract, and exhaust Al Qaeda's adversaries. There are two components: one is economic; the other, operational. Al Qaeda has rarely claimed it could or would defeat the U.S. militarily. Instead, it hopes to wear the United States down economically by forcing it to spend more on domestic security and remain involved in costly overseas military commitments. Given the current global economic downturn, this message arguably has greater resonance now with Al Qaeda s followers and supporters, and perhaps even with recruits. The operational dimension seeks to flood already stressed intelligence and law enforcement agencies with "noise": low-level threats from "lone wolves" and other *jihadist* "hangers-on." This "low-hanging fruit" is designed to distract law enforcement and intelligence personnel from more serious terrorist operations, allowing such plots to go unnoticed beneath the radar and thereby succeed.[81]

Four of Al Qaeda's Strengths[82]

One strength is that the group's ideological influence on other *jihadist* groups is on the rise in South Asia. One of the key leaders of the Taliban as it surged in strength several years after 9/11 was Mullah Dadullah, a thuggish but effective commander who, like his counterpart in Iraq, Abu Musab al-Zarqawi, thrived on killing Shi'a, beheading his hostages, and media celebrity.[83] In interviews in 2006, Dadullah conceded what was obvious as the violence dramatically expanded in Afghanistan between 2005 and 2006: that the Taliban had increasingly morphed together tactically and ideologically with Al Qaeda. "Osama bin Laden, thank God, is alive and in good health. We are in contact with his top aides and sharing plans and operations with each other.[84] The Taliban also adopted the playbook of Al Qaeda in Iraq wholesale, embracing suicide bombers, but only began deploying suicide attackers in large numbers from 2005 forward after the success of such operations in Iraq had become obvious to all. Where once the Taliban had banned television, now they boast an active video propaganda operation named Umar, which posts regular updates to the Web mimicking those of Al Qaeda's production arm, Al-Sahab.

Second, Al Qaeda's influence has continued to extend beyond South Asia, as it inspires and gives guidance to Al Qaeda affiliates in eastern Africa, North Africa, Iraq, Yemen, and Saudi Arabia.

A third key pillar of Al Qaeda's resilience stems from the simple fact that its top leadership is still intact. Osama bin Laden and his deputy, Ayman al-Zawahiri, are still at liberty. This matters for several reasons. First, there is the matter of justice for the almost 3,000 people who died in the 11 September attacks and for the thousands of other victims of Al Qaeda's attacks around the world. Second, every day that bin Laden remains at large is a propaganda victory for Al Qaeda. Third, although bin Laden and al-Zawahiri are not managing Al Qaeda's operations on a daily basis, they guide the overall direction of the *jihadist* movement around the world, even while they are in hiding, through videotapes and audiotapes that they continue to release on a regular basis.

Those messages from Al Qaeda's leaders have reached untold millions worldwide via television, the Internet, and newspapers. The tapes have not only instructed Al Qaeda's followers to continue to kill Westerners and Jews, but some also carried specific instructions that militant cells then acted on. In March 2008, for instance, bin Laden denounced the publication of cartoons of the Prophet Mohammed in the Danish newspaper, which he said would soon be avenged. Three months later, an Al Qaeda suicide attacker bombed the Danish embassy in Islamabad, killing six.

A final strength is that Al Qaeda and affiliated groups can provoke a massive amount of overwrought media coverage based on attacks that do not even succeed—such as the near-miss on Christmas Day 2009. The person who seems to best understand the benefits of American overreaction is bin Laden himself, who in 2004 said on a tape that aired on Al-Jazeera, "All that we have to do is to send two mujahedeen to the furthest point east to raise a piece of cloth on which is written al Qaeda, in order to make generals race there to cause America to suffer human, economic and political losses without their achieving anything of note other than some benefits for their private corporations."[85]

American officials and the wider public should realize that, by the law of averages, Al Qaeda or an affiliate will succeed in getting some kind of attack through in the next years, and that the best response would be to demonstrate that the United States as a society is resilient and is not being intimidated by such actions.

Four Operational and Four Strategic Weaknesses Trouble Al Qaeda

First, drone attacks in Pakistan have degraded the group's central leadership and operational capability in Pakistan. In 2007, there were three reported drone strikes in Pakistan; in 2008, there were 33; and, by the end of September 2010, the Obama administration had already authorized 127.[86] Since the summer of 2008, U.S. drones have killed scores of lower-ranking militants and at least a dozen mid- and upper-level leaders within Al Qaeda or the Taliban in Pakistan's tribal regions.

Officials in both the Bush and Obama administrations have been leery of discussing the highly classified drone program on the record, but a window into their thinking was provided by the remarks of then-CIA director Michael Hayden on 13 November 2008, as the drone program was in full swing. "By making a safe haven feel less safe, we keep Al Qaeda guessing. We make them doubt their allies; question their methods, their plans, even their priorities."[87] This strategy seems to have worked, at least up to a point. Since the summer of 2008 when the drone program was ramped up, law enforcement authorities have uncovered only two plots against American targets traceable back to Pakistan's tribal regions (the Zazi and Shahzad cases mentioned earlier). However, Western militants have continued to travel to the tribal regions where, by one estimate, as many as 150 Westerners have sought training in recent years, including dozens of German citizens or residents.[88]

The drone program has certainly put additional pressure on Al Qaeda's propaganda arm and its top leaders. Al Qaeda takes its propaganda operations seriously; bin Laden has observed that 90 percent of his battle is waged in the media, and al-Zawahiri has made similar comments. In 2007, al Qaeda's video production arm Al-Sahab had a banner year, releasing almost 100 tapes. But in 2008, the year the drone program was dramatically expanded, the number of releases dropped by half, indicating that the group's leaders were more concerned with survival than public relations. According to IntelCenter, a Washington-based group that tracks *jihadist* propaganda, in the first nine months of 2010 al-Zawahiri released the fewest tapes in seven years—only two audiotapes, as opposed to nine audiotapes and one video in 2009—while other Al Qaeda leaders such as Abu Yahya al-Libi similarly fell relatively silent in 2010. Bin Laden resurfaced in early October 2010 after several months of silence.

According to a counterterrorism official, the fact that bin Laden and al-Zawahiri are keeping such a low profile is causing some criticism of the leaders within Al Qaeda itself. These critics say it is worrisome that their leaders are saying so little and are not managing the organization. Some have gone so far as to say "it would be helpful if the boss gave a damn," according to this counterterrorism official.[89]

When Faisal Shahzad traveled to Pakistan to link up with the Taliban in the winter of 2009, he spent a total of 40 days in the Taliban heartland of Waziristan but only five days actually being trained, which likely accounts for his lack of skills as a bombmaker.[90] This abbreviated training schedule may have been the result of the pressure that the drone program is putting on militants in Pakistan's tribal regions, including Waziristan.

The well-known fact that the drones have killed hundreds of militants in Pakistan's border regions is also having an effect on where Western militants—including from the United States—are seeking training, as some are opting to go to Somalia or Yemen, according to a counterterrorism official.[91]

Second, Pakistanis have increasingly negative attitudes about the militants based on their territory, and Pakistan has made more concerted efforts to take on the extremists militarily. If there is a silver lining to the militant atrocities that have plagued Pakistan in the past several years, it is the fact that the Pakistani public, government, and military are increasingly seeing the *jihadist* militants there in a hostile light. The Pakistani Taliban's assassination of Benazir Bhutto, the country's most popular politician; Al Qaeda's bombing of the Marriott hotel in Islamabad; the attack on the visiting Sri Lankan cricket team in Lahore; the widely circulated video images of the Taliban flogging a 17-year-old girl—each of these has provoked real revulsion among the Pakistani public, which is, in the main, utterly opposed to the militants.[92]

In fact, historians will likely record the Taliban's decision to move in early 2009 from the Swat Valley into Buner District, only 60 miles from Islamabad, as the tipping point that finally galvanized the sclerotic Pakistani state to confront the fact that the *jihadist* monster it had helped to spawn was now trying to swallow it.[93]

The subsequent military operation to evict the Taliban from Buner and Swat was not seen by the Pakistani public as the army acting on behalf of the United States, as was often the case in previous such operations, but something that was in their own national interest. Support for Pakistani army operations against the Taliban in Swat has increased from 28 percent two years ago to 69 percent today. Support for suicide bombings has dropped from 33 percent to 8 percent in Pakistan over the past several years, while the number of Pakistanis who feel that the Taliban and Al Qaeda operating in Pakistan are a "serious problem" has risen from 57 percent to 86 percent since 2007.[94]

After having suffered three defeats in the tribal region of South Waziristan over the previous five years, the Pakistani army went in again in October 2009, this time with a force of at least 30,000 troops, following several months of bombing of Taliban positions.[95] These operations were conducted with the support of at least half of the Pakistani public.[96]

The changing attitude of the Pakistani public, military, and government constitutes arguably the most significant strategic shift against Al Qaeda and its allies in the past several years, as it will have a direct impact on the terrorist organization and allied groups that are headquartered in Pakistan. However, the changing attitudes do not mean, for the moment, that the Pakistani military will do much to move against the Taliban groups there that are attacking U.S. and other NATO forces in Afghanistan, such as Mullah Omar's Quetta Shura, the Haqqani Network, and Gulbuddin Hekmatyar s Hezb-i-Islami.

Pakistan's massive and prolonged flooding, to which the military is responding on a large scale, is likely to give the militants on the Afghanistan—Pakistan border some breathing room.

A third key weakness of Al Qaeda is the increasingly hostile attitude toward the group and its allies in the Muslim world in general. This is because most of the victims of these groups are Muslim civilians.[97] This has created a dawning recognition among Muslims that the ideological virus that unleashed 11 September and the terrorist attacks in London and Madrid is the same virus now wreaking havoc in Muslim countries such as Pakistan and Iraq. Until the terrorist attacks of May 2003 in Riyadh, for instance, the Saudi government was largely in denial about its large-scale Al Qaeda problem. There have been some 20 terrorist attacks since then in the kingdom and, as a result, the Saudi government has taken aggressive steps—arresting thousands of suspected terrorists, killing more than a hundred, implementing an expansive public information campaign against them, and arresting preachers deemed to be encouraging militancy.

Polling around the Muslim world also shows sharp drops in support for Osama bin Laden personally and for suicide bombings in general. Support for suicide bombings has dropped in Indonesia, for instance, from 26 percent to 15 percent in the past eight years and in Jordan from 43 percent to 20 percent.[98]

A fourth problem for Al Qaeda is that some *jihadist* ideologues and erstwhile militant allies have now *also* turned against it. They include religious scholars and militants whom the organization had relied upon in the past for various kinds of support. Around the sixth anniversary of 11 September, Sheikh Salman al-Awdah, a leading Saudi religious scholar, addressed Al Qaeda's leader on MBC, a widely watched Middle East TV network: "My brother Osama, how much blood has been spilt? How many innocent people, children, elderly, and women have been killed . . . in the name of Al Qaeda? Will you be happy to meet God Almighty carrying the burden of these hundreds of thousands or millions [of victims] on your back?" What was noteworthy about Awdah's statement was that it was not simply a condemnation of terrorism, or even of 11 September, but that it was a personal rebuke of bin Laden himself.[99]

Similarly, leaders of the Libyan Islamic Fighting Group, which was once loosely aligned with Al Qaeda, in 2009 officially turned against Al Qaeda's ideology of global *jihad* and made a peace deal with the Libyan government.

In addition to the four operational problems facing Al Qaeda, the group has four key strategic issues that foreshadow its long-term implosion. First, Al Qaeda keeps killing Muslim civilians. This weighs especially heavily in the diminishing support for Al Qaeda among Muslims, since the Koran forbids killing civilians and fellow Muslims.[vi] Second, Al Qaeda has not created a genuine mass political movement. Third, Al Qaeda's leaders have constantly expanded their list of enemies. Al Qaeda has said at various times that it is opposed to all Middle Eastern regimes; Muslims who do not share their views; the Shi'a; most Western countries; Jews and Christians; the governments of India, Pakistan, Afghanistan, and Russia; most news organizations; the United Nations; and international nongovernmental organizations. It's very hard to think of a category of person, institution, or government that Al Qaeda does not oppose. Making a world of enemies is never a winning strategy. And finally, Al Qaeda has no positive vision. It is known what bin Laden is against, but what's he really for? If you asked him, he would say the restoration of the caliphate. In practice that means Taliban-style theocracies stretching from Indonesia to Morocco. A silent majority of Muslims do not want that. Al Qaeda is, in short, losing the war of ideas in the Islamic world. Still, even terrorist groups with little popular support or legitimacy can continue to carry out infrequent but often highly consequential attacks, as the Red Army Faction demonstrated in West Germany in the 1980s and 1990s.

Potential Future *Jihadist* Attacks: Strategic Calculations, Operations, and Tactics

Strategic Calculations: Risk Assessment

Several disquieting trends converged in Times Square on 1 May 2010.[100] First, a foreign terrorist group, with a hitherto local agenda and otherwise parochial aims, once more stretched its wings and sought to operate on a broader, more ambitious global canvas. Second, the conventional wisdom, which has long held that the threat to the United States was primarily external, involving foreigners coming from overseas to kill Americans in this country as on 11 September 2001, was once again shattered. Third, the comforting stereotype that terrorists are poor, uneducated, provincial loners, and thus are both different from everyone else and can be readily identified, was again refuted. Fourth, the

[vi] It is a positive development that Al Qaeda's killing of Muslim civilians has turned popular opinion away from the group. However, historically, even when terrorist groups have killed more of their ethnic or religious brethren than their enemy—such as in Algeria in the 1950s, Northern Ireland in 1968–98, and Palestine since 1968—it has not really harmed their fortunes. The National Liberation Front came to power after torturing and killing far more Muslim Algerians that the French ever did; the Provisional Irish Republican Army killed over 2,000 civilians, the majority of whom were Roman Catholics, compared with only a few hundred British soldiers, police, and Protestants, yet its political wing, Sinn Fein, is now part of Northern Ireland's governing body. Palestinians have always killed far more of one another (not least during the past few years in Gaza infighting between Fatah and Hamas) than Israelis and Jews.

belief that the American "melting pot" would provide a firewall against radicalization and recruitment, given the historical U.S. capacity to readily absorb new immigrants, fell by the wayside. Finally, it became apparent that Al Qaeda and its allies have embraced a strategy of attrition that is deliberately designed to overwhelm, distract, and exhaust its adversaries. The Times Square incident, despite initial claims to the contrary, was not a "one-off" event perpetrated by a "lone wolf" but rather is part of an emerging pattern of terrorism that directly threatens the United States and presents new challenges to U.S. national security.[101]

This was precisely the message that Faisal Shahzad sought to convey when he appeared before a U.S. District Court in New York in June 2010. Declaring himself a "holy warrior" (*mujahid*) and a "Muslim soldier" who had been deployed by the Tehrik-e-Taliban Pakistan (Pakistani Taliban) to wage what he called a "war" in the United States, Shahzad described himself as "part of the answer to the U.S. terrorizing Muslim nations and the Muslim people." He further promised that if Washington did not cease invading Muslim lands and did not withdraw from Iraq, Afghanistan, and other Muslim countries, more attacks on the United States would follow. Americans, Shahzad explained, "don't see the drones killing children in Afghanistan. . . . [They] only care about their people, but they don't care about the people elsewhere in the world when they die." In his view, this means that attacks on children and innocents are both justified and should be expected.[102]

While it is perhaps tempting to dismiss Shahzad's threats as the irrelevant ranting of an incompetent wannabe terrorist, he and his likely successors present the most serious challenge to the security of the United States and the safety of its citizens and residents since the 11 September 2001 attacks. There are at least four good reasons for taking Shahzad at his word.

Cost-Benefit Analysis. Shahzad's attack may have been a failure, but the potential for damage was substantial. One can be certain that the terrorist movement responsible for deploying the next attacker to the United States will try to provide that person with the requisite training to ensure the success of that attack. Terrorists play the odds, thus perhaps explaining the seeming "amateurish" dimension of the Times Square plot. What appeared "amateurish" to many Americans may in fact be more a reflection of the attack having been rushed and the perpetrator too hastily deployed. At a time when the capabilities of the Pakistani Taliban and Al Qaeda in Pakistan are being relentlessly degraded by U.S. drone attacks, this make sense. Both groups may feel pressed to implement an operation either sooner or more precipitously than they might otherwise prefer. Fears of the would-be attacker being identified and interdicted by authorities may thus account for what appears to be a more compressed operational tempo and faster "soup to nuts" process by which a recruit is radicalized, trained, and operationally deployed.

The Pakistani Taliban as well as Al Qaeda may be prepared to accept the tradeoff of shorter training periods leading to accelerated plots though less reliable operations in order to dispatch "clean skin" recruits before they can be identified, detected, and stopped. For the terrorist groups behind such plots, this arguably represents an acceptable risk for a potentially huge return on a modest investment. They will have expended little effort and energy training operatives like Shahzad who present them with new, attractive low-cost opportunities to strike in the United States.

These groups may also pin their faith and hopes on eventually simply getting lucky. Over a quarter of a century ago, the Irish Republican Army famously taunted then—Prime

Minister Margaret Thatcher after its bombers failed to kill her at the 1984 Conservative Party conference in Brighton, England, with the memorable words: "Today we were unlucky, but remember we only have to be lucky once. You will have to be lucky always."[103] Al Qaeda, the Pakistani Taliban, and their allies doubtless have embraced the same logic.

Terrorism Is Inexpensive. A Times Square—style plot is by no means an expensive proposition for any terrorist group to undertake. The grand jury indictment details how two payments totaling approximately $12,000—roughly the same cost of the 7 July 2005, suicide attacks on London's public transportation system—were effortlessly transferred from overseas bank accounts to Shahzad via locations in Massachusetts and New York State. Given the minimal cost of orchestrating such an operation, foreign terrorist groups will likely continue to regard U.S. homeland operations as both desirable and at least financially feasible options. They also understand that even failed plots, such as Shahzad's bungled effort, can still pay vast dividends in terms of publicity and attention.

An Ongoing Campaign. As mentioned earlier, Shahzad's attempted attack should not be considered a "one-off," but as a single component of an ongoing effort by Al Qaeda and its allies to target the U.S. homeland.

Smaller-Scale Attacks. As one counterterrorism official put it, "Abdulmutallab is not a very high barrier for terrorist groups to surmount. His attack demonstrated to other terrorists that you don't have to be [9/11 operational commander] Khalid Sheikh Mohammed to carry out an attack." Another counterterrorism official said terrorist groups now see the United States as more "gettable" because of the failed plots on Christmas Day 2009 and in Times Square in 2010. Smaller-bore plots and attacks by a wider range of *jihadist* groups are the likely pattern going forward, closer to the attacks that killed 52 commuters in London on 7 July 2005, than anything on the scale of 9/11.

Potential Future Targets

Commercial Aviation. A cell of British Pakistanis, some trained by Al Qaeda, plotted to bring down seven passenger jets flying to the United States and Canada from Britain during the summer of 2006. During the trial of the men accused in the "planes plot," the prosecution argued that some 1,500 passengers would have died if all seven of the targeted planes had been brought down, and most of the victims would have been Americans, Britons, and Canadians.[104]

The U.K.-based planes plot did not stand alone. Four years earlier, an Al Qaeda affiliate in Kenya had almost succeeded in bringing down an Israeli passenger jet with a surface-to-air missile,[105] while in 2003 a plane belonging to the DHL courier service was struck by a missile as it took off from the Baghdad airport.[106] The same year militants cased the Riyadh airport and were planning to attack British Airways flights into Saudi Arabia.[107] In 2007, two British doctors with possible ties to Al Qaeda in Iraq tried unsuccessfully to ignite a car bomb at the Glasgow airport.[108] And if the Nigerian Umar Farouk Abdulmutallab had brought down the Northwest Airlines flight over Detroit on Christmas Day 2009, it would have been Al Qaeda's most successful attack on an American target since it destroyed the World Trade Center towers and part of the Pentagon.

According to several counterterrorism officials the authors spoke to, the skilled Yemeni-based bombmaker who built Abdulmutallab's explosive is still at large. He is likely to try to bring down another commercial jet with a concealed bomb that is not detectable by metal detectors. And Al Qaeda or an affiliate could also try to down a jet with a surface-to-air missile, as was attempted in Kenya in 2002.

Distinctive Western Brand Names, in Particular American Hotel Chains. Since the 9/11 attacks, Al Qaeda and its affiliated groups have increasingly attacked economic and business targets. The shift in tactics was in part a response to the fact that the traditional pre-9/11 targets, such as American embassies, warships, and military bases, are now better defended, while so-called soft economic targets are both ubiquitous and easier to hit. In 2002, a group of 11 French defense contractors were killed as they left a Sheraton hotel in Karachi, which was heavily damaged.[109] In 2003, suicide attackers bombed the J.W. Marriott hotel in Jakarta; bombers struck it again six years later, simultaneously also attacking the Ritz Carlton hotel in the Indonesian capital.[110] In October 2004, in Taba, Egyptian *jihadists* attacked a Hilton hotel. In Amman, Jordan, in November 2005, Al Qaeda attacked three hotels with well-known American names—the Grand Hyatt, Radisson, and Days Inn.[111] Five-star hotels that cater to Westerners abroad are a perennial target for *jihadists:* in 2008 the Taj and Oberoi in Mumbai, the Serena in Kabul, and the Marriott in Islamabad, and in 2009 the Pearl Continental in Peshawar. Such attacks will likely continue, as hotels are in the hospitality business and cannot turn themselves into fortresses.

Israeli/Jewish Targets. This is an Al Qaeda strategy that has only emerged strongly post-9/11. Despite bin Laden's declaration in February 1998 that he was creating the "World Islamic Front against the Crusaders and the Jews," Al Qaeda only started attacking Israeli or Jewish targets in early 2002. Since then, Al Qaeda and its affiliated groups have directed a campaign against Israeli and Jewish targets, killing journalist Daniel Pearl in Karachi, bombing synagogues and Jewish centers in Tunisia, Morocco, and Turkey, and attacking an Israeli-owned hotel in Mombasa, Kenya, killing 13. Al Qaeda's North African affiliate attacked the Israeli embassy in Mauritania in 2008.

American Soldiers Fighting Wars in Two Muslim Countries. A few months before Army Maj. Nidal Malik Hasan's murderous spree in Texas, Abdulhakim Mujahid Muhammad, an African-American convert to Islam, attacked two U.S. military recruiters in Little Rock, Arkansas, killing one and wounding the other. Despite the fact that the FBI had had him under surveillance following a mysterious trip that he had recently taken to Yemen, Muhammad was still able to acquire guns and attack the recruiting station in broad daylight. When Muhammad was arrested in his vehicle, police found a rifle with a laser sight, a revolver, ammunition, and the makings of Molotov cocktails.[112]

Daniel Boyd, the alleged leader of the *jihadist* cell in North Carolina, obtained maps of the Quantico Marine base in Virginia, which he cased on 12 June 2009, for a possible attack. He also allegedly possessed armor-piercing ammunition, saying it was "to attack Americans," and said that one of his weapons would be used "for the base," an apparent reference to the Quantico facility.[113]

Potential Future Tactics

Suicide Operations. The fact that American citizens engaged in suicide operations in Somalia raises the possibility that suicide attacks could start taking place in the United States itself. To discount this possibility would be to ignore the lessons of the British experience. On 30 April 2003, two Britons of Pakistani descent launched a suicide attack in Tel Aviv; the first British suicide bomber, Birmingham-born Mohammed Bilal, blew himself up outside an army barracks in Indian-held Kashmir in December 2000.[114] Despite those attacks, the British security services had concluded just months before the 7 July 2005, bombings of the London transport system that suicide bombings would not be much of a concern in the United Kingdom itself.[115] The London attacks ended that complacent attitude.

Nidal Malik Hasan, a Palestinian-American medical officer and a rigidly observant Muslim who had made no secret to his fellow officers of his opposition to America's wars in Iraq and Afghanistan, went on a shooting spree at the giant Army base at Fort Hood, Texas, on 5 November 2009, killing 13 and wounding many more. This attack seems to have been an attempted suicide operation in which Hasan planned a *jihadist* "death-by-cop." In the year before his killing spree, Hasan had made Web postings about suicide operations and the theological justification for the deaths of innocents, and had sent more than a dozen e-mails to Anwar al-Awlaki, the American-born cleric living in Yemen who is playing an operational role in the Al Qaeda affiliate there.[116] Awlaki said he first received an e-mail from Hasan on 17 December 2008, and in that initial communication Hasan "was asking for an edict regarding the [possibility] of a Muslim soldier [killing] colleagues who serve with him in the American army."[117]

"Fedayeen" Attacks. The "success" of Lashkar-e-Taiba's 60-hour assault on Mumbai in late November 2008, which involved 10 gunmen all willing to die, is producing similar copycat operations known as "Fedayeen" (self-sacrificer) attacks. The long, drawn-out assault in Mumbai produced round the clock coverage around the globe, something other terrorist groups want to emulate. There are examples in attacks on Afghan government buildings and in a similar attack in October 2009 against GHQ, the Pakistani military headquarters in Rawalpindi. And an alleged plot disclosed in the fall of 2010 is said to have involved teams of Al Qaeda–linked militants planning "Mumbai-style" attacks in major European cities.[118] Some reports suggest bin Laden personally approved the Europe plot.[119]

Assassinations of Key Leaders and U.S. Officials, and Those Who Are Perceived as Insulting Islam. Because Al Qaeda and allied groups are rightly thought of as preoccupied by inflicting mass-casualty attacks, one tends to ignore their long history of assassinating or attempting to assassinate key leaders and American officials. Two days before 9/11, Al Qaeda assassinated the storied Afghan military commander Ahmad Shah Massoud; in December 2003 it tried to kill Pakistani President Pervez Musharraf on two occasions; and in 2009, the top Saudi counterterrorism official, Prince Mohammed bin Nayef, narrowly escaped being killed by an Al Qaeda assassin bearing a concealed bomb. Afghan President Hamid Karzai has been the subject of multiple Taliban assassination attempts, and the leading Pakistani politician, Benazir Bhutto, was killed by a Taliban suicide bomber in 2007. In 2002 American diplomat Leonard Foley was murdered in Amman by Al Qaeda in Iraq, and six years later the Taliban killed Stephen Vance, an American working in Peshawar on an aid project funded by the U.S. Agency for International Development. It is worth noting here that since 9/11 the U.S. consulate in Karachi has been the subject of three serious attacks;[120] the U.S. consulate in Jeddah the subject of one large-scale attack[121] and the U.S. embassy in Sana, Yemen, the subject of two such attacks.[122] And as has been seen, Scandinavian artists who have drawn cartoons of the Prophet Mohammed are now frequently targeted by *jihadists.* For Al Qaeda and allied groups, the Danish cartoon controversy has assumed some of the same importance that Salman Rushdie's fictional writings about the Prophet did for Khomeini's Iran two decades earlier.

Attacks That Are Unlikely to Happen

Mass-Casualty Attacks Involving True Weapons of Mass Destruction. As discussed in more detail earlier, despite Al Qaeda's long interest in acquiring chemical, biological, radiological, and nuclear (CBRN) weapons, on the infrequent occasions that it or affiliated groups have tried to deploy crude versions of these weapons their efforts have fizzled.

An Attack on a Mall in Some Midwestern Town or Other Less Populous Region of the U.S. For the Muslims around the globe whom Al Qaeda is trying to influence, an attack on an obscure town in the Midwest, for example, would have relatively little impact, which explains Al Qaeda's continuing fixation on attacks on cities and targets well known in the Islamic world. It explains Zazi's travel to Manhattan in September 2009 from his then home base in Colorado and Al Qaeda's many attempts in the past decade to bring down American passenger jets. That is not, of course, to say that someone influenced by bin Laden's ideas—but not part of Al Qaeda or one of its affiliates—might not attempt an attack in some obscure American town, but the terrorist organization and its affiliates remain focused on symbolic targets: New York, Washington, D.C., Los Angeles, and commercial airliners.

Preparedness Questions for the U.S. Government

It is fundamentally troubling, given this collection of new threats and new adversaries directly targeting America, that there remains no federal government agency or department specifically charged with identifying radicalization and interdicting the recruitment of U.S. citizens or residents for terrorism. As one senior intelligence analyst lamented, "There's no lead agency or person. There are First Amendment issues we're cognizant of. It's not a crime to radicalize, only when it turns to violence. There are groups of people looking at different aspects of counter-radicalization. [But it] has to be integrated across agencies, across levels of government, public-private cooperation"[123]—which, unfortunately, it is not. America is thus vulnerable to a threat that is not only diversifying, but arguably intensifying.

The long-held belief that homegrown terrorism could not happen here has thus created a situation where the United States is today stumbling blindly through the legal, operational, and organizational minefield of countering terrorist radicalization and recruitment occurring here. Moreover, rather than answers, there is now a long list of pressing questions on this emerging threat, on the U.S. response, and on the capacity of the national security architecture currently in place to meet it.

On the Threat

What can be done when the terrorists are like everyone else? When they conform to the archetypal American immigrant success story? When they are American citizens or U.S. residents? When they are not perhaps from the Middle East or South Asia and in fact have familiar-sounding names? Or, when they are self-described "petite, blue-eyed, blonde" suburban housewives who, as Colleen LaRose, a.k.a. Jihad Jane, boasted, "can easily blend in"?[124]

On the U.S. Response

Who in fact has responsibility in the U.S. government to identify radicalization when it is occurring and then to interdict attempts at recruitment? Is this best done by federal law enforcement (e.g., the Federal Bureau of Investigation) or state and local jurisdictions working closely with federal authorities? What is the role of state and local governments? Is it a core mission for a modernized, post-9/11 FBI? Or for the Department of Homeland Security? Can it be done by the National Counterterrorism Center, even though it has only a coordinating function and relies on other agencies for intelligence collection, analysis, and operations? What is the role of the Office of the Director of National Intelligence in homegrown terrorism and recruitment and radicalization? Will coming to grips with these challenges be the remit of the next FBI director given the incumbent's impending retirement?

On the U.S. Current National Security Architecture

Despite the reforms adopted from the 9/11 Commission's report and recommendations and the 2004 Intelligence Reform and Terrorism Prevention Act, have terrorists nonetheless discovered the Achilles's heel of the United States in that it currently has no strategy to counter the type of threat posed by homegrown terrorists and other radicalized recruits? Did "the system work" on 1 May 2010, when Faisal Shahzad attempted to detonate explosives in Times Square? Or was a lot of luck involved because of the plot's rushed nature? And finally, can Al Qaeda and its affiliates and associates be deterred from attacking in the United States? If even a "hard target" like New York City continually attracts terrorist attention, what does this say about vulnerabilities elsewhere in the country?

Conclusion

The conventional wisdom has long been that America was immune to the heady currents of radicalization affecting both immigrant and indigenous Muslim communities elsewhere in the West.[125] That has now been shattered by the succession of cases that have recently come to light of terrorist radicalization and recruitment occurring in the United States. And while it must be emphasized that the number of U.S. citizens and residents affected or influenced in this manner remains extremely small, at the same time the sustained and growing number of individuals heeding these calls is nonetheless alarming.

Given this list of incidents involving homegrown radicals, lone wolves, and trained terrorist recruits, the United States is arguably now little different from Europe in terms of having a domestic terrorist problem involving immigrant and indigenous Muslims as well as converts to Islam. The diversity of these latest foot soldiers in the wars of terrorism being waged against the United States underscores how much the terrorist threat has changed since the 11 September 2001 attacks. In the past year alone the United States has seen affluent suburban Americans and the progeny of hard-working immigrants gravitate to terrorism. Persons of color and Caucasians have done so. Women along with men. Good students and well-educated individuals and high school dropouts and jailbirds. Persons born in the United States or variously in Afghanistan, Egypt, Pakistan, and Somalia. Teenage boys pumped up with testosterone and middle-aged divorcees. The only common denominator appears to be a newfound hatred for their native or adopted country, a degree of dangerous malleability, and a religious fervor justifying or legitimizing violence that impels these very impressionable and perhaps easily influenced individuals toward potentially lethal acts of violence.

The diversity of this array of recent terrorist recruits presents new challenges for intelligence and law enforcement agencies, already over-stressed and inundated with information and leads, to run these new threats to ground. There seems no longer any clear profile of a terrorist. Moreover, the means through which many of these persons were radicalized—over the Internet—suggests that these days you can aspire to become a terrorist in the comfort of your own bedroom.

In short, the threat that the United States is facing is different than it was nine years ago. It has also changed and evolved since the 9/11 Commission presented its report six long years ago. Today, America faces a dynamic threat that has diversified to a broad array of attacks, from shootings to car bombs to simultaneous suicide attacks to attempted in-flight bombings of passenger aircraft.

In the aftermath of 11 September 2001, the consensus within the national security and intelligence communities was that when it came to attacks on the U.S. homeland, Al Qaeda was intent on matching or besting the loss of life and destruction it caused that day. Since catastrophic-scale attacks require high levels of planning and coordination to succeed, they also generate more opportunities for detection and intervention. Now it is clear that terrorist groups see operational value in conducting more frequent and less sophisticated attacks that can place severe stress on finite intelligence and law enforcement resources. In addition, Al Qaeda has concluded that these attacks can have strategic value by generating a "big bang for the buck," given that even a near-miss (e.g., the Christmas Day 2009 plot) can generate so much media and political fallout.

Improving the odds of effectively countering today's increasingly dynamic and diversified terrorist threat will require a much greater degree of engagement of state and local public safety officials. As the ranks of U.S. recruits have grown, the new frontlines have become the streets of Bridgeport, Denver, Minneapolis, and other big and small communities across America. Making sure that the nation's 50,000 public safety agencies are kept apprised of the changing face of terrorism poses a significant training and information-sharing challenge, but one that America neglects at its peril.

However, even if America's intelligence, law enforcement, and homeland security communities are far better prepared to counter this new collection of adversaries, it still will not be enough. On Christmas Day 2009, it was not a federal air marshal, but the courageous actions of the passengers and flight crew aboard Northwest Flight 253 that helped disrupt the attack once it was underway. In Times Square, it was a sidewalk T-shirt vendor, not the New York Police Department patrolman sitting in a squad car directly across the street, who sounded the alarm about Faisal Shahzad's explosive-laden SUV. It is reckless to leave the task of combating terrorism only to the professionals when the changing nature of the threat requires that ordinary Americans play a larger support role in detecting and preventing terrorist activities.

It is also important to acknowledge that how Americans respond to terrorist attacks can influence the worrisome trend by terrorist groups to radicalize and train recruits to carry out less sophisticated operations on U.S. soil. If any attack can succeed in generating significant political and economic fallout, then there is a greater motivation for undertaking these attacks. Alternatively, terrorist attacks that have limited potential to inflict serious casualties or cause disruption become less attractive if Americans display a greater degree of resilience by being better prepared to respond to and recover from these attacks. Since as a practical matter it is impossible to prevent every terrorist attack, the United States should be working in any event to improve the capacity of its political system, along with citizens and communities, to better manage how America deals with such attacks when they occur.

When the United States demonstrates its national resilience in the face of terrorism, terrorist groups will have little to gain by attacking the American homeland. When federal agencies work well with one another and their counterparts at the state and local levels, and reach out to everyday Americans, the United States will be far better able to detect and prevent future attacks. In short, nine years after the 11 September 2001, attacks on New York and Washington, the changing nature of the terrorist threat makes clear that the United States must be willing to reexamine many of its counterterrorism assumptions and approaches. Only then can America succeed at maintaining the upper hand in the face of an adversary who continues to demonstrate the ability to learn and adapt.

Appendix A: Terrorist Incidents in the United States in 2009[126]

The following 11 terrorist incidents in 2009 are divided into the following categories: terrorist attacks, serious plots, and Americans conspiring to take part in *jihadist* training or campaigns overseas. A "serious plot" is defined as involvement in a concrete plan to commit a terrorist attack, with specific chosen targets and other preparations, including target surveillance and the preparation of explosives or other weapons and travel or attempted travel to join a *jihadist* group.

- Terrorist attacks (2)
    - **Abdulhakim Mujahid Muhammad (Carlos Bledsoe)**—In June 2009 Muhammad, known as Carlos Bledsoe before his conversion to Islam, killed one soldier and wounded another at a U.S. military recruiting station in Little Rock, Arkansas. Muhammad had spent time in Yemen and claimed to be a member of the group Al Qaeda in the Arabian Peninsula.
    - **Nidal Malik Hasan**—On 5 November 2009, Maj. Hasan, a military psychologist stationed at Fort Hood, Texas, opened fire on the base with two handguns, killing 13 and wounding 43 before security officers shot and disabled him. Hasan was born in Virginia to Palestinian parents, and currently awaits trial in the military justice system.
- Serious plots (5)
    - **Michael Finton**—Finton, a convert to Islam, was arrested in September 2009 after attempting to set off an inert car bomb in front of a federal government building in Springfield, Illinois. Federal agents posing as Al Qaeda members supplied Finton with a fake bomb, and a friend working as an FBI informant

recorded conversations where Finton expressed his hatred of the United States and his desire to engage in *jihad.*

- **Hosam Maher Husein Smadi**—Smadi, a 19-year-old Jordanian, was arrested in a sting operation after trying to set off an inert car bomb in September 2009 in front of the Fountain Place office tower in Dallas. As with Finton, the FBI had been investigating Smadi, supplied him with harmless materials disguised as explosives, and recorded Smadi's conversations with undercover agents where he discussed his plan to commit a terrorist attack in the United States.
- **Najibullah Zazi et al.**—Zazi, an Afghan immigrant and permanent U.S. resident, was arrested in September 2009 while preparing to attack targets including the New York City subway system. Zazi had stockpiled chemicals, including hydrogen peroxide, needed to make an explosive compound known as TATP. He pleaded guilty in February 2010 to conspiring to commit a terrorist act using a "weapon of mass destruction." He also admitted to having received training in Pakistan. Zazi had gone originally to fight American forces in Afghanistan, but Al Qaeda leaders convinced him to return to the United States. Zazi's friend Zoran Ahmedzay pleaded guilty to involvement in the plot, while another friend, Adis Medunjanin, is currently awaiting trial on charges of involvement.
- **David Coleman Headley**—Headley, a Pakistani-American who changed his name from Daood Gilani, was arrested along with Tawahhur Rana in October 2009 on charges that he helped scope out targets for the 2008 Mumbai attacks, conducted by the Pakistani militant group Lashkar-e-Taiba. Headley pleaded guilty in March 2010, also admitting to having helped plot an attack that never took place against the Danish newspaper *Jyllands-Posten,* in retaliation for the paper's publication of cartoons depicting the Prophet Mohammed.
- **Umar Farouq Abdulmutallab**—Abdulmutallab, a 23-year-old Nigerian affiliated with Al Qaeda in the Arabian Peninsula, botched an attempt to explode a bomb with plastic explosives on Northwest Airlines Flight 253 over Detroit on Christmas Day 2009. Abdulmutallab boarded the flight in Amsterdam, bound for Detroit with some 300 passengers and crew on board. As the plane neared Detroit, the young man tried to detonate his bomb with a chemical initiator, setting himself on fire and suffering severe burns. Some combination of his own ineptitude, faulty bomb construction, and the quick actions of the passengers and crew who subdued him and extinguished the fire prevented an explosion that might have brought down the plane near Detroit. Immediately after he was arrested, Abdulmutallab told investigators that the explosive device "was acquired in Yemen along with instructions as to when it should be used." He has been charged in a six-count criminal indictment including attempted use of weapons of mass destruction and attempted murder, and faces life in prison if convicted.[127]

- Americans seeking to join or aid foreign terrorist organizations (4)
  - **The "DC 5"**—In November 2009 five young Americans of Pakistani, Arab, and African descent were arrested in Pakistan after their families reported

them missing and found what appeared to be at least one "martyrdom video." The five reportedly had tried to join multiple Pakistani militant groups, without success, before being picked up by Pakistani police. They were charged in Pakistan and convicted in June 2010 of criminal conspiracy and funding a banned terrorist organization. The five are Umar Chaudhry, Ramy Zamzan, Waqar Hassan Khan, Ahmad Abdullah Minni, and Amein Hassan Yemer.

- **Minnesota Somalis**—Federal prosecutors in 2009 indicted two groups of men (eight in one indictment, six in another) for recruiting young men in Somali communities in Minnesota and fund-raising for the Al Qaeda—linked group al-Shabab. Some of the men are currently believed to be in Somalia, and seven of those charged as part of the ongoing investigation were indicted in August 2010 on additional charges of providing material support to Shabab. Those indicted include Abdow Munye Abdow, Khalid Abshir, Salah Osman Ahmad, Adarus Abdulle Ali, Cabdulaahi Ahmed Faarax, Khalid Abshir, Salah Osman Ahmad, Kamal Hassan, Mohamed Hassan, Abdifatah Yusef Isse, Abdiweli Yassin Isse, Zakaria Maruf, Omer Abdi Mohamed, Ahmed Ali Omar, Mahanud Said Omar, and Mustafa Salat.
- **North Carolina Cluster**—Daniel Boyd, a convert to Islam, was arrested in July 2009 along with six others, including two of his sons, and charged with plotting to wage "violent *jihad*" abroad. He allegedly performed reconnaissance on the U.S. Marine base at Quantico, Va., while planning a possible attack on the base. Members of the "North Carolina Cluster" allegedly traveled to Gaza, Israel, and Jordan in the past several years in the hope of fighting Israeli forces. Besides Boyd, those arrested were his sons Zakariya and Dylan, Anes Subasic, Mohammad Omar Aly Hassan, Ziyad Yaghi, and Hysen Sherifi.
- **Tarek Mehanna**—Boston resident Mehanna was arrested in October 2009 on charges that he had plotted to join insurgents fighting U.S. troops abroad, attack a shopping mall in the United States, and kill two U.S. politicians. Mehanna was also charged in June 2010 with seeking to provide material support to Al Qaeda. An alleged accomplice in Mehanna's nascent plots, Ahmed Abousamra, is currently believed to be in Syria.

Appendix B

2009 and 2010* terrorism-related arrests and indictments of American citizens or residents in the U.S. and abroad[128]

Last name	First name	Ethnicity (where known)
2009–43		
Abousamra	Ahmad	Arab
Abdow	Abdow Munye	Somali
Abshir	Khalid	Somali
Ahmed	Salah Osman	Somali
Ali	Adarus Abdulle	Somali
Boyd	Daniel	Caucasian
Boyd	Dylan	Caucasian
Boyd	Zakaria	Caucasian
Chaudhry (Farooq)	Umar	South Asian
Cromitie	James	African American
Faarax	Cabdullaahi Ahmed	Somali
Finton	Michael	Caucasian
Hammami	Omar	Arab
Hasan	Nidal Malik	Arab
Hassan	Mohammad Omar Aly	–
Hassan	Kamal	–
Hassan	Mohamed	Somali
Headley	David Coleman	Pakistani father, Am.mother
Isse	Abdiweli Yassin	Somali
Isse	Abdifatah Yusuf	Somali
Kaziu	Betim	Albanian
Khan	Waqar Hussain	South Asian
LaRose	Colleen R.	Caucasian
Maruf	Zakaria	Somali
Mehanna	Tarek	Arab
Minni	Ahmad A.	African American (Eritrean)
Mohamed	Omer Abdi	Somali
Muhammad	Abdulhakim Mujahid	African American
Omar	Ahmed	Somali
Omar	Mahamud Said	Somali
Payen	Laguerre	Haitian
Rana	Tahawwur Hussain	South Asian
Salat	Mustafa	Somali
Sherifi	Hysen	Kosovar

Smadi	Hosam Maher Husein	Arab
Subasic	Anes	Serbian
Vinas	Bryant Neal	Hispanic
Williams	David	African American
Williams	Onta	African American
Yaghi	Ziyad	Arab
Yemer	Aman Hassan	Arab
Zamzam	Ramy	Arab
Zazi	Najibullah	South Asian
2010–20		
Abdi	Abdikader Ali	Somali
Ahmedzay	Zarein	South Asian
Alessa	Mahmoud	Arab
Almonte	Carlos	Hispanic
Beledi	Farah Mohamed	Somali
Bujol	Barry	–
Chesser	Zachary	Caucasian
Hasanoff	Sabirhan	–
Medunjanin	Adis	Bosnian
Ouazzani	Khaled	Arab
Rockwood	Paul	Caucasian
Shahzad	Faisal	South Asian
al-Hanafi	Wasam	–
Ali	Abdisalam Hussein	Somali
Masri	Shaker	–
Mostafa	Jehad	Caucasian
Ali	Amina	Somali
Hassan	Hawo	Somali
Khan	Raja Lahrasib	South Asian
Mobley	Sharif	Somali-American

*Through 10 September 2010.

A version of this article was first written for the Bipartisan Policy Center's National Security Preparedness Group, which intends to assess progress on the initial 9/11 Commission recommendations. The authors thank NSPG co-chairs Lee Hamilton and Tom Kean and its director, Michael Allen, for the opportunity to write this report; NSPG member Stephen Flynn for his input on the conclusion; Gene Thorp for the detailed map and Keith Sinzinger for his review; Andrew Lebovich, Laura Hohnsbeen, Nicole Salter, and Sophie Schmidt from the New America Foundation, and Professor William Banks, Alyssa Procopio, Jason Cherish, Joseph Robertson, Matthew Michaelis, Richard Lim, Laura Adams, and Drew Dickinson from the Maxwell School at Syracuse University for their research on recent anti-American terrorism.

Address correspondence to Bruce Hoffman, Director, Center for Peace and Security Studies and Security Studies Program, Georgetown University, Mortara Building, 3600 N Street NW, Washington, DC 20007, USA. E-mail: brh6@georgetown.edu

Critical Thinking Questions

1. In your view, do today's policymakers and media provide an accurate portrayal of the threat posed by Al Qaeda?
2. Does the diversified nature of Al Qaeda diminish or elevate the potential threat this movement poses to the U.S. homeland?
3. At what point in the future will we no longer consider Al Qaeda a threat to homeland security?

Notes

1. Dina Temple-Raston, "Missing Somali Teens May Be Terrorist Recruits," *National Public Radio: Morning Edition,* 28 January 2009. Available at http://www.npr.org/templates/story/story.php?storyId=99919934.
2. AbdizirakBihi, a community activist who represents the families of the six young men quoted in Oren Dorell, "Somalis may be Leaving Minn. for Jihad," *USA Today,* 18 December 2008. Available at http:www.usatoday.com/news/nation/2008-12-18-somalis_JN.htm
3. Ibid. See also Elizabeth Mohr, "Missing Somalis Families Speak Out: They Fear Males Were Brainwashed For Jihad Overseas," *St. Paul Pioneer Press,* 7 December 2008; and, Abdi Aynte, "Are Jihadist Groups Luring Minnesota Somalis Back to Fight?" *The Minnesota Independent,* 23 December 2008. Available at http://minnesotaindependent.com/21144/did-jihadist-recruiters-lure-local-men-home-to-fight
4. Associated Press, "Young Somali Men Missing from Minneapolis," *USA Today,* 26 November 2008. Available at http://www.usatoday.com/news/nation/2008-11-26-missing-somali_N.htm
5. Quoted in ibid.
6. Al-Shabaab also has used, or is known by, the following names: Harakat al-Shabaab al-Mujahideen; Hisb'ul Shabaad; Hizbul Shabaab; Al-Shabaab al-Islam; Al-Shabaab al-Islamiya; Al-Shabaab al-Jihad; Harakat Shabaab al-Mujahidin; Mujahideen Youth Movement; Mujahidin Al-Shabaab Movement; Unity of Islamic Youth; The Youth; Youth Wing; and Popular Resistance Movement in the Land. See Office of Intelligence and Analysis, *Reference Aid: Foreign Groups in Focus: Al-Shabaab,* IA-0110-09, Unclassified//For Official Use Only, p. 5. Note: only material from this DHS report marked unclassified has been cited in this testimony.
7. Spencer S. Hsu, "Concern Grows Over Recruitment of Somali Americans by Islamists," *Washington Post,* 4 October 2009.
8. One was killed in the Little Rock shooting and 13 in the Ft. Hood shooting.
9. James McKinley and Julia Preston, "U.S. Can't Trace Foreign Visitors on Expired Visas," *New York Times,* October 12, 2009. Available at http://www.nytimes.com/2009/10/12/us/12visa.html?_r=1&pagewanted=print
10. Dirk Johnson, "Suspect in Illinois Bomb Plot 'Didn't Like America very Much,'" *New York Times,* 27 September 2009. Available at http://www.nytimes.com/2009/09/28/us/28springfield.html
11. Leon Panetta, "This Week," 27 June 2010. Available at http://blogs.abcnews.com/politicalpunch/2010/06/cia-at-most-50100-al-qaeda-in-afghanistan.html
12. David E. Sanger and Mark Mazzetti, "New Estimate of Strength of Al Qaeda is Offered," *New York Times,* 30 June 2010. Available at http://www.nytimes.com/2010/07/01/world/asia/01qaeda.html

13. Glenn Greenwald, "The Crux of Our Endless War on Terror," Salon.com, 6 July 2010. Available at http://www.salon.com/news/opinion/glen_greenwald/2010/07/06/terrorism; Kevin Drum, "How Dangerous is Al Qaeda in Afghanistan?" MotherJones.com, 2 July 2010. Available at http://motherjones.com/kevin-drum/2010/07/how-big-al-qaeda-afghanistan
14. Peter Bergen interview with FBI Special Agent Daniel Coleman, a leading U.S. government expert on Al Qaeda in 2004 in Washington, DC.
15. Sami Yousufzai and Ron Moreau, "The Taliban in Their Own Words," *Newsweek,* 25 September 2009. Available at http://www.newsweek.com/2009/09/25/the-taliban-in-their-own-words.html
16. "U.S.: Taliban has Grown Fourfold," *Al Jazeera English,* 9 October 2009. Available at http://english.aljazeera.net/news/americas/2009/10/20091091814483962.html
17. Joby Warrick and Pamela Constable, "CIA Base Attacked in Afghanistan Supported Airstrikes against Al Qaeda, Taliban," *Washington Post,* 1 January 2010; "Bomber Fooled CIA, Family, Jordanian Intelligence," Associated Press, 6 January 2010.
18. "An Interview with the Shaheed Abu Dujaanah al Khorshani (Humam Khalil Abu-Mulal al-Balawi)," 28 February 2010, NEFA Foundation.
19. Mustafa Abu al-Yazid, "Infiltrating the American Fortresses," 31 December 2009, NEFA Foundation. Available at http://www.nefafoundation.org/miscellaneous/nefaAbul-Yazid0110.pdf
20. Stephen Farrell, "Video Links Taliban to CIA Attack," *New York Times,* 9 January 2010. Available at http://www.nytimes.com/2010/01/10/world/middleeast/10balawi.html
21. United States District Court Eastern District of New York, United States of America v. Adis Medunjanin, Abid Nasser, Adnan El Shukrijumah, Tariq Ur Rehman, and FNU LNU, 7 July 2010.
22. Carrie Johnson and Spencer Hsu, "Najibullah Zazi Pleads Guilty in New York Subway Bomb Plot," *Washington Post,* 23 February 2010. Available at http://www.washington post.com/wp-dyn/content/article/2010/02/22/AR2010022201916.html; Department of Justice, "Zarein Ahmedzay Pleads Guilty to Terror Violations in Connection with Al Qaeda New York Subway Plot," 23 April 2010. Available at http://www.justice.gov/opa/pr/2010/April/10-ag-473.html
23. United States District Court Eastern District of New York, United States of America v. Adis Medunjanin, Abid Nasser, Adnan El Shukrijumah, Tariq Ur Rehman, and FNU LNU, 7 July 2010.
24. Luis Martinez and Martha Raddatz, "Al Qaeda Operations Planner Saleh al-Somali Believed Dead in Drone Strike," ABC News, 11 December 2009. Available at http://abcnews.go.com/print?id=9314585
25. Spencer S. Hsu, "Al Qaeda Operative Led N.Y. Subway Plot, U.S. Says," *Washington Post,* 8 July 2010.
26. Asif Farooqi, Carol Grisanti, and Robert Windrem, "Sources: U.K. Terror Suspect Forced to Talk," NBC News, 18 August 2006. Available at http://www.msnbc.msn.com/id/14398423/
27. Jeremy Page, "How Pakistan can Help to Stop Terrorist Camps Training Britons," *Times of London,* 25 March 2009. Available at http://www.timesonline.co.uk/tol/news/uk/article5971074.ece
28. Interview with NSPG, 8 July 2010.
29. United States of America v. Daniel Patrick Boyd et al, Indictment, Eastern District of North Carolina, 2 July 2009.

30. On Christmas Day: Anahad O'Connor and Eric Schmitt, "Terror Attempt Seen as Man Tries to Ignore Device on Jet," *New York Times,* 26 December 2009; Carrie Johnson, "Explosive in Detroit Terror Case could have Blown Hole in Airplane, Sources Say," *Washington Post,* 29 December 2009; "Bomb Suspect Umar Farouk Abdulmutallab on UK Watch-List," BBC, 29 December 2009; "Key Dates Surrounded the Christmas Day Attack," *Associated Press,* 30 December 2009. Available at http://www.wtop.com/?nid=116&sid=1851004; Richard Esposito and Brian Ross, "Photos of the Northwest Airlines Flight 253 Bomb," ABC News, 28 December 2009. Available at http://abcnews.go.com/print?id=9436297
31. "Yemeni Diplomat: Yemen can Carry Out Airstrikes against Al Qaeda," CNN.com, 30 December 2009. Available at http://www.cnn.com/2009/WORLD/meast/12/30/U.S..yemen.strikes/index.html
32. Peter Bergen, "Similar Explosive Used in Saudi Attack," CNN.com, 27 December 2009. Available at http://www.cnn.com/2009/U.S./12/27/bergen.terror.plot/index.html
33. Peter Bergen, "Saudi Investigation: Would-Be Assassin Hid Bomb in Underwear," CNN.com, 30 September 2009. Available at http://edition.cnn.com/2009/WORLD/meast/09/30/saudi.arabia.attack/index.html
34. Summary of the White House Review of the 25 December 2009 Attempted Terrorist Attack, p. 2. Available at http://www.whitehouse.gov/the-press-office/white-house-review-summary-regarding-12252009-attempted-terrorist-attack
35. Interview with NSPG, 26 January 2010.
36. John Brennan, White House press conference, Washington, DC, 7 January 2010. Available at http://www.whitehouse.gov/the-press-office/briefing-homeland-security-secretary-napolitano-assistant-president-counterterroris
37. Jake Tapper, Karen Travers, and Huma Khan, "Obama: System Failed in a 'Potentially Disastrous Way,'" ABC News, 5 January 2010. Available at http://abcnews.go.com/print?id=9484260
38. See Nur Dianah Suhami, "Local Muslim Preachers Need to Modernize Ways," *Straits Times* (Singapore), 31 July 2010; and Rachel Lin, "Twisted Teachings, Twisted Logic," *Straits Times* (Singapore), 31 July 2010.
39. This section draws on Peter Bergen, "Reassessing the Evolving al Qaeda Threat to the Homeland," Testimony before the House Committee on Homeland Security, 19 November 2009.
40. "Somalia's Shabab Proclaim Allegiance to bin Laden," Agence France-Presse, 22 September 2009.
41. Osama bin Laden tape, translated by NEFA Foundation, 19 March 2009. Available at http://www.nefafoundation.org/miscellaneous/nefaubl0309-2.pdf
42. Sudarsan Raghavan, "Foreign Fighters Gain Influence in Somalia's Islamist al-Shabab Militia," *Washington Post,* 8 June 2010.
43. Mohammed Ibrahim and Jeffrey Gettlemen, "Somalis Protest against Shabab in Mogadishu," *New York Times* 29 March 2010. Available at http://www.nytimes.com/2010/03/30/world/africa/30shabab.html
44. Spencer Hsu and Carrie Johnson, "Somali Americans Recruited by Extremists," *Washington Post,* 11 March 2009. Available at http://www.washingtonpost.com/wp-dyn/content/article/2009/03/10/AR2009031003901.html; *USA vs Cabdulaahi Ahmed Faarax, Abdei-weli Yassin Isse,* criminal complaint filed 8 October 2009 in U.S. District Court Minnesota. Available at http://graphics8.nytimes.com/packages/pdf/U.S./20091124_TERROR_DOCS/faarax.pdf

45. "FBI Investigating Seattleite in Suicide Bombing," Associated Press, 25 September 2009. Available at http://www.msnbc.msn.com/id/33025395/ns/world_news-tenOTism/
46. Spencer Hsu, "Concern Grows over Recruitment of Somali Americans by Islamists," *Washington Post,* 4 October 2009. Available at http://www.washingtonpost.com/wp-dyn/content/article/2009/10/03/AR2009100302901.html
47. Sudarsan Raghavan, "Islamic Militant Group al-Shabab Claims Uganda Bombing Attack," *Washington Post,* 12 July 2010. Available at http://www.washingtonpost.com/wp-dyn/content/article/2010/07/12/AR2010071200476.html
48. CNN.com, "Danish Cartoonist Hid in 'Panic Room' during Attack," 2 January 2010. Available at http://articles.cnn.com/2010-01-02/world/denmark.cartoonist_1_danish-police-suspect-attacked?_s=PM:WORLD
49. Adrian Croft, "Al Qaeda in Iraq 'Never Closer to Defeat': U.S. Envoy," Reuters, 24 May 2008. Available at http://www.reuters.com/article/idUSCOL46197920080524
50. National Counterterrorism Center, WITS database. Parameters: 1 January 2010 to 1 July 2010, IN: Iraq.
51. Quoted in Peter Bergen, "Where You Bin?" *The New Republic,* 29 January 2006.
52. William Maclean, "Ransoms Boost Al Qaeda in Africa," Reuters, 31 August 2010. Available at http://www.reuters.com/article/idUSLDE67U1C420100831
53. See, for example, Karin Brulliard and Pamela Constable, "Militant Factions with Global Aims are Spreading Roots throughout Pakistan," *Washington Post,* 10 May 2010; and Anne E. Korn-blut and Karin Brulliard, "U.S. Blames Pakistani Taliban for Times Square Bomb Plot," *Washington Post,* 10 May 2010.
54. Jean-Pierre Perrin "Al-Qa'ida Has Lost Its Footing: Interview with Jean-Pierre Filiu," *Liberation* (Paris), 6 May 2010; and Douglas Farah, "Analysis of the Spanish Suicide Bombers Case," *NEFA,* 22 February 2008.
55. *United States of America v. Faisal Shahzad,* Defendant, Case 1:10-mj-00928-UA Filed 4 May 2010.
56. Express Tribune, "Video Shows Faisal Shahzad with HakimullahMehsud." Available at http://tribune.com.pk/story/30356/video-shows-faisal-shahzad-with-hakimullah-mehsud/
57. Armed with that training and $8,000 in cash: *United States of America v. Faisal Shahzad,* Plea agreement, Southern District of New York, 21 June 2010.
58. Interview with NSPG, 8 July 2010.
59. Headley indictment and plea.
60. Much of this section draws on Paul Cruickshank, "The Militant Pipeline," New America Foundation, February 2010. Available at http://counterterrorism.newamerica.net/publications/policy/the_jmilitant_pipeline
61. Craig Whitlock, "Flow of Terrorist Recruits Increasing," *Washington Post,* 19 October 2009.
62. Associated Press, "Islamist Terrorists Planned to Blow Up U.S. Base in Germany," 4 March 2010. Available at http://www.guardian.co.uk/world/2010/mar/04/islamic-jihad-union-bomb-plot
63. Associated Press, 4 March 2010.
64. Cruickshank, "The Militant Pipeline."
65. Melissa Eddy, "U.S. Strike Kills Five German Militants in Pakistan," Associated Press, 4 October 2010.
66. Michael Leiter, Aspen, Colorado, 30 June 2010.

67. Andrea Elliott, "The Jihadist Next Door," *New York Times Magazine,* 27 January 2010. Available at http://www.nytimes.com/2010/01/31/magazine/31Jihadist-t.html.
68. See Walter Laqueur, *The Age ofTerrorism* (Boston and Toronto: Little, Brown, 1987), p. 7; idem, *The New Terrorism: Fanaticism and the Arms of Mass Destruction* (New York and Oxford: Oxford University Press, 1999), p. 8; and Claude Berrebi, "Evidence About the Link Between Education, Poverty and Terrorism Among Palestinians," 2003, pp. 5–7. Available at http://www.irs.princeton.edu/pubs/pdfs/477.pdf
69. See, for instance, Scott Atran, "Who Wants to Be a Martyr," *New York Times,* 5 May 2003; BBC News, "Poverty 'Fuelling Terrorism,'" *bbc.co.uk,* 22 March 2002. Available at http://news.bbc.co.uk/2/hi/1886617.stm; and, Nicholas D. Kristof, "Behind The Terrorists," *New York Times,* 7 May 2002. Available at http://query.nytimes.com/gst/fullpage.html?res=9A0CE1DA1730F934A35756C0A9649C8B63&sec=&spon=&pagewanted=1
70. Online Newshour, "President Bush's Speech at the United Nations Financing for Development Conference," Monterrey, Mexico, 22 March 2002, PBS.org. Available at http://www.pbs.org/newshour/updates/march02/bush_3-22.html
71. Saadia Khalid, "Illiteracy Root Cause of Terrorism, Extremism: PM," *The International News,* 21 February 2009. Available at http://www.thenews.com.pk/daily_detail.asp?id=163751
72. "We're learning more about the suspect," the President explained. "We know that he traveled to Yemen, a country grappling with crushing poverty and deadly insurgencies. It appears that he joined an affiliate of Al Qaeda and that this group, Al Qaeda in the Arabian Peninsula, trained him, equipped him with those explosives and directed him to attack that plane headed for America." Quoted in Peter Baker, "Obama Says Al Qaeda in Yemen Planned Bombing Plot, and He Vows Retribution," *New York Times,* 2 January 2010.
73. BBC News, "Profile: Umar Farouk Abdulmutallab," 7 January 2010. Available at http://news.bbc.co.uk/2/hi/8431530.stm
74. Walter Laqueur, *No End To War: Terrorism in the Twenty-First Century* (New York and London: Continuum, 2003), p. 17.
75. Andrew Lebovich, New America Foundation/Syracuse terrorism database.
76. Department of Justice, "TahawwurRana and David Headley Indicted for Alleged Roles in India and Denmark Terrorism Conspiracies," 14 January 2010. Available at http://www.justice.gov/opa/pr/2010/January/10-nsd-038.html
77. *United States of America v. Colleen LaRose,* Indictment, United States District Court, Eastern District of Pennsylvania, 4 March 2010.
78. Interview with NSPG, 8 July 2010.
79. Aspen Security Forum 2010 "Counterterrorism Strategy with the Hon. Michael E. Leiter, Director, National Counterterrorism Center," 30 June 2010.
80. Joseph Tanfani, John Shiffman, and Kathleen Brady Shea, "American Suspect in Mumbai Attack was DEA Informant," *Philadelphia Inquirer,* 14 December 2009. Available at http://www.mcclatchydc.com/2009/12/14/80622/american-suspect-in-mumbai-attack.html
81. In recent years, writings as diverse as the 1,600-page treatise of Mustafa bin Abd al-Qadir SetmariamNasar (writing under the pseudonyms of either Abu Mus'ab al-Suri or Umar Abdal-Hakim) titled *The Call to Global Islamic Resistance* and Anwar al-Awlaki's "44 Ways to Support Jihad" have forcefully explicated this strategy, amplifying and building on the similar call to arms in this respect first issued by Ayman al-Zawahiri in *Knights Under the Prophet's Banner* nearly nine years ago.

82. This section draws on Peter Bergen, "Confronting al Qaeda: Understanding the Threat in Afghanistan and Beyond," Testimony before the Senate Foreign Relations Committee, 7 October 2009 and Peter Bergen, "Reassessing the Evolving al Qaeda Threat to the Homeland," Testimony before the House Committee on Homeland Security, 19 November 2009.
83. Author interview of U.S. military official, Kabul Afghanistan, September 2006.
84. BBC News, "Afghanistan: Taleban Second Coming," 2 June 2006. Available at http://news.bbc.co.uk/2/hi/south_asia/5029190.stm; CBS News, CBS Evening News with Katie Couric, 29 December 2006.
85. Full text of Osama bin Laden's videotape message directed at the American people. Al Jazeera website, 1 November 2004, translated by Federal News Service and accessed via Lexis Nexis, 27 August 2010.
86. Available at http://counterterrorism.newamerica.net/drones
87. Michael Hayden, "State of Al Qaeda Today," Atlantic Council, 13 November 2008, Washington, DC. Available at http://www.acus.org/http:/%252Fwww.acus.org/event_blog/cia-director-event-transcript
88. Lolita C. Baldor, "Terror Training Camps Are Smaller, Harder to Target," Associated Press, 9 November 2009.
89. NSPG interview, 2010.
90. Aaron Katersky, "Faisal Shahzad Pleads Guilty in Times Square Car Bomb Plot, Warns of More Attacks," ABC News, 21 June 2010. Available at http://abcnews.go.com/print?id=10970094
91. Eric Schmitt and David Sanger, "Some in Qaeda Leave Pakistan for Somalia and Yemen," *New York Times,* 11 June 2009. Available at http://www.nytimes.com/2009/06/12/world/12terror.html
92. This section draws on Peter Bergen and Katherine Tiedemann, "The Drone War," *The New Republic,* 3 June 2009.
93. Jane Perlez, "Taliban Seize Vital Pakistan Area Closer to the Capital," *New York Times, 22* April 2009.
94. Available at http://pewglobal.org/files/pdf/Pew-Global-Attitudes-2010-Pakistan-Report.pdf, p. 96.
95. Karin Bruillard, "Pakistan Launches Full-Scale Offensive," *Washington Post,* 18 October 2009. Available at http://www.washingtonpost.com/wp-dyn/content/article/2009/10/17/AR2009101700673.html
96. For an account of those operations see Sameer Lalwani, "The Pakistani Military's Adaptation to Counterinsurgency in 2009," *CTC Sentinel,* January 2010, and for Pakistani public support of these operations see "Military Action in Waziristan: Opinion Poll," Gilani Poll/Gallup Pakistan, 3 November2009. Available at www.gallup.com.pk/Polls/03-11-09.pdf
97. Combating Terrorism Center, "Deadly Vanguards: A Study of Al Qaeda's Violence Against Muslims," December 2009. Available at http://www.ctc.usma.edu/deadly%20vanguards_complete_l.pdf
98. Pew Global Attitudes Project, "Muslim Disappointment," 17 June 2010. Available at http://pewglobal.org/2010/06/17/obama-more-popular-abroad-than-at-home/8/#chapter-7-attitudes-toward-extremism-among-muslim-publics, Q96.
99. This section draws on Peter Bergen and Paul Cruickshank, "The Unraveling," *The New Republic,* 11 June 2008.

100. See *United States of America v. Faisal Shahzad,* Defendant, Case 1:10-mj-00928-UA Filed 4 May 2010.
101. See the statements by Homeland Security Secretary Janet Napolitano, "'This Week' Transcript: McKay, Napolitano, Salazar and Allen," *ABC News,* 2 May 2010. Available at http://www.abcnews.go.com/print?id=10532649; Denis McDonough, Chief of Staff of the National Security Council on "News Hour," *Public Broadcasting System,* 5 May 2010. Available at http://www.pbs.org/newshour.bb/law/jan-june10/timessquare2_05-05.html; and General David H. Petraeus in Yochi J. Dreazen and Evan Perez, "Suspect Cites Radical Iman's Writings," *Wall Street Journal,* 6 May 2010. See also, Joseph Berger, "Pakistani Taliban Behind Times Sq. Plot, Holder Says," *New York Times,* 9 May 2010. Available at http://www.nytimes.com/2010/05/10/us/politics/10holder.html; and Associated Press, "Gen. Petraeus: Times Square Bomber Acted Alone," 7 May 2010. Available at http://www.google.com/hostednews/ap/article/ALeqM5iXN8wcxfFxkTe1TWhZtNClI5XW3QD9FI85E00.
102. Quotes taken from Jerry Markon, "Guilty Plea in Failed Times Square Bombing; Shahzad Warns of More Attacks Unless U.S. Leaves Muslim Countries," *Washington Post,* 22 June 2010; Ron Scherer, "Failsal Shahzad Calls Times Square Bomb Plot 'War, Please Guilty," *Christian Science Monitor* (Boston), 21 June 2010; and "Shahzad Pleads Guilty to Times Square Bombing Charges," *CNN.com*, 21 June 2010.
103. Quoted in Peter Taylor, *Brits* (London: Bloomsbury, 2001), p. 256.
104. Some fifteen hundred passengers would have died: Richard Greenberg, Paul Cruickshank, and Chris Hansen, "Inside the Plot that Rivaled 9/11," Dateline NBC, 14 September 2009. http://www.msnbc.msn.com/id/26726987/
105. "Al Qaeda Claims Kenya Attacks," BBC, 3 December 2003.
106. Agence France-Presse, "Civilian Plane Hit by Missile over Baghdad," 23 November 2003.
107. "British Airways Suspends Flights to Saudi Arabia after Threats," *New York Times,* 14 August 2003.
108. Raymond Bonner, Jane Perlez, and Eric Schmitt, "British Inquiry of Failed Plots Points to Iraq's Qaeda Group, points to Iraq's Qaeda Group," *New York Times,* 14 December 2007, http://www.nytimes.com/2007/12/14/world/europe/14london.html
109. BBC News, "France Remembers Car Bomb Victims," 13 May 2002. Available at http://news.bbc.co.uk/2/hi/europe/1984376.stm
110. Berni Moestafa and Widya Utami, "Marriott Jakarta Attack May Be Linked to Bali Bombers," Bloomberg, 18 July 18, 2009. Available at http://www.bloomberg.com/apps/news?pid=newsarchive&sid=aZHC0FMYX6K4
111. Scott Macleod, "Behind the Amman Hotel Attack," *Time,* 10 November 2005. Available at http://www.time.com/time/world/article/0,8599,1128209,00.html
112. U.S. military recruiting station: District Court of Little Rock, Arkansas, County of Pulaski, Affidavit for Search and Seizure Warrant. Available at http://www.investigativeproject.org/documents/case_docs/988.pdf.
113. *USA v. Daniel Patrick Boyd et al,* Indictment in U.S. District Court for the Eastern District of North Carolina, filed 22 July 2009. Available at http://www.investigativeproject.org/documents/case_docs/1029.pdf; and the superseding indictment in the same case dated 24 September 2009. Available at http://www.investigativeproject.org/documents/cas_docs/1075.pdf

114. Emma Brockes, "British Man Named as Bomber Who Killed 10," *The Guardian,28* December 2000. Available at http://www.guardian.co.uk/uk/2000/dec/28/india.kashmir
115. Peter Bergen, "The Terrorists among us," *ForeignPolicy.com*, 19 November 2009.
116. Sudarsan Raghavan, "Cleric Says He was Confidant to Hasan," *Washington Post, 16* November 2009. Available at http://www.washingtonpost.com/wp-dyn/content/article/2009/11/15/AR2009111503160_pf.html
117. Anwar al Awlaki, interview by Abdelela Haidar Shayie, AlJazeera.net, 23 December 2009. Translation by Middle East Media Research Institute. Available at http://www.memrijttm.org/content/en/report.htm?report=3859%26param=GJN
118. "Officials Warn EU Terror Plot is Still Active," Associated Press, 29 September 2010. Available at http://online.wsj.com/article/SB1000142405274870411600457552176322 1143580.html
119. Nic Robertson and Paul Cruickshank, "Official: Terror Plot Included Possible Attacks in 5 European Countries," CNN.com, 29 September 2010. Available at http://articles.cnn.com/2010-09-29/world/us.europe.terror.plot_terror-plot-law-enforcement-counterterrorism?_s=PM:WORLD
120. In March 2006, http://news.bbc.co.uk/2/hi/south_asia/4765170.stm, February 2003, http://news.bbc.co.uk/2/hi/south_asia/2807301.stm, and June 2002, http://news.bbc.co.uk/2/hi/south_asia/2045045.stm
121. In December 2004, http://www.cnn.com/2004/WORLD/meast/12/06/jeddah.attack/.
122. In September 2008, http://www.guardian.co.uk/world/2008/sep/18/yemen.usa and January 2009, http://news.bbc.co.uk/2M/middle_east/7852481.stm
123. Interview with NSPG, 8 July 2010.
124. Quoted in Carrie Johnson, "Jihad Jane, an American woman, Faces Terrorism Charges," *Washington Post,* 10 March 2010.
125. See for example "America's Muslims after 9/11," VOANews.com, 10 September 2006. Available at http://www1.voanews.com/english/news/news-analysis/a-13-Muslims2006-09-10-voa17.html; "Overview of Muslims in America," PBS series, "The Muslims in America." Available at http://www.pbs.org/weta/crossroads/about/show_muslim_americans.html#top; and, "Pew Study Sees Muslim Americans Assimilating," Barbara Bradley Hagerty, National Public Radio, "All Things Considered," 22 May 2007. Available at http://www.npr.org/templates/story/story.php?storyId=10330400
126. Count by Andrew Lebovich, New America Foundation, September 2010.
127. Department of Justice, "Umar Farouk Abdulmutallab Indicted for Attempted Bombing of Flight 253 on Christmas Day," 6 January 2010. Available at http://detroit.fbi.gov/dojpressrel/pressrel10/de010610.htm
128. Count by Andrew Lebovich, New America Foundation, September 2010.

Najibullah Zazi's Plot to Bomb the New York City Subway System

A Case Study of How U.S. Domestic Counterterrorism Operates

Joshua Sinai

Najibullah Zazi's plot to bomb the New York City subway system in mid-September 2009 was timed to coincide with the 8th anniversary of 9/11. In the plot, Zazi and two of his high school friends planned to strap explosives to their bodies and head for the Grand Central and Times Square stations, where they would board packed trains at rush hour and blow themselves up to inflict maximum fatalities.[1] In addition to his two associates, Zazi's plot also involved links to high ranking al Qaida operational managers in Pakistan who directed the operation, as well as those of fellow operatives in Britain and Norway who were in the process of carrying out their own attacks in those countries. Had Zazi's plot succeeded, it would have been the most lethal terrorist attack in the U.S. homeland since 9/11. Estimated casualties would have eclipsed the March 2004 Madrid train bombings, which killed 191 people and wounded 1,800, and the July 2005 London bombings, which killed 52 people and wounded more than 700. Like Zazi's plot, the Madrid and London attacks followed the al Qaida "script" of coordinated and simultaneous terrorist attacks (although al Qaida's involvement in the London operation was more indirect).[2]

This particular case study is important because it represents a transformational paradigm shift[3] in the types of questions that need to be asked, structured, and probed for answers, as well as what is to be observed, scrutinized and interpreted by U.S. counterterrorism agencies in responding to the types of terrorist threats the U.S. is facing today. This threat largely involved American residents with a nexus to al Qaida and its affiliates who are involved in planning and launching attacks domestically. Specifically, with the increasing difficulty for foreign terrorist operatives to enter the country, due to the tightening of U.S. airport and border controls, what are termed "homegrown extremists" among U.S. legal residents and citizens have become increasingly attractive recruitment "assets" for foreign terrorist groups that seek to launch attacks on American soil. Further, preventing Zazi and his colleagues from executing their plot required an array of federal, state, and local efforts, while also working in close coordination with allied government counterparts, including the British, Canadian, Pakistani and Scandinavian intelligence and security services. Thus, this case also demonstrates how responding to this type of threat requires information and intelligence sharing across domestic agency levels as well as transnationally.

This case study is based entirely on available open source information about the case, which is utilized to aid in understanding how government counterterrorism agencies likely went about tracking and investigating the plot during its pre-incident phases.

"The Talker": Zazi's Radicalization

Najibullah ("Najib") Zazi was born in Afghanistan's Paktia province, a middle child with two sisters and two brothers. His family is part of the large Afghani Zazi tribal clan, which is primarily located in Afghanistan's Paktia and Khost provinces, including the country's capital, Kabul, and in Pakistan's Kurram Agency of the North-West Frontier Province. The violence of Afghanistan's civil war and the long struggle to oust the Soviets eventually drove Zazi's family in the early 1990s to settle to Pakistan's Peshawar area, where other Zazis resided. Around 1992, Najib's father Mohammed Wali Zazi moved to America and found employment as a taxi driver,[4] eventually becoming a naturalized U.S. citizen. This enabled him in 1999 to arrange for his family, including 14-year old Najibullah, to settle in New York City, where they became legal residents. The family lived in a two bedroom apartment in Flushing, Queens, in a mostly Afghani immigrant neighborhood. Two years later, the attacks of 9/11 drove a wedge among members of the Afghani community in Queens. This was most notably seen at the mosque where the Zazi family worshipped, when its imam Mohammad Sherzad began openly criticizing the Taliban government that had shielded al Qaida in Afghanistan. The Zazi family joined a faction within the mosque that left in protest of Sherzad's anti-Taliban sermons.

At age 16, Najibullah—an indifferent student at Flushing High School, more interested in playing basketball than studying—dropped out and from about 2004 to 2008 he worked at his father's coffee cart near Wall Street, as well as driving a cab, earning about \$800 a month.[5] It was during this period that Zazi also became increasingly religiously devout, spending considerable time at the Masjid Hazrat Abu Bakr mosque, which was attended by Afghans, and even volunteering to work there as a janitor. As a demonstration of his increased religious fervor he would become stern with friends, chastising them for their interest in popular music, calling it "dishonest to your religion." He also began replacing his Western-style clothes with a traditional Afghan tunic, and he let his beard grow. As a neighbor remarked, "'Najib [became] completely different. He looks like a Taliban. He has a big beard. He's talking different."[6]

According to a friend, among the contributing factors to his overt religious and political radicalization were his four trips to Pakistan between 2004 and 2008.[7] One such trip in 2006 was to consummate an arranged marriage with his 19-year-old cousin, and he traveled to Pakistan again in 2007 and 2008 to spend time with his wife. On these annual visits, Zazi would spend about three months of a year in Pakistan.[8] Although publicly available information is not available, it can be surmised that during those visits Zazi likely came into contact with radicalized relatives and friends who further radicalized him. It was also during this time period that Zazi's wife gave birth to two children. Zazi would return to New York to earn money for his family, although he constantly fell deeply into debt.[9] Further, he opened 15 new credit card accounts between April and August 2008.[10] Despite his indebtedness, Zazi told friends he hoped to bring his family to the U.S. someday.[11]

His radicalization was also influenced by YouTube videos featuring Dr. Zakir Naik, an extremist Muslim televangelist, who preached an unorthodox Muslim theology that endorsed polygamy and harsh Islamic criminal law.[12] Dr. Naik's sermons spoke favorably of Usama bin Laden, stating that "If [bin Laden] is fighting enemies of Islam, I am for him."[13] Najib became enchanted with Naik's preachings, which according to Silber "may have given Zazi a mirror for his own confused feelings as he struggled to start a family and make ends meet."[14]

"Going Operational": The Plot to Blow Up NYC's Subway System

Beginning around late-2007, Zazi became intensely angry over the U.S. war in Afghanistan and began thinking about taking action. Adis Medunjanin and Zarein Ahmedzay, two of his friends who also attended Flushing High School had similar sentiments, and the three of them began discussing their opposition to the war in Afghanistan. Like Zazi, Ahmedzay was also born in Afghanistan. In 2007, he took a civil service test to become a New York City firefighter, but became a cab driver, instead. Medunjanin was a Bosnian immigrant who came to the U.S. in 1994, was naturalized in 2002, and was a student at Queens College, majoring in Economics.

Years later, Zazi recounted that his friends "were bitter over the deaths of civilians in his homeland."[15] The three friends, who also worshiped together at a mosque in Queens, were further radicalized by recordings of Anwar al-Awlaki, the extremist imam who was based at the time in Yemen.[16] As they crossed the threshold from radicalization into violent action, they came up with a plan "to join the Taliban—to fight alongside the Taliban against the United States"[17] in Afghanistan. Although exact details are not publicly known, it has been hypothesized that Zazi's credit cards allowed the three of them to fly on Qatar Airlines from Newark International Airport August 28, 2008 to Doha, Qatar (via Geneva, Switzerland), where they boarded another flight to Pakistan, with Peshawar as their final destination.[18]

At Medunjanin's trial in April 2012, Ahmedzay stated that he had been to Afghanistan before and was familiar with the areas where a strong Taliban presence would enable them to join the fight against the American forces.[19] Once they arrived in Peshawar, however, their plans changed. According to several accounts, prior to their plan to hook up with the Taliban, once in Peshawar the three friends attempted to cross into Afghanistan via the Torkham border crossing in order to link up with the Taliban, but were foiled at a Pakistani army checkpoint when they were ordered back into Pakistan.[20] They were turned back, it is reported, because the guards had suspected their foreign origin.[21] In earlier court testimony in July 2011 by Amanullah Zazi, Najibullah's cousin, claimed that once the three associates had returned to Peshawar, while he was living with his parents in Pakistan in 2008 he introduced Zazi to a Pakistani cleric who arranged for them to hook up with al Qaida operatives to receive military training at one of their safe houses in Pakistan's northern Waziristan region.[22] It was upon their return to Peshawar, therefore, that Zazi's cousin had facilitated their change-of-plan to link up with al Qaida.

Upon their arrival at an al Qaida safe house in Waziristan in early September, a man known as "Yusuf" (aka Ferid Imam)[23] played a key role in arranging for their military training and religious indoctrination, with the three friends staying at his house for about two weeks.[24] According to a debriefing of Medunjanin, Imam "provided religious instructions on the rewards of fighting and dying together."[25] Imam also showed them videos of several prominent attacks linked to al Qaida, such as 9/11, Madrid, and London, "and various other suicide or martyrdom operations."[26] Imam, a 30-year-old Canadian from Winnipeg, had emigrated from East Africa with his family at age seven, and had been a student at the University of Manitoba. He left for Pakistan's Peshawar in March 2007 with Maiwand Yar, aged 27, a former mechanical engineering student at the University of Manitoba, and Muhannad al-Farekh, also a University of Manitoba student.[27] All three had grown up in Winnipeg after their families arrived in the city from other countries. They met and became friends at the university, but disappeared before completing their studies.[28] On March 15, 2011, Imam was indicted by U.S. authorities for providing material support to al Qaida and aiding and abetting their training.[29] Terror conspiracy charges were also filed against him in Canada, in a criminal investigation known as Project Darken.[30]

Court records of the Zazi case indicate that while the three associates underwent military training at one of al Qaida's training camps in the mountains of Pakistan's Waziristan region by September 2008, in November of that year, Zazi was taken aside and given special bomb-making training because of his knowledge of the New York City subway system.[31] Zazi took lengthy notes and scanned and emailed them to himself at an Internet café in Peshawar,[32] so he could access them upon his return to the U.S.[33] Al Qaida's operatives then tasked them to return to the U.S. and conduct a suicide martyrdom operation on the New York City subway system. It is likely that it was during this period that at the al Qaida camp Zazi's bomb-making instructor had asked him to tape a martyrdom video.[34] In this last will and testament, Zazi stated that "This is the payback for the atrocities that you [America] do" for the wars in Iraq and Afghanistan.[35] The video was to be released by al Qaida following their suicide attack.[36]

It is also reported—although not confirmed—that Zazi may have met Bryant Neal Vinas at one of al Qaida's training camps.[37] Vinas, an American, was captured in November 2008 by Pakistani authorities and turned over to American law enforcement. Vinas, of Long Island, NY, a convert to Islamist extremism, is reported to have revealed extensive information to his American interrogators about al Qaida's network in Pakistan, so it is possible that he may have tipped them off to Zazi's activities during this period, since it has been reported that it was during this period that the CIA may have picked up on Zazi's presence in Peshawar, a city used by al Qaida to arrange meetings with potential foreign operatives.[38] Even if Zazi and his associates had not met Vinas, they likely interacted with some of the same al Qaida commanders that Vinas had met in Pakistan's tribal areas.[39]

At some point during this trip, Zazi also met with a low level al Qaida "fixer" or facilitator in Peshawar, who used the names Sohaib, Ahmad and Zahid. After returning to the U.S. Zazi communicated several times with this individual in late August-early September 2009, most of the time seeking advice on mixing chemicals.[40] Attesting to the international makeup of the terrorist networks that were being established at the same time, two of the 12 Pakistani students from Manchester, Britain, had also met this same al Qaida facilitator in Peshawar in November 2008.[41]

During their time in Waziristan, Zazi and his two associates also reportedly met high ranking al Qaida operatives, such as Rashid Rauf, Saleh al-Somali, and Adnan Shukrijumah. At the time, al-Somali was al Qaida's chief of international operations, and in charge of plotting attacks worldwide.[42] Although he was killed in a U.S. drone strike in 2009, he was instrumental in three plots that had already been set in motion by the time of his death.[43] Rauf was also a key al Qaida operative.[44] Meanwhile, Shukrijumah, a 35-year old Saudi-born al Qaida veteran, had grown up in Florida, but had left the U.S. just before the 9/11 attacks. Attesting to Shukrijumah's importance, he was viewed as the successor to replace al-Somali.[45] Both Shukrijumah and Zazi's "facilitator" became directly involved in plotting the New York City subway operation.[46] The "facilitator" was also involved in managing plots in Manchester and Scandinavia.[47] The Scandinavian cell, which was tasked with bombing the Danish newspaper *Jullands Posten* over publication of cartoons of the Prophet Mohammed and the Chinese embassy in Oslo, was arrested in July 2010.[48]

"Operationalizing the Plot and Its Preemption"

Of three young men who traveled from Newark to Peshawar in August 2008, Adis Medunjanin left on a return flight home to New York on September 25, 2008.[49] His sudden return may have resulted from a feud with Zazi, who frequently chastised him about his personal and religious beliefs, accusing him of "drinking tea from a Pepsi bottle, [which he told him] wasn't the right way."[50] This conflict caused one of al Qaida's leaders at the camp to suggest that they should not travel together.[51] Meanwhile, Zazi and Zarein Ahmedzay remained in Peshawar or thereabouts until returning to the U.S. in mid-January 2009 on separate flights.[52]

While Zazi may have been under some sort of surveillance by U.S. authorities while in Pakistan—and this is unconfirmed—his actual plot may have been initially uncovered by Scotland Yard in early 2009 as part of "Operation Pathway," when it intercepted an e-mail from a senior al Qaida operative in Pakistan to Zazi, instructing him how to implement his attack.[53] Scotland Yard then notified the FBI, which began its surveillance operation against Zazi, including listening to his phone conversations.

Upon his return to the U.S. in mid-January 2009 Zazi began the plot's "pre-operational phase." Within days of his return, he moved to Aurora, Colorado, to live with his aunt and uncle. Later, Zazi reportedly told law enforcement officials that he moved to Colorado because it was cheaper to live there than New York.[54] Zazi began working for several airport shuttle companies, driving a 15-person airport shuttle van between Denver International Airport and downtown Denver. He proved highly industrious and hardworking, routinely working 16-to-18-hour shifts. "He was a regular kind of guy, but he worked hard, and he wanted money," said Hicham Semmaml, a fellow driver. In June, however, his uncle kicked him out of the apartment for not paying rent. His parents then moved to Aurora from New York, and the three took a residence together, with his father obtaining employment as a cabdriver.

Interestingly, while there are indications of al Qaida motivation and instruction, the evidence suggests only limited (if any) financial support was given to Zazi and his colleagues. He did not even have enough cash to purchase hydrogen peroxide-based products for the bombs, so in order to fund his operation Zazi piled debt onto several credit cards. Further, while many seasoned terrorist and criminal operatives have become quite skilled at concealing their finances from authorities, Zazi filed for bankruptcy in New York State on March 26, 2009, with records showing accumulated debts of $51,000. By the time his bankruptcy was discharged on August 17, 2009, it is likely that this raised an additional warning flag with U.S. authorities, who had already begun surveillance of Zazi (as described below).

Beginning around June 2009, Zazi began the plot's "operational phase" by accessing his bomb-making notes and researching sites on the Internet to find ingredients for the explosives. He conducted several internet searches for hydrochloric acid, and used his bomb-making notes to construct an explosive based on hydrogen peroxide, acetone, and acid, which are readily available in beauty supply stores, and are components used in the powerful explosive Triacetone triperoxide (TATP, also known as acetone peroxide). TATP-based bombs were used in the 2005 London subway bombings, and by Richard Reid, the "shoe bomber," in his abortive 2003 attempt to blow up an airliner en-route from Paris to Boston.

He also took several trips to New York, meeting with his associates to discuss the plan, the attack's timing, and where to make the explosives. At the trial of Medunjanin,

Ahmedzay revealed that as the three agreed to proceed with the operation, Zazi was tasked with making the bomb, while Ahmedzay, a cabdriver, was to scout locations for the attack, and Medunjanin would join them in its execution.[55] They had decided to strap on bombs to blow themselves up at three different locations inside Manhattan's subway system during the morning rush hour to cause maximum panic and casualties.[56] During the course of the FBI's surveillance, it was discovered that in July and again in August, Zazi and several associates who had traveled from New York to Colorado began shopping at various beauty-supply stores in Denver, purchasing large quantities of hydrogen peroxide and acetone products. His associates reportedly used stolen credit cards to purchase these and other bomb-making materials.[57] At the Beauty Supply Warehouse on East Sixth Avenue in Denver, investigators found Zazi's image on security tapes, pushing a cart full of hydrogen peroxide–based products down the aisle. Additional supplies were purchased in early September 2009 as well. Later in the investigation, a search of Zazi's laptop indicated that he also searched the Internet for locations of a home-improvement store in Queens, New York where he could purchase muriatic acid, a diluted version of hydrochloric acid.[58]

In August 2009 Zazi informed his al Qaida contact in Pakistan that the plot was "operational."[59] On August 28 and again on September 6 and 7, Zazi checked into a local motel suite, where he experimented with heating and mixing the chemicals to create a bomb using the stove in the room's kitchenette.[60] Later, when law enforcement authorities examined the kitchenette, they discovered traces of acetone, which they believe was from a nail polish remover. During this August 2009 period, as the FBI listened in on his telephone calls Zazi was heard talking about 'chemical mixtures and other things.' It is reported that around this time Zazi's bomb making efforts hit a glitch when he discovered that he was missing a page of his notes that had detailed the quantities of ingredients required to build a large bomb.[61] This led him to contact his al Qaida instructor in Pakistan via e-mail, but no reply was received.[62]

Shortly thereafter, FBI electronic surveillance revealed that Zazi had sent text and e-mail messages to his intermediary, the aforementioned "facilitator" known as "Ahmad," suggesting (in code) that the plot was nearing the attack stage,[63] using phrases like "The wedding cake is ready,"[64] and "the marriage is ready" shortly before he drove from Colorado to New York City carrying the bomb-making components,[65] although for smaller bombs that Zazi and his associates would strap to themselves to detonate in the subway cars.[66] (In previous al Qaida plots, operatives have often used references to weddings to disguise upcoming terrorist attacks.)

Early in the morning on September 9, Zazi left home in a car that he and his father had rented the night before, and began driving east toward New York City, 1,800 miles away. Inside the car were detonators, explosives, and other materials used for building bombs. He was followed by a team of FBI agents. In the evening of September 10, Zazi's car was stopped on the George Washington Bridge as he was entering New York City, and was told it was a random drug checkpoint (other cars were stopped, as well). Zazi then arrived in New York City and spent the night at the residence of his childhood friend Naiz Kahn, in Flushing, Queens. According to his later testimony, he had intended to obtain and assemble the remaining components to build a bomb over the weekend.[67] Later that day, Zazi and several associates attempted to rent a U-Haul moving van in Queens, possibly for transporting the operatives and their backpacks to the subway stations chosen for the operation.[68]

Also on September 10, in a related development, two New York City Police Department (NYPD) Intelligence Division detectives interviewed imam Ahmad Wais Afzali, a Muslim cleric whom they had used as an informant over the years, for information about Zazi and three of his associates. It is not known, however, if this interview had been coordinated with the FBI, whose agents were trailing the suspects. Afzali admitted that he knew them and that Zazi had prayed at his Queens mosque. On September 11, Afzali called Zazi's father, who then spoke with Zazi, telling him that "they" had shown Afzali his photos and photos of others. Zazi's father added, "So, before anything else, speak with [Afzali]. See if you need to go to [Afzali] or to make . . . yourself aware, hire an attorney." Afzali also called Zazi, and told him that the authorities had asked him about "you guys." He also asked Zazi for the telephone number of one of the other men whose photos he had been shown, and set up a meeting with him.

On September 11, Zazi's rental car, which was parked near his friends' residence in Queens, was towed on a "purported" parking violation, and FBI agents then conducted a legally-authorized search during which they found his laptop computer and copied (or "mirrored") its contents.[69] Their investigation found images of nine pages of notes in Zazi's handwriting on how to make initiating explosives, main explosive charges, detonators, and fuses.[70] The recipe for homemade explosives found on Zazi's computer would have produced bombs of the same size and type used in the July 2005 London attacks.[71] The laptop also revealed that Zazi had researched baseball and football stadiums and locations of the recent Fashion Week event in New York City.[72] Subsequent investigations and court testimony later revealed that the plot's objective was to assemble the remaining bomb components as soon as they were ready for Zazi and his two associates to conduct the coordinated suicide bombings on September 14 (the most likely date), 15, or 16. They planned to detonate backpack bombs on New York City Subway trains near New York's two busiest subway stations, the Grand Central and Times Square stations in Manhattan, during rush hour. They planned to board the middle of packed trains on the 1, 2, 3, and/or 6 lines, to cause maximum casualties.

Zazi was supposed to return his rental car in New York on September 14, but after being tipped off by his father that he was under surveillance, he decided to abort the operation. He and his associates began taking steps to dispose of the detonator explosives and other materials. Zazi, for example, went to Ahmedzay's home to hide the detonator explosives, and he and Ahmedzay then proceeded to flush the remaining chemicals at a mosque's toilet.[73] Then on September 12, he flew home from La Guardia Airport in Queens, New York, to Denver, Colorado, and there he enlisted his family to help him dispose of the bomb's ingredients. They believed, correctly, that the FBI was eavesdropping, and referred to the potential evidence by the code word "medicine."[74] His father, Mohammed, ordered his family members to get rid of his son's bomb-making materials which were stored in the garage and lie to FBI agents if they were questioned.[75] This was revealed by Amanullah Zazi, Najibullah's cousin, who testified at Mohammed's trial.

On September 14, two days after Zazi had left New York, FBI investigators executed search warrants on several addresses in New York City, including one where Zazi had stayed with his friends. In one of the apartments, they found 14 newly purchased backpacks, an electronic "black scale," and batteries with Zazi's fingerprints.[76] Electronic scales of this kind can be used to measure chemicals for hydrogen peroxide-based explosives, which the federal authorities suspect was the purpose. An alert was then issued to American law enforcement officials to be on the lookout for hydrogen peroxide-based bombs.

On September 16, a few days after returning to Denver, Zazi and his attorney Art Folsom met with federal agents at the FBI office in Denver, where he was asked to submit DNA, hair, and handwriting samples.[77] During his eight-hour interview, he denied knowing anything about the nine-page handwritten document found on his hard drive, and then claimed they were innocent chemistry drawings he had downloaded from a book online.[78] In subsequent interviews on September 17 and 18, however, he acknowledged receiving explosives and weapons training in the tribal areas of Pakistan. On September 19, 2009, the FBI arrested Zazi and his father (for conspiring to destroy evidence) in Denver, while Ahmad Afzali was arrested in New York City (charged with tipping off Najibullah Zazi). On September 21, Zazi was formally charged with making false statements involving international and domestic terrorism. His father was released on $50,000 bond to his home in Aurora under house arrest, where he wore an electronic bracelet. On March 4, 2010, Afzali accepted a plea deal in which he pleaded guilty to a reduced charge and agreed to be deported to Saudi Arabia with his wife. Meanwhile, on January 7, 2010, knowing he was about to be arrested, Adis Medunjanin intentionally crashed his car on the Whitestone Expressway in Queens, New York, ultimately failing in his objective to kill himself and other drivers.[79] In his 911 call from his cellular phone, he told the operator: "We love death."[80]

On February 22, 2010, Zazi pled guilty to conspiring to use weapons of mass destruction (explosive bombs), conspiracy to commit murder in a foreign country, and providing material support to a terrorist organization. His guilty plea was the result of a plea bargain with the prosecution. In July 2011, Zazi's uncle Naqib Jaji pled guilty to his role in conspiring to destroy evidence against his nephew, and agreed to cooperate with the government as part of his guilty plea.[81] Following his indictment in January 2010, Ahmedzay pled guilty to terrorism charges in April of that year. In April 2012, Medunjanin was convicted of terrorism charges for participating in the plot, following a two-week trial in which Zazi and Ahmedzay had testified as government witnesses against him.[82]

Implications for Domestic Counterterrorism

Najibullah Zazi's thwarted plot to bomb the New York City subway system was part of the religiously fundamentalist wave of terrorism threatening America and its allies, with militantly religious "homegrown" individuals, also known as a "bunch of guys," joining up with foreign terrorist groups that are part of the global "jihad."[83] Unlike the 9/11 plot—which involved al Qaida "Central's" top operational managers in direct command-and-control over all aspects of the operation, including deploying their highly trained and well-funded foreign-based cells who kept a low profile once in the targeted country—Zazi and his associates were second-rate, 'dispensable' al Qaida operatives directed to mount and fund an operation pretty much on their own, although the choice of weaponry and targets was likely selected by their "controllers" in Pakistan. They were preempted due to the robust counter-terrorism intelligence and law enforcement infrastructure established following 9/11, including the close cooperation between the CIA and FBI and their allied security service counterparts, in this case, Britain, Canada, Scandinavia, and Pakistan, which led to uncovering Zazi's plot during its early stages. As such, this case highlights the challenges faced by modern counterterrorism agencies, and provides some important lessons for responding effectively.

While tracking Zazi and his associates in what became known as Operation Highrise,[84] the U.S. government's counterterrorism agencies worked seamlessly and in an integrated manner to physically and electronically place them under surveillance and preempt their operation at the appropriately early moment. Unlike the pre-9/11 law enforcement-dominated paradigm, intelligence gathering was given due consideration. Zazi's conspiracy was allowed to proceed through its later stages to enable authorities to uncover and then apprehend the entire network.

One of the first times Zazi's name (and likely those of his associates) reportedly drew the attention of federal authorities—due to the potentially suspicious nature of his travel destination—was on August 20, 2008, when he took off from Newark to Pakistan, with his name entered into the Passenger Name Record (PNR) database.[85] PNR data includes a passenger's itinerary, payment method, and contact information, so such data would have provided valuable information about Zazi's travel arrangements.[86] It surely came to their notice again when he returned on January 15, 2009 at Kennedy Airport.[87] But had this information not been shared, important signals of the plot could have been missed.

In terms of federal—local counterterrorism relations, the FBI worked closely with local law enforcement agencies. On September 9, when Zazi started driving his rental car from Denver to New York City, the FBI obtained the cooperation of a Colorado State Patrol trooper to pull him over "purportedly" for speeding, in order to inquire about his destination, with the same cooperation extended by New York State troopers as he was crossing the George Washington Bridge into New York.[88] Although journalistic accounts claim that the NYPD's detectives' interview with Afzali, the Queens imam, tipped off Zazi that the authorities were on to him and could have thwarted potential prosecution,[89] perhaps it actually was part of a coordinated plan with the FBI and NYPD to "smoke out" other potential associates, such as the imam, Zazi's father and others. It ended up working because both were eventually arrested as co-conspirators, with other members of Zazi's family not only implicated, but ending up as government witnesses against them. In any case, it is fortunate that Afzali's tipping off Zazi was not sufficient to give him enough time to destroy evidence that revealed how close he had come to building his bombs and leading his team to carry out the operation.

The FBI's role in the investigation also demonstrated how it had transformed its domestic law enforcement and intelligence capabilities, becoming more of a combination of Britain's vaunted MI-5 and Scotland Yard. The FBI's field offices in Denver and New York City, which are part of the Bureau's 56 field offices nationwide, were involved operationally in countering Zazi and his associates by sifting through information and then disseminating it locally and nationally, including to the more than 100 Joint Terrorism Task Forces (JTTF) nationwide, and a National JTTF at FBI Headquarters with 40 member agencies. As explained by Department of Homeland Security Secretary Janet Napolitano in praising the investigation of Najibullah Zazi, several FBI field offices and their JTTFs (including the New York JTTF) contributed to efforts in identifying Zazi, conducting surveillance of him, and arresting Zazi before he could execute his attack, while also identifying Zazi's associates.[90]

According to Director Robert Mueller, the FBI has adopted a threat-based, intelligence-driven framework that patiently tracks networks of associates over appropriate lengths of time, noting in his congressional testimony that "the new approach prioritizes the collection and utilization of intelligence to develop a comprehensive threat picture, enabling strategic disruptions of terrorist networks before they act."[91] The case also illustrates the critical importance of intelligence sharing between the FBI and state and local law enforcement agencies. Countering the Zazi case was successful, according to Senator Susan Collins, because it "underscore[d] the incredible value of information sharing," and coordination among agencies with their law enforcement and intelligence counterparts.[92] A key component of this information sharing involved the Colorado Information and Analysis Center (CIAC), which provided analytic support to the Denver FBI and DHS, including personnel to assist the Denver FBI in the investigation and support the field operations. According to the DHS website, "CIAC analysts also assisted in the review and analysis of the evidence obtained during the execution of the search and arrest warrants. CIAC leadership addressed media inquiries regarding the investigation, the threat to Colorado residents, and the threat to national security."[93] In this particular investigation, the Colorado fusion center's databases were used by the FBI's Denver office to quickly assess information obtained through an FBI search warrant on Zazi.[94]

The FBI has also established partnerships throughout the intelligence, law enforcement, and allied nations' security communities, where FBI legal attachés maintain liaison relationships with foreign counterparts, which must have been the case in Zazi's investigation. Other FBI divisions likely involved include the FBI's Terrorist Screening Center (TSC), established in December 2003, which maintains the U.S. Government's consolidated Terrorist Watchlist—a single database of identifying information about individuals known or suspected of being involved in terrorist activity, the Terrorism Financing Operations Section (TFOS), which tracks terrorist financing, including, when possible, utilizing such information to identify previously unknown terrorist cells, and the Foreign Terrorist Tracking Task Force (FTTTF), established in 2003, which provides—once an investigation is authorized—a spectrum of new or confirming information generated from government and public databases about individuals with a nexus to terrorism who may be operating in the United States. Once identified, leads on such terrorists and their associates are provided to appropriate law enforcement agencies to initiate or sustain investigatory and judicial actions against them.

Although not considered a domestic counterterrorism agency, the National Security Agency (NSA) was also likely involved in the Zazi investigation. The NSA collects overseas signals intelligence (SIGINT), which in counterterrorism consists of intercepting, processing, analyzing, and disseminating information derived from electronic communications and other signals employed by terrorist groups, their associates, and state sponsors. The NSA works closely with the FBI on cases involving Americans and foreign counterparts.

Also involved in helping to preempt Zazi's operation was the National Counterterrorism Center (NCTC).[95] It was set up following the September 11, 2001 attacks, after it emerged that vital data on the pending strikes was not shared swiftly between various U.S. intelligence agencies. Its mission is to synchronize the fight against terrorist threats within the United States and abroad, and to coordinate and share data on individuals with a nexus to terrorism and pending strikes with U.S. government departments and agencies and U.S. foreign partners, including the coordination of intelligence collection and analysis efforts between federal, state, and local government agencies. The NCTC's role in the Zazi investigation was recognized by President Barack Obama, who stated, "You [NCTC] stitched together the intelligence. You worked together, across organizations, as one team. And then—arrests in Denver and New York."[96]

Working with these and other intelligence and law enforcement partners enabled the FBI to deploy a discreet, yet robust, physical and electronic surveillance of Zazi once he returned to the U.S. in January 2009, ensuring that he and his associates never posed, at any point, an immediate threat. This was also due to British intelligence's interception of his e-mails early on and sharing them with the FBI, and the FBI's tapping of his calls and reading his e-mails before he began building bombs. As soon as he attempted to leave Denver for New York City to carry out his operation, he was placed under constant surveillance along the route by the FBI and local law enforcement agencies. As in other cases, such as Faisal Shahzad's aborted attempt to bomb Times Square in early May 2010, Zazi was inept—constantly e-mailing his al Qaida contacts to plead for advice in constructing the bombs. Moreover, publicly declaring personal bankruptcy and even buying bomb materials with maxed out and stolen credit cards, must have sent numerous red flags through the counterterrorism financial tracking system.

A final noteworthy success in thwarting Zazi's operation was the highly selective way in which information about the case was released to the public, with extensive gaps in information about Zazi and his associates that may never be publicly revealed. Such restrictions are justified in order to protect possible on-going related investigations flowing from this and other cases, such as the one involving Vinas, who had reportedly met Zazi at one of al Qaida's training camps in Pakistan in Fall 2008.

As discussed in the introduction of this paper, Zazi's case study represents a transformational paradigm shift in the nature and magnitude of terrorist threats the U.S. faces from American residents who become radicalized into violent extremism and decide to join al Qaida and its affiliates. Even if their recruitment path was circuitous, and not direct, Zazi and his associates were the types of recruits al Qaida's operational planners were seeking: legal residents, acculturated in American society (even if ambivalent and even hostile to its culture), and seemingly innocuous (although their activities would have raised red flags along the way). As such, the Zazi case suggests that al Qaida's network, weakened though it might be from its expulsion from Afghanistan after 9/11 and constant attacks against its operatives in Pakistan's lawless regions, could still project its terrorist violence into the U.S., with its motivation to do so as high as ever following the targeted killings of its leader, Usama bin Laden, in May 2011 and one of its chief ideologues (and operational managers) Anwar al-Awlaki in September of that year.

As a result of this paradigm shift, the U.S. now faces threats by the prototypical homegrown terrorist—a legal U.S. resident who is sufficiently radicalized, motivated, connected, and capable of executing terrorist attacks, even if they may not approximate the catastrophic magnitude of 9/11. Other types of terrorist threats will persist, such as the continuous attempts by foreign terrorists to enter the U.S. to conduct operations against the homeland, but which will be difficult to execute because of the comprehensive anti-terrorism infrastructures instituted after 9/11.

The Zazi plot not only represented a dangerous new phase in the terrorist threat against America due to its homegrown nature, but its operational planners were part of a multi-national network of al Qaida and its affiliates. These terrorist networks stretched from Pakistan's Taliban-dominated regions—where al Qaida's operatives found sanctuary—to al Qaida in the Arabian Peninsula's (AQAP) strongholds in Yemen, as represented by two follow-up, highly organized and separate attacks launched in the span of eight months that would have caused catastrophic damage had they not failed in their execution phase.

These were the AQAP-trained and directed Umar Abdulmutallab's abortive operation to blow up Northwest flight 253 bound for Detroit on Christmas Day and the Taliban-trained and directed Faisal Shahzad operation to detonate his explosive laden van in Times Square on May 1, 2010. These and other similar plots demonstrate that al Qaida and its affiliates have made a strategic decision not to solely pursue attacks on the scale of 9/11 that kill thousands, but to launch smaller-scale attacks inside the U.S. to achieve at least some tactical success in inflicting tens or hundreds of casualties. As explained by former FBI agent Jack Cloonan, "They want to see bodies, blood sprayed all over the place. They want to punish us . . . . It accomplishes a number of things aside from body count. It reaffirms that they are alive and well."[97]

Further, the 'do-it-yourself' aspect of the Zazi case underscores the kind of strategic effect al Qaida needs in order to remain a relevant terrorist threat in the face of several setbacks in recent years. To some degree, even failed plots are seen as advantageous by al Qaida's leaders, because with minimal investment, they remain on the radar screen of powerful Western countries like the U.S. and demonstrate a continued capability to inspire others to lethal action on behalf of their global jihadist ideology. From this perspective, it is logical to expect that we will see other terrorist plots of this type in the foreseeable future.

Critical Thinking Questions

1. What were the most critical elements of the local, state, and/or federal response to this terrorist threat?
2. What could be done, if anything, to prevent this potential attack from reaching the nearly operational stage that it did?
3. Do you believe an attack similar to this will be successful at some point in the future? Why or why not?

Notes

1. John Marzulli, "Zazi, Al Qaeda pals planned rush-hour attack on Grand Central, Times Square subway stations," *Daily News,* April 12, 2010.
2. For an account of the extent of al Qaida's involvement in the March 2003 Madrid bombings, see Mitchell D. Silber, *The Al Qaeda Factor: Plots Against the West* (Philadelphia: University of Pennsylvania Press, 2011), pp. 184–205.
3. This formulation is based on Thomas Kuhn, *The Structure of Scientific Revolution* (Chicago: The University of Chicago Press, 1966).
4. Kerry Burke, et al., "How the feds caught Najibullah Zazi, pieced together the 9/11 terror plot," *Daily News,* September 27, 2009.
5. James Gordon Meek, et al., "A dozen on constant watch including Najibullah Zazi in FBI's terrorist probe," *Daily News,* September 18, 2009, and Kerry Burke, et al., "How the feds caught Najibullah Zazi, pieced together the 9/11 terror plot."
6. Aryn Baker, "An Enemy Within: The Making of Najibullah Zazi," *Time,* October 1, 2009.
7. Aki Peritz and Eric Rosenbach, *Find, Fix, Finish: Inside the Counterterrorism Campaigns That Killed Bin Laden and Devastated Al Qaeda* (New York: Public Affairs, 2012), p. 169; and Silber, *The Al Qaeda Factor,* p. 159.

8. Dayle Cedars, "Zazi Question By FBI For Hours," *The DenverChannel.com,* September 17, 2009.
9. Aryn Baker, "An Enemy Within: The Making of Najibullah Zazi."
10. James gordon Meek, et al., "A Dozen on Constant Watch Including Najibullah Zazi in FBI's Terrorist Probe."
11. *Ibid.*
12. Silber, *The Al Qaeda Factor,* p. 159
13. *Ibid.*
14. *Ibid.*
15. Tina Susman and Richard A. Serrano, "Guilty plea in New York terrorism case," *Los Angeles Times,* February 23, 2010.
16. Mosi Secret, "Witness Details Plot to Attack Subways," *The New York Times,* April 16, 2012.
17. *Ibid.*
18. "United States of America v. Najibullah Zazi," *Criminal Complaint,* [United States District Court for the District of Colorado], September 19, 2009, p. 2.
19. Mosi Secret, "Witness Details Plot to Attack Subways."
20. Silber, *The Al Qaeda Factor,* pp. 159–160.
21. Paul Cruickshank, "The Militant Pipeline: Between the Afghanistan-Pakistan Border Region and the West," National Security Studies Program Policy Paper, New America Foundation, [Second Edition], July 2011, p. 36.
22. Tom Hays, "Father of NYC subway bomb plotter is convicted," *Associated Press,* July 22, 2011, Denverpost.com, and John Marzulli, "Father of would-be terrorist Najibullah Zazi hid bomb materials, relative testifies," *Daily News,* July 18, 2011.
23. *Ibid.,* p. 160.
24. John Marzulli, "Ferid Imam provided terror training to three high school friends trying to join the Taliban: feds," *Daily News,* March 15, 2011.
25. *Ibid.*
26. *Ibid.*
27. "Ferid Imam, Canadian Fugitive Charged in NYC Subway Plot," *Associated Press,* March 15, 2011.
28. "Terror charges laid against former Winnipeggers," *CBC News,* March 15, 2011.
29. Warren Richey, "Canadian charged with helping Najibullah Zazi in New York bomb plot," *Christian Science Monitor,* March 15, 2011.
30. *Ibid.* Also, see "RCMP Lay Terrorism Related Charges," Royal Canadian Mounted Police, March 15, 2011, http://www.rcmp-grc.gc.ca/news-nouvelles/2011/03-15-darken-eng.htm.
31. John Marzulli, "Zazi, Al Qaeda pals planned rush-hour attack on Grand Central," Times Square subway stations, *Daily News,* April 12, 2010.
32. Mosi Secret, "Witness Describes Bomb-Making Process for Thwarted Subway Plot," *The New York Times,* April 18, 2012.
33. "Najibullah Zazi reveals chilling details on Al Qaeda training and terrorist plot to blow up subways," *NY Daily News* (Feb. 23, 2010) Online at: http://www.nydailynews.com/news/crime/najibullah-zazi-reveals-chilling-details-al-qaeda-training-terrorist-plot-blow-subways-article-1.169311
34. Phil Hirschkorn, "Would-be Subway Suicide Bomber Najibullah Zazi Speaks," *CBS News,* April 19, 2012.

35. *Ibid.*
36. Mosi Secret, "Witness Describes Bomb-Making Process for Thwarted Subway Plot."
37. Sebastian Rotella, "Fear of Homegrown Terror Up," *Chicago Tribune,* December 7, 2009. http://articles.chicagotribune.com/2009-12-07/news/0912070064_1_al-qaida-qaida-radicalization.
38. Brian Ross, et al., "FBI Arrests Three Men in Terror Plot that Targeted New York," *ABC News,* September 20, 2009, http://abcnews.go.com/Blotter/men-arrested-fbi-nyc-terror-plot/story?id=8618732.
39. Paul Cruickshank, "The Militant Pipeline: Between the Afghanistan-Pakistan Border Region and the West," p. 35.
40. Duncan Gardham, "New York Subway Plot Was Five Days From Success," *The Telegraph,* December 14, 2010, http://www.telegraph.co.uk/news/worldnews/northamerica/usa/8202709/New-York-subway-plot-was-five-days-from-success.html.
41. Duncan Gardham, "New York Subway Plot Was Five Days From Success," *The Telegraph,* December 14, 2010, http://www.telegraph.co.uk/news/worldnews/northamerica/usa/8202709/New-York-subway-plot-was-five-days-from-success.html.
42. Silber, *The Al Qaeda Factor,* p. 160.
43. Ian MacDougall, et al., "Norway bomb plot connected to U.S., British threats," *Associated Press,* July 9, 2010.
44. Silber, *The Al Qaeda Factor,* p. 160.
45. James Gordon Meek, "Subway plotter Najibullah Zazi met with key al Qada player Adnan Shukrijumah, feds believe," *Daily News,* July 1, 2010.
46. Tom Hays and Matt Apuzzo, "New York subway bomb plot linked to British cell," *Associated Press,* July 8, 2010.
47. Duncan Gardham, "Manchester bomb plot students were planning co-ordinated attacks in New York and Scandinavia," *The Telegraph,* December 16, 2010.
48. *Ibid.*
49. "United States of America Against Adis Medunjanin, Abid Naseer, Adnan el Shukrijumah, Tariq ur Rehman, and FNU LNU," *Indictment,* No Date, JHK: DMB/JPL/BWB, F. # 201oR00057, p. 8.
50. Mosi Secret, "Witness Details Plot to Attack Subways."
51. *Ibid.*
52. Brian Ross, et al., "FBI Arrests Three Men in Terror Plot that Targeted New York": and "United States of America Against Adis Medunjanin, Abid Naseer, Adnan el Shukrijumah, Tariq ur Rehman, and FNU LNU," p. 8.
53. *Daily Telegraph,* 2009,
54. Peritz and Rosenbach, *Find, Fix, Finish,* p. 171.
55. Mosi Secret, "Witness Details Plot to Attack Subways."
56. Tom Hays,"Zazi in Subway Plot Trial: We Also Eyed NYSE," *The Associated Press,* April 18, 2012.
57. Bruce Finley and Felisa Cardona, *The Denver Post,* September 24, 2009.
58. *Ibid.*
59. Mosi Secret, "Homegrown Bomb Plot Is Rarity for Open Court," *The New York Times,* April 15, 2012.
60. *Ibid.*
61. Mosi Secret, "Witness Describes Bomb-Making Process for Thwarted Subway Plot."
62. *Ibid.*

63. Duncan Gardham, "Manchester bomb plot students were planning co-ordinated attacks in New York and Scandinavia."
64. Brian Ross, et al., "FBI Arrests Three Men in Terror Plot that Targeted New York."
65. Tom Hays and Matt Apuzzo, "Najibullah Zazi's Al Qaeda Bomb Plot Likely Part of Larger Operation," [Associated Press], *The Herald Sun,* July 7, 2010,
66. Mosi Secret, "Witness Describes Bomb-Making Process for Thwarted Subway Plot."
67. Garret M. Graff, "Homegrown Terror," *5280 The Denver Magazine* (November 2011), online at: http://www.5280.com/magazine/2011/11/homegrown-terror?page=0,0
68. Dan Fletcher, "Terrorism Suspect Najibullah Zazi," *Time,* September 22, 2009.
69. "United States of America v. Mohammed Wali Zazi," *Criminal Complaint,* United States District Court for the District of Colorado, September 19, 2009, p. 6.
70. Peritz and Rosenbach, *Find, Fix, Finish,* p. 178.
71. Brian Ross, et al., "FBI Arrests Three Men in Terror Plot that Targeted New York."
72. *Ibid.*
73. Mosi Secret, "Witness Describes Bomb-Making Process for Thwarted Subway Plot."
74. Garret M. Graff, "Homegrown Terror," *5280 The Denver Magazine* (November 2011), online at: http://www.5280.com/magazine/2011/11/homegrown-terror?page=0,1
75. John Marzulli, "Father of would-be terrorist Najibullah Zazi hid bomb materials, relative testifies."
76. James Gordon Meek, et al., "Feds unsure if arrest of Najibullah Zazi and two others has foiled Al Qaeda terror plot," Daily News, September 20, 2009, http://articles.nydailynews.com/2009-09-20/news/17933259_1_najibullah-zazi-al-qaeda-fbi.
77. "Najibullah Zazi Denies Any Ties To Terrorist Groups," *TheDenverChannel.com,* October 2, 2009.
78. Garret M. Graff, "Homegrown Terror," *5280 The Denver Magazine* (November 2011), online at: http://www.5280.com/magazine/2011/11/homegrown-terror?page=0,3
79. "United States of America Against Adis Medunjanin, Abid Naseer, Adnan el Shukrijumah, Tariq ur Rehman, and FNU LNU," p. 9.
80. *Ibid,* p. 8.
81. Adam Reiss, "Trial begins for father of NYC bomb plotter accused of misleading FBI," *CNN,* July 18, 2011.
82. Mosi Secret, "Terror Defendant Convicted in New York Subway Plot," *The New York Times,* May 1, 2012.
83. cf. David C. Rapoport, "The Four Waves of Terrorism," in *Attacking Terrorism: Elements of a Grand Strategy,* edited by Audrey Kurth Cronin and James M. Ludes (Washington, DC: Georgetown University Press, 2004); Brian Michael Jenkins, "Would-Be Warriors: Incidents of Jihadist Terrorist Radicalization in the United States since September 11, 2001." Santa Monica, CA: RAND Corporation, 2010; and Bruce Hoffman, "American Jihad," *the National Interest* (April 20, 2010).
84. Silber, *The Al Qaeda Factor,* p. 165.
85. Zrausnitz, "DHS defends passenger data collection amid E.U. privacy concerns," *Fierce Homelandsecurity,* October 5, 2011.
86. Zrausnitz, "DHS Defends Passenger Data Collection Amid E.U. Privacy Concerns," *Fierce Homeland Security,* October 5, 2011.
87. Kerry Burke, et al., "How the feds caught Najibullah Zazi, pieced together the 9/11 terror plot."

88. Sara Burnett, "Colorado Zazi's coded e-mail started agencies plan to stop N.Y. subway attack," *The Denver Post,* October 2, 2011.
89. See Kerry Burke, et al., "How the feds caught Najibullah Zazi, pieced together the 9/11 terror plot."
90. Testimony of Secretary Janet Napolitano Before the United States House of Representatives Committee on Homeland Security, "Understanding the Homeland Threat Landscape—Considerations for the 112th Congress," February 9, 2011, http://www.dhs.gov/ynews/testimony/testimony_1297263844607.shtm.
91. Robert S. Mueller, "Ten Years After 9/11: Are We Safer," Statement Before the Senate Committee on Homeland Security and Governmental Affairs, September 13, 2011, http://www.fbi.gov/news/testimony/ten-years-after-9-11-are-we-safer.
92. Statement of Ranking Member, Susan M. Collins, "Information Sharing in the Era of Wikileaks: Balancing Security and Collaboration", March 10, 2011, http://www.fas.org/irp/congress/2011_hr/031011collins.pd.
93. Department of Homeland Security, "Fusion Center Success Stories: Fusion Center Supports Zazi Investigation," September 2009, http://www.dhs.gov/files/programs/gc_1296488620700.shtm.
94. Dana Priest and William M. Arkin, *Top Secret America: The Rise of the New American Security State* (New York: Little, Brown and Company, 2011), p. 148.
95. "Obama vows to flush out Al Qaeda," *Agence France Presse,* October 6, 2009.
96. Remarks by President Obama at the National Counterterrorism Center (NCTC), October 6, 2009, http://www.dni.gov/speeches/20091006_speech.pdf
97. Pierre Thomas, "NYC Subway Plot: Dangerous new Phase in Threat by Al Qaeda," *ABC News.com,* February 23, 2010, http://abcnews.go.com/GMA/najibullah-zazi-nyc-subway-plot-al-qaeda-threat/story?id=9917485.

Lessons from Mumbai

Assessing Armed Assault Threats to the United States

James Jay Carafano

For three bloody days in November 2008, Indian police and military forces battled heavily armed and well-organized groups of terrorists who fanned out across the city of Mumbai. Armed terrorist assaults against populated areas will be neither an unprecedented nor a remote threat in the future, and Mumbai offers lessons for the United States in how to respond to such threats.

Effective counterterrorism, intelligence, and information-sharing programs are the best way to prevent organized conspiracies from undertaking armed assaults, using vehicle-borne explosives, or employing other common terrorist tactics. The best way to minimize the likelihood that such attacks will be successful is to develop an integrated approach: a homeland security enterprise that promotes joint action linking law enforcement, emergency responders, and federal capabilities (such as the U.S. military) in a common effort to save lives and property.

Unthinkable But Possible

While November's armed assaults in Mumbai were horrific, they are not unprecedented. Russia, for instance, has experienced a string of similar incidents undertaken by Chechen separatists.

- In 1995, 1,000 hospital patients were held captive at Budyonnovsk, near the border with Chechnya. Russian troops stormed the hospital twice, and more than 100 civilians died during the effort to retake the hospital grounds.
- In October 2002, 50 heavily armed Chechen rebels seized a Moscow theater, holding hundreds hostage. They booby-trapped entrances with mines, strapped explosives to some of the hostages, and rigged a large bomb in the center of the theater. Russian Special Forces pumped the theater full of gas, and more than 100 hostages died from the effects of that gas.
- On September 1, 2004, a well-armed group of Chechen rebels stormed a school at Beslan in the North Caucasus. Armed with automatic weapons and explosives, they took more than 1,000 hostages. After a bloody stand-off, 334 hostages were killed.

Even the United States has not been immune to the danger of planned armed assaults. In August 2005, a Pakistani national was arrested in a terrorism investigation of a possible plot to attack the Israeli consulate, California National Guard facilities, and other targets in Southern California. In 2007, the FBI arrested six men from Cherry Hill, New Jersey, for planning an armed assault on Fort Dix.

Talking Points

- Armed terrorist assaults against populated areas such as the recent attacks in Mumbai are neither an unprecedented nor a remote threat. They offer critical lessons for the United States in preventing and responding to such attacks.
- The number of publicly known arrests related to organized terrorist attacks demonstrates that terrorist groups have not relinquished their essential goals of assault on the U.S.
- The best defense against organized armed assaults is to stop them before they occur by developing and maintaining effective counterterrorism, intelligence, and information-sharing programs.
- If attacks are successful, prior preparation is essential in dealing with the aftermath. This preparation must include an effective and integrated national homeland security system that brings together law enforcement, emergency responders, and federal assets.

Threat and Response

Armed assault is a category of threat that includes a range of weapons and tactics traditionally associated with terrorist activities, from car bombs to kidnapping, sabotage, and assassination, to weapons rarely employed in the United States such as surface-to-air man-portable missiles, rocket-propelled grenade (RPG) launchers, and suicide bombers.

Traditionally, bombs—particularly surface-delivered bombs—have been the weapon most often employed in terrorist attacks. Bombs can deliver significant destruction at modest cost, require little technical skill, can be assembled with commercially available materials, and leave a minimal operational signature that might compromise security and surprise. Indeed, numerous illicit Web sites include instructions on everything from assembling improvised explosives to large-truck bombs.[1]

The United States has been far from immune to the threat of bombing since long before 9/11. Bombs have long been a favored tactic for criminals and domestic terrorists. The Department of the Treasury recorded 2,757 bombing incidents in the U.S., resulting in over $50 million in damage, in 1996 alone.[2]

With each major bombing attempt, new security measures are adopted, making public infrastructure, high-profile objectives, and government facilities less accessible targets. Nonetheless, many assets remain vulnerable to terrorist strikes. Even as additional defensive measures are employed, rather than discarding a highly desirable and proven form of attack, enemies may adjust their courses of action by refining previously used tactics; seeking new creative means for delivering weapons, such as various forms of suicide attack (even hiding explosives internally in human bodies); attempting to generate explosions by sabotaging hazardous material; searching out critical weaknesses in security systems; or shifting to unprotected targets with high potential for economic disruption or psychological effect such as entertainment venues, cultural icons (museums, monuments, historic sites), office buildings, universities, or shopping malls.

One terrorist conspiracy attempted just such an innovation. In 2007, authorities arrested four men for plotting a significant explosion at John F. Kennedy airport in New York City by igniting the pipelines carrying jet fuel to the airport.

Terrorists might well seek alternative forms of attack to demonstrate their ability to strike America. Acts of sabotage, kidnapping, raids, and assassination may increase in frequency. They also might attempt to introduce weaponry not normally used in the United States, employing tactics and devices used frequently elsewhere including rocket-propelled grenades; shoulder-fired surface-to-air missiles; suicide bombers; small, ground-launched rockets; or improvised mortars fired by timers.

Again, some have already tried. In 2003, the U.S. government successfully intercepted an attempted arms sale of a shoulder-fired Igla SA-18 missile capable of downing commercial aircraft three miles in range and two miles in altitude.[3] The novelty of such attacks in the United States would probably deliver added psychological damage out of proportion to the physical destruction inflicted.

There are some legal and international restrictions that may make it harder to obtain certain weapons suitable for armed assault. In December 2000, 33 nations signed the Wassenaar Arrangement to stem the proliferation of man-portable air-defense systems.[4] Various statutes and federal and state regulations also affect the import of weapons and the sale of explosives.[5] But the opportunities to sidestep these barriers, particularly for obtaining small arms and limited amounts of explosives, are numerous. In addition, weapons and explosives can be fashioned from many common materials, and individual armed assaults are not beyond the ability of almost any terrorist group.

While the United States is highly vulnerable to individual attacks, staging an integrated campaign of frequent, major strikes faces serious obstacles. The more ambitious and well-organized a campaign is, the more difficult it will be to support. The more operational activities required to prepare and mount an operation, the more vulnerability there will be to sacrificing security and surprise. U.S. law enforcement has gained much experience addressing large-scale conspiracies from years of battling organized crime. Similar tactics can work in combating transnational terrorist conspiracies.[6]

Armed terrorist assaults might be useful in any number of scenarios. They could be part of an anti-access campaign, sabotaging key facilities in the United States to prevent the deployment of U.S. forces.[7] They might be used as a threat to deter or coerce the United States. Alerting authorities to potential attacks, however, could sacrifice the element of surprise and allow time for countermeasures to be taken. On the other hand, since it is relatively easy to create a credible armed assault threat, deception and hoaxes could be effective instruments for a cost-imposing strategy designed to force the United States to adopt excessive responses, such as expensive new security measures.

Armed assaults could also be an integral part of a protracted war strategy designed to weaken the country over time. For example, terrorist groups might launch a series of strikes, hoping for an aggressive response by law enforcement authorities that might be seen by the American population as threatening civil rights. This in turn could generate a backlash against the government and create social unrest.[8]

The challenge for any terrorist employing armed assaults in the United States is that the attacks are unlikely to prove decisive by themselves. Individual attacks are among the least likely ways to "bring America down." A protracted campaign, on the other hand, could represent a significant danger, particularly if it capitalizes on other serious economic or social problems. Transnational terrorist organizations are shifting away from calibrated, limited acts of terrorism, designed to shape public opinion or provoke a specific response from the targeted state, to the unconstrained use of violence intended to inflict maximum carnage and fundamentally change society. Attacks cease to be a psychological weapon to influence behavior and become a means to another end: physical destruction. A distinctive feature of these strikes is that their purpose is justified and articulated in extremist messianic, apocalyptic, or millenarian terms.

There is little question that this trend is real. By some counts, the number of groups claiming to base their actions on religious or ideological extremism grew from two in 1980 to 11 in 1992 to 26 in 1995. In 1995, worldwide, a religiously motivated group perpetrated every terrorist act resulting in eight or more fatalities. There was also a sharp increase in attacks, beginning in 1999. Destruction and casualties from attacks by non-state enemies, even before 9/11, had risen steadily.

By most measures, the lethality inflicted per attack has increased over the past decade.[9] According to the Human Security Project, the rate and number of transnational terrorist attacks, as well as the appeal of radical extremist agendas, have been declining in recent years, but the number of casualties per attack is on the rise.[10]

The trend toward higher levels of violence is most significant because the increasing lethality of terrorist strikes has been achieved not with weapons of mass destruction, but with the instruments of armed assault. For enemies looking for an easy way to inflict fear and casualties, armed assault is among the best options.

A revival of state-sponsored terrorism could provide new sources of sanctuary and support as well. One possibility is that a state may opt to conduct covert armed assaults against the American homeland in support of a regional competition with the United States.

Iran offers a case in point. Iran routinely employs terrorism as a means to advance its regional security interests and reaffirm its commitment to the founding principles of the Iranian revolution. Its support for terrorism has waxed and waned over the course of the past three decades. There is no evidence that the country has sponsored or is contemplating attacks on the U.S. homeland, but it still views terrorism as a legitimate weapon and has sponsored acts to advance its own interests at the risk of regional stability. If Iran perceived supporting attacks against the United States as being in its interest and calculated that it could avoid attribution or otherwise protect itself from U.S. retaliation, it might well represent a serious threat to the homeland.[11]

Preventing Battlefield America

The best way to deal with the threat of armed assaults on the United States is to prevent attacks from being planned in the first place. Since 9/11, effective counterterrorism, intelligence, and information-sharing operations have proven to be the best means to keep the nation safe from terrorist attacks of all kinds.[12]

Criticisms of post-9/11 efforts to protect the United States from attack range from claims that America is more vulnerable than ever to the contention that the transnational terrorist danger is vastly overhyped.[13] A review of publicly available information about at least 19 terrorist conspiracies thwarted by U.S. law enforcement suggests that the truth lies somewhere between these two arguments.[14]

The list of publicly known arrests of alleged terrorists demonstrates conclusively that the lack of another major terrorist attack is not a sign that organizations have relinquished their essential goals. A number of plots conducted by individuals have been prevented as a result of the increase in effective counterterrorism investigations by the United States in cooperation with friendly and allied governments. Continuing these operations, which include sound, effective, and lawful intelligence, surveillance, and investigations, is one of the best weapons in America's arsenal for the long war.

Clearly, some of the most controversial measures since 9/11 have proven to be the most effective. These measures have neither undermined the health of American civil society nor undermined constitutional liberties as many critics contended they would. In particular, Congress and the Administration should continue to:

- **Rely on the investigative authorities established in the USA Patriot Act.** In the wake of the terrorist attacks on Washington and New York on September 11, 2001, Congress passed the USA Patriot Act.[15] Among other things, the act provided additional authorities for the sharing of information between law enforcement and intelligence agencies and granted additional powers to fight terrorism, primarily law enforcement tools that had already been used to fight other serious crimes. Congress stipulated that these powers would expire unless reauthorized by law. In 2006, Congress extended the investigative authorities in the Patriot Act. These powers have been used to conduct counterterrorism investigations. Congress and the Administration should not change or undermine these authorities.
- **Exploit the authority to monitor terrorist** communications worldwide as provided under the FISA Amendments Act of 2008.[16] The capacity to monitor terrorist communications is essential for building an intelligence picture of the threat and focusing investigations.
- **Develop the Information Sharing Environment (ISE) under the office of the Director of National Intelligence.** Established by the Intelligence Reform and Terrorism Prevention Act of 2004, the ISE exists to create a "trusted partnership among all levels of government in the United States, the private sector, and our foreign partners, in order to detect, prevent, disrupt, preempt, and mitigate the effects of terrorism against the territory, people, and interests of the United States by the effective and efficient sharing of terrorism and homeland security information."[17] The ISE is essential in promoting effective integration and cooperation among federal, state, and local anti-terrorism efforts.

Fighting Back

It is unrealistic to believe that all homeland security measures will thwart every attack, every time. In particular, armed assaults and vehicle-borne explosive attacks are tactics that are within reach of any modestly funded and committed terrorist group. But if the U.S. government takes the offensive, it can take the initiative away from the terrorists, lessen their chances of success, and mitigate the damage they cause. Washington should therefore:

- **Retain an integrated approach to homeland security.** When an explosion happens, the government cannot delay its response until it knows whether it is a terrorist attack or an industrial accident. The nation needs to respond with alacrity, and that means taking an integrated "all-hazards" approach from the local level to the national level. Therefore, the Federal Emergency Management Agency (FEMA) must remain an integral part of the Department of Homeland Security (DHS). Removing FEMA from DHS would re-create gaps and vulnerabilities that were eliminated when the Homeland Security Act of 2002 created DHS.[18]

- **Stop wasting money.** The lion's share of financial and material support should be targeted toward state and local public-preparedness programs in those areas of the country that are at greatest risk—where terrorist attacks and catastrophic natural disasters are most likely to occur. Legislated mandatory distribution of resources based on fixed percentages to states and major urban areas must finally be eliminated. Congress should consider a forced federal funding model similar to the Base Realignment and Closure (BRAC) process where agencies work with an independent nonpartisan commission that develops a proposal. Congress and the President have the power only to accept or reject the whole proposal without amendment.

  States should take the lead in codifying the Targeted Capabilities List (TCL) established by DHS to identify the highest-priority needs for disaster response. They should require biennial risk and capabilities assessments to identify capability gaps and ensure that grant fund applications do not request any capability not listed in the TCL or exceed the capabilities that are deemed essential. Because every state or locality faces unique challenges, it is critical to develop a tier structure that helps states and localities to identify the appropriate level of security they need so that jurisdictions neither overinvest nor underinvest in capabilities.

  All communities must be assisted in developing a base level of preparedness. All communities face the threat of pandemic diseases and recurring natural disasters. The federal government should highlight best practices and develop and promote baseline community preparedness standards. A good example is the Council for Excellence in Government's "Readiness Quotient" index.[19]

- **Revise national disaster scenarios to include armed assaults.** The Department of Homeland Security uses 15 disaster planning scenarios that include both natural disasters and terrorist attacks to identify common capabilities needed by responders and to serve as a focus for planning and training exercises at the federal, state, and local levels. These scenarios should be revised to include armed assault responses.[20]

The Best Response

In the future, terrorists may use armed assaults or any number of other tactics to murder innocents and disrupt the peace and prosperity of America. The best response to these potential dangers is persistent vigilance through counterterrorism programs as well as continuing to build a national homeland security system that can deal equally well with both natural and manmade disasters.

Critical Thinking Questions

1. How prepared is the United States for the kind of attack that occurred in Mumbai in November 2008?
2. Consider a large city near you, or where you have lived previously. If you were an armed group intent on inflicting the kind of damage seen in Mumbai, what specific targets and tactics would you choose, and why?
3. What, if anything, could be done to improve our local, state, and federal agencies for this kind of terrorist attack?

Notes

1. See, for example, Gabriel Weimann, *Terror on the Internet: The New Arena, The New Challenges* (Washington, D.C.: U.S. Institute of Peace Press, 2006), p. 123.
2. U.S. Department of the Treasury, "1996 Selected Explosive Incidents,"1996, at *http://www.atf.treas.gov/pub/fire-explo_pub/eir/cover.htm* (December 3, 2008).
3. James Jay Carafano, Ph.D., and Jack Spencer, "Facts About the Shoulder-Fired Missile Threat," Heritage Foundation *WebMemo* No.328, August 14, 2003, at *http://www.heritage.org/Research/BallisticMissileDefense/wm328.cfm.*
4. U.S. Department of State, Statement by Richard Boucher, Spokesman, "Wassenaar Arrangement Agreement: Man-Portable Air Defense Systems Export Controls Man-Portable Air Defense Systems Export Controls," December 5, 2000, at *http://secretary.state.gov/www/briefings/statements/2000/ps001205b.html* (December 4, 2008).
5. For a summary of regulations, see U.S. Department of the Treasury, Bureau of Alcohol, Tobacco, and Firearms, Web site, at *http://www.atf.treas.gov/regulations/index.htm* (December 4, 2008).
6. See Michael A. Sheehan, *Crush the Cell: How to Defeat Terrorism Without Terrorizing Ourselves* (New York: Crown, 2008).
7. This scenario was tested in a simulation conducted at the U.S. Army War College. See Richard Brennan, *Protecting the Homeland: Insights from Army Wargames* (Santa Monica, Cal.: RAND, 2002).
8. For an example of the discussion of these issues, see transcript, "Fighting Terrorism, Preserving Civil Liberties," Cato Institute Policy Forum, October 2, 2001, at *http://www.cato.org/events/transcripts/011002et.pdf* (December 4, 2008).
9. For the supporting statistical analysis, see Bruce Hoffman, "Terrorism Trends and Prospects," in *Countering the New Terrorism,* ed. Ian O. Lesser, Bruce Hoffman, John Arquilla, David Ronfeldt, and Michael Zanini (Santa Monica, Cal.: RAND, 1999), at *http://www.rand.org/publications/MR/MR989/MR989.chap2.pdf* (December 4, 2008). There is some debate about the reasons for the statistical trends of the past two decades. Worldwide, the number of terrorist incidents overall declined during the 1990s, but this may not indicate a long-term trend. Some analysts argue that increases in terrorist incidents strongly correlate with periods of war, major regional crises, and divisive international events. There are so many variables, they contend, that identifying long-term trends is virtually impossible. See Rex A. Hudson, *The Sociology and Psychology*

of Terrorism: Who Becomes a Terrorist and Why? A Report Prepared by the Federal Research Division, Library of Congress, September 1999, at *http://www.loc.gov/rr/frd/pdf-files/Soc_Psych_of_Terrorism.pdf* (December 4, 2008); Bruce Hoffman, "Old Madness, New Methods: Revival of Religious Terrorism Begs for Broader U.S. Policy," *RAND Review,* Winter 1998–99, pp. 14–15; David Tucker, "Combating International Terrorism," in *The Terrorism Threat and U.S. Government Response: Operational and Organizational Factors,*ed. James M. Smith and William C. Thomas (Colorado: U.S. Air Force Academy, USAF Institute for National Security Studies, March 2001), pp. 130–139; Richard A. Falkenrath, Robert D. Newman, and Bradley A. Thayer, *America's Achilles' Heel: Nuclear, Biological, and Chemical Terrorism and Covert Attack* (Cambridge, Mass.: MIT Press, 1998), pp. 179–202.

10. Human Security Report Project, "Human Security Brief 2007," May 21, 2008, at *http://www.humansecuritybrief.info* (December 4, 2008).
11. Ely Karmon, "Counterterrorism Policy: Why Tehran Starts and Stops Terrorism," *The Middle East Quarterly,* Vol. V, No. 4 (December 1998), at *http://www.meforum.org/meq/dec98/elyk.shtml* (December 4, 2008). Karmon argues that only a confrontational approach will deter Iranian terrorist activity. For a different analysis of Iranian decision-making and the prospects for the future, see Daniel L. Byman *et al., Iran's Security Policy in the Post-Revolutionary Era* (Santa Monica: RAND, 2001), pp. 99–104.
12. James Jay Carafano, Ph.D., "Securing the Homefront," *The Journal of International Security Affairs,* No. 12 (Spring 2007), at *http://www.securityaffairs.org/issues/2007/12/carafano.php*. (December 4, 2008).
13. For analysis contending that the United States remains vulnerable, see Clark Kent Ervin, *Open Target: Where America Is Vulnerable to Attack* (New York: Palgrave Macmillan, 2006). For a study claiming that the transnational threat is far less severe than is commonly assumed, see John Mueller, "Is There Still a Terrorist Threat? The Myth of the Omnipresent Enemy," *Foreign Affairs,* Vol. 85, No. 5 (September/October 2006), at *http://www.foreignaffairs.org/20060901facomment85501/john-mueller/is-there-still-a-terrorist-threat.html* (December 4, 2008).
14. James Jay Carafano, Ph.D., "U.S. Thwarts 19 Terrorist Attacks Against America Since 9/11," Heritage Foundation *Backgrounder* No. 2085, November 13, 2007, at *http://www.heritage.org/Research/HomelandDefense/bg2085.cfm#_ftn1.*
15. See Paul Rosenzweig, Alane Kochems, and James Jay Carafano, Ph.D., "The Patriot Act Reader," Heritage Foundation *Special Report* No. 01,September 13, 2004, at *http://www.heritage.org/research/homelandsecurity/The-Patriot-Act-Reader.cfm.*
16. For the importance of this authority, see General Michael Hayden, Principal Deputy Director of National Intelligence, address to the National Press Club, January 23, 2006.
17. Office of the Director of National Intelligence, "Information Sharing Environment Implementation Plan," November 2006, at *http://www.ise.gov/docs/reports/ise-impplan-200611.pdf* (December 4, 2008).
18. Jena Baker McNeill, "Removing FEMA from DHS Would Be a Terrible Mistake," Heritage Foundation *WebMemo* No. 2071, September 22, 2008, at *http://www.heritage.org/Research/HomelandSecurity/wm2071.cfm.*

19. David Heyman and James Jay Carafano, Ph.D., "Homeland Security 3.0: Building a National Enterprise to Keep America Safe, Free, and Prosperous," Heritage Foundation *Special Report* No. 23, September 18, 2008, pp. 7–8, at *http://www.heritage.org/Research/HomelandDefense/sr23.cfm.*
20. Homeland Security Council, "Planning Scenarios: Executive Summaries," July 2004, at *http://www.scd.state.hi.us/grant_docs/National_Planning_Scenarios_ExecSummaries_ver2.pdf* (December 4, 2008).

Preventing Lone Wolf Terrorism

Some CT Approaches Addressed

Edwin Bakker and Beatrice de Graaf[1]

Abstract

After a brief discussion of the epistemological and phenomenological difficulties associated with the concept of lone wolf terrorism, a number of possible counter-terrorist approaches are discussed. Lone operator terrorist acts should be considered 'black swan' occurrences that are almost impossible to categorize or systematize, let alone forecast. Thus, not the profile of the perpetrator, but the modus operandi offer clues for a better response to this particular threat. Furthermore, almost all lone operators do display a degree of commitment to, and identification with, extremist movements—providing leads for preventing new rounds of radicalization within this potential group of sympathizers or followers. With the apparent increase of Islamist lone wolf terrorism and fears for right-wing extremists wanting to follow the example of the Norwegian mass murderer A.B. Breivik, new questions need to be posed, addressing the role of virtual communities with which lone operators identify themselves.

Introduction

After the cold-blooded murder of 77 people in Oslo and Utoya (Norway) on 22 July 2011, the threat of lone wolf terrorism has quickly moved (further) up on the agenda of counter terrorism officials. Two questions were raised in the aftermath of the horrible killings by Anders Breivik: (i) could it have been prevented? and (ii) how to discover new plots, possibly by individuals who want to answer Breivik's explicit call to follow his example? Both questions are difficult to answer. The Norwegian authorities are investigating the first question, which has already resulted in the arrest of the owner of an online trading business who is suspected of supplying chemicals to the Norwegian killer. Finding satisfactory answers to the second question—is it possible to discover and prevent future cases—is even more difficult. 'Probably not' is perhaps the most frank and honest answer, but an unacceptable one at that. In this article, we address seven possible counter-terrorist approaches to the threat posed by lone wolf terrorism with an eye on reducing chances of deadly attacks like the one experienced in Norway. First, however, we have to define lone wolf terrorism.

Defining the Concept

The term 'lone wolf' was popularized in the late 1990s by white supremacists Tom Metzger and Alex Curtis as part of an encouragement to fellow racists to act alone for tactical security reasons when committing violent crimes.[2] Other terms that have been used to describe similar or comparable forms of political violence include 'leaderless resistance,'[3] 'individual terrorism'[4] and 'freelance terrorism.'[5] In this article the definition proposed by Burton and Stewart in a STRATFOR essay functions as the point of departure. They define a lone wolf as "a person who acts on his or her own without orders from—or even connections to—an organization."[6] They stress the difference with sleeper cells, arguing that sleepers are operatives who infiltrate the targeted society or organization and then remain dormant until a group or organization orders them to take action. In contrast, "A lone wolf is a stand alone operative who by his very nature is embedded in the targeted society and is capable of self-activation at any time."[7] However, by stressing the absence of connections with a broader network or organization, Burton and Stewart neglect the ideological connections individuals might have with other networks or organizations, either through personal contacts or inspirational content on the Internet.

We focus our attention in this article on the operational aspect of lone wolf terrorism. Even though some lone wolves have been linked to larger (underground) networks, such as Baruch Goldstein (who has been linked to Kach) and Timothy McVeigh (who has been linked to several right wing-groups), they decided, planned and performed their act on their own, rather than as having followed instructions from some hierarchical command structure.[8] In our view, a definition of lone wolf terrorism has to be extended to include individuals that are inspired by a certain group but who are not under the orders of any other person, group or network. They might be members of a network, but this network is not a hierarchical organization in the classical sense of the word.[9]

No Single Profile

Infamous examples in the United States, Israel and Europe include Baruch Goldstein, an American-born Israeli citizen who was responsible for the death of 29 Muslims praying in the Cave of the Patriarchs in Hebron; the Austrian Franz Fuchs who used letter bombs to kill four persons and injure 15 more; U.S. army major Nidal Malik Hassan who is accused of a mass shooting at Fort Hood where 13 people died and 30 others were wounded, and the American mathematician Theodore Kaczynski, also known as the 'Unabomber,' who engaged in a mail bombing spree that killed three persons and wounded 23 others. In addition, there have been several assassinations of political leaders committed by lone wolves. Think of Yigal Amir, the assassin of Prime Minister of Israel Yitzhak Rabin, or Volkert van der Graaf who killed the Dutch politician Pim Fortuijn.

These individuals and their violent acts exemplify the variations in targeting and modus operandi within lone wolf terrorism, as well as the variety of political and ideological backgrounds of the perpetrators. Anarchist revolutionaries, religious zealots, environmental and animal rights extremists, white supremacists and jihadists all have engaged in lone wolf attacks. When it comes to religious backgrounds we also see a variety of motivations. Among those who claim or justify their acts in the name of a religion are individuals of all faiths. Muslim lone wolves like Nidal Malik Hassan and Abdulhakim Mujahid Muhammad who opened fire on a U.S. military recruiting office, as well as *anti-Semitic/Christian-identity adherents like Buford Furrow who* attacked a Jewish Community Center *and Eric Rudolph, also known as* the Olympic Park Bomber, who killed two people and injured at least 150 others. Lone wolf terrorism also includes *radical Roman Catholics like James Kopp and radical Protestants like Scott Roeder* who both killed a physician who performed abortions.

Obviously, there is no single profile for a lone wolf. Nonetheless, it is possible to distinguish between different categories of lone wolf terrorists based on their ideological or religious background. In addition to this distinction, there are a few common characteristics shared by many lone wolves. One of the problems for both counterterrorism practitioners and academics is the relatively low number of terrorists who act their own without orders from—or even connections to—an organization. According to a study by COT/TTSRL, a total number of 72 lone wolf terrorist incidents accounted for only 1.28 percent of the total number of terrorist incidents in the U.S., Germany, France, Spain, Italy, Canada and Australia.[10] This statistical *quantité négligable* turns these incidents into the typical 'black swan' occurrences that are almost impossible to categorize or systematize, let alone preview.[11] However, the number of incidents linked to lone operator terrorists seems to be on the rise.

Encouraging Lone Wolf Terrorism

The increase in lone wolf terrorism in the United States in the last three decades can partly be explained by the adoption and dissemination of the lone wolf tactic by and amongst right wing extremists.[12] For example, in the late 1990s the white supremacists Tom Metzger and Alex Curtis explicitly encouraged fellow extremists to act alone when committing violent crimes. A few years earlier, white supremacist Louis Beam, a former Ku Klux Klan and Aryan Nations member, popularized the strategy of *leaderless resistance.*[13] He envisaged a scenario where 'all individuals and groups operate independently of each other, and never report to a central headquarters or single leader for direction or instruction.[14] Also, in Islamist circles the idea of support for small-scale, loosely organized terrorist attacks can hardly be called new. In 2003, an article was published on the extremist Internet forum *Sada al Jihad* (Echoes of Jihad), in which Osama bin Laden sympathizers were encouraged to take action without waiting for instructions.[15] In 2004, Abu Musab al-Suri (or: Mustafa Setmarian Nasar), a dual citizenship Spanish-Syrian who had been in the inner circle around Bin Laden but fell out with him after 9/11 due to differences on strategic issues, published a "Call for Worldwide Islamic Resistance," on the Internet. In this sixteen hundred pages manuscript, al-Suri proposes a next stage of jihad, characterized by terrorism created by individuals or small autonomous groups, which he also labelled "leaderless resistance." These individuals will wear down the enemy and prepare the ground for the far more ambitious aim of waging war on "open fronts"—an outright struggle for territory.[16] In 2006, Al Qaeda leader Abu Jihad al-Masri followed suit with a call to arms, entitled "How to fight alone" circulated widely in jihadist networks.

The 1,518 page-long manifesto of Anders Breivik can also be regarded as a guide into the workings of lone operator terrorism. In one part of his manifesto, Breivik explains how to publish documents on the Internet and how to use social media for recruiting purposes. Moreover, he shows the tricks he himself used to circumvent European custom agents and describes in detail how he manufactured the explosives he used to blow up the government building in Oslo. Breivik also points at the possibilities of the use of unconventional weapons, such as Radiological Dispersal Devices, or so-called dirty bombs.

The Challenge of Fighting Lone Wolf Terrorism

Attacks by lone operator terrorists provide the most puzzling and unpredictable form of terrorism. Lone wolf terrorists are a nightmare for the counterterrorism organizations, police and intelligence communities as they are extremely difficult to stop.

First of all, lone wolves are solitary actors, whose intentions are hard to discern since they usually avoid contact with others. This makes identifying, monitoring, and arresting a lone wolf extremely difficult. Compared to (conventional forms of) group terrorism or network-sponsored terrorists, lone operators have a critical advantage in avoiding identification and detection before and after their attacks since most of them do not communicate their plans with other people. When militants operate in a cell consisting of more than one person, chances increase substantially that law enforcement authorities will be able to foil a terrorist plot. Breivik was well aware of this. He even warns other potential terrorists they will increase their chance of being apprehended by 100% for every other person they involve in their plans: "Don't trust anyone unless you absolutely need to (which should never be the case). Do absolutely everything by yourself," he writes in his manifesto.[17]

Second, even if lone wolves like Breivik make references to existing political or ideological discourses, they remain very hard to pinpoint as political terrorists/activists. This pose some problems to CT practitioners since insights into the disenfranchised, alienated or frustrated movement behind individual terrorists often provides clues as to their modus operandi, target preferences or outreach and/or propaganda activities. Lone wolfs, by definition, are idiosyncratic. They display a variety of backgrounds with a wide spectrum of ideologies and motivations: from Islamists to right wing extremists, and from confused suicidal psychopaths to dedicated and mentally healthy persons. This vast array of expressions and visions, ranging from ideological ramblings on the Internet and hate mail to fully-fledged acts of terrorism, hardly gives away anything in the sense of patterns or recurring methods behind lone wolf's attacks.

Third, it is particularly difficult to differentiate between those lone operator extremists who intend to commit attacks and those who simply express radical beliefs or issue hollow threats (hoaxes). In Western countries in general and in the United States in particular, the freedom of speech is a fundamental freedom which limits possibilities to investigate radical scenes unless they are violent. While most terrorists are radical but not all radicals are terrorists, it is extremely difficult to single out lone wolves who will carry out an actual attack before they strike, even with the help of the most sophisticated technical intelligence gathering tools.

Fourth, lone wolves inspire copycat behavior and become role models for other alienated youngsters; they often invite bandwagon attacks. Kazcynski's manifesto still circulates on the Internet, as do Bouyeri's letters. And it is likely that we will see the same of Breivik's 'European Declaration of Independence' ten to twenty years from now. In addition to this, certain tactics—shooting sprees, bomb letters, arson attacks or anthrax letters—also have a tendency to continue over a long period of time—although not necessarily by the same perpetrator.

Finally, although lone operator terrorists have the disadvantage of lacking the means, skills, and 'professional' support of terrorist groups or networks, their attacks nonetheless have proven to be very lethal—Anders Breivik and Timothy McVeigh are cases in point.

Possible CT Responses

How to deal with the threat of lone wolf terrorism and the challenge of identifying, targeting, and arresting persons who act entirely on their own? The question has not yet been sufficiently answered and poses the problem of how to reconcile fundamental principles of open societies with guaranteeing security to citizens. One thing, however, is clear: the challenge is enormous, especially when confronted with a person like Anders Breivik who used years to meticulously prepare his horrible attacks—the Oslo bombing (8 killed) and the Utoya massacre (69 killed).

Nonetheless, the above described commonalities and challenges provide some clues as to where to start with CT responses.

First of all, according to Alex Shone of the Henry Jackson society, a British-based think-tank, the key factor of the UK's CT response concerning locating lone wolf attacks is in knowing not *who* will carry out an attack (almost an impossibility) but rather in knowing *how* such attacks are formulated. In his essay, Shone stresses the need to learn about the radicalization processes of lone wolves. He shows that insight into these processes open up possible avenues for effective CT measures to prevent or counter the threat of lone wolf terrorism.[18]

Knowing how lone operator attacks are formulated requires a far more sensitive detection system at the tactical, sharp-end of operations than most CT organizations currently use. According to Shone, CT services need to be far more attuned to those signals, as minimal as they might be, that any individual with a terrorist intent will inevitably give off in preparing his attack. This requires not only effective data capture and exploitation enabled by efficient overall information management, but also fused intelligence products. This requires intelligence analysts and collectors to work in far closer union.[19]

Secondly, given the 'commonality' shared by many lone wolves that there is a degree of commitment to, and identification with, extremist movements and that their radicalization process does not take place in a vacuum, it is important to both investigate and cooperate with afflicted communities. And given the general agreement that an effective counter radicalization strategy depends on effective community engagement, it is essential to promote passive and active aversion towards the terrorist seed in these communities with the help of influential community members.

In the third place, even a seemingly spontaneous combustion of violence is often triggered by some catalyst event. It could be rewarding to study and compare the nature of potential triggers or catalyst events in the radicalization processes of lone wolves. Are they located within the private domain or are they provided by outside political developments? Or are triggers even mastered by 'entrepreneurs of violence' who use them to call upon their anonymous followers to become active?

In the fourth place, exactly because lone wolves—although operating alone—draw inspiration from other extremists or ideologues, disseminating counter narratives ought to be an important element of an effective CT strategy. A crucial ingredient of counter narratives is the de-legitimisation of perpetrators and their acts and the falsification of their ideologies.

In the fifth place, although lone wolves are not part of hierarchical organisations, they do formulate their acts in a certain context. Awareness programs for parents, schools, universities are worth considering—obviously without launching large-scale public campaigns that only serve to create a moral panic.

A sixth clue as to where to start with CT responses also involves communication processes. On the one hand, communicating the potential threat of lone wolves to relevant target audiences is very important. At the same it is important to refrain from handing them the public theatre they strive for. Handling lone wolves without giving them any positive public status should be one core principle. Of course, much depends on the channels used by the perpetrator. In the days of Kaczynski, one could, at least for a while, successfully prevent the publishing of his manifesto. Today, the Breivik case in Norway has shown that a lone wolf can send an email to possible supporters and post his video and the 1,500 pages of his manifesto on the Internet in the last remaining hour before he detonates the explosives and heads for his destination to engage in mass murder.

Lastly, perhaps the most concrete clue concerning lone wolf operators and their tactics is their modus operandi. In recent cases of shooting sprees (including high school shootings and mall shootings) all perpetrators were male and all had a license to possess (semi-automatic) firearms. This specific group of people who are allowed to keep firearms—of which the overwhelming majority are law-abiding citizens who use their weapon for hunting or sport shooting—needs special scrutiny. The same holds for the procedures for applying for a weapon permit and membership of a shooting club.

Final Remarks

As stated above, the challenge to prevent lone wolf terrorism is enormous and any CT response can only partly reduce this particular threat or limit its impact. As with other forms of terrorism, it is not possible to reach 100% security against this threat. Obviously, there is still a long way to go in preventing lone wolf terrorism. Potential answers on the 'how?' question regarding the modus operandi of lone wolf terrorists and their radicalization processes are still preliminary, needing further investigation. And with the apparent increase of Islamist lone wolf terrorism and fears for right-wing extremists wanting to follow the example of Breivik, new questions need to be posed, for instance about the role of the Internet or the possible impact of attacks on minority groups in society. The fact that there are—fortunately—few cases we can learn from does not make the task to know more about the '*how*' of lone wolf terrorism any easier. Therefore, sharing experiences, data and ideas regarding this particular terrorist threat between practitioners, policy makers and researchers is essential to be able to develop at least some viable responses to lone wolf terrorism.

Critical Thinking Questions

1. Is the term "lone wolf" misleading? Why or why not?
2. How important is the Internet to the future of "lone wolf" terrorism?
3. What policies or strategies should be implemented to mitigate or diminish the threat of this kind of terrorism?

Notes

1. This article is based on a ICCT article on lone wolf terrorism by the same authors; it is available at www.icct.nl. *With profound thanks to Liesbeth van der Heide for her research assistance.* http://www.icct.nl

2. *COT/TTSRL, Lone-Wolf Terrorism, Transnational Terrorism Security and the Rule of Law, July 2007. Cf: http://www.transnationalterrorism.eu/tekst/publications/Lone-Wolf%20Terrorism.pdf*, p. 13.
3. Jeffrey Kaplan. 'Leaderless Resistance', *Terrorism and Political Violence,* vol. 9 (1997), no. 3, pp. 80–95.
4. Ze'ev Iviansky. 'Individual Terror: Concept and Typology', *Journal of Contemporary History,* vol. 12, no. 1 (January 1977), p. 45.
5. H. W. Kushner. *Encyclopedia of Terrorism,* Thousand Oaks: Sage 2003, pp. 144–145; C. Hewitt. *Understanding Terrorism in America. From the Klan to al Qaeda,* London and New York: Routledge 2003, p. 79.
6. Scott *Stewart and Fred Burton, 'The Lone Wolf Disconnect', 30 January 2008, Stratfor, Cf:* http://www.stratfor.com/weekly/lone_wolf_disconnect.
7. Ibid.
8. L. van der Heide. 'Individual Terrorism: Indicators of Lone Operators', 30 August 2011, http://igitur-archive.library.uu.nl/student-theses/2011-0902-02354/MA%20Thesis%20Liesbeth%20van%20der%20Heide.pdf p.24.
9. Marc Sageman, *Understanding Terror Networks,* Philadelphia: University of Pennsylvania Press, 2004.
10. COT/TTSRL, 2007, op. cit., pp. 16–17.
11. N. N. Taleb. *Fooled by Randomness: The Hidden Role of Chance in Life and in the Markets.* New York: Random House, 2005.
12. Mark S. Hamm, *In Bad Company. America's Terrorist Underground,* Northeastern University Press, 2002.
13. Louis Beam. 'Leaderless Resistance', *The Seditionist,* Issue 12, 1992, cf: http://www.louisbeam.com/leaderless.htm.
14. COT/TTSRL, 2007, op. cit. p. 13.
15. Integrated Threat Assessment Center (Canada), "Lone-Wolf Attacks: A Developing Islamist Extremist Strategy?", 29 June 2007, cf: *http://www.nefafoundation.org/miscellaneous/FeaturedDocs/ITAC_lonewolves_062007.pdf*, p. 4.
16. Lawrence Wright, 'The Master Plan', in: *The New Yorker,* 11 September 2006, cf: *http://www.newyorker.com/archive/2006/09/11/060911fa_fact3?printable=true#ixzz1f7mqzvZe*; cf. 'Major Al Qaeda Leader Arrested in Pakistan', on *Foxnews,* 2 May 2006.
17. Andrew Berwick, *2083—A European Declaration of Independence,* London, 2011, p. 844.
18. Alex Shone, 'Countering lone wolf terrorism: sustaining the CONTEST vision', *Henry Jackson Society,* 17th May 2010, Cf. *http://www.henryjacksonsociety.org/stories.asp?id=1582.*
19. Ibid.

Section 1.3

Specific Areas of Vulnerability

Flight of Fancy? Air Passenger Security Since 9/11

K. Jack Riley[1]

The phrase "touch my junk" became part of the lexicon of air passenger security in late 2010 thanks to the controversial decision by the U.S. Transportation Security Administration (TSA) to increase the physical scrutiny of air travelers. John Tyner, attempting to fly from San Diego, uttered the now-famous words when he refused to walk through a whole body image (WBI) scanner and subsequently also refused to submit to a full-body frisk. The latter would have involved a TSA agent touching his "junk," or genitals.

That national attention focused on the anatomy of a private citizen is one small indication of how distracted the country has become in its efforts to ensure air passenger security. The focus of these efforts should be on what works best and at least cost, but the traveling public remains doubtful that the focus has been put in the proper place. Although many travelers do not object to the use of WBI scans and frisks, many others do, grumbling about airport security issues in lines, lounges, and planes around the world.

TSA has moved toward this kind of screening in reaction to the December 2009 attempted bombing of an airplane over Detroit by Umar Farouk Abdulmutallab, the so-called "Christmas bomber," who had concealed explosive material in his underwear. The intent of TSA is to make WBI and frisks the primary methods by which all passengers are screened.[2] Those selected for a WBI scan who are unwilling or unable to complete it will have a TSA agent touching private parts of the body as part of intensified pat-downs.

The objections to the WBI scanning are varied.[3] The machines do not detect explosives but use x-rays or millimeter waves to generate an image of a person's body. Denser objects—such as metal, multiple folds of clothing, medical devices, or diapers—show up as darker areas (called anomalies) on the image. There is debate as to whether the machines, had they been in use, would have detected the explosive material that Abdulmutallab had concealed.[4] Health concerns have also been raised about these backscatter machines, which generate their images from x-rays.[5] Some travelers object to the slow speed of the WBI scans, which are demonstrably slower than earlier screening methods. Other objections include the fact that travelers with external medical devices (including wheelchairs) or certain medical conditions (including a need for portable oxygen or an inability to stand without a cane or similar implement) are ineligible for such scans and instead must be patted down.[6] At many airports, WBI machines are configured in a way that creates personal insecurity: Travelers standing in the WBI cannot watch their personal goods go through the scanning machines, creating a risk of theft as goods exit the machines.[7]

Further objections arise from the fact that the "anomalies" detected are frequently false alarms that must be resolved with a pat-down.[8] Finally, many people object, usually on Fourth Amendment (unreasonable search and seizure) or privacy grounds, to the fact that the WBI scans generate detailed images of the traveler's body that are viewed—and perhaps stored—by government employees.[9] TSA has begun testing software modifications that use cartoon body images while still showing anomalies. While these methods address some privacy concerns, they do not alleviate the Fourth Amendment, health, effectiveness, speed, personal insecurity, or false-alarm concerns.

In addition to the growing discontent with this new form of security, there are looming financial constraints. Passenger security is one of the most visible and expensive components of the overall transportation security system. Given the costs associated with the new screening methods—an estimated $1.2 billion per year in capital, equipment, and operating costs by 2014[10]—it is worthwhile to ask three questions: How has passenger security performed since 9/11? What opportunities and innovations have been missed or not pursued? What steps should the United States be considering?

Air Travel Is Safe and Secure

In the ten years since 9/11, about 6 billion enplanements (instances of passengers boarding a commercial plane) have occurred in the United States, and perhaps an additional 14 billion have occurred worldwide. Among those 20 billion passengers, according to the Aviation Safety Network, 7,019 died in aviation accidents between 2001 and 2009.[11] In addition, roughly 200 more have died on airplanes or at airports as a result of terrorism since 9/11.[12] Terrorists have succeeded in bringing down planes since 9/11, but they have been incapable of extending the damage by hijacking a plane and using it against a supplemental target. And since 9/11, no passengers have died in terrorist acts from enplanements originating in the United States. In short, despite the tragedy and loss of life on 9/11, air transportation is overwhelmingly a secure means of transportation, especially in the United States.

At least three factors contribute substantially to the improved security since 9/11.[13] First, and perhaps most importantly, passengers know now that they must be vigilant. The attacks of 9/11 were a wake-up call for a traveling public previously unaccustomed to suicide attacks. The lessons of 9/11 were learned within minutes of the first attack, as evidenced by the fact that the passengers and crew on Flight 93 realized that the attackers were on a suicide mission and fought to regain control of the plane.[14] Since then, passengers and crew have helped disrupt a number of additional incidents, including the attempted attacks by Richard Reid (the "shoe bomber") in 2001 and by Abdulmutallab.

Second, airlines have reinforced cockpit doors in a way that strictly limits access to the cockpit. Most crews have also modified their procedures to ensure that there is a barrier between the cockpit door and the passengers when the cockpit door needs to be opened. These steps mean that it is much more difficult, if not impossible, to commandeer an airplane and to conduct an attack similar to those of 9/11.

Third, changes to the visa approval process represent a relatively unheralded but important contribution to air transportation security. All 19 of the terrorists involved in the 9/11 attacks were in the United States on legitimate visas. Hence, the visa process was one target of policy reforms.[15] Currently, residents of 36 countries can travel to the United States without obtaining a visa, but those traveling from other nations, such as Pakistan, Saudi Arabia, and Yemen, must obtain one.[16] Obtaining a visa involves providing extensive documentation (of the individual and, in some cases, family members, business associates, and the sponsor) that is investigated using homeland security, intelligence, and law enforcement databases and resources. Applicants also undergo an in-person consular interview. Overall, the number of nonimmigrant visas granted to residents of such countries fell sharply after 9/11 and, with some exceptions, has remained well below the number recorded in 2001.[17] In addition, the number of visa denials because of suspected links to terrorism increased from 47 (none of which were overturned as a result of subsequent evaluation) in 2002 to 683 (387 of which were overturned after additional investigation, leaving 296) in 2010. Thus, there has been a greater than sixfold increase in visa denials because of suspected links to terrorism.

Granted, the dramatic increase in visa denials entails costs beyond the visa process itself. By making it harder to come to the United States, we in America deter not only terrorists but also a large number of legitimate travelers—foreign tourists, foreign students, and qualified foreign workers—whose presence provides great benefits to our economy and the vibrancy of our culture. This opportunity cost needs to be accounted for when considering the security value of visa changes.

In the meantime, the three improvements cited above should help keep future aviation security incidents from being as catastrophic as the 9/11 attacks. In fact, future incidents are more likely to be on the scale of aviation *safety* incidents rather than *security* incidents. Thus, even if future attacks are successful, they need not lead to the loss of confidence in the air travel system that the American public experienced on 9/11.

Despite the improvements made to air transportation security involving passengers, cockpits, and visas, the vast majority of U.S. transportation security money is spent at the airport to prevent passengers from bringing potentially dangerous goods on board. Although there are many prohibited items, including firearms and knives exceeding a certain length, the primary concern is with explosives. TSA annually spends about $5 billion on a workforce numbering an estimated 60,000. These screeners man the walk-through metal detectors, operate the baggage x-ray systems, search for liquids that exceed the established thresholds, man the WBI devices, conduct pat-downs, implement behavioral profiling, and conduct other screening functions. One reason for the workforce and expenses being so large is the fact that the screening functions are imposed virtually uniformly on every traveler entering an airport in the United States.

Missed Opportunities

The high level of scrutiny to which U.S. airline passengers are subjected is a curious departure from the levels implemented in other areas of transportation and border security that use more risk-based approaches, such as the highly selective screening of shipping containers and the limited placement of federal air marshals aboard U.S. commercial flights. Until recently, though, the starkest contrast of all to the treatment of U.S. airline passengers was the treatment of U.S. commercial cargo on those *same flights* boarded by the passengers. It was not until August 2010 that all of the commercial cargo loaded onto domestic passenger planes was scanned or searched. Shipments on cargo jets from international destinations are not all currently screened, although the date for implementing the plan for screening them has been moved up from 2013 to 2011.

Another departure from the "inspect everyone and everything" approach involves TSA's own workforce at the airports. TSA employees are not screened when they enter the secure area of an airport throughout the course of the day, because they are trusted employees who have had a background check. They are thought to be at particularly low risk for coercion or conversion to radicalism. At many airports, certain other employees also have all-access badges that allow them to bypass security.

Thus, what is considered the "sterile area" of the airport is in fact not sterile. Substantial volumes of people (and, until recently, cargo) have made it into the sterile area without inspection. There have been no terrorist incidents associated with these leakages, however, suggesting that the *cargo* and *employee* risks have been appropriately managed for years (even before full cargo screening began) and begging the question of what kinds of risk management improvements might be available for *passengers.*

There are two main opportunities for improving the risk management system for passengers. First, flights originating in the United States are at much lower risk of being attacked by terrorists than are flights originating overseas. Second, enough is known about many passengers—their occupations, the security clearances they hold, their traveling profiles—to trust them to a greater degree than the current system does.

There is very little reason to be concerned about suicide bombers being present on flights *originating in the United States.* The security improvements noted above—passenger vigilance, cockpit security, and visa screening—go a long way toward preventing radical jihadists from entering the country or, having entered, from being able to commandeer a plane to conduct a spectacular attack. Moreover, the radical threat resident in and willing to conduct a suicide attack on the United States is extremely small.

Thus, the first opportunity for improving passenger risk management would be to differentiate between the domestic and international enplanements. One way to do this is to subject travelers who wish to come to the United States to a higher level of scrutiny than those already in the United States. This could be accomplished by maintaining current levels of inspection of travelers coming to the country and reducing the use of advanced equipment and intrusive methods inside the United States, where the threat is lower. Such a step would yield big savings in equipment and personnel by reducing the number of machines and agents required at U.S. airports. It would also reduce the deadweight losses that domestic travelers incur from arriving at airports early, waiting in lines, and undergoing intensive scrutiny.

The second opportunity, specifically for domestic enplanements (at least initially), would be to develop a trusted traveler program. The current security regime applies the same procedures to all 700 million passengers who board planes each year in the United States.[18] That we have not developed a reasonable way to reduce that inspection workload is perhaps the biggest missed opportunity of the past decade.

A trusted traveler program could be configured in a variety of ways. Recent conversations with airline industry executives suggest that a very small fraction of fliers account for a very large proportion of trips. In all likelihood, then, a trusted traveler program could be relatively small (with 5 million enrollees or less) and could still provide significant benefits. No program will be bulletproof, but such a program does not need to be given the extremely low odds of encountering a suicide terrorist on a flight originating in the United States. A trusted traveler program could initially be organized around these characteristics or combinations of characteristics:

- *Possession of a security clearance issued by a U.S. government agency.* Security clearances are issued after a comprehensive background investigation that includes an examination of foreign ties. These clearances are also far more stringent than the criminal background checks conducted on TSA agents. Individuals with security clearances are extremely unlikely to be involved in terrorist activities. The *Washington Post* reported in 2010 that more than 850,000 people held Top Secret clearances, which require an investigation covering the preceding ten years that includes contact with employers, co-workers, and others; involves investigation of education, employment, and personal and civic affiliations; and includes agency checks of spouses and significant others.[19] Several additional million individuals hold Secret clearances that involve a similar level of investigation. The cost of these clearances has already been incurred, so the marginal cost of starting a trusted traveler program with this group would be low.

- *A profile that involves frequent travel.* An individual traveling 100,000 miles per year is, conservatively, spending 200 hours on airplanes a year. That is 10 percent of a standard 2,000-hour work year, suggesting that such travelers can be trusted with the basic screening that was in place prior to the deployment of WBI machines and pat-downs. Airlines generally do not make information on the size of their frequent flyer pools publicly available, but such individuals are thought to number in the tens to hundreds of thousands. Even at the lower end of the range, they would still be responsible for a large portion of the 630 million annual enplanements in the United States. The costs of a program based on frequent travel, and who would bear them, are unclear.
- *Willingness to submit to the equivalent of a security-clearance process.* Some travelers would find it well worth the time and expense to obtain such a credential in exchange for the ability to move through an airport more quickly. Several programs, including Global Entry, NEXUS, and SENTRI, already allow certain travelers to be pre-approved for expedited clearance for entry at U.S. borders. Global Entry members pay a fee, undergo an interview and background check, and provide fingerprints as part of seeking approval. SENTRI and NEXUS operate in a similar fashion at Mexican and Canadian ports of entry, respectively. The combined programs cover hundreds of thousands of frequent travelers. The marginal costs of implementing this approach would be relatively low, since more than a million travelers have already paid for these entry/exit credentials. Extending the privileges of these programs from entry into the United States to security at U.S. airports would be a relatively trivial and easily justified action.

I am not advocating that trusted travelers be *exempt* from security screening, in part because terrorists would make attempts to exploit the program. Rather, trusted travelers should be eligible for a level of primary screening that is not as restrictive, intrusive, and time-consuming as WBI and frisks—or even what was in place prior to the Abdulmutallab attempt. If U.S. trusted travelers were eligible for the pre-Abdulmutallab screening, they could see their processing further simplified by the development of special lanes where they would not be required to remove their shoes or computers and other electronics and where they would also be allowed to carry on liquids. These trusted traveler screenings would be supplemented by random applications of more intensive secondary screening to small portions of the trusted population. The random secondary screenings would help prevent contraband and risk from creeping into the process. In the meantime, the more intensive methods could be used more effectively on people about whom little is known.

Recognizing the security of flights originating in the United States and thus returning *all* passengers to the domestic procedures that existed before the recent additions would save, at minimum, about $1.2 billion annually. Additional savings could be achieved by eliminating the supplemental searches of passengers that now occur as they board planes and the use of roving teams to test passengers' beverages for explosive residue in the secure parts of airports.

The savings from a trusted traveler program would depend largely on how it was configured, on what fraction of the traveling public was qualified to be trusted travelers, and whether security procedures were already relaxed for U.S. enplanements. If procedures were relaxed for all U.S. enplanements, the incremental savings from a trusted traveler program would be smaller. Again, the savings would come from the need for marginally fewer personnel and machines. However, if procedures were not relaxed for all U.S. enplanements, the savings from a trusted traveler program could be substantially greater. The savings would rise with the fraction of travelers who are trusted and could easily approach those associated with relaxing the standards for all U.S. enplanements. Even greater savings could be achieved if trusted traveler status were something for which travelers had to pay.

Had these steps been implemented in the years after 9/11, the savings would now likely total in the tens of billions of dollars, with no discernible reduction in security.

The Decade Ahead

Beyond their financial costs, the current screening methods, which are slower than those they replaced, impose additional losses on travelers, who could use the time they spend waiting for airport security more productively. In addition, the new security measures seem likely to deter some people from traveling at all and to push some toward using other modes of transportation. Deterring travel will impose additional losses on the economy, and travelers who are now choosing to drive instead of fly may be placing themselves at greater risk.

Researchers have estimated that the 9/11 attacks generated nearly 2,200 additional road traffic deaths in the United States through mid-2003 from a relative increase in driving and reduction in flying resulting from fear of additional terrorist attacks and associated reductions in the convenience of flying.[20] If the new security measures are generating similar, or even smaller, substitutions and the driving risk has grown as hypothesized, the new methods could be contributing to more deaths *annually* on U.S. roads than have been experienced *cumulatively* since 9/11 from terrorism against air transportation targets around the world.

Returning to the domestic air security procedures that had existed prior to December 2009 and creating a trusted traveler program are two relatively short-term steps that can be taken. What other changes should we be looking at for the longer term?

While by no means a trivial change, TSA should be required to analyze proposed security measures and regulations, using clear, transparent, peer-reviewed risk management principles. Congress can help in this regard by requiring TSA to use such methods in reporting on significant policy changes to passenger security. One reason for the current situation is that security measures have been grafted on or layered on in response to specific incidents, with little regard to an integrated assessment of cost, effectiveness, and impact.

Risk management modeling can be used to assess these variables.[21] It is possible to calculate how much a policy would need to reduce the annual losses from terrorism to cover the cost of implementing it. For example, a recent study, using conservative assumptions, found that WBI machines would have to disrupt more than one attack involving body-borne explosives *and* originating from U.S. airports every two years to be cost-effective.[22] Given that these joint conditions are not currently present, it is fair to conclude that the new methods are not worth the tradeoff of public expenditures and costs to travelers.

As noted in other chapters in this volume, terrorists are unlikely to go away, and they seem intent on developing new and more inventive ways of disrupting our society. Their intent, however, does not justify the blind application of restrictive security measures that impede commerce, compromise privacy, and imperil civil liberties. Yet, for most of the past decade, the United States has pursued policies with very little regard to the costs they impose on travelers or the net reduction in risk that they generate. It is imperative that we use the next decade to develop smarter, more sustainable, and more practical solutions to air passenger security. We should start by rolling back the procedures that were implemented in late 2010, which appear to exceed any reasonable test of regulatory cost-effectiveness. Further savings can likely be gained by subjecting other security measures—such as shoe removal, the ban on liquids, gate inspections, and the use of behavioral-detection officers—to careful scrutiny.

Critical Thinking Questions

1. Do you agree with the author that our nation's homeland security efforts over the past ten years have reduced the terrorist threat to aviation? Why or why not?
2. Despite these efforts, it is important to note that recent terrorist plots (particularly in 2006 and 2009) have still targeted airplanes. What does this signify about our terrorist adversaries?
3. What kinds of "sustainable, more practical" solutions to air passenger security would you recommend?

Notes

1. I am indebted to the many individuals who contributed ideas to this essay, including Bob Poole of the Reason Foundation and the vocal and informed participants on Flyertalk's Travel Safety and Security forum. I am also grateful to the anonymous travelers who have given their opinions about airport security issues in lines and lounges and on planes all over the world.
2. It is not possible to reliably estimate the fraction of travelers on which these methods are being used. TSA has deployed approximately 400 WBI scanners, but they are not always in use at the airports where they are deployed.
3. Pilots and flight crews objected when the machines were first introduced. Pilots have now been exempted.
4. Steve Lord, *TSA Is Increasing Procurement and Deployment of the Advanced Imaging Technology, but Challenges to This Effort and Other Areas of Aviation Security Remain,* testimony before the Subcommittee on Transportation Security and Infrastructure Protection, Committee on Homeland Security, House of Representatives, Washington, D.C: U.S. Government Accountability Office, GAO-10-484T, March 17, 2010, p. 9.

5. In April 2010, four researchers from the Department of Biochemistry and Biophysics at the University of California, San Francisco, made their concerns public in a "letter of concern" to the Assistant to the President for Science and Technology (as of May 27, 2011: http://www.npr.org/assets/news/2010/05/17/concern.pdf). Health concerns are magnified by the lack of transparency in the maintenance schedule (Allison Young and Blake Morrison, "TSA to Retest Airport Body Scanners for Radiation," *USA Today,* March 14, 2011).
6. The TSA letter provides a list of all the conditions that prohibit use of the WBIs. It can be found, as of May 27, 2011, at: http://www.cfnewsl3.com/static/articles/images/documents/TSA-letter-to-disability-community-1123.pdf
7. This is a problem with the backscatter machines in particular, as they have solid, non-transparent walls. The millimeter-wave machines have clear walls that better enable passengers to track personal items. However, some machines are configured in a way that prevents passengers from maintaining constant visual contact with their goods.
8. Perhaps the highest-profile recent example comes from Sharon Cissna, a representative in the Alaska legislature. A previous bout with breast cancer left her with scarring that was visible on the WBI and therefore led to pat-downs. An account of her recent experience can be found at Scott McMullen, "TSA Bars AK State Rep. Sharon Cissna from Flying," Alaska TravelGram blog, February 21, 2011. As of May 27, 2011: http://www.alaskatravelgram.com/2011/02/21/tsa-bars-ak-state-rep-sharon-cissna-from-flying/

   TSA does not publish statistics on anomaly detection rates, but reporting on a test of machines deployed in Germany indicates high false-alarm rates from folded clothing, pleats, and other issues (Ulrich Gassdorf, *Hamburger Abendblatt,* February 11, 2011).
9. It is unclear whether the machines can store images. Specifications in the procurement documents seem to require the machines to be able to store images, but TSA reports that they can store images only when the machine is in "test" mode (letter from Gale D. Rossides, TSA Acting Administrator, to Rep. Bennie G. Thompson, February 24, 2010; as of May 27, 2011: http://epic.org/privacy/airtravel/backscatter/TSA_Reply_House.pdf). In August 2010, the U.S. Marshals Service (part of the Department of Justice) acknowledged that more than 30,000 images were stored on a machine used at a courthouse in Orlando (letter from William E. Bordley, Associate General Counsel/FOI/PA Officer, Office of the General Counsel, U.S. Marshals Service, to John Vetdi, Esq., Electronic Privacy Information Center, August 2, 2010; as of May 27, 2011: http://epic.org/privacy/body_scanners/Disclosure_letter_Aug_2_2010.pdf). The Electronic Privacy Information Center filed a declaration against DHS in the U.S. District Court for the District of Columbia on May 27, 2010, that, among other requests, sought to compel the Department of Homeland Security (TSA) to produce 2,000 images stored for training purposes. This request was blocked on January 12, 2011, on the grounds that it would reveal vulnerabilities of the body-scanning technology.
10. Mark G. Stewart and John Mueller, *Risk and Cost-Benefit Analysis of Advanced Imaging Technology Full Body Scanners for Airline Passenger Security Screening,* University of New Castle, Australia, Research Report No. 280.11.2010, January 2011.
11. See the "Statistics" web page at the Aviation Safety Network website. As of May 27, 2011: http://www.aviation-safety.net/statistics
12. National Consortium for the Study of Terrorism and Responses to Terrorism, Global Terrorism Database, no date. As of May 27, 2011: http://www.start.umd.edu/gtd/

13. Another augmentation of security has probably crept in, albeit inadvertently: An increasing fraction of domestic enplanements consists of small regional jets that are incapable of causing the kind of damage that occurred with the larger planes hijacked on 9/11.
14. See, for example, Susan Sward, "The Voice of the Survivors: Flight 93, Fight to Hear Tape Transformed Her Life," *San Francisco Chronicle,* April 21, 2002. See also pp. 10–14 of the 9/11 Commission Report (*Final Report of the Commission on the Intelligence Capabilities of the United States Regarding Weapons of Mass Destruction,* Washington, D.C: U.S. Government Printing Office, 2005. As of May 24, 2011: http://www.gpoaccess.gov/wmd/index.html
15. *Final Report of the Commission on the Intelligence Capabilities of the United States Regarding Weapons of Mass Destruction,* Washington, D.C: U.S. Government Printing Office, 2005. As of May 24, 2011: http://www.gpoaccess.gov/wmd/index.html
16. TravelState.gov, "Visa Waiver Program (VWP)," no date. As of May 27, 2011: http://travel.state.gov/visa/temp/without/without_1990.html#countries
17. These statistics come from the FY2010 and FY2002 reports of the U.S. Department of State's Visa Office, Tables XVII and XX. As of May 27, 2011: http://travel.state.gov/visa/statistics/statistics_1476.html
18. Bureau of Transportation Statistics, Research and Innovative Technology Administration, *Transportation Statistics Annual Report, 2010,* Table 2-2-5, "Domestic Enplanements at U.S. Airports: 1999-2009," p. 122.
19. Dana Priest and William M. Arkin, "A Hidden World, Growing Beyond Control," in "Top Secret in America: A Washington Post Investigation," *Washington Post,* July 19, 2010.
20. Garrick Blalock, Vrinda Kadiyali, and Daniel H. Simon, "Driving Fatalities After 9/11: A Hidden Cost of Terrorism," *Applied Economics,* Vol. 41, No. 14, 2009, pp. 1717–1729.
21. *Review of the Department of Homeland Security's Approach to Risk Analysis,* Committee to Review the Department of Homeland Security's Approach to Risk Analysis, National Researsh Council, 2010. As of June 21, 2011: http://www.nap.edu/catalog.php?record_id=12972
22. Mark G. Stewart and John Mueller, "Risk and Cost-Benefit Analysis of Advanced Imaging Technology Full Body Scanners for Airline Passenger Security Screening," University of New Castle, Australia, Research Report No. 280.11.2010, January 2011.

Related Reading

Riley, K. Jack, Bruce W. Bennett, Mark Hanson, Stephen J. Carroll, Lloyd Dixon, Scott Gerwehr, Russell W. Glenn, Jamison Jo Medby, and John V. Parachini, *The Implications of the September 11 Terrorist Attacks for California: A Collection of Issue Papers,* Santa Monica, Calif.: RAND Corporation, IP-223-SCA, 2002. As of May 24, 2011: http://www.rand.org/pubs/issue_papers/IP223.html

Stevens, Donald, Thomas Hamilton, Marvin Schaffer, Diana Dunham-Scott, Jamison Jo Medby, Edward W. Chan, John Gibson, Mel Eisman, Richard Mesic, Charles T. Kelley Jr., Julie Kim, Tom LaTourrette, and K. Jack Riley, *Implementing Security Improvement Options at*

Los Angeles International Airport, Santa Monica, Calif.: RAND Corporation, DB-499-1-LAWA, 2006. As of May 24, 2011: http://www.rand.org/pubs/documented_briefings/DB499-1.html

U.S. Government Accountability Office, *TSA Is Increasing Procurement and Deployment of the Advanced Imaging Technology, but Challenges to This Effort and Other Areas of Aviation Security Remain,* Washington, D.C.: U.S. Government Printing Office, March 17, 2010. As of May 24, 2011: http://www.gao.gov/new.items/d10484t.pdf

Wilson, Jeremy M., Brian A. Jackson, Mel Eisman, Paul Steinberg, and K. Jack Riley, *Securing America's Passenger-Rail Systems,* Santa Monica, Calif.: RAND Corporation, MG-705-NIJ, 2007. As of May 24, 2011: http://www.rand.org/pubs/monographs/MG705.html

Soft Targets, Hard Choices

James S. Robbins

On November 9, 2005, three blasts rocked hotels in the Jordanian capital of Amman. The near simultaneous suicide attacks bore all the hallmarks of an al Qaeda attack, and the terrorist group soon took credit. Yet, while the attacks were tactically adept, their immediate impact was to inspire fury among Jordanians and to damage al Qaeda's reputation across the region. The next day angry Jordanians crowded the streets in protest, chanting "Burn in hell, Abu Musab al-Zarqawi!" and calling the incident Jordan's 9/11. Political scientist Fares Breizat, who conducts opinion research in Jordan, found that among survey participants who had previously viewed al Qaeda in Iraq as a "legitimate resistance organization," nine out of ten had changed their minds.[1] Another survey found al Qaeda with a 90 percent disapproval rating in the country.[2] This incident illustrates in microcosm the ambiguities of the soft-target attack; it is a tactical option that rarely translates into strategic gains for terrorists, but which remains popular with them because it is within their means, guarantees publicity, and helps keep them relevant on the world stage.

Trends in Attacking Soft Targets

At base, soft targets can be defined as locations either difficult to defend, or usually undefended. They are typically nongovernment sites and, more often than not, places where people congregate in large numbers. Ideally, from the terrorist's point of view, the target also has some other value, such as the possibility of secondary effects beyond those caused by the attack itself. The types of soft targets discussed in this volume are typical of the category and include national monuments, hospitals, schools, sporting arenas, and hotels.

The broad definition of soft targets is itself flexible when applied to specific cases; the line between "soft" and "hard" is at best indistinct. Any target of the above-mentioned categories may be "hardened" by putting defenses in place, and since there are many types and gradations of defenses, hardness may be in the eye of the attacker. Terrorists have exhibited great imagination finding flaws in defensive schemes—one might ask if a hard target really is hard if it has an unknown fatal defensive flaw. They have also demonstrated an ability unilaterally to redefine targets and methods. For example, aircraft hijackings were traditionally considered a means of taking large numbers of hostages for purposes of negotiation, something usually thought characteristic of soft-target attacks. However, on 9/11 airliners became weapons for attacking other targets, both hard and soft, and the passengers were incidental, except insofar as they added to the casualty count, or as in the case of United Airlines Flight 93, they forced the mission to fail at the cost of their own lives.

Soft target threats are nothing new; they have been on the terrorist menu for as long as there have been those with the means and intent to commit violence against innocents. The United States has experienced many such attacks. One prominent early example of domestic soft-target terrorism was the September 16, 1920, horse-cart bombing in Lower Manhattan by a group called the American Anarchist Fighters, which killed 30 and injured 200. Domestic terror bombings by violent protest groups in the early 1970s raised threat perceptions to the point that when architect James Loftis was asked to design a new federal building for Oklahoma City in 1973, one of the structural requirements was that the building be able to withstand a substantial blast. The Alfred P. Murrah Federal Building was finished five years later, and when it was in fact bombed on April 19, 1995, by Timothy McVeigh and Terry Nichols, what was noteworthy about the subsequent destruction was how much more damage would have been done had the building not already been hardened.

Since the 9/11 attacks there have been periodic alerts based on soft-target threats, such as in May 2002 when al Qaeda detainee Abu Zubaydah told investigators that the terror group was discussing an attack on apartment buildings, malls, restaurants, and places where large numbers of people gather. Likewise, in March 2005, reports circulated of planned strikes by Abu Musab al Zarqawi's al Qaeda network on soft targets inside the United States, including movie theaters, restaurants, and schools. While no attacks materialized (perhaps because of the alert status), such reported threats were and must be taken seriously. Many recent high-profile terrorist attacks have been against soft targets, such as the above-mentioned bombings in Jordan, the transportation system bombings in Madrid (March 3, 2004) and London (July 7, 2005), the multiple soft-target attacks in Casablanca (May 16, 2003), and the two Bali bombings (2002 and 2005).

Aggregate data on terror attacks since 1968 (Table 2.1) show that categories of targets that tend to be soft are more often attacked than those that tend to be hard. Further, as demonstrated in Figure 2.1, when the data are examined in more detail and ambiguous cases are removed, soft targets account for 73 percent of the attacks.

Since 2001, soft targets have accounted for about two-thirds of global attacks (see Table 2.2 and Figure 2.2). What is noteworthy is the relative decrease in soft targeting over the same period, from 77.4 percent of all attacks in 2001 to 53.2 percent in the first nine months of 2005. This may indicate that since the war on terrorism has become overt—that is, since it became a "war"—terrorists are more willing to take risks attacking regime targets directly.

While soft targets still account for the overwhelming majority (90 percent) of attacks inside the United States over the same period, the overall number of incidents has declined dramatically since 2001 (see Table 2.3 and Figure 2.3). This can no doubt be attributed to

TABLE 2.1 Global Terror Attacks by Target[3], 1968-2005

Target*	Incidents	Injuries	Fatalities
Infrastructure	2,787	15,139	4,663
Regime	8,887	27,797	10,384
Property	7,755	28,695	11,825
Other	4,626	11,314	5,420
Total	24,055	82,945	32,292

*Note: Infrastructure targets include telecommunication, transportation, utilities, food or water supply, maritime, and airports and airlines. Regime targets include diplomatic, government, military, and police targets. Property and commercial targets include business, tourists, private citizens, and property targets. Other targets include abortion related, educational institutions, nongovernmental organizations, terrorists, religious figures / institutions, other, and unknown targets.

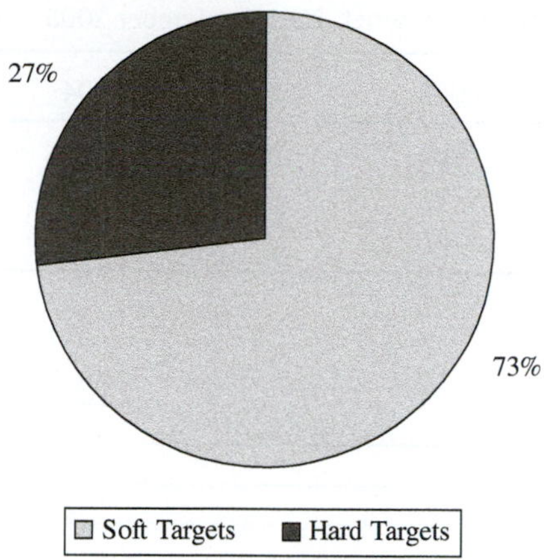

FIGURE 2.1 Global Terror Attacks by Type, 1968–2005

TABLE 2.2 Global Terror Attacks by Type, 2001–September 2005

	2001	2002	2003	2004	Jan.-Sept. 2005	Total
Soft target	1,341	1,948	1,291	1,701	1,830	8,111
Hard target	391	701	606	937	1,613	4,248
Total	1,732	2,649	1,897	2,638	3,443	12,359

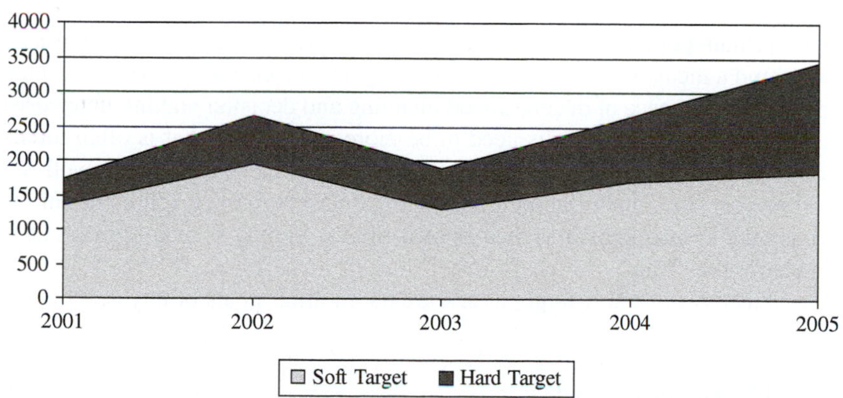

FIGURE 2.2 Global Terror Attacks by Type, 2001–September 2005

the national response to 9/11—new tools for law enforcement and intelligence, a strategy to defeat terrorists abroad before they reach the homeland, and, most importantly, a general awareness of the threat and willingness to take coordinated preemptive action that had been lacking in the years before 9/11.

TABLE 2.3 U.S. Domestic Attacks by Target, 2001–September 2005

	2001	2002	2003	2004	2005	Total
Soft target	36	15	15	5	2	73
Hard target	3	1	3	1	0	8
Total	39	16	18	6	2	81

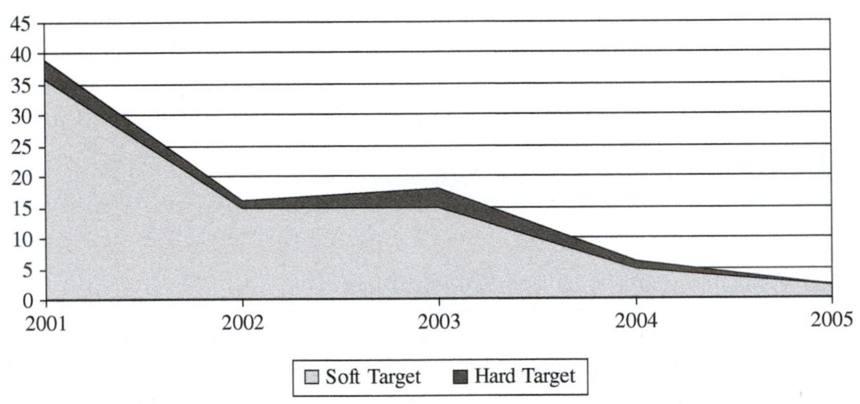

FIGURE 2.3 U.S. Domestic Attacks by Target, 2001–September 2005

Why Attack Soft Targets?

Soft targets remain popular because of their tactical logic—the comparatively weak terrorist needs to find a means of attack, and the soft target is the easiest one to hit. Soft targeting can also be a consequence of decentralized planning and decision making in terrorist organizations. Small, independent cells need to be more opportunistic; it is often too difficult for them to undertake complex attacks on their own, especially against well-defended targets. Therefore, the smaller, more dispersed and underground a cell is, the more likely it will undertake an attack that matches its capabilities. Simply stated, terrorists attack soft targets because they can.

The objectives of a soft-target attack are the familiar goals of any acts of terrorism; *inter alia:*

- kill and injure people,
- sow chaos,
- create a climate of fear and insecurity,
- deter the regime,
- damage the economy,
- exploit symbolism,
- gain publicity, and
- prove relevance.

Killing and injuring people are routine objectives for terrorists. Human beings are the original and ultimate soft target. They may be targeted for killing or for hostage taking, the latter of which was the dominant paradigm for decades and still is in some parts of the world. Terrorists target people in order to inspire the fear that perhaps any other citizen could be the next victim. Terrorists motivated by a sense of revenge or an eschatological vision frequently desire a large body count, which draws them toward areas where people congregate, such as sporting events or shopping centers. If nothing else, body counts serve as a way to keep score, and because they are quantifiable they have attracted inordinate attention from both terrorists and analysts alike. However, numbers of casualties are not proportional to the fear inspired; a more important factor is persistence and momentum—the idea that more killings lie in the future. For example the October 2002 Washington, D.C., sniper attacks did not result in an inordinately large number of casualties in aggregate (ten killed and three wounded), but very effectively inspired fear because the attacks were random and sustained over a three-week period.[4]

A related direct effect of an attack is the chaos that it creates in the attack zone. Transportation networks can be shut down, businesses disrupted, fires started, and so forth. These effects are, however, temporary. In broader terms, terrorists seek to create a climate of fear and insecurity among the general population, not just among those in the target zone. Soft targets serve an important role in this because they are where most people live, work, and recreate. Thus in striking at the soft target, the terrorist is really attacking the country's way of life. Yet, as noted above, this type of fear can dissipate quickly without follow-on attacks. The terrorist threat is not credible without momentum to sustain it. And even with follow-on attacks, populations may become adjusted to the level of violence terrorists inflict and place it in the category of acceptable risk. Much of the effect of terrorism is subjective; Tom Marks, a professor at the National Defense University, notes that the violent death rate in Jammu and Kashmir, which faces an active insurgency, and which Indians describe as "Hell on Earth," is about the same as in Baltimore.[5] In addition, the sense of fear may be accompanied by anger, which can be mobilized by the regime to give support for unprecedented action in the name of public safety.

Effects on the economy also play an important role in soft-target selection. The economy is a primary target for terrorism; Osama bin Laden stated in December 2001 that it is possible to achieve victory over the United States only "through hitting the economic structure, which is basic for the military power. If their economy is destroyed, they will be busy with their own affairs rather than enslaving the weak peoples. It is very important to concentrate on hitting the U.S. economy through all possible means."[6] Targeting the economy, particularly the consumer sector, makes sense in cost-benefit terms, because terrorists can impose millions of dollars of social costs (through increased security, depressed consumer spending, higher insurance, etc.) with a very small investment. The ideal target is the shopping mall or the large chain store, anywhere that is familiar to the average consumer and will make him less likely to go out and spend. The ideal time for such attacks would be the holiday shopping season, when many businesses, especially small companies, make most of their annual profit.

The attack on the symbolic target, such as a national monument, is more esoteric. Such attacks may not result in economic disruptions or high casualties, but they can serve to inspire the terror group's followers and demoralize the foe. Washington, D.C. went on local alert on October 7 and 13, 2005, when threats were made against the Washington

Monument. One might ask what difference it would make if it were attacked, especially if empty and resulting in no casualties. Terrorists could not destroy the structure unless they used a very powerful explosive. However, they might be attracted to the imagery alone, showing that not even the most cherished symbols of American pride are safe from violence. El Sayyid Nosair, who was convicted of gun violations relating to the 1990 murder of Zionist Rabbi and Jewish Defense League leader Meir Kahane, and who was also complicit in the 1993 World Trade Center bombing, wrote, "We had to thoroughly demoralize the enemies of God. This is to be done by means of destroying and blowing up the towers that constitute the pillars of their civilization, such as the tourist attractions they're so proud of and the high buildings they're so proud of."[7] Terrorists might seek to multiply the effect by combining a symbolic target with a holiday. For example, in 1983 Iranian-backed Shiite extremists were reportedly plotting to ram the White House with a truck bomb on Thanksgiving Day.[8]

Publicity is a natural objective of any terrorist attack, whether on a hard target or soft. In a letter intercepted by authorities in 2005, al Qaeda second in command Ayman al Zawahiri admonished Abu Musab al-Zarqawi to keep in mind that "we are in a battle, and that more than half of this battle is taking place in the battlefield of the media. And that we are in a media battle in a race for the hearts and minds of our people."[9] Timothy McVeigh said that he and Terry Nichols chose to attack the Murrah Building in part because it had "plenty of open space around it, to allow for the best possible news photos and television footage."[10] Any such attack will gain publicity, no matter how large, and the amount of coverage will rise exponentially as follow-on attacks occur.[11] Finally, soft-target attacks are an ideal method for terror groups to demonstrate their relevance. Hitting hard targets takes time and effort; the group may have to lie dormant a long time, and there is no guarantee of success once the plan is executed. Hitting a soft target gives the terror group not only publicity, thus raising its profile, but relevance within the broader movement of which it may be a part. This helps with fund-raising and recruitment to the cause.

The Soft-Target Attacks and Terror Strategy: The Chechen Case

The question remains how effectively soft-target attacks translate into achieving strategic goals. After all, a terror attack is rarely an end in itself; terrorists have a political agenda to implement, and ideally the means are related to and help facilitate the ends. But the record for soft-target attacks is not auspicious. They rarely if ever lead to the changes the terrorists desire and frequently have the opposite effect.

Chechen insurgents have made something of a specialty of soft-target attacks over the last decade. They have sought to gain initiative, publicize their cause, and bring a measure of the same kind of suffering to the Russian people that they themselves have suffered. But these attacks, even when successful, have not always translated into strategic gains. In June 1995, Chechen guerillas seized control of a hospital in the southern Russian town of Budyonnovsk, taking over 1,500 hostages. The four-day siege led to an agreement that suspended military actions in Chechnya. This was a notable success. But a corresponding strategic failure attended the September 1999 multiple attacks on apartment blocks in Moscow, Buy-naksk, and Volgodonsk. The bombings killed 292 people. Then-Prime Minister Vladimir Putin used the attacks as a pretext for renewed military intervention in Chechnya, which had driven out Russian forces in August 1996. In February 2000, the capital city Grozny was recaptured and razed.

Other Chechen soft-target attacks have generated substantial media coverage, but had little positive long-term impact for their cause. On October 23, 2002, rebels seized a theater in Moscow—the House of Culture of the State Ball-Bearing Plant Number One—and held 763 people hostage. Their stated rationale was that

> people are unaware of the innocent who are dying in Chechnya: the sheikhs, the women, the children and the weak ones. And therefore, we have chosen this approach. This approach is for the freedom of the Chechen people and there is no difference in where we die, and therefore we have decided to die here, in Moscow. And we will take with us the lives of hundreds of sinners. If we die, others will come and follow us—our brothers and sisters who are willing to sacrifice their lives, in God's way, to liberate their nation.[12]

The terrorists sought publicity for their cause, for the crimes they accused Russia of committing, and to inspire others who might follow in their wake. After a three-day standoff, Russian security forces sought to end the crisis by pumping a chemical anesthetic into the theater. In the rescue attempt 120 hostages died, along with all the terrorists, many of whom were shot in the head while incapacitated.[13] The attack was used to justify further action inside Chechnya, as well as to tighten controls on the media for terrorism coverage.

The Chechens did not give up. In 2003, there were an estimated 11 bombings in Russia by Chechen groups. But the most determined and spectacular Chechen campaign against soft targets took place late in the summer of 2004. On August 24, two Russian commercial airliners flying several hundred miles south of Moscow crashed nearly simultaneously. One of the flights had sent an alert that it was being hijacked. Explosive residue found at the scene indicated hexogen, an explosive used in the 1999 Msocow apartment block bombings. Both planes had left from the domestic terminal of Domodedovo International Airport, and an investigation concluded that two women, Amanata Nagayeva and Satsita Dzhebirkhanova, were probably responsible for bringing down the aircraft using suicide bombs. Both were ethnic Chechens who had lost relatives in the conflict and had family ties to terrorists groups. A group calling itself the Islambouli Brigades of al Qaeda claimed responsibility for both crashes, and later Chechen guerilla leader Shamil Basayev, who had masterminded the theater takeover in 2002, also took credit. On that same day as the aircraft bombings, a bus stop was blown up on Kashirskoye Highway near Moscow, as a bus was pulling away. Four people were injured.

On August 31, 2004, Rosa Nagayeva, sister of airline bomber Amanata Nagayeva, blew herself up outside of the entrance to the Rizhskaya subway station and the Krestovskiy shopping center in Moscow. She had apparently intended to detonate her two-kilogram bomb inside the underground station to maximize casualties, but had to ignite the weapon early when she unexpectedly encountered a police checkpoint near the entrance, a response to the bombings earlier in the week. Even detonating the bomb outside the station, 11 people were killed and 50 wounded. The Islambouli Brigades of al Qaeda and Basayev again claimed credit.

The next day, September 1, 2004, Basayev's group perpetrated one of the most notorious soft-target terrorist attacks in recent history, taking over an entire elementary school. Three dozen guerillas, men and women, Chechens and foreign fighters, took between 1,000 and 1,500 people hostage in a daylight raid on School Number One in the southern Russian town of Beslan. The hostages included children, parents, and teachers who had gathered for traditional first day of school ceremonies. The attack had been long planned; weapons and explosives had been prepositioned under the floorboards and in the walls of the school. The incident may have been an attempt to recreate the earlier success at Budyonnovsk.

A three-day siege followed. The hostage takers presented a list of demands, including that Russian forces withdraw from Chechnya and that Chechnya be admitted to the Commonwealth of Independent States as a sovereign country. Children were lined up at windows to serve as human shields, and the terrorists threatened to kill 50 kids for every hostage taker killed (or 20 for every one injured). The hostages were held in the gymnasium in searing heat, without food or medical attention. On September 2, terrorists opened fire on a vehicle that passed too close to the school, and the next day a truce was arranged to remove the bodies from near the school. While this was going on an explosive that had been rigged to a basketball hoop fell to the ground and exploded, prompting one of the militants to open fire on the Russians. A general melee followed in which Russian forces blew a hole in the side of the gym and rushed the building, urging the hostages to run for cover as they exchanged fire with the terrorists, who had begun killing hostages. The fierce firefight left over 300 dead and many more hospitalized. Most of the terrorists were killed, though a number seem to have escaped.

The net result of the late summer 2004 campaign was publicity for the Chechen cause, but little else. The attacks failed to sway the Russian government to change its policies or the Russian people to have more sympathy for the Chechen cause. Any gains the terrorists made in terms of publicity, revenge, or demonstrations of strength were countered by Russian anger and use of the attacks as pretext for more resolute action against the threat.

Protecting Ourselves from Soft-Target Attacks

A free society is naturally full of soft targets, and its citizens are wary of and resistant to the idea of defensive measures that inhibit their liberty. For example, metal detectors were first widely employed in prisons to prevent prisoners from transporting weapons, and they were used to screen airline passengers in Hong Kong as early as 1948.[14] When FBI Director J. Edgar Hoover suggested in the 1960s that metal detectors at airports might help reduce the possibility of hijacking, his proposal was denounced as an unconscionable and unworkable intrusion on the flying public. Today they are commonplace worldwide, and few would feel safe flying without them.

Cost is another issue. Defensive measures can be expensive, particularly those that involve adding personnel to the budget. Over time, facing a determined foe, the costs of terrorism to an economy can be significant. A 2004 study of the effects of terrorism in Israel showed a 15 percent decline in gross domestic product, caused mostly by government diversion of funds for defensive measures.[15]

A third issue deals with the symbolism of defenses against terrorism, the perception that taking any action at all hands them a victory. In the late 1970s, counterterrorism officials in the Carter Administration argued that diverting resources to defensive measures was playing into the hands of the terrorists, imposing costs on the United States while making the terror groups feel more powerful because they forced the U.S. to flinch.[16] But after the Beirut barracks bombing on October 23, 1983, large vehicles were positioned around the White House, later replaced by concrete barriers used as flower planters, to prevent similar domestic vehicle bombings. President Reagan's critics made light of the defensive "flower pots," but on November 7, 1983, the Capitol was bombed by a group calling itself the Armed Resistance Movement. The bombing did little damage, but spurred the Congress to take action. New defensive measures included concrete barriers used as planters, similar to those installed at the White House to prevent vehicle bombs; metal detectors; more sophisticated ID cards; and bulletproof inserts in the backs of the chairs on the floor of the House of Representatives.[17] Predictably, some initially saw these precautionary measures as a terrorist victory in themselves, in that they closed off the government from the people and impinged on our traditional access of the governed to the government.[18] However, over time the defensive measures became part of life and of the landscape. People worked them into their routines, and they became less burdensome over time.

Hardening targets is a good option in some cases. Common defensive means of protection include barriers, surveillance, checkpoints, ID protocols, establishing choke points for people or traffic flow, limiting or restricting vehicle access to buildings or areas near them, and antiterrorism training for personnel. These measures seek to defend, but more importantly to deter. They filter out some forms of attack and make others harder to execute. Hardened targets may still be attacked, of course, but deterrence comes into play—because the target is harder, the terrorist may seek one that is not as hard. And given the number of potential targets, there will always be another, softer one available.

This situation suggests a paradox in adopting defenses against terrorism. There is a favorable cost-benefit ratio in individual cases—almost any resource commitment will make a target tougher to hit. High priority locations can readily be made less attractive as targets. Figure 2.4 shows an illustrative curve—initial investments in passive defenses can go a long way to secure targets, and costs escalate when more active defenses requiring full-time staff are employed and as defenses become more onerous to daily life of those who frequent the target (workers, tourists, et al.).

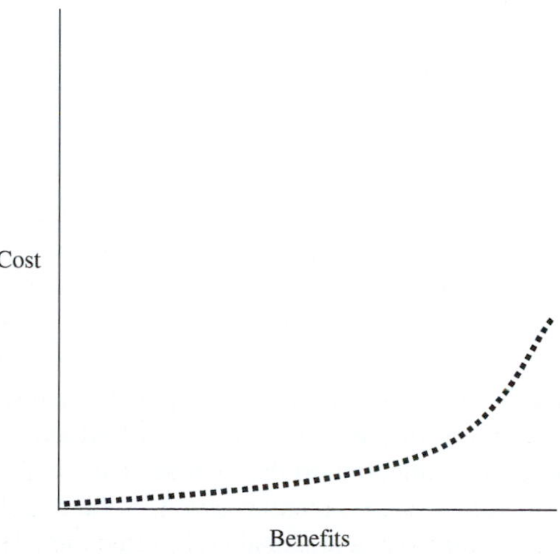

FIGURE 2.4 Cost Versus Benefit Hardening Individual Targets

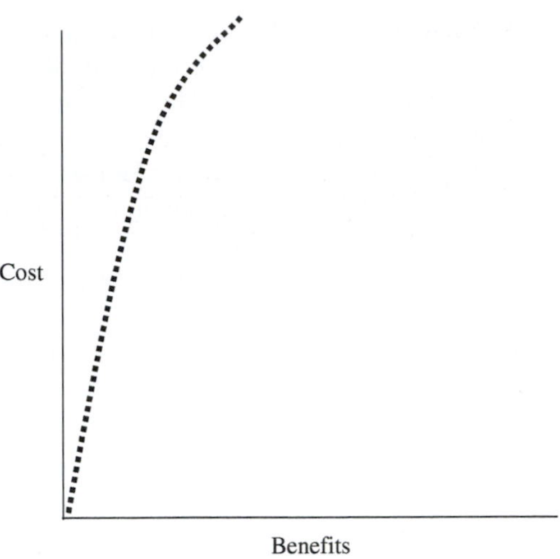

FIGURE 2.5 Cost Versus Benefit Hardening Aggregate Targets

Yet, there is an unfavorable cost-benefit ratio when targets are taken in aggregate because there are too many to defend all of them. If benefits are measured in terms of reducing overall threats, security can be achieved only with excessive resources and major inconveniences (because of the number of targets and the ease with which terrorists can find another). Figure 2.5 illustrates this relationship. This indicates the need for risk balancing and prioritization in spending resources for hardening targets—seek to find the greatest security for the greatest number among a predetermined set of targets based on terrorist targeting priorities (potential number of casualties, symbolism, disruption potential, etc.). At the same time, decision makers and the general population should understand that a degree of risk must inevitably be accepted because it is impossible to protect everyone everywhere from every type of threat.

Conclusion

The recent failure of terrorists to exploit soft targets in the United States should not be seen as indicative of a trend, but rather as evidence of effective counterterrorism and antiterrorism efforts in the wake of the 9/11 attacks. If more time passes without further attacks, political pressure will grow to divert attention and resources from the efforts against terrorism to other priorities. As complacency grows, so too does the tendency to accept more risk, or, more properly, to allow more risk without realizing it. The constant in the equation is the determination of the enemies of the United States to find and exploit gaps in the system and to use violence to bring attention to their cause. The United States will never be in a position to be able to secure every potential target in the country; such an ambition is not only unfeasible, it would mean a practical end to freedom. Thus, the soft-target challenge will always be with us.

Critical Thinking Questions

1. In your view, does the United States prioritize the protection of so-called "soft targets" against the threat of terrorism? Why or why not?
2. Is there a particular kind of soft target that you would prioritize as needing more protection? If so, why, and what specifically would you recommend?
3. How can local, state, and federal authorities better educate the general public that, as the author describes, "a degree of risk must inevitably be accepted"?

Notes

1. Jonathan Finer and Nasser Mehdawi, "Hotel Bombings in Jordan Fuel Anger at Exiles," *The Washington Post,* November 17, 2005, A17.
2. "Ipsos Stat Survey Shows: 90 Percent of Jordanians Say Al-Qa'ida Terrorist Organization" *Al-Ghadd* (Web edition), November 16, 2005.
3. All data used in this section are from the Memorial Institute for the Prevention of Terrorism Terrorism Knowledge Base (TBK). The TKB database is derived from a number of official and semiofficial sources, and it covers incidents from 1968 to 2005. The database can be accessed at http://www.tkb.org/Home.jsp.
4. Cf. James S. Robbins, "Terrorism, the Media, and Homeland Security," *Homeland Security: Readings and Interpretations,* ed. Russell Howard, James Forest, and Joanne Moore (New York: McGraw-Hill Publishers, 2005).
5. Tom Marks, comments at "Religion as Ideology in Terrorist and Insurgent Movements," Symposium on Religious Factors and the Global War on Terrorism, Pew Forum on Religion and Public Life, School for National Security Executive Education, National Defense University, Washington, DC, July 29, 2005.
6. Osama bin Laden statement of December 27, 2001, as broadcast by the Al Jazeera network.
7. Quoted in Benjamin Netanyahu, *Fighting Terrorism* (New York: The Noonday Press, 1995), 94.
8. Ronald Kessler, "Shiites Purportedly Planned to Blast White House," *The Washington Post,* December 7, 1983, A18.
9. Letter from Ayman al-Zawahiri to Abu Musab al-Zarqawi, Office of the Director of National Intelligence News Release No. 2-05, October 11, 2005.
10. Quoted in "Terrorism Q&A: Terrorism and the Media," Council on Foreign Relations information sheet, 2004.
11. Cf. Robbins, "Terrorism, the Media, and Homeland Security."
12. "Gunmen Release Chilling Video," *CNN.com*, October 24, 2002.
13. Rescue Ended Days of Horror And Uncertainty, *The Washington Post,* October 27, 2002, A1. A Russian commando was quoted as explaining, I understand that this is cruel, but when there are two kilos of plastic explosives hanging on a person, we saw no other way of rendering them safe.
14. "Detectors Probe for Air Pirates," *The Washington Post,* September 19, 1948, R12.
15. Zvi Eckstein and Daniel Tsiddon, "Macroeconomic Consequences of Terror: Theory and the Case of Israel," CEPR discussion paper, June 2004.

16. Cf. Arthur T. Hadley, "America's Vulnerability to Terrorism," *The Washington Post,* December 4, 1977, 79.
17. Allison Muscatine, "Capitol Securely Greeting Tourists," *The Washington Post,* June 1, 1984, C1.
18. See, for example, Nicholas O. Berry, "Good Fences, Bad Idea," *The New York Times,* December 19, 1983, A19.

Cyber Threats

Ten Issues To Consider

Frank Cilluffo and Paul Byron Pattak

As the United States hurtles into the Information Age, we are forced to grapple with a new set of national security problems heretofore not contemplated. Distance, time, and geography have been reduced to the point of irrelevancy. Information networks have given the United States an unrivaled, perhaps unsurpassable, lead over the rest of the world in virtually every facet of modern life. To an unprecedented degree American national security and economic well-being depend upon critical infrastructures, such as banking and finance, electric power, information and communications, oil and gas production, transportation, water supply, emergency services, and the continuity of government services. These infrastructures in turn depend upon telecommunications and networked information systems. Along with the clear rewards of information systems come new risks and a host of unintended consequences that need to be better understood by corporate and government leaders.

The United States faces threats from peer nations, trading partners, hostile countries, non-state actors, terrorists, organized crime, insiders, and teenage hackers. While few adversaries would attempt to confront the United States in a conventional war on the traditional battlefield, its adversaries recognize that terrorism and other asymmetric forms of conflict, such as cyber attacks, are more effective methods of striking the United States where it is most vulnerable. Bits and bytes will never completely replace bullets and bombs, but they can be synergistically combined. Imagine if the Oklahoma City bombing had been accompanied by electronic disruptions of federal, state, and local emergency and public safety communications systems, including Emergency-911.

The ability to network has far outpaced the ability to protect networks. When the Internet was created, it was designed with "openness" and accessibility as guiding principles. Most information systems have been engineered in the most economically efficient manner, and are therefore dependent upon a small number of critical nodes, making them vulnerable to attack. As computer systems become increasingly interdependent, damage to one can potentially cascade and impact others.

America's vulnerabilities were dramatized during a 1997 Joint Chiefs of Staff exercise, code-named "Eligible Receiver." The purpose of the exercise was to test the United States' ability to respond to cyber attacks. The results opened the eyes of skeptics. Using software widely available from hacker websites, the thirty-five-person team showed how they could have disabled elements of the U.S. electric power grid by exploiting Supervisory Control and Data Acquisition (SCADA) systems (which allow remote control of the systems). They also demonstrated how to incapacitate portions of U.S. military command-and-control systems in the Pacific and Emergency-911 systems in the United States.

In response to the emerging threat of cyber terrorism, on May 22, 1998, Presidential Decision Directive (PDD-63) authorized the creation of a National Infrastructure Protection Center (NIPC). The NIPC is now housed within the Federal Bureau of Investigation (FBI) and serves as a lookout for attempted intrusions and to monitor cyber attacks. PDD-63 also led to the establishment of the Critical Infrastructure Assurance Office (CIAO) within the Department of Commerce to serve as a policy coordination staff for infrastructure assurance issues within the Executive Branch.

While the U.S. government has taken these important steps, a more holistic, high-level policy debate is required. Information warfare, cyber crime, and cyber terrorism all overlap, yet require different domain expertise and varied responses. At present it is impossible to refer to clearly delineated rules. Before committing ourselves to policies with enormous potential for adverse results and misspent taxpayer dollars, the United States must first fully understand the dangers of cyber threats. Ten issues require thoughtful consideration.

1. Defining Conflict in Cyberspace

Cyber warfare raises serious questions about how future conflicts and wars are prosecuted. What constitutes an act of war? How does one differentiate between a terrorist attack and a financial crime committed with a computer? What is the adequate balance between protecting civil liberties, businesses, and national security? To a large extent, determining whether the United States is at war depends on the antagonist. A cyber attack by China's People's Liberation Army requires a substantially different series of responses than an attack by teenagers from China, although American victims of an attack might never know the difference.

In late January and early February 1998, as the United States considered deploying forces to the Persian Gulf, hackers attacked scores of Defense Department networks. Pentagon and FBI investigators thought that these intrusions might have been launched in response to a military build-up in the Persian Gulf. Fearing the worst, senior Defense officials informed the White House that an Iraqi information warfare campaign may have been underway. Their fears were substantiated because the hackers used foreign Internet service providers, including one located in the United Arab Emirates, as a staging point for their attacks.

After several days of investigating, the FBI learned that two California-based teenagers, mentored by an eighteen-year-old Israeli national, had conducted the attack. They were able to preserve the anonymity of their attack by routing it through a host of computer systems around the world. They successfully breached U.S. military computer defenses and gained access to the Defense Department's unclassified (yet important) logistics networks. The attack and the subsequent investigation, dubbed "Solar Sunrise," were characterized by John Hamre, Deputy Secretary of Defense, as "the most organized and systematic attack" on U.S. defense networks discovered thus far.

Cyber warriors can systemically attack vital American networks in relative anonymity. The person on the other end could just as easily be a child, a competitor, or a foreign intelligence service. A few months after "Solar Sunrise," a Massachusetts teenager was charged with disabling the FAA control tower at Worcester Regional Airport for six hours. Incoming planes could not use the runway lights. Later in 1998, a man in Toborg, Sweden managed to disable major portions of South Florida's Emergency-911 system.

To date, most of these denial-of-service incidents have either been perpetrated by insiders or hackers and are best characterized as annoyances. Hackers, largely thrill-seeking young people, have demonstrated that vulnerabilities can be exploited by those with hostile intent. Any one of the increasing number of groups and individuals hostile to U.S. interests could exploit these vulnerabilities to harm those interests.

Current U.S. policy does not draw clear distinctions between these various scenarios. Without established rules of engagement, there is no battle plan in place to address the dangers raised by the various attacks. Likewise, because of the virtual nature of cyberspace, conventional force projection will not pre-empt or prevent cyber assaults. As we are by and large dealing with "actors without addresses," conventional military projection will not prevent a cyber assault. But a well-defined policy and an established strategy would go a long way towards showing our adversaries that the United States is willing and able to respond both in kind and conventionally. In the final analysis, the nation's best deterrent may be the ability to quickly reconstitute our damaged systems, regardless of the perpetrator.

2. Rules of Engagement

National planners need to define carefully the criteria for U.S. rules of engagement for cyberspace. In short, they must determine how the United States selects information warfare targets, as well as who and what are fair game. In turn, this may be a harbinger of how U.S. systems will be targeted by adversaries.

According to U.S. media reports, President Clinton issued a highly classified finding authorizing the CIA to use covert means to undermine Serbian President Slobodan Milosevic. The President allegedly authorized government agencies to conduct cyber operations against Mr. Milosevic by tapping into his bank accounts. Intelligence sources believe Mr. Milosevic secreted money in Swiss, Russian, Greek, Cypriot, and Chinese banks. A compelling reason to support this effort is that it personalized the target and did not result in collateral damage-in this case innocent Serbian civilians.

The problem with this particular "covert" action is that it ceased to be covert upon the public's awareness of its occurrence. Accordingly, it is substantially more difficult to execute this type of plan when the would-be target is aware of the action. The first rule of covert action is to keep it clandestine and maintain plausible deniability. An information arms race does not bode well for the United States given its unparalleled dependence on critical infrastructures. In many ways, it is the reverse of Cold War nuclear deterrence policy—America's ability to defend ourselves is now more important than its ability to project power.

3. Non-State Actors

The increased availability of advanced technology has strengthened the capabilities of hostile non-state actors. The situation will only worsen as the requisite level of knowledge and skill decreases while the power and technological sophistication of these cyber attack tools increase exponentially. As a result, terrorists have become empowered and have moved away from the fringes of world affairs toward the center stage.

Cyber warfare can also be a tool to collect intelligence in support of terrorist operations and campaigns, and to communicate and disseminate propaganda. Given today's state of technology and dual-use applications, terrorist groups can easily acquire an inexpensive, yet robust communications intelligence (COMINT) collection capability. First, terrorists can intercept valuable political, economic, and military secrets; run counter-surveillance on law enforcement; and perform profiling analyses to identify individuals who can be bribed, co-opted, coerced, or "neutralized." Much of this work can be done anonymously, diminishing the risk of reprisal and increasing the likelihood of success. Second, terrorists can use advanced technology for communication and tradecraft. The Internet and other information systems provide terrorist groups a global and near real-time command, control, and communications capability. The availability of sophisticated encryption devices and anonymous re-mailers also provides relatively secure communications or stored data.[1]

Nearly all major terrorist organizations have a website, including the Shining Path, HAMAS, the Revolutionary Armed Forces of Columbia (FARC), the Liberated Tamil Tigers of Eelam (LTTE), and the Irish Republican Army (IRA). They look to the Internet largely to disseminate communiques, fundraise, and recruit. The United States' most-wanted transnational terrorist, Osama bin Laden, uses laptops with satellite uplinks and encrypted messages to conduct operations and maintain links across national borders with his terrorist network.

There is no shortage of terrorist "cookbooks" on the Internet, step-by-step recipes for hackers, crackers (criminal hackers), and cyber terrorists.[2] An adversary can circumvent national militaries completely, armed only with automated "weapons of mass disruption." It is only a matter of time before there is a convergence between those with hostile intent and those with techno-savvy—where the real bad guys exploit the real good stuff.

4. Public Opinion

Malfeasants can easily hide in cyberspace's void and lash out either precisely or indiscriminately. The Internet also provides the perfect medium for people to communicate their ideas, organize initiatives, and execute activities on a distributed basis.[3] This raises the possibility that adversaries could organize covertly on an unprecedented scale. The activities of "hacktivists" such as the J18 and the Electronic Disturbance Theater (EDT) begin to illustrate the potential for global organization and mobilization.

On June 18, 1999, demonstrators organized a global protest, with manifestations in major cities on several continents and along a broad spectrum of agendas. Groups were implored to demonstrate against the rubric of globalization, but without a unified theme or format.

The result was simultaneously orchestrated global disruptions and Internet attacks. In London, individuals described in the media as "evil savages" and "masked thugs" assembled in the financial district in a rampage against capitalism. Stilt-walkers, magicians, jugglers, and musicians lined the streets, targeting the London International Financial Futures and Options Exchange. Dismissed locally as a drunken mob, the "New Age guerrillas" managed to disrupt the ebb and flow of business.

Meanwhile, on the same day in Austin, Texas, a bicycle ride by a group called Critical Mass arrived at a particular coffee shop to be part of a global "reclaim the street" project. As the first set of bikers started to arrive, they encouraged others to stand in the street, which had been barricaded to interrupt traffic. The organizers managed to briefly address the crowd and hand out fliers before the police arrived and dispersed them.

While people protested, the Electronic Disturbance Theater organized a "virtual sit-in," a denial-of-service attack that called on people around the world to point their

Internet browser toward the Zapatista Floodnet URL between 4:00 p.m. and 10:00 p.m. (GMT). The computers continually sent reload commands to the Floodnet site. Floodnet then redirected these requests to the Mexican Embassy in London. Thus, much like the previous two examples, the Internet "streets" were crowded with "people." The results of the virtual sit-in were even more impressive than the physical demonstrations: 18,615 unique contributors from forty-six countries were part of the assault.

The events of June 18, 1999 raise frightening possibilities. Protesters in more than forty countries mobilized on the same day, physically and virtually. If the protests had existed for a single organized purpose, the results could have been devastating. These events further illustrate that the Internet can be both a tool and a target. J18 passed largely unnoticed by the media, which to date has focused only on highly visible activities, while ignoring many of cyber warfare's subtle dangers.

The November 1999 World Trade Organization (WTO) meetings became the site of the most recent iteration of Internet-mobilized protests. Under the same anti-globalization banner, chief organizer Michael Dolan used the Internet to organize and mobilize a large unrelated group of protesters under the collective banner of "NO2WTO." The protesters represented a panoply of issues. Everyone from animal rights activists to supporters of the Zapatistas in Mexico came from all across North America to voice their grievances. The result was the "Battle in Seattle." Individual messages were lost in the ensuing violence. Through their website, a group calling themselves the "Electrohippies" organized a virtual sit-in, shorthand for a denial-of-service attack, just as other groups had done with J18.

J18 and NO2WTO were successful protests in that they succeeded in disrupting that day's, and even that week's, events. They illustrate a new model or principle dubbed "disorganization," or decentralization by experts. This precept encourages many simultaneous local protests addressing specific concerns. Protesters thereby benefit from "demonstrations of scale."

NO2WTO also introduced new faces to the protest crowd. It showed the appeal of being not only able to reach a wider audience, but also in drawing from a larger pool. In many ways, however, this was a one-trick pony. Groups with an established constituency and a defined message, like the AFL-CIO, clearly suffered some loss in legitimacy by association with violent protests. While future protests may lose several better-known organizations, the more radical elements have everything to gain by joining forces and in this paradoxical global-local protest.

Already many of the groups that brought the world J18 and NO2WTO, including the Direct Action Network (DAN) and People's Global Action (PGA), are planning MayDay2000. As May Day has a tradition of protests, chances are that MayDay2000 will be larger in scope than J18 and NO2WTO. Local governments and emergency responders need to be aware of the potential for the type of disruption displayed in Seattle and plan accordingly.

5. Media Misunderstanding

The most visible attacks on American systems result in a disproportionate amount of media attention. Indeed, there has been no shortage of headlines with the recent battle between federal officials and computer intruders. Websites maintained by the Senate, the FBI, the Interior Department, the White House, the U.S. Army, and the North Atlantic Treaty Organization (NATO), to name a few, were defaced in 1999. The transgressions were usually nothing more than graffiti and unsightly annoyances. Meanwhile, a number of truly dangerous incidents have passed relatively unnoticed.

The recent spate of hacker events has drawn a great deal of publicity. The media focused on the attacks against the FBI and Senate web pages and dutifully reported that a top U.S. Justice Department official labeled the attacks as "serious." On June 2, 1999, apparently in retaliation for FBI raids against their peers, hackers overwhelmed the agency's Web site and left messages criticizing the FBI's investigation of the hacker incidents. They were limited to the web pages and did not penetrate the FBI's main computer systems. These attacks were serious in that they disrupted the government's ability to effectively communicate its message to the population at large, but they are not the most serious threats. While the perpetrators should be punished, they do not warrant the highest level of coverage or attention.

Young hackers want to show off, and hacktivists seek to use the Internet as simply another means to draw attention to their respective causes. What both groups have in common is a desire for attention, and the media is happy to oblige. Insufficiently covered in press reports are the discreet and often silent efforts by serious adversaries to develop tools, techniques, and doctrines for conducting information warfare against the United States and its interests. The imbalance of reporting must change in order for the American public to better understand the extent of the emerging threats.

Despite the extensive coverage of web hacks and Web site vandalism, they amount to mere graffiti in cyberspace. While it is essential that the media act responsibly and not panic the citizenry, they play a crucial role in educating the public as to the dangers, both overt and subtle, presented by information warfare.

6. Lessons from Y2K

Insiders and internal saboteurs, either disgruntled employees or moles, are perfectly positioned to wreak havoc within organizations. Moreover, these people know where the most sensitive information is stored, how to access it, and what to steal or damage. Insiders are ideal candidates for subversion by foreign governments or terrorist organizations. Pressure to solve the Y2K dilemma led the United States government and private industry to emphasize expediency over safety in many cases. As a result, thousands of Y2K consultants have been given unprecedented access to systems that are otherwise strictly protected.

Most crisis managers knew a lot about the Y2K problem, but not enough about its possible consequences. There are some issues that have not generated much media interest, but which present possible national security hazards. Aside from the counterintelligence concerns, backdoor Y2K access can be exploited for theft or disruption. Some of the programmers contracted to exterminate the Y2K bug may have exploited their position by leaving a "backdoor," granting them the ability to subsequently access the system undetected. The profile of likely perpetrators in such a scenario would be a highly skilled software engineer who worked on Y2K remediation efforts and understands both the information systems and the business processes of the enterprise that hired them.

Ideally, the Y2K experience should serve as both a wake-up call and a training exercise so that industry and government can use the lessons learned to become better informed about the potential effects and consequences of cyber threats. Hopefully, Y2K will inspire both industry and government to strengthen information protection and infrastructure assurance. Success is possible with plans in place and a course of action.

7. Cyber Invasion

Currently, several countries possess offensive information warfare capabilities comparable to those of the United States. Most of these nations, however, would be foolish to take down U.S. systems, as this would compromise a valuable intelligence collection method for them. Nevertheless, they are conducting surveillance, mapping critical nodes that can be exploited during future crises.

The ability to identify and reconnoiter such targets is today possible due to the Internet and powerful search engines on the World Wide Web. Moreover, information warfare extends the battlefield to incorporate all of society. In the same way that we can no longer rely upon Fort Knox's steel and concrete to protect U.S. financial assets, Americans can no longer rely upon the two oceans to prevent a mainland invasion.

The myth persists that the continental United States has not been invaded since 1812. In reality, invasion through cyberspace has become a daily occurrence. Currently, an Internet-connected computer or server in the United States is broken into every twenty seconds. While an assailant can penetrate borders in a matter of nanoseconds, the law enforcement official charged with their apprehension must stop at these borders and cannot adequately pursue the attacker. In essence, we have created a "global village" without a police department.

Enemies also have the luxury of choosing between civilian and military targets. As military targets become better protected, assailants will naturally turn to more vulnerable prey. Industry and government need to solidify their partnership in the face of this reality.

8. Public and Private Overlap

Due to financial considerations and efficiency principles, military and civilian sectors are interdependent. The U.S. military is becoming increasingly dependent on applications developed by the civilian world. Specifically, U.S. forces rely on Commercial Off-The-Shelf (COTS) technology, and commercial systems and services. U.S. forces also count on commercial transportation services and facilities for mobilization and logistics support. These all have an information technology component, be they air traffic control or ground transportation. These systems are largely under civilian control and are responsible for ensuring the delivery of people and machines from place to place.

About 95 percent of Defense Department communications travel over commercial networks, services, and lines. The substance of the communiques can be protected through encryption, which can better protect confidentiality of information, and to a lesser extent, the integrity of the information. All of the encryption in the world, however, cannot prevent denial-of-service attacks. The physical connections—the satellite links, glass fibers, metal wires, and microwave stations—go relatively unprotected. Additionally, in embracing COTS, the Pentagon is now more likely to purchase hardware, software, and firmware from various domestic and overseas sources. Similar risks occur in business with just-in-time delivery and reliance on electronic information transfers.

9. Privacy vs. National Security

The delicate balance between privacy and security is an ever-present tension in American society. One hundred years ago, government employees did not undergo background investigations for security clearances in the same manner as today. However, over the course of the tumultuous twentieth century, background investigations, security clearances, and loyalty oaths became the necessary price that many Americans paid to serve in critical civilian and military positions.

As government and other organizations compile databases to track everything from driver's licenses to medical histories, Americans have become more sensitive to privacy issues and the specter of numerous "Little Brothers" in addition to "Big Brother." Serious debates are also raging on such matters as encryption technology and the ability to track and trace cellular phones.

Tools that ensure privacy and convenience for the United States do the same for its adversaries. The encryption software that protects sensitive financial information also allows a terrorist to conceal a destructive plot. The ability to track cellular phones may prove critical in stopping or capturing those who are conducting hostile operations. The key issue here is not whether a line must be drawn, but rather, where it will be drawn. The United States must reallocate and manage intelligence assets in order to ensure that policymakers develop an accurate, comprehensive understanding of the threat posed by information warfare. Information must not be trapped in narrow channels, but should instead flow to all sources that may be affected, including business concerns. We do not have to choose between privacy and national security—we can have both.

10. The Rule of Law

Almost all of the issues discussed in this article have legal implications, yet the United States has only just begun to consider the necessity of amending existing laws and passing new ones. Laws that do not necessarily appear to have a direct application to national security are relevant. Unless changes are made to the Freedom of Information Act and certain anti-trust statutes, it will be virtually impossible for industry and government to share information that would help defend against cyber threats.

Almost all U.S. national security legislation is based on American operations in air, on land, on water, and in space. And it is not surprising that a large percentage of U.S. laws concern physical property and associated rights. Many of these laws, and the entities that enforce them, have their authority based upon, and limited by, geography. But with the movement of conflict to the electronic domain, the United States, without delay, must conform its statutes to reflect the corresponding jurisdictional issues. Our legislative and legal mechanisms are admittedly cautious in a world that is moving with ever-increasing speed. Mindful of the tradeoff between these deliberative processes and the rapid development of cyber threats, the United States cannot effectively address twenty-first-century crimes armed only with nineteenth-century laws.

Concluding Thoughts: Community and Defense

The United States has faltered in the face of cyber threats because, despite considerable efforts, the national focus is strategically misplaced. The media misdirects the nation's attention, using more ink to report hacker exploits than the substantive national security threats made possible by information technology. This same technology has also enhanced the role of individuals in the national security arena. Gone are the days when one needed to raise an army, build a command structure, train soldiers, and purchase weapons to attack an adversary. The price of entry is at an all-time low. Widespread destruction can be perpetrated from the comfort of one's living room with inexpensive tools, or over telecommunications networks designed, ironically, for collective convenience.

Industry and government must establish a genuine partnership. In some way, we must introduce the "sandals" to the "wingtips." The Department of Defense should not be the only entity concerned with defending American interests in cyberspace. Government no longer has the luxury of having all the knowledge or assuming that it will be in a position to provide all of the answers. If we are to ensure that all relevant parties have a seat at the table, a bigger table must be furnished.

The administration should be applauded for its initial first efforts with PDD-63. However, to truly enhance national security, such efforts must extend beyond the government-centered parameters of PDD-63. The United States must make an irrevocable commitment in terms of education, awareness, sensible application of technology, and decisive action.

Perhaps the old notion that security begins in the communities-neighbors watching out for each other-is more significant now than ever before. Interconnectedness will become the sine qua non of everyday life now that everyone has a vested interest in community protection. As interdependence among institutions and individuals grows, particularly in the realm of cyberspace, the distinctions between public and private, industry and government, and "your" and "my" responsibility fade, and are replaced by "our" responsibility.

President John F. Kennedy once said, "The best time to fix the roof is when the sun is shining." The time to begin thinking about, and addressing, the challenges posed by cyber threats is now.

Critical Thinking Questions

1. While there are clearly vulnerabilities in cyberspace, do you agree with the common use of the term "cyberterrorism"? Why or why not?
2. What kinds of cyber attacks should we be most concerned about?
3. What can/should our local, state, and federal agencies, as well as the private sector, do to mitigate or diminish this kind of threat to our homeland?

Notes

The authors would like to acknowledge the substantial contributions made by George C. Salmoiraghi, a third-year student at the University of Richmond Law School.

1. For a more in-depth review, see Frank J. Cilluffo and Curt H. Gergely, "Information Warfare and Strategic Terrorism," *Terrorism and Political Violence,* Vol. 9, No. 1 (Spring 1997): 84–94.
2. For a more in-depth review, see CSIS, *Cybercrime, Cyberterrorism, and Cyberwarfare: Averting and Electronic Waterloo,* Global Organized Crime Project 1998.
3. For a more in-depth review, see John Arquilla and David Ronfeldt (eds.), *In Athena's Camp: Preparing for Conflict in the Information Age* (Santa Monica, CA: the RAND Corporation, 1997).

Homeland Security on the Hyperborder

U.S.-Mexico Drug War Interactions

John P. Sullivan

The nearly 2,000 mile-long frontier (*frontera*) separating the United States (U.S.) and Mexico is one of the most complex border zones in the world.[1] The border is bounded by the U.S. states of California, Arizona, New Mexico, and Texas and the Mexican states of Baja California, Sonora, Chihuahua, Coahuila, Nuevo León, and Tamaulipas.[2] Commerce and people—licit and illicit—go through 45 legal border crossings with nearly five million cars and trucks transiting each year. An estimated half million illegal entries into the U.S. occur each year.[3]

A complex web of federal, state, local, and tribal law enforcement agencies (LEAs) protect the U.S. side of the border. These include elements of the Department of Homeland Security, such as Customs and Border Protection (CBP), Immigrations and Customs Enforcement (ICE), the Bureau of Alcohol, Tobacco, Firearms and Explosives (ATF), the United States Coast Guard, and the Border Patrol (an element of CBP). Over 20,000 border patrol agents guard the U.S. side of the frontier (at points of entry and interior checkpoints).[4] These agencies are joined by Department of Justice components, including the Federal Bureau of Investigation (FBI) and Drug Enforcement Administration (DEA).

In addition, Border Enforcement Security Task Forces (BEST) and Alliance(s) to Combat Transnational Threats (ACTT) linking numerous federal, state, local and tribal agencies—police and sheriffs—are augmented by a Southwest Border Task Force, National Guard forces from border states, and Department of Defense support LEAs in the form of the U.S. Northern Command's Joint Task Force North (JTF-North), the El Paso Intelligence Center (a specialty fusion center) and the U.S. Intelligence Community. Mexican federal police, customs (*adjuana*), army (SEDENA) and naval (SEMAR) forces, as well as numerous state and municipal police patrol the Mexican side of the frontier.

The border has two major functions, in addition to delineating the boundaries of national space: controlling access and facilitating the flow of commerce. The functions often result in tension, and a balance between the two is necessary. Key concerns in the border zone include security (national and public security), immigration/migration, energy security (protecting critical infrastructure including pipelines and petroleum extraction capacities), water supply, environmental preservation, communications, and transport infrastructure (including points of entry). Within these broad concerns, authorities face several criminal and homeland security challenges including:

- Illegal/undocumented immigration/migration
- Human trafficking (and slavery)
- Drug trafficking
- Smuggling
  - Small arms
  - Contraband/piracy

    - Weapons of Mass Destruction (especially fissile materials and nuclear components)
    - Terrorist penetration
- Money laundering
- Cross-border violence
- Kidnapping
- Home invasion robberies

Spillover of border violence and corruption are also key concerns, as is the threat that terrorists will enter the porous border to conduct attacks in the U.S. Together these issues involve crime control (local, cross-border, and transnational) and homeland security. At times the terrorist and national security dimensions of cartel violence may require homeland defense and military options as well.

Smuggling involves the movement of people and illicit goods across the border. This activity is facilitated by tunnels, trains, vehicles, ultralights, vessels (*pangas* and narco-submarines)[5], and human-borne means. In reaction to these concerns (which are facilitated by transnational organized crime and cross-border gangs) the once quiet 'borderland' or 'borderworld' has become a contested place. As one commentator put it, " What was once little more than a line on the map has become a theater of operations."[6]

The 'Hyperborder'

This theater of operations is a complex mix of commerce, contention and cooperation—as Rodger Hodge notes, "Patrolled by Predator drones, radar blimps, dogs, and scanners, the U.S./Mexico border is now a state unto itself: Borderworld."[7] U.S.-Mexico border communities are inherently tied together by history, culture, and socio-economics. Frequently these communities are referred to as 'border pairs,' 'sister cities,' and 'borderplex regions.' Given the importance of these bilateral population centers to economic activity (licit and illicit), an understanding of Mexico's border population is important, inasmuch as it provides the context for framing the southwest border region's criminal underworld within its legitimate communities.

According to the U.S.-Mexico Border Counties Coalition,[8] Mexico's border populations are concentrated primarily in the same regions as their U.S. counterparts.[9] There are 35 border *municipios* (similar to U.S. counties) in Mexico; three in Baja California, six in Coahuila, six in Chihuahua, one in Nuevo León, ten in Sonora, and nine in Tamaulipas.[10]

In addition, "The two most important border economies with the largest concentration of *maquiladora* (manufacturing) employment are split between Tijuana, Baja California and Ciudad Juárez, Chihuahua."[11] In addition to crime, key cross-border policy issues that influence homeland security policy include the economy, labor, income, education, the environment, health, trade and traffic, immigration (in a broad sense), housing, and public funding and taxation. All of these issues influence border and homeland security policy, operations, and human space on both sides of the frontier.

Because of the complexities, the U.S.-Mexico border zone has been termed the 'hyperborder." The designation is from the seminal 'geosocial' ethnography of architect Fernando Romero.[12] Romero asserts that the "roving vigilantes, fear-mongering politicians, hysterical pundits, and the looming shadow of a 700-mile-long fence [make] the United States-Mexico border . . . one of the most complex and dynamic areas on the planet today."[13]

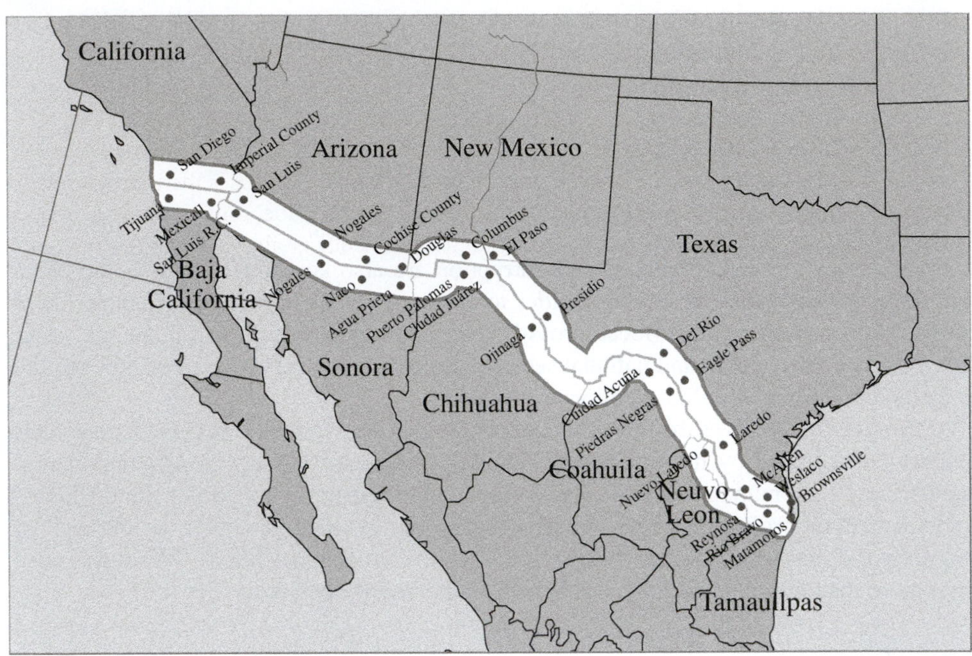

FIGURE 1 Map of U.S.-Mexico Border and Sister Cities

Source: http://www.epa.gov/usmexicoborder/indicators/images/border2012-sister-city-map.jpg

According to Romero, "Crime, corruption, free trade, urbanization, resource scarcity, migration, border control, death, and environmental degradation . . . define the nature of the hyperborder, making the boundary unique in the contemporary world for the breadth of issues confronting it."[14] According to Romero (and others) the economic disparity of the border zone breeds illegal activity. The zone is estimated to be home to 24 million persons (90% of which live in the zone's 14 twin cities)[15] in 2012.[16] Narcotraffickers, enticed by the huge and lucrative demand for drugs in the U.S., bring corruption, instability, and violence to the otherwise robust cross-cultural crucible.

The border region is fueled by cross-border remittances, shared cultural references (such as *narcocorridos* – drug ballads), family ties, and in notable cases cross-border gangs (discussed later) and cross-border tribal nations. One example of a cross-border tribal nation is the Tohono O'odham Nation located west of Tucson and ranging across mountains into Mexico (Sonora). The tribe controls a sovereign enclave the size of Connecticut. Elements of the nation are believed to have facilitated narco-trade ties to the Sinaloa Federation and/or the porous sovereignty of the enclave, presenting a unique bi-lateral (or tri-lateral) security challenge.[17]

The border zone includes a variety of terrain features—urban wastelands, rivers, lakes, arid desert, and pastureland. The boundary ranges from modern, sensor-embedded walls and fences, to wooden picket fences, to strands of barbwire, to a virtual fence, to no barrier at all. The frontier transverses coastline and littoral space, desert, cities, and stark cliffs; all-in-all a challenging operational space to control, interdict transgressors and deter smugglers of people (*coyotes*) and contraband.

The 'hyperborder' is also contiguous with the 'Drug War Zone' (DWZ), which is a terrain of social and political transformation. Anthropologist Howard Campbell coined the term 'drug war zone' to describe the cultural world of drug traffickers (narco-culture or *narcocultura*) and the law enforcement agents that counter it. The DWZ is the transnational, fluid space where contending forces battle over the meaning, value, and control of drugs. For Campbell, the DWZ is not only a geographic space, but is also a symbolic domain where drug producers, drug smugglers and drug consumers are connected to their police, military, and intelligence counterparts in a strategic, tactical, and ideological fight.[18]

Frontier Threats

Border zones are assessed by many analysts to be areas subject to weak state control. Frontiers, as a result of their complex cross-border connections, are sometimes incubators of criminal instability and violence. Weak state presence in many frontier areas and the lucrative drug trade is combining to challenge state sovereignty in acute ways. Cross-border criminal networks engage in a range of crimes, including drug trafficking and counterfeiting (the most lucrative according to the United Nations Office on Drugs and Crime) and human trafficking with about 2.4 million victims at any given time.[19] Globally, cross-border crime is estimated to be worth about $870 billion per year (about 1.5 percent of the world's gross domestic product).[20] These economic drivers demonstrate the links of U.S. border and homeland security to broader global economic factors. Weak state presence in areas proximate to the U.S. Southern Border enable potential cross-border threat groups to find a secure base for sustaining their cross-border operations into the U.S. In the simplest case, drug cartels with a secure foundation in Mexican border states can stage drugs and people for transshipment into the U.S. Weak state institutions allow them to operate these staging areas with minimal interference. The vast size of these global economic flows gives these actors sufficient resource capability to wage operations that challenge U.S. homeland security and border security efforts.

Further, as Sullivan and Elkus observed, "Border zones are potential incubators of conflict. Criminal gangs exploit weak state presence to forge a parallel state and prosecute their criminal enterprises sustained by fear, violence and brutality."[21] Border-zones are natural transit corridors. When enforcement pressures in neighboring states increase, criminal activity and violence are also prone to spill over. Border zones, such as Guatemala's Petén province are incubators of instability and ideal venues for refueling, repackaging product, and warehousing drug stockpiles. While this was first realized in Guatemala and Honduras, all Central America to the south and the U.S. 'hyperborder' zone are currently at risk of being caught in the 'cross-border' spillover of Mexico's drug wars. Controlling these border zones is a key homeland security function for Mexico and a parallel national security concern for the U.S., since weakness here impacts the U.S. Southern Border; in addition, a strong Mexican Southern Border is necessary to contain the freedom of movement of transnational gangs and cartels. Helping Mexico contain its *frontera del sur* (Southern Border) will enhance U.S. border security and efforts to stem illicit flows.

Frontier crime management is also imperative to control the grey and illicit informal economies that thrive around Latin American border zones and the U.S.-Mexico 'hyperborder'. U.S. homeland security could be strengthened by extending our sense of perimeter to a layered defense where we support key allies and homeland security efforts for Central American countries along the supply chain of illicit goods. This approach is currently being implemented as part of the CBP 'Illicit Pathways Attack Strategy (IPAS' where CBP homeland security investigations personnel go beyond physical U.S. borders to attack illicit pathways and breakdown transnational criminal networks that operate in the U.S.[22]

Contemporary border security is an integral component of both homeland and national security due to the impact of transnational crime and terrorism. Indeed both can be considered components of global security.[23] Border security initiatives which were typically restricted to the frontier and border zone now augment police and homeland security operations throughout the U.S. and abroad. ICE currently deploys 7,000 agents to 200 cities throughout the U.S. and has 71 offices in 47 countries worldwide. This wide-ranging deployment is designed to disrupt the illicit pathways of transnational crime.[24]

Mexico's Drug War

Mexico is embroiled in a complex drug war where a series of battles to control a hyper-competitive drug market brings a range of criminal enterprises and the state into conflict. Mexico's criminal markets are key nodes in the network of global illicit economic circuits. Drug trafficking is one major niche in this illicit trade, but other illicit goods and services are also involved. The drug market is a key point of contention in the battle among cartels and gangs.[25] Deaths attributed to the drug war (which started under Vicente Fox, but matured under the *sexenio*—six-year term—of Felipe Calderón) are estimated at between 47,000 and 71,000 persons.[26] An additional 24,000 persons are listed as missing (*desaparecidos*); of the known dead, 16,000 are unidentified.[27] Violence isn't the only concern; barbarism and battle prowess exemplified by new weaponry (*narcotanques* or improvised infantry fighting vehicles), grenade attacks, beheadings, and information operations (including *narcomensajes* [coercive public messages] in the form of *narcomantas* [banners], *narcopintas* [graffiti messages], *narcobloqueos* [street blockades], and 'corpse-messaging'—leaving a message on a mutilated corpse) help to shape the operational space.

Kidnappings—including kidnappings for ransom, express kidnappings (*levantons*), cross-border kidnappings, and kidnap-torture-murders—and attacks on journalists, mayors, police, and civil society in general punctuate the inter-cartel battles. *Narcocultura* [narco culture] in the form of alternate belief systems such as the cult of Santa Muerte and Jesus Malverde and reinforced by *narcocorridos* [drug ballads] support the narco worldview. Mass graves (*narcofosas*) and social cleansing (mass targeted murders within cartel zones of influence) provide brutal context for the violence. It has been estimated that over half of all Mexico's municipalities are influenced by organized crime, with 60–65% of Mexican municipalities impacted by cartels, gangs and narco-trafficking groups. Drug cartels have reportedly infiltrated over 1,500 Mexican cities, and use them as the base for kidnappings, extortions, and vehicle thefts. In addition, or perhaps as a consequence, 980 'zones of impunity' where criminal bands operate unchecked were reported in 2009. In these 980 'zones of impunity' or 'criminal enclaves,' organized crime has more control than the Mexican State.[28]

While many view this as insecurity, high intensity crime, or organized crime as usual, other analysts have characterized this as 'criminal insurgency.' Criminal insurgency is different from conventional terrorism and insurgency because the criminal insurgents' sole political motive is to gain autonomy and economic control over territory. They do so by creating criminal enclaves in which they can freely maneuver. The result is a "hollowing" of many state functions or hollow state.[29] Criminal insurgencies challenge the state by generating high intensity criminal violence that erodes the legitimacy and solvency of state institutions.[30]

According to David Shirk, director of the Trans-Border Institute at the University of San Diego, the security crisis in Mexico is a reflection of the country's decades-long economic struggles. Shirk observes that Mexico's underground (informal or gray and black) economy—including street vendors, pirate taxis, and contraband goods—accounts for 40 percent of all economic activity.[31] In addition, the illegal drug trade (production and trafficking) provides employment for an estimated 450,000 people and constitutes about 3–4 percent of Mexico's greater than $1 trillion GDP.[32] Jobs filled by the drug trade include a range of specialties: pilots, drivers, logisticians, lookouts, enforcers, *sicarios* (assassins), etc. The hyper competition to control these markets when confronted with enforcement from the state, fractionalization of cartels, proliferation of violence, and decentralization of cartel-gang operations results in a chaotic and unpredictable pattern of violent conflict in Mexico.[33] Much of this violence is centered within the Northern Border States of Mexico and is focused on the *plazas* (or key transshipment points)—many of which are in twin cities on the U.S.-Mexican border.

The Mexican Drug Trade

Mexico's drug trade includes the production and transshipment of heroin and marijuana, the production of methamphetamine, and the transshipment of South American cocaine and heroin. As these narco products (*i.e.,* illicit pharma) move through the supply chain there is an opportunity to extract profit. The transport corridors, staging areas, markets and *plazas* provide an opportunity for a range of criminal actors to extract financial gain.

As a result, money laundering and corruption become key adjuncts to the drug trade. The global drug trade has significant destabilizing effects on society, nations, communities, crime, and policy. For the United States, illegal drugs are a "$60 billion-dollar-per-year industry patronized by at least 16 million Americans."[34] Violence and drug trafficking are an intersecting problem. Drug profits fuel corruption and violent conflict. They introduce and reinforce existing conflicts and social fissures, empower gangs and criminal enterprise, and contribute to an erosion of state authority and legitimacy.

The size of the U.S. market for illicit drugs, combined with the inflationary pressure of prohibition on prices allows Mexican gangsters to earn enormous profits, estimated at $6–$7 billion annually.[35] Ironically, the profit margin increases as the border becomes more secure. Traffickers can add a premium to the cost of transshipping drugs and contraband across secured space. The northbound drug trade is augmented by a range of criminal enterprises, foremost money laundering and illicit financial transactions to reinvest narco-profits, the illegal southbound weapons trade in small arms, and human trafficking.

Human trafficking, such as trafficking for the purposes of sexual exploitation and labor exploitation (including child labor) often involves slavery and brutalization. Smuggling of migrants is another dimension of shadow migration. No solid estimates of the size of the cross-border trade exist, but cartels (such as the Zetas) and gangs (such as

MS-13) are believed to be active in this trade. The Zetas are believed to have committed multiple acts of atrocity against migrants—many transversing Mexico to reach the U.S. from Latin America. In one notable act of barbarity 72 migrants (58 men and 14 women) were executed in Tamaulipas in August 2010. The executions are believed to be based upon a refusal of the migrants to pay extortion fees to the gangsters or alternatively become conscripts for the gang. Similar massacres have led to the discovery of mass graves (*fosas*) on a recurrent basis.[36] Refugees (and internally displaced persons-IDPs) present a similar challenge, as people flee narco-violence (and social cleansing by gangs) to the U.S. and other parts of Mexico.[37]

As a consequence of Mexico's proximity to the United States (which has a huge illicit drug market), Mexico is a key transshipment zone in the movement of narcotics from South America. As a key node in the distribution chain, Mexico serves as a staging area, and a transshipment node, produces its own illicit pharma, and increasingly has its own growing internal market for drug use. This confluence of geographic and economic factors has placed Mexico at the center of global narcotic flows. As a result, a range of criminal, armed non-state actors contend for dominance within the economic space. This places these actors at odds with the government and each other. Battles for supremacy and freedom of action have led to significant drug violence.

Key border cities—functioning as *plazas*—are lucrative nodes in this global distribution chain.[38] Border cities such as Tijuana (bordering San Diego), Ciudad Juárez (bordering El Paso), and Nuevo Laredo (bordering Laredo, Texas) are key strategic nodes where battles for cartel supremacy have been waged. These battles for the *plazas* involve brute force, area denial, deterrence and punishment as tactical tools of the cartels and their gang proxies. Ambushes, attacks on police, beheadings, dismemberments, car bomb attacks, and infantry style attacks are among the tactics, techniques and procedures (TTPs) utilized in cartel conflict. Barbarization is a strategic approach to ward off interference. Rival gangsters, the police, journalists, mayors, soldiers, and at times the public fall prey to the brutal narco-warriors known as *sicarios.*

Cross-Border Crime and Gangs: Impact of Transnational Gangs in the U.S.

Containing cross-border crime at the border is difficult if not impossible. The large financial gains made by smuggling drugs, weapons, people, and contraband across the border attract gangsters on both sides of the border. As a result, transnational gangs forge alliances with criminal enterprises on both sides of the border to facilitate their illicit flows. Gangs in the U.S. are increasingly linked to cross-border activities. As a result, traditional local law enforcement is now linked to border and homeland security in new ways. For example, CBP has implemented an Anti-Gang Initiative (AGI) involving liaison and cooperative investigations with the FBI, DEA, U.S. Bureau of Prisons, and ICE. These linkages can be expected to expand as the transnational criminal threat matures, making the relationship between local U.S. and foreign law enforcement agencies a homeland security policy issue for the foreseeable future.

Gangs on the Southwest Border pose a significant on-going criminal threat. The frontier is rugged, rural, and porous. Nearly 2,000 miles of contiguous U.S.-Mexican territory is an active home for a range of criminal activity, including drug and arms trafficking, alien smuggling, human trafficking, extortion, kidnapping, and corruption. U.S.-based gangs, Mexican cartels (drug trafficking organizations, or DTOs), and other criminal enterprises in both the United States and Mexico exploit this fluid region to extract profit. To do so they employ wide-reaching hybrid drug/crime networks; smuggling drugs, arms, and illegal immigrants; and serving as enforcers for cartel interests on both sides of the U.S.-Mexico border.

U.S. gangs on the border are increasingly 'trans-border' gangs with links to the cartels. This is not surprising, as cartels require armed/violent structures to counter threats and challenges from other illicit enterprises and the state. Specifically cartels and their illicit networks need to protect operations (plazas, transport routes, clandestine labs, business processes, and personnel), they need to protect clients who purchase protection, they need personnel to extract 'street taxes,' and they need personnel to attack adversaries and exert their will. These personnel can be internal operatives or allies and outsourced enforcers (contractors, *sicarios,* and gangs).

Notable cross-border (or transnational) gangs[39] include Mara Salvatrucha (MS-13),[40] 18th Street,[41] the Logan Heights gangs, Barrio Azteca/Los Aztecas and La Línea. La Línea is notable because it is a hybrid entity, networked with a range of non-state criminal actors in Mexico's drug war. It serves as an enforcement and tax collection cell for the Juárez cartel but is also linked to corrupt police and various Azteca factions. It essentially appears to be a mercenary variant of a third generation gang.[42] Table 1 lists U.S. gangs with links to Mexican DTOs.

The 2011 National Gang Threat Assessment (NGTA) notes that many U.S. gangs have strong working links with Central American and Mexican gangs. Since Mexican drug trafficking organizations (MDTOs) control most of the cocaine, heroin, methamphetamine and marijuana shipped into the U.S., this is significant. The U.S. gangs play key enforcer roles in this transshipment.[43] These enforcer roles penetrate past the border zone. For example, according to the NGTA, the Sinaloa Cartel uses local Los Angeles gang members as proxies for participating in kidnappings, selling and obtaining drugs, and collecting the proceeds from drug transactions.[44]

In addition, law enforcement agencies reported to the National Gang Intelligence Center (NGIC) that gangs in their jurisdictions have ties to Mexican criminal organizations. These were summarized as:[45]

- Well-established U.S. prison gangs such as the Hermanos de Pistoleros Latinos (HPI), *la Eme* [the California Mexican Mafia], the Texas Syndicate, Barrio Azteca and the Tango Blast are reportedly aligned with or connected to MDTOs;
- Street gangs such as the Latin Kings, MS13, Sureños, and Norteños maintain working relationships with MDTOs;
- Sureños in California and South Carolina maintain an association with the Los Zetas Cartel in Mexico;
- According to 2010 California Department of Corrections and Rehabilitation (CDCR) and open source reporting, some Aryan Brotherhood and *la Eme* prison gang members—bitter rivals inside prison—work together with MDTOs to smuggle drugs into California and prisons, steal vehicles, smuggle illegal weapons into Mexico, and intimidate rivals of the Mexican cartels.

TABLE 1 U.S.-based Gangs with Ties to Mexican DTOs

Arizona New Mexican Mafia
Aryan Brotherhood
Avenues
Bandidos
Barrio Azteca
Barrio Westside
Black Guerilla Family
Bloods
California Mexican Mafia (Eme)
Crips
Hardtimes 13
Happytown Pomona
Hells Angels
Hermanos de Pistoleros Latinos (HPL)
La Nuestra Familia
Latin Kings
Lennox 13
Mara Salvatrucha (MS-13)
Mexican Mafia
Mongols
Norteños
Satins Disciples
Sureños
Tango Blast
Texas Mexican Mafia (Mexikanemi)
Texas Syndicate
Tri-City Bombers
Vagos Vatos Locos
Westside Nogalitas
Wetback Power
Wonder Boys
18th Street Gang

Source: 2011 National Gang Threat Assessment

According to the 2011 NGTA, "Hispanic prison gangs along the Southwest border region are strengthening their ties with MDTOs [Mexican Drug Trafficking Organizations] to acquire wholesale quantities of drugs, based upon National Drug Intelligence Center (NDIC) reporting. In exchange for a consistent drug supply, U.S.-based gangs smuggle and distribute drugs, collect drug proceeds, launder money, smuggle weapons, commit kidnappings, and serve as lookouts and enforcers on behalf of the MDTOs. MDTOs subsequently profit from increased drug circulation in the United States, while U.S.-based gangs have access to a consistent drug supply which expands their influence, power, and ability to recruit."[46]

Collaboration between U.S. gangs and Mexican Cartels varies widely but according to the 2011 National Drug Threat Assessment (NDTA) generally involve one of three types of relationships—business, partnership, or franchise.[47] Most U.S. gangs with

Mexican cartel ties are in a business relationship that involves purchasing drugs from cartel members or associates for distribution by the gang. Some U.S. gangs form partnerships with Mexican traffickers and distribute drugs for the cartels; they often provide warehousing, security, and/or transportation services as well. A few U.S. gangs act as franchises of Mexican cartels, operating as extensions of the organizations in the United States. For example:[48]

- Members of California's 38th Street gang operating in Los Angeles have established business relationships with traffickers in Mexico to distribute methamphetamine and cocaine in southern California.
- The California Mexican Mafia (*la Eme*) in San Diego maintains a close partnership with members of the Tijuana Cartel for purchasing multi-kilogram quantities of cocaine and marijuana for distribution throughout southern California.
- The Barrio Azteca, a Texas prison gang, serves as a franchise for the Juárez Cartel—gang leaders use members to carry out enforcement operations as well as to smuggle, transport, and distribute cocaine and methamphetamine in the United States and to smuggle cash and weapons to Mexico.

The Tijuana Cartel (Arellano-Félix Organization) in Baja California is key to trade into California. It currently is believed to have a power sharing arrangement with the Sinaloa Cartel. Cross-border links in Tijuana include links with San Diego Street gangs (such as Logan Heights), Sureño gangs, Mara Salvatrucha (MS-13) and *Eme* (the Mexican Mafia). Ciudad Juárez, contested by the Juárez cartel, Sinaloa Cartel, and Los Zetas (as well as a number of transborder gangs) has been the site of high intensity violence. The 2011 NDTA reported that "Mexican-based cartels dominate the supply, trafficking, and wholesale distribution in the United States."[49] Documented links between Mexican Cartels and U.S. gangs are displayed in Table 2.

Securing the 'Hyperborder'

Securing the border involves a range of operations. Broadly speaking, these are centered on *interdiction* (disrupting illegal movements across borders), aimed at *deterrence* of cross-border crime (that is, dissuading would be smugglers, criminals and terrorists from making illegal border crossings). These are supported by *intelligence* (increasingly networked in nature) to collect, fuse, analyze, and disseminate operational warning.[50] These operations must occur at border crossings (ports of entry) and in between along the frontier.

Human patrols and human operated checkpoints (such as those at border crossings) are a major element of this interdiction. These involve dismounted and vehicle borne patrols, patrols on horseback,and riverine and maritime patrols supported from the air in helicopters, planes, and increasingly unmanned aerial vehicles (UAVs). For the U.S., most border checks involve inspecting northbound persons, vehicles, and cargo. The Mexican government also conducts checks. Explosive and narcotics detection canines (K-9s) are currently used on both sides of the border, as are a dynamic mix of customs, immigration, border patrol, police, and military operations.

In Texas, the Texas Department of Public Safety (which is comprised of the Highway Patrol and Texas Rangers, who were formed to address the cross-border violence of an

TABLE 2 Mexican Cartel-U.S. Gang Alliances

Cartel	Aligned with
The Sinaloa Cartel (aka Guzman-Loera Organization or Pacific Cartel)	Hermanos de Pistoleros Latinos
	New Mexico Syndicate
	Los Carnales
	Latin Kings
	Mexican Mafia (Eme) (California)
	Sureños
	MS-13
	Arizona Mexican Mafia (Old & New)
	Wet Back Power
	Sinaloa Cowboys
	West Texas Tangos
	Border Brothers (California)
	Border Brothers (Arizona)
La Familia Michoacana Cartel (Formerly part of los Zetas under the authority of the Gulf Cartel)	Sureños
	MS-13
	West Texas Tangos
Los Zetas	Barrio Azteca
	Hermanos de Pistoleros latinos
	Mexikanemi
	Texas Syndicate
	MS-13
Cardenas-Guillen Cartel (Gulf Cartel)	Hermanos de Pistoleros Latinos
	Partido Revolutionary Mexicano
	Raza Unida
	Texas Chicano Brotherhood
Vincente Carrillo-Fuentes Cartel (Juárez Cartel)	Hermanos de Pistoleros Latinos
	Barrio Azteca
	New Mexico Syndicate
	Los Carnales
Arellano-Félix Cartel (Tijuana Cartel)	Mexican Mafia (Eme) (California)
	Sureños
	Arizona Mexican Mafia (Old & New)
	Border Brothers (California)

Source: National Gang intelligence Center, 2011 National Gang Threat Assessment, APPENDIX B. MDTOs Alliances and Rivals.

earlier era) recently initiated riverine gunboat patrols of the Rio Grande (Rio Bravo) and Intercoastal Waterway. A total of six lightly armored 34' fast patrol vessels, each equipped with six M-240, 30-caliber automatic machine guns will be deployed.[51] According to the *Wired* magazine *Danger Room* blog, "As many as 40 percent of car chases in populated Hidalgo County across from the Mexican border city of Reynosa end up with the suspects escaping, many of them in "splashdowns" after dumping their vehicles in the river."[52]

The gunboats also address concerns about cross-border cartel violence. Falcon Lake, a water reservoir along the river, has been the site of several violent incidents, involving shootouts between Mexican security forces and Zeta gunmen. In one incident in May

2011, a Mexican marine was killed along with 13 gunmen during a firefight on an island in the lake. Earlier on 30 September 2010, pirates (believed to be *Zetitas,* so-called "baby Zetas") operating in Falcon Lake shot and killed U.S. citizen David Hartley while he was vacationing with his wife. Hence the gunboats.[53]

On the U.S. side for example, border patrol deployments grew from 2,900 agents in 1980 to around 4,000 agents in 1994 (at the start of the North American Free Trade Area-NAFTA). As U.S. concerns about the drug trade and undocumented migrants grew, so did border security. New fencing and high-tech surveillance systems (sensors, cameras, etc.) were added to the human patrols and by 2000 the border patrol had more than doubled in size, fielding over 9,000 agents. After the 9/11 attacks again reinforced public and administration concerns over the border, and by the end of President Obama's first year in office, the border patrol had once again more than doubled in size, deploying more than 20,000 agents; total border security spending grew to more than $40 billion annually (up from about $20 billion in 2002 and about $10 billion in 1996).[54] Unintended consequences of heightened interdiction include traffic congestion at border crossings leading to obstructions of legitimate commerce and movement and the increased sophistication of cross-border smuggling operations as exemplified by the complex network of illicit cross-border tunnels operated by the cartels.[55]

The Mérida Initiative

The Mérida Initiative is a U.S. initiative to support Mexico's battle against organized crime. It has four pillars: 1) disrupt organized crime groups, 2) strengthen institutions (such as the police, judiciary, and corrections), 3) build a "21st Century Border," and 4) build strong and resilient communities. Building a 21st Century border essentially means bringing high technology support to interdiction operations through the use of high-tech sensor platforms and digital information processing to facilitate operations and intelligence. Since the initiative began in FY 2008, the U.S. has appropriated $1.6 billion to the program.[56]

Bi-Lateral/Cross-Border Cooperation

Addressing the complex issues of the 'hyperborder' require enhancing the already unprecedented levels of cooperation by U.S.-Mexican authorities. This should include joint initiatives by the United States Government (USG) and Government of Mexico (GOM), as well as a range of sub-national 'state' and local initiatives. These must include cooperation by customs authorities, LEAs, and potential expanded joint border patrols (and potentially the development of a reformed Federal Frontier Police for Mexico).

The complexity of U.S. government agencies working on border security within the homeland security domain potentially complicates operations. Complication could arise from bureaucratic competition, poor liaison, or the ambiguity of jurisdictional boundaries. Future homeland security policy debate can be expected over both organizational configuration and jurisdictional boundaries.

One simple suggestion for reorganizing bureaucratic alignments was suggested by border scholar David Danelo, who observed that the jurisdictional boundaries of the wide range of U.S.-Mexico, state and local enforcement and security services on the border had a complex set of asymmetric boundaries. In Danelos' own words:[57]

> One strategic security solution may begin with organizing U.S. and Mexican forces, as well as state and local counterparts, along the same terrain into parallel zones of operation. The U.S. Border Patrol deploys units on the southwest border into nine sectors—which have not changed since 1924 when the Border Patrol was formed in response to U.S. demands for illegal alcohol during Prohibition. In Texas, the boundaries of the Border Patrol sectors do not correspond with the Texas Department of Public Safety's six sectors (developed in 2002), let alone Mexico's four military sectors (which represent Mexico's only security structure on their northern border).

Communications, cooperation and intelligence sharing (and 'co-production' of intelligence) along the border involving the range of enforcement and security agencies and responders must be enhanced. Avenues of bi-lateral cooperation that could be expanded or leveraged to reform the border and build a truly functional and resilient 21st Century border include the U.S.-Mexico Bi-Lateral Commission (especially the Working Group on Homeland Security and Border Cooperation), the U.S.-Mexico Military Commission, the Border Governors Conference, the Conference of Border Attorneys General, border state consular officials, and a range of civil society non-governmental organizations.

Technology, including enhanced trusted traveler (*e.g.,* Secure Electronic Network for Traveler's Rapid Inspection-SENTRI) and commercial cargo (e.g., Free and Secure Trade Program-FAST) initiatives need to be expanded and augmented with a cross-border communications system and non-intrusive detection that balance security, congestion management, and ease of flow.

Conclusion

The policy dimensions of U.S. border security are constantly evolving. On the Southern Border, we have seen a simple access control issue mature into a homeland security frontier, where securing the border goes beyond checkpoints at points of entry to securing the entire border zone and beyond. Future homeland security analysts and practitioners are thus faced with calibrating border security with broader homeland security efforts. Certainly immigration policy will continue to be part of this debate, but in all likelihood containing transnational illicit flows and transnational gangs and cartels will be a growing part of this security equation. Homeland security, national security and law enforcement (domestic and transnational) are likely to interact more often and in new ways, fueling the potential growth of a global security approach. This will demand new skills for individual practitioners and organizations, as well as potential reorganization of organizational structure and relationships.

Securing the complex U.S.-Mexico 'hyperborder' is a complicated, yet essential task. The border zone is more than a line *(la línea)* demarking state boundaries and containing threats, it is a vital and economically essential component of both nations and an essential node in the global flow of commerce (unfortunately illicit and well as licit). Developing the much heralded '21st Century' border will require continuing trust by all the agencies working to secure and manage the border enterprise. This will require the development of clear policy, negotiation and much on-going work both at the frontier and in the border zone, and indeed throughout both nations. Transnational criminal organizations are early beneficiaries of the global economy. Their illicit flows of commerce and finance fuel conflict and violence far from the twin border cities. Their reach extends into inner cities and suburbs throughout both the U.S. and Mexico and, while Mexican cartels and the drug traffic have a border nexus, their threat penetrates much deeper. Hence border security needs to be prioritized as a critical element of both U.S. and Mexican public and national security policy and practice, and better integrated into the comprehensive security structure of both nations.

Critical Thinking Questions

1. What are the most pressing challenges in protecting our nation's borders?
2. While these challenges are clearly important to border states, do they matter to the rest of the U.S.? Why or why not?
3. What can local, state, and federal authorities do about border security that is not already being done?

Notes

1. The border is actually 3,189 km or 1,969 miles in length. It follows the middle of the Rio Grande—according to the 1848 Treaty of Guadalupe Hidalgo between the two nations, "along the deepest channel"—from its mouth on the Gulf of Mexico a distance of 2,019 km (1,255 mi) to a point just upstream of El Paso and Ciudad Juárez. It then follows an alignment westward overland and marked by monuments a distance of 858 km (533 mi) to the Colorado River, during which it reaches its highest elevation at the intersection with the Continental Divide. Thence it follows the middle of that river northward a distance of 38 km (24 mi), and then it again follows an alignment westward overland and marked by monuments a distance of 226 km (140 mi) to the Pacific Ocean.
2. See David J. Danelo, *The Border: Exploring the U.S.-Mexico Divide,* Mecanicsburg, PA: Stackpole Books, 2008 for a vivid view of the border's terrain and humanscape.
3. These figures are found at Wikipedia: *http://en.wikipedia.org/wiki/Mexico–United_States_border*
4. The U.S. Department of Homeland Security, Customs and Border Protection (CBP) Budget Request for FY 2013 would deploy 21,3000 Border patrol agents 1,200 CBP Air and Marine Agents, and 21,100 CBP officers, See Donna Bucella, Assistant Commissioner, Office of Intelligence and Investigation, U.S. Customs and Border Protection, Testimony to U.S. House of Representatives, Committee on Homeland Security, Subcommittee on Border and Maritime Security, 19 June 2012.
5. Narco-submarines are actually Self-Propelled Semi-Submersible (SPSS) and have a low profile waterline.
6. Roger D. Hodge, Borderworld: "How the U.S. Is Reengineering Homeland Security," *POPSCI,* 17 January 2012 at *http://www.popsci.com/technology/article/2011-12/how-us-reengineering-homeland-security-borders*
7. Ibid.
8. See U.S.-Mexico Border Counties Coalition, "Chapter 3: Mexico Border Populations and Policy Linkages," in *At the Cross Roads: U.S./Mexico Border Counties in Transition,* March 2006 at *http://www.bordercounties.org/vertical/Sites/%7BB4A0F1FF-7823-4C95-8D7A-F5E400063C73%7D/uploads/%7B222A54B6-2E09-4A91-9D8B-70FA1E9C8269%7D.PDF*

9. The exception is the Middle Rio Grande on the Mexico side which has a substantial population not matched by a U.S. counterpart.
10. The concept of *municipios* is similar to that of a U.S. county. Within *municipios* are *localidades,* which themselves are similar to the concept of cities.
11. "Chapter 3: Mexico Border Populations and Policy Linkages," p. 3–3.
12. Feranando Romero/LAR, *Hyperborder: The Contemporary U.S.-Mexico Border and It's Future,* New York: Princeton Architectural Press, 2008.
13. Ibid, cover matter.
14. Ibid, p. 42.
15. The twin or sister cities are west to east (U.S.-MX): San Diego-Tijuana, Calexico-Mexicali, Yuma-San Luis Rio Colorado, Nogales-Nogales, Naco-Naco, Douglas-Agua Prieta, Columbus-Las Palomas, El Paso-Ciudad Juárez, Presido-Oinaga, Del Rio-Cd. Acuña, Eagle Pass-Piedras Negras, Laredo-Nuevo Laredo, Mc Allen-Reynosa, and Brownsville-Matamoros.
16. Ibid, p. 44.
17. See Samuel Logan, "Crime, Innovation, & the Mexican Border," *The Counter Terrorist,* December 2011/January 2012, p. 31–32.
18. Howard Campbell, *Drug War Zone,* Austin: University Of Texas Press, 2009.
19. Reuters, "Cross-Border Organized Crime a $870 Billion Yearly Industry," 16 July 2012.
20. Ibid.
21. John P. Sullivan and Adam Elkus, "Border zones and insecurity in the Americas," OpenDemocracy, 24 November 2009 at *http://www.opendemocracy.net/opensecurity/john-p-sullivan-adam-elkus/border-zones-and-insecurity-in-americas*
22. James A. Dinkins, Executive Director of Homeland Security Investigations, U.S. Immigration and Customs Enforcement, Testimony to U.S. House of Representatives, Committee on Homeland Security, Subcommittee on Border and Maritime Security, 19 June 2012.
23. See Peter Katina, Michael D. Intriligator, and John P. Sullivan, Countering terrorism and WMD: Creating a global counter-terrorism network, London: Routledge, 2006 for a discussion of building a global security network.
24. James A. Dinkins, Congressional Testimony, 19 June 2012.
25. Mexico's drug trafficking organizations (DTOs) are popularly called cartels. While they are not cartels in an economic sense the narcos use the term to describe their own organizations. Mexican mafias are linked to transnational economic circuits in a range of activities beyond drug trafficking so many are properly described as transnational criminal organizations (TCOs).
26. The lower figure is attributed to the associated Press, as reported by the *San Diego Union-Tribune.* The higher figure was reported by the Tijuana weekly *Zeta.* See AP, "In drug war, dead go nameless," *San Diego Union-Tribune,* 23 July 2012 and "Sexenio de Calderón: 71 Mil Ejecuciones," *Zeta,* 31 May 2012.
27. Olga R. Rodriguez, "Mexico Violence: Unidentified Bodies, Missing Cases Mount," *Huffington Post,* 23 July 2012 at *http://www.huffingtonpost.com/2012/07/23/mexico-violence_n_1695788.html*
28. John P. Sullivan, "From Drug Wars to Criminal Insurgency: Mexican Cartels, Criminal Enclaves and Criminal Insurgency in Mexico and Central America, and their

Implications for Global Security," *Vortex Working Paper No. 6,* Bogotá: Scientific Vortex Foundation, p. 9.

29. 'Hollow states' are defined by John Robb at his web blog *Global Guerrillas;* see *http://globalguerrillas.typepad.com for elaboration.*
30. For a detailed discussion of criminal insurgency see for example John P. Sullivan and Robert J. Bunker, *Mexico's Criminal Insurgency: A Small Wars Journal-El Centro Anthology,* Bloomington: iUniverse, 2012; John P. Sullivan, "Criminal Insurgencies in the Americas," *Small Wars Journal,* 13 February 2010; John P. Sullivan and Adam Elkus, "Cartel v. Cartel: Mexico's Criminal Insurgency," *Small Wars Journal,* 01 February 2010; John P. Sullivan and Adam Elkus, "Red Teaming Criminal Insurgency," *Red Team Journal,* 30 January 2009 at *http://redteamjournal.com/ 2009/01/red-teaming-criminal-insurgency-1/.*
31. David A. Shirk, "Transnational Crime, U.S. Border Security, and the war on Drugs in Mexico," Testimony to the U.S. House of Representatives Sub-Committee on Oversight, Investigations and Management, 31 March 2011. Shirk cites Jose Brambila Macias, *Modeling the Informal Economy in Mexico: A Structural Equation Approach,* Munich 2008 at *http://mpra.ub.uni-muenchen.de/8504/*
32. Shirk, "Transnational Crime." Shirk cites Howard Campbell, *Drug War Zone,* Austin: University Of Texas Press, 2009.
33. See George Grayson, "Mexico transborder crime and governance," *Great Decisions 2012,* Foreign Policy Organization, 2012, pp. 33–44 for an excellent overview of crime on Mexico's *frontera del norte* (Northern Border).
34. This amount is in the upper range of illicit narcotic industry estimates. See Jonathan P. Caulkins, Peter Reuter, Martin Y. Iguchi and James Chiesa, *How Goes the 'War on Drugs'? An Assessment of U.S. Drug Problems and Policy,* Santa Monica, CA: RAND, Drug Policy Research Center, 2005.
35. Shirk, "Transnational Crime."
36. See for example AP, "Zetas suspected in Tamaulipas migrant massacre," *The Monitor,* 26 August 2010.
37. The Internal Displacement Monitoring Centre issued a report stating that there are an estimated 120,000 internally displaced people (IDPs) as a result of the violence from the Mexican Drug War and other factors. See Internal Displacement Monitoring Centre, *Internal Displacement: Global Overview of Trends and Developments* in 2010. *http://www.internal-displacement.org/publications/global-overview-2010.pdf.* For additional discussion on this critical issue see Paul Rexton Kan, *Mexico's "Narco-Refugees": The Looming Challenge for U.S. National Security,* Carlisle Barracks, Strategic Studies Center, October 2011.
38. See John P. Sullivan and Adam Elkus, "Plazas for Profit: Mexico's Criminal Insurgency," *Small Wars Journal,* 26 April 2009.
39. See John P. Sullivan, "Transnational Gangs: The Impact of Third Generation Gangs in Central America," *Air & Space Power Journal—Spanish Edition,* Second Trimester 2008 at *http://www.airpower.maxwell.af.mil/apjinternational/apj-s/2008/2tri08/sullivaneng.htm*
40. See John P. Sullivan and Samuel Logan, "MS-13 Leadership: Networks of Influence," The Counter Terrorist, August/September 2010 at *http://digital.ipcprintservices.com/display_article.php?id=428186* and Samuel Logan, This is for the *Mara Salvatrucha: Inside the MS-13, America's Most Violent Gang.* New York: Hyperion, 2009.

41. Both MS-13 and 18th Street (M-18), collectively known as *maras* are often as mistakenly referred to as Central American gangs. This is a misnomer as both originate in Los Angeles and gained a Central American presence and transnational status as an unintended consequence of criminal alien deportation.
42. See John P. Sullivan and Samuel Logan, "La Línea: Network, Gangs, and Mercenary Army," *The Counter Terrorist,* August/September 2011 at *http://onlinedigitalpublishing.com/display_article.php?id=766740*
43. 2011 National Gang Crime Assessment-Emerging Trends, Washington, DC: National Gang Intelligence Center, p. 26 at *http://www.f.bi.gov/stats-services/publications/2011-national-gang-threat-assessment/2011-national-gang-threat-assessment-emerging-trends*
44. Ibid, p. 26.
45. Ibid, p. 26.
46. "2011 National Gang Crime Assessment-Emerging Trends," p. 39.
47. "2011 National Drug Threat Assessment," Washington, DC: U.S. Department of Justice, p. 12.
48. Ibid, p. 12.
49. Ibid, p. 2.
50. See Henry H. Willis, Joel B. Predd, Paul K. Davis, and Wayne P. Brown, *Measuring the Effectiveness of Border Security Between Ports-of-Entry,* Santa Monica: RAND 2010.
51. Doug Miller, "Heavily-armed Texas gunboats now patrol Rio Grande," KHOU-11, 28 June 2012 at *http://www.khou.com/news/Heavily-armed-Texas-gunboats-patrol-Rio-Grande-160760375.html*
52. Robert Beckhusen, "Texas's New Weapon Against Cartels: Armored Gunboats," *Wired Danger Room,* 01 March 2012 at *http://www.wired.com/dangerroom/2012/03/texass-gunboats/*
53. Ibid.
54. Shirk, "Transnational Crime."
55. The first cross-border tunnel was discovered by the border patrol in 1990. Since then, CBP has seen and increase in tunneling with 154 tunnels discovered on the Southern border through 31 March 2012 according to Congressional Testimony by Bucella.
56. U.S. Department of State Fact Sheet at *http://www.state.gov/j/inl/merida/* (July 2012).
57. David J. Danelo, "Disorder on the Border," *Proceedings,* October 2009, Vol. 135 at *http://www.usni.org/magazines/proceedings/2009-10/disorder-border*

Unit Two

Response and Resilience

In UNIT TWO, we turn our focus toward understanding how the United States is responding to the threats and challenges identified in the first part of this book. Much has been written in recent years about what various federal, state, and local agencies do to support the homeland security mission, so the selections provided here are meant to amplify and expand—rather than duplicate—that knowledge. In the first section, authors examine national dimensions of U.S. homeland security efforts. This is followed by a section on state and local dimensions, and the final section explores the critically important topic of resilience.

In the first selection, Erik Brattberg of Johns Hopkins University offers an analytical framework for assessing the effectiveness of post-9/11 homeland security reforms. He notes that while new interagency network mechanisms were established, many suffer from problems relating to implementation. Further, while efforts have been made to establish a national exercise planning program, problems with regard to program leadership remain unresolved. Overall, he argues, U.S. homeland security is in far better shape today than it was prior to 9/11, but improvements are needed. He concludes with some suggestions on how we might further strengthen the capacity of the U.S. homeland security system.

In the next selection, Joanne Moore, a senior officer in the U.S. Army, describes how the Department of Defense charts a narrow path based on traditional roles of the military in the United States, legal restrictions, continuing commitments to expeditionary roles, and preparing for missions on American soil. She explains how the principal exceptions of the Posse Comitatus Act paves the way for DoD to balance its mission to defend the homeland with the expectation that it will assist other agencies when needed. Three areas of activity of particular interest are homeland defense against external threats; defense support to civil authorities, mainly in times of crisis (hurricanes, earthquakes, etc.); and the WMD Civil Support Teams that provide detection, identification, and dispersal capability for incidents involving chemical, biological, radiological, or nuclear materials. She concludes by noting that federal law only prohibits federal armed forces from performing law enforcement duties in the United States and that improvements can be made in how DoD plans and positions its capabilities throughout the United States in ways that will be more effective in responding to future homeland security incidents.

This is followed by a reading from Brian Jenkins of the Rand Corporation in which he notes that al-Qaeda has never possessed a nuclear weapon, yet the fear of a nuclear attack has given the terrorist network a degree of psychological influence that is unwarranted. He draws an important distinction between nuclear terrorism—the possibility that terrorists will acquire and use nuclear weapons—and nuclear terror, which is about the anticipation of that event. Nuclear terrorism is driven by terrorist capabilities, while nuclear terror is driven by our imagination. Americans, he argues, have been avid consumers of nuclear terror, adding another layer to our already considerable national anxieties and demanding obedience to an orthodoxy that cannot be challenged without provoking accusations of being dangerously naïve or soft on terrorism. At the very least, the threat of nuclear terrorism, real or imagined, has led to increased security for nuclear weapons and fissile material, which is a positive development. But the United States must find a way to balance the fear of a nuclear attack with the facts, and the facts are that no terrorist group anywhere in the world has come even close to crossing the nuclear threshold.

Fear is a prominent theme in the next selection as well, in which Frank Harvey of Dalhousie University (Nova Scotia, Canada) offers a critical analysis of what he considers a serious homeland security dilemma: the greater the financial costs, public sacrifice and political capital invested in security, the higher the public's expectations and corresponding standards for measuring performance, the more significant the public's sense of insecurity after each failure, and, paradoxically, the higher the pressure on governments and citizens to sacrifice even more to achieve perfect security. His central argument can be summed up by the following counterintuitive thesis: The more security you have, the more security you will need, not because enhancing security makes terrorism more likely, but because enormous investments in security inevitably raise public expectations and amplify public outrage after subsequent failures. Unfortunately, he concludes, the key policy implications derived from this analysis are not encouraging; there are no solutions, because the most rational and logical policy options are part of the problem.

In the final selection of the first section, senior defense economists David Trybula and John Whitley examine the value proposition that having a single Department of Homeland Security (DHS) provides better protection against terrorism than any alternative approach. The establishment of the DHS was followed by a substantial increase in funding. However, this increase in funding could have occurred without establishing the Department. The value proposition in establishing the Department was that it would lead to greater coordination and unity of effort across the disparate activities that had been combined. They introduce and apply a cost-benefit analysis to demonstrate how policymakers can determine whether the benefits of DHS outweigh its costs. Their approach can also provide useful insights to decision makers when assessing policy choices in other areas as well.

In the second part of UNIT TWO, authors focus on state and local dimensions of the response to the homeland security threat landscape. First, SUNY Albany Professor James Steiner explores several dimensions of state-level intelligence activities that support law enforcement and executive level (governor's office) homeland security decision making. State-level intelligence has three primary functions and customers—providing counterterrorism intelligence support to law enforcement, ensuring situational awareness for state-level executive and legislative decision makers, and providing critical infrastructure threat analyses to executive decision makers and policy implementation staff. State-level intelligence also provides unclassified information and assessments to the private sector and to the public when it is possible and appropriate to do so. Homeland security efforts in New York State are used as a case study to illustrate key themes and challenges for state authorities throughout the United States.

Former Oklahoma Governor Frank Keating reminds us that not all terrorist attacks are conducted by international non-state actors such as al-Qaeda. Based on his experience as governor during the April 19, 1995, Oklahoma City bombing and his later participation in the *Dark Winter* exercise in 2002, Governor Keating provides useful conclusions and findings and makes recommendations for first responders to follow in the event of a terrorist attack. And in the last reading of this section, former FBI Special Agent Kevin Eack explores the challenges faced by state and local intelligence fusion centers. For most states, these fusion centers were natural expansions of existing law enforcement intelligence analysis centers, where information was gathered and analyzed on violent gangs, drug trafficking, prostitution, child exploitation, weapons smuggling, theft rings, and other crimes. The involvement of the DHS and FBI in these fusion centers has, at times, complicated—rather than improved—state and local efforts to combat terrorism. Eack concludes that staffing, training, intelligence-handling procedures, benchmark capabilities, and sustained funding are all critical issues that must be addressed in a much-needed effort to improve the effectiveness of fusion centers nationwide.

The third and final section of UNIT TWO provides different perspectives on the critically important topic of resilience. First, Stephen Flynn and Sean Burke of Northeastern University describe how the key to assuring security, safety and prosperity in the 21st century will be possessing resilience in the face of chronic and catastrophic risks. Building resilience, they note, requires a broad and sustained engagement of citizens, companies and communities. In essence, it requires creating capabilities from the bottom up. Further, our nation's critical infrastructure needs substantial investment to improve its resilience in the face of major disasters. They conclude that fostering community and critical infrastructure resilience should be a national priority.

Then Michael Kindt, a senior officer of the U.S. Air Force, notes that resilience plays a critical role in how people respond to traumatic incidents. He examines in detail the concept of resilience and techniques to enhance the resilience of the public. He then describes the model of resilience preparation provided by the military, explores past national efforts to prepare for an attack, and examines related initiatives that have not yet borne fruit in terms of their ability to enhance our resilience. Finally, he offers recommendations to improve the overall resilience of the United States to terror attacks and disasters. And in the final reading, Robert Bach and David Kaufman of the Naval Postgraduate School's Center for Homeland Defense and Security argue that the American public should be engaged in new ways that invite their participation in understanding, assessing, and mitigating risk. From their assessment, new community-oriented techniques are needed that draw heavily on community policing models and public health philosophies. Further, the federal government needs to alter its strategic planning and funding processes, and leverage the restructuring of the Federal Emergency Management Agency (FEMA) and other priorities as opportunities to put communities first. In sum, the reading identifies a dire need to invest in a social infrastructure for homeland security that will bring the American people fully into strengthening their own preparedness.

The readings in UNIT TWO illustrate how securing the homeland is one of the most complex missions, requiring a coordinated and integrated effort from all levels of society—the federal government, state, and local governments, and the private and non-profit sectors. The research and perspectives provided here are meant to provoke thoughtful discussion among the homeland security professionals of today and tomorrow, and frame a useful backdrop for the discussion of legal and ethical challenges addressed in UNIT THREE.

Learning Objectives

The readings in UNIT TWO will help students develop an appreciation for the complexities of homeland security and an ability to articulate the importance of a coordinated and integrated effort from all levels of society—the federal government, state, and local governments, and the private and nonprofit sectors. Students will also come to understand key concepts of community and national resilience, and the centrality of these concepts in efforts to improve homeland security.

Recommended Resources

Booz, Allen, Hamilton. (2010). *Risk and crisis communications: Best practices for government agencies and non-profit organizations.* Retrieved October 13, 2011, from http://www.boozallen.com/media/file/Risk-and-Crisis-Communications-Guide.pdf

Chenoweth, Erica. "Vulnerabilities and Resilience in America's Financial Services," in James Forest (ed.), *Homeland Security: Protecting America's Targets* (Westport, CT: Praeger, 2006).

Department of Homeland Security (2010), DHS Report to Congress: Quadrennial Homeland Security Review. Online at: http://www.dhs.gov/quadrennial-homeland-security-review-qhsr

Department of Homeland Security (September 2011), *Presidential Policy Directive / PPD-8: National Preparedness Guidelines.* Online at: http://www.fema.gov/pdf/prepared/npg.pdf

Department of Homeland Security. (2011). *If you see something, say something campaign.* Retrieved January 6, 2012, from http://www.dhs.gov/files/reportincidents/see-something-say-something.shtm

Federal Emergency Management Agency (November 2010), *Developing and Maintaining Emergency Operations Plans: Comprehensive Preparedness Guide 101.* Online at: http://www.fema.gov/pdf/about/divisions/npd/CPG_101_V2.pdf

Ferro, Carmen, David Henry, and Thomas MacLellan, *A Governor's Guide to Homeland Security,* National Governor's Association (November 2010). Online at http://www.nga.org/files/live/sites/NGA/files/pdf/1011GOVGUIDEHS.PDF.

Ford, Christopher. "Twitter, Facebook and Ten Red Balloons: Social Network Problem Solving and Homeland Security," *Homeland Security Affairs,* Vol 7, Article 3 (February 2011) Available from www.hsaj.org.

German, Michael and Jay Stanley. *"What's Wrong with Fusion Centers"* Dec. 2007. Online at http://www.aclu.org/pdfs/privacy/fusioncenter_20071212.pdf.

Hunt, David. *They Just Don't Get It: How the Washington Political Machine is Compromising Your Safety—And What You Can Do About It* (Crowne Press: New York, 2005).

Mailer, Gideon. "Individual Perceptions and Appropriate Reactions to the Terrorist Threat in America's Public Spaces," in James Forest (ed.), *Homeland Security: Protecting America's Targets* (Westport, CT: Praeger, 2006).

Meade, Charles and Roger C. Molander, Considering the Effects of a Catastrophic Terrorist Attack, Santa Monica, Calif.: RAND Corporation, TR-391-CTRMP, 2006. Online at: http://www.rand.org/pubs/technical_reports/TR391.html

Miskel, James F. *Disaster Response and Homeland Security: What Works, What Doesn't,* (Stanford University Press: Stanford, CA, 2008).

Mueller, John, and Mark G. Stewart. "Balancing the Risks, Benefits, and Costs of Homeland Security." *Homeland Security Affairs* 7, Article 16 (August 2011). Online at: http://www.hsaj.org/?article=7.1.16

National Security Council (July 2004), *Planning Scenarios: Executive Summaries.* Online at: http://www.voiceoffreedom.com/archives/homelandsecurity/15-attacks_the_hawiaa_disclosure.htm

Office of the President. (2010). *Nuclear detonation preparedness: Communicating in the immediate aftermath, approved for interim use.* Retrieved September 24, 2011, from http://www.remm.nlm.gov/NuclearDetonationPreparedness.pdf

Preparedness, Response, and Resilience Task Force, "Interim Task Force Report on Resilience." Homeland Security Policy Institute, The George Washington University (May 16, 2011). Online at http://www.gwumc.edu/hspi/policy/report_Resilience1.pdf.

Stehr, Steven D. "The Changing Roles and Responsibilities of the Local Emergency Manager: An Empirical Study," *International Journal of Mass Emergencies and Disasters* Vol. 25, No. 1 (March 2007), pp. 37–55.

Williams, Cindy. "Paying for Homeland Security: Show Me the Money." MIT Center for International Studies Audit of the Conventional Wisdom, 07-08 (May 2007)

Wilner, Alexandre S. "Deterring the Undeterrable: Coercion, Denial, and Delegitimization in Counterterrorism," *Journal of Strategic Studies,* Vol. 34, No. 1, pp. 3–37.

Section 2.1

National Response

Coordinating for Contingencies

Taking Stock of Post-9/11 Homeland Security Reforms

Erik Brattberg

Over a decade after September 11, American citizens are still asking themselves: 'how much safer are we today?' This question is also pertinent for scholars seeking to understand the post-September 11 homeland security reforms. This paper, drawing on the public administration literature and using Don Kettl's 'contingent coordination' framework, sets out to discuss how well these efforts have addressed the central coordination challenges posed by homeland security. In doing so, it makes two contributions: one methodological (e.g., operationalizing the contingent coordination framework) and one empirical (e.g., assessing the effectiveness of post-9/11 homeland security reforms). The paper concludes with an overall assessment of how to find ways to further strengthen the capacity of the US homeland security system.

1. Introduction

The September 11, 2001 terrorist attacks placed homeland security at the very top of the national public policy agenda. A decade after the attacks, homeland security remains one of the top missions for the US government. But, as the National Strategy for Homeland Security argues, securing the homeland is also an extremely complex mission, requiring a coordinated and integrated effort from all levels of society—ranging from the federal government to state and local governments to the private and non-profit sectors. How to achieve coordination between these various actors has been the focal point of recent years' homeland security reforms. The September 11 terrorist attacks revealed coordination problems between federal agencies, and varying levels of response capacity among local authorities (Perrow, 2007; 9/11 Commission, 2005). These events thus created strong impetus for reorganization of the national homeland security system. As a result, a number of initiatives to 'connect the dots' between organizations, address common management and response principles and develop common planning frameworks, saw daylight.

But when faced with another large-scale disaster—Hurricane Katrina hitting the Gulf Coast in August 2005—the new preparedness and response mechanisms proved toothless (Cooper & Block, 2006; Daniels, Kettl, & Kunreuther, 2006; Parker, Stern, Pagila, & Brown, 2009). Hurricane Katrina illustrated competing decision-making structures, information-sharing obstacles between federal, state and local officials, a lack of effective preparedness among officials across the governance spectrum and implementation resistance at the local level (Perrow, 2007; Cooper & Block, 2006). The flawed response to Hurricane Katrina led to additional organizational reshuffling and further efforts to improve the federal government's ability to coordinate its efforts with those of state and local authorities in the event of large-scale disasters.

While no new major homeland security emergency have yet forced the current system into extreme test, experts remind us that it is only a matter of time before the next 'big one' is likely to occur. Unprecedented crises and disasters—whether terrorism attacks, natural disasters or the outbreak of serious pandemic influenzas—are on the rise, both in frequency and intensity. Taking stock of the current efforts to establish a unified management of the national crisis and disaster response is therefore a pertinent undertaking, especially in light of the 10-year anniversary of the 9/11 attacks. One major limitation of this study is that it will primarily focus on the role of the Department of Homeland Security (DHS), leaving out the issue of reform in the intelligence community.

This paper employs a public administration perspective to assess how well the post-September 11 and the post-Katrina policy reform efforts have addressed the central coordination challenges posed by homeland security, thus making America safer in an era of 'new vulnerabilities'. Don Kettl's 'contingent coordination approach', which presents five analytical dimensions, allows us to make such an assessment. These are: (1) how to match place and function, (2) how to define a floor, (3) how to build a reliable learning system, (4) how to balance the old with the new and (5) how to meet citizens' expectations in a fragmented system. These dimensions provide useful metrics for identifying challenges in providing for homeland security and assessing institutional vulnerability in the US homeland security system. I conclude with an overall assessment of how to find ways to further strengthen the capacity of the US homeland security system.

2. Homeland Security As a Coordination Puzzle

While coordination challenges are inescapable in any modern society, the institutional fragmentation and organizational complexity characterizing the American federalist system is known to present exceptional coordination challenges (see, for example, Kaufman, 1960; Peters, 2006, pp. 185–187). Developments of complex government and intergovernmental systems since the 1960s have rendered a complicated set of coordination challenges. These challenges are further exacerbated by the more recent task of providing for homeland security (Kettl, 2003a, 2007).

Having historically lacked a comprehensive national response and emergency system, US emergency preparedness and response responsibilities have traditionally rested primarily on state and local governments and have tended to focus on natural disasters rather than on terrorist attacks (see CRS Report to Congress, 2006). Moreover, the role of the federal government has historically been limited to supporting emergency preparedness and management by providing resources before large-scale disasters, and to offer response and recovery assistance after such disasters when local resources are exhausted (Lindsay & O'Hanlon, 2002; Sauter & Carafano, 2006).

The September 11, 2001 attacks, however, would change the US national response and emergency system fundamentally. The passing of the Homeland Security Act of 2002, calling for the establishment of the DHS to consolidate the essential agencies charged with securing US borders and national infrastructure, created impetus for a more coordinated national preparedness and response approach. The White House (2002) declared DHS responsible for comprehensive vulnerability assessments for critical infrastructure and key assets, by merging intelligence and information analysis in order to focus on long-term preventive measures and coordinating and sharing of information with other executive branch agencies, local and state actors and with non-federal entities.

Today, a decade after the September 11 attacks, surprisingly few attempts have been made to systematically assess to what extent the massive homeland security overhaul initiated after 9/11 has addressed the central homeland security challenge; namely, how to obtain an adequate level of coordination between the numerous actors at federal, state and local levels involved in this complex national mission. To assist us in making this assessment, we turn to the public administration literature, which has a long track record of dealing with the issue of coordination in public policy.

2.1. Coordination in the Public Administration Literature

Sometimes referred to as 'the philosopher's stone of public administration' (see Seidman, 1998), coordination is a classic topic in the public administration literature (Morris & Morris, 2007, p. 95) and one that is notoriously difficult to define[1] (Helsloot, 2008, p. 174). Public administration scholars have argued that this is possible to bring under control the challenges posed by complex governmental systems as long as the right formula for coordination is found (see for example Seidman, 1998, p. 142). On the question of what the central coordination obstacles are, and what the best formula for addressing them is, we can distinguish between two separate conceptual approaches.

The first of these is the traditional 'hierarchical approach'. Stemming from Max Weber's classic bureaucratic model of public administration and built on the work of Gulick (1937), Taylor (1911) and Dahl (1947), this approach depicts organizations as being divided into specialized functional units. Coordination in a hierarchical organization is thus viewed as 'a carefully crafted, clear, and unambiguous set of relationships delineated for each element of the system, with clear lines of authority developed to link the various pieces together in a rational manner' (Morris & Morris, 2007, p. 95). Effective coordination, from this perspective, is about dividing responsibilities within an organization and establishing clear links between functions. Or if we are speaking of interagency coordination, this view sees coordination as something occurring between units rather than between individual workers (Morris & Morris, 2007).

Contrary to this view, the more recent 'network approach' depicts coordination as the interaction between multiple interdependent organizations existing apart from traditional hierarchical mechanisms (Chisholm, 1992; O'Toole, 1997; Wise, 2002, p. 133; Wise, 2006, p. 311). Instead of being based on top-down authority and position, network coordination between organizations is based on a mutual need for sharing resources, authority, knowledge and technology, using negotiation and mutual adjustment instruments (Morris & Morris, 2007, p. 95).

Thus, depending on how one conceptualizes the core coordination issue—whether it is essentially a hierarchical challenge or a network one—different solutions to the coordination dilemma follow accordingly. However, when it comes to the complex task of providing for homeland security, neither model is entirely appropriate. The hierarchal approach suffers from the fact that managers in multi-organizational settings often lack authority over other organizations, making it also difficult to establish such clear top-down linkages. An additional problem is that the hierarchies can be too rigid and slow to adapt to the sudden changes and unanticipated problems typically characterizing modern security threats (Wise, 2006, p. 311). While network approaches, on the other hand, might be better suited to address the lack of authority common in many multi-organizational settings, they also fall short when it comes to accountability and measuring of performance (Wise & Nader, 2002)—two very important elements of homeland security.

Relying too heavily on one ideal type conceptualization of coordination to identify the central coordination gaps in homeland security accordingly risks overlooking a certain set of challenges, and consequently also the instruments, by which these challenges can be addressed. In order to assess the central coordination challenges in homeland security, and discuss suitable models for addressing these, it is therefore important that the relative insights from both approaches are given equal weight.

Fortunately, doing precisely this is Don Kettl in the article 'Contingent Coordination', which appeared in the *American Review of Public Administration* in 2003. In this article, Kettl presents a framework that is specifically tailored to using coordination for addressing homeland security threats, drawing on the comparative strengths of both the hierarchical and the network approaches. This framework will constitute the basis for our assessment of how the post-9/11 homeland security reforms have addressed the central coordination gaps.

3. The Contingent Coordination Framework

Having learned that coordination is both the diagnosis of, and the solution to, the homeland security problem, what we now need is a clearer understanding of the nature of homeland security problems and how coordination can address these through better identifying and connecting the dots between the organizations and actors involved in this mission. According to Kettl, coordinating for homeland security in the United States poses five principal problems, which the government must address. This homeland security-specific framework will in turn constitute the metrics for assessing the homeland security coordination efforts in the United States following 9/11 in this paper.

3.1. Dimension 1: How to Match Place and Functions

Agencies responding to homeland security problems tend to be functionally organized, as opposed to place-based, rendering coping with incidents affecting specific locations particularly challenging. Many homeland security functions, such as law enforcement, transportation, food safety and public health, information technology and emergency management, are dispersed across a vast array of different actors ranging from the federal government to different state and local authorities to the non-profit and private sectors (Lindsay & O'Hanlon, 2002; Sauter & Carafano, 2006). Homeland security coordination must therefore occur simultaneously on the horizontal and vertical levels. Horizontally, coordination may entail establishing an executive office coordination office or networks between the various federal departments and agencies carrying homeland security responsibilities. Vertical coordination, on the other hand, could be local officials cultivating working relationships with their state and federal counterparts.

Proposing that coordination is obtainable both under hierarchical and network forms of authority, Kettl suggests that different actors, both within and outside of traditional hierarchical organizational structures, must collaborate with each other in the event of a crisis situation (Morris & Morris, 2007, p. 96). However, a common misinterpretation, he argues, is that improving homeland security coordination through the connecting place-based and function-based capacities inevitably requires physical reorganization and relocation of functions. Improving coordination through decision making is more effective than structural reorganization since the latter is typically slow to adapt to sudden changes. Noting that any system dealing with homeland security needs to be 'lithe and flexible', Kettl suggests that establishing inter-organizational networks, that is informal network approaches bridging the gap between structural and individual approaches, is one practical way of better balancing place-based and function-based capacities. Using information technology, such networks can assist in identifying, linking and connecting organizations (Kettl, 2003b, p. 273). Furthermore, along the lines of the 9/11 Commission report, Kettl recommends strengthening regional emergency planning and establishing state-wide mutual aid agreements to reinforce local capacities in the event of major crises.

3.2. Dimension 2: How to Define a Floor

In many government circles, there is a growing consensus that efforts should be result-oriented rather than focusing on inputs and processes. From a theoretical point of view, this perspective puts an emphasis on effectiveness, efficiency and accountability in boosting an organization's capacity to fulfil its mission, and this requires that efforts are continually evaluated (Kaimen, 2005, p. 226). Naturally, this requires some sort of basis to evaluate progress against. Since all homeland security events begin as local events, the federal government's response plan must necessarily be integrated with state and local ones (Kettl, 2003b, p. 283). Because homeland security incidents can occur virtually anywhere, it is also imperative to set up at least a minimum level of local preparedness across the nation. Moreover, as Lee Clarke reminds us, such plans must also be attainable and not mere 'fantasy documents' (Clarke, 1999). But how to best do this with limited federal power over state and local authorities, and with a difficult process of setting up and enforcing federal minimum standards for intergovernmental programmes in emergency management?

While observing that state and local government have considerably enhanced their homeland security planning following September 11, Kettl advocates stronger coordination in areas where local officials have yet been reluctant to yield autonomy to the federal government. To achieve this, Kettl proposes a two-way track. First, the federal government should identify clear key baseline goals for homeland security and measure the performance of state and local actors against these goals through establishing strong and clear federal performance reporting standards.[2] Along the same lines, Perrow argues that it is essential that these federal standards be higher than local ones, and that state and local authorities can exceed these minimum standards (Perrow, 2007, p. 36). Second, the goals of state and local authorities should be assisted by the federal government in funding high-priority needs to implement these through uniform federal grant tools (Kettl, 2003b, pp. 273–274). Such a federal block-grant system would appropriate funding, while states retain responsibility for developing statewide plans. Local governments should also be given substantial power to manage their resources within the statewide strategy.

3.3. Dimension 3: How to Build a Reliable Learning System

Establishing a well-coordinated routine response system based on previous experiences is particularly difficult when it comes to the area of homeland security because of its many intrinsic irregularities and unpredictabilities. Since homeland security incidents seldom occur, actors responsible for providing homeland security need to develop other ways of learning from past experiences. Although the United States experienced several crises and disasters during the 1990s[3], it was not until the September 11 attacks and Hurricane Katrina that the lack of effective coordination routines were brought into the limelight of public discourse. Many authors have argued that Hurricane Katrina highlighted the need for better exercises and simulations (see, for instance, Samaan & Verneuil, 2009). Kettl here suggests that effective routines can be reinforced through joint simulations, exercises and field drills.

3.4. Dimension 4: How to Balance the Old with the New

Following the September 11 attacks and the surge of interest in beefing up the nation's crisis management system, government agencies previously assigned homeland security functions now had to develop new ways of linking their activities with those of other actors. At the same time, other agencies were handed additional homeland security responsibilities on top of their already existing missions. Many of the early proposals for homeland security reform, including the Hart-Rudman report and the 9/11 Commission report, proposed that federal homeland security functions should be consolidated under one single organizational umbrella. Consolidating a vast number of diverse federal agencies into one single cabinet-level agency (i.e., DHS) naturally gave rise to a series of new concerns: how should DHS continue to meet the existing missions of these agencies while also strengthening the new homeland security missions and at the same time integrate these various missions without increasing government spending? To address these challenges, Kettl suggests that DHS leaders must seek to balance outside and inside organizational demands, including managing expectations of key external actors, and foster a well-functioning organizational culture.

3.5. Dimension 5: How to Meet Citizens' Expectations in a Fragmented System

Since protection against homeland security threats is never absolute, and since some homeland security efforts inevitably bring trade-offs between risk protection on the one hand and individual freedoms on the other, it is pivotal that leaders clarify to citizens what the acceptable level of risk is and how to balance freedom and security under a certain risk level (Kettl, 2003b, p. 274). In recent years, a considerable body of literature on risk communication has sprung up. This literature suggests that individuals must have experienced or been exposed to risks in order to respond effectively to disasters (Kaimen, 2005, p. 352). Since homeland security incidents are rare, the perceived need for preparedness also tends to decline in the absence of a major disaster (Kaimen, 2005, p. 352). Additionally, individuals are more likely to take action when they have been forewarned about a disaster. According to Kettl, governments should concentrate on fostering a culture of preparedness that incidents will occur, develop a perception of risk and provide risk communication.

4. Assessing Vulnerability in the US Homeland Security System

In this section, I gauge how the reforms of the US homeland security system measures on the five dimensions of coordination introduced above. After discussing each dimension in detail, I assess how the US is best characterized on that dimension, looking at the key policy developments in each area.[4] I finally explore how that characteristic may affect its capacity to cope with future crises.

4.1. Matching Place and Functions

4.1.1. Inter-organizational Networks versus Structural Reorganization The main approach to post-9/11 homeland security reform can be described as structural insofar as sweeping reorganization has been favoured over inter-organizational network solutions. In the immediate aftermath of the 9/11 attacks, however, President George W. Bush took an inter-agency approach, establishing two new entities: the Office of Homeland Security (OHS) tasked with coordinating federal, state and local homeland security efforts within the executive branch (Davis, 2002), and the Homeland Security Council (HSC) tasked with coordinating policies among the top national leaders. Amid growing congressional criticism over the ability of these entities to manage the nation's homeland security efforts, the President eventually shifted sands towards an interdepartmental solution; a move which would pave the way for the establishment of the DHS in January 2003 (Newmann, 2002).

The establishment of DHS came to mark the most significant transformation of the US government in several decades (Relyea, 2003). Bringing together 22 agencies[5]—containing over 100 bureaus, branches, sub-agencies and sections ((Lindsay & O'Hanlon, 2002), and employing approximately 180,000 workers—the new department became responsible for a variety of missions, including identifying and developing plans for protecting critical infrastructure; conducting intelligence gathering and analysis; exercising the mechanisms to enhance emergency preparedness; and coordinating and sharing of information with other executive branch agencies, local and state actors and with non-federal entities. Today, DHS is the third largest federal government department with more than 200,000 employees and an annual budget of more than $40 billion.

The creation of the DHS represented a structural approach to the nation's homeland security problem through physically connecting many (although not all) of the agencies carrying homeland security responsibilities and promoting new command and control structures between these. Critics have argued DHS have lacked a flexible and more nimble process to ensure that it can adjust to the ever-changing circumstances of homeland security. According to Wise (2006), network management (e.g., processes that encourage the sharing of information both horizontally and vertically and more collaboration that would foster organizational learning and facilitate adaptation and improvization) has been the missing capability in the DHS organization. Some evidence of network collaboration exists though, such as the efforts to utilize technology towards connecting agencies dealing with intelligence and information as a part of so-called 'fusion centres'.

Although the role of DHS when it comes to intelligence is mainly limited to assessment and dissemination of intelligence information collected by other agencies, some DHS offices, such as Customs and the Coast Guard, have retained some capabilities to gather intelligence information. Following the so-called 'Second State Review' completed in mid-2005, DHS has seen its intelligence capabilities grow somewhat though. More specifically, a reinforced Office of Intelligence and Analysis (I&A) was set up to provide intelligence information supporting DHS and disseminating information and intelligence to state and local actors, and assist the fusion centres in providing operational and intelligence support as well as personnel to enable the National Fusion Center Network (CRS Report to Congress, 2006, p. 2; Stimson Center, 2008, p. 11). These so-called 'fusion centres' function as regional hubs through which information and expertise can be accessed by federal authorities. According to the QHSR, fusion centres play a key role 'in bridging information gaps among federal, state, and local governments' (Nelson, 2010). As of July 2009, there were 72 designated fusion centres scattered across the country. Fusion centres thus represent one prominent example of 'connecting the dots' in the absence of structural reorganization.

In addition, a number of technology platforms serve to assist fusion centres in gathering and disseminating information such as the Joint Fusion Center Program Management office (JCF-PMO) (Harwood, 2009). To improve the sharing of 'sensitive but unclassified' material between federal, state, local, private sector and international partners, DHS has also established the Homeland Security Information Network (HSIN), a secure Internet platform (Kaimen, 2005, pp. 407–408). An integrated network called Homeland Secure Data Network (HSDN) was also set up to allow the federal government to disseminate information and intelligence with the states and to give fusion centre staff access to terrorism-related information from the National Counterterrorism Center (NCTC), which maintains a classified portal of the most current terrorism-related information, and from the DoD Secret Internet Protocol Router Network (SIPRNet), a secure network used to send classified data. Currently, HSDN has been deployed to 27 fusion centres. However, the fusion centres are not exclusively a success story. Documented shortcomings include ineffectiveness at counterterrorism activities, the potential to be used for secondary purposes unrelated to counterterrorism and alleged violations of civil liberties of American citizens (Monahan & Palmer, 2009; German & Stanley, 2008; Fox News.com, 2009).

4.1.2. Clarifying Organizational Relationships In this section, we zoom in closer on two major attempts to clarify the organizational relationships in homeland security—the National Response Framework (NRF) and the National Incident Management System (NIMS). To remedy the problem associated with the lack of relationships between the plethora of actors typically involved in emergency management incidents, Homeland Security Presidential Directive 5 of February 2003 called for the development of the National Response Plan (NRP), as part of a comprehensive national incident management system to replace a previously existing plan. In the aftermath of Hurricane Katrina, this instrument was heavily criticized for overemphasizing federal preparedness and response over state and local efforts (CRS Report to Congress, 2008). Other cited problems were the emphasis on terrorism at the expense of other hazards (see Flynn & Prieto, 2006), the failure to adequately clarify the roles of the various actors partaking in the overall response effort (Parker et al., 2009, p. 213) and to specify multi-state disaster management (Wise, 2006, p. 303), the face that some parts of the document, such as the annexes, were still incomplete at the time of the disaster (Daniels et al., 2006, p. 258) and a lack understanding of the requirements of the plan among DHS leaders (White House, 2007). In January 2008, the NRP was replaced by a new document incorporating the lessons learned from the Katrina disaster called the NRF (CRS Report to Congress, 2008). While the main focus of the NRF is on short-term recovery, the document also stipulates the guiding principles for national response actions as well as the roles and responsibilities of the various actors involved throughout all phases of emergency management. The response to recent disasters such as Hurricanes Gustav and Ike and the 2008 Midwest floods suggest that the NRF has at least been more successful than its predecessor (see Fowler, 2008a,b,c).

Homeland Security Presidential Directive-5 also called for NIMS to serve as 'a structured framework used nationwide for both governmental and nongovernmental agencies to respond to natural disasters and or terrorist attacks at the local, state and federal levels of government' (CRS Report to Congress, 2008). The benefits of NIMS supposedly include a unified approach to incident management, standard command and management structures and emphasis on joint preparedness (including planning, training, qualifications and certifications), mutual aid and resource management. Also providing common terminology, NIMS is designed to foster more effective communication among agencies and organizations jointly responding to incidents. All federal agencies are required to adopt and apply NIMS, and since 2006 federal preparedness assistance (e.g., grants, contracts and other activities) for state and local preparedness is also tied to compliance with the NIMS. Nevertheless, state and local governments are not 'preemptively' compelled to adopt and use the NIMS but are merely encouraged to do so (Sylves, 2008, p. 150). The flawed response to Hurricane Katrina casted light on several implementation problems regarding NIMS. For example, the existence of parallel command structures between federal and state personnel operating in the state of Louisiana had given rise to questions such as 'who is in charge', complicating responsibility and accountability (Daniels et al., 2006, p. 251). It was also evident that state authorities lacked knowledge about NIMS, preventing them from effectively taking advantage of it (see Lester & Krejci, 2007). NIMS has also been subject to criticism for failing to adequately address other types of jurisdiction, authority and leadership issues. Yet, such criticism has often missed the point as NIMS was designed to merely provide an effective vehicle for joint command but not imposing centralized command. Naturally it will take some time before leaders become accustomed with the NIMS through more training and practice. Perhaps even more important though is that the implementation of the NIMS is accompanied by further attempts to foster a common vision and mission between major player involved in disaster response, and that organizational cultures undergo change.

4.1.3. Mutual Aid Agreements Mutual aid agreements predate DHS but have increasingly become prioritized in recent years as mutual aid has become an integrated part of the NIMS (see above). Moreover, in an effort to enhance regional planning, DHS has allocated funds to encourage mutual aid agreements across local public sectors to enhance coordination. In particular, large urban areas can access funding from the Urban Area Security Initiative (UASI). One recent study found that 'regional collaboration as a consequence of both federal UASI guidance and UASI networks may increase the participation of different types of organizations to take part in homeland security and preparedness activities, such as regional exercises and training' (Jordan, 2010). A prominent example here is the Metropolitan Washington Council of Governments (COG), which has taken several critical steps to further develop a regional emergency coordination plan based on UASI grants (Kaimen, 2005, pp. 297–310).

While the UASI initiative has allowed for increased state access to regional planning funding, several implementation problems are also noted. A task force report to Congress recently concluded that moving forward on establishing and funding 'a national comprehensive mutual aid system based on the National Incident Management System (NIMS) to enable all levels of government to tap into assets and capabilities around the country before, during, and after incidents remains a priority'. Another potentially problematic aspect of UASI is that it demands that states disperse 80% of homeland security funding to local governments, thus limiting state authorities' freedom to spend the money where they think they are needed the most.

4.2. Defining a Floor

4.2.1. Federal Baseline Goals and Standards Several documents stipulating federal baseline goals and standards have been adopted since 9/11. The principal of these is the National Strategy for Homeland Security. The first such strategy was published in 2002. In July 2007, an updated version incorporating lessons from Hurricane Katrina was released. Besides this document, DHS also has its own strategic plan laying out the department's mission and identifying its key goals. These goals have a number of objectives against which performance can be measured. DHS' Office of Inspector General (OIG) also releases an Annual Performance Plan, presenting performance information as well as information about resources management.[6] The 2003 Homeland Security Presidential Directive 8 called for DHS to develop a national domestic all-hazards preparedness goal. As a result, the National Preparedness Guidelines—stating the vision, capabilities and priorities for national preparedness—was adopted. At its disposal, the Guidelines have four critical elements: the National Preparedness Vision, providing a concise statement of core national preparedness goals; the National Planning Scenarios, depicting 15 different potential terrorist attacks and natural disasters; the Universal Task List (UTL), a list of 1,600 different tasks that can facilitate efforts in the National Planning Scenarios; and the Target Capabilities List (TCL), defining 37 different capabilities that all actors should possess in order to respond to disasters. According to a Heritage Foundation report, while 'the scenarios and capabilities list [in the TCL] addressed a long-standing glaring shortfall in national leadership by providing standards for performance and capabilities that could be used to assess the readiness of responders and to identify additional capabilities that are needed to make Americans safer', problems remain when it comes to ensuring that federal, state and local authorities put these into action (Carafano & Mayer, 2007).

4.2.2. High-Priority Federal Grants Since 2003, DHS homeland security assistance programmes are administrated by the DHS' Office of Grant Programs (OGP). OGP allocates homeland security assistance to different states and local actors to bolster national preparedness capabilities and protect critical infrastructure (CRS Report to Congress, 2008). Its primary funding mechanism is the Homeland Security Grant Program (HSGP), which consolidated six programmes into one application in order to improve coordination of funding and administration (Haddow, Bullock, Coppola, & Yeletaysi, 2006). HSGP presents a number of priorities for DHS' risk-based funding and the capability-based planning process. In addition to this programme, OGP also administers non-competitive grants programmes, which are allocated to different agencies or jurisdictions using threat and risk assessments. Finally, UASI exists 'to address the unique planning, organization, equipment, training, and exercise needs of high-threat, high-density urban areas, and assists them in building an enhanced and sustainable capacity to prevent, protect against, respond to, and recover from acts of terrorism' (CRS Report to Congress, 2006).

While overall federal funding to DHS has grown quite modestly ($42.4 billion in FY 2003 to $56.3 billion in FY 2011) over the past decade, federal homeland security assistance to state and local authorities has skyrocketed. Still, merely spending more money does not guarantee that the money is well spent. After all, one of the 9/11 Commission report's recommendations for setting priorities in national preparedness was the importance of basing homeland security assistance strictly on assessments of risk and vulnerabilities. In a June 2005 report, the Congressional Research Service noted that DHS had yet to allocate funding to state and local actors based on risk. Congress has also repeatedly voiced concern over that DHS funding has focused on terrorism at the expense of other priorities (see Washington Post, 2006b). For example, most of the homeland security grants under the Patriot Act to the states take no consideration whatsoever to risk or needs assessment (Scavo, Kearney, & Kilroy, 2007). Since then, DHS has begun applying a risk methodology 'to identify critical areas eligible for homeland security grants, accounting for threats, population, economic output, and prevalence of critical infrastructure.' In the fiscal year of 2009, DHS identified five grants based on risk as well as an initiative to measure the impact and effectiveness of homeland security federal grant funds. However, the Government Accountability Office has directed criticism against its risk-based grant methodology, which it concludes lacks a proper way to measure variations in vulnerability (GAO Report to Congressional Committees, 2008). Another study conducted by the Heritage Foundation criticizes Congress for treating homeland security grants 'as simply another entitlement, not as a national security instrument . . . by crafting legislative grant formulas that guarantee every state and city some federal role for homeland security, Congress ensures that it spends a little on everything and does nothing well' (Carafano & Mayer, 2007). In other words, what appear to be lacking is clear priorities. Countless examples also exist of federal homeland security funding going to the wrong 'stuff' or places. Criticism of the HSGP includes its distribution of funds, which for most parts is evenly allocated across all recipients regardless of population. As a result, Wyoming has received more than four times the amount of funding per citizen given to either California or New York (Haddow et al., 2008, p. 103). Despite increased federal homeland security funding for state and local authorities over the past decade, problems with ensuring that state and local authorities use the TCL as a blueprint their homeland security grants have been widespread. More specifically, DHS reportedly still lacks the ability to determine how well state and local governments abide by its standards (Carafano & Mayer, 2007). The UASI has applied its own risk-formula slashed funding in 2006 for New York City and Washington DC while significantly boosting support for such 'urban areas' as Louisville, Omaha and Charlotte (Mayer, 2009).

4.2.3. Federal Performance Reporting In February 2010, DHS published its first Quadrennial Homeland Security Review (QHSR), a comprehensive assessment of the National Strategy for Homeland Security (see above) outlining the long-term strategy and priorities for homeland security and guidance on DHS' programmes, assets, capabilities, budget, policies and authorities. It subsequently also produced a 'bottom-up review' (BUR), with the purpose of systematically linking strategy to programme to budget. The overall goals of the QHSR are to prevent and disrupt terrorist attacks; protect citizens, critical infrastructure and key resources; respond to and recover from incidents that do occur and continue to strengthen the foundation to ensure our long-term success (White House, 2002). While both certainly helpful documents in taking stock of the DHS performance to date, the QHSR and BUR, according to the Government Accountability Office, lacked assessments about DHS' management systems, budget and accounting systems, human resource systems and procurement systems.

4.3. Building a Reliable Learning System

The current national emergency preparedness doctrine has evolved over time. The Post-Katrina Emergency Management Reform Act introduced new efforts to establish a national exercise planning programme (CRS Report to Congress, 2008). A number of activities have also been taken to strengthen preparedness through training and exercises, including the establishment of a National Exercise Program (NEP) to improve the delivery and organization involved with planning for, developing and executing preparedness-related exercises for the federal government. In addition, the National Integration Center (NIC) implements an integration-focused strategy for training and exercises within the Federal Emergency Management Agency (FEMA); the Center for Domestic Preparedness (CDP) prepares state, local, federal and the private sector first responders for dealing with all-hazards and weapons of mass destruction threats through training, education, technical assistance and general support activities; and the Training and Exercise Integration (TEI/TO) train first responders in preparing the nation to prevent, protect against, respond to and recover from incidents of terrorism and catastrophic events. Besides these activities, the Homeland Security Exercise and Evaluation Program (HSEEP) functions as a capabilities and performance-based exercise programme intended to provide a common exercise policy and programme guidance constituting a national exercise standard, building on the NRF and NIMS. FEMA also manages the Comprehensive Exercise Program (CEP) to develop and implement comprehensive, all-hazards, risk-based exercise programme. While the development of a reliable learning system certainly appears to have gone forward, especially after Hurricane Katrina, problems with regard to the leadership of these programmes, particularly the role of FEMA, remain unclear. Moreover, NEP has been criticized for excluding non-federal participants (CRS Report to Congress, 2009).

4.4. Balancing the Old with the New

Naturally, a major challenge for DHS has been to foster a new 'mission culture', replacing—or at least complementing—those of the individual departments and agencies it absorbed—many of which already had a strong 'esprit de corps' of their own (e.g., the Coast Guard, the Transportation Security Administration, FEMA, etc.). As a Homeland Security Council Task Force report from 2007 reports, 'it will require a continuum of progress over a period of many years before optimum cultural unity and affinity can be achieved. It must be further acknowledged that establishing and maintaining a cultural "esprit de corps" is not a one-time or incident-based process—it is an unceasing journey' (White House, 2007). One complicating factor is that most DHS staff are not concentrated in the DHS headquarters in Washington, DC but scattered across the country, thus making the task of fostering a single organizational culture even more difficult. Employee morale at DHS is catastrophically low, with DHS employees accused of fraud and waste (New York Times, 2006). In the 2007 federal workforce survey, DHS was listed as worst place in the federal government to work. Commenting on the survey findings, a former inspector general at DHS said that 'it is still the case that the department is just a collection of disparate, dysfunction agencies . . . [t]here is yet to be an integrated, cohesive whole' (ABC .com, 2007). Since then, things appear to have improved somewhat. In the Partnership for Public Service's 2010 rankings of Best Places to Work in the Federal Government, DHS had climbed to 28 out of 32 agencies on scores for employee satisfaction and commitment.[7]

Few agencies have struggled with balancing old and new responsibilities as much as FEMA. After 9/11, when the need for prevention, mitigation and response to terrorist attacks gained attention, FEMA's traditional focus on natural disasters was reoriented to responding to terrorism events (Waugh & Streib, 2006, p. 136). After the 2004 Florida hurricanes and Hurricane Katrina, FEMA was criticized for having revamped national response capabilities around terrorism while neglecting natural disasters (Cilluffo, Janiewski, Lane, Lord, & Keith, 2009). These events also demonstrated that FEMA's traditionally strong working relationships with state and local counterparts had deteriorated. Some critics even argued that FEMA should be taken out of DHS altogether, allowing it to report directly to the President (see Washington Post, 2006a). Following the enactment of the Post-Katrina Emergency Management Reform Act of 2006, a new Preparedness Directorate within DHS, comprising all the functions of FEMA, elevating the status of FEMA within the agency and providing a direct line to the President, FEMA came to remain within DHS (GAO Report to Congressional Committees, 2009). After Katrina, further proposals were put forward to establish regional offices and roles for DHS (Heyman & Carafano, 2004; Meese, Carafano, & Weitz, 2005).

4.5. Meeting Citizen's Expectations in a Fragmented System

4.5.1. Fostering a Culture of Preparedness Although the United States had a culture of civil defence during the Cold War, much of this was lost after the disappearance of the Soviet threat. Still, recent disasters point to the need for citizens to be well prepared to face an emergency. Since 9/11, one major early attempt to better communicate preparedness to citizens is through a readiness website operated by the DHS called Ready.gov. Through this website, which was heavily advertised across the Internet, DHS sought to communicate preparedness measures to ordinary citizens and businesses. However, Ready.gov has also been intensely criticized—even ridiculed—for being overly alarmist. For example, one of the first announcements that garnered widespread public attention of this campaign was the advice that, in the case of a chemical attack, citizens should use duct tape and plastic sheeting to build a homemade bunker, or 'sheltering in place' to protect themselves. A detailed report by the Federation for American Scientists (FAS) from 2006 concluded that problems included 'generic advice, unnecessarily lengthy descriptions, and verbatim repetition of details on multiple pages, all encapsulated within a confusing navigational structure' (Homeland Security Weekly, 2006). According to FAS, in some cases the advice given was even incorrect, such as the recommendation to take cover underground in the case of a nuclear attack; despite the fact the nuclear explosions do not provide the luxuries of time or evasion.

4.5.2. Informing the Public about Risks Since 9/11, the federal government has sought to step up its risk communication capabilities. Nevertheless, no single integrated system of risk communication is yet in place. Up until recently, DHS' primary public service tool was the National Homeland Security Advisory System (HSAS), first created in 2002. Using a five-step colour guide, this system was meant to direct law enforcement and alert citizens about the current homeland security risk level. However, HSAS has been subject to heavy criticism. According to the Secretary of Homeland Security, Janet Napolitano, the colour-coded system fell short when it came to risk communication, often presenting 'little practical information' to the public and using ambiguous threat levels (Washington Post, 2011; CNN.com, 2011). Shapiro and Cohen argue that the system has utterly failed to adequately increase beliefs about the value of protection, and to generate predictable outcomes that match the purposes for an alert (Shapiro & Cohen, 2007). In January 2011, plans were announced to replace the HSAS with a new system called the

National Terrorism Advisory System (NTAS). Using a two-level terrorism advisory scale, this system is intended to provide the public with alerts 'specific to the threat' and 'with a specified end date'. The objective is to provide information about actions to be taken to ensure public safety and recommended steps that individuals, communities, businesses and governments can take to help prevent, mitigate or respond to the threat. The public alerts will be based on the nature of the threat, which can in some cases be sent directly to law enforcement or affected areas of the private sector, while in others, alerts will be issued more broadly to the public through both official and media channels. The NTAS thus have a much stronger eye towards risk communication than the previous system. Still a nascent system, there are few examples to evaluate the effectiveness of the new system. Still, there seems to have been improvements.[8]

A final aspect of risk communication is how to strike a balance between freedom and security, which certain levels of risk entails. In particular, controversies surrounding the enhanced use of control and detection measures (such as so-called 'body scans') at the nation's airports have been widespread. Critics claim that such measures as full body scans infringe personal liberties, while DHS representatives argue they are necessary to ensure security on board. It seems fair to say that regardless of which side of the debate one is on, federal authorities have clearly not been effective in explaining all its actions to the public.

4.6. Concluding Discussion

The US government's efforts to enhance coordination in the area of homeland security after 9/11 have yielded mixed results. When it comes to the first dimension, 'matching place and functions', several new initiatives were recorded, including the establishment of new interagency network solutions. Many of these, however, still suffer from problems relating to implementation. On the second dimension, 'defining a floor', the federal government has defined new standards and sought to follow up with appropriate funding to address shortcomings relating to these standards. Examples of 'wasteful' or misguided federal homeland security grants are plentiful however. In terms of the third dimension, 'building a reliable learning system', while efforts have been made to establish a national exercise planning programme, problems with regard to leadership of these problems remain unresolved. As to the fourth dimension 'balancing the old with the new', the DHS in general and FEMA in particular, still suffer from a lack of mission, culture and morale. Finally, when it comes to 'meeting citizens' expectations', public information campaigns appear in many cases to have been insufficient. In summary, the overall assessment of the homeland security reorganization's effects on coordination accordingly appears, despite notable achievements and a plethora of new initiatives, to be far from adequately addressed.

5. Conclusions

The 11 September 2001 terrorist attacks immediately placed homeland security at the very top of the national public policy agenda in the United States. Ten years later, homeland security remains one of the top missions for the US government. Securing the homeland is also one of the most complex missions, requiring a coordinated and integrated effort from all levels of society—ranging from the federal government to state and local governments to the private and non-profit sectors. Coordination is therefore both the diagnosis of the homeland security problem as well as the diagnosis of the solution. This paper has employed a public administration perspective to assess how the post-September 11 reforms have addressed the central coordination challenges posed by homeland security. In doing so, it made use of Don Kettl's 'contingent coordination' framework in order to identify areas where progress has been made and point to areas where more work still needs to be done.

In short, this study confirms that US homeland security is indeed in far better shape today than it was 10 years ago, prior to 9/11. Important efforts have been undertaken, frequently mixing both structural and network approaches. However, while the dots between relevant homeland security actors at the federal, state and local levels are better connected today, several shortcomings remain unsolved. The key findings are summarized below.

First, while the major post-9/11 homeland security reform efforts have centred on the structural merger of federal departments and agencies with homeland security responsibilities into the new DHS—examples of inter-organizational coordination are also present, particularly in the intelligence field. More specifically, progress has been made in terms of creating new inter-organizational networks (such as the fusion centres) between federal, state and local officials. While several attempts have been made to clarify organizational relationships (such as NIMS and the NRF), organizational confusion remains a perennial problem. Since both NIMS and the NRF remain works in progress, further assessments are needed though before we can draw any general conclusions regarding the success of these efforts. Finally, in terms of mutual aid agreements, some progress can be discerned in terms of boosting regional emergency management collaboration.

Second, new federal baseline goals and standards for homeland security have been adopted since 9/11, including the National Preparedness Guidelines. Some problems with the implementation of this document were found, however. Moreover, while high-priority federal grants have provided assistance to state and local authorities, problems with regard to applying risk methodology and the distribution of assistance were noted. Finally, new federal performance reporting has been introduced, although these still lack information about certain areas of the federal performance on homeland security.

Third, while the federal efforts to build a reliable learning system has made much progress over the past decade, for example by creating new training and evaluation programmes, the United States has yet to implement a national planning and exercise programme fully equal to the task of preparing for catastrophic disasters.

Fourth, it has proven difficult fostering an entirely new organizational culture from scratch for the Department of Homeland Security. The diversity and deep-rooted history and strong culture of many of its constituent organizations naturally meant that DHS would face hurdles in imposing a 'single culture' within the new department. Although some efforts have been made, including leadership reforms, it is clear that DHS is still struggling with developing an overarching and blended organizational culture based on common values, goals and focus of mission, both within DHS headquarters and between its component organizations.

Fifth, efforts to improve public communication after 9/11 have proved largely ineffective. In response, the old system was eventually abandoned and a new one—intended to address these shortcomings—was introduced. While this development mark a step forward in theory, only time will tell whether it will be seen as a more effective tool than its predecessor.

These findings may allow us to say that although homeland security coordination has improved effectiveness has not necessarily followed automatically. This conclusion challenges the underlying assumption that more and more coordination is necessary while previous research suggests that there are limits to the effectiveness one might expect from more coordination. For example, in a study of crisis management in the Netherlands, Berlin and Carlstrom (2008) found that (during exercises) collaboration is typically limited (and hence also the need for coordination), while Scholtens (2008) stated that directing front line units during incidents is almost impossible (and thus coordination is of limited value). Better collaboration should accordingly be obtained in the preparation phase. While coordination is doubtlessly important, it would be naïve to think of it as the 'magic silver bullet' which alone can solve all problems involved in the challenge of providing for homeland security.

The findings of this paper have identified the biggest coordination challenges facing the US government in the area of homeland security. The US federal government would do well to pay heed to these findings, seeking to improve these coordination shortcomings in order to strengthen homeland security. Further studies should build on these findings to improve our understanding of past and present homeland security developments.

Acknowledgements

The author would like to thank Mark Rhinard, the anonymous reviewers and the editor of this issue for helpful comments on previous drafts. All errors remain solely with the author however.

Critical Thinking Questions

1. How can or should the effectiveness of homeland security efforts be assessed?
2. What are the most daunting challenges confronting efforts to implement homeland security reforms, and how can they be overcome?
3. Beyond the recommendations offered by this author, what other kinds of things could be done to "strengthen the capacity" of the U.S. homeland security system?

Notes

1. Following Wollmann (2003, p. 594) this paper defines coordination as 'the attempt to optimize the coherence and consistency of political decisions as well as policy implementation across policies, actors and stakeholders, and levels'.
2. Similarly, the 9/11 report recommended the establishment of national priorities for homeland security, based on an assessment of risks and vulnerability.
3. Examples include the World Trade Center bombings in 1993, the Oklahoma bombings in 1994, the Atlanta Olympics shootings in 1995 and Hurricane Mitch in 1998.
4. To assess progress in these policy initiatives, this paper draws heavily on reports from the Congressional Research Office and the Government Accountability Office.
5. For a complete list of the agencies incorporated by DHS, see http://www.dhs.gov/xabout/history/editorial_0133.shtm
6. For 2009's Annual Performance Plan, see http://www.dhs.gov/xoig/assets/OIG_APP_FY09.pdf

7. See http://bestplacestowork.org/BPTW/rankings/overall/large
8. See DHS website: http://www.dhs.gov/files/publications/ntas-public-guide.shtm

References

9/11 Commission. (2005), *9/11 Commission Report: Final Report of the National Commission on Terrorist Attacks Upon the United States,* W.W. Norton & Company, New York.

ABC.com. (2007), *'Homeland Security Employees Rank Last in Job Satisfaction Survey',* 8 February 2007, http://abclocal.go.com/wls/story?section=news/national_world&id=5017688 (accessed 28 December 2011).

Berlin, J.M. and Carlstrom, E.D. (2008), 'The 90-Secnd Collaboration: A Critical Study of Collaboration Exercises at Extensive Accident Sites', *Journal of Crisis Management and Contingencies,* Volume 16, Number 4, pp. 1771–65.

Carafano, J.J. and Mayer, M. (2007), *Pending Smarter: Prioritizing Homeland Security Grants by Using National Standards and Risk Criteria,* Heritage Foudnation, Washington DC.

Chisholm, D. (1992), *Coordination without Hierarchy: Informal Structures in Multiorganizational Systems,* University of California Press, Berkeley, CA.

Cilluffo, F.J., Janiewski, D.J., Lane, J.P., Lord, G.C. and Keith, L.P. (2009), *Serving American's Disaster Victims: FEMA—Where Does It Fit?,* Homeland Security Policy Institute, George Washington University, Washington DC, http://www.gwumc.edu/hspi/policy/IssueBrief_FEMA.pdf (accessed 28 December 2011).

Clarke, L.B. (1999), *Mission Improbable: Using Fantasy Documents to Tame Disasters,* University of Chicago Press, Chicago, IL.

CNN.com. (2011), *'U.S. Replaces Color-Coded Terror Alerts',* 27 January 2009, http://edition.cnn.com/2011/TRAVEL/01/27/terror.threats/ (accessed 26 December 2011).

Cooper, C. and Block, R. (2006), *Disaster: Hurricane Katrina and the Failure of Homeland Security,* Times Books, London.

CRS Report to Congress. (2006), *Department of Homeland Security Reorganization: The 2SR Initiative,* Congressional Research Service, Washington DC.

CRS Report to Congress. (2008), *The National Response Frame-work: Overview and Possible Issues for Congress,* Congressional Research Service, Washington DC.

CRS Report to Congress. (2009), *Homeland Emergency Preparedness and the National Exercise Program: Background, Policy Implications, and Issues for Congress,* Congressional Research Service, Washington DC.

Dahl, R. (1947), 'The Science of Public Administration', *Public Administration Review,* Volume 7, pp. 1–11.

Daniels, R.J., Kettl, D. and Kunreuther, H. (2006), *On Risk and Disaster: Lessons from Hurricane Katrina,* University of Pennsylvania Press, Philadelphia, PA.

Davis, L.E. (2002), *'Organizing for Homeland Security',* Rand Corporation Issue Paper, http://www.rand.org/pubs/issue_papers/IP220.html (accessed 28 December 2011).

Flynn, S.E. and Prieto, D.B. (2006), *Neglected Defense: Mobilizing the Private Sector to Support Homeland Security,* Council of Foreign Relations Special Report, NewYork.

Fowler, D. (2008a), *'Effective Response to Gustav—Courting Complacency or Heralding a Habit?',* CQ Press, 3 September 2008.

Fowler, D. (2008b), *'Who's in Charge Still a Disaster-Response Question Mark',* CQ Homeland Security, 22 September 2008.

Fowler, D. (2008c), *'Federal Response to Recent Hurricanes Termed "So Far, So Good"'*, CQ Homeland Security, 23 September 2008.

Fox News.com. (2009),*'Fusion Centers' Expand Criteria to Identify Militia Members*, 23 March 2009.

GAO Report to Congressional Committees. (2008), *Homeland Security: DHS Risk-Based Grant Methodology Is Reasonable, But Current Version's Measure of Vulnerability Is Limited,* U.S. Government Accountability Office, Washington DC.

GAO Report to Congressional Committees.(2009*),Urban Area Security Initiative: FEMA Lacks Measures to Assess How Regional Collaboration Efforts Build Preparedness Capabilities,* U.S. Government Accountability Office, Washington DC.

German, M. and Stanley, J. (2008), *Fusion Center Update,* American Civil Liberties Union, New York, http://www.aclu.org/pdfs/privacy/fusion_update_20080729.pdf (accessed 28 December 2011).

Gulick, L.H. (1937), 'Notes on the Theory of Organization', in Gulick, L.H. and Urwick, L.F. (eds), *Papers on the Science of Administration,* Institute of Public Administration, NewYork, pp. 3–35.

Haddow, G., Bullock, J., Coppola, F. and Yeletaysi, S. (2008), *Introduction to Homeland Security,* Butterworth-Heinemann, Burlington, MA.

Harwood, S. (2009), 'DHS *to Create New Office to Support Intelligence Fusion Center',* Security Management, 10 January 2009, http://www.securitymanagement.com/print/6287 (accessed 28 December 2011).

Helsloot, I. (2008), 'Coordination Is a Prerequisite for Good Collaboration, Isn't It?', *Journal of Crisis Management and Contingencies,* Volume 16, Number 4, pp. 173–176.

Heyman, D. and Carafano, J.J. (2004), *DHS 2.0.: Rethinking the Department of Homeland Security,* Heritage Special Report, Heritage Foundation, Washington DC.

Homeland Security Weekly (2006), *Changing of the Guards: The Federation of American Scientists Has Serious Issues with ready.gov,* http://www.homelandsecurityweekly.com/features/dhs-fas-readygov-082906/ (28 December 2011).

Jordan, A.E. (2010), 'Collaborative Relationships Resulting from the Urban Area Security Initiative', *Journal of Homeland Security and Emergency Management,* Volume 7, Number 1, pp. 1–19. Article 38.

Kaimen, D. (2005), *The McGraw-Hill Homeland Security Handbook,* McGraw-Hill, NewYork.

Kaufman, H. (1960), *The Forest Ranger,* Johns Hopkins University Press, Baltimore, MD.

Kettl, D. (2003a), *The States and Homeland Security: The Missing Link,* Century Foundation, New York.

Kettl, D. (2003b), 'Contingent Coordination: Practical and Theoretical Puzzles for Homeland Security', *American Review of Public Administration,* Volume 33, Number 3, pp. 253–277.

Kettl, D. (2007), *Systems under Stress: Homeland Security and American Politics,* CQ Press, Washington DC.

Lester, W. and Krejci, D. (2007), 'Business "Not" as Usual: The National Incident Management System, Federalism, and Leadership, *Public Administration Review,* Volume 67, Special Issue, pp. 84–93.

Lindsay, J.M. and O'Hanlon, M.E. (2002), *Protecting the American Homeland,* Brookings Institution Press, Washington DC.

Mayer, M.A. (2009), *An Analysis of Federal, State, and Local Homeland Security Budgets,* Heritage Foundation, Washington DC.

Meese, E., Carafano, J.J. and Weitz, R. (2005), *Organizing for Victory: Proposals for Building a Regional Homeland Security Structure,* Heritage Backgrounder, Heritage Foundation, Washington DC.

Monahan, T. and Palmer, N.A. (2009), 'The Emerging Politics of DHS Fusion Centers', *Security Dialogue,* Volume 40, Number 6, pp. 617–636.

Morris, J.C. and Morris, E.D. (2007), 'Reaching for the Philosopher's Stone: Contingent Coordination and the Military's Response to Hurricane Katrina', *Public Administration Review,* Volume 67, Special Issue, pp. 94–106.

Nelson, R.O. (2010), *First Quadrennial Homeland Security Review,* Center for Strategic and International Studies, Washington DC, http://csis.org/publication/first-quadrennial-homeland-security-review (accessed 28 December 2011).

New York Times (2006), 'Homeland Security Department Is Accused of Credit Card Misuse', New York Times, 19 July 2006.

Newmann, W.W. (2002), 'Reorganizing for National Security and Homeland Security', *Public Administration Review,* Volume 62, Special Issue, pp. 126–137.

O'Toole, L.J. (1997), 'Treating Networks Seriously: Practical and Research-based Agendas in Public Administration, *Public Administration Review,* Volume 57, Number 1, pp. 45–52.

Parker, C.F., Stern, E.K., Pagila, E. and Brown, C. (2009), 'Preventable Catastrophe? Hurricane Katrina Disaster Revisited', *Journal of Contingencies and Crisis Management,* Volume 17, Number 4, pp. 206–220.

Perrow, C. (2007), *The Next Catastrophe: Reducing Our Vulnerabilities to Natural, Industrial, and Terrorist Disasters,* Princeton University Press, Princeton, NJ.

Peters, B.G. (2006), 'Concepts and Theories of Horizontal Policy Management, in Peters, G. and Pierre, J. (eds), *Handbook of Public Policy,* Sage Publications, Thousand Oaks, CA.

Relyea, H.C. (2003), 'Organizing for Homeland Security', *Presidential Studies Quarterly,* Volume 33, Number 3, pp. 602–624.

Samaan, J.-L. and Verneuil, L. (2009), 'Civil-Military Relations in Hurricane Katrina: A Case Study on Crisis Management in Natural Disaster Response', in Steets, J. and Hamilton, D.S. (eds), *Humanitarian Assistance: Improving U.S.-EU Cooperation,* The Johns Hopkins University, Washington DC, pp. 413–435.

Sauter, M. and Carafano, J. (2006), *Homeland Security: A Complete Guide to Understanding, Preventing, and Surviving Terrorism,* McGraw-Hill, NewYork.

Scavo, C., Kearney, R.C. and Kilroy, R.J. (2007), 'Challenges to Federalism: Homeland Security and Disaster Response', *Publius: The Journal of Federalism,* Volume 38, Number 1, pp. 81–110.

Scholtens, A. (2006), 'Controlled Collaboration in Disaster and Crisis Management in the Netherlands, History and Practice of an Overestimated and Underestimated Concept, *Journal of Crisis Management and Contingencies,* Volume 1 6, Number 4, pp. 195–207.

Seidman, H. (1998). *Politics, Position, and Power: The Dynamics of Federal Organization* (5th edn), Oxford University Press, New York.

Shapiro, J.N. and Cohen, D.K. (2007), 'Color Blind: Lessons from the Failed Homeland Security Advisory System', *International Security,* Volume 32, Number 2, pp. 121–154.

Stimson Center. (2008), *New Information and Intelligence Needs in the 21st Century Threat Environment,* Stimson Center, Washington DC, http://www.stimson.org/images/uploads/research-pdfs/SEMA-DHS_FINAL.pdf (accessed 28 December 2011).

Sylves, R. (2008), *Disaster Policy and Politics: Emergency Management and Homeland Security,* CQ Press, Washington DC.

Taylor, F.W. (1911), *Principles of Scientific Management,* Harper and Brothers, New York.

Washington Post (2006a), 'Can Congress Rescue FEMA?', Washington Post, 26 June 26 2006.

Washington Post (2006b), 'Have Fewer Requirements', Washington Post, 6 November 2006.

Washington Post (2011), 'Obama Administration to Replace Color-Coded Terror Alerts with New Warning System', Washington Post, 27 January 2011.

Waugh, W.L., Jr and Streib, G. (2006), 'Collaboration and Leadership for Effective Emergency Management', *Public Administration Review,* Volume 66, Special Issue, pp. 131–140.

White House. (2002)*, 'National Strategy for Homeland Security',* Washington DC.

White House. (2007)*, 'Report of the Homeland Security Culture Task Force',* Washington DC.

Wise, C.R. (2002), 'Organizing for Homeland Security', *Public Administration Review,* Volume 62, Special Issue, pp. 131–144.

Wise, C.R. (2006), 'Organizing for Homeland Security after Katrina: Is Adaptive Management What's Missing?', *Public Administration Review,* Volume 66, Number 3, pp. 302–318.

Wise, C.R. and Nader, R. (2002), 'Organizing the Federal System for Homeland Security: Problems, Issues, and Dilemmas', *Public Administration Review,* Volume 62, Special Issue, pp. 44–57.

Wollmann, H. (2003), 'Coordination in the Intergovernmental Setting', in Peters, G.B. and Pierre, J. (eds), *Handbook of Public Administration,* Sage Publications, London, pp. 594–604.

Tradition v. Efficiency

What Role for DoD in the Homeland Security?

Joanne Moore

In the late 1990s, the Department of Defense (DoD) began considering its roles and missions in light of the increasing terrorist threat to the U.S. homeland. For almost a century prior to that, the military preferred to concentrate on its expeditionary role and had arranged its structures to do so. Considering missions in the homeland brought greater attention to legal and policy considerations that frame military activities at home, in some cases causing suspicion and confusion. The events of September 11, 2001 marked the beginning of DoD's renewed significant activities in the homeland, while Hurricane Katrina brought on new approaches to perennial legal, policy and process issues for DoD operations at home. Today, DoD states that protecting the homeland is its top priority.[1] Backing these words with action requires DoD to chart a narrow path based on traditional roles of the military in the U.S., legal restrictions, continuing commitments to expeditionary roles, and preparing for missions on American soil. This chapter will review the legal environment, DoD initiatives taken in the last ten years, and areas yet to be addressed in order strengthen the military's ability to defend the homeland from organized state or nonstate attackers, and to support civil authorities.

On September 11, 2001 parts of the North American Aerospace Defense Command (NORAD) tracked aircraft and scrambled fighter jets to protect the skies over New York and Washington, DC when it was unclear how many commercial aircraft had been hijacked and what planes still in the air might have hostile intentions.[2] In the tense days and weeks after those attacks, U.S troops provided additional security in the skies, on the borders, at airports and at sea. As needed, they assisted with recovery efforts at crash sites, chiefly providing security and helping with labor-intensive rubble removal. Named Operation Noble Eagle,[3] the military ultimately employed over 100,000 people in providing continued security presence in the air, on land, and in the maritime approaches to the homeland. Many people were taken aback by the presence of uniformed soldiers on our borders, in our airports, and guarding critical infrastructure. Some were surprised because such military activities seemed to violate the Posse Comitatus Act, a federal law that prohibits federal military troops from performing law enforcement activities within the United States.

In 2003, following the recommendations of the Hart-Rudman Commission and the 2001 Quadrennial Defense Review, DoD established the Assistant Secretary of Defense for Homeland Defense and Americas' Security Affairs. This office mirrored the federal restructuring that created the Department of Homeland Security, and gave other federal agencies a single point of entry into the DoD to work out evolving relationships within the homeland security enterprise. Within a few years, the approach of an active, layered defense was officially adopted,[4] and DoD carved out a mission that honored its traditional homeland role as well as its relationship with DHS.

However, it was not the terrorist attacks on September 11, 2001 that spurred the federal government's increasing reliance on DoD during catastrophic domestic disasters, but the performance of DoD during the response to Hurricane Katrina. At the height of the response over 15,000 active duty personnel had been deployed to the disaster area, but federal law limited the role of the active duty troops to rescue, evacuation, emergency medical treatment, emergency power restoration, debris removal, food distribution, roadway control and emergency communications.[5] Over 50,000 National Guard troops also deployed to the disaster area, conducting a wide variety of functions including assisting local police in restoration of civil security.[6] What roles DoD and the federal government could undertake created some confusion, as the Louisiana State Governor requested that the federal government "send everything you've got," and specifically requested federal troops, but was unwilling to release control of National Guard troops from herself to the federal government. This led to some discussion in the White House as to whether the response could be federalized despite the governor's objections (citing the Insurrection Act as the basis for such a step). Ultimately, the Bush Administration did not federalize all troops on the ground, which complicated command and control of the massive operation. In the flurry of reports and lessons learned after Katrina, the national government re-examined the federal law restricting DoD actions in a domestic response, and DoD undertook a concerted effort to support the planning efforts of DHS and other agencies. In a speech on September 15, 2005, President Bush stated, "It is now clear that a challenge on this scale requires greater federal authority and a broader role for the armed forces—the institution of our government most capable of massive logistical operations in a moment's notice."[7]

Understanding the roles of the armed forces in the cases of a catastrophic terrorist attack and a major natural disaster required careful analysis of the federal law and the roles that the DoD can perform versus the roles that the nation desires DoD to perform. Understanding the Posse Comitatus Act and its principal exceptions paves the way for DoD to balance its mission to defend the homeland, the expectation that it will assist other agencies when needed, and will honor the American traditional skepticism of military forces operating domestically. To develop that understanding, it is essential to review the military's major homeland operations since 1880, and especially since 2001.

Reviewing the Law and Tradition of Posse Comitatus

The US Constitution states that one of the roles of government is to "provide for the common defense" in that a federally controlled military would defend the entire nation, but elsewhere in the same document, the nation's aversion to large standing armies is clear. The Third Amendment prohibits quartering soldiers in private homes—colonial households were often required to provide room and board for British soldiers without their consent and without payment. Likewise the Constitution requires that the budget that pays for federal troops can be funded for only two years at a time. In Federalist 26, Alexander Hamilton explained that the Article II provision would require the legislature to "to deliberate upon the propriety of keeping a military force on foot" and formally vote upon it "in the face of their constituents."[8] No such controls were placed upon the Navy, which was viewed as essential to protect commerce, or the several States' militias—a precursor to the National Guard.

The Constitution gives the President wide berth in his control of federal troops, in his role as Commander in Chief, and in his role to "faithfully execute the laws." It was this combination that allowed President Washington to use several States' militias to quell the Whiskey Rebellion of 1794. The President's role was further strengthened by the Insurrection Acts, first passed in the early 1800s, which allowed President Grant to use federal troops to impose order in several southern States before and during the election of 1876. At several points during the Reconstruction period, federal troops were deployed to Louisiana and Mississippi to enforce legislative election results. In the months before the 1876 Presidential Election, the governor of South Carolina appealed to the President to assist in dealing with particularly violent Ku Klux Klan activities that amounted to targeted killings of the newly enfranchised blacks. Southerners viewed these actions as federal imposition of martial law, and federal interference with the states' electoral processes. Resentful Southern Senators introduced the Posse Comitatus Act (PCA) as an amendment to the National Defense Authorization Action of 1878 to ensure their states would never again be subjected to martial law at the hands of US troops.[9]

The PCA is often cited as the reason federal troops cannot carry out a variety of activities on U.S. soil. First, the law itself stipulates that Congress may create exceptions to *posse comitatus*. Second, the law does not exclude non-federalized troops. That is, any State National Guard acting in a state capacity is not constrained by the PCA. Finally, examining the reasons for the act's passage sheds light on whether its application should be further reviewed given today's environment. Immediately following the Civil War, Congress required each Southern State to ratify the 14th Amendment. When they failed to comply immediately, the Southern States were divided into five military districts, with a general officer commanding each district. Beginning in March 1867, federal troops were given authority to supervise elections, maintain order, and enforce the law. Later that same year they were granted authority to turn away potential voters from the polls and to discharge elected officials.

The Army had to quell violence on several occasions when Southern States were unable to peaceably transfer political power. In Louisiana and Arkansas, the Army was used to quell violence in the legislatures resulting from contested elections. In South Carolina, the Army was used to stop violence and political intimidation being perpetrated by the Ku Klux Klan, arresting over 500 people. Finally, in several Southern states, the published Democratic campaign plan for 1876 included intimidation, bribery and violence to deter blacks from voting. It even went so far as to suggest that a black man's death was better than allowing him to vote.[10] The use of federal troops to maintain order at the polls during the 1876 election was highly controversial, and became more so when the presidential contest was so close that an electoral commission had to be established to determine the election results. Some insisted that the presence of federal troops at the polls in Southern states was an attempt by the Grant administration to influence the election results, while Reconstruction governors determined it was necessary to ensure that newly enfranchised blacks had an opportunity to vote.

PCA is a federal criminal law that prevents the use of federal troops to enforce civil laws, under penalty of fine or imprisonment. Southern Senators added it as an amendment to the National Defense Authorization Action of 1878 to redress Southern grievances regarding the Army's employment during Reconstruction. The proximate cause of the PCA is usually cited as the use of the Army to maintain order at the polls during the 1876 presidential election. The original law reads:

> From and after the passage of this act it shall not be lawful to employ any part of the Army of the United States, as a posse comitatus [a power or force of the county], or otherwise, for the purpose of executing the laws, except in such cases and under such circumstances as such employment of said force may be expressly authorized by the Constitution or by act of Congress.[11]

The PCA applies only to "federal troops." Although not apparent to most Americans, this means that the PCA does not apply to members of the States' National Guard or their leaders. Wearing the same uniform and operating in the same places as their federal counterparts, State Guardsmen can execute the laws of their State if need be. This flexibility uniquely positions the National Guard to be useful in a homeland security situation. These troops can offer federal, state and local officials the capabilities of the Department of Defense—information sharing, technical assistance, logistical assistance and law enforcement assistance—as needed, so long as they work under the control of a state governor. When they are ordered to federal service by the President, they only lose the ability to provide direct law enforcement assistance—that is, the ability to conduct searches, seizures and arrests.

There are several exceptions to the PCA in which federal law provides alternative ways for the president to exercise his constitutional authority to "faithfully execute the laws." Most notable is the Insurrection Act; this section of the federal code was most recently amended in the wake of Hurricane Katrina (10 U.S.C. § § 331–335). These five sections of federal law provide circumstances in which the president may federalize the National Guard, or authorize federal troops to provide civil law enforcement if required. Past examples of using the Act provide some insight regarding future policy implications

Section 331 allows the President to suppress an insurrection upon the request of a governor. President George H.W. Bush invoked this section of the Act in 1992 when the governor of California requested federal assistance during the Los Angeles riots. The President issued an executive order 'authorizing the Secretary of Defense to use the armed forces to suppress "domestic violence and disorder . . . in Los Angeles . . . endangering life and property and obstructing execution of the laws . . . and to restore law and order."'[12] However, the military leadership of Joint Task Force-Los Angeles vetted every request for assistance from civilian authorities, refusing all requests to perform law enforcement duties. This confusion actually reduced the number of people available to perform law enforcement because the presidential decree also federalized the California National Guard in order to maintain unity of command. This lesson was quickly learned; President Bush did not federalize the Nation Guard later that year when military forces were requested to stop looting after Hurricane Hugo.

Section 332 gives the President the authority to deploy federal troops to enforce the laws when there is an obstruction of justice or when federal laws cannot be enforced. As with all parts of the law, the President must make a declaration addressing the issue and directing that all people involved peaceably return to their homes. In several cases during the 1950s and 1960s, Presidents used federal troops to enforce court decisions regarding desegregation. In 1957, President Eisenhower federalized all Louisiana National Guard troops, taking them away from the purview of the governor, who was using National Guardsmen to block integration of Little Rock High School. Then, he used active component troops to enforce a federal District Court ruling that implemented the 1954 U.S. Supreme Court decision that declared racially separate public education illegal. Federal troops spent a year stationed in Little Rock ensuring that seven black students were able to safely attend the previously all-white high school.

In 1992, President George H.W. Bush most likely relied on Section 333 of the law to allow federal troops to prevent looting after Hurricane Hugo because that portion of the law gives the president a general authority to suppress any insurrection or domestic violence that hinders or impedes the execution of the laws of the U.S. This section also identifies actions in a state that violate the civil rights of a class of people. It does not require a request from the governor or a ruling by a federal court; it could have been used more recently by the White House during Hurricane Katrina. However, during Hurricane Katrina the Governor of Louisiana would not give up control of the National Guard, or overall control of the response. Evidently, in this case the president's attorneys did not make a sufficiently compelling case for invoking the Insurrection Act, therefore none of the nearly 15,000 active component troops deployed for Katrina could perform law enforcement duties, such as assisting the National Guard troops in Louisiana and Mississippi with enforcing curfews and preventing looting.

A report issued by the White House following Katrina criticized the limitations on the Department of Defense's ability to use "military capabilities during domestic incidents, specifically citing "limitations in Federal law and DoD policy" that required state governors to request military assistance. In light of these concerns, President Bush requested that Congress determine whether or when a domestic disaster of a certain size would be turned over to the DoD to lead the response.[13] Following a period of considerable debate, Congress instead amended the language of the Insurrection Act as part of the National Defense Authorization Act of 2007. The Senate Armed Services Committee Report characterized these changes as a "provision that would update the Insurrection Act to clarify the President's authority to use the armed forces, including the National Guard in federal service, to restore order and enforce federal laws in cases where, as a result of a terrorist attack, epidemic, or natural disaster, public order has broken down.[14] The committee report speculated that the law's antiquated language and lack of specificity may have contributed to initial confusion during Hurricane Katrina. The amended law went further, changing the name of the chapter of the US Code in which the statutes appear from "Insurrection" to "Enforcement of the Laws to Restore Public Order."[15]

The Insurrection Act, as amended in 2007 in the wake of Hurricane Katrina, grants the president broad authorities to employ federal forces domestically in the event of a major domestic disaster, whether natural or manmade. Checks to constrain executive branch abuse of this new language rely on traditional reluctance to employ federal troops and burdensome Congressional reporting (every two weeks). As the DoD seeks to fulfill its mission to protect the homeland, the legal considerations of the Posse Comitatus Act and the statutory exceptions to it that are found in the Insurrection Act remain influential. In additional to the legal constraints that arise principally from these two laws, DoD has drawn clear distinctions between what its military role is in defending the homeland, and what support it may provide to civil authorities—by law, and by policy.

First, the DoD separated its homeland roles into two distinct categories: homeland defense and defense support to civil authorities (DSCA). "Homeland defense" consists of those defensive actions that DoD might take to prevent or respond to a direct attack by a state or a nonstate actor. DSCA provides assistance to domestic civil authorities in the event of a natural or manmade disaster, potentially in response to a very significant or catastrophic event. The lead agency for disaster response is usually the Department of Homeland Security (DHS). Further, DoD provides technical assistance and occasionally manpower for National Security Special Events (NSSE) such as a major summit or a major sporting event in which local and federal authorities have insufficient capacity for the required security presence. The lead agency for these events might be the Department of Justice or the Secret Service.

Homeland Defense

DoD defines homeland defense as the "protection of US sovereignty, territory, domestic population and critical defense infrastructure against external threats and aggression, or other threats as directed by the President."[16] The category of activities that DoD uses to describe homeland defense has one central issue at its core: an external threat. DoD is only the lead federal agency in response to that threat in very particular cases when a law enforcement response is insufficient: 1) air threats in North American airspace in which the aircraft must be defeated; 2) maritime threats in US waters or the approaches in cases in which the vessel must be defeated; 3) a ground attack against the U.S. by another state. In all cases, DoD strives for an active and layered defense—one which layers the air, land and sea domains—and which strives to identify threats as early as possible. DoD seeks to identify and counter air and maritime threats at a safe distance, primarily through persistent air and maritime awareness and the ability to intercept aircraft and vessels as required.[17]

To protect the nation from air threats, DoD receives assistance from the Federal Aviation Administration (FAA) and DHS assets to identify anomalous air activity which may threaten the United States, but DoD has sole responsibility for defeating air threats once they are identified as hostile. Further, the United States has partnered with Canada since the 1950s to provide integrated air warning and airspace control for all of North America. The organization, known as the North American Aerospace Defense Command (NORAD), renewed its bilateral agreement in 2006 and added maritime warning to its missions. Soon after September 11, 2001, NORAD began flying missions under the auspices of Operation Noble Eagle to intercept suspicious aircraft, protect restricted airspace, and if required, defeat hostile aircraft.

The maritime domain is particularly complex because it is multi-jurisdictional, with various U.S. civil agencies at multiple levels which are responsible for tracking maritime traffic—including vessels, cargo and people. To help identify suspicious vessels, DoD should seek to establish shared maritime sensors with such agencies, conceptually similar to the radar assets shared with the FAA. To counter maritime threats at a safe distance from U.S. shores, DoD already partners with DHS. Both organizations rely on well-practiced agreements for quickly transferring control of Navy and Coast Guard assets as the Navy intercepts emergent maritime threats,[18] and then transfers leadership of the incident to the Coast Guard, and provides support to them.

Early identification of potential threats is critical for preventing a terrorist attack on the homeland. In this arena, DoD offers support to U.S. civil counterparts through intelligence sharing. DoD also maintains response capabilities to help counter improvised Explosive Devices (IEDs), and to detect and prevent terrorists' use of weapons of mass destruction (WMD) in the homeland. DoD has developed unique and expansive counter-IED capabilities in Iraq and Afghanistan. These capabilities have significant applicability to the civilian-led law enforcement mission in the homeland. As the U.S. contemplates the possibility of future domestic threats, improvised explosives are a proven terrorist tool. The averted Times Square bombing in May 2010 is an example—an IED planted in a car. DoD's counter IED capabilities provide a significant asset which can be employed in the homeland if required, and can be shared with law enforcement agencies ahead of a crisis, improving federal, state, tribal and local authorities' ability to detect, prevent and neutralize IEDs.

In the homeland, DoD would not normally be the lead agency to prevent a terrorist (WMD) attack. Under specific exceptions to the Posse Comitatus Act specifying the use of military forces in the U.S. to prevent or respond to nuclear attacks, DoD can provide a wide range of support capabilities to federal law enforcement agencies. Currently, the military provides logistical, informational and operational support as requested. Additional planning and coordination among the relevant agencies is required to ensure timely response and appropriate knowledge of what assets could be made available. DoD should also pursue changes to the federal law that stipulates whether National Guard forces can be mobilized in a nuclear, chemical radiological or biological threat crisis.

DoD also strives to prevent terrorism in the homeland by supporting civil law enforcement authorities with rapid acquisition, analysis and dissemination of threat information; by adopting effective programs within the military to counter insider threats and notify civil authorities as appropriate. Overall, the capabilities DoD uses to prevent terrorist attack in the homeland are limited to providing technical expertise, information sharing, and protection of DoD assets. Improved information sharing has aided both military investigators and civil authorities. For example, in August 2012, military authorities at Fort Stewart, Georgia and civil law enforcement shared information leading to the arrest of several ex-service members who were plotting to overthrow the government. Information sharing generally occurs through military participation within the various FBI Joint Terrorism Task Forces, with over 120 uniformed personnel serving in those regional task forces by the end of 2013. Continuing to ensure appropriate policy and mechanisms are in place to rapidly share information is important for both routine cooperation as well as crises.

While the homeland defense mission is important, it remains nearly invisible to most of the American public. It is founded on inherently military tasks that take place in the skies of North America and at sea. But because these activities remain low-visibility, the majority of American public remains relatively unaware and, thus, does not object. However, when something happens that requires troops, questions quickly arise about the legal and policy basis for using troops. Americans remain deeply suspicious of a militarized homeland despite the relatively narrow set of activities that the PCA restricts, and the large number of activities that the military can perform upon request of U.S. civil government authorities—usually a state governor or another federal agency.

Defense Support of Civil Authorities

State and local authorities have extensive emergency management and first responder capabilities, but they may be overwhelmed in certain situations and request federal assistance. Likewise, federal civil agencies have significant capacity to execute mission assignments developed by the Federal Emergency Management Agency (FEMA) for responding to a State's requests for assistance, but they also may formally request DoD assistance based on the scope or scale of the incident and the related response requirements.

Historically DoD support to civil authorities (DSCA) in the homeland most often follows a major natural disaster such as wildfires, hurricanes and earthquakes. Responding to a natural disaster usually first involves the affected state's National Guard, which is usually activated when the governor makes a state disaster declaration.[19] At that point the Guard members work for the state governor and can provide additional law enforcement support if needed. The affected state may also have a series of agreements with other states regarding reciprocal support. These Emergency Management Assistance Compacts (EMACs) allow states to request personnel, equipment and commodities from other states on a reimbursable basis. If the capability is a state-owned service it can be requested under pre-arranged EMACs. If at any time the state needs specific assistance from the military it can make a formal request. Heavy lift helicopters are among the most frequent requests because these assets can be used for anything from delivering supplies to search and rescue to firefighting. For states, knowing what capabilities to request can be daunting in the midst of a crisis. For that reason, DoD has developed pre-crisis planning mechanisms to partner with federal agencies and states in identifying potential services and capabilities DoD might be able to provide. For more detailed plans, the parties may develop prescripted mission assignments so both the state and the Department know what to expect.

One of the major criticisms of DoD response to requests for assistance is the amount of time such actions take. Typically, it takes 96 hours from the time a request for assistance is made to the time federal troops arrive.[20] DoD recognizes this challenge and has begun taking steps to be more responsive. First, a statutory change in the 2012 National Defense Authorization Act changes involuntary mobilization rules for Federal (non National Guard) Reservists to allow involuntary mobilization for domestic disaster response. This authority increases DoD's pool of available medical, engineering, decontamination, mortuary and logistics capabilities, and may place those capabilities closer to the incident area, as Reserve units are spread throughout the country.

DoD is also exploring whether to make better use of existing policy and law that allows installation commanders to provide immediate assistance to the surrounding community—within 72 hours of an incident. Short of providing law enforcement support, this would allow military personnel from neighboring installations to help save and sustain lives, protect property and mitigate suffering during catastrophic events. Such assistance may include emergency evacuation, search and rescue, fire-fighting, medical assistance, and providing essential emergency shelters. Policy barriers to providing this assistance must be removed, and some legal issues will need to be addressed if this is to become a reality. As of 2012, installation commanders have little incentive to aid local authorities unless there is significant duress because the installation would bear the full cost of all assistance rendered; second, installation commanders also have to determine whether military personnel will be free to assist without endangering their own base or significantly impacting their readiness. Finally, for those skills that require state licensure—such as emergency medicine—states would need to be willing to provide temporary waivers to allow military medical personnel to assist local medical authorities.

CBRN Response in the Homeland

Since 2005, DoD has taken steps to greatly expand its ability to detect, protect against, and respond to a chemical, biological, radiological or nuclear (CBRN) act of terrorism in the homeland. The Hart-Rudman Commission Report identified terrorist use of weapons of mass destruction as a potential threat that DoD was uniquely positioned to address due to the capability it had developed for overseas employment. As of 2012, DoD maintains small, specialized elements capable of CBRN agent detection, identification and dispersion modeling in every state and some national territories. It also maintains larger forces capable of those tasks plus casualty extraction, mass decontamination, emergency medical treatment, patient triage, trauma care, security, engineering, logistics and transportation, and command and control elements. Altogether, DoD has nearly 18,000 service members capable of deploying to an incident site within 96 hours of an event.[21] These personnel are dedicated to this particular mission; if they are assigned to do something else for anything other than a temporary basis, DoD replaces them with other units. Two-thirds of this force are National Guard units, with smaller portions of Federal Reserve and Active Component personnel. To be highly responsive, the CBRN Response Enterprise relies on being geographically dispersed; at least a portion of the force is stationed within driving distance of every major and medium metropolitan area in the continental U.S. However, the capabilities and responsiveness of the various elements detracts from the potential effectiveness of the overall package.

DoD has restructured National Guard units into several types of organizations for the CBRN Response Enterprise. The oldest type units are 57 WMD Civil Support Teams which provide the detection, identification and dispersal capability. These are light 22-person teams with little ability to sustain themselves for more than a few days, and require up to three hours to be prepared to deploy. All these teams are resident in the National Guard; each state has at least one team and but governors can access additional teams through EMAC agreements. Likewise, there are 17 somewhat larger units spread throughout the country with some search and extraction capability, a small decontamination element and a small emergency medical unit. These 186-member units have up to twelve hours to be prepared to deploy—which means it could be up to twenty hours before a unit is on the scene of an incident. States without such a unit under their control would have to request assistance through the EMAC program. The last National Guard unit is called a Homeland Response Force (HRF), made up of 556 personnel who have a twelve-hour window to prepare to deploy. These units provide the same type of capabilities as the smaller organizations, with some additional security forces and a command and control element. Again, it could be up to twenty hours before a HRF is on-scene. Federal response units tend to include additional general purpose forces, a significant medical capability, helicopters and ground casualty evacuation and logistics support for all DoD forces. These forces could take up to two days to prepare to deploy, and another two days to be operational on the ground, surging the response force by over 5,000 people. A final package of entirely active component forces with capabilities similar to those previously listed can be on the ground on the fifth day after it is requested, bringing the total force to just under 18,000 personnel.

Since 2009, DoD has made a significant investment in these forces, with total spending approaching $1 billion in 2012 alone.[22] Both the 2010 Quadrennial Defense Review and the 2012 Defense Strategic Guidance emphasize the need to maintain this capability.[23] For now, DoD seems committed to ensuring the Enterprise has sufficient supplies and equipment prepared to deploy at a moment's notice; this is reflected in the fact that it maintains and improves its specialized agent detection capability, and that both specialized and general purpose forces are capable of operating in a contaminated environment. DoD recognizes that this skill is imperative if the Enterprise will be sufficiently able to perform the most critical life-saving tasks and maintain the safely of the troops who are responding. However, even as the DoD improves its response times, the number of personnel available will remain incremental over the 96 hour period—and perhaps longer because those times represent the time each element has to prepare to deploy; this does not include time required to request assistance or travel time, both of which can be causes of delay. DoD would have to take highly specific and unique steps in conjunction with DHS to mitigate delays and retain decision-making space required by the Secretary of Defense and the President.

A terrorist incident of the size that was part of several recent national planning scenarios—the proverbial "dirty bomb"—most likely would require additional assets beyond those that DoD has on standby. Both national-level exercises and lessons learned from the Fukushima nuclear reactor incident in Japan point to a sustainability issue. Working in a contaminated environment is exhausting, and even with specialized gear, personnel can only work in that environment for a limited time before they cannot continue without serious health risks. Further, decontaminating workers, equipment, and casualties requires the same level of care as does working in the contaminated environment. Ensuring contaminated materials do not leave the incident area and spread a trail of contamination is a significant concern. Finally, U.S. authorities do not have commonly understood protocols for handling contaminated human remains. Dealing with all these issues before a CBRN threat requires time and resources. Ultimately the U.S could make considerable investments to protect from, respond to and mitigate a threat deemed as relatively unlikely.

A CBRN threat in the homeland is a low-probability, high consequence event. Such an event would make the response to Hurricane Katrina look small. Even with 18,000 troops on hand, and sufficient resources to conduct robust periodic training events, DoD and the rest of the government will need to continue to make significant investments and to conduct national level exercises in order to respond effectively to such a catastrophic event. The degree of commitment to this type of preparedness also calls for regular re-assessment of the threat and relative adjustment of the planned response. Each type of threat—chemical, biological, radiological or nuclear—places significantly different stressors on the national response and requires evaluation of the assessment and attribution processes.[24] In the case of a CBRN incident in the homeland, DoD's greatest contribution may be the upfront commitment of capabilities and the planning of how to employ them, rather than the actual contribution of the CBRN Response Enterprise.

As DoD looks to the future of Homeland Defense and Defense Support of Civil Authorities, there are several issue areas that are ripe for additional examination. First is the structure of the National Guard. National Guard forces operating under state control provides the most flexibility for the affected state, and it is the most common way uniformed personnel provide assistance during a crisis. National Guard personnel are more likely to be near the incident area; their armories can be found throughout the U.S. As long as they work for the state governor, they can supplement law enforcement authorities without running afoul of the Posse Comitatus Act. They have robust mutual aid agreements with neighboring states. But, aside from the CBRN Response Enterprise, there has been little appetite to ensure National Guard structures provide skills that are useful for both domestic assistance and war (dual use capabilities). For example, there are no Federal Reserve infantry, tank, or artillery units. But there are many National Guard units with this specialty. With very limited exceptions, these organizations bring no organizational capabilities to a domestic emergency other than manpower. However, if these organizations were converted to engineers, military police, medical, aviation, and myriad logistics units, their military specialty would be useful in both wartime and domestic operations. A tank or field artillery unit has very little military equipment that is helpful for response to a hurricane or tornado, but construction engineers have bulldozers, backhoes and other equipment that would be immensely useful. The Hart-Rudman Commission recognized that the National Guard was best fit for domestic response operations and recommended "that the National Guard be given homeland security as a primary mission, as the U.S. Constitution itself ordains. The National Guard should be reorganized, trained, and equipped to undertake that mission."[25] Of the approximately 350,000 Army National

Guard personnel, approximately 10,000, or 2.8%, have been specifically restructured and designated as homeland response forces. The current structure needs to be re-examined to ensure the service members who are closest to a domestic incident and can be most flexibly employed also possess the skills, equipment and training that can be best leveraged in a disaster response. This undertaking will be difficult due to the competing interests of state executive powers and the Secretary of Defense. But for governors who want their Guardsmen to be well-trained and well-equipped to aid the state in an emergency, it is an opportunity waiting to be seized.

Second, as DoD continues in its trend of consolidating military bases, it should add a criteria that takes its homeland role into account. Military bases dot the nation; Chicago is the only major US city without a military base within a few hours' drive. These locations represent a ready-made distribution system through which DoD could respond to major disasters without overburdening the local infrastructure. Moreover, proximate military bases provide military personnel and capabilities that could response to an event quickly. Military installations as far away as Atlanta provided temporary shelter to Hurricane Katrina victims. With a little bit of planning and investment, military installations could be organized and supplied to provide temporary housing to the displaced, as well as supplies and equipment to those responding to the incident. DoD should explore how to establish greater ties at the state and local levels to leverage military installations' services and infrastructure when disaster strikes, and ensure that base closure decisions include determinations of a base's role in protecting the homeland, both as a staging area for responding DoD forces and also as a part of the locality's response plan.

Placing the right forces with the right capabilities closer to the incident will help DoD response times when it is called upon. So will comprehensive planning with states and federal agencies in order to establish common practices, a joint understanding of what may be needed, and the organizational leadership structures that will ensure all entities on the ground after an incident work together to save lives, mitigate suffering and protect property. DoD has committed to strengthening ties with federal agencies—particularly FEMA—and state emergency management organizations in order to ensure that disaster planning considers DoD assets, and that there are established and practiced means for rapid communications when disaster strikes.

Conclusion

The Posse Comitatus Act is often cited as a limiting factor in DoD's role in homeland defense and homeland security. In fact, federal law only prohibits federal armed forces from performing law enforcement duties in the United States. This is a small part of DoD's overall mission to protecting the homeland and assisting civil authorities when required. Further, the National Guard is not subject to the Posse Comitatus Act except when working as a federalized military force. Additionally, exceptions to the Posse Comitatus Act are already written into law, and Presidents invoke those exceptions in a variety of circumstances. It is only public perception that constrains more frequent presidential decrees through the Insurrection Act—the section of the federal code in which it appears is now renamed "Enforcement of the Laws to Restore Public Order."

In a homeland setting DoD can bring a wide range of capabilities and great capacity to bear when a disaster requires a large infusion of resources and manpower. And

DoD can do more to streamline state requests for assistance by conducting planning with them well ahead of the actual incident. DoD needs to continue to find innovative ways to be positioned to rapidly respond to a disaster when called upon, with the first goal to help save lives, safeguard property, and mitigate further damage. Pursuing this end should necessitate that DoD re-evaluates the types of capabilities it places in the National Guard—already the most responsive and flexible homeland force DoD provides. National Guard capabilities should be restructured with the intention of creating forces with skills and equipment that are in high demand for use in the homeland, and can be used in wartime as well. Right now, only a small fraction of the National Guard is dedicated to homeland missions while it retains significant equipment and training capabilities that are exclusively for wartime use.

DoD seems content to protect the nation from as far away from the homeland as feasible, to watch the approaches to the U.S., and to provide its unique material, personnel skills, and organizational controls to a catastrophic disaster response effort. Its emphasis on saving lives and mitigating suffering when civil authorities need assistance clearly works within U.S. law, policy and tradition regarding maintaining a large standing army in the homeland.

Critical Thinking Questions

1. What are the most important factors constraining DoD's effectiveness in responding to homeland security incidents?
2. What financial costs might be associated with the policy and organizational recommendations offered in this article?
3. What kinds of policy, legal, or practical barriers must be addressed before U.S. military installations can be truly ready to provide assistance in the event of a major local catastrophe?

Bibliography

Bronner, Michael. "9/11 Live: the NORAD Tapes" in *Vanity Fair,* August 2006.

Currier, Donald J. "The Posse Comitatus Act: A Harmless Relic from the Post-Reconstruction Era or a Legal Impediment to Transformation?" Strategic Studies Institute, Carlisle PA, September 2003.

Department of Defense, *Strategy for Homeland Defense and Civil Support*, GPO, June 2005.

——— *Defense Strategic Guidance*, GPO. January 2012.

——— Publication 3-27, *Homeland Defense*. GPO, July 2007.

——— *Defense Strategic Guidance*, January 2012. http://www.defense.gov/news/Defense_Strategic_Guidance.pdf.

Hamilton, Alexander, James Madison and John Jay. *The Federalist Papers.* http://thomas.loc.gov/home/histdox/fedpapers.html

Hart, Gary, et al. Roadmap for National Security: Imperative for Change. Phase III Report of the US Commission on National Security in the 21st Century. Government Printing Office, February 15, 2001.

United States Congress, Senate Committee on the Armed Services. *Senate Report No 109-254.* Government Printing Office, Washington, D.C. May 9, 2006.

———, *National Defense Authorization Act of 2012.* http://armedservices.house.gov/index.cfm/files/serve?File_id=7953f7b8-84cb-49ef-ab26-9ed7078c9d6c

VandeHei, Jim and Josh White, Bush Urges Shift in Relief Responsibilities, The Washington Post, Sept.26, 2006.

White House, *The Federal Response to Hurricane Katrina: Lessons Learned*, Government Printing Office, Washington, D.C. February 2006.

——— Executive Order 12804 (May 1, 1992).

——— Press Release on the Ongoing Response to Hurricane Katrina, September 15, 2005. http://georgewbush-whitehouse.archives.gov/news/releases/2005/09/20050915-8.html.

Notes

1. Hart, Gary, et al. *Sustaining U.S. Global Leadership: Priorities for the 21st Century,* January 2012. Retrieved from http://www.defense.gov/news/Defense_Strategic_Guidance.pdf, August 20, 2012.
2. Vanity Fair broke NORAD's minute-by minute tapes of actions taken on September 11th. For a complete account see: Bronner, Michael. "9/11 Live: the NORAD Tapes" in *Vanity Fair,* August 2006. Retrieved from http://www.vanityfair.com/politics/features/2006/08/norad200608 August 2012.
3. Though greatly scaled down since its height in the fall of 2001, Operation Noble Eagle continues as of August 2012, primarily providing the ability to put military aircraft in the sky to interdict civilian aircraft that act in a suspicious manner or enters restricted airspace. Military personnel also provide additional security during major public or government events such as summits or major sporting events.
4. Department of Defense, *Strategy for Homeland Defense and Civil Support*, 2005. Retrieved from http://www.hsdl.org/?view&did=454976 on August 20, 2012.
5. The Federal Response to Hurricane Katrina: Lessons Learned, p.43, February 2006. Retrieved from http://permanent.access.gpo.gov/lps67263/katrina-lessons-learned.pdf on August 20, 2012.
6. Ibid.
7. White House press release. Retrieved from http://georgewbush-whitehouse.archives.gov/news/releases/2005/09/20050915-8.html on August 20, 2012.
8. Hamilton, Alexander, James Madison and John Jay. *The Federalist Papers.* Retrieved from http://thomas.loc.gov/home/histdox/fed_26.html on August 22, 2012.
9. Currier, Donald J. "The Posse Comitatus Act: A Harmless Relic from the Post-Reconstruction Era or a Legal Impediment to Transformation?" Strategic Studies Instituted. September 2003. Retrieved from http://www.carlisle.army.mil/ssi/ on August 20, 2012.
10. Ibid.
11. 1. Posse Comitatus Act, U.S. Code, Title 18, sec. 1385, 1878.
12. Executive Order 12804 (May 1, 1992) Retrieved from http://www.presidency.ucsb.edu/ws/index.php?pid=23739 on August 20, 2012.
13. Jim VandeHei and Josh White, Bush Urges Shift in Relief Responsibilities, The Washington Post, Sept.26, 2006, available at http://www.washingtonpost.com/wp-dyn/content/article/2005/09/25/AR2005092501224.html.
14. Senate Report No. 109-254, Comm. On The Armed Services (May 9, 2006). http://www.gpo.gov/fdsys/pkg/CRPT-109srpt254/pdf/CRPT-109srpt254.pdf
15. Ibid.

16. Joint Pub 3-27.
17. As part of the DoD's homeland defense role, the Department has primary responsibility to defend the homeland from a ground attack by a state actor. Because this scenario is quite unlikely at present, DoD is not expressly postured for this eventuality. Other federal agencies have responsibility for border security absent an imminent threat of ground attack.
18. The Coast Guard retains law enforcement authorities when it works under the control of DHS. Once a vessel is intercepted in US territorial waters, the Coast Guard can conduct boardings, and make arrests if required. In accordance with the Posse Comitatus Act and DoD policy, the Navy is prohibited from engaging in the actual law enforcement activity.
19. A state disaster declaration moves responsibility for coordinating a response from the locality to the state. A disaster declaration is not required for state governors to access and employ their State National Guard forces.
20. Preparation time is one reason why there has been a trend in recent years to "go big, go early" as the American public's expectations of government response to disasters has risen in recent years. Precautionary call ups of the National Guard and other response and recovery assets are expensive for Governors, but are increasingly the norm when dealing with potentially disastrous weather patterns. This will be an exceptionally difficult standard when faced with unexpected events—whether natural or manmade.
21. http://www.defense.gov/news/HRFCERFP.pdf, or http://smallwarsjournal.com/blog/the-cbrn-response-enterprise-in-the-homeland, accessed Aug 31, 2012.
22. National Defense Authorization Act of 2012. Accessed from http://armedservices.house.gov/index.cfm/files/serve?File_id=7953f7b8-84cb-49ef-ab26-9ed7078c9d6c on Sep 1, 2012.
23. Defense Strategic Guidance, January 2012. Accessed from http://www.defense.gov/news/Defense_Strategic_Guidance.pdf, on Sep 1, 2012.
24. For example, a biological attack is much less likely to begin with an explosion in a metropolitan area. Instead it may be discovered through pattern analysis conducted by the medical community organizations such as the Centers for Disease Control.
25. Hart, Gary, et al. *Roadmap for National Security: Imperative for Change.* Phase III Report of the US Commission on National Security in the 21st Century. p 9. February 15, 2001.

Have We Succumbed to Nuclear Terror?

Brian Michael Jenkins

We live at the edge of doom. President Obama has declared that "the single biggest threat to U.S. security, . . . near-term, mid-term, and long-term, would be the possibility of a terrorist organization obtaining a nuclear weapon."[1] According to Harvard University political scientist Graham Allison, who has emerged as the nation's leading voice of concern about nuclear terrorism, there is "better than a 50 percent chance that terrorists will detonate a nuclear bomb in the United States within ten years"[2] (that is, by 2014). A national commission on weapons of mass destruction concluded that there is a "better than even chance that terrorists will use biological or nuclear weapons within five years"[3] (that is, by 2013). The CIA's top analyst on terrorist use of weapons of mass destruction, Rolf Mowatt-Larssen, writes that now, in 2011, "we cannot exclude the possibility of nuclear terrorism. It is not tomorrow's threat; it is with us here today."[4] As former CIA Director Michael Hayden has warned: "Al-Qaeda is the CIA's top nuclear concern."[5]

These are not the rantings of cranks with signs warning that the end is nigh; they are crafted public statements by some of America's highest-ranking, most highly respected, most thoughtful people. And yet al Qaeda, with no known nuclear capability, has ascended to the level of a virtual nuclear power, one that the CIA apparently ranks ahead of Iran, whose suspected nuclear-weapons ambitions are backed up by a large contingent of nuclear scientists and an extensive network of nuclear facilities; ahead even of North Korea, which we know possesses nuclear weapons. Al Qaeda has become the world's first terrorist nuclear power without, insofar as we know, possessing a single nuclear weapon.

A Psychological Triumph

There is very little concrete evidence upon which to base such dire forecasts. The threat of nuclear terror floats far above the world of known facts. How has al Qaeda managed to pull off this stunning feat of psychological legerdemain?

The dramatic impact of terrorism provides part of the answer. What distinguishes terrorism from other modes of armed conflict is the separation between the actual targets of terrorist violence and the targets of the psychological terror. Because terrorists cannot hope to defeat their foes in open battle, they deliberately aim spectacular attacks at vulnerable civilian targets, hoping to create an atmosphere of terror, which will induce the public audience to exaggerate the terrorists' strength and dissuade governments from pursuing policies opposed by the terrorists because of the perceived price. Terrorist attacks also create political crises, provoking overreaction and compelling governments to divert vast resources to security in order to maintain public confidence that they will be protected, even while knowing that absolute security is not possible. This is the very essence of terrorism. And it often works.

The trajectory of contemporary terrorist violence also has contributed to fears of mass destruction. Nearly 40 years ago, observing that most terrorist violence was symbolic, I suggested that "terrorists want a lot of people watching, not a lot of people dead."

Those earlier generations of terrorists seemed to worry that wanton slaughter would alienate their constituencies and be counterproductive to their political causes. While today's terrorists still argue about the appropriate level of violence, self-imposed constraints clearly have eroded.

As war has become less lethal, terrorism has become more lethal. In the decades since World War II, military power has moved away from the industrial-scale slaughter of total war, placing greater emphasis on reducing collateral casualties to a minimum. The development of increasingly precise weapons has facilitated this effort. Domestic genocide, particularly the targeting of specific ethnic groups, has been the exception to this rule. Meanwhile, contemporary terrorists have moved in the opposite direction, toward large-scale indiscriminate violence, escalating from small, mostly symbolic bombings involving few casualties in the 1970s to truck bombs aimed at killing hundreds in the 1980s and 1990s to the attacks on September 11, 2001, that killed thousands. From this cataclysmic event, it was easy to extrapolate the idea of Osama bin Laden using a nuclear weapon if he had one.

The 9/11 terrorist attacks fundamentally altered perceptions of plausibility. With box cutters and mace, terrorists turned commercial airliners into guided missiles that brought down skyscrapers. People feared that al Qaeda would try to launch more 9/11-scale attacks if it could, or perhaps even more-ambitious attacks. Terrorist scenarios that had been deemed far-fetched before 9/11 became operative presumptions after 9/11. In this environment, no terrorist scheme could be dismissed. Nuclear terrorism ascended to a clear and present danger.

There are vast differences between chemical, biological, radiological, and nuclear weapons. In its final report, written before 9/11, the National Commission on Terrorism chose wisely to avoid the collective term "weapons of mass destruction."[6] Aggregating such weapons confuses a low threshold for occurrence—terrorists already have employed chemical and biological weapons, with modest results—with a high potential for theoretical casualties, thereby exaggerating both probability and likely consequences. Realistically, only biological and nuclear weapons have a capacity for true mass destruction. And nuclear weapons differ from biological weapons in that biological weapons also may be used to kill just a few, as the anthrax letters did. It is hard to imagine a minor nuclear attack.

Ambitions, Not Capabilities

The assessment of al Qaeda's nuclear capabilities is based on very little information. Everyone agrees that al Qaeda's leaders have nuclear ambitions. Osama bin Laden, while still in Sudan, may have had contact with some radicalized U.S. scientists, and according to one informant, he tried unsuccessfully to acquire nuclear material. Al Qaeda's abundant cash and lack of nuclear expertise made it an easy mark for scams. There were several reported cases in which al Qaeda thought it was purchasing nuclear-weapons components or fissile material but instead got nothing more than low-grade fuel, car parts, or other useless junk.

Al Qaeda's interest in nuclear weapons continued in Afghanistan. Documents left behind as al Qaeda retreated from the country included descriptions and even crude diagrams of nuclear weapons. A knowledgeable physicist who was asked to examine these documents said that they did not indicate the knowledge necessary to make a nuclear bomb.[7] Although their author apparently understood general theory, a bomb based on the diagrams would not have produced a nuclear explosion. Given time, the terrorists might figure out how to assemble a nuclear device, but they would still need fissile material and technical expertise. (Some more conspiracy-minded individuals opined that al Qaeda deliberately left behind amateurish documents to deceive authorities about just how far along its nuclear-weapons efforts actually were.)

Aware of al Qaeda's technological shortcomings, bin Laden sought the assistance of two sympathetic Pakistani scientists with whom he spoke in Afghanistan shortly before 9/11. They told him that he could not build a device with the material he had. It is not clear how much more technical advice the Pakistanis were able to provide, however. Within a few months, al Qaeda was on the run, and the two scientists ended up in the custody of Pakistani authorities.

How serious were al Qaeda's nuclear efforts? When he was interrogated about al Qaeda's nuclear weapons, Khalid Sheikh Muhammad, al Qaeda's chief operational planner and the architect of the 9/11 attacks, reportedly said the efforts never went beyond downloads from the Internet. There is also a report that some in al Qaeda doubted that the organization could develop true weapons of mass destruction but nonetheless agreed to continue to use the term because it would give the movement psychological influence.[8] Subsequent public reports suggest that even as al Qaeda's senior leaders were on the run, with their capability to launch large-scale terrorist operations diminished, efforts to acquire nuclear weapons continued. But despite numerous sensational "revelations" of the organization's purported nuclear arsenal, there is no evidence that al Qaeda has ever acquired a stolen nuclear weapon or the fissile material to make one.

Beyond these very few known facts about al Qaeda's nuclear aspirations, everything else falls into the realm of surmise and speculation, and there is plenty of that. Intelligence analysts, frustrated at the lack of hard evidence but unwilling to risk being accused of another "failure of imagination" as they were after 9/11, cannot exclude the possibility that al Qaeda or some other terrorist group might acquire nuclear weapons in the future. The absence of concrete evidence, therefore, does not diminish perceptions of the threat. Instead, the inability to say "it will never happen" can be taken a step further as confirmation that nuclear terrorism is inevitable—to use the now famous phrase, a matter of "not if, but when."

Absence of Warning

Paradoxically, the absence of evidence heightens the threat. Many believe that the public will have no warning of an impending terrorist nuclear attack. Although there are two diametrically opposite views of U.S. intelligence capabilities, both fuel nuclear terror.

The first view of U.S. intelligence credits it with omniscience but remains suspicious that Washington is deliberately withholding information to avoid causing public panic. This is a popular theme among conspiracy-driven books and articles on nuclear terrorism that promise to tell the reader what the government will not. In fact, since 9/11, the government has routinely passed threat information—some of it vague, even dubious—on to the public. Yet it is also true that since the 1970s, there have been scores of undisclosed nuclear threats to American cities. The Federal Bureau of Investigation (FBI) and U.S. Department of Energy nuclear emergency teams have mobilized to conduct secret searches. All of the threats were found to be apparent hoaxes, but none of this was published at the time. As an example, just after 9/11, the CIA received intelligence from a source appropriately code-named Dragonfire that terrorists had planted a nuclear device in

New York City. The federal government initiated a search without informing the public or local authorities. Nothing was found—the source was mistaken. But given this record, it is conceivable that if the government received credible intelligence that al Qaeda or another terrorist organization had acquired a nuclear weapon, it might not reveal it.

The second view of U.S. intelligence is that it cannot be depended upon to provide advance warning of a terrorist nuclear attack. We will know it only when we see the bright yellow flash. After all, American intelligence officials were surprised to discover in 1991 that Iraq had come closer to developing nuclear weapons than they had imagined.

U.S. intelligence did not foresee 9/11. It failed to predict the testing of nuclear weapons by India, Pakistan, and North Korea, but prior to the Iraq War, it reported with confidence that Iraq had weapons of mass destruction when it had none. While this recitation is not entirely fair to the intelligence community, perceived past failures of intelligence do not inspire confidence.

Lacking hard evidence that terrorists have nuclear weapons or material, intelligence analysts instead pore over al Qaeda's public statements for warnings or other clues about its interest in nuclear weapons. They argue over whether *fatwas*—religious rulings—authorizing al Qaeda to kill millions should be interpreted as the obligatory warning required by Islamic concepts of warfare. They debate whether terrorists might be deterred from acquiring or using nuclear weapons. These are legitimate lines of inquiry, but they also reify the threat, treating a hypothetical—al Qaeda's or any terrorists' possession of nuclear weapons—as if it were a concrete fact, or at least an inevitable development.

Hypothetical Possession, Vivid Consequences

"A 10-kiloton nuclear bomb detonated in Times Square in New York City could kill a million people," noted U.S. Secretary of State Hillary Clinton in April 2010. "Beyond the human cost, a nuclear terrorist attack would also touch off a tsunami of social and economic consequences across our country."[9]

How is it that such alarming pronouncements come to be made, despite their having the predictable effect of exaggerating the likely threat and contributing to the terrorists' goal of instilling fear? As indicated by the string of quotes that began this essay, Secretary Clinton is hardly alone in her use of such pronouncements, nor was her calm discussion of nuclear arms reduction, nuclear proliferation, and nuclear terrorism intended to be scare-mongering. There is no sinister intent. The dilemma, generically, is that to do sensible things, political leaders must engage the enthusiasm of those charged with the "doing," must obtain funding from the fickle U.S. Congress, and must convey a sense of seriousness. They cannot do that with meek speeches that say, "Well, of course, there is also the outside threat of nuclear terrorism, but I don't lose sleep over it." They would lose credibility and stature, would be seen by the citizenry as soft and ineffectual, and could demoralize those on whom the country is counting to hunt down the bad guys.

Nuclear terrorism has thus created its own orthodoxy. Regardless of its likelihood, to question it is to risk being seen as soft. Whatever the intention, the formula of presentation is by now well established: A hypothetical event produces historically confirmable consequences.

Historically confirmable they are. While the threat of nuclear terrorism remains clouded in uncertainty, we know a lot about nuclear explosions. Hiroshima and Nagasaki and decades of Cold War experience in calculating nuclear blast effects provide detailed and vivid accounts of them. Analysts generally assume—the operative word—that a terrorist bomb would produce a 10-kiloton nuclear explosion, but it is by no means certain that terrorists could build a nuclear device with that yield. A crude nuclear device might just as likely be in the tenths-of-a-kiloton range, but that does not convey the desired dramatic impact.

A typical article on the subject begins with the assumption that terrorists can steal or build a nuclear bomb, then proceeds to describe in detail the intense fireball, blinding flash, diameter of immediate destruction, widespread firestorms, charred flesh, death by radiation, and social chaos that would emanate from a 10-kiloton blast at city center. That the underlying premise of terrorist possession of a nuclear weapon is hypothetical gets lost among the "reality" of its effects. Likewise, hypothetical worst-case scenarios generate consequences that outweigh their low probabilities of occurrence. With a presumed million fatalities—the equivalent of 300 9/11s—how low must the odds be to be considered acceptable?

Spinning Nuclear Fantasies

Al Qaeda's efforts to obtain nuclear weapons were accompanied by an active communications effort, which implied that the terrorist group was further along in its quest than it actually was. This public communications campaign intensified as al Qaeda's central leadership came under increasing pressure after 9/11.

In earlier interviews, Osama bin Laden, when asked by reporters about weapons of mass destruction, coyly responded that their acquisition was a religious duty. But in an interview with a Pakistani reporter in November 2001, as the Taliban and al Qaeda were being bombed by American warplanes, bin Laden and Ayman al-Zawahiri were said to have claimed that al Qaeda had chemical and nuclear weapons, although the reporting of this interview raised doubts. The first published version had bin Laden saying only that al Qaeda would survive even if the United States used chemical or nuclear weapons against it; subsequent versions of the same interview introduced the claim that al Qaeda itself already had such weapons.

Neither of al Qaeda's two top leaders made many public mentions of nuclear weapons after the 2001 interview, but in 2002, an al Qaeda spokesman posted a message on the Internet claiming that because the United States was responsible for the deaths of millions of Muslims, al Qaeda, in accordance with Islamic law, had the right to kill 4 million Americans.[10] This was amended by a fugitive Saudi cleric who issued a religious ruling in 2003 authorizing al Qaeda to kill 10 million Americans.[11]

Exactly why al Qaeda elicited the two statements about killing millions of Americans is not known, but the statements excited the organization's followers and alarmed analysts in the United States. The two communications prompted a lively discourse among jihadists about al Qaeda's nuclear posture and strategy, as if its possession of nuclear weapons were real. Analysts in the United States, meanwhile, interpreted the two statements as providing the necessary warning before attack required by the Islamic code of warfare. They noted that the only way al Qaeda could achieve this magnitude of casualties was with nuclear, or possibly biological, weapons. It was seen as a signal.

Al Qaeda's communications campaign was not a centrally directed effort but, rather, a distributed project, a new phenomenon made possible by the Internet. A chorus of online jihadists carried on the campaign, issuing threats and adding lurid landscapes of fireballs and mushroom clouds over Manhattan and Washington. These were the fantasies of the powerless, vicarious participation in al Qaeda's terrorist campaign. Psychologically satisfying to their jihadist authors, they kept Western government officials on edge.

Al Qaeda's nuclear threats also commanded the attention of the U.S. news media, which, for reasons of commercial competition, has veered off into the realm of shock and entertainment in the years since 9/11. Editorial constraint yielded to drama. The line between news and fiction blurred. Here was the stuff of suspense novels, with Western civilization hanging in the balance. What could make for a better story? Nuclear terror acquired a life of its own.

Driven by Our Imagination

A receptive audience, Americans have been avid consumers of nuclear terror. It has revived Cold War anxieties. It has resonated with many who anticipate the Apocalypse, confirming their belief that we are in the end times. It has acted as a condenser for the nation's broader apprehensions about economic and political decline, its fear of being taken over by alien cultures.

"Nuclear terrorism" and "nuclear terror" have different domains of meaning. Terrorism is action, and it can include the mere threat of action, which can produce its own powerful effect. Terror is the effect. Nuclear terrorism today is about the possibility that terrorists will acquire and use nuclear weapons, while nuclear terror is about the *anticipation* of that event. Nuclear terrorism is driven by terrorist capabilities. Nuclear terror is driven by our imagination.

The history of nuclear terrorism can be quickly summarized: It hasn't happened. Terrorists are not known to have acquired and certainly have not used nuclear weapons—although many would hasten to add "yet." But nuclear terror is real, and it has become deeply embedded in our popular culture and policymaking circles.

This fear does not come free. It adds another layer to our already considerable national anxieties. It fans xenophobia. It corrodes our commitment to liberty. It demands obedience to an orthodoxy that cannot be challenged without provoking accusations of being dangerously naïve or soft on terrorism. And yet, paradoxically, despite the widespread apprehension that within a very few years, terrorists armed with nuclear weapons will destroy an American city, we still live in those cities. Even those who warn us that nuclear terrorists are coming have not removed themselves from danger.

The government did not invent the bogeyman of nuclear terrorism to compensate for the end of the Cold War or to perpetuate the military-industrial complex, as some cynics suggest. Concern about the nuclear threat is genuine, and we should be grateful for the many officials who work tirelessly to prevent nuclear attacks from any quarter. But we should also be careful about how we allow the threat of nuclear terrorism to be harnessed to serve a variety of purposes, some of which are more useful than others.

Harnessing the Power

Ironically, the dramatic excesses in nuclear terror since 9/11 may be having some useful consequences. The heightened fears, in particular, may be stimulating nations worldwide, and factions within them, to become more unified in demanding and supporting stringent measures to control nuclear weapons and related materials, thereby strengthening the consensus that nuclear weapons are to be avoided, reduced, and maybe even eliminated. The merits of any policy moving toward the latter are debatable for complex reasons, including verification, but such a broad consensus would bode well for mankind.

The threat of nuclear terrorism might be used to counter arguments that because some countries have nuclear weapons, others are entitled to have them. While countries may disagree on how to treat suspected *proliferators*, they can more easily agree that too many nuclear-weapons programs, too many nuclear-weapons designers, too much fissile material, and too many nuclear weapons increase the threat of nuclear terrorism and therefore agree that proliferation itself is dangerous to the entire world. Even if proliferation cannot be stopped in its tracks, raising concerns about nuclear terrorism can open space for cooperation on increasing controls, reducing access, and implementing other positive measures.

The threat of nuclear terrorism can just as easily be employed to argue for nuclear disarmament on grounds that the elimination of existing nuclear arsenals, or at least significant reductions in them, will reduce the threat of loose nuclear weapons and therefore of nuclear terrorism. Whether the threat of nuclear terrorism is real, and whether preventing further proliferation or disarmament would reduce that threat, is not the issue. It is a matter of manipulating widespread perceptions for the greater good.

At the very least, the threat of nuclear terrorism, real or imagined, has led to increased security for nuclear weapons and fissile material. That must be counted as a positive development, however it comes about.

If nuclear terror has prompted measures that are good in and of themselves, that is to be applauded, but has it prevented nuclear terrorism? Some assert that by raising the alarm, Armageddon has been averted—at least, deferred—but this circular argument treats its own presumptions as fact. One cannot prove that the threat of nuclear terrorism has been exaggerated or, absent evidence, that it has ever existed. Nor can one prove that it is now more likely or less imminent.

So far, at least, nuclear terrorism has occurred only in novels. Nuclear terror, on the other hand, is a fact. What matters now is whether we are its victims or its masters.

Critical Thinking Questions

1. What, if anything, should be done to balance the public fear of nuclear terror with what we know about terrorist capabilities?
2. How do we know what we know about terrorist capabilities?
3. Who, if anyone, is best positioned to lead a sophisticated national discussion about the true nature of the nuclear terror threat, and why?

Related Reading

Ackerman, Gary A., Charles P. Blair, Jeffrey M. Bale, Victor Asal, and R. Karl Rethemeyer, *Anatomizing Radiological and Nuclear Non-State Adversaries: Identifying the Adversary.* College Park, Md.: National Consortium for the Study of Terrorism and Responses to Terrorism, 2009.

Bass-Golod, Gail V., and Brian Michael Jenkins, *A Review of Recent Trends in International Terrorism and Nuclear Incidents Abroad,* Santa Monica, Calif: RAND Corporation, N-1979-SL, 1983. As of May 24, 2011: http://www.rand.org/pubs/notes/N1979.html

Daly, Sara A., John V. Parachini, and William Rosenau, *Aum Shinrikyo, Al Qaeda, and the Kinshasa Reactor: Implications of Three Case Studies for Combating Nuclear Terrorism,* Santa Monica, Calif: RAND Corporation, DB-458-AF, 2005. As of May 24, 2011: http://www.rand.org/pubs/documented_briefings/DB458.html

Davis, Paul K., and Brian Michael Jenkins, *Deterrence and Influence in Counterterrorism: A Component in the War on Al Qaeda,* Santa Monica, Calif.: RAND Corporation, MR-1619-DARPA, 2002. As of May 24, 2011: http://www.rand.org/pubs/monograph_reports/MR1619-html

DeLeon, Peter, Bruce Hoffman, Konrad Kellen, and Brian Michael Jenkins, *The Threat of Nuclear Terrorism: A Reexamination,* Santa Monica, Calif: RAND Corporation, N-2706, 1988. As of May 24, 2011: http://www.rand.org/pubs/notes/N2706.html

Jenkins, Brian Michael, "Georgia Dispute Derails Bid to Stop Nuke Terrorism," *Providence Journal,* October 6, 2008.

———, *The Likelihood of Nuclear Terrorism,* Santa Monica, Calif: RAND Corporation, P-7119, 1985. As of May 24, 2011: http://www.rand.org/pubs/papers/P7119.html

———, "A Nuclear 9/11?" CNN.com, September 11, 2008.

———, "Nuclear Terror: How Real?" *Washington Times,* May 13, 2007.

———, *The Potential for Nuclear Terrorism,* Santa Monica, Calif: RAND Corporation, P-5876, 1977. As of May 24, 2011: http://www.rand.org/pubs/papers/P5876.html

———, *Terrorism and the Nuclear Safeguards Issue,* Santa Monica, Calif.: RAND Corporation, P-5611, 1976. As of May 24, 2011: http://www.rand.org/pubs/papers/P5611.html

———, *Will Terrorists Go Nuclear?* Los Angeles, Calif: Crescent Publications, 1975.

———, *Will Terrorists Go Nuclear?* Amherst, N.Y.: Prometheus Books, 2008.

———, "Will Terrorists Go Nuclear?" *United Press International,* September 11, 2008.

Levi, Michael A., *On Nuclear Terrorism,* Cambridge, Mass.: Harvard University Press, 2007

Masse, Todd M., *Nuclear Jihad: A Clear and Present Danger?* Dulles, Va.: Potomac Books, Inc., 2011.

Meade, Charles, and Roger C. Molander, *Considering the Effects of a Catastrophic Terrorist Attack,* Santa Monica, Calif: RAND Corporation, TR-391-CTRMP, 2006. As of May 24, 2011: http://www.rand.org/pubs/technical_reports/TR391.html

Mueller, John, *Atomic Obsession: Nuclear Alarmism from Hiroshima to Al-Qaeda,* Cambridge: Oxford University Press, 2009.

Parachini, John V., David E. Mosher, John C. Baker, Keith Crane, Michael S. Chase, and Michael Daugherty, *Diversion of Nuclear, Biological, and Chemical Weapons Expertise from the Former Soviet Union: Understanding an Evolving Problem,* Santa Monica, Calif: RAND Corporation, DB-457-DOE, 2005. As of May 24, 2011: http://www.rand.org/pubs/documented_briefings/DB457-html

Wenger, Andreas, and Alex Wilner, *Deterring Terrorism: Theory and Practice,* forthcoming.

Wilner, Alexandre S., "Deterring the Undeterrable: Coercion, Denial, and Delegitimization in Counterterrorism" *Journal of Strategic Studies,* Vol. 34, No. 1, pp. 3–37.

Notes

1. "U.S. President Barack Obama Warns of Nuclear Terrorism," BBC, April 12, 2010.
2. Graham Allison and Joanne J. Myers, *Nuclear Terrorism: The Ultimate Preventable Catas-trophe,* New York: Times Books, 2004.
3. Bob Graham, Jim Talent, Graham Allison, Robin Cleveland, Steve Rademaker, Tim Roemer, Wendy Sherman, Henry Sokolski, and Rich Verma, *World at Risk: The Report of the Commission on the Prevention of WMD Proliferation and Terrorism,* New York: Vintage Books, 2008, p. xv.
4. Rolf Mowatt-Larssen, *Islam and the Bomb: Religious Justification For and Against Nuclear Weapons,* Cambridge, Mass.: Harvard Kennedy School, January 2011, p. 9.
5. "CIA Chief: Al-Qaida Is Top Nuclear Concern," Associated Press, September 16, 2008.
6. L. Paul Bremer and Maurice Sonnenberg, *Countering the Changing Threat of International Terrorism,* Report from the National Commission on Terrorism, June 2000. As of June 16, 2011: http://www.fas.org/irp/threat/commission.html
7. David Albright, "Al Qaeda's Nuclear Program: Through the Window of Seized Documents," *Policy Forum Online,* Nautilus Institute, Special Forum, No. 47, November 6, 2002.
8. Peter L. Bergen, *An Oral History of al Qaeda's Leader, The Osama bin Laden I Know,* New York: Free Press, 2006, p. 343.
9. Hillary Rodham Clinton, "Remarks on Nuclear Proliferation at the University of Louisville," Louisville, Ky., April 9, 2010.
10. Suleiman Abu Gheith, "In the Shadow of the Lances," June 2002, translation at *MEMRI Special Dispatch Series,* No. 388, June 12, 2002.
11. Nasser bin Hamad al-Fahd, "Risalah Fi'istjkhdam 'asliha Al-Dammar Al-Shamil Did Al-Kuffar," May 2003. For a discussion, see Reuven Paz, "Global Jihad and WMD; Between Martyrdom and Mass Destruction," *Current Trends in Islamist Ideology,* Vol. 2, September 2005.

The Homeland Security Dilemma

Imagination, Failure and the Escalating Costs of Perfecting Security

Frank P. Harvey

Introduction

Besieged by insurgencies in Afghanistan and Iraq and gripped by mounting pressure to enhance security and public safety at home, officials in Washington and Ottawa are now confronted with a serious homeland security dilemma: *the greater the financial costs, public sacrifice and political capital invested in security, the higher the public's expectations and corresponding standards for measuring performance, the more significant the public's sense of insecurity after each failure, and, paradoxically, the higher the pressure on governments and citizens to sacrifice even more to achieve perfect security.*

Some of the best work on security dilemmas appears in the field of international relations and typically builds on excellent research by Herz (1950, 1951), Jervis (1976, 1978), Snyder (1984), Posen (1993), Glaser (1997), Collins (1997, 2000, 2004), Taliaferro (2000), and Christensen (1999, 2002). "When states seek the ability to defend themselves," Jervis explains, "they get too much and too little—too much because they gain the ability to carry out aggression; too little because others, being menaced, will increase their own arms and so reduce the first state's security" (1976: 64). It is the uncertainty of an opponent's intentions, Collins adds, that compels states to "pursue the prudent option of procuring arms, yet since others can witness this acquisition and feel menaced by it, they too respond in order to safeguard their security" (2004: 31). The paradox at the international level explains why perfectly rational decisions to enhance power actually diminish security by promoting unstable spirals in competitive defence spending—a common account of escalating military budgets throughout much of the Cold War.

The homeland security dilemma represents the post-9/11 equivalent for domestic politics in the war on terrorism. The paper's central argument can be summed up by the following counterintuitive thesis: *the more security you have, the more security you will need,* not because enhancing security makes terrorism more likely (although the incentive for terrorists to attack may increase as extremists feel duty bound to demonstrate their ongoing relevance), but because enormous investments in security inevitably raise public expectations and amplify public outrage after subsequent failures.

This dilemma will continue to shape American and Canadian domestic and international security priorities for decades, with combined effects that are no less historically significant than those associated with security dilemmas preceding the Cold War. The key policy implications derived from the arguments and evidence presented in this report are not encouraging; there are no solutions, because the most rational and logical policy options are part of the problem.

Confidence, Trust and Approval: Public Evaluations of the War on Terrorism

If public assessments of Washington's (or Canada's) performance in the war on terrorism were based, at least in part, on the government's multibillion dollar commitment to homeland security (Figure 1) we would logically expect confidence, trust and approval ratings to be higher rather than lower.

We should also expect positive public evaluations in light of the *perfect* homeland security record since 2001. The absence over the last six years of a single terrorist attack on US soil is quite remarkable for at least four reasons. First, there is no question that terrorists are highly motivated to attack western targets, as demonstrated in Bali (2002), Madrid (2004), London (2005) and Toronto (2006), and there is no compelling logical reason why American cities would be excluded from this list. In fact we have every reason to believe US targets represent the gold standard for a successful, high-value terrorist attack. The fact that none has occurred is particularly noteworthy given the powerful incentives for terrorist groups to demonstrate ongoing relevance in response to regime changes in Afghanistan and Iraq; impressive turnout rates in democratic elections in both countries (surpassing turnouts in recent American, Canadian and many European elections); arrests (and deaths) of senior Al-Qaeda (Abu Musab Al-Zaraqwi), Taliban and former Iraqi leaders; an important counter-terrorist alliance with Pakistan; the unprecedented decision by Libya's Muammar Al-Qadhafi to renounce the country's weapons of mass destruction program and comply with robust International Atomic Energy Agency inspections; and so on. With these successes in mind (and many other media reports of successful counterterrorist operations listed in endnote 1), the absence of a US-based attack over the last six years is arguably quite impressive.

Second, several very explicit threats have been repeatedly issued by Osama Bin Laden, Aymen al-Zawahiri and Abu Musab al-Zarqawi declaring their intentions to launch attacks in

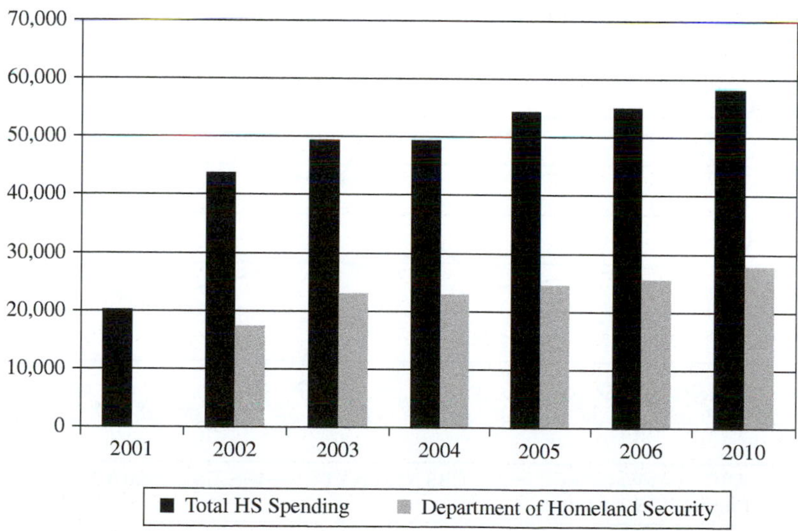

FIGURE 1 Security Commitment: Total Homeland Security Spending and Total Department of Homeland Security Spending (in millions)

the US like those in London and Madrid. Since these threats are costly signals that ultimately speak to their credibility (and status) as terrorist leaders, they must be taken seriously.

Third, there is a prevailing belief among senior terrorist operatives (as stipulated in their own strategic documents) that attacking American, Canadian and European targets is essential to their primary goal of extracting US and NATO troops from Iraq and Afghanistan (Brachman and McCants, 2006: 6) Despite the motivations, explicit threats and strategic rationale for killing Americans in their own cities, we have gone 1825 days (as of September 2006) without a single failure. It is useful to recall here that in the aftermath of 9/11 no one with any measure of responsibility for defence, security or public safety, and certainly no well-informed terrorist expert, came anywhere close to predicting this level of success (or luck). If such a prediction was issued in 2001 there would have been many reasons to dismiss it as wishful thinking, and there are as many reasons in 2006 to be impressed with this record. While it is certainly difficult to establish a direct causal linkage between the billions invested in homeland security and the absence of a US-based attack it is not unreasonable to expect a majority of the public would draw this connection.

Fourth, there are literally hundreds (perhaps thousands) of other reasons why a moderately informed public would assign higher rather than lower confidence and approval ratings for Washington's security performance—namely, the mounting evidence that law enforcement and intelligence organizations in Washington, Ottawa and allied governments around the world have succeeded in launching hundreds of successful counterterrorist operations that have thwarted planned attacks in the US, Asia, Europe and Australia.[1] If only a portion of the facts emerging from these many reports is accurate, these successes have arguably saved thousands of lives.

Yet, notwithstanding Washington's very robust commitment to protecting American citizens by spending billions every year on homeland security, a perfect record of success (so far) with respect to preventing other attacks on US and Canadian soil, and several other significant achievements since 2001, public confidence, trust and satisfaction have steadily declined over the past five years (Figures 2[2] and 3[3]).

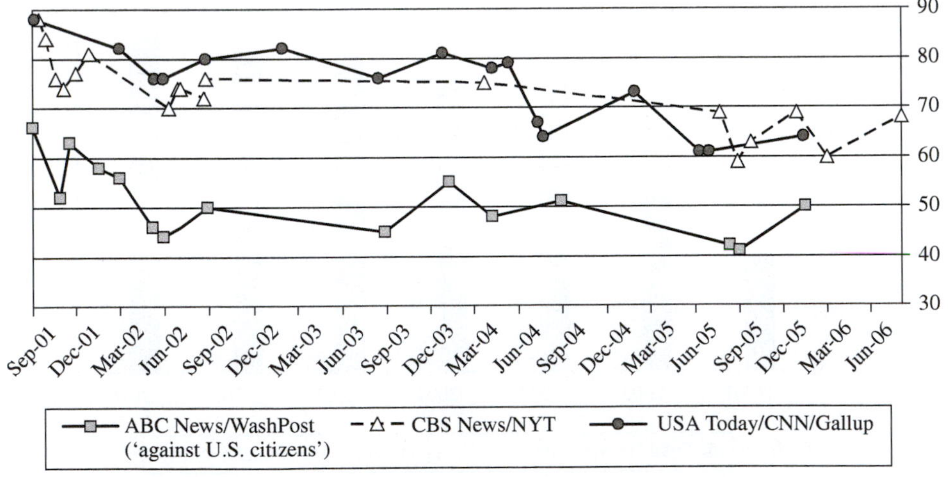

FIGURE 2 Public Confidence in US Government's Ability to Prevent Another Terrorist Attack ('great deal'/'moderate amount')

These downward trends are confirmed by dozens of other polls between 2001 and 2006 measuring overall public "approval" of the global war on terrorism (Figure 4[4]).

The polling information compiled in Figures 2, 3, and 4 goes well beyond the typical snapshot of opinions offered by the press and other media. The data and trends are derived from tens of thousands of responses to hundreds of terrorism-related opinion polls administered over the last six years by dozens of the largest American polling organizations, think tanks and news outlets.[5] When these trends are juxtaposed against the rising costs of

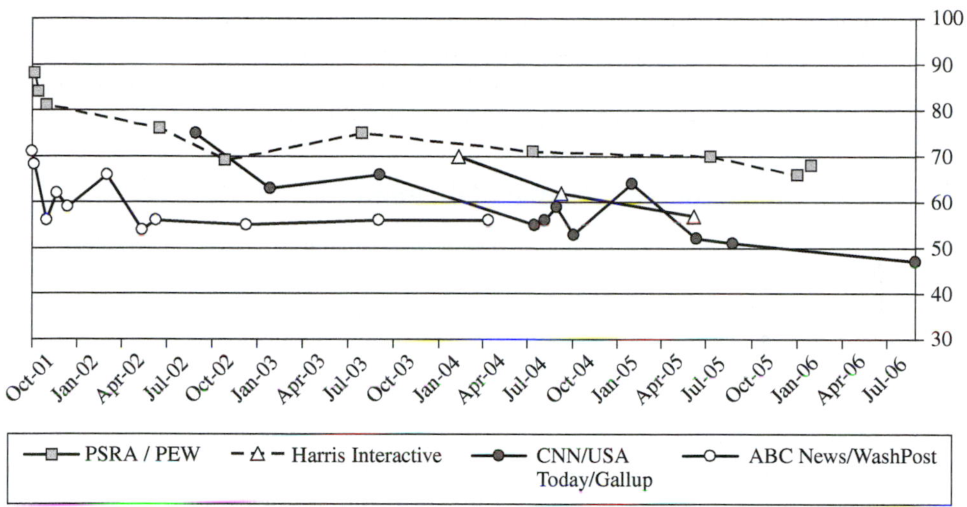

FIGURE 3 Public Support for President George W. Bush and US Government in Global War on Terror

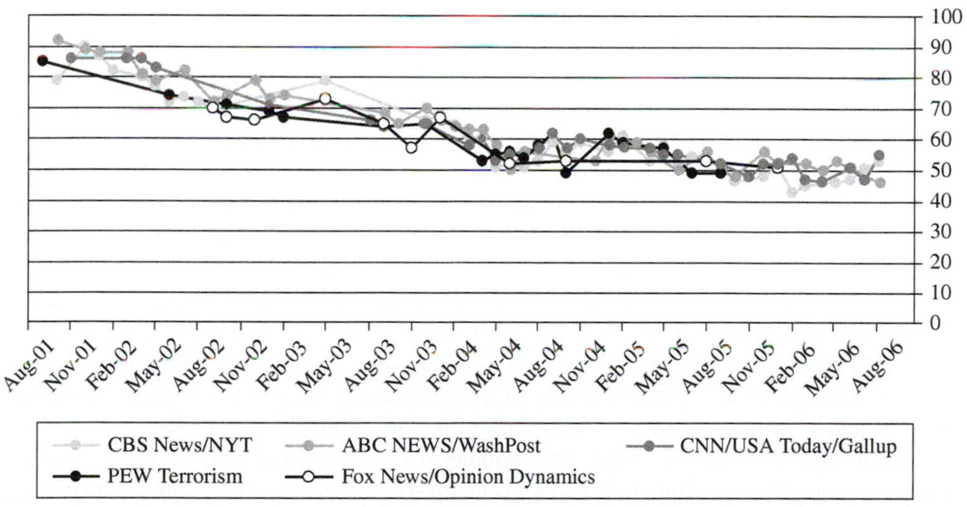

FIGURE 4 Public Approval of US Approach to Global War on Terror (GWOT)

homeland security (from Figure 1) the evidence clearly shows an expanding gap between, on the one hand, Washington's obviously very strong commitment to protecting American citizens and, on the other, a steady decline in public appreciation for the impressive results generated by that commitment.[6] How do we reconcile the absence of US-based terrorist attacks since 9/11 (and other major successes) with diminishing approval?

Among the more popular explanations is that Americans have become increasingly more distrustful of President Bush and his administration. At this point, anything the president does runs into heavy water, and the polls on homeland security reflect this general malaise—as do the results in the 2006 American midterm election. While this explanation is partially correct, it is also incomplete. The homeland security dilemma, described in detail below, provides a more thorough account of the complex mechanisms through which declining approval ratings are not only inevitable but largely irreversible, paradoxically, because of the very policies and programs designed to elevate those same ratings.

Explaining the Homeland Security Dilemma

Five factors explain why increasing investments (spending), political commitments (policy) and public sacrifice in the name of homeland security produce diminishing returns over time, each of which encompasses an important component of the current dilemma: (a) rising public expectations and standards for measuring government performance, (b) the power of failure (failures trump successes, and smaller failures trump larger successes over time), (c) public imagination and exaggerated perceptions of terrorist threats, (d) political-military imagination and official overestimations of terrorist risks, and (e) declining public support for sacrificing civil liberties.

Rising Public Expectations and Standards for Measuring Performance

The dilemma is, in part, a logical outgrowth of the substantial, though perfectly rational, security expenditures in the United States following the 9/11 attacks (see Figure 5).

The proportion of annual spending to secure airports, seaports, borders, government buildings and critical infrastructure has increased significantly since the 2001 attacks. Without exception, every agency associated with the Department of Homeland Security (DHS) and any department with links to homeland security and public safety have received annual funding increases (United States, 2004a, 2006). The 2007 Federal Budget Authority for Homeland Security was $58.3 billion—which represents an impressive 185 per cent increase over the $20.3 billion allocated in October 2001 when the DHS was established by presidential executive order (United States, 2001). The scope of these very sizeable investments can best be illustrated by comparing the performance of homeland security/defence stocks (Spade Defence Index, DXS) with those listed on the DOW (DJI), NASDAQ (IXIC) and the S&P 500 (GSPC) indices over the last five years (Figure 6).

In addition to the tens of billions of dollars spent each year to improve homeland security and continental defence, Washington has now invested well over $400 billion (and counting) to fund two wars, two counterinsurgencies and two massive post-war reconstruction efforts in Iraq and Afghanistan, all to improve international security in the midst of a global war on terrorism. Moreover, the public is being asked to make several other significant personal and social sacrifices, including military and civilian casualties in

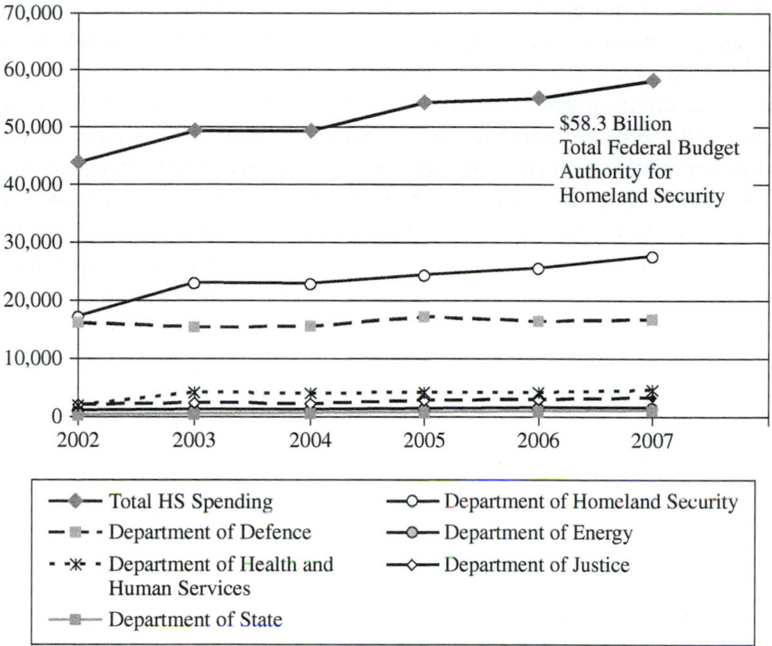

FIGURE 5 Spending by Select Key Departments (in Millions) http://www.gao.gov/new.items/d06161.pdf

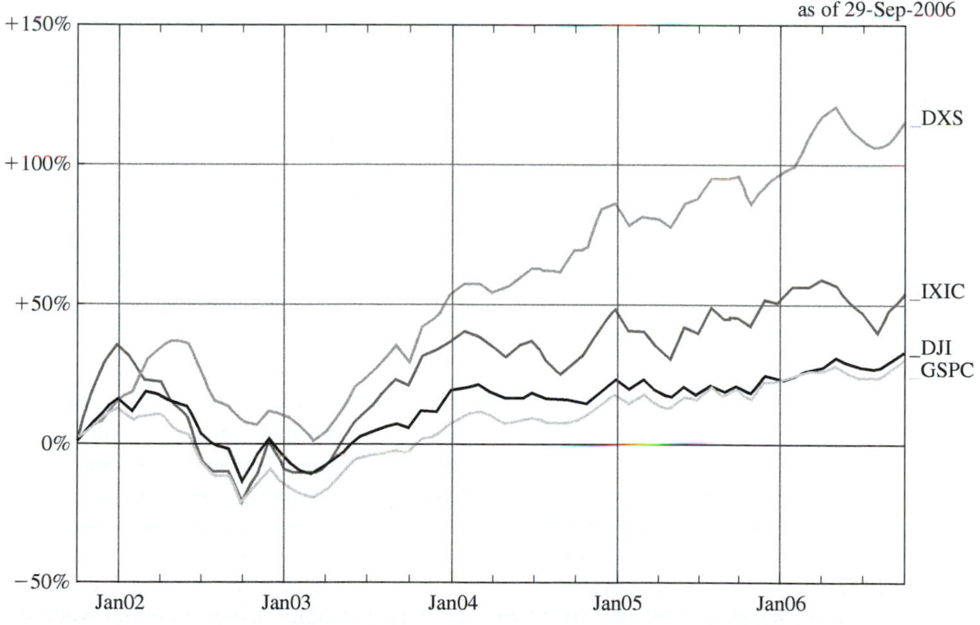

FIGURE 6 Security Stocks (DXS) versus Dow (DJI), NASDAQ (IXIC) and S&P 500 (GSPC)

Iraq and Afghanistan, diminishing civil liberties as a consequence of anti-terrorism legislation, expanding National Security Agency surveillance of domestic telephone, email and internet communications, rising levels of anti-Americanism throughout Europe, Asia and the Middle East, inflation and other cost-of-living increases tied to rapidly escalating oil prices and so forth. Finally, many businesses have been forced to enhance their own critical infrastructure while covering the costs of new trade regulations and security standards to maintain a relatively free flow of goods and services across the Canada-US border.

Consistent with the first key tenet of the homeland security dilemma, standards for assessing government performance will shift to accommodate rising expectations, and those expectations shift upwards in accordance with the sacrifices already made. Any discrepancy between the security the public expects in return for its investments and the actual level of security the government appears to be delivering will increase public threat perceptions and political pressure to spend more to fix the problem (Harvey, 2004a: 37). In essence, as expectations rise, failures become increasingly painful and unacceptable.

By way of illustration, if a repeat of the 9/11 attacks occurred today the corresponding loss in public perceptions of security would be even more pronounced (and potentially disruptive) than was the case after the original attack. This is precisely *because* billions of dollars have been spent to prevent an attack from happening, and *because* expectations are so much higher today in view of the unprecedented number of institutional reforms and improvements in critical infrastructure that, ostensibly, were designed to resolve the problem.

Similarly, the ripple effects of hurricane Katrina were greater in 2005 *because* the American public and media expected emergency preparedness, evacuation plans and public safety to be considerably stronger after spending billions of dollars on these very programs from 2001 to 2005. The scope of Katrina's post-hurricane failure was so unexpected (and the standards for assessing government performance so much higher) that criticism was understandably relentless. Had Katrina occurred on September 10, 2001, the backlash, political fallout, financial costs and political motivation to respond would likely have been far lower.[7]

In his address to the nation immediately following hurricane Katrina President George W. Bush provided the clearest illustration of the dilemma at work.

> Four years after the frightening experience of September the 11th, Americans have every right to expect a more effective response in a time of emergency. When the federal government fails to meet such an obligation, I, as president, am responsible for the problem, and for the solution. . . . This government will learn the lessons of Hurricane Katrina (by mounting) one of the largest reconstruction efforts the world has ever seen. . . . We're going to review every action and make necessary changes, so that we are better prepared for any challenge of nature, or act of evil men, that could threaten our people. . . . In a time of terror threats and weapons of mass destruction, the danger to our citizens reaches much wider than a fault line or a flood plain. I consider detailed emergency planning to be a national security priority, and therefore, I've ordered the Department of Homeland Security to undertake an immediate review, in co-operation with local counterparts, of emergency plans in every major city in America. (United States, 2005)

Of course, every one of the president's entirely laudable policy recommendations raises the obvious questions: what were the federal government, the Federal Emergency

Management Agency (FEMA) and the Department of Homeland Security doing over the past five years if not developing programs to deal with public safety and emergency preparedness? Is not this precisely what the spending, sacrifices and government transformations were designed to accomplish? More alarmingly, if Katrina represents the best we can do *with* clear warnings, what are we likely to experience after a terrorist attack no one expected? Would public confidence not continue to drop under these circumstances, regardless of whatever successes the government has managed to achieve to date? In fact, approval levels are likely to drop even further as various Senate and House committees detail every minute of decision making prior to Katrina, highlight every failure and scrutinize every missed opportunity in a report that will inevitably pose thousands of questions the White House, governor and mayor will not be able to satisfactorily answer. These committee findings, much like the 9/11 Report, will no doubt recommend spending more money to fix the problem.

The point here is not to establish a direct causal relationship between spending and confidence; spending does not automatically *cause* approval ratings to go down. If it was that simple, then the dilemma could be easily resolved by spending nothing on security, an absurd policy recommendation that does not flow logically from the arguments outlined here. Obviously, the absence of security spending and related commitments would increase threat perceptions and decrease public confidence as the media and opposition groups slam the government for its failure to heed the lessons of 9/11. The main point, rather, is that increased spending (along with other sacrifices described earlier) creates expectations the government can never meet, but spending any less is an option the government can never accept. Both reactions are perfectly rational, and that is the problem. As expectations for higher levels of security increase, and as corresponding thresholds for acceptable levels of pain decrease, both parties will compete to convince the American public that *their* party's programs are different, more comprehensive, and more likely to succeed (Harvey, 2004: 27). Washington is becoming "addicted to security" because spending will never be sufficient to achieve absolute success in the war on terror, yet perfection will remain the standard politicians will claim to be trying to reach.

The Dubai Ports World fiasco (February 2006) is the most recent manifestations of this emerging competition. For a brief period of time the crisis seriously threatened to loosen the Republicans' grip on security policy by providing Democrats with the opportunity to gain political traction on a key security file. Of course, the risks associated with the United Arab Emerates' operational control of six American ports were exaggerated by both Democrats and Republicans to enhance their security credentials in preparation for midterm elections. But the message that will no doubt be picked up by friends and exploited by enemies in the region is obvious: the US is not prepared to trust Arab/Muslim states or companies. The potential for these mixed signals to undermine, rather than enhance, American security over the long run was not lost to the US senators who quickly travelled to Dubai to apologize for their actions. The ports crisis provides a very clear illustration of the unintended, counterproductive and paradoxical consequences of the dilemma.

The Power of Failure

The predisposition we have to overvalue the negative effects of failures and undervalue (if not completely ignore) the positive effects of successes is a second important component of the homeland security dilemma. There are several reasons for our bias in this regard.

First, our sense of security after an attack or natural disaster is rarely (if ever) based on how many lives are saved but rather on how many are lost. Few of us can recall the number of people successfully evacuated from the World Trade Center and Pentagon on 9/11 but we can all recite the number of deaths. Similarly, we never see pictures of houses tornadoes or hurricanes miss.

Second, we typically perceive a greater loss in security from a minor failure than a corresponding gain in security from news that a major attack was prevented or that a significant counterterrorist success was achieved; the arrests of 17 terrorist suspects in the Toronto area in June 2006 increased rather than decreased threat perceptions in Canada (for reasons outlined below). Consider the following: a relatively minor terrorist attack in the United States today resulting in, say, five deaths from a suicide bomb in a Wal-Mart would have a profoundly more negative impact on American perceptions of their security than all of the terrorist attacks and casualties in Iraq and Afghanistan combined. Yet the absence of a single post-9/11 attack on US soil—essentially a perfect record in preventing the worst kind of security failure—is almost completely excluded from the public's success-failure balance sheet. If the US government achieved the same measure of success in preventing terrorist attacks in Iraq as it has on American soil, we would be hailing the 2003–2006 Iraq intervention as one of the most impressive and important military victories since the Second World War. But no such credit is being assigned to Washington's homeland security performance. As Joseph Nye (1995) observed, "security is like oxygen. You do not tend to notice it until you begin to lose it."

Third, when successes occur nothing really happens, so we have no reference points, no facts or images to include in the balance sheet.[8] Conversely, security failures are all inclusive and encompass an ever-expanding list of conceptually disparate images and facts readily identifiable and far easier to incorporate into our calculations. The blurring of homeland security and the global war on terrorism means that almost any type of foreign or domestic policy failure becomes relevant to perceptions of security. Everything from abuse at the Abu Ghraib prison to the bombing of the Golden Mosque in Samara, fears of a civil war in Iraq to images of angry Muslims involved in violent protests around the world following the publication of caricatures of the prophet Mohammad, images of kidnap victims (most of whom have been released in return for ransom) and suicide bombings in Iraq and Afghanistan to news about American ports being controlled by Dubai, and so forth, all combine to tip the balance in favour of failure. Even non-terrorist events, such as Katrina, SARS or warnings of an avian flu pandemic get inserted into our lists of real or potential security problems. It is perfectly reasonable to argue, for example, that the levees in New Orleans could just as easily have been damaged by a terrorist attack, so the collapse of disaster relief efforts following Katrina are legitimately interpreted as a breakdown in homeland security. Similarly, the many challenges we face with a SARS or potential bird flu crisis are not unlike those we would expect to encounter in the midst of a biological terrorist attack, so any evidence that the government is failing to prepare for, manage or control these viruses are easily incorporated into our sense of insecurity.

Fourth, we tend to believe failures more readily than we do successes and often ascribe some measure of political motivation to the latter. When President Bush delivers a series of televised speeches revisiting a "success" in 2001 involving the arrest of Zacharias Moussawi, the only person arrested and tried for his alleged involvement in the 9/11 attacks, the public and media are naturally suspicious. The consensus in this case was that Bush was simply bolstering White House arguments defending warrant-less National Security Agency surveillance practices in the midst of a national debate about whether the president can claim these as constitutional powers.

Fifth, the press and other media tend to focus heavily on our side's failures, often for perfectly rational reasons tied to ratings, circulation and profits. But the more difficult challenge for those trying to make a case for progress in the war on terrorism is the tendency for the press to overlook obvious (and significant) failures on the part of terrorists and their state sponsors. The global response to 9/11, for example, has led to hundreds of new multilateral and bilateral laws and agreements, enhanced co-ordination across intelligence organizations, and counterterrorist victories that have significantly improved our capacity to monitor and control terrorist funding, recruitment and other illegal activities. The precise benefits emerging from all of this may be difficult to measure, but the obvious costs to terrorists receive almost no sustained coverage in the press.

Sixth, counterterrorist successes are easily (and logically) reinterpreted by the public, media and opposition groups as failures. Consider the rise in Canadian threat perceptions immediately following the June 2006 arrests in Toronto of 17 terrorists suspects (Figure 7). Clearly the most interesting poll results are those compiled *after* the arrest. Canadian threat perceptions escalated to 71 per cent following what was believed at the time to be one the most important counterterrorist *successes* in Canadian history. Oddly enough, threat perceptions after this success were higher than those following a major failure in London a year earlier (July 2005).

These percentages should concern security officials in Ottawa who obviously would prefer a more balanced public assessment of the government's security performance and

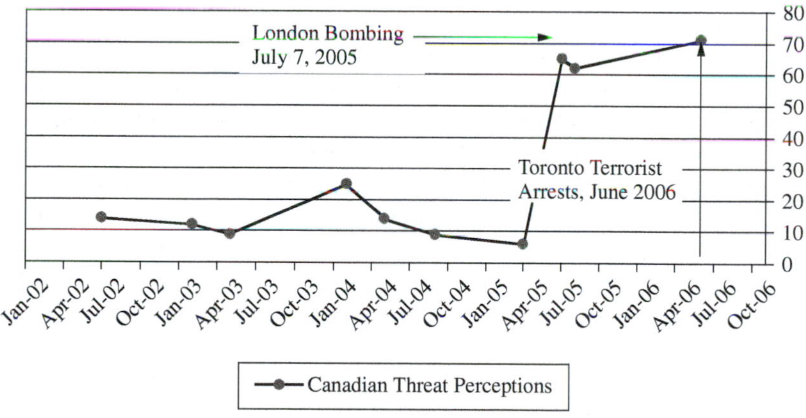

FIGURE 7 Canadian Threat Perceptions Terrorist Attack in Canada Likely

Data points for Figure 7 were compiled from the following sources. http://www.pollara.ca/Library/News/terrorsubsiding.html; http://www.ipsos-na.com/news/pressrelease.cfm?id-1614; http://www.wilsoncenter.org/topics/pubs/threats.pdf; http://www.ctv.ca/servlet/ArticleNews/story/CTVNews/20040208/terror_poll040206?s_name=&no_ads=; http://www.ipsos-na.com/news/pressrelease.cfm?id-2736; http://www.angus-reid.com/polls/index.cfm/fuseaction/viewItem/itemID/8227; http://www.pollara.ca/Library/QI/JUL05.pdf; http://www.angusreid.com/polls/index.cfm/fuseaction/viewItem/itemID/8491; http://www.ctv.ca/servlet/ArticleNews/story/CTVNews/20060609/terrorism_poll_060609/20060609/; http://www.angus-reid.com/polls/index.cfm//fuseaction/vieItem/itemID/12213.

no doubt expected at least some credit for their accomplishment (Nagy, 2006). Judging by the impact of the arrests, however, those responsible for Canadian security and public safety are facing serious impediments to critical risk management and communication.

When news of the arrests began to filter through the media, many Canadians realized (perhaps for the first time) that their country is not immune to the same security challenges plaguing our American, Australian and European allies: homegrown terrorists motivated by a collection of extremist causes that spawn levels of anger and hatred most Canadians are only now beginning to partially grasp.

The Canadian media fed public fears by explaining the threat with reference to, among other things, the inevitable backlash against Canada's commitment to Afghanistan, serious gaps in Canada's immigration and refugee policies, fundamental flaws with Canadian multilculturalism, and so forth. A few American senators used the success to hammer home the crucial importance of border security and began repeating the same post-9/11 assertions about Canada's reputation as a haven for terrorists plan- ning to attack US targets. And, of course, opposition groups in Canada, rationally motivated by a political mandate to exploit every instance of government incompetence, began to draw connections between the apparent "decline" in Canadian security and our counterinsurgency efforts in the Kandahar region of Afghanistan.

Paradoxically, the very rational reactions we would expect to see following a major security failure emerged after a significant counterterrorist success. It should come as no surprise to anyone, therefore, that two separate polls by Angus Reid and IPSOS taken shortly after the arrests confirmed that 57 per cent and 58 per cent of Canadian respondents, respectively, believed the group of 17 suspected terrorists is just the "tip of the iceberg" (Angus Reid Global Monitor, 2006b; Ipsos-Reid, 2002).

These perceptions are likely to become even more entrenched in light of an unclassified Canadian Security and Intelligence Service report concluding that an al-Qaeda attack in Canada is now "probable" (Chronicle Herald, 2006), CIA estimates that terrorist threats are rising as a consequence of ongoing insurgencies in Iraq and Afghanistan, and a more recent MI5 report confirming that British intelligence agencies are currently tracking up to 30 different terrorist groups. And Canada's ongoing battle against a growing al-Qaeda/Taliban insurgency in Afghanistan will do little to alleviate public concerns (Linzer and Pincus, 2006). The pressure on Ottawa to spend more on security will rise accordingly, as will public expectations and standards for measuring their performance—standards the government will be increasingly incapable of satisfying, either in Afghanistan or here at home.

Finally, the tendency for failures to trump successes is strongly supported by empirical evidence from the polls described in Figure 4. When relevant post-9/11 events are juxtaposed onto these "approval" ratings (illustrated in Figure 8) the results reveal much stronger negative effects from failures (downward trends) than any positive effects from successes (upward trends).

Consider for example how quickly the trend lines begin to decline after Bush's "mission accomplished" declaration on the USS Abraham Lincoln (May 2003), the capture of Saddam Hussein (December 2003), the positive boost from Bush's 2004 re-election campaign (August–November 2004), and the Iraqi elections (January 2005). When compared with the negative impact of the Madrid bombings (March 2004), the Abu Ghraib prisoner abuse scandal (April 2004), the London bombings (July 2005), or hurricane Katrina (August 2005), the decline in approval is more pronounced and permanent.

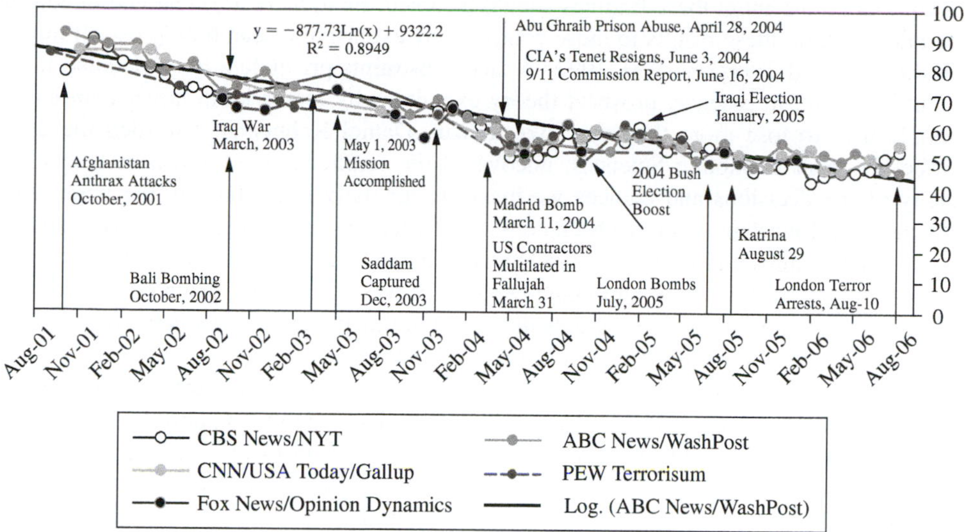

FIGURE 8 Public Approval of US Approach to Global War on Terror (GWOT)—Marked by Key Events

In terms of the overall trend, the steady decline in confidence and approval from 2001–2006 indicates that successes (no matter how many or how significant) are never strong enough to reverse the downward spiral. To use the analogy of a scale, when balanced against successes the combined weight of failures is always heavier and more resilient, a phenomenon that can be demonstrated using the ABC News-Washington Post polls from Figure 4 (arrow, upper left). A logarithmic linear regression line (arrow, upper left) provides a graphic illustration of the best fit and slope through the data.[9] If the ebb and flow in public approval ratings were event driven (that is, characterized by peaks and valleys after successes and failures, respectively), then the data would naturally produce a relatively straight logarithmic regression line (with very little slope) and a correspondingly low regression coefficient (R2) that would approach zero. On the other hand, if failures are more negative than successes are positive, as predicted by the homeland security dilemma, we should see a steady linear decline in approval over time and a correspondingly very high regression coefficient approaching one. As expected, the coefficient for the ABC News-Washington Post data over the last six years is very strong at 0.8949. Without exception, the coefficients for the data compiled by each of the other media outlets are also uniformly high.

Polling Series	Log R^2
ABC News/Washington Post	*0.8949*
CNN/USA Today/Gallup	*0.8671*
CBS News/New York Times	*0.8575*
PEW Research Center	*0.7976*
Fox News/Opinion Dynamics	*0.7076*

Two final points about these findings should be noted. First, there are clear and important parallels linking these results to those compiled by extensive research on prospect theory (Kahneman and Tversky, 1979, 1992). Space constraints preclude a more detailed treatment here, but, in essence, prospect theory explains why losses loom larger than gains: people hate to lose more than they like to win. Daniel Kahneman, awarded the 2002 Nobel Prize in Economic Sciences, uncovered the implications of prospect theory for many of the decisions and choices we make in our daily lives. Indeed, the underlying psychological mechanisms have been consistently demonstrated in repeated experimental trials in economics and psychology (Kahneman and Tversky, 1979, 1992). The research presented here explains how important elements of prospect theory, when combined with other political and economic pressures described in this paper, are producing a homeland security dilemma political officials will be unable to control.

Second, the findings presented here are relevant to another important debate in the literature on the relationship between casualties and US public support for the war in Iraq (Mueller, 2005; Gelpi, Feaver and Reifler, 2005/6; and Gelpi and Mueller, 2006). According to Mueller, the decline in public approval for the Iraq war is essentially a function of casualty figures (for example, the Vietnam syndrome revisited). Gelpi and Feaver claim that Mueller's explanation is incomplete because it ignores an important link between casualty acceptance (or aversion) and the public's assessment of victory and/or defeat—casualties are generally more acceptable if the war is going well. Although Gelpi and Feaver's observations are more consistent with those developed here, their thesis is also incomplete. The homeland security dilemma represents a more comprehensive account of declining approval ratings for the war in Iraq, Afghanistan and the larger war on terrorism. These three wars cannot be studied in isolation, and a thorough accounting of the insurmountable dilemma Canadian and American policy officials are facing today will not be possible if this point continues to be overlooked. The problem, in other words, is significantly more complex and challenging than Mueller, Gelpi and Feaver acknowledge.

Public Imagination: Exaggerated Perceptions of Terrorist Risks and Threats

A third catalyst driving the homeland security dilemma is the public's inability to accurately evaluate the probability of a terrorist attack. Consider the following evidence from Figures 9[10], 10[11] and 11.

Clearly, a very large percentage of Americans remain overly concerned about another attack: the range has been between 55 and 75 per cent over the last five years. The percentage of respondents who fear that they or a family member will personally be a target of an attack drops to between 30 and 50 per cent, but even that number is considerably higher than any reasonable measure of the risks and probabilities would indicate. If we were to combine the effects of 9/11, the anthrax attacks, the Bali, Madrid and London bombings, and throw in every other terrorist attack in the world (Iraq and Afghanistan included) over the last two decades, the probability of being a target of a terrorist attack would be infinitesimally tiny. Yet the level of fear and anxiety in the US today remains disproportionately very high.

Understanding why these percentages remain so high is essential to appreciating the dilemma political officials are facing today. Research into the social and psychological

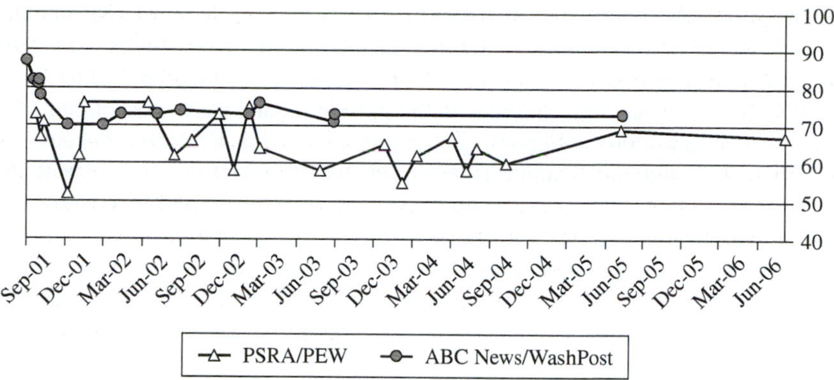

FIGURE 9 Polling Question: "How Worried/Concerned Are You about 'Another Attack'?" ('very worried'/'somewhat worried')

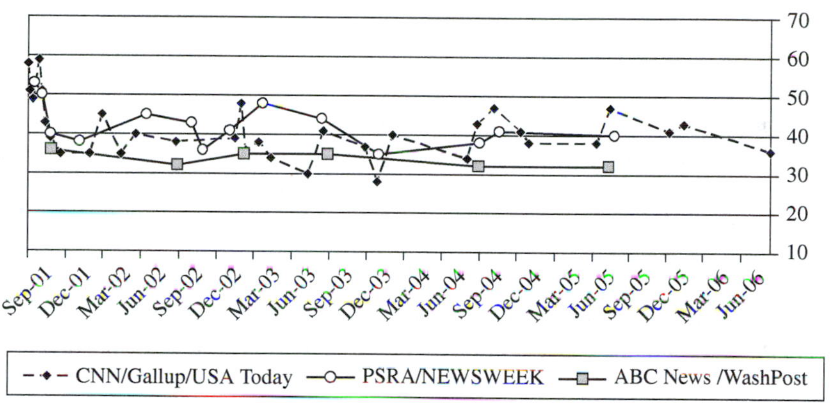

FIGURE 10 Polling Question: "How Worried Are You or Someone in Family Will be a Victim of Terrorism?" (very worried/somewhat worried)

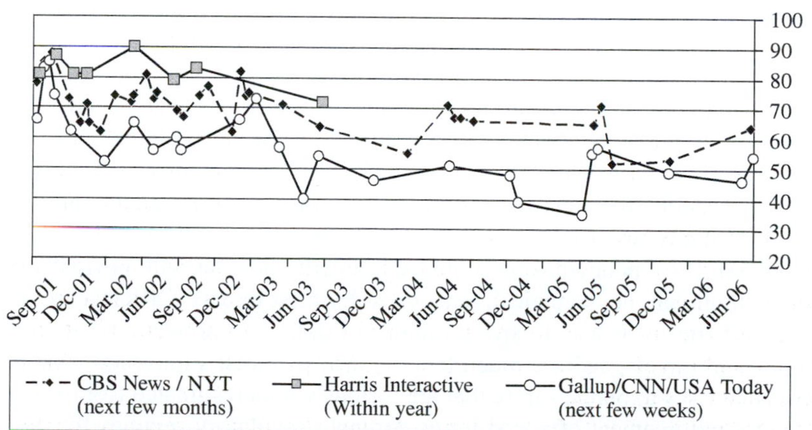

FIGURE 11 Polling Question: Likelihood of Attack in Next Several 'Weeks'/'Months' (very likely/likely)

origins of threat perceptions has consistently shown that the level of risk people assign to specific events or behaviours is a function of, among other things, *familiarity* and *controllability;* it is almost never a function of facts, statistics or probabilities.[12] "If a risk is an old, well-established one, familiar to the individual and easily detectable," Croxford explains, "it will tend to be underestimated compared to a risk of the same actual magnitude which is new, unfamiliar and difficult to detect" (2005: 3). Easily controllable risks associated with personal choices or habits are usually perceived as less serious than those over which we have no real control. We fear things that could happen suddenly and play down risks that have a high probability of developing over time. All of which explains why familiar and controllable risks related to smoking, drinking or driving a car are typically underestimated, despite the fact that each of these activities virtually guarantees thousands of deaths each year.

Research on the subject also clearly indicates that we tend to fear what is most readily available in memory, so the risks tied to events that receive extensive media and press coverage are likely to be overestimated by the public:

> Horrific images of a DC-10 catapulting across the Sioux City runway, or the Concorde exploding in Paris, or of United Flight 175 slicing into the World Trade Center, form indelible memories. And availability in memory provides our intuitive rule of thumb for judging risks. . . . We can know that unprovoked great white shark attacks have claimed merely 67 lives worldwide since 1876. Yet after watching *Jaws* and reading vivid accounts of last summer's Atlantic coastal shark attacks, we may feel chills when an underwater object brushes our leg. . . . We comprehend the 266 passengers and crew on those four fated flights. We don't comprehend the vast numbers of accident-free flights—16 million consecutive fatality-free takeoffs and landings during one stretch of the 1990s. Dramatic outcomes capture our attention; probabilities we hardly grasp. The result: we overvalue lottery tickets, overestimate flight risk, and underestimate the dangers of driving. (Myers, 2001)

Terrorist threats are unfamiliar and uncontrollable, so most of the public consistently exaggerates and overestimates the real risks, as confirmed by very high threat perceptions noted in Figures 8 and 9. In addition, declining trust and confidence in the government's homeland security performance (Figures 2–4) does not help. Confidence is directly related to perceptions of controllability; it is only natural for us to be more concerned about a threat if we have very little faith in the government's ability to keep us safe. Moreover, relentless negative media coverage of every dimension of an expanding list of security failures also helps to sustain the very strong belief by large segments of the population that terrorism is among the most serious threats they face, notwithstanding all of the facts and statistics to the contrary.

The dilemma for policymakers is obvious: security policies will inevitably prioritize the public's emotional, not statistical, reaction to terrorist threats. Officials are politically motivated, for better or worse, to spend billions of dollars to protect citizens from exaggerated risks and threats, and are much less inclined to invest similar amounts to reduce highly probable risks to public safety that are seriously underestimated (for example, paying for stricter enforcement of speed limits, stronger regulatory regimes for the tobacco and fast food industries, public awareness campaigns to encourage healthier diets and eating habits, and so forth). If close to 75 per cent of the public believes terrorists will attack again, political leaders will be reluctant to downplay the threat or openly question public perceptions for two straightforward and perfectly rational reasons. First, it is easier to accept and exploit the public's fears than it is to invest the time and resources to control those perceptions. Second, if any attack does occur (no matter how unlikely or how small) the political costs will be significant for those who downplayed the threat or called for a more balanced view of the facts and risks. Terrorists do not deserve either the status or the credit for being that powerful, but even weak and insignificant terrorists become relevant in light of the public's higher standards: any attack is unacceptable.

Political-Military Imagination: Official Overestimation of Risks and Threats

A fourth component of the dilemma emerges from the enormous pressure political and military leaders face to find and fill gaps in security. Consider the following conclusions from the final report of the 9/11 commission (9/11 Commission Report, 2005b):

> We believe the 9/11 attacks revealed four kinds of failures: in *imagination,* policy, capabilities, and management. (339, emphasis added)
>
> *The most important failure was one of imagination.* We do not believe leaders understood the gravity of the threat. (14, emphasis added)
>
> *Imagination* is not a gift usually associated with bureaucracies . . . *It is therefore crucial to find a way of routinizing, even bureaucratizing, the exercise of imagination.* . . . Considering what was not done suggests possible ways to *institutionalize imagination.* (344–346, passim, emphasis added)

When the most powerful nation on earth is tasked with a policy directive to routinize, bureaucratize and institutionalize the exercise of "imagination," and when this authoritative recommendation is assigned to multiple federal, state and municipal organizations by one of the most important bipartisan committees in decades (a committee widely supported by an American public scarred by the trauma of 9/11), no one should be surprised by how overwhelming and expensive the task has become. But the application of imagination as a key policy guideline has added yet another important dimension to the homeland security dilemma.[13]

Officials have answered the call by imagining thousands of different threats, potential vulnerabilities and existing or evolving gaps in security, and just as many ways to spend money to fill the holes. Resolving this incredibly complex security puzzle has become the government's primary preoccupation in a post-9/11 world. Also, the lists of threats and solutions are endless, ranging from airline passengers with paper clips and tweezers to the need to launch 43,000 air force sorties since 9/11 to stop hijacked airplanes from slamming into buildings. Yet five years after the 9/11 attacks senior homeland security officials testifying on various committees continue to express serious reservations about vulnerability at airports. Similarly, any military briefing focussing on maritime security today will inevitably outline the following facts about the world's 46,222 shipping fleet: as of January 1, 2005, the fleet includes 18,150 general cargo ships, 11,356 tankers, 6,136 bulk carriers, 5,679 passenger ships (carrying thousands of civilian tourists), 3,165 container ships and 1,733 ships in the "other" category. (Shipping Facts, 2005) More alarmingly, only 2 per cent of the 10,000,000 containers shipped into the US annually are physically inspected (Clawson, 2006). These figures are not meant to inform the public about the scope of maritime transportation, trade or tourism, they are offered as examples of thousands of potential threats. Also, politicians have become very adept at imagining the political fallout if they fail to prevent an attack they were warned about—an important lesson from hurricane Katrina.

The real problem today, then, is not the failure of imagination; it is the imagination of failure that continues to entrench into American domestic politics the main elements of the homeland security dilemma. Paradoxically, routinzing, bureaucratizing and institutionalizing imagination undermines the public's sense of security while simultaneously pushing the government to spend more.

Declining Support for Sacrificing Civil Liberties

In light of the public's exaggerated threat perceptions and the tendency for political officials to overestimate the risks, one would expect to see sustained public support for government surveillance activities. These, after all, are the tools the government claims it needs to improve intelligence gathering and counterterrorist operations. But public support for surveillance has steadily declined since 2001, which accounts for the fifth and final component of the homeland security dilemma (see Figure 12).

The paradox here is obvious: the government is losing public support for operations it believes are essential for success in the war on terrorism at a time when public expectations for security are rising. In the absence of another attack (ironically, thanks to a perfect homeland security record), a creeping complacency kicks in whereby the public begins to reject policies that appear to diminish their rights and civil liberties. Unlike the other four aspects of the dilemma, however, this one can be partially corrected, if not reversed, but only after another attack. Now that's a dilemma.

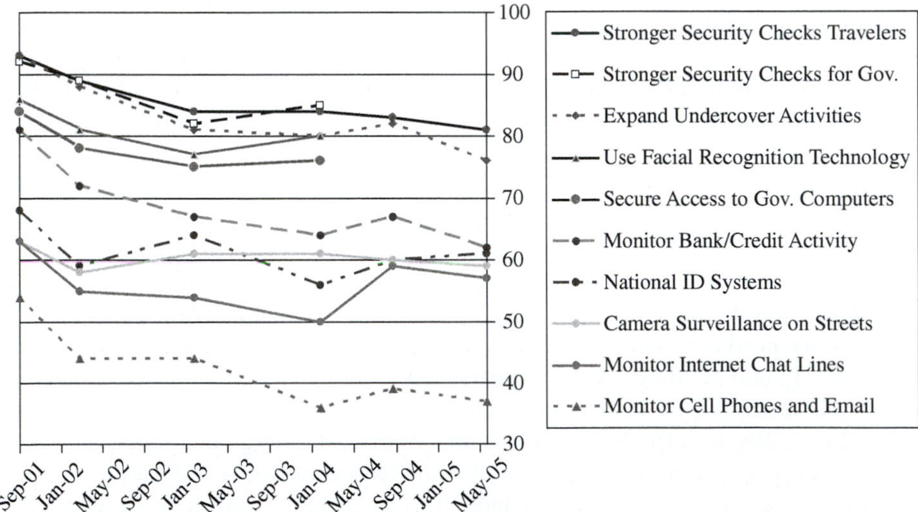

FIGURE 12 Declining Support for Government Surveillance/Monitoring Powers (Harris Interactive)

There Are No Policy Recommendations, Only Policy Dilemmas

The most important policy implication flowing from the preceding analysis is that there are no straightforward policy recommendations to offer. In fact, the more compelling the logic, arguments and evidence offered to support the existence of a homeland security dilemma, the more obvious the challenges for identifying a coherent set of policy alternatives because the most rational options are part of the problem. If solutions were obvious there would be no dilemma. The fact that we are in the midst of a "dilemma" defines the nature of the policy conundrum: "A state of uncertainty or perplexity especially as requiring a choice between equally unfavorable options"; "a situation from which extrication is difficult especially an unpleasant or trying one"; "a problem that seems to defy a satisfactory solution"; "an argument that presents two alternatives, each of which has the same consequence, (or) a situation that requires a choice between options that are mutually exclusive."

This is not to imply that policy makers are incompetent boobs who just don't get it. While this may be a standard (and convenient) assumption in much of the literature (Mueller, 2006), it is both simplistic and exceedingly insulting to the many very bright people tasked with the challenge of security and public safety. The point here is that there are no simple or easy solutions for policy makers to identify and implement. Being caught on the horns of a dilemma does not mean that we are subject to non-rational decisions; it simply means that we are forced to select from several rational policy options that are equally costly, potentially counterproductive, or largely irrelevant to resolving the problem.

If we were to compare the homeland security dilemma with other familiar policy challenges it would be much closer to the intractable puzzle of Middle East peace than it would be to the softwood lumber dispute between the US and Canada. To use another analogy, any request to end this article with a list of clear cut policy recommendations is not unlike asking those who wrote about security dilemmas in the 1950s and 1960s to resolve the Cold War.[14] There are no silver bullets, and those who think there are easy answers are probably wrong.

Perhaps the best way to illustrate the nature of the policy paradox is to evaluate three common recommendations through the prism of the homeland security dilemma.

Example 1: In light of the public's tendency to overestimate if not completely exaggerate the risk of terrorism, several prominent scholars (Mueller, 2006), observors and policy analysts have recommended developing better programs to inform people about the facts and risks of terrorism. Clarifying the statistics and probabilities, they argue, should be sufficient to resolve at least part of the homeland security dilemma. An informed public with a better understanding of the risks would obviously have a more reasonable and balanced set of expectations. Myers' recommendations are typical in this regard. "To be prudent is to be mindful of the realities of how humans die. By so doing, we can take away the terrorists' most omnipresent weapon: exaggerated fear. When terrorists strike again, remember the odds. If, God forbid, anthrax or truck bombs kill a thousand Americans, we will all recoil in horror. Small comfort, perhaps, but the odds are 284,000 to 1 that you won't be among them" (2001: 1).

John Mueller's (2006: 2) book *Overblown* is among the more popular on the subject of U.S. overreactions to 9/11. According to Mueller, "International Terrorism generally kills a few hundred people a year worldwide—not much more, usually, than the number who drown yearly in bathtubs in the United States. . . . (T)he lifetime probability that a resident of the globe will die at the hands of international terrorists is 1 in 80,000, about the same likelihood that one would die over the same interval from the impact on earth of an especially ill-directed asteroid or comet."

In keeping with this line of reasoning, Brian Flemming, former chairman of the Canadian Air Transport Security Authority, warns that "only by surrendering to fear will we lose our civilization and our souls," and goes on to offer the following quote from Alfred Hitchcock to highlight his point: "There is no terror in the bang, only in the anticipation of it" (2006: 11). Aside from forgetting that the terror produced by the "bang" of 9/11 transformed the world, Flemming, like Myers, assumes that understanding our fears is the answer. There are hundreds of other books, articles, editorials and "expert" opinions, and now thousands of internet blogs, that arrive at the same obvious conclusions about the public's exaggerated fears and repeat the same sage advice to look at the numbers, understand the facts and risks, relax (or, more poetically, don't surrender to fear) and get a life.[15]

The problem with this conventional view is that it is largely irrelevant because it misses the following fundamental point: the fact that we overestimate the risks of terrorism is less relevant than the tendency to consistently do so *despite the facts and evidence to the contrary*. Repeating the extremely low statistical odds of dying in a plane crash will not change the fact that air travel will be *mis*perceived by most people (most of the time) as posing a significantly greater risk than driving a car. Informing the public about the safety of nuclear energy will never be sufficient to dissipate fears (and images) associated with the Three Mile Island or Chernobyl disasters. Also, the very small odds that any given individual will experience a catastrophic accident in their lives will not alter the general consensus that life insurance is well worth the investment. If facts, statistics and rational probabilities alone were sufficient to guide perceptions and choices, then insurance companies, lotteries, and the tobacco, fast food and gambling industries would not be among the most profitable businesses in the world.

In sum, a clearer understanding of the origins of our fears is not the solution to the security dilemma; it is the best explanation for the problem.

Example 2: Another very common policy recommendation is for the government to design more effective critical risk management and communication skills to prepare the public for the next crisis. Some of the best work on the topic is by Peter Sandman who offers the following comprehensive list of best practices, guidelines and recommendation for effectively managing fear (Table 1):

While the list is impressive, consider how many of these guidelines and recommendations are likely to be applied in practice by politicians. How many are being applied today to address fears in the US or Canada? As one works through the list it becomes quite apparent that political officials are more likely to do exactly the opposite, for obvious political reasons: they are pre-programmed to highlight what they are doing right, not what they are doing wrong or why we should be concerned about the things they simply can not do.

Ironically, applying these best practices in Canada is even more challenging because Canadian officials are often inclined to issue a completely different set of pre-programmed messages that many Canadians find appealing: messages that reinforce often false perceptions that Canadians are not Americans and, therefore, *don't* share the same security risks, threats or priorities. This popular myth is not only counterproductive from the point of Sandman's recommended guidelines, but it represents a view that will be much harder to sustain in the future in light of Canada's ongoing counter-insurgencey efforts in Afghanistan.

TABLE 1 Critical Risk Management and Communications: Guidelines and Recommendations for Action

Guidelines

1. Candour versus secrecy
2. Speculation versus refusal to speculate
3. Tentativeness versus confidence
4. Being alarming versus being reassuring
5. Being human versus being professional
6. Being apologetic versus being defensive
7. Decentralization versus centralization
8. Individual control versus expert decision-making

Recommendations

1. Don't over-reassure.
2. Err on the alarming side.
3. Acknowledge uncertainty.
4. Share dilemmas.
5. Acknowledge opinion diversity.
6. Be willing to speculate.
7. Don't over-diagnose or over-plan for panic.
8. Don't aim for zero fear.
9. Don't ridicule the public's emotions—legitimize people's fears.
10. Tolerate early over-reactions.
11. Establish your own humanity.
12. Tell people what to expect.
13. Offer people things to do, but let people choose their own actions.
14. Acknowledge errors, deficiencies, and misbehaviours.
16. Apologize often for errors, deficiencies, and misbehaviours.
17. Be explicit about changes in official opinion, prediction, or policy.
18. Don't lie, and don't tell half-truths.
19. Aim for total candour and transparency. (Sandman, 2001)

Example 3: Acquiring a much better understanding of how the public thinks about successes and failures in the war on terrorism is one of the most important but neglected dimensions of contemporary security policy. If we fail in this regard then the long war will be very difficult to manage, let alone win. In the absence of systematic research on how these stories, images and events interact to push perceptions in one or the other direction, leaders will continue to face a difficult uphill battle in their efforts to establish some balance in public perceptions of victory and defeat. And unless governments find innovative ways to clearly communicate credible signs of success, the only direction support will go is down, especially if the experts are busy imagining larger numbers of threats that need containing. The problem, as demonstrated in Figure 4, is that peaks in confidence and approval are short lived and valleys are virtually impossible to reverse. Even a major success in the war on terrorism, for example the capture and trial of Osama Bin Laden, will not be suffieient to push the trend in the opposite direction for any length of time.

Conversely, it is very easy to imagine hundreds of different types of failures that will continue to push the approval lower. Herein lies the dilemma for policy makers: if successes are simply too difficult to identify (or prove) and failures so easy to exploit, the only real policy option governments have left is to spend more to feed the illusion that something important is being accomplished. Paradoxically, this is precisely the strategy that continues to raise expectations the government is increasingly incapable of meeting. The one thing that was made abundantly clear in congressional reports on 9/11, Iraq's WMD program and hurricane Katrina is that "perfect" security is emerging as the only acceptable standard. But no combination of policies or strategies will ever come close.

Summary and Policy Implications for Canada

In sum, investing more in security simultaneously increases public expectations and the political and economic fallout after each failure. Successes are ignored while an expanding list of failures pushes public approval lower. Despite the facts, the public continues to exaggerate terrorist threats while both political parties compete to defend their security credentials by imagining longer lists of security gaps. Doing anything less is too risky, and doing more (or too much), while counterproductive, can become a badge of honour.[16]

Now, if all of these pressures continue to unfold in a relatively benign security environment with a perfect homeland security record, imagine how much more pressure Washington will experience after the next terrorist attack on US soil. This is the context in which a discussion of Canadian interests, policies and priorities becomes most relevant, because the homeland security dilemma establishes the parameters Washington, the US media and the American public will use when evaluating Canada's contribution to security after the next failure.

The official estimate of Canada's post-9/11 security spending is about $11 billion (including figures in Prime Minister Harper's 2007 federal budget). Over the past few years periodic increases in Canada's defence budget included hundreds of millions of dollars pegged to security and public safety programs. Another $2 billion (and counting) has been spent on Canada's contribution to the war in Afghanistan. Most of the money has been used to create or enhance existing programs through the departments of Public Safety, National Defence, Immigration, Transport, the Canada Border Services Agency, the Royal Canadian Mounted Police (RCMP), Canadian Security and Intelligence Service (CSIS) and other key agencies tied to Canada's security establishment.

With the preceding analysis in mind, the important question is not whether Canadian investments and related programs have enhanced North American security, but whether it really matters *even if they have.* When the next attack occurs Washington will evaluate Canada's commitment in much the same way (and through many of the same biases) that the US public and media evaluate Washington's performance. No matter what Ottawa has accomplished so far, the next failure will create the overwhelming impression (even if false) that more could and should have been done.

The policy implications for Canada are obvious and disturbing. If standards continue to rise and if failures (including real and imagined gaps in security) trump successes, then it really doesn't matter how many organizational, administrative or infrastructure changes Ottawa has institutionalized since 9/11 at a cost of $11 billion,[17] or how strong our anti-terrorism legislation has become, or how much of our rising defence budget we have allocated to continental security program, or how rigid we think our immigration policy might be[18] or how much we've enhanced border security while protecting the free flow of goods and services (Collacott, 2006). None of the successes listed in government briefings today—for example, the Security and Prosperity Partnership, Western Hemisphere Travel Initiative, the Smart Border agreement, Integrated Border Enforcement Teams, the Integrated Threat Assessment Program, bilateral and trilateral intelligence sharing agreements, the expansion of NORAD's mandate to include maritime security, the creation of CANADACOM, the many programs and initiatives outlined in Canada's new National Security Policy or International Policy Statement, and so forth (Canada, 2003, 2006)—will carry much weight in Washington after the next failure, *whether or not these programs are essential, produced significant successes in the past, or ultimately contribute to saving lives after the next attack.*[19] That is Canada's homeland security dilemma.

Critical Thinking Questions

1. If strategies and policies aim for "perfect security," are we setting up our intelligence and law enforcement agencies for inevitable failure and condemnation when an attack takes place? If so, can anything be done about this?
2. Who within our local, state, or federal government should be responsible for educating the public about the impossibility of "perfect security" or other misleading expectations?
3. Does the absence of a major terrorist attack since 9/11 lead to a false sense that enormous investments made by government at all levels have provided "near-perfect security"?

Notes

1. Several prominent examples of media reports detailing successful conter-terrorist operations include Argetsinger and Geis, 2005; Evans, 2004; CTV, 2004; CBC News, 2005; Limbacher, 2006; Limbacher, 2006; Fox News, 2004; Zakis and Macko, 2002; BBC News, 2003; Gilbert, 2004; BreakingNews.ie, 2003; CBS News, 2005; Saunders, 2004; Baker and Eggen, 2006; Gilbert, 2004; Bacon, 2003; Dunnigan, 2005; Heritage Foundation, 2005; Hughes, 2005; Baker, 2004; Tendler, 2006; USAToday.com, 2006; Nagy, 2006.
2. For a comprehensive compilation of terrorism-related polling results for each organization, see Bowman (2006). The specific wording used in the surveys listed in Figure 2 asked "How much confidence do you have in the US government to protect its citizens from future terrorist attacks?" The table combines percentages for respondents selecting "a great deal" and "a fair amount."
3. Specific wording for the surveys (Bowman, 2006) listed in Figure 3 follows. ABC News/*Washington Post:* "Do you think the United States is doing all it reasonably can do to try to prevent further terrorist attacks, or do you think it should do more?" Percentages responding "doing all it can" were registered. CNN/*USA Today*/Gallop: "How satisfied are you with the way things are going for the US in the war on terrorism?" Percentages responding "very satisfied" and "somewhat satisfied" were registered. Harris Interactive: "How would you rate the job the Bush administration has done in preventing a terrorist attack in the United States since September 11, 2001?" Respondents who selected "excellent" and 'pretty good" were registered in the table.

4. The following question was asked (Bowman, 2006): "Do you approve or disapprove of the job President Bush is doing handling the issue of terrorism?" The percentage of respondents selecting "approve" were registered.
5. The reasons for highlighting these specific events and for noting the logarithmic linear regression line for the ABC News/*Washington Post* data will be explained toward the end of section "The Power of Failure" (and in endnote 12).
6. Despite the steady decline in public confidence, George W. Bush won the 2004 election, in part, because Republicans consistently generated higher approval ratings than Democrats on security issues.
7. With respect to emerging standards for measuring success and failure, the 9/11, Iraq WMD and Katrina reports all provide illustrations of public expectations, regardless of whether those standards and benchmarks can ever really be met. For a detailed review of the mutually exclusive recommendations flowing from these reports, see Harvey (2005).
8. Few observers are likely to recall any of the reports of successful counterterrorist operations listed in endnote 2, not because they are irrelevant to a balanced account of successes and failures, but because we expect successes and tend to quickly forget them. In contrast, images of failures are vivid and usually linger.
9. A logarithmic linear regression model is ideal, because the decline in support (measured by confidence, trust, approval, etc.) is expected to taper off—it will never approach either extreme over time (i.e., 0% or 100%). There will always be a core group of Republican (or Democratic) respondents who would support their party regardless of the scope or number of failures.
10. The surveys asked, "How worried are you that there will soon be another terrorist attack in the United States?" The percentage of respondents selecting "very worried" and "somewhat worried" were combined and included in the table. With respect to the ABC News/*Washington Post* survey, the question was; "How concerned are you about the possibility there will be more terrorist attacks in the United States?" Those selecting "a great deal" and "somewhat" are represented in the figure.
11. The ABC News/*Washington Post* poll asked, "How concerned are you about the chance that you personally might be the victim of a terrorist attack?" Percentages answering "a great deal" and "somewhat" were noted in the figure. For the CNN/Gallup/*USA Today* poll: "How worried are you that you or someone in your family will become a victim of terrorism?" Those selecting "very worried" and "somewhat worried" were registered. For the PSRA/*Newsweek* poll: "All in all, how worried are you that you or someone in your family will become a victim of a terrorist attack?" Respondents selecting "very worried" and "somewhat worried" were included in the figure.
12. Several other factors are cited in the literature to explain why certain risks are over- and under-estimated, although "controllability" and "familiarity" are commonly accepted as instrumental. For an excellent treatment of these issues, see Sandman (2001). In addition to controllability and familiarity, for example, Sandman lists the following factors to explain why risks are overestimated (all of which apply to the post-9/11 experience): catastrophic potential, lack of understanding, uncertainty, voluntary exposure, effects on children, effects on future generations, victim identity, effects dreaded, absence of trust in institutions, media attention, costs/benefits, reversibility. See also Croxford, 2005.
13. Critics of the Iraq war should consider that prior to the invasion the primary directive for security and intelligence communities was to find and connect the dots, because

failures to do so could be catastrophic. Consequently, the potential pitfall of connecting too many dots, as with Iraq's WMD program, was not a serious concern.

14. For example, the apparently rational decision in 1972 to sign the Anti-ballistic Missile Treaty (a co-operative arms control and disarmament agreement prohibiting the deployment of large-scale ballistic missile defence systems) actually undermined security by creating the conditions for the most rapid vertical proliferation of nuclear weapons in history. On the surface the ABM treaty seemed to make perfect sense, but the Cold War security dilemma forced American and Soviet leaders to expand their respective inventories of offensive weapons as a way of establishing a reliable second strike retaliatory capability. For a comprehensive treatment of these trends and other problem with multilateral arms control and disarmament agreements, see Harvey, 2004a.
15. The following are among the more prominent examples of authors who seem to have missed this basic point: Dyer, 2006; Schneier, 2003; Ranum, 2004; Minter, 2005; Delvoie, 2005; Myers, 2001; Leitenberg, 2006; Glassner, 2000; Altheide, 2002; Siegel, 2005; Furedi, 2002a, 2002b; Lemons, Purtschert and Winter, 2003.
16. For example, in response to demands that he resign for mismanaging the Iraq war, Secretary of Defense Donald Rumsfeld defended his record in these terms: "I have a sense of urgency. I get up every morning and worry about protecting the American people and seeing if we are doing everything humanly possible to see that we do the things that will make them safe." Calls for his resignation slowly dissipated.
17. Other examples include the Critical Infrastructure Assurance Program; National Disaster Mitigation Strategy; Canadian Emergency Preparedness College; Joint Emergency Preparedness Program; Government Operations Centre; Canadian Cyber Incident Response Centre; Disaster Assistance Inventory; Provincial/Territorial Emergency Management Organization; Disaster Financial Assistance Arrangements.
18. Collacott (2006) describes serious security gaps in Canada's approach to identifying and accepting refugees. As he concludes, "failure to exercise adequate control over the entry and the departure of non-Canadians on our territory has been a significant factor in making Canada a destination for terrorists. The latter have made our highly dysfunctional refugee determination system the channel most often used for gaining entry. A survey that we made based on media reports of 25 Islamic terrorists and suspects who entered Canada as adults indicated that 16 claimed refugee status, four were admitted as landed immigrants and the channel of entry for the remaining five was not identified. Making a refugee claim is used by both terrorists and criminals as a means of rendering their removal from the country more difficult" (2006: 2).
19. Recent US Government Accountability Office (GAO) reports of undercover agents smuggling radioactive material across the BC-Washington State and the Mexico-US borders is but the latest example of a failure that will trump any of the successes so far. While this was obviously a failure at the US border, the smugglers came in from Canada and could just as easily have entered Canadian territory first—a point US Congressman will likely exploit in their search for scapegoats in the next crisis. According to one report, "On Dec. 14, two teams of investigators—one on the Canadian border, the other on the Mexican border—put radioactive material in rental cars and attempted to cross over into the US. Kristi Clemens, a spokeswoman for US Customs and Border Protection, said the radiological material was cesium-137. Detection equipment alerted authorities at both borders of the radioactive materials.

When questioned, the investigators said they needed the material to calibrate construction equipment, a common use. The investigators presented the authorities with counterfeit Nuclear Regulatory Commission licenses and freight inventories." For additional details, " 'Dirty Bomb' Material Smuggled to US, GAO Says," Bloomberg.com, 2006; See also De Sola, 2006; "Border Breach," news.bbc.co.uk, 2006; "Border Breach," UnionLeader.com, 2006.

References

Altheide, David. 2002. *Creating Fear: News and the Construction of Crisis.* New Jersey: Aldine Transaction.

Angus Reid Global Monitor. 2006a. *Polls & Research.* http://www.angus-reid.com/polls/index.cfm/.

Angus Reid Global Monitor: Polls & Research. 2006b. "Canadians Concerned After Terror Arrests." http://www.angus-reid.com/polls/index.cfm/fuseaction/viewItem/itemID/12213 (June 13, 2006).

Argetsinger, Amy and Sonya Geis. 2005. "4 Charged With Terrorist Plot in California." *Washington Post,* September 1, A02.

Bacon, William. 2003. "Scorecard on the War on Terrorism." FrontPageMagazine.com, http://www.frontpagemag.com/Articles/ReadArticle.asp?ID=8687 (July 3, 2003).

Baker, Gerard. 2004. "The war on terror has been a great success—but still Bush can't sell it." *The Times Online,* October 7, http://www.timesonline.co.uk/article/0,,1072-1297604,00.html (August 10, 2006).

Baker, Peter and Dan Eggen. 2006. "Bush Details 2002 Plot to Attack L.A. Tower." *Washington Post,* February 10, A04.

BBC News. 2003. "Major al-Qaeda attack foiled." http://news.bbc.co.uk/2/hi/europe/2690629.stm (January 14, 2003).

BBC News. 2006. "Border Breach: Hey, it's only a little radioactive material." http://news.bbc.co.uk/2/hi/americas/4852410.stm (March 29, 2006).

BBC News. 2006. "Blair backs MI5 terrorism warning." http://news.bbc.co.uk/2/hi/uk_news/6137188.stm (November 10, 2006).

Bloomberg.com. 2006. "'Dirty Bomb' Material Smuggled to US, GAO Says." http://www.bloomberg.com/apps/news?pid=10000103&sid=a.6ODqglGQO0&refer=us (March 28, 2006).

Bowman, Karlyn H. 2006. "America and the War on Terror." American Enterprise Institute, http://www.aei.org/publications/pubID.22819/pub_detail.asp (October 13, 2006).

Brachman, Jarret M. and William F. McCants. 2006. "Stealing Al-Qaeda's Playbook." *Studies in Conflicts and Terrorism* 29: 309–321.

BreakingNews.ie. 2003. "Top al-Qaida terrorist blows himself up in Saudi." http://archives.tcm.ie/breakingnews/2003/07/03/story104790.asp (July 3, 2006).

Canada. Foreign Affairs and International Trade Canada. 2003. The Canada-U.S. Smart Border Declaration. http://www.dfait-maeci.gc.ca/anti-terrorism/actionplan-en.asp.

Canada. Foreign Affairs and International Trade Canada. 2006. *A Strong Partnership: Canada-U.S. Relations,* http://www.dfait-maeci.gc.ca/can-am/main/menu-en.asp.

CBC News. 2005. "Australian arrests foiled 'catastrophic' attack: police." http://www.cbc.ca/world/story/2005/11/08/australia-plot051108.html (November 8, 2005).

CBS News. 2005. "Morocco Arrests 17 Terror Suspects." http://www.cbsnews.com/stories/2005/11/20/world/main1060357.shtml (November 20, 2005).

Christensen, Thomas J. 1999. "China, the US-Japan Alliance, and the Security Dilemma in East Asia." *International Security* 23: 49–80.

Christensen, Thomas J. 2002. "The Contemporary Security Dilemma: Deterring a Taiwan Conflict." *The Washington Quarterly* 25: 7–21.

Chronicle Herald. 2006. "CSIS Reports Al-Qaeda attack 'probable.'" May 10, A6.

Clawson, Greg. 2006. "Using Passive RFID to Meet Container Tracking and Personnel Security." *Symbol Technologies, Inc.* http://www.aeanet.org/AeACouncils/txjJDbXivUH.pdf (January 13, 2006).

Collacott, Martin. 2006. *Inadequate Response to Terrorism: The Need for Policy Reform.* Fraser Institute Digital Publication, February 2006. http://www.fraserinstitute.ca/admin/books/files/TerrorismResponse4.pdf.

Collins, Alan. 1997. *The Security Dilemma and the End of the ColdWar.* Edinburgh: Keele University Press.

Collins, Alan. 2000. *The Security Dilemmas of Southeast Asia.* Basingstoke: Macmillan.

Collins, Alan. 2004. "State-Induced Security Dilemma: Maintaining the Tragedy." *Cooperation and Conflict* 39: 27–44.

Croxford, Tracy. 2005. "Public Perceptions in a ChangingWorld." Presentation to the World Nuclear Transport Institute, February 13–15, Paris, http://www.wnti.co.uk/attachment/publications/speeches/presentationpapers/WP_PIME_TCR_Poster.pdf.

CTV News. 2004. "US unjustified in deporting Arar, poll finds." http://www.ctv.ca/servlet/ArticleNews/story/CTVNews/20040208/terror_poll040206 (February 8, 2004).

CTV News. 2004. "Pakistan arrests damage al Qaeda network: report." http://www.ctv.ca/servlet/ArticleNews/story/CTVNews/20040807/Pakistan_alQaeda_040807 (August 7, 2004).

CTV News. 2006. "71% believe terrorists will hit Canada: poll." http://www.ctv.ca/servlet/ArticleNews/story/CTVNews/20060609/terrorism_poll_060609/20060609 (June 9, 2006).

De Sola, David. "Government investigators smuggled radioactive materials into US." 2006. CNN.com, http:/edition.cnn.com/2006/US/03/27/radioactive.smuggling/index.html.

Delvoie, Louis A. 2005. "Terrorism: Global Insecurity or Global Hyperbole?" *Canadian Military Journal* 6: 103–104.

Dunnigan, James. 2005. "Keeping Score against al Qaeda." StrategyWorld.com, https://www.strategyworld.com (February 20, 2005).

Dyer, Gwynne. 2006. "Lying for jihad: The '20th hijacker' shows terrorists were a bunch of bumblers." *Winnipeg Free Press.* http://www.winnipegfreepress.com/westview/story/3420216p-3954600c.html (April 3, 2006).

Evans, Michael. 2004. "Al-Qaeda agent's laptop yields vital intelligence clues." *London Times On Line,* http://www.timesonline.co.uk/article/0,,2-1205983,00.html (August 7, 2004).

Flemming, Brian. 2006. "Dispatches from the War on Terror." Presentation delivered for the Calgary Chamber of Commerce, the Van Horne Institute and CDFAI, March 14, Calgary, Alberta.

Fox News. 2004. "Major Anti-Terror Bust in UK." http://www.foxnews.com/story/0,2933,115587,00.html (March 30, 2004).

Furedi, Frank. 2002a. *Culture of Fear: Risk Taking and the Morality of Low Expectation.* London: Continuum International Publishing Group.

Furedi, Frank. 2002b. "Epidemic of fear" Spiked-Online.com, http://www.spikedonline.com (March 15, 2002).

Gelpi, Christopher, Peter D. Feaver and Jason Reifler. 2005–2006. "Success Matters: Casualty Sensitivity and the War in Iraq." *International Security* 30: 7–46.

Gelpi, Christopher and John Mueller. 2006. "The Cost of War." *Foreign Affairs* 85: 139.

Gilbert, Nina. 2004. "Hamas mega-attack thwarted." *Jerusalem Post Online Edition,* http://www.jpost.com/ (June 16, 2004).

Glaser, Charles L. 1997. "The Security Dilemma Revisited." *World Politics* 50: 171–201.

Glassner, Barry. 2000. *The Culture of Fear:Why Americans Are Afraid of the Wrong Things.* New York: Basic Books.

Harvey, Frank P. 2004a. "Addicted to Security: Globalized Terrorism and the Inevitability of American Unilateralism." *International Journal* Winter 2004: 27–57.

Harvey, Frank P. 2004b. *Smoke and Mirrors: Globalized Terrorism and the Illusion of Multilateral Security.* Toronto: University of Toronto Press.

Harvey, Frank P. 2005. "Canada's Addiction to American Security: The Illusion of Choice in the War on Terror." *American Review of Canadian Studies* 35: 265–294.

Heritage Foundation. 2005. "Bush's War Score Card Has More Pluses than Minuses." http://heritage.com (August 15, 2005).

Herz, John. 1950. "Idealist Internationalism and the Security Dilemma." *World Politics* 2: 157–180.

Herz, John. 1951. *Political Realism and Political Idealism: A Study in Theories and Realities.* Chicago: Chicago University Press.

Hughes, John. 2005. "Four years after 9011, terror's hold is loosening." *Christian Science Monitor,* http://www.csmonitor.com/2005/0831/p09s02-cojh.html (August 31, 2005).

Ipsos-Reid. 2002. *Polls and Research.* http://www.ipsos-na.com/news/results.cfm.

Jerusalem Post OnLine. 2004. "UAE stops suspected sale of nuclear secrets." http://www.jpost.com/ (July 20, 2004).

Jervis, Robert. 1976. *Perception and Misperception in International Politics.* Princeton: Princeton University Press.

Jervis, Robert. 1978. "Cooperation under the Security Dilemma." *World Politics* 40: 167–214.

Kahneman, Daniel and Amos Tversky. 1979. "Prospect Theory: An Analysis of Decision under Risk." *Econometrica* 47: 313–327.

Kahneman, Daniel and Amos Tversky. 1992. "Prospect Theory: An Analysis of Decision under Risk." *Journal of Risk and Uncertainty* 5: 297–323.

Leitenberg, Milton. 2006. "Bioterrorism, hyped." *Los Angeles Times,* http://LAtimes.com (February 17, 2006).

Lemons, Katherine, Patricia Purtschert and Yves Winter. 2003. "Feeding Fear: The New Security Culture." AlterNet, http://www.alternet.org (December 3, 2003).

Limbacher, Carl. 2006. "Major Terror Plot Against US Ignored." NewsMax.com, http://www.newsmax.com/archives/ic/2006/1/5/101649.shtml (January 5, 2006).

Linzer, Dafna and Walter Pincus. 2006. "Taliban, Al-Qaeda Resurge in Afghanistan, CIA Says." *Washington Post,* November 16, 2006, A22. http://www.washingtonpost.com/wpdyn/content/article/2006/11/15/AR2006111501622.html.

Minter, Richard. 2005. *Disinformation: 22 Media Myths That Undermine the War on Terror.* Washington: Regnery Publishing Inc.

Mueller, John. 2005. "The Iraq Syndrome." *Foreign Affairs* 84: 44.

Mueller, John. 2006. *Overblown: How Politicians and the Terrorism Industry Inflate National Security Threats, and Why We Believe Them.* New York: Free Press.

Myers, David G. 2001. "Do We Fear the Right Things?" *Observer: Journal of the American Psychological Society* 14, http://www.psychologicalscience.org/observer/1201/prescol.html.

Nagy, Sasha. "Massive terror attack averted: RCMP." 2006. *Globe and Mail,* http://www.theglobeandmail.com/servlet/story/RTGAM.20060603.wwarrants0603_3/BNStory/National/home (March 6, 2006).

Nye, Joseph S., Jr. 1995. "Strategy for East Asia and the US-Japan Security Alliance." Presentation at the Pacific Forum Center for Strategic and International Studies/Japanese Institute of International Affairs Conference, San Francisco. http://www.defenselink.mil/speeches/1995/s19950329-nye.html.

Pollara. 2002. *Public Opinions and Research.* http://www.pollara.ca/library.html.

Posen, Barry. 1993. "The Security Dilemma and Ethnic Conflict." *Survival* 35: 27–47.

Ranum, Marcus J. 2004. *The Myth of Homeland Security.* Indianapolis: Wiley Publishing.

Sandman, Peter. 2001. "Anthrax, Bioterrorism, and Risk Communication: Guidelines for Action." www.psandman.com/col/part1.htm.

Saunders, Doug. 2004. "Al-Qaeda raid in Pakistan led to arrests in London—British officials say information gathered is not enough to raise terror alert levels." *Globe and Mail.* August 6, A9.

Schneier, Bruce. 2003. *Beyond Fear: Thinking Sensibly About Security in an Uncertain World.* New York: Copernicus Books.

Schweller, Randall L. 1996. "Neorealism's Status-Quo Bias: What Security Dilemma?" *Security Studies* 5: 90–121.

Shipping Facts. 2005. "Shipping and World Trade: Number of Ships (by total and trade)." http://www.marisec.org/shippingfacts/keyfactsnoofships.htm.

Siegel, Marc. 2005. *False Alarm: The Truth about the Epidemic of Fear.* Toronto: John Wiley and Sons.

Snyder, Glenn H. 1984. "The Security Dilemma in Alliance Politics." *World Politics* 36: 461–495.

Taliaferro, Jeffrey W. 2000. "Security Seeking under Anarchy: Defensive Realism Revisited." *International Security* 25: 128–161.

Tendler, Stewart. 2006. "Foiled transatlantic bomb plot 'was ready to go in days.'" *The Times Online,* http://www.timesonline.co.uk/article/0,,29389-2306721,00.html (August 10, 2006).

The 9/11 Commission Report. 2004b. United States. National Commission on Terrorist Attacks upon the United States. http://www.9-11commission.gov/report/911Report.pdf.

UnionLeader.com. 2006. "Border Breach: Hey, it's only a little radioactive material." http://www.unionleader.com/ (March 30, 2006).

United States. Department of Homeland Security. 2001. Presidential Executive Order. October 8, http://www.whitehouse.gov/news/releases/2001/10/20011008-2.html.

United States. Department of Homeland Security. 2004a. "Fact Sheet: Department of Homeland Security Appropriations Act of 2005." Press Release, http://www.dhs.gov/dhspublic/display?content=4065 (October 18, 2004).

United States. Department of Homeland Security. 2006. *Department of Homeland Security Budget-in-Brief.* http://www.dhs.gov/xlibrary/assets/Budget_BIB-FY2006.pdf.

United States. The White House. 2005. "President Discusses Hurricane Relief in Address to the Nation." http://www.whitehouse.gov/news/releases/2005/09/20050915-8.html (September 15, 2005).

USAToday.com. 2006. "Canada nabs 17 terror suspects in Toronto." http://www.usatoday.com/news/world/2006-06-03-toronto-terror-suspects_x.htm. (June 3, 2006).

Zakis, Jeremy and Steve Macko. 2002. "Major Terrorist Plot in Singapore Discovered." *EmergencyNet News,* http://www.emergency.com/2002/Singapore_terror02.htm (January 12, 2004).

DHS

Assessing the Value Proposition

David Trybula and John Whitley

Introduction

When the Department of Homeland Security (DHS) was created, Public Law 107-96, also known as the Homeland Security Act, provided the following rationale:

> The primary mission of the Department is to—
>
> (A) prevent terrorist attacks within the United States;
> (B) reduce the vulnerability of the United States to terrorism;
> (C) minimize the damage, and assist in the recovery, from terrorist attacks that do occur within the United States;
> (D) carry out all functions of entities transferred to the Department, including by acting as a focal point regarding natural and manmade crises and emergency planning;
> (E) ensure that the functions of the agencies and subdivisions within the Department that are not related directly to securing the homeland are not diminished or neglected except by a specific explicit Act of Congress;
> (F) ensure that the overall economic security of the United States is not diminished by efforts, activities, and programs aimed at securing the homeland; and
> (G) monitor connections between illegal drug trafficking and terrorism, coordinate efforts to sever such connections, and otherwise contribute to efforts to interdict illegal drug trafficking.[1]

The value proposition inherent in this statement is that having a single DHS provides better protection against terrorism while ensuring that any negative economic impact is minimized. As described later in this chapter, funding was also significantly increased for the collection of activities that were combined to form DHS following its creation. When Congress passed the Homeland Security Act and the President signed it into law, and through the subsequent increases in funding, they implicitly determined that this value exceeded the investment required to establish and grow the Department of Homeland Security.

Good governance requires assessments of investments both prior to making the investment and on an on-going basis while the investment continues. The Office of Management and Budget (OMB) provides the framework for agency investment decisions in OMB Circular A-94.[2] More generally, this type of analysis is known as cost-benefit analysis or net present value analysis.

This chapter provides a brief overview of cost-benefit analysis and applies it to DHS. The numerous challenges in conducting such an analysis are outlined and suggestions are made for where further analysis would be valuable. The goal of this chapter is not to arrive at a specific answer to the question of whether the benefits of DHS outweigh its costs, but instead to introduce the reader to the tools necessary for analyzing this question and illustrate how they can be used.

Cost-Benefit Analysis

The premise behind cost-benefit analysis is that when deciding whether or not to make a specific investment, the decision should be based on the result of comparing the costs to the benefits. If the benefits exceed the costs then the investment is advantageous, if not then the investment should be avoided. To begin with, we will assume that decisions are binary. You will make a choice whether or not to invest (or buy). Furthermore, we will assume that the choice of not investing has no value, either negative or positive. Once we have some basic understanding, we will relax these assumptions.

The simplest case for a cost-benefit analysis is when there is only one option under consideration and the costs and the benefits are easily measured in monetary terms (i.e., dollars or some other currency), and occur immediately and simultaneously. Classical arbitrage opportunities are an example. For example, John wants to sell a book to you for $5 and you know Sally will pay $20 for it. Assuming there is no risk and no other costs involved, you calculate the cost as $5 and the benefit as $20.

$$\text{Value} = \text{Benefits} - \text{Costs}$$
$$= \$20 - \$5 = \$15$$

This results in a net gain of $15, so the investment is beneficial to you.

If the benefits are not easily measured in monetary terms, a cost-benefit analysis becomes more complicated because the benefits must be imputed. These situations occur in everyday life, all the time, and are undertaken by each of us almost without thought. Examples include paying highway tolls, eating at a restaurant, staying at a hotel, going to a movie, and almost anything else that provides nearly immediate benefit for its cost. Let's use going to see a movie as an example. When we make the decision to go see the latest movie at the movieplex, we can see the cost and implicitly compare that to the value that we will gain from watching the movie. In this still simple case, we purchase the ticket to watch the movie if our personal value of watching the movie exceeds the cost of the ticket to watch the movie.

To pull the thread on the simple movie case, we know that the value we place on the movie prior to seeing it may not be the same value that we ascribe to the experience after seeing the movie. That sleeper hit is more valuable than expected after watching the movie, while the mega blockbuster flop is less valuable than expected after the experience. This introduces two very important concepts when thinking about cost-benefit analysis: expected value and the difference between *ex ante* (i.e., prior to the decision) and *ex post* (i.e., after the decision) analysis.

Expected value incorporates the fact that the value of something is unlikely to be known with certainty before it is experienced. In the case of the movie, a friend with similar tastes may provide a reliable estimate of how much we will value the film, but the theater could be overcrowded, forcing us to sit on the end of the first row (where viewing is less than optimum), or we could be unfortunate enough to be in the row with the moviegoer that has to get up and go past us every fifteen minutes to get more snacks or go to the facilities. Given the movie, the time we are going to it, the weather, and other relevant experiences, we implicitly factor how these will impact the value of our movie experience when we make the decision to pay to watch the movie.[3]

Understanding expected value is important to understanding the difference between *ex ante* and *ex post* analysis. *Ex ante* analysis must rely on expected value because there is uncertainty involved. In an *ex post* analysis there is no expected value; once the event has occurred, a specific benefit has been realized, regardless of what the probability was that it would occur. This means that it is possible that based on a correct *ex ante* analysis the decision was made to see the movie and *ex post* we determine that the movie[4] was not worth the cost. Assuming that the *ex ante* analysis was based on the actual probabilities and their associated values, the next time you are faced with the same decision,[5] the cost-benefit analysis would again favor seeing the movie.

In all the examples so far, the only cost was the dollar cost of a transaction. This ignores the singularity of time which means that the decision to do something implicitly is also a decision not to do something else during that time or with that money. The next best alternative is therefore a cost in addition to the monetary cost, since it is something that is foregone. This additional cost is referred to as the opportunity cost because it is the cost, often in foregone value, of taking the opportunity. If the best alternative to seeing the movie was going to work and making $20, then the opportunity cost of seeing the movie would be $20 in addition to the cost of the movie. The cost-benefit analysis should include the $20 opportunity cost. Similarly, the use of the money for the movie has an opportunity cost; it could have been invested or used for another purpose. The opportunity cost associated with money is generally referred to as the time value of money.

Costs and benefits are rarely nearly instantaneous and simultaneous. Often either the cost or the benefits, or both, are realized over a period of time. This means that the cost-benefit analysis must take into account the time value of money. The time value of money is based on the notion that one dollar today is more valuable than one dollar a year from now. How can this be? As mentioned above, the dollar could be deposited in an insured savings account[6] where it will earn interest. This means that today's dollar will be worth one dollar plus interest a year from now, clearly more than just a dollar in a year. Furthermore, having the dollar in the savings account may also provide liquidity that can be its own value. History is riddled with companies that have gone bankrupt not because they are not profitable but because their cash flow did not provide them the liquidity needed to pay their creditors. This illustrates the value that money in hand provides. Additionally, humans are mortal and therefore live for undetermined but finite periods. This means that there is a natural and rational human proclivity to value today more than tomorrow. Thus the time value of money has several components which when aggregated are normally expressed as a percentage that reflects how much an individual discounts the future on an annual basis, and is therefore termed a discount rate.[7] If my savings account pays 5%,[8] I value relieving liquidity constraints at 3%, and my preference for today over tomorrow is another 4%, then my discount rate would be 12%.[9] Since we have added a time dimension, our cost-benefit analysis becomes a net present value (NPV) analysis:

$$NPV = Today's\ value + Next\ Year's\ value\ (discounted\ to\ today) + Second\ Year's\ value\ (discounted\ to\ today) + \ldots$$

$$NPV = (Benefits_{today} - Costs_{today}) + \frac{(Benefits_{next\ year} - Costs_{next\ year})}{(1 + discount\ rate)} + \frac{(Benefits_{2nd\ year} - Costs_{2nd\ year})}{(1 + discount\ rate)^2} + \ldots$$

$$NPV = \sum_{i=1}^{n} \frac{(Benefits_i - Costs_i)}{(1 + discount\ rate)^i}$$

This general depiction of net present value is useful across the full range of potential cost-benefit analyses. It is even useful when we add more complexity by analyzing multiple alternatives at the same time. This is often referred to as an analysis of alternatives. The obvious way to conduct this analysis is to calculate the net present value of each alternative and compare the result. The one with the highest net present value is the best among the alternatives. That said, if none of them result in a positive value, then they all provide less benefit than they cost. When analyzing alternatives, there are often costs that are the same across all alternatives. These are referred to as wash costs because they need not be calculated; as they add the same cost to all alternatives, they have no net effect on the ranking of the alternatives—i.e., they "wash" out. Remember that there is a time dimension to our analysis, so wash costs must not only be the same magnitude but also must occur at the same time. Just as costs can wash out across alternatives, so too can benefits. It is important to carefully list all of these wash costs and benefits during the analysis because while they have no impact on which alternative is better, they may impact whether or not any alternative is net beneficial. Thus if all of the alternatives' costs are the same, we can show their relative value by only analyzing their benefits, but this does not directly provide us with the information of whether or not the best alternative is worthwhile and therefore requires the analyst to explicitly provide the wash costs in reporting the finding of the net present value analysis.

With this general understanding of cost-benefit analysis, we can turn to assessing the value proposition of the Department of Homeland Security. To do this we will begin by understanding the costs involved, move to a discussion of the benefits, and then look at some examples.

Department of Homeland Security Costs

The best place to start looking at Department of Homeland Security (DHS) costs is at the top or highest level of aggregation; how much money did the Department spend? Because we are dealing with the federal government, there are actually several ways to examine this question, each with its advantages and disadvantages. Every year Congress appropriates money for the Department that approves a budget and provides the authority to spend money up to that budget. This is referred to as the Department's budget authority.

Budget authority contains both mandatory and discretionary elements. Mandatory budget authority is, as its name suggests, mandatory and the Department simply manages the provision of these funds; the Department is significantly limited in the decisions it can make regarding these funds. Discretionary budget authority provides the Department funding to execute the preponderance of its mission, and, within limits, the ability for discretion in how these funds are spent.

In addition to budget authority, spending is also captured as outlays. Outlays represent the disbursement of funds and may therefore more directly capture actual costs. This is not necessarily the case because the outlays associated with a project or acquisition could possibly extend beyond the time horizon being analyzed.

Using data from the President's Fiscal Year 2013 budget submission,[10] Figure 1 depicts the cost of DHS from 1977 through 2011 with estimates for the years through 2017. Since DHS was not in existence for the majority of this time period, an obvious question is what does the pre-DHS data represent? The data are taken directly from the Fiscal Year 2013 President's Budget submission's historical tables and are purported to reflect those agencies and functions that later were consolidated in the Department of Homeland Security. This is far easier said than done and certainly reflects many judgment calls that are not explicitly described. That said, the way the data were combined should be consistent and while omitting or including elements that shouldn't have been, the combining process should not have added any extra noise.

The solid line in Figure 1 represents the total budget authority for DHS in constant fiscal year 2005 billions of dollars. Constant dollars are used to remove the impact of inflation and provide a more straight forward comparison across years. Budget authority was \$8–10 billion per year from 1977 through 1990 and then began to increase, reaching \$18 billion in 2001. The 2002 through 2004 time period is shaded to differentiate this transition period. We know that the events of September 11, 2001 had a dramatic impact on the United States' approach to homeland security. What is not clear is when that impact made its way into the formal budget process.

The dashed line in Figure 1 represents the discretionary budget authority. The discretionary budget authority closely mirrors total budget authority. The obvious difference is in fiscal year 2006, which started October 1, 2005. This difference is due primarily to the recovery efforts provided by the Federal Emergency Management Agency (FEMA) for Hurricane Katrina and flood insurance payouts.

The dash-dot-dash line in Figure 1 reflects total outlays. Total outlays generally follow total budget authority but may also lag behind, or if some of the budget authority is

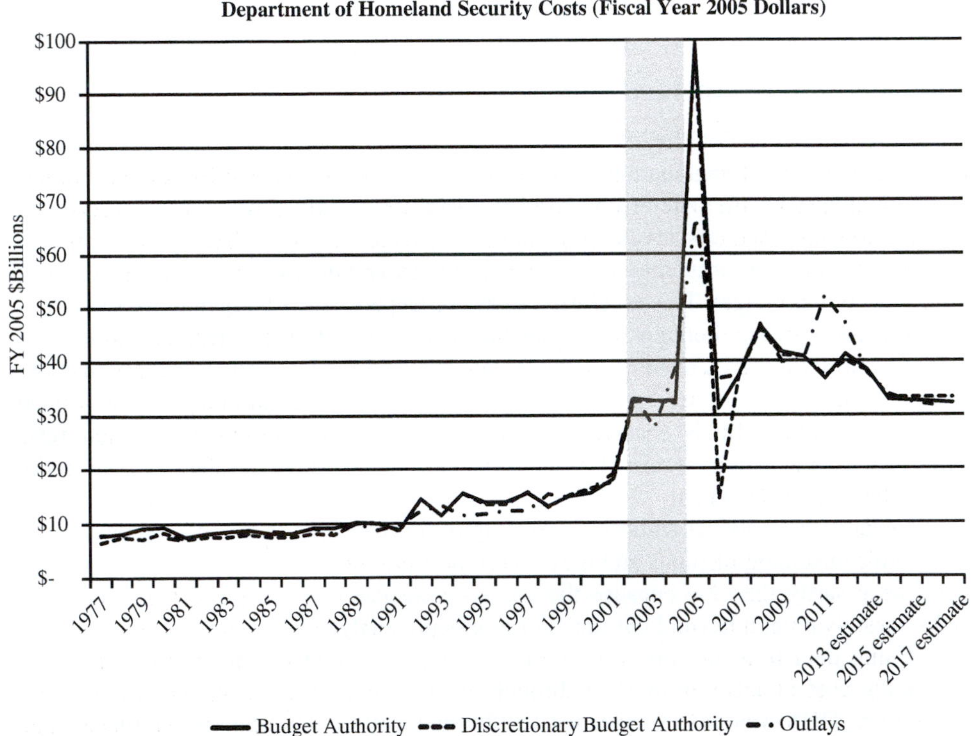

FIGURE 1

TABLE 1 Five Year Annual Averages (FY 2005 $Millions)

	Budget Authority		Discretionary Budget Authority		Outlays	
1977–1981	$ 8,436		$ 7,371		$ 8,000	
1982–1986	$ 8,386	−0.6%	$ 7,666	4.0%	$ 8,030	0.4%
1987–1991	$ 9,482	13.1%	$ 9,947	29.8%	$ 8,910	11.0%
1992–1996	$13,919	46.8%	$13,729	38.0%	$11,712	31.4%
1997–2001	$15,417	10.8%	$15,550	13.3%	$14,246	21.6%
2002–2006	$46,054	198.7%	$42,138	171.0%	$37,143	160.7%
2007–2011	$40,550	−12.0%	$40,372	−4.2%	$40,203	8.2%

not used, simply be smaller. It appears that in the mid-1990s, not all of the budget authority was used, while from 2004 forward outlays appear to lag behind the budget authority.

Given the year-to-year changes in all three measures of spending, picking any particular year to ascertain the cost of DHS is problematic. Instead, given that the Department is now a permanent structure within the federal government, it is more appropriate to use an average over several years. Table 1 depicts five year annual averages for each of the three measures of spending.

Given the discussion previously about the transition period, we will use the last five-year period and compare it to the 1997–2001 period. When this is done, the increased cost of the Department is calculated at $25–26 billion per year.

Department of Homeland Security Benefits

The Department of Homeland Security (DHS) provides many benefits for the United States. Given that we are looking at the difference between 2007–2011 and 1997–2001, all of the benefits provided previous to 2002 and still provided today wash out in our analysis. These benefits are the same in the later period as in the former and are also included in the $14–15 billion spent annually that has already been deducted from the cost assessment.

According to its implementing legislation, the intended benefits of the creation of—and presumably the subsequent increase in spending by—DHS are to ensure that another attack like that of September 11, 2001 does not happen, and to minimize the economic impact of additional security measures. So the benefit is to avoid the costs—monetary, emotional, and in human lives—of similar attacks in the future. That leads to the question of what did the attacks in 2001 cost the United States? The Institute for the Analysis of Global Security estimated that the direct costs were $100 billion, which increases to $2 trillion if economic impacts on markets are taken into account.[11]

The attacks in 2001 also led to the wars in Iraq and Afghanistan. Allocation of the cost of these wars is thus another factor to be considered. Some of the cost was a direct result of the terrorist attacks and some was an investment in preventing a future attack. It would be hard to allocate those costs but two reference points can be created to examine their impact—allocating all of the cost of the wars as a cost of the terrorist attacks and allocating none of the cost of the wars as a cost of the terrorist attacks. Estimates of the total cost of the wars vary and one of the largest is from Nobel Laureate Joseph Stiglitz at

$3–5 trillion, not including the economic impacts on the markets.[12] These considerations provide a range of estimates of $100 billion dollars to $7 trillion.[13]

When we consider the benefits, the frequency of attack is important; how often do we realize the benefit? James Carafano, Steve Bucci, and Jessica Zuckerman concluded in *Fifty Terror Plots Foiled Since 9/11: The Homegrown Threat and the Long War on Terrorism* that counterterrorism efforts have stopped at least fifty plots from since September 11, 2001 through January 2012.[14]

Assessing the Value Proposition

Now that we have a high-level understanding of the costs and benefits of the new Department of Homeland Security, we can begin to assess the value proposition. Since we have a wide range of estimates of benefits we will attempt to bound the problem by using three specific estimates: the lowest estimate of $100 billion that just includes the direct costs of the 2001 attacks, a middle estimate of $2 trillion that includes the economic impact (but not the subsequent wars in Iraq and Afghanistan), and the highest estimate of $7 trillion that attributes the entire cost of the wars as a cost of the 2001 attacks.

To begin, we will use the lowest estimate for benefits of $100 billion. This converts to $110 billion in fiscal year 2005 dollars.[15] Since we have already shown the annual cost is $25–26 billion, it is obvious that if one attack the size of those of September 11, 2001 is stopped each year then the benefits far exceed the costs. A more interesting question is at what frequency is the cost equal to the benefit. To determine this we need to use cost-benefit analysis. The cost benefit analysis requires a discount rate in addition to knowing the costs and benefits. The Office of Management and Budget provides discounts rates for analysis in Appendix C of OMB Circular A-94.[16] Given that we are examining a permanent change to the U.S. government, the time horizon of our analysis is infinite, which means that we will use the thirty year rate from the real interest rate table. In the current version of the appendix, updated December 2011, this means that a rate of 2.0% is the appropriate discount rate.

To keep things simple we will use a trial and error method to determine when the net present value goes from positive to negative. There is no need to calculate the first several iterations because the result is obvious, so we will begin assuming an attack is stopped every fourth year:

$$\text{NPV} = (\$0-\$26\text{B}) + \frac{(\$0-\$26B)}{1.02} + \frac{(\$0-\$26B)}{1.02^2} + \frac{(\$110-\$26B)}{1.02^3}$$

$$\text{NPV} = -\$26\text{B} - \$25.5\text{B} - \$25\text{B} + \$79\text{B}$$

$$\text{NPV} = \$2.5\text{B}$$

Assuming an attack is stopped every fifth year provides:

$$\text{NPV} = -\$26\text{B} - \$25.5\text{B} - \$25\text{B} + \frac{(\$0-\$26B)}{1.02^3} + \frac{(\$110-\$26B)}{1.02^4}$$

$$\text{NPV} = -\$26\text{B} - \$25.5\text{B} - \$25\text{B} - \$24.5\text{B} + \$77.6\text{B}$$

$$\text{NPV} = -\$23.4\text{B}$$

Thus, if the lower bound of benefits is used, the Department of Homeland Security's value is positive if it stops one terrorist attack of the scale of those on September 11, 2001 every four years or more frequently. If the frequency is less, then the costs exceed the benefits.

Next we will examine the breakeven point if the indirect economic impact is included resulting in \$2 trillion of benefits in 2001, that equates to nearly \$2.2 billion in fiscal year 2005 dollars. Computers make the analysis much easier than the manual trial method above. The result is that the NPV of a foiled attack every 49 years is \$25.3 billion and the NPV of a foiled attack every 50 years is −\$1.2 billion. Thus, if the direct and indirect benefits of two trillion dollars are used, the Department of Homeland Security's value is positive if it stops one terrorist attack of the scale of those on September 11, 2001 every forty-eight years or more frequently. If the frequency is less, then the costs exceed the benefits. We leave the calculation including the benefits of avoiding wars (the seven trillion dollar cost estimate) to the reader.

This example is purposely simple yet it shows how the changing of one assumption can have very large impacts on the assessment. To this point, some of our key assumptions have been implicit and we now need to make them explicit. In conveying a cost-benefit analysis, explicitly listing and reviewing assumptions is critical to support decision making because a decision maker may have information or a bias that means what you think is a perfectly reasonable assumption may not be. The key assumptions underlying this analysis include the following. First, the analysis assumed that all of the costs of countering terrorism in the homeland are captured by the Department of Homeland Security's spending. Similarly, since the benefits are attributed to the Department, the implicit assumption is that no other entity contributes to the benefit. In addition, the costs and benefits of the new DHS are all assumed to focus on counter terrorism while minimizing the economic impact related to counter terrorism activities and not other areas of responsibility for the newly created Department. Finally, the possibility of any distributional effects for either the costs or the benefits has been ignored.

One way to begin relaxing these assumptions and examining their impact on the results is to conduct a sensitivity analysis. For example, an assumption was made that DHS alone was responsible for preventing future terrorist attacks when, in fact, the United States invested in a wide range of efforts to prevent future attacks. In addition to establishing and increasing the funding for DHS, the United States increased funding for intelligence and established the Director of National Intelligence, increased diplomatic engagement on terrorism issues, and conducted the wars in Iraq and Afghanistan. The cost benefit question can thus be refined to include what the individual contribution of DHS was to the prevention of future attacks.

In the chart below we vary three key assumptions: a) the contribution of DHS to preventing an attack (the vertical axis); b) the frequency of potential future attacks (the horizontal axis); and c) the low and medium cost estimates of an attack. The plus and minus signs indicate where benefits exceed costs of establishing and increasing the funding for DHS. For example, using the two trillion dollar cost of an attack (direct and economic effects), if an attack is prevented every 10 years then DHS would have to contribute approximately 15% to the effort preventing the attack for its benefits to exceed its costs.

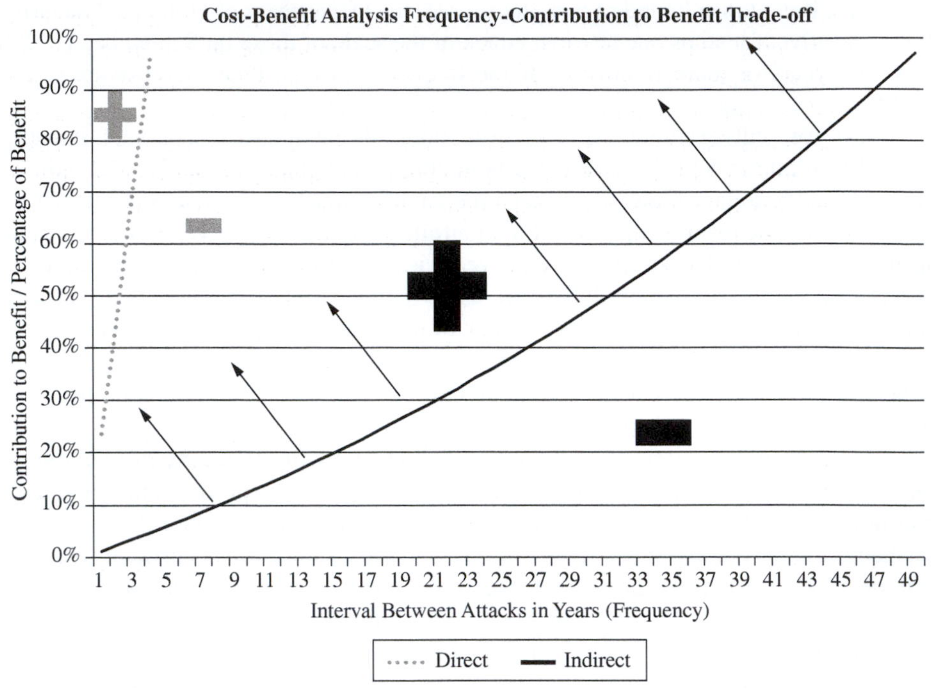

Further Refinement of the Analysis

Another key assumption identified above was that the establishment of and increased funding for DHS was entirely focused on countering terrorism. In fact, when DHS was created it had many areas of responsibility that vary in the degree to which they are related to countering terrorist threats. So, instead of examining DHS in its entirety, an alternative is to examine individual portions. The Department of Homeland Security's first Quadrennial Homeland Security Review (QHSR) in 2009–2010[17] laid out a mission structure that organized and rationalized the missions of the Department. The primary missions of DHS are to prevent terrorism, secure borders and manage immigration, secure cyberspace, and oversee disaster management. This section provides a brief overview of these mission areas and discussion on how cost benefit analysis might proceed with them.

Prevent terrorism:

> This is the first mission of DHS and formally titled "Preventing Terrorism and Enhancing Security" in the QHSR report. Although it is the Department's highest priority, there is surprisingly little direct programmatic DHS activity in this mission set. Much of the direct engagement to prevent terrorism overseas is led by the Department of Defense or the State Department. Much of the intelligence effort focused on preventing terrorism is led by non-DHS members of the Intelligence Community. In a peculiar artifact of the establishment of DHS, much of the law enforcement effort at preventing terrorism remained with Department of Justice while non-security related law enforcement (e.g., child pornography and bank fraud) was transferred to DHS. Finally, state and local governments are heavily involved in preventing terrorism.

DHS does have important responsibilities in this mission area, however, and does play an important role in coordination of terrorism prevention efforts across the federal government and with state and local government. Programmatic activities conducted by DHS focused directly on preventing terrorism include transportation security (e.g., airport screeners), domestic Weapons of Mass Destruction detection (e.g., biological and nuclear screening and detection), and infrastructure protection (e.g., patrolling ports and waterways). The overarching cost benefit analysis described in the previous sections was focused on the combined effect of these activities (along with the indirect terrorism prevention contributions made by DHS activities in other areas). Individual analyses could also be conducted on specific programmatic activities to evaluate their effectiveness in preventing terrorism. For example, DHS scans all inbound containerized cargo for a certain level of radioactive material. The cost of this scanning equipment and the impact of the process on economic activity could be evaluated against the benefit of the program. Challenging policy questions that could be informed with this type of analysis include the cost-benefit of scanning all cargo versus a sample and the cost-benefit of using the existing equipment or upgrading to more sensitive equipment that might be more successful in detecting shielded nuclear material.

Secure borders and manage immigration:

This area includes the second and third QHSR missions of DHS formally titled "Securing and Managing our Borders" and "Enforcing and Administering our Immigration Laws". DHS directly operates most of the government's programmatic activity in this mission area. Areas of DHS responsibility include patrolling and preventing illegal entry across the land, air, and maritime borders of the United States, investigating and apprehending unlawful immigrants within the United States, managing the deportation process of illegal immigrants, and conferring immigration benefits (e.g., citizenship). Some areas outside of DHS responsibility include some policy setting (e.g., establishment of legal immigration quotas) and some administrative law functions (e.g., the deportation hearing process administered by the Department of Justice).

This area has been one of the primary recipients of the increased funding identified above. During the period examined above, the United States Border Patrol doubled in size (from approximately 10,000 agents to over 20,000 agents), 670 miles of border fence was constructed, and significant investments in sensing technology (e.g., radars, ground sensors, and unmanned aerial vehicles) were made. Obvious cost benefit analysis questions in this DHS mission area include comparison of these border security investments with the benefits received in controlling illegal immigration, drug smuggling, and other border crime (including terrorism risk at the border).

Secure cyberspace:

This is the fourth QHSR identified DHS mission and is formally titled "Safeguarding and Securing Cyberspace". DHS responsibilities include civilian Federal systems (e.g., the ".gov" domain) and promoting security in private domains. The military is responsible for cybersecurity in military and national security systems. Programmatic activity conducted by DHS includes the detection and protection against intrusions into civilian Federal systems. As DHS increases its spending in this mission area, cost benefit analysis is an important tool to assist policy makers in prioritizing investments.

Oversee disaster management:

The fifth primary mission of DHS identified in the QHSR is formally titled "Ensuring Resilience to Disasters". The primary responsibilities that DHS oversees or implements in disaster management are mitigation of hazards, preparedness for disasters, emergency response, and longer term recovery efforts. DHS programmatic activity ranges from the establishment and manning of response teams to development of flood maps to the provision of grants for preparedness, mitigation, and disaster assistance. As the spike in the above figures illustrate in 2005 and 2006 from Hurricane Katrina, this can become a very large portion of DHS spending. Cost benefit analysis is appropriate for the full range of activities DHS engages in, e.g., do the benefits of preparedness grants justify their costs and, similarly, for flood maps?

Each of these mission categories allows for a more in-depth analysis if desired. The cost-benefit analysis methodology is still fully applicable. While this may allow for more in-depth analysis, studies at the mission category level still have many of the same challenges, perhaps most importantly how to measure benefits.

One place to start for the measurement of benefit is with the Department's performance measures. The U.S. Department of Homeland Security Annual Performance Report Fiscal Years 2011–2013[18] is the Department's internal mechanism to assess performance across a spectrum of goals. The Government Accountability Office (GAO) also regularly assesses the Department's progress. In 2011, GAO found progress had been made but work remained in implementing homeland security missions.[19] These types of reports provide useful insights to assess the Department, its effectiveness at accomplishing individual missions or goals, or to assess a sub-component of the Department.

Separately Analyzing the Establishment of DHS

Until now, the analysis of this chapter has combined the establishment of the DHS with the substantial increase in funding that occurred in the years immediately following its establishment. The increase in funding could have occurred without establishing the Department. The value proposition in establishing the Department was that it would lead to greater coordination and unity of effort across the disparate activities that had been combined.

Cindy Williams[20] and Jessica Zuckerman[21] try to analyze the specific question of establishing the Department by assessing its effectiveness in adapting the budget to priorities that are different today than they were fifteen years ago. The general notion is that if consolidation provided efficiency or more holistic oversight, then that should show up in an examination of how budget shares for the sub-components have changed over time or how funding is taken from lower priorities and applied to higher priorities. Trying to get at this more specific question in isolation is more challenging but is an important area for analysis.

Conclusions

There are a multitude of options regarding how to assess the Department or its components. While the theory to assess the value proposition of the Department of Homeland Security is straightforward, the analysis is complex and requires many assumptions. Assessments are easier and more transparent if the measures needed to make the assessment are considered in the planning phase and the data is collected throughout the process. Even in these cases, however, the analysis is normally limited. The limitation comes from the unidirectionalism of time. Yes, time only goes forward, making comparisons to alternative policy decisions full of assumptions necessary to create the counter factual. This means that effective assessments need to be updated regularly and all assumptions revalidated with each update. Finally, the method chosen for the analysis should be based on the particular policy question being analyzed and the data available; this may turn out to be a balancing act. With a full understanding of the question and the relevant data and facts, the various analysis methods described here can provide useful insights to decision makers when assessing policy choices.

Critical Thinking Questions

1. What do you think of the central value proposition that a central Department of Homeland Security makes us safer, and is thus a smarter investment, than any other alternative arrangement of government resources?
2. How can we assess whether qualitative improvements have been made in coordination and "unity of effort" among security professionals engaged in homeland security?
3. Are the "costs" and "benefits" asserted in this article accurate and complete, or have the authors overlooked some other critical dimensions?

Notes

1. Public Law 107-96, Section I, available at http://www.gpo.gov/fdsys/pkg/PLAW-107publ296/pdf/PLAW-107publ296.pdf.
2. Office of Management and Budget, *Circular A*-94 (Washington, DC: undated), available at http://www.whitehouse.gov/sites/default/files/omb/assets/a94/a094.pdf.
3. More formally, the value and associated probability of each of these various outcomes could be estimated and the expected value would be calculated by the weighted sum-product of each of these outcomes and their probability of occurring.
4. Perhaps more correctly, the movie experience.
5. "Same decision" in this context means that the values and their associated probabilities are identical to the original decision.
6. Generally Federal Deposit Insurance Corporation insured savings are assumed to be riskless.
7. For simplicity throughout we use constant discount rates, but there is no need to do so if additional detail is known.
8. Discount rates can include inflation (nominal) or exclude it (real). In this case the savings rate includes inflation, so it is a nominal rate. Either real or nominal rates can be used, what is important is that all components of the analysis either include the effects

of inflation or exclude them. If the effects of inflation are measured correctly, the decision does not depend upon whether real or nominal values are used.

9. This example of the components of an individual discount rate is illustrative only. In practice, discount rates can generally only be inferred from observing behaviors and then only in an aggregate form.
10. Office of Management and Budget, *Budget of the United States Government, Fiscal Year 2013, Historical Tables* (Washington, DC: 2012), available at http://www.whitehouse.gov/omb/budget/Historicals.
11. Institute for the Analysis of Global Security (IAGS), *How much did the September 11 terrorist attack cost America?* (Potomac, MD: 2003), available at http://www.iags.org/costof911.html.
12. Joseph Stiglitz, *The Price of 9/11* (New York, NY: Project Syndicate, September 11, 2011), available at http://www.project-syndicate.org/commentary/the-price-of-9-11.
13. Note that these estimates are not in fiscal year 2005 dollars and will need to be converted when the analysis is conducted.
14. Carafano, James Jay, Steve Bucci, and Jessica Zuckerman, *Fifty Terror Plots Foiled Since 9/11: The Homegrown Threat and the Long War on Terrorism* (Washington, DC: The Heritage Foundation, April 25, 2012), available at http://report.heritage.org/bg2682.
15. The Gross Domestic Product (GDP) deflator was used to convert the 2001 costs into 2005 dollars. This conversion is explained in macroeconomic text books and is widely available online.
16. Office of Management and Budget, *Circular A-94 Appendix C* (Washington, DC: December 2011), available at http://www.whitehouse.gov/omb/circulars_a094/a94_appx-c.
17. Department of Homeland Security, *Quadrennial Homeland Security Review Report: A Strategic Framework for a Secure Homeland* (Washington, DC: February 2010), available at http://www.dhs.gov/xlibrary/assets/qhsr_report.pdf.
18. Department of Homeland Security, *U.S. Department of Homeland Security Annual Performance Report Fiscal Years 2011–2013* (Washington, DC 2012), available at http://www.dhs.gov/xlibrary/assets/mgmt/cfo_apr_fy2011.pdf.
19. Dodaro, Gene L., *Department of Homeland Security Progress Made and Work Remaining in Implementing Homeland Security Missions 10 Years after 9/11* (Washington, DC: Government Accountability Office, September 8, 2011), available at http://www.gao.gov/products/GAO-10-940T.
20. Williams, Cindy, *Paying for Homeland Security: Show Me the Money* (Cambridge, MA: Center for International Studies, Massachusetts Institute of Technology, May 2007), available at http://web.mit.edu/cis/pdf/Audit_05_07_Williams.pdf.
21. Zuckerman, Jessica, *The 2013 Homeland Security Budget: Misplaced Priorities* (Washington, DC: The Heritage Foundation, March 14, 2014), available at http://www.heritage.org/research/reports/2012/03/the-2013-homeland-security-budget-misplaced-priorities.

Section 2.2

State and Local Response

Information Sharing

Exploring the Intersection of Policing with National and Military Intelligence

Gary Cordner and Kathryn Scarborough

This article explores the intersection of (1) policing and police intelligence (2) with national intelligence and military intelligence. The premise is that for more than 150 years, prior to the events of September 11, 2001, police intelligence had little connection to national or military intelligence. Basically, national intelligence focused on serious world-wide political and economic threats to the nation's well-being; military intelligence focused specifically on military threats to the national security; the police focused their intelligence work on criminals who posed threats to individuals and local communities. A fairly clear division of labor was in place, based largely on the type and scale of threats.

Since 9/11, however, it has become plausible that a small group of non-state actors, such as terrorists, could launch a serious attack against the nation using weapons of mass destruction, or even small arms, as in Mumbai. These individuals might live in a local U.S. community or halfway across the world, yet plan and execute a massive and violent attack against a local U.S. community. They might also commit ordinary crimes to help finance their larger intentions. In this new context of terrorism and asymmetric threats, a local police department might develop intelligence of significant interest to national and military intelligence, or vice versa.

Important historical, conceptual, and policy issues associated with the intersection of national, military, and police intelligence are discussed more fully elsewhere.[1] This article presents the results of a small-scale study in which subject matter experts were asked to respond to several scenarios related to intelligence and information sharing, asking both what *should* happen and what *would* actually happen.

U.S. Policing

Policing in the United States is civilian (non-military), predominantly local (funded and directed by local governments), and extremely fragmented. It is not just that police are distributed all around the country[2]—they mostly answer to local elected officials. The U.S. has almost 18,000 separate law enforcement agencies, roughly 16,000 of which are local. Of the remaining 2,000 agencies, the vast majority represent special jurisdictions (university police, transit police, park police, etc.), followed by state agencies, and lastly by federal non-military agencies. Out of 837,000 full-time sworn police personnel (armed with arrest authority), 74 percent work for local agencies, 13 percent work for federal law enforcement, and 13 percent work for state or special jurisdiction law enforcement agencies.[3]

The two largest components of U.S. policing are both local: municipal police departments (cities, towns, townships, boroughs, villages) and county sheriff's offices.[4] Two characteristics of these types of law enforcement agencies are absolutely essential for understanding their capabilities and contexts: most are small (77 percent have fewer than twenty-five full-time sworn officers)[5] and they are all independent of each other. There is no chain of command in the police industry—within individual agencies, yes, but among and between the 18,000 agencies, no.[6]

Along with industry structure, it is important to note a thing or two about police work and police culture. Particularly at the local and state levels, police officers in the field frequently act alone and without immediate supervision. Much of their work involves making "low visibility decisions"—especially when an officer's decision does not result in a report or an arrest (and most police actions and decisions do not), it is rarely subject to review. If an officer's decision does not result in a report or arrest, it probably will not produce any official information for later analysis. As Peter Manning notes, "information in police departments can best be characterized as systematically decentralized. Often, primary data known to one officer are not available to other officers" because they are stored in the officer's head or personal notes. Moreover, "all essential police knowledge is thought to be contextual, substantive, detailed, concrete, temporally bounded, and particularistic" while information in official reports and files is often viewed by officers and investigators as trivial, having been created and manipulated mainly for bureaucratic purposes.[7]

Additionally, police agencies and police culture tend to celebrate and reward good arrests. Information and intelligence, by themselves, are not traditional units of police work, they are not measured, and producing them is not rewarded. Also, information that is not directly connected to an incident, crime, or case does not have a natural home in the typical police records system—there is no file to put it in. Incidents, crimes, and cases are traditionally assigned to individual officers (or detectives) who are evaluated on how well they handle and dispose of these events. Consequently, the tendency is for officers and detectives to hold information closely in order to use it later to enhance their own productivity.

It is also important to recognize that U.S. police, not just the military and federal law enforcement agencies, engaged in intelligence-related abuses in the 1960s and 1970s.[8] Informants, undercover operations, and electronic surveillance were often used to gather information about civil rights and anti-war groups. Subsequent inquiries showed that many of the targets of these intelligence operations were not involved in any serious criminal behavior, but rather were engaged in political activities in opposition to prevailing government policies, such as the Vietnam War. Local police intelligence capabilities were significantly curtailed in the wake of exposes of these abuses, and in some jurisdictions have yet to recover.[9]

The point of these observations is that the structure of U.S. policing, the nature of police work, some historical stumbles, and common features of police culture all seem to conspire against an intelligence-led approach to policing and the free flow of information.[10] To this we can add the traditional tensions between levels of policing in our federal system. State and federal law enforcement are often represented or perceived as more important and more professional than local police—much to the resentment of local police. Local police sometimes also fear state and federal agencies, because those agencies have the authority to investigate public corruption and civil rights violations in local communities. Specifically on the issue of information sharing, a common complaint is that it is a one-way street—local police provide information to their state and federal "partners" but get little or nothing in return. The following anecdote from one of the subject matter experts who participated in this project illustrates the common local police experience and perspective:

> Person is stopped off I-35 North of Georgetown, TX. Subject has possession of numerous photographs of large venue HVAC systems, such as stadia and arenas. Subject is a Middle Eastern engineering student. First photos are of subject inside Reunion Hotel in Dallas, obviously shot by someone else. Subject alone when stopped. Digital photographs copied by police. Local police notify Secret Service because of proximity to Western White House. Secret Service tails subject until they lose him. THEN they notify FBI, which enters information into Threat Matrix. Local police notified after subject left the country.

Frustration with federal-local information sharing has led the New York Police Department (NYPD) to station overseas personnel in eleven posts, including London, Paris, Abu Dhabi, and Amman.[11] Their post-9/11 reasoning is that (1) their city is a likely target of international terrorism, (2) they are not confident that the Federal Bureau of Investigation (FBI) or Central Intelligence Agency (CIA) or other federal agencies will share important information with them immediately, and therefore (3) they want their own people on the ground around the world in the places where key intelligence might be uncovered. They also argue that local police in Tel Aviv or Madrid are more likely to share information with U.S. local police than with U.S. federal officials.

In spite of all these longstanding and fundamental challenges, since 9/11 there is evidence of improved intelligence gathering and information sharing. Local police have been encouraged to collect and forward a new type of document, Suspicious Activity Reports (SAR).[12] State-level fusion centers have been created to serve as the link between local agencies and federal/national agencies and networks;[13] some of these have even been granted access to classified Department of Defense information systems.[14] Local and state agencies have reported increased contacts with the likes of the FBI, CIA, Centers for Disease Control (CDC), Federal Aviation Administration (FAA), and National Guard.[15] At the national level, reorganization of the intelligence community, increased emphasis on counter-terrorism in the FBI, creation of the National Counterterrorism Center, and establishment of an Information Sharing Environment all reflect serious attention toward intelligence and information sharing.[16] Numerous obstacles still exist,[17] but the consensus is that information sharing is improving.

This Study

This study examines how terrorism-related intelligence and information is shared between local police, on the one hand, and state police, federal law enforcement, intelligence agencies, and the military in the post-9/11 era. It was understood that federal laws, state laws, secrecy provisions, and security clearances all affect what can be shared in different situations.[18] Also, it was presumed that most local police had longstanding communication channels with state and federal law enforcement (whether effective or ineffective), but not with intelligence agencies or the military. Thus, if local police came into possession of information that might be of interest to a federal agency, intelligence agency, or the military, what would they do? Similarly, if the military or CIA came upon some information in Central Asia with ramifications for a local community in Middle America, what would they do?

Methodology

Six short scenarios/vignettes were sent to a small non-random sample of subject matter experts in 2008. The scenarios were designed to represent a variety of realistic situations in which information sharing might be desirable and might or might not occur. The common ingredient in each scenario was a Kentucky connection, only because both authors taught at Eastern Kentucky University at the time. The main purpose was to ground the scenarios in a typical and realistic setting, without introducing the complexity that might ensue if the location was New York, Los Angeles, or Washington, DC.

Responses to the scenarios were obtained from fourteen experts. Of these, ten were police executives (identified hereafter as PE) or police intelligence (PI) practitioners, two were associated with military intelligence (MI), one was associated with federal law enforcement (FE), and one was an academic expert (AE). The police respondents represented six different states while the other respondents were also distributed around the country.

The small size of the sample significantly limits any claims of statistical validity, as does the weighting of the sample toward police respondents. It is best to think of this study as an initial exploration of information sharing among police, intelligence agencies, and the military without any pretense that it accomplished a scientific measurement of the phenomenon.

Scenarios

We asked the subject matter experts to respond to several hypothetical scenarios that combined crime, terrorism, and information sharing issues. Six scenarios were presented following some general instructions:

> Listed below are several hypothetical scenarios that might involve information sharing among local, state, and federal law enforcement, intelligence agencies, and military agencies. Each scenario has a Kentucky connection, but you may feel free to apply it to your own local jurisdiction. We would appreciate any insight you could provide regarding two things in each scenario:
>
> - What *would* probably happen today in regard to information sharing?
> - What *should* happen, in your opinion?
>
> **Scenario A:** U.S. Army forces in Afghanistan find a computer in a terrorist camp that contains images of a chemical plant in Ashland, KY.
>
> **Scenario B:** A CIA agent in Africa observes a U.S. citizen meeting with elements of Al Qaeda. It is determined that the U.S. citizen lives in Elizabethtown, KY, which is near Fort Knox.
>
> **Scenario C:** A police officer in Hopkinsville, KY, near Fort Campbell, is told by a citizen that she (the citizen) knows an active duty soldier who has

rocket-propelled grenades (RPG) in his garage. She says that he (the soldier) often talks about how easy it would be to shoot down a passenger airplane near the Nashville airport.

Scenario D: A police officer in Lexington, KY, while handling a domestic dispute call at a residence in the city, sees quite a few interesting pieces of art. Casual inquiry reveals that the husband in the house is an Army reserve doctor recently returned from a tour of duty in Iraq. The officer wonders whether the pieces of art might be stolen antiquities.

Scenario E: A police officer in Louisville, KY responds to a call at a private residence. The parents of a 15-year-old boy show the officer the boy's computer, on which they found an elaborate plan to assemble a fertilizer truck bomb and explode it outside an Army recruiting station in Cincinnati, OH.

Scenario F: An FBI analyst develops an intelligence report that indicates that organized groups are smuggling significant quantities of cigarettes out of Kentucky for resale in northern states where taxes are higher, and then sending the profits overseas to groups that are affiliated with Hezbollah.

Sharing by and with Local Police

The post-9/11 focus on local police has mainly been on their role as "eyes and ears" in local communities throughout the nation. In this respect they are seen as very important collectors of information, of raw data that can be fed into the intelligence process in order to help analysts and others "connect the dots." Community policing is seen by some as an ideal local police strategy because it helps officers get to know their communities and builds trust, making it more likely that residents will share important information with the police.[19] It has become common to refer to local police as "first preventers" who are most likely to be in a position to prevent a terrorist act, both by gathering information and by taking action, when appropriate. This first preventer role is paired with the more familiar "first responder" role to make a logical and meaningful package that (1) demonstrates the synergy between effective crime reduction tactics and counterterrorism and (2) encourages local police to take their counterterrorism role more seriously.[20]

The *National Strategy for Information Sharing* reiterated this expanded role for local police and provided a few specific examples:

> These partners are now a critical component of our Nation's security capability as both "first preventers" and "first responders," and their efforts have achieved concrete results within their communities, as the following examples illustrate:
>
> - A narcotics investigation—conducted by Federal, State, and local law enforcement officials and resulting in multiple arrests—revealed that a Canadian-based organization supplying precursor chemicals to Mexican methamphetamine producers was in fact a Hezbollah support cell.
> - A local police detective investigating a gas station robbery uncovered a homegrown jihadist cell planning a series of attacks.

- An investigation into cigarette smuggling initiated by a county sheriff's department uncovered a Hezbollah support cell operating in several States.[21]

Scenarios C, D, and E all focused on suspicious activity discovered by local police. None apparently involved international terrorism, but one or two might involve domestic terrorism, one might involve transnational crime, and all three involved the military in some way.

Most project interviewees agreed that the local police department in Scenario C should, and would, forward its information about the soldier with the RPG to federal and/or military authorities. There was some disagreement over details, such as whether the investigation should be handled by the appropriate Joint Terrorism Task Force (JTTF) or the military. Some variation in responses might have resulted because the scenario did not clearly specify whether the soldier's garage was on or off the military base. One respondent indicated that the proper response *should* involve both information sharing and collaboration:

> The local police should investigate the soldier with members of the FBI and the military in a joint investigation since both criminal and possible terrorism activity may be involved. If follow up is warranted with the TSA and the Nashville airport, it should be the responsibility of the FBI. But in this case both criminal and national security intelligence may be obtained and can be disseminated to sworn law enforcement in the Nashville Airport area if a reasonable suspicion of an attack on a plane is detected. If the reason for wanting to shoot the plane is one of terror as opposed to some personal animosity, then the subject should also be entered into VGTOF (the Violent Gang and Terrorist Organization File in NCIC). (PI)

This same respondent, though, indicated that what *would* happen might be less collaborative—the local police would conduct an investigation and they might contact the Transportation Security Administration (TSA) or the Nashville airport. From an information-sharing and intelligence standpoint, the possibility of the local police department conducting its own investigation without informing any other authorities would be the least desirable response, but also problematic could be joint investigations if they were initiated outside post-9/11 information-sharing procedures. For example, if the police and the Fort Campbell MPs conducted an investigation, or if the police and the local FBI office conducted an investigation, the raw information might never make it to the local agency's intelligence unit, the state fusion center, the applicable JTTF, or the National Counterterrorism Center (NCTC). One respondent noted:

> Sharing of information with the military is always a problem. There are also problems associated with local information that is sent to the FBI first instead of traveling through normal local reporting structures first. If suspect information goes directly to the FBI, or other federal entity, the information is not generally disseminated down to the local level in a timely manner. Unfortunately, when this occurs, local intelligence information is often lost. Additionally, vulnerability assessments could be updated and local law enforcement resources could be allocated towards prevention efforts when local intelligence is received in a timely manner. (PI)

Scenario D was at most criminal in nature (possible possession of stolen art from Iraq) but involved a military service member. Respondents seemed to be split about evenly on whether the matter would be handled strictly by the local police or referred to either military or federal law enforcement. Since the evidence that a crime had occurred was limited, some thought the likelihood of any action was minimal. Most seemed to agree, though, that the proper action would be to share the information with the military. For example:

> Contact with military investigators should be made by the local agency sharing what the officer observed. Military should investigate and provide a follow up call back to the initiating agency as to whether or not the art is possibly stolen. In this case, if the military determines that there is reasonable suspicion that the paintings are stolen, possession of those paintings is then a crime and intelligence reports on the subject can be shared between the military police and the initiating agency. (PI)

Scenario E involved a possible threat to a military recruiting station. Because it involved the threat of explosives, it elicited a familiar difference of opinion about whether the proper federal agency to contact should be the FBI or the Bureau of Alcohol, Tobacco, Firearms and Explosives (ATF). These two agencies have feuded for years over the lead federal role in explosives investigation, resulting in conflict between the agencies, competition over specific cases, and mixed signals sent to state and local law enforcement. A 2009 U.S. Department of Justice Inspector General's report indicates that this situation still persists.[22]

There was also a split of opinions on whether the local police would conduct their own investigation, whether they would hand it off to the FBI, whether the military would be notified in a timely manner, and whether a joint investigation would ensue. Two examples:

> My guess is this would be handled completely by local authorities. It appears to be only peripherally related to the military. Ideally, the recruiting commander would be contacted, which would probably result in contact from Army CID. The information should be shared here, but it may never get out of CID. (MI)

> The local agency would share the information with the FBI and in turn the FBI would most likely investigate the boy directly prior to contacting the military. If the FBI determines that the subject is indeed a possible threat, he would be entered into VGTOF. (PI)

There was more agreement about what *should* happen in this scenario—information should be shared and a joint investigation should be conducted. Responses varied on whether the conduit for information sharing should be a regional or state fusion center or some other network such as the Terrorism Early Warning Groups (TEWG) that have been set up in some areas of the country. Since the scenario involved two local police departments in different states, as well as the military connection, established channels would seem to be important in making sure that information and intelligence sharing crossed state borders as well as agency boundaries.

One respondent provided detailed information on additional steps that would be taken in his jurisdiction. This response strayed from the basic questions about information and intelligence sharing, but is worth reviewing because it illustrates the kinds of concerns that local agencies have beyond just investigating a possible crime; they also tend to worry about others who might be involved, others who might have similar ideas, copycats, as well as fallout in the local community.

> The local police agency School Resource Officer (SRO) would be briefed and analysis would be conducted as to evidence of theft or purchase of various items needed to carry out any attack. Local police would also update local military recruiting stations and look for pre-incident indicators. A coordinated follow up with the military would be conducted.
>
> Since this type of information involves the internet and therefore could permeate our schools, our computer crimes unit would be used to monitor this type of activity as it relates to this suspect. Chances are if one student has this type of information, there are many more out there that may also be involved in criminal activity and not discovered by parents, schools, or others. The local police agency would not be satisfied with catching one student, but rather they would embark on an effort to educate parents and schools on how to be more vigilant at detecting these types of crimes. Specific computer and internet investigations into this activity may be warranted. (PI)

State Police

The post-9/11 environment has had potentially significant consequences for state police agencies.[23] Each state has set up some type of homeland security apparatus to advise the governor and the legislature, oversee statewide threat assessment and infrastructure protection, receive and distribute DHS funds, provide training and assistance to local jurisdictions, etc. In many if not most states, the state police have naturally assumed a large role in these activities, since they are usually the largest state public safety agency (other than corrections, which has limited expertise on the counterterrorism issue and little responsibility for terrorism prevention, response, or investigation). The development of state fusion centers has also typically been with substantial state police involvement—the state police usually had a pre-existing intelligence unit,[24] and they were often already serving as a principal point of contact for federal law enforcement and national intelligence agencies.

Interestingly, though, none of the scenarios used in this project elicited many responses that involved state police *per se.* One or two responses included the state police among the range of agencies that should be notified about some information or threat revealed in the scenario. One respondent referred several times to the fact that the state police in his state dominate the new fusion center but that information sharing is no better than in the past.

> Our state police Intelligence Branch has been a failure for decades for agencies other than themselves. Even past state police intel commanders will admit that, because of the very nature of the state police to horde information and not share it with others. I have witnessed local intelligence meetings where the state police and at times the FBI have attended and the meeting starts with asking them what they have brought to share. After hearing each of them (mostly state police) say they have nothing to report the group goes around the room

> and everyone says the same thing. A few words are given of thanks and the meeting has adjourned only to reconvene after the state police have left the building. Then the real information is shared among the locals with a vow of not giving anything to the state police.
>
> We have many statutes that require us to report to the state police but none to require them to share information back to anyone. To state the problem simply: the state police have an inherent distrust for local LE and all local LE does is mirror that distrust right back at them. (PE)

Several factors may account for the apparent low level of state police involvement in the new information sharing environment. One possibility is that the scenarios simply did not incorporate elements that would have made state police participation more relevant. A second is that state police are a relatively small slice of the law enforcement pie. Also, state fusion centers may have superseded state police agencies as the principal state-level cogs in the system—if so, this probably just reflects how the new system is supposed to operate. Additionally, though, it is probably the case that many local agencies have their own direct connections to the JTTF, FBI, or other federal agencies, so that no state-level involvement is initiated in many situations. From an efficiency standpoint this may seem desirable; however, it might limit information sharing and intelligence development if pertinent information does not also find its way to broader networks such as the state fusion centers or the NCTC.

Federal Law Enforcement

Scenario F used for this project specifically involved intelligence developed by an FBI analyst relating cigarette smuggling and an international terrorist group. The general consensus of respondents was that the FBI would either keep the intelligence to itself and conduct an investigation, or they would collaborate with other federal/national/military agencies for additional information gathering and investigation. Two interviewees thought that the FBI would work with the ATF due to the cigarette (tobacco) angle. Three mentioned that the FBI would involve the appropriate JTTF, which might be a means of limited information sharing with local police, although the intelligence would probably be classified and therefore not widely shared. Also, one respondent indicated that the frequency of JTTF meetings might not be sufficient to count on them for timely information sharing.

> It is likely this will be a strictly FBI operation. Although it would be good for local authorities to know about the investigation, I don't see it as necessary. It should be something that gets briefed in the next JTTF meeting. The difference in *probably* and *should* here is the frequency of the JTTF meetings. They should be no longer than quarterly (monthly is better) but I have heard that some JTTFs are meeting only rarely now. (MI)

This scenario raises a typical "need to know" vs. "need to share" issue. The new information-sharing environment is supposed to put greater emphasis on need to share.[25] One method for doing that, in this scenario, would be for the FBI to forward the intelligence report to the NCTC, which would presumably share it with other agencies as deemed appropriate. Another avenue would be to enter pertinent information in the NCIC VGOTF file. The former method would theoretically be more proactive, since it might result in intelligence about cigarette smuggling being widely shared with agencies that could then use it in a variety of ways. The latter method would be more reactive—if an officer stopped a vehicle or person somewhere and made a NCIC query, they could be notified of the possible terrorism connection.

One respondent pointed out the importance of collaboration with local police in a situation of this type: "the local agency should be involved to assist with intelligence information they may have on the location, undercover vehicle stops, etc." (PI). Another potential value of following the "need to share" philosophy in this scenario was outlined by a different respondent.

> This type of generic information has been widely circulated for some time now; however, instead of working closely with local law enforcement agencies, this type of crime is typically worked solely by the FBI/JTTF for follow up.
>
> Since these types of crimes are not worked by local law enforcement officers, they lack the knowledge needed to effectively investigate crimes of this nature. It would be beneficial if more training was provided to local law enforcement in this area. Local law enforcement needs to recognize when this type of information should be forwarded to the appropriate intelligence agencies. More importantly, critical information on these types of crimes comes not only through reports or information analysis, but also through human sources. Human source development training should be enhanced to help local police officers develop homeland security sources at the local level. The private sector should also be better trained and utilized for recognition and timely reporting of suspicious criminal activity related to our homeland security. (PI)

Information sharing by and with federal law enforcement agencies was potentially involved in all the other scenarios used in this project. As previously noted, one concern is that information shared directly by a local police agency with the FBI, while appropriate for handling a particular investigation, may not get the wider dissemination or availability it deserves unless it is also sent to the local agency's intelligence unit, a fusion center, the NCTC, and/or the VGOTF. Also, cases involving explosives or cigarette smuggling should probably trigger collaboration between the FBI and ATF, but this may not always occur.

Scenario A involved military discovery of information in Central Asia with a possible terrorism link back to the U.S. (images of a chemical plant). Several respondents indicated that this information would probably be transmitted to the FBI, but whether it would then be shared with local or state police in the threatened jurisdiction might be problematic. Among the responses were these:

> May make the FBI Threat Matrix, but will not be released to local law enforcement unless authorized at the "Secret" level. I do not expect that local law enforcement would be notified, albeit they should. (PE)
>
> The State Fusion Center will receive the information—if it is not classified as "Top Secret;" and if they do they will most likely only share with their state police. At this point in time, the likelihood of the local police department or county sheriff being notified is slim to none. (PE)

> The information *would* flow from military channels to the FBI. The information would be classified and passed through to the local JTTFs. The information would stay at that level with no notification of the local agency . . . the [local] agency *should* be contacted and the substance of the information *should* be passed on. The source information does not need to be included. (PI)
>
> If the military chose to share this information, they would be forced to share it at the federal level which usually means the FBI. The FBI would assume responsibility for follow up and investigation. Local police agencies would have to rely on the release of information from a local FBI/JTTF office in order for the local police to be involved. Many local police departments do not have direct contact with FBI/JTTF offices. (PI)

As responses to these scenarios illustrate, there remains a good bit of skepticism about the free flow of information from federal law enforcement agencies. Improved systems for information sharing have been established but they are not always used. The 2007 *National Strategy for Information Sharing* and 2008 *Information Sharing Environment* provide additional enhancements that should continue the improvements already made. Traditional obstacles and barriers certainly remain even though progress has been made.

> Since 9/11, information sharing between the federal government and state and locals has improved. Most of the improvement has come through the FBI's Joint Terrorism Task Force (JTTF), which has tripled in number from 34 before September 11 to 100 today. In Los Angeles and other large departments across the country, there are active levels of communication and cooperation with the Department of Homeland Security and the FBI.
>
> Despite this progress, the level of cooperation seems to vary greatly, depending on the personalities of individual bureau and police chiefs. Too often, the FBI cuts itself off from local police manpower, expertise, and intelligence. More than 6,000 state and local police now have federal security clearances, but the historical lack of trust is still an issue. For example, many police chiefs complain of calls they get from their JTTF' alerting them to a potential threat, but when they ask for the detailed information needed to launch an investigation, they are told by the bureau: "We can't tell you" or "You don't need to know."[26]

National Intelligence Agencies And The Military

This project's Scenario B posed the situation of a CIA agent in Africa observing a U.S. citizen meeting with elements of Al Qaeda. This is a situation involving international terrorism, a covert observation made overseas, and information collected by a national intelligence agency. The respondents were mixed on whether the information would be kept by the CIA, shared with the military, or shared with the FBI. Most were fairly certain that local and state police in the citizen's hometown and state would probably not be informed.

> Unless the CIA agent has a friend in the FBI in Kentucky, it is likely this information will not go beyond the CIA. What *should* happen is that both

> the KY FBI and Army Intelligence should be notified of the person and a joint investigation conducted to determine if there is any link to activities occurring in Kentucky. The FBI would likely run the investigation, but Fort Knox security should be notified and kept up on any potential links/threats to the base. (MI)

> A peripheral check into the subject's background *would* be performed by the CIA and without further results would cause the subject to be entered into a database accessed only by the CIA or Military. This information might be shared with Fort Knox but not with local agencies surrounding the base . . . The subject *should* be thoroughly investigated by the FBI including contacting local agencies to see if the subject might be wanted on criminal charges unrelated to terrorism. Often an arrest and follow up interview can provide an opportunity to obtain further information regarding the terrorism angle. The subject should also be entered into VGTOF through NCIC to alert local police once they have contacted the subject that he may be involved in terrorism activities. (PI)

> Currently, the information would not necessarily be disseminated to local law enforcement agencies in a timely manner. Information sharing on U.S. Citizens abroad is usually limited to local law enforcement sending local information up the intelligence chain about subject activities while they were in the U.S. Local police would not receive information directly from the CIA, but would rely on information passed from the CIA to the FBI and then hopefully to the local police. Information collected abroad would need to be sanitized to enable timely dissemination to local law enforcement. (PI)

A consequence in this scenario of restricted information sharing *up* from the local police level was also anticipated by one police executive.

> The information will stay with the CIA and maybe will be shared with the FBI. I do not believe the information will be pushed down to any lower levels at this time. However, due to the nature of information not going up from the local level to the Fusion Center, there may be valuable information about this citizen in local police data bases and because of the lack of trust, lack of cooperation and lack of quality information sharing back and forth between local LE and state police, the information will therefore never be shared with the CIA. (PE)

Scenario A is the only one that began with the military, in this case soldiers discovering a computer in a cave in Central Asia containing images of a U.S. chemical plant. Several respondents suspected that the information would be retained by the military, while others believed it would be shared with the FBI.

> The information *should* be forwarded by the DOD intelligence component through the National Counterterrorism Center (NCTC), which would forward it to the KY fusion center who then share it with all appropriate LE agencies in KY [but] there is a good chance the NCTC would not receive the information. (AE)

> Given there is no information in the scenario about pending attack (only images), it is likely nothing would be done and no information shared until after [final analysis of the computer]. Usually, the Army/DOD is pretty good about getting information like this to the FBI. It would likely flow to the SAC with responsibility for Ashland. From there, it all depends on the relationship between the Kentucky FBI and local entities. (MI)

> This would be classified by the military at the Secret, most likely Top Secret level, and sent to analysis by Central Command. I do not expect to hear anything further on this in time to be actionable. May make the FBI Threat Matrix, but will not be released to local law enforcement unless authorized at the Secret level. I do not expect that local law enforcement would be notified, albeit they should. (PE)

None of the project interviewees expected any prompt information sharing with the local police in the chemical plant's jurisdiction. Notification to the chemical plant's corporate security seemed about as likely as to local police. One specific problem interfering with sharing of the information was its likely classification as secret or top secret.

> The issues are two-fold: first, although necessary for national security, the laws pertaining to sharing intelligence information between law enforcement and the military (*posse comitatus*) have not been updated and do not adequately address the loss of information in the critical need to exchange information. Secondly, instead of sanitizing information so it can be easily disseminated to law enforcement officers, similar information would usually be over-classified and therefore would never be disseminated to those who need the information the most. (PI)

Despite the fact that this information would most likely be held closely and not promptly shared with local authorities (if shared at all), several respondents felt wider sharing would be beneficial.

> The differences between what is likely and what should be are these: (1) the information about the images should be initially released as soon as they are discovered (initial analysis). Doesn't have to be extensive, but the authorities in Ashland should know about it early; (2) there should be some formal information sharing arrangements between DOD and FBI about cases like this (if they don't already exist); (3) there should be an investigation opened by the FBI and locals to determine if there is something that should be investigated further indicating a potential attack and why the images were gathered. (MI)

> This information should be shared with the FBI to evaluate as national security intelligence. Follow up should be completed by the FBI with any law enforcement agencies which may respond to a call for service in the event something happens to the plant. Since the information does not center around a person (yet), the right to privacy is not an issue and the intelligence generated from it may be shared. (PI)

> This type of information should be shared and analyzed at a variety of levels in order to obtain a better view of its relevance to local criminal activities. The information should be shared through timely channels and analyzed not only by the military, but at the national, state, regional, county, tribal and local levels. By viewing the information from a variety of perspectives, there would be a greater chance of filling the intelligence gap and turning information into actionable intelligence. Sharing information would also foster greater cooperation between agencies rather than local law enforcement learning about local threats through the National media. Timely sharing of information would also allow local law enforcement officers to implement a more effective collection plan of new information, which may generate more pieces of intelligence related to local threats. (PI)

Discussion

It seems apparent that procedures and protocols for counterterrorism information sharing have not achieved full implementation. Subject matter experts responding to six scenarios often differed in what they thought *should* happen, and often judged that what *would* happen would be less than full-scale information sharing. Most expected that investigations would be narrower and less collaborative than desirable. In many cases the experts thought information sharing would not be as systematic as it should, between and among intelligence agencies and especially with local police. Some opportunities to engage local police in intelligence gathering were not expected to be utilized because doing so might require intelligence agencies to take police into their confidence. Over-classification of intelligence was expected to interfere with information sharing. Often, the likelihood of information sharing was seen as dependent on the existence of personal contacts and relationships.

Part of the explanation for differences in what *should* happen follows from the complexity of the inter-organizational environment surrounding counter-terrorism. The police system has 18,000 separate agencies, including 18,000 CEOs and, potentially, 18,000 terrorism liaison officers. The number of national intelligence and military intelligence agencies is much smaller but each of these agencies is large and complex in its own right. This extremely large inter-organizational set exists within a maze of federal and state law, bureaucratic rules, traditions, customs, and politics.

Another part of the explanation is that the situation is new and evolving. Local police have little experience at counterterrorism or domestic/homeland security intelligence. Before 9/11 they had little reason to interact with national intelligence or military intelligence agencies. The notion of transnational crime was exotic enough for most police agencies—international terrorism seemed even less likely to affect Main Street, city hall, or hometown security. Now, suddenly, there are state fusion centers and a complicated information sharing environment of new alphabet-soup federal agencies including the Office of the Director of National Intelligence (ODNI), NCTC, and the Interagency Threat Assessment and Coordination Group (ITACG).

Besides complexity and newness, though, there seems to be a great deal of residual resentment and tension clogging counterterrorism information-sharing channels, affecting what *would* happen in various scenarios. The "need to know" mentality still seems to outweigh the "need to share" mentality. Petty inter-agency jealousies seem to remain, as evidenced most recently between the FBI and the NYPD (whose counterterrorism chief is a former CIA official) in the Najibullah Zazi case.[27] Local agencies still think of information sharing as a one-way experience, lacking confidence that state police, fusion centers, or federal agencies will share information with local agencies and officials when they should.

At the state level, it seems absolutely essential in the new information sharing environment that fusion centers learn to function as state-wide entities rather than state police entities. In the former mode, they stand a chance of being perceived as serving all agencies in the state, and if they in fact disseminate useful information and products to all agencies, they should become critical assets for both intra-state and national information sharing.[28] On the other hand, if they come to be seen as glorified state police units serving state police interests first and foremost, then they will provide little added value and will not substantially improve information sharing. Local agencies will tend not to participate, they will create their own fusion centers when possible, and they will continue to create their own individual relationships with federal agencies in an ad hoc manner. This seems to be a very crucial distinction that is still being worked out around the country, with no guarantee of success.

Beyond the state level, it is interesting that only two of the respondents consistently referred to the NCTC and information sharing environment throughout the scenarios, and none referred to the ITACG. The NCTC was established in 2004 and includes federal law enforcement agencies, national intelligence agencies, and the military among its partner organizations. As described on the NCTC website:

> NCTC serves as the primary organization in the United States Government for integrating and analyzing all intelligence pertaining to terrorism possessed or acquired by the United States Government (except purely domestic terrorism); serves as the central and shared knowledge bank on terrorism information; [and] provides all-source intelligence support to government-wide counterterrorism activities.[29]

The NCTC is assisted by the ITACG, which specifically represents the interests of state and local law enforcement and related officials. Its purpose is to enable and facilitate the production of "federally-coordinated" terrorism-related information and products that are shared "through existing channels" with state and local agencies. The ITACG is billed as a temporary step in coordinating federal law enforcement and national intelligence communication with state and local agencies, "until such time as the ISE matures organizationally and culturally to satisfy those needs as a normal part of doing business."

Together, these new entities, along with the 2007 *National Strategy for Information Sharing* and the *Intelligence Community Information Sharing Strategy,*[30] are supposed to assure that terrorism-related information and intelligence are shared more effectively among all the counterterrorism players, including state and local police, federal law enforcement, federal and state homeland security operations, the national intelligence community, and the military. The fact that much of this new architecture and strategy was not cited by most project respondents may reflect its newness, or it may indicate that old habits have yet to be replaced by new ones.[31]

Recommendations

This small exploratory study is not a firm foundation from which to offer any strong recommendations for improving intelligence and information sharing. Moreover, the complexity of the inter-organizational environment of law enforcement-related and homeland security-related information sharing is daunting, comprised as it is of thousands of local, state, and federal agencies, plus the military. One would be hard pressed to design a more complicated or challenging system. Fundamentally, of course, it is a system intended to limit the power of the government rather than maximize its effectiveness.

A 2001 Government Accountability Office (GAO) report on information sharing for critical infrastructure protection emphasized the importance of building trust between officials and agencies.[32] Recommended techniques for building trust included regular interaction, consistent representation, appropriate vetting of participants, creation of an atmosphere of mutual respect, and enforcement of information sharing norms. Additional recommendations included timely and secure communication, top management support, leadership continuity, penalties for failing to share information, and rewards for sharing.

Beyond these basic principles, a few specific intelligence-sharing suggestions can be offered:

- State fusion centers have to figure out how to serve their entire state, not just the state police. DHS might insist that these centers have governing boards with majority local representatives. That would help get local law enforcement buy-in and participation. State police could still house or run the centers, but they would have to be responsive to local interests in order to maintain the support of their governing board.
- Model agreements between local law enforcement agencies and state fusion centers should be developed and implemented. These agreements could stipulate that the local agency will complete and submit SAR in a systematic and timely manner, but also mandate the fusion center to report back on SAR utilization and generally obligate the fusion center to operate on a "need to share" basis.
- All agencies should adopt the "tear line" practice as a means of implementing "need to share." This practice puts non-classified information found in intelligence reports below a "tear line" so that it can be disseminated more quickly and more broadly. Information that would compromise intelligence sources and methods remains "above the tear line" and still does not get disseminated except to qualified recipients who "need to know."
- JTTF meetings need to be held with reasonable frequency to keep local chiefs and commanders in the intelligence loop and to build and maintain the trust needed to encourage information sharing. If these meetings are held frequently, and if "need to share" is the operating philosophy, then local law enforcement suspicion and resentment can easily be minimized.

As simplistic as some of these recommendations sound, they would probably be sufficient to resolve much of the gridlock associated with local law enforcement's participation in counterterrorism intelligence and information sharing. That is because, with the exception of the NYPD and a very few other big city agencies, local police agencies do not see themselves in competition with each other or with state and federal agencies in the intelligence game. Most of them would like to play their role and do their part, as long as state and federal agencies cooperate and treat them fairly.

At the federal level, the situation is different. Federal law enforcement and intelligence agencies often do seem to regard each other as the competition. They also seem to regard local law enforcement agencies as inferior or perhaps untrustworthy (or, in the case of the NYPD, as competition). Beyond systematic and persistent efforts at trust building, forceful action by the president, attorney general, DHS secretary, and Congress would seem necessary to overcome longstanding traditions and the political/bureaucratic pathologies that currently inhibit significant improvement in information sharing among the heavyweight agencies in the national intelligence community, and between those agencies and their more humble counterparts in state and local law enforcement.

Gary Cordner *is professor of criminal justice at Kutztown University in Pennsylvania and a commissioner with the Commission on Accreditation for Law Enforcement Agencies (CALEA). Previously, he was police chief in St. Michaels, Maryland and Dean of the College of Justice & Safety at Eastern Kentucky University. Dr. Cordner earned his PhD from Michigan State University. He may be contacted at cordner@kutztown.edu.*

Kathryn Scarborough *is on leave from her position as professor in the Department of Security, Safety, and Emergency Management at Eastern Kentucky University. She is co-author of textbooks on police administration and women in law enforcement and has directed several projects focused on law enforcement technology, cyber crime, and police intelligence. Dr. Scarborough worked as a police officer in Virginia and earned her PhD in criminal justice from Sam Houston State University.*

Acknowledgments: This article is derived from a study funded by the Homeland Security Defense Education Consortium (now the Homeland Security Defense Education Consortium Association). Any errors or misrepresentations in the paper are solely the responsibility of the authors. Points of view expressed in the paper are the authors' and do not represent the views of HSDEC or the Department of Defense. The authors are grateful for the support of HSDEC and specifically for encouragement and assistance provided by Houston Polson and Lance Robinson.

Notes

1. Gary Cordner and Kathryn Scarborough, "Connecting Police Intelligence with Military and National Intelligence," in Keith Logan, ed., *Homeland Security and Intelligence* (New York: Praeger, forthcoming 2010).
2. The terms "police" and "law enforcement" are used interchangeably in this article. Neither is meant to exclude sheriffs/deputy sheriffs, sworn investigators, or other similar officials.
3. Brian A. Reaves, *Census of State and Local Law Enforcement Agencies* (Washington, DC: Bureau of Justice Statistics, 2007), http://www.ojp.usdog.gov/bjjs/pub/pdf/csllea04.pdf.

4. The relative strength and roles played by municipal police, sheriffs, state police, and federal law enforcement vary from state to state. Louisiana is the most sheriff-dominated state (sheriffs as a proportion of all police), Delaware is the most state police dominant, and Arizona is the most federal law enforcement dominant. See Gary Cordner, "The Architecture of U.S. Policing: Variations Among the 50 States," *Police Practice and Research: An international Journal* (forthcoming, 2010) for more detailed description of this variation.
5. Half of the 18,000 police agencies in the United States have ten or fewer sworn officers.
6. Federal and/or state law sometimes assigns lead responsibilities and specific jurisdictions, as in the case of National Special Security Events (NSSEs). In most cases, though, the law does not specify who is in charge, and the relative standing of various agencies with concurrent jurisdiction is unspecified or at least ambiguous.
7. Peter K. Manning, "Information Technologies and the Police," in Michael Tonry and Norval Morris, eds., *Modern Policing* (Chicago: University of Chicago Press, 1992), 370.
8. David L. Carter, *Law Enforcement Intelligence: A Guide for State, Local, and Tribal Law Enforcement Agencies* (Washington, DC: Office of Community Oriented Policing Services, 2004).
9. "Reopen SFPD's Intelligence-Gathering Unit," *San Francisco Examiner,* October 15, 2009, http://www.sfexaminer.com/opinion/Examiner-Editorial-Reopen-SFPDs-intelligence-gathering-unit-64317377.html#.
10. Jerry H. Ratcliffe, *Intelligence-Led Policing* (Devon, UK: Willan Publishing, 2008).
11. Lydia Khalil, "Is New York a Counterterrorism Model?" *Expert Brief* (New York: Council on ForeignRelations, September 10, 2009), http://www.cfr.org/publication/20174/counterterror model in progress.html?breadcrumb=%2F; "NYPD Holds Security Briefing Ahead of High Holy Days," New York Police Department Press Release, September 14, 2009, http://www.nyc.gov/html/nypd/html/pr/pr 2009 ph22.shtml; Sullivan, John P. Sullivan and James J. Wirtz, "Global Metropolitan Policing: An Emerging Trend in Intelligence Sharing," *Homeland Security Affairs* 5, no. 2 (May 2009), http: //www.hsaj.org/?fullarticle=5.2.4.
12. Bureau of Justice Assistance (BJA), *Nationwide Suspicious Activity Reporting (SAR) Initiative* (Washington, DC: Bureau of Justice Assistance, 2009), http://www.iacptechnology.org/LEIM/2009Presentations/Nationwide%20SAR%20Initiative.pdf
13. John Rollins and Timothy Connors, "State Fusion Center Processes and Procedures: Best Practices and Recommendations," *Policing Terrorism Report No. 2* (New York: Manhattan Institute for PolicyResearch, 2007), http://www.manhattan-institute.org/html/ptr 02.htm.
14. U.S. Department of Homeland Security, "DHS Announces New Information-Sharing Tool to HelpFusion Centers Combat Terrorism," Press Release, September 14, 2009, http://www.dhs.gov/ynews/releases/pr 12.52955298184.shtm.
15. Chad Foster and Gary Cordner, *The impact of Terrorism on State Law Enforcement: Adjusting to New Roles and changing conditions* (Lexington, KY: Council of State Governments, 2005).
16. ISE, *Information Sharing Environment* (2008), http://www.ise.gov/; White House, *National Strategy for information Sharing: Successes and challenges in improving*

Terrorism-Related information Sharing (washington, DC: white House, 2007), http://www.whitehouse.gov/nsc/infosharing/NSIS book.pdf.

17. Kevin D. Eack, "State and Local Fusion Centers: Emerging Trends and Issues," *Homeland Security Affairs,* Supplement No. 2 (2008), http://www.hsaj.org/pages/supplement/issue2/pdfs/supplement.2.3.pdf; Jerry Markon, "FBI, ATF Battle for Control of Cases," *The Washington Post,* May 10, 2008, http://www.washingtonpost.com/wp-dyn/content/article/2008/05/09/AR2008050903096.html; Richard B. Schmitt, "FBI is Called Slow to Join the Terrorism Fight," *Los Angeles Times,* May 9, 2008, http://www.latimes.com/news/nationworld/nation/la-na-intel9-2008may09,0,7865641.story; Nancy Bernkopf Tucker, "The Cultural Revolution in Intelligence: Interim Report," *The Washington Quarterly* (Spring 2008): 47–61.
18. Carter, *Law Enforcement intelligence.*
19. Police Executive Research Forum (PERF), *Local Law Enforcement's Role in Preventing and Responding to Terrorism* (washington, DC: Police Executive Research Forum, 2001), http://www.policeforum.org/upload/terrorismfinal%5B1%5D 715866088 12302005135139.pdf; Matthew Scheider and Robert Chapman, "Community Policing and Terrorism," *Journal of Homeland Security* (April 2003), http://www.homelandsecurity.org/newjournal/articles/scheider-chapman.html; International Association of Chiefs of Police (IACP), *From Hometown Security to Homeland Security* (Alexandria, VA: International Association of Chiefs of Police, 2005), http://www.theiacp.org/leg policy/HomelandSecurityWP.PDF.
20. George L. Kelling and William J. Bratton, "Policing Terrorism," *Civic Bulletin* No. 43 (New York: Manhattan Institute for Policy Research, 2006), http://www.manhattan-institute.org/html/cb 43.htm.
21. White House, *National Strategy for Information Sharing,* 10.
22. Devlin Barrett, "Law Enforcement Feuding Persists: Efforts to End FBI-ATF Disputes Unsuccessful, Mueller Says," *The Washington Post,* September 17, 2009, http://www.washingtonpost.com/wp-dyn/content/article/2009/09/16/AR2009091603211.html; Theo Emery, "It's Official: The ATF and the FBI Don't Get Along," *Time,* October 24, 2009, http://www.time.com/time/nation/article/0,8599,1932091,00.html.
23. The term "state police" is used to refer to each state's primary state law enforcement agency. Actual names include state police, state patrol, highway patrol, and department of public safety. The jurisdiction and responsibility of these agencies varies from state to state. See Foster and Cordner, *The impact of Terrorism.*
24. Eack, "State and Local Fusion Centers."
25. ISE, *information Sharing Environment.*
26. Kelling and Bratton, "Policing Terrorism."
27. Michael A. Sheehan, "The Hatfields and McCoys of Counterterrorism," *The New York Times,* September 26, 2009, http://www.nytimes.com/2009/09/27/opinion/27sheehan.html? r=1&th&emc=th.
28. Rollins and Connors, "State Fusion Center Processes and Procedures;" Eileen R. Larence, "Federal Efforts Are Helping to Address Some Challenges Faced By State and Local Fusion Centers," Testimony before the Ad Hoc Subcommittee on State, Local, and Private Sector Preparedness and Integration, Committee on Homeland security and Governmental Affairs, U.S. Senate, GAO-08-636T (Washington, DC: Government Accountability Office, 2008).

29. Information available at http://www.nctc.gov/.
30. Director of National Intelligence, *Intelligence Community Information Sharing Strategy* (Washington, DC: Office of the Director of National Intelligence, 2008), http://www.dni.gov/reports/IC Information Sharing Strategy.pdf.
31. Schmitt, "FBI is Called Slow to Joint the Terrorism Fight"; Tucker, "The Cultural Revolution in Intelligence."
32. Government Accountability Office (GAO), *information Sharing: Practices That can Benefit critical infrastructure Protection,* GAO-02-24 (washington, DC: GAO, 2001), http://www.gao.gov/new.items/d0224.pdf. The authors are indebted to one of *Homeland Security Affairs'* manuscript reviewers for suggesting this source.

Catastrophic Terrorism

Local Response to a National Threat

Frank Keating

In June of 2001, I had the honor of taking the role of a state governor in an exercise that simulated the intentional release of the deadly virus smallpox in three U.S. cities. During the simulated thirteen days of the game, titled *Dark Winter*, the disease spread to 25 states and 15 other countries. Fourteen participants playing roles—including that of the president, the National Security Council, and a seated Governor (played by me)—and 60 observers witnessed terror warfare in slow motion. Discussions, debates, and decisions focused on the public health response, lack of an adequate supply of smallpox vaccine, roles and missions of federal and state governments, civil liberties associated with quarantine and isolation, the role of the Department of Defense, and potential military responses to the anonymous attack. The scenario of that exercise was different from the real-life crisis we faced in Oklahoma on April 19, 1995, but the fundamental principles were the same. In both instances, our tasks as leaders of local, state, and federal agencies were to respond to a terrorist assault in ways that protected and preserved lives and property, ensured accountability and justice for those responsible for the attack, and protected the national security. I was honored to share my own experiences from Oklahoma City with the group, and I am equally honored to share my perspective with the American public.

In that respect, I want to review briefly what happened in Oklahoma City in 1995 and then relate the lessons we learned there to the experiences we shared at the *Dark Winter* exercise and to the issues surrounding an incident of this magnitude.

You will recall that a massive terror bomb was detonated at 9:02 a.m. on April 19, 1995, in front of the Alfred P. Murrah Federal Office Building in the heart of our community. It killed 168 people, injured hundreds more, and severely damaged many dozens of buildings. The rescue and recovery efforts that followed, along with the criminal investigation, were the most massive of their kind in American history. These efforts threw together, literally overnight, more separate agencies from the local, state, and federal governments than had ever worked cooperatively on a single task. The outcome could have been chaotic—it has been before when far fewer agencies tried to coordinate their efforts on much more discrete and manageable tasks. But the outcome in Oklahoma City was not chaos. Later, observers would coin the label "The Oklahoma Standard" to refer to the way our city, state, and nation came together in response to this despicable act.

I think that what happened in Oklahoma City in 1995 served as a model for the *Dark Winter* participants, and I believe it should also help guide the deliberations on a national policy for responding to catastrophic events on the American homeland. Simply put, we did it right in 1995. The principles behind the Oklahoma Standard can help govern our nation's future course in responding to the terrorist threat.

On April 19, 1995, every injured person was cared for promptly and with great skill and compassion—in fact, at the closest hospital to the blast site, every arriving ambulance was met by an individual physician assigned to a specific victim. Of several dozen victims deemed critically injured on that day, only one who made it to the hospital alive subsequently died.

Every deceased victim was recovered, and all remains were restored to the families for burial, promptly and with great sensitivity.

Key evidence that would lead to the apprehension, conviction and eventual execution of the primary perpetrator of the crime was in law enforcement hands within minutes after the explosion. A local deputy sheriff found and recorded the serial number from the bomber's vehicle at almost the same moment that a state trooper was arresting the suspect some miles away. The criminal case built over the next few weeks was simply overwhelming. It assured our victims, and our society, of justice.

Finally, our national security was protected. In the months and years after the Oklahoma City bombing, local and federal authorities directed new attention to potentially dangerous domestic insurgent groups, defusing a number of similar terrorist plots before anyone was hurt. Congress also passed stronger antiterrorism legislation.

The *Dark Winter* scenario involved a foreign source of terrorism, not one of our own citizens. In *Dark Winter*, the weapon was bacterial rather than explosive. But in virtually every other respect, these two scenarios shared these key goals and principles:

- To protect, preserve, and save lives and property
- To hold accountable those responsible for terrorism
- To protect and advance America's interests and security

Those are the three fundamental challenges presented by any terrorist attack, from a bomb to a biological assault to the nightmare of a clandestine nuclear confrontation. I think it is instructive to compare how we pursued those goals in Oklahoma City with the outcomes of the *Dark Winter* scenario and to look at how that comparison might reflect on future policy.

The conclusions drawn by a series of after-action analyses from Oklahoma City are remarkably similar. I will consolidate those conclusions into five basic findings, compare them to what we did (or did not do) at *Dark Winter*, and suggest resulting policy implications:

The Local Response

Recognize that in virtually every possible terrorism scenario, first responders will be local. In Oklahoma City, the true heavy lifting of the initial rescue and recovery operations, as well as the key evidence collection that led to a successful criminal prosecution, was the task of local fire, police, and emergency medical personnel. In fact, the real first responders were not even public employees; they were bystanders and co-workers of the trapped and injured, who often shrugged off their own injuries and got up out of the rubble to help others. The first Federal Emergency Management Agency (FEMA) Urban Search and Rescue Task Force did not reach Oklahoma City until late on the night of April 19—several hours after the last living victim had been extracted from the wrecked building. That task force, and the ten that followed it, were absolutely essential to the successful recovery operations that followed, but it is important to note that even those FEMA Urban Search and Rescue Task Forces are drawn from local police and fire departments.

As an example, many of those task forces brought structural engineers to Oklahoma. They were able to work closely in planning the search and recovery operation with the local architect who had designed and built the Murrah Building in the 1970s. Who was better prepared and qualified for this crucial task? Neither party was; it was a true cooperative effort, blending federal and local resources to achieve outstanding results that allowed many hundreds of rescue workers to labor around the clock in a devastated and unstable structure without serious injury to any of those involved.

In the *Dark Winter* scenario, as in virtually any real-world terrorist assault, the first responders will also be local. The federal government does not maintain rapid response teams in any area of expertise close enough to any potential terrorist target, save perhaps the White House, to allow them to be first on the scene. In *Dark Winter*, local private physicians and public health officials were the first to detect cases of smallpox. Local government and law enforcement agencies were the ones with the power to impose and enforce quarantines, curfews, and states of martial law, to disseminate information through local media, and to collate and forward epidemiological data to federal agencies such as the Centers for Disease Control in Atlanta. Local law enforcement would be the ones to discover, preserve, and secure any available crime scenes or evidence. As in Oklahoma City, the preponderance of personnel, vehicles, equipment and even the volunteer force of blood donors, Salvation Army canteen operators, and the people who showed up to do laundry for the FEMA Urban Search and Rescue Task Force members will necessarily be drawn from local resources.

Teamwork

Insist that teamwork is not just desirable—it is possible. The after-action reports from Oklahoma City noted that agencies from various levels and jurisdictions that had not traditionally worked closely in the past did so to a remarkable extent at the Murrah Building site, and in the ensuing criminal investigation. They even did so in overcoming what was a huge potential initial hurdle—the conflicting purposes of those who were working through the rubble to extract the dead and those who saw the same rubble pile as a vast crime scene to be processed for evidence.

This is not to say that there were no conflicts. There were, but they were resolved, in virtually every case, to the mutual satisfaction of all of those concerned. We have seen too many cases in the past where an investigative agency or a rescue unit squabbled in private (and sometimes in public) over "my crime scene" or "our rescue mission." That this natural source of conflict did not overwhelm or dissipate the Oklahoma City effort is a tribute to the good sense and reason of those involved.

The one central problem that emerged in Oklahoma City was that of communications. From the first response through the final body recovery, it was noted that the many radio frequencies and institutional policies in play all too often left many participants in the effort in the dark concerning vital decisions that should have been shared universally. This was remedied in part—but only in part—by the creation of a unified command center, which invited key representatives from all the agencies involved to frequent information briefings and discussions on tactics.

Ironically, local agencies were in some ways better equipped to overcome this communications gap than their federal counterparts, thanks to a quirk of geography. Because central Oklahoma is located dead center in what is called "tornado alley," our public safety and emergency medical agencies had planned and even drilled for a mass-casualty incident in the past. They had on hand mobile command posts with some (though not all) interlocking radio capabilities. They also had the distinct advantages of familiarity with each other's basic operating procedures, local geography, even which local companies might be able to bring a large crane to the site on that first night to begin the search for buried victims. Time after time, I saw federal officials turn to local fire and police personnel and ask for assistance that only they could give.

I want to encourage the readers of this chapter, and the general public, to visit the Oklahoma City National Memorial Institute for the Prevention of Terrorism (www.mipt.org), which was a direct outgrowth of our experiences in Oklahoma City and a co-sponsor of the *Dark Winter* exercise. No one has more information drawn directly from field experience of how to blend the many levels of responders in as seamless a way as possible to react to a terrorist attack.

Information Assurance

The rapid and accurate flow of information—both internally among government agencies and externally to the public—is absolutely essential. Because the Murrah Building was located in downtown Oklahoma City, for all to see, we immediately stumbled into the right answer to the eternal question "How much do we tell the public?" That answer is simple—We tell them everything that does not need to be safeguarded for valid reasons of security.

I know you will all recall the steady, 24-hour broadcasts and news dispatches that came from Oklahoma City in the first days after the 1995 bombing. Our policy was to conduct regular media briefings on everything from body counts to alerts involving the composite drawings of the principal suspects in the bombing, and the results were in virtually all cases positive. Certainly many aspects of the criminal investigation were not disclosed in those early days. The Oklahoma City Fire Department and the Office of the Chief Medical Examiner carefully controlled release of information concerning the dead to ensure that families were fully notified before victim identities were made public. We did not allow open media access to the interior site itself for reasons of safety and efficiency. But in almost every other instance, our decision was in favor of openness and candor, and the results are very clear. I continue to receive letters, more than six years later, from Americans who have a permanently positive impression of how the bombing was handled.

In the *Dark Winter* exercise, many decisions concerning the release of information went in a different direction. From my own service in Washington, I know there exists an instinct for secrecy, an urge to classify, that often bears little relation to the realities of the moment. This happened in *Dark Winter* too. I believe that was, and is, a mistake, especially in a situation where bioterrorism was involved. Americans expect and deserve to be told the truth by government at all levels when their safety is at stake. Certainly I do not counsel revealing matters that would endanger national security or ongoing criminal investigations, but when the question is one between candor and secrecy in a matter of enormous public interest, and absent a clear and compelling reason for secrecy, candor should be the chosen option.

Our *Dark Winter* participants too often opted to conceal or obscure where openness would have done no harm—and where it would have increased public confidence. To cite a clear and compelling example of why this is true, contrast the high public approval of the FBI's successful identification and prosecution of Timothy McVeigh in the Oklahoma City bombing with the Bureau's present image problems related, in large part, to inept handling of documentation in that case. Simply put, the FBI was remarkably open—and praised—as it identified, caught, and prosecuted McVeigh; it was closed, and justifiably mistrusted, when it misplaced the files.

Government at all levels earns the trust of those it serves every day. It does not merit that trust if it is overly secretive.

Using Experts

Experts are called experts for a reason—rely on them. In Oklahoma City, the agency best equipped to handle the removal, identification, and processing of the 168 people killed in the bombing was the Office of the Chief Medical Examiner, which did an outstanding job. I recall at least one federal official with some experience in mass-casualty incidents assuring the staff from the medical examiner's office that they would "never" be able to identify all the victims. In fact, they did so, with vast cooperation from local funeral directors, dentists, physicians, and many others who worked countless hours at a most heartrending and often distasteful task. They were the experts, and they did their job well.

That was also true of the crane operators who helped remove the rubble, the federal agents who identified the explosive components, and many others. People work for many years to acquire skills; agencies involved in responding to a terrorist attack should let them do their jobs.

In *Dark Winter*, the obvious agency with the expertise to isolate and identify the smallpox microorganism was the Centers for Disease Control in Atlanta. The experts in potential delivery systems were chemists and physicists. Those best equipped to identify Iraqi origins for the terrorist act were from the intelligence field.

Conversely, those best qualified to assess what (and how) information is to be publicly released are the communications professionals. When a building is badly damaged by a bomb, engineers and architects play a central role; when germs are released on the public, doctors must be involved. In responding to any terrorist attack, supervising agencies should rely on the experts in their respective fields, and not seek to concentrate decision-making powers above and removed from the level where those experts can be heard.

Federal vs. Local Responses

Resist the urge to federalize everything. Perhaps the strongest lesson from Oklahoma City—and perhaps the most worrisome outcome from the *Dark Winter* exercise—concerns the almost instinctive urge common to officials of federal agencies and the military to open the federal umbrella over any and all functions or activities. Simply put, the federal government all too often acts like the 500-pound gorilla.

In *Dark Winter*, we encountered this tendency as soon as state National Guard units were activated in response to the bioterrorist attack. The functions of those units—imposing curfews and quarantines and keeping public peace—were exclusively local. Still, many of the participants sought to call the Guard into federal service immediately. I want to thank Senator Nunn, who played the role of the president in the exercise, for resisting this temptation and deciding not to federalize the Guard.

Federalizing makes sense when the mission is largely federal—for example, a combat environment or an overseas deployment—but not when the mission remains largely local. I noted that I failed to see how a National Guard company, led by a local captain and staffed by local residents who had assembled at the local armory for duty, would perform in any different manner if it were formally inducted into federal service. My experience following the Oklahoma City bombing was that members of the Oklahoma Army and Air National Guards called to service did an excellent job under state control. In fact, the very first makeshift memorial to the dead was created near the Murrah Building site, along a security fence line, by Air Guard personnel who were mourning the deaths of their neighbors. The Guard blended well with other agencies, both local and federal. Its members took special pride in serving their Oklahoma neighbors as members of the *Oklahoma* Guard.

Certainly if a Guard formation cannot perform well, or if it requires specialized training or equipment to discharge its role in response to a terrorist incident, it should be promptly federalized. Equally surely, many components of the national response to an attack like that proposed in *Dark Winter* must be largely federal—from the gathering of intelligence that pointed to an Iraqi connection to the formulation for diplomatic and military responses. But that does not mean that every part of the broad response must or should originate at the federal level, or that federal officials should assume supremacy in every aspect of the response, or that the military response should trump the humanitarian response. It was a deputy sheriff who jotted down the number from a mangled truck axle that, ultimately, brought McVeigh to justice. It was a surgeon from a state hospital who crawled into the Murrah rubble to amputate a trapped victim's leg as local police officers and firefighters held lights and moved obstacles. Oklahomans carried the first injured out of the building on April 19, and three weeks later they recovered the last of the dead. They continue to staff mental health and counseling services—funded in part by federal sources—to help with the healing.

Conclusion

My experiences in Oklahoma City in 1995, and my participation in *Dark Winter* this year, both taught me some valuable lessons:

- Train and equip your first responders, for they are the front line in meeting the terrorist threat
- Search for ways to support teamwork *before* an incident, and emphasize that teamwork after
- Tell the truth, and be candid with the people we are working to protect and serve
- Trust the experts to do what they know best

And remember that the response to terrorism does not begin and end in Washington. Trust local governments, local agencies, and local citizens to do the right thing, because in the end, they are the real targets of terrorism, whether it's a bomb in front of a building filled with ordinary Americans or a germ unleashed on their neighbors.

Critical Thinking Questions

1. What kinds of efforts are essential for local municipalities to prepare for an effective response to a terrorist attack?
2. Both Gov. Keating and the 9/11 Commission Report describe communication challenges as undermining the effectiveness of first responders. Do these challenges persist, or have we derived and implemented lessons learned?
3. Is it truly the case, as Gov. Keating suggests, that local and state agencies share as much information with the public as they can, while at the federal level there is an emphasis on constraining information? Why or why not?

State and Local Fusion Centers

Emerging Trends and Issues

Kevin D. Eack

Introduction

The proliferation of state and local fusion centers and the efforts to partner them with the intelligence community have been compared to organizing a new little league baseball team. Just as each team in a league has different strengths and weaknesses each center has a different set of skills, abilities, and equipment.[1] This paper provides a brief overview of the present status of state and local fusion centers, as well as the current policy issues and obstacles these centers face.

Counter Terrorism: Not a New Mission for State and Local Law Enforcement

Combating terrorism in the United States is not a new concept for state and local law enforcement. There are a number of examples where state and local law enforcement have played a key role in detecting terrorist activity. A simple traffic stop of a subject on April 19, 1995, by an Oklahoma state trooper, for driving a vehicle without a license plate resulted in the arrest of Timothy McVeigh for the bombing of the Alfred P. Murrah Federal Building.[2] On May 31, 2003, a local patrolman arrested the notorious Eric Robert Rudolph, a domestic terrorist who was on the Federal Bureau of Investigation's (FBI) Ten Most Wanted List for a series of bombings including one at the 1996 Olympics. Rudolph was the subject of a tenacious manhunt in the Appalachian Mountains for several years before being arrested by a local police officer on routine patrol in the small town of Murphy, North Carolina. Rudolph specifically targeted police and other first responders with secondary devices in some of his bombings.[3] On April 4, 1980, the deadly Fuerzas Armadas de Liberacion Nacional (FALN), a small, heavily armed terrorist organization responsible for over 100 bombings in major cities including Chicago, New York, and Miami suffered its most serious setback when its members were arrested by patrolmen in Evanston, Illinois, as they assembled in a park with several stolen vehicles, thirteen weapons, disguises, and false identifications, preparing to heist an armored truck at the prestigious Northwestern University.[4]

Intelligence Not New to State and Local Law Enforcement

While the concept of "fusion centers" is certainly new, many states have had a centralized intelligence system of some sort for decades. Typically, these have been housed in state police agencies, as a central repository on intelligence related to violent gangs, drug trafficking, prostitution, child exploitation, weapons smuggling, theft rings, and other crimes. In those states with a major city or county police department (such as New York, Los Angeles and Chicago) those agencies have also operated intelligence units. For many states today's fusion center is simply an extension of these intelligence units, with a higher degree of vertical (federal intelligence community) and horizontal (state/local) collaboration. Some have compared today's fusion centers with "state police intelligence units on steroids."[5]

What is new is the mission of preventing international terrorist attacks on U.S. soil and law enforcement is adjusting to a new enemy with new methods. Law enforcement organizations are also adjusting to new operational issues that were previously not areas of concern. According to Congressional testimony these include:

1. The absence of a cohesive federal strategy regarding information sharing,
2. Too many federal information sharing networks, and
3. An inability or unwillingness on the part of the Department of Homeland Security (DHS) and the FBI to work effectively together.[6]

One example of an obstacle created by the lack of coordination between DHS and the FBI is security clearances. State and local fusion centers are required to have security clearances in order to receive, analyze, store, and disseminate classified material. Yet, in many cases it is reported the FBI is unwilling to accept those with DHS security clearances. In still other cases, DHS requires verification that someone from a state or major city possesses an FBI clearance through a process where the clearance is "passed" or certified to DHS from the FBI. Such problems can prove frustrating to state and local partners who are doing all they can to perform their role in homeland security.[7]

Another example is the apparent mission overlap between DHS and the FBI. A primary mission for many state and local fusion centers is collecting, analyzing, and disseminating critical infrastructure data to DHS. Since the creation of the department, DHS has conducted several data calls in order to populate the national critical infrastructure database. It also adopted the Automated Critical Asset Management Systems (ACAMS) system from the Los Angeles Police Department as a nationwide system to manage this data, urging state fusion centers to utilize this system.

Yet the FBI has continued to operate a critical infrastructure protection program of its own, called Infraguard, which is quite popular in some states among the private stakeholders. This presents a number of challenges for state and local fusion centers, which often find they are "caught in the middle," trying to show a cooperative spirit between both agencies while also trying to maintain credibility with their private stakeholders who own, operate, and have a vested interest in protection of critical infrastructure. Some in the private sector complain that the "federal government needs to get its act together" on this important issue soon, as its efforts appear to be disjointed and uncoordinated.[8]

State and local stakeholders who operate fusion centers are often frustrated with trying to provide the necessary information to both agencies. In order to be effective, fusion centers need to work with both the FBI and DHS; the FBI is a critical partner and DHS provides needed funding. According to one state fusion center commander, "we are anticipating this to be very challenging."[9]

As a recent Congressional report highlights, the evolution of state and local fusion centers leaves a number of looming issues.[10] One issue is that many state and local fusion centers are in some ways less familiar with civil liberties issues and the federal regulations regarding intelligence storage, handling, and dissemination. As a result, more privacy concerns are likely to develop due to unintentional violations of intelligence rules.

Fusion centers also face a number of long-term issues. Congress provided substantial resources to support the DHS grant program in the years following the 9/11 attacks. As time passes, such funding may taper off, leaving insufficient funding for fusion center operations.[11] As those who have opened and operated such centers know, while funding sources have varied widely from state to state the majority of states have leveraged homeland security funds for equipment and analysts, subject to certain limitations imposed by DHS.[12]

One of the most significant issues found in the Congressional research has been the absence of a well-defined long-term role for state and local fusion centers. According to testimony by Eileen Larence, Director of Homeland Security and Justice Issues

> The federal government has not clearly articulated the long term role it expects to play in sustaining fusion centers. It is critical for center management to know whether to expect continued federal resources, such as personnel and grant funding, since the federal government, through an information sharing environment, expects to rely on a nationwide network of centers to facilitate information sharing with state and local governments.[13]

According to Congressional findings, there are currently fifty-eight fusion centers at the state and local level. Forty-three are considered operational, while fifteen are in various stages of development. Nine centers opened shortly after the attacks of September 11, 2001. Thirty-four became operational after January, 2004. At least thirty-four fusion centers report employing federal personnel.[14]

While many efforts have been made by the federal government to support fusion centers, many fusion center officials report challenges accessing and managing multiple information systems. The FBI's Law Enforcement Online (LEO) system and the DHS Homeland Security Information Network (HSIN) are mentioned prominently in the Congressional reports. These multiple systems are reported to be causing "information overload" at many centers, often with redundant information.[15] To compound the problem, DHS continues to change the information-sharing platform, making it a challenge to establish stability among the fusion centers. Initially many fusion centers were operating on the Joint Regional Information Exchange System (JRIES), but then DHS directed they move to the HSIN system. Recent announcements suggest that platform will also soon be changing.[16]

For many fusion center officials at the state and local level, the single biggest concern is sustainability. Van Godsey, director of the Missouri Information and Analysis Center (MIAC) states it this way:

> With this tremendous focus on fusion centers, my concern is sustainability of these centers and the national effort. Currently, any federal funding for fusion centers is located within the federal allocation to the states. The use of these funds is subject to local demands, politics and views that may not always be supportive of the fusion center effort. If the federal government is going to look at the fusion centers and expect minimum capabilities, then I believe there are going to have to be controls to ensure a minimum level of funding.[17]

Godsey advocates specific line item funding for fusion centers instead of the present method of funding.[18]

As Congressional reports point out, ultimately the federal government needs to make a policy decision about the future of state and local fusion centers. As one report states, a number of questions need to be answered including the following:

1. Do fusion centers solve the pre-9/11 information sharing problems, and as such, make Americans safer?
2. Can fusion centers work if they aren't part of an integrated philosophy of intelligence and security?
3. Who benefits from fusion centers? Who should staff, fund, and oversee them? What role, if any, should fusion centers play in the Intelligence Community (IC)? What role should federal agencies play in fusion centers, to include funding?
4. Is some basic level of common standards necessary in order for fusion centers to offer a national benefit? Does the federal government have an integrated national fusion center strategy? How is their performance to be measured?
5. Is the current configuration of forty-plus fusion centers, with multiple centers in some states the most efficient way to structure them?[19]

2007 National Strategy for Information Sharing

The recent release of the *National Strategy for Information Sharing* in October, 2007, certainly supports earlier Congressional findings that more federal leadership with regard to fusion centers is needed.[20] Referencing Guideline 2 of the president's December 16, 2006 *Memorandum to Heads of Executive Departments and Agencies,* the strategy calls for a "common framework" to be developed governing the roles and responsibilities between the federal government, state, local, and tribal governments, and private sector entities.[21]

The strategy also acknowledges the important role of state and local fusion centers as follows: "State and major urban area fusion centers are vital assets critical to sharing information related to terrorism. They will serve as the primary focal points within the State and local environment for the receipt and sharing of terrorism-related information."[22]

The strategy also contemplates how state and local fusion centers may scrub and further disseminate classified terrorism-related intelligence to others in the region.

> Federal departments and agencies will provide terrorism-related information to State, local and tribal authorities primarily through these fusion centers. Unless specifically prohibited by law, or subject to security classification restrictions, these fusion centers may further customize such information for dissemination to satisfy intra- or inter State needs.[23]

Additionally, the *National Strategy* addresses the important issue of public and private collaboration to protect critical infrastructure. "This Strategy builds on these efforts to adopt an effective framework that ensures a two way flow of timely and actionable security information between public and private partners." It also acknowledges the sensitivity of critical infrastructure information provided by the private sector and the importance of maintaining the confidentiality of such data when it is provided to governmental units.[24]

Conclusion

With proper support and guidance of state and local fusion centers, one can easily imagine a time when the U.S. has a significantly stronger situational awareness within its borders than we presently have today. To be sure, there are many issues on the road ahead. Staffing, training, intelligence-handling procedures, benchmark capabilities, and sustained funding are among those issues. However, from the perspective of state and local fusion centers, great strides are being made in creating a lasting network across the nation through which terrorism-related threat intelligence can be effectively shared. In some cases that capability extends to "all crimes" and "all hazards." Those in the intelligence community who may have at first doubted these centers would ever play a role in our national security, now see these fusion centers gaining in strength and sophistication. In some cases, these centers are breaking new ground in the use of new and innovative methods for effective intelligence collection, analysis, and dissemination.[25] It is important to remember that state and local law enforcement have always had a public safety mission, dating back to the first county sheriffs. Given the tragic events of September 11, 2001, no one should underestimate the resolve and determination of state and local public safety agencies to do their part in keeping Americans safe.

Critical Thinking Questions

1. Do you agree with the author's assertion that the involvement of federal entities (like DHS and FBI) brought fewer benefits and more complications to previously established state and local intelligence analysis centers? Why or why not?
2. Have the capabilities and missions of state and local fusion centers changed during the recent economic recession? Why or why not?
3. If you were to design a training program to improve the effectiveness of a fusion center, what would it contain?

Notes

1. Matthew M. Johnson, "Number of Databases Bogging Down Fusion Centers," *Congressional Quarterly,* October 9, 2007, www.cq.com. See also General Accounting Office, *Federal Efforts Are Helping to Alleviate Some Challenges Encountered by State and Local Information Fusion Centers, GAO-08-35,* October 2007, http://www.gao.gov/new.items/d0835.pdf.
2. Trial testimony, http://www.law.umkc.edu/faculty/projects/ftrials/mcveigharrest.html.
3. Maryanne Vollers, "Lone Wolf, Eric Rudolph: Murder, Myth and the Pursuit of an American Outlaw," (Harper Collins, 2006); see also www.cnn.com/2003/us/05/31/rudolph.main/.
4. CBS News, April 7, 1980, http://openweb.tvnews.vanderbilt.edu/1980-4/1980-04-07-CBS-22.html.
5. Todd Masse and John Rollins, *A Summary of Fusion Centers: Core Issues and Options for Congress* (Congressional Research Service, September 19, 2007).
6. Johnson, "Number of Databases Bogging Down Fusion Centers." See also GAO, *Federal Efforts Are Helping to Alleviate Some Challenges.*

7. Interview with Major Monte McKee, Indiana Intelligence Fusion Center, November 26, 2007.
8. Interview with Michael Crane, co-chair of the Illinois Terrorism Task Force Private Sector Committee, and Vice President and General Counsel for IPC International, a private security firm whose clients include most major malls in the U.S., and those in four other countries, November 26, 2007.
9. Interview with Major Monte McKee.
10. Masse and Rollins, "A Summary of Fusion Centers."
11. Ibid.
12. Electronic survey of Midwest fusion center commanders by author, July 2007.
13. Testimony of Eileen R. Larence, September 27, 2007 Before the Subcommittee on Intelligence, Information Sharing and Terrorism Risk Assessment, Committee on Homeland Security, House of Representatives, GAO-07-1241T.
14. Ibid.
15. Ibid, 8.
16. Federal Computer Week, *DHS to Modify Info-Sharing Network,* January 21, 2008, http://fcw.com/online/news/151380-1.html.
17. Interview with Director Van Godsey, Missouri Information and Analysis Center, November 26, 2007.
18. Ibid.
19. Masse and Rollins, "A Summary of Fusion Centers," 4.
20. *National Strategy for Information Sharing, October 2007.* http://www.whitehouse.gov/nsc/infosharing.
21. Ibid, 17.
22. Ibid, 20.
23. Ibid, 21.
24. Ibid, 21.
25. Microsoft Corporation, *Microsoft and Illinois State Police Collaborate on Best Practices and Information Technology Architecture for Homeland Security Fusion Centers,* December 5, 2007, http://www.microsoft.com/presspass/press/2007/dec07/12-05MSILPolicePR.mspx.

Section 2.3

Fostering Resilience

Critical Transportation Infrastructure And Societal Resilience

Stephen E. Flynn and Sean P. Burke

I. Introduction

The key to assuring security, safety and prosperity in the 21st century will be possessing resilience in face of chronic and catastrophic risks. The years ahead will be marked by turbulence, fueled by unconventional conflict, likely changes in climate, and the sheer complexity and interdependencies of modern systems and networks. This places a premium on assuring that individuals, communities, and critical infrastructure have the capacity to withstand, respond, rapidly recover, and adapt to man-made and natural disturbances.

Building resilience requires a broad and sustained engagement of citizens, companies, and communities. For individuals and families, it requires a commitment to a greater degree of self-reliance. At the neighborhood and community level, it requires civic engagement and volunteerism. Businesses must recognize that their ability to operate in good times as well as bad is dependent on the capabilities of the communities that host them. Thus, close collaboration between the private and public sector becomes essential to the success of both.

Resilience building requires creating capabilities from the bottom-up. Concrete policy actions must be shaped by stakeholders from the private and public sectors, drawn primarily from outside the usual Washington, DC policy circles. This will require both a shift in approach and emphasis to the post-9/11 homeland response. The civilian population and private sector will need to be enlisted as full partners in strengthening societal and infrastructure resilience. This effort must be extended beyond the task of detecting and intercepting terrorists in advance of an attack. In the aftermath of the attacks of September 11, 2001, too little time and energy was assigned to the elements of homeland security most relevant to *resilience—protection, response,* and *recovery.* It was largely only due to pressure from Congress that DHS started to pay real attention to critical infrastructure protection. It was not until 2006 that the first "National Infrastructure Protection Plan" was issued—and the plan only established a process for setting priorities and provided a suggested action plan for protection activities.

When President Barack Obama came into office, he made a commitment to recraft the homeland security mission in important ways. First was to explicitly incorporate homeland security into national security; second, to broaden the focus of the homeland security mission to include natural and man-made disasters; and third to identify resilience as strategic element of homeland and national security.

One outcome of broadening the homeland security mission to include natural disasters and placing greater emphasis on resilience is that it has begun the process of recalibrating public expectations about the inherent limits of preventing all catastrophic risks, including the risk of terrorism. The U.S. government is powerless when it comes to preventing a hurricane, earthquake, or tornado. However, American society possesses the means to mitigate the consequences of these events, recover quickly, and adapt. In other words, the actions that are necessary to deal with natural disasters can also support building the kind of resilience that will make man-made threats far less consequential. By including natural disasters and other catastrophic risks, homeland security generally, and resilience specifically, becomes much more relevant to communities and companies.

To overlook the resilience imperative is to put in peril the future prosperity of the nation. When critical systems such as transportation and logistics do not have the robustness and nimbleness to recover, they present attractive targets for those who are intent on inflicting harm. This is because it offers America's current and potential adversaries a big potential destructive and disruptive bang for their buck. Furthermore, vulnerable systems amplify the deadly and costly consequences that can be wrought by natural disasters. Companies striving to be grow strong and prosperous and then remain so, don't stay in societies that are easy to knock down and slow to get up. These companies know that if they are a part of a supply chain or depend on one that lacks resilient elements, they will wither and die. So they move to safer harbors that can better assure business continuity. And people with the means to do so, will generally select to live in places that demonstrate a capacity to cope with chronic disruptions.

Given the benefits of resilience—and the direct and indirect risks associated with fragile communities and systems—it is very much in the interest of Americans to embrace it. This will require developing policies and incentives that encourage community resilience at the local level, and within and across networks and infrastructure sectors such as transportation at all levels. It also requires acknowledging that safety and security efforts that aim to eliminate risks will always reach a point of diminishing returns. In most cases, a more prudent and realistic investment is to manage risks by building the skills and capabilities to do three things: (1) maintain continuity of function in the face of chronic disturbances, (2) develop the means for graceful degradation of function when placed under severe stress, and (3) sustain the ability to quickly recover to a desired level of functionality when extreme events overwhelm mitigation measures.

An emphasis on resilience provides a compelling rationale for greater levels of cooperation and collaboration between the public and private sectors. When it comes to assuring the continuity of operations for essential systems and networks, the users, designers, operators, managers, and regulators all have a shared interest in infrastructure resilience and each has an important role to play. There should be no higher priority than engaging and integrating the multiplicity of parties into a common effort that ensures that society's critical foundations such as transportation are resilient.

The simple fact is that there never will be enough professionals at the right place at the right time when terrorists or disasters strike. The United States has vast transportation networks that operate at the local, state, regional, continental, and global levels. Intelligence and technologies are fallible and Mother Nature cannot be deterred. As appealing as it might be to leave security and emergency preparedness and response to professionals, when it comes to detecting and intercepting terrorist activities or dealing with a catastrophic natural event, the first preventers and first responders will almost always be civilians and system operators who by circumstance find themselves unwitting targets of terrorists or in the path of a disaster when it strikes.

II. A Counterterrorism Imperative

The tactical and strategic value of emphasizing resilience as a counterterrorism imperative has been reinforced by a report on "Assessing the Terrorist Threat" that was released on September 10, 2010 by the National Security Preparedness Group. The report highlights how the diversifying nature of the terrorist threat has been motivated in part by a growing recognition by al Qaeda and associated organizations that terrorist attacks on the West and especially the United States do not have to be spectacular or catastrophic to be effective. As the attempted bombing of Northwest Airlines Flight Number 563 on Christmas Day 2009 dramatically illustrated, even near-miss attacks can generate considerable political fallout and a rush to impose expensive and economically disruptive new protective measures. Since relatively small and unsophisticated attacks have the potential to generate such a big-bang for a relatively small investment, the bar can be lowered for recruiting terrorist operatives, including those who belong to the targeted societies.

A succession of recent cases that have come to light within the United States and elsewhere in the West has highlighted that terrorist radicalization and recruitment is indeed growing. The process of training is being facilitated by an increasing diverse array of global bases from which terrorist groups are operating. There seems no longer any clear profile of a terrorist. Moreover, the means through which many of these persons have been radicalized over the Internet, suggests that the ranks will continue to be filled by those who are drawn to radical causes from the privacy of their own homes. Among the newest operatives drawn from Western countries, the only common denominator appears to be a new found hatred for their native or adopted country; a degree of dangerous malleability; and a religious fervor justifying or legitimizing violence that impels these very impressionable and perhaps easily influenced individuals towards potentially highly lethal acts of violence.

The diversity of this array of recent terrorist recruits presents new challenges for intelligence and law enforcement agencies that are already over-stressed and inundated with information and leads, to run these new threats to ground. Sophisticated attacks such as those carried out on New York and Washington on September 11, 2001 require a larger group of operatives, communications with those overseeing the planning, and time to conduct surveillance and rehearse the attack. Money, identification documents, safe-houses for operatives, and other logistical needs have to be supported. All this effort ends up creating opportunities for detection and interception by intelligence and law enforcement officials.

Less sophisticated attacks on the other hand, particularly those being conducted by homegrown operatives and lone wolves are almost impossible to prevent. In the May 2010 bombing attempt on Times Square it was a sidewalk T-shirt vendor, not the NYPD patrolman sitting in a squad car directly across the street, who sounded the alarm about Faisal Shahzad's explosive-laden SUV. Shahzad was not in any federal or NYPD database that identified him as a suspected terrorist.

The October 2010 air cargo incident involving explosives hidden in ink cartridges shipped from Yemen is consistent with this trend towards smaller attacks, but with the added element of aspiring to create significant economic disruption. The would-be bombers had no way of knowing that the cartridges would end up on a commercial airliner with hundreds of passengers or a dedicated air cargo carrier with a small crew. That was not important since they understood that destroying any plane in midair would trigger U.S. officials and others to undertake an extremely costly and profoundly disruptive response that would undermine the movement of global air cargo.

Given that smaller-scale terrorist attacks are being motivated because they are harder to prevent and can yield a response by the targeted society that is extremely harmful to that society, it follows that there is tactical and strategic value from investing in the means to sustain critical functions and better respond to and rapidly recover from attacks when they occur. If attacks have limited potential to disrupt in any meaningful way critical infrastructure and networks such as transportation systems that support the movement of people and the flow of supply chains, those attacks become less attractive to cany out. In other words, when the United States demonstrates that it has the ability to withstand attacks without inflicting damage on the essential systems that underpin our economy and way of life, terrorism becomes a less attractive weapon for America's adversaries. Alternatively, a lack of resilience that results in unnecessary loss of life, destruction of property, and disruption of key networks and functions is reckless. It is also a strategic vulnerability in an era when non-state actors will continue to elect to wage their battles in the civil and economic space rather than the conventional military space.

III. Return on Investment

Most natural disasters and large-scale accidents are far more routine than people are generally willing to acknowledge. Individuals, community, and corporate leaders often convince themselves that disasters reside in the realm of chance and fate. But the reality is that the risk of disaster is generally predictable. In addition, the overwhelming costs associated with disasters are almost always associated with failures to prepare for them upfront. Losses and damages rise exponentially when risk mitigation measures that assure adequate robustness are not in place, when responses to disasters are poorly planned and executed, and when efforts to speed recovery and implement changes based on lessons learned receive too little attention.

Accordingly, while the danger that disasters will occur is inescapable, boosting resilience will always provide a positive return on investment. On a micro scale, it is far more cost effective to make an upfront investment in safeguards that mitigate risk and consequences, than to pay the price for response and recovery after a foreseeable hazard manifests itself. To illustrate this point, one need look no further than the *Deepwater Horizon* disaster in the Gulf of Mexico in 2010 where inadequate attention to preventative measures and lack of planning for dealing with the aftermath of what was widely viewed as a low probability event ended up leading to a massive ecological disaster and a significant disruption of the offshore drilling industry. The failure of the crucial emergency vents at the Fukushima Daiichi nuclear facility following the March 2011 earthquake and tsunami provides another compelling example. The hydrogen explosions that occurred after the loss of power rendered the vents inoperable triggered not just a local nuclear disaster. It also caused cascading consequences to international transportation networks, global supply chains, and the worldwide investment into new nuclear power plants.

From a macro standpoint, a society's level of resilience will increasingly be a source of its global competitiveness. The one thing that can be safely predicted with confidence is that the 21st century will be marked by major disruptions arising from man-made and natural threats. There is the risk of terrorist attacks, pandemics, earthquakes and volcanoes, and more frequent and destructive storms associated with climate change. In addition, as the world witnessed with the near meltdown of global financial markets in the fall of 2008 and the Japanese earthquake and tsunami in 2011, with increasingly complex and interdependent networks supporting modern global economic activity, problems in one part of the system can quickly have cascading consequences across the entire system. The countries, communities, and systems that are most able to manage these risks and bounce back quickly will be the places where people will want to live, work, and invest. Those that are so brittle that they break instead of bend in the face of familiar and emerging risks will become the national and global backwaters.

IV. Intermodal Transportation System & Supply Chain Security vs. Resilience

When resilience is the overarching strategic imperative, it generates a different assessment of risk, and highlights a wider range of solutions for dealing with that risk. Comparing the current assumptions and policy prescriptions associated with transportation security on the one hand, with the assumptions and optimal policy prescriptions for advancing transportation and supply chain resilience on the other, makes the case. Simply put, the security focus with respect to transportation and cargo can be boiled down to two concerns: (1) how transportation and logistics system might be used as a conduit for smuggling dangerous people and weapons, and (2) how planes, trains, and other conveyances might be targeted to kill and injure passengers, operators, and bystanders. Alternatively, resilience places an emphasis on the core function of transportation; i.e., to provide the mobility our economy and society requires in order to function and prosper. In other words, those who have been looking through a security lens have been largely seeing transportation as something a terrorist might exploit so as to endanger the lives of people. But when we shift to adopting a resilience lens, our focus ends up centering on the fact that transportation is a critical infrastructure whose continuity must be assured in the face of potential threats that would disrupt it.

In the immediate aftermath of the 9/11 attacks, the transportation security response was to ground aviation and divert international flights from U.S. airspace. Maritime traffic into New York and other seaports was halted, and many of the land border crossings were effectively closed due to the intensive vehicle inspection process immediately put in place. The effect was akin to a self-imposed embargo on the U.S. economy.[1]

There was a straightforward reason for the decision by Washington to throw the equivalent of a transportation "kill-switch" after the 9/11 attacks. Faced with tremendous uncertainty about the nature of the threat and possessing little confidence in the pre-9/11 checks that inspectors routinely used to screen passengers and cargo, the White House had few options. The hijacked passenger airliners were proof-positive that the passenger-screening process had failed and immediately placed that process along with inspection protocols for other transportation conveyances under scrutiny. Those operations and protocols did not hold up to critical review. As a consequence, new requirements were rushed into place, especially at airports, that were costly and disruptive. The added expense in time and resources associated with these new mandates was justified by the assertion that facilitating trade and travel must be "balanced" with the imperative of security.

On its face, the contention seems compelling that there is an inherent tension between advancing the requirements of security and advancing reliable and affordable mobility. Prior to 9/11, the security imperative was largely overlooked, so the scales presumably need to now be tipped in the direction of protecting the transportation system and its users from threats. But advancing both security and the functionality of transportation can and should be complementary. Since an act of sabotage on transportation infrastructure can mechanically undermine the function of a transportation system and dissuade people from using it, providing adequate security is clearly supportive of the goal of safeguarding the continuity of the mobility. But jeopardizing the purpose of transportation so as to better protect it makes no sense. When a threat to transportation infrastructure leads officials to take actions that are costly and disruptive, it can have the unintended consequence of actually elevating the security threat. This is because the goal of terrorism is to cause a reaction that is harmful to the targeted society. If every terrorist act or near-miss leads to new government measures that make transportation systems more inefficient, then an adversary gets a much bigger dividend than the actual attack could deliver. This fuels the incentive to cany out more of these attacks in the future. In other words, national security and homeland security are ultimately best advanced when primacy is assigned to safeguarding the important service that transportation infrastructure provides should it be attacked or exploited. The emphasis on resilience necessarily incorporates appropriate protection measures, but it does so in order to minimize the risk of disruption. The more resilient transportation systems become, the greater will be the deterrent for an adversary to target those systems.

There are significant policy implications associated with making transportation infrastructure resilience a strategic imperative. To begin with, it should compel a critical examination of current transportation security efforts, centered on three questions: First, are the protective measures unduly disruptive to the function being protected? An extreme example of this would be prohibiting all vehicles from using a bridge in order to protect the bridge from a potential act of sabotage. Second, will the protective measures be seen as credible following a major breach of security; i.e., will they survive a "morning-after-test" and be judged as reasonable safeguards given what we know about threat, vulnerability, and consequence? Or will they be assessed to be largely cosmetic, ill conceived, or woefully inadequate, leading the public to believe that the risks associated with using the system might outweigh its benefits? Third, should prevention and protection measures fail, are there adequate plans in place to rapidly respond and recover transportation systems in the aftermath of a major security incident?

An objective assessment of the current cargo security measures for the intermodal transportation system leads to three sobering conclusions. First, if these security measures were being fully implemented in strict accordance with current official agency protocols or as the law requires,* global supply chains would face considerable risk of disruption. Second, if put to the test, these measures will not survive the post-mortem assessment of their effectiveness. The public will be justifiably outraged that U.S. officials oversold the limited steps they have been taking while downplaying the ongoing vulnerability of the cargo system to being exploited and targeted by a determined adversary. The resultant collapse in public trust and recriminations will create a toxic political environment that could result in freezing portions or all of the intermodal transportation system until

* The position that Customs Border and Protection (CBP) has taken since the passage of the 2007 9/11 Recommendations Act is to publicly oppose and take little to no action to meet the Act's legislated mandate to have the contents of all U.S.-inbound cargo containers subjected to non-intrusive inspection technology at overseas ports.

new measures are devised and implemented. Finally, the U.S. government and the other major trade nations still have no plan to respond and recover from a major security incident involving the global intermodal transportation system. As a result, there could be a weeks-long period where the international system of trade and logistics grind to a halt with devastating consequences for the global economy.

1. The Disruptive Risk of the Current Cargo Security Regime

The U.S. government's cargo security measures that were put in place after the attacks of September 11, 2001, have had as their primary aim to more effectively police the intermodal transportation system for suspicious cargo. Customs and Border Protection (CBP) has been the lead agency in developing these measures. The U.S. Coast Guard, the Domestic Nuclear Detection Office (DNDO), and the Department of Energy have also been playing an important support role. The underlying approach depends on CBP's ability to assess risk and target containerized cargo for inspection. If a container is determined to pose a higher risk for potential smuggling, it is subjected to closer scrutiny by customs inspectors. If it is deemed to be a low risk, it is allowed to move through the global logistics system with little or no intervention by government officials.

The process for determining risk begins with an analysis of the cargo manifest and other commercial data provided by transportation providers, importers, and companies involved with logistics. The ocean carrier drawing on information it receives from a shipper provides cargo manifest information to CBP at least 24 hours in advance of a shipment being loaded for transport to the United States. Since the container is sealed, neither the marine terminal where the container is stored in advance of loading, nor the ocean carrier is in position to confirm the veracity of the declarations it receives from its customers. Essentially, it is an honor system.

CBP analyzes the data it receives using rules-based software to identify containers that are at risk of tampering by terrorists. If software triggers an alert, the agency can access a variety of databases to get an impressive array of additional information to help determine whether the contents of a container should be subjected to closer scrutiny. However, except in very rare instances when there is specific intelligence, the software that sounds the alert relies on the truthfulness of the data originally provided by an importer and ocean carrier. This is problematic given that historically, cargo manifest and trade data have been notoriously incomplete and inaccurate.

After the September 11 attacks, CBP instituted the Container Security Initiative (CSI) in 58 ports around the world. Under the CSI protocol, U.S. customs inspectors partner with their overseas counterparts on conducting these examinations using non-intrusive inspection (NII) technology to scan the contents of cargo containers for radiation and to create an x-ray or similar image of what is inside. If these examinations cannot be completed overseas, they are typically undertaken once they arrive at a U.S. port. But this is less desirable from a security standpoint because both the ship and the arriving U.S. port could be placed in jeopardy if the container indeed has a weapon and that weapon is detonated prior to the U.S.-based inspection.

If CBP strictly complied with it own protocol, virtually all U.S.-bound containers determined to present a high risk and warranting an inspection, would have that inspection done at the port of loading. But this rarely happens. Instead, the overwhelming majority of containers that CBP determines to pose a risk are inspected *after* they arrive in a U.S. port. According to congressional testimony provided by a senior CBP official on February 7, 2012, a total of 45,500 containers were examined in the 58 CSI ports in 2011. This represents 0.5% of the 9.5 million manifests CBP reviewed in advance of overseas loading. When 45,500 is divided by the 58 CSI ports and 365 days per year, the result is CSI inspectors are examining with their foreign counterparts on average, just 2.15 containers per loading port per day.[2]

There are practical problems associated with implementing the official protocol of using non-intrusive inspection technology to scan U.S.-bound cargo containers that are targeted as high risk. Cargo containers are typically pre-positioned a few days before shipment in a container yard at a marine terminal in stacks of up to six. If a container is selected for inspection after CBP receives cargo manifest data 24-hours before loading as the agency requires, the container must be located, removed from the stack, and transported to an inspection facility. Performing this labor intensive process often results in the container missing its voyage even if its contents were deemed to be legitimate. This is because the container typically cannot be brought back from the inspection facility with sufficient time to be placed aboard the ship in accordance with a carefully devised loading plan.

According to a simulation conducted by the Wharton Risk Management and Decision Process Center at the University of Pennsylvania, no more than 3 percent of U.S. outbound cargo could be inspected using the CSI protocol at a large marine terminal in South China, without generating a significant backlog. The simulation assumed that local inspectors and cargo scanning equipment would be available to examine U.S.-bound cargo 24-hours per day, 7 days per week. Even under this unlikely circumstance, within 30 days of trying to inspect just 5 percent of U.S. outbound cargo, the accumulated backlog of containers waiting to be examined would fill 2.9 acres, with containers stacked three high. At a 20-percent inspection rate, the backup would fill 31.4 acres.[3] The requirement to inspect more than 3 percent of U.S-bound cargo would not be unrealistic, particularly in the event of an elevated alert level following a terrorist incident or based on intelligence warnings of a likely threat originated from or transiting through a major seaport. In short, CBP's current CSI protocol presents a significant disruptive risk to supply chains. The reason why that risk has not been apparent to date is only because CBP has quietly avoided executing the protocol. This practice exposes the intermodal transportation system to an even greater disruptive risk—the near certainty that container security practices will fail the "morning-after-test."

2. Failing the "Morning-After-Test"

The test of any security measure is how well it survives an attempt to breach it. Even if it does not successfully foil a determined adversary, it can stilled be judged to be a reasonable safeguard based on the available information about the threat and the anticipated consequences. But in some instances, bureaucracies succumb to the temptation to adopt cosmetic measures that they believe will reassure an anxious public, even though they know the measures are likely to prove ineffective in stopping or deterring the anticipated threat. For instance, following the detonation by a suicide bomber of a panel-truck full of explosives in a crowded area, having cement barriers placed outside of train stations would likely be reassuring to daily commuters. But if the barriers were not anchored to the ground, which is a costly and time-consuming process, a terrorist at the wheel of an explosive-laden truck would be able to push them aside and drive up to or through the station's entrance. In the aftermath of such a scenario, families of the victims would be rightfully outraged that security officials who should have known better, deployed the barriers without ensuring those barriers could actually stop a truck.

As a stopgap, a case can sometimes be made for taking actions that are more about appearance than substance, given that perceptions play a role in how people—and adversaries—think about risk. But in the end, providing security is a core function of government and preserving public trust is essential to government legitimacy. While the secrecy that surrounds security can help shield an agency from critical review in advance of an incident, after an attack there will be a day of reckoning. If the public concludes that they were deceived into complacency by officials who were aware of the danger but only went through the motions of addressing it, there will be hell to pay.

In short, in order for a security measure to advance versus undermine resilience, it must be able to survive a "morning-after test"; that is, it should be judged as credible if a capable bad guy decides to take it on. If it fails this test, new measures will have to be devised quickly in an atmosphere of heightened anxiety and against a backdrop of damaged public trust. This will substantially slow down the ability to recover after a major security event.

It is extremely unlikely that the current container security regime would survive a security incident involving a weapon of mass destruction. Sadly each of the key elements of that regime poses no meaningful barrier to a determined adversary intent on using a cargo container to ship a dirty bomb or a nuclear device and detonating it within the intermodal transportation and global logistics system. Consider the following hypothetical scenario that is based on a composite of security breaches involving the smuggling of contraband:[4]

> A container of athletic footwear for a name brand company is loaded at a manufacturing plant in Surabaya, Indonesia. The container doors are shut and a mechanical seal is put into the door pad-eyes. These designer sneakers are destined for retail stores in malls across America. The container and seal numbers are recorded at the factory. A local truck driver, sympathetic to al Qaeda picks up the container. On the way to the port, he turns into an alleyway and backs up the truck at a nondescript warehouse where a small team of operatives pry loose one of the door hinges to open the container so that they can gain access to the shipment. Some of the sneakers are removed and in their place, the operatives load a dirty bomb wrapped in lead shielding, and they then refasten the door.

The driver takes the container now loaded with a dirty bomb to the port of Surabaya where it is loaded on a coastal feeder ship carrying about 300 containers for the voyage to Jakarta. In Jakarta, the container is transferred to an Inter-Asia ship that typically carry 1200–1500 containers to the port of Singapore or the Port of Hong Kong. In this case, the ships goes to Hong Kong where it is loaded on a super-container ship that carriers 5000–8000 containers for the trans-Pacific voyage. The container is then off-loaded in Vancouver, British Columbia. Because it originates from a trusted-name brand company that has joined the Customs-Trade Partnership Against Terror, the shipment is never identified for inspection by the Container Security Initiative team of U.S. customs inspectors located in Vancouver. Consequently, the container is loaded directly from the ship to a Canadian Pacific railcar where it is shipped to a railyard in Chicago. Because the dirty bomb is shielded in lead, the radiation portals currently deployed along the U.S.-Canadian border do not detect it. When the container reaches a distribution center in the Chicago-area, a triggering device attached to the door sets the bomb off.

There would be four immediate consequences associated with this attack. First, there would be the local deaths and injuries associated with the blast of the conventional explosives. Second, there would be the environmental damage done by the spread of industrial-grade radioactive material. Third, there would be no way to determine where the compromise to security took place so the entire supply chain and all the transportation nodes and providers must be presumed to present a risk of a potential follow-on attack. Fourth—and perhaps most importantly—all the current container and port security initiatives would be compromised by the incident.

In this scenario, the container originated from a one of the thousands of companies that belong to the Customs-Trade Partnership Against Terrorism. It would have transited through multiple ports—Surabaya, Jakarta, Hong Kong, and Vancouver—that have been certified by their host nation as compliant with the post-9/11 International Ship and Port Facility Security (ISPS) Code that went into effect on 1 July 2004. Because it came from a trusted shipper, it would not have been identified for special screening by the Container Security Initiative team of inspectors in Hong Kong or Vancouver. Nor would it have been identified by the radiation portal. As a consequence, governors, mayors, and the American people would have no faith in the entire risk-management regime erected by the Bush Administration and continued under the Obama Administration. There will be overwhelming political pressure to move from a 0.5 percent inspection rate at overseas ports to a 100-percent inspection rate mandated by the 2007 9/11 Recommendations Act, effectively shutting down the flow of global commerce. The almost certain consequence would be to push the world back into global recession.

Avoiding this sobering scenario requires first a frank admission by the White House, CBP, the Coast Guard, the Department of Energy, and other agencies involved with container security of the shortcomings of the existing measures. Next, it requires aggressive planning to manage a major terrorist incident while new measures are being developed and implemented. Finally, the new measures should be designed to not just protect the intermodal transportation system, but to enhance the capacity to respond surgically and recover the system quickly should the new protective efforts fail.

3. No Plan For Recovery of the Intermodal Transportation System

Immediately following the attacks of September 11, 2001, the White House and the Secretary of Transportation were in direct contact with the top executives of the major airlines. Once commercial aviation was grounded, the challenge was how to get it up and running again. This involved both operational issues as well as convincing the public that it would safe for them to return to the skies. The government had to work closely with the airlines to make this happen and in just three days, the airports began to reopen.

Today, the U.S. government has no contingency plan for managing the aftermath of a major disruption to the global intermodal transportation system. In June 2007, former

Secretary of Homeland Security Michael Chertoff rolled out "The Strategy to Enhance International Supply Chain Security" that includes a chapter that outline a response and recovery plan in the aftermath of a major security incident involving a U.S. port. The plan makes no mention of coordination with overseas port authorities and marine terminal operators, ocean carriers, or even America's continental neighbors, Mexico and Canada.[5] In January 2012, the Obama Administration released its National Strategy for Global Supply Chain Security. Three years in the making, the strategy is just under five pages long. It calls for "Fostering a Resilient Supply Chain" by "galvanizing action" and "managing supply chain risk." Given the brevity of the document, not surprisingly, there are few details of how it will achieve these outcomes beyond a commitment "to update our threat and risk assessments; align programs and resources; and engage government, private sector, and international stakeholders." The stated objective of this engagement is: "to seek specific recommendations to inform and guide our collaborative implementation of the Strategy."[6]

The weakness of these strategy documents points to how underprepared the U.S. government is to deal with the operational aspects of managing a disruption of the global maritime transportation system. For instance, Washington has not established any coordinating mechanisms to work with the four largest global marine terminal operators or the major ocean carriers who move the overwhelming majority of containerized cargo to the United States and elsewhere around the world. Sixty percent of the world's maritime containers are currently at sea. That translates into 10–12 days of shipping traffic underway in the Pacific Ocean and 8–10 days of traffic in the Atlantic Ocean right now. Many of these container ships are post-Panamax which means that they can only be received at the largest seaports and cannot be easily rerouted. A response and recovery plan that identifies no mechanism to directly engage the leaders of the global maritime community is not truly a response and recovery plan.

4. The "Industry-Centric" Inspection Regime: An Alternative Approach for Building Intermodal Transportation System and Supply Chain Resilience

Building more resilient transportation systems and supply chains requires that there be enough transparency to accomplish four things. First, to credibly validate that low-risk cargo shipments are indeed low risk. Second, to expeditiously resolve whether high-risk cargo shipments actually pose a risk. Third, to support a surgical response to a security breach; i.e., the risk revealed by the incident can be quickly isolated. Fourth, to facilitate a rapid restart of the disrupted portion or portions of the system after a security incident.

The most efficient way to accomplish these four goals is to routinely scan all cargo containers with non-intrusive inspection technology as they enter a marine terminal at the port of loading. This can be accomplished by adapting an "industry-centric" inspection scheme. Such a scheme was assessed by a simulation conducted by the Wharton School using real-world data on container movements in two of the world's busiest ports.[7] The simulation model was informed by experts in terminal operations and experts in fielding and operating container inspection technology within international seaports. The Wharton study concludes that an inspection scheme that integrates non-intrusive inspection technology into the entry gate and as a part of terminal operations is capable of being scaled-up to accomplish nearly universal scrutiny of the contents containerized cargo.

Under the industry-centric scheme, marine terminal operators purchase and install the inspection equipment. That equipment is then maintained and operated by certified third-parties who are overseen by government officials. The equipment and operational costs would be recovered by establishing a universal $15 per-container terminal security fee, much like the security fee included as a part of purchasing a passenger airline ticket. The potential economy and robustness of the industry-centric scheme results from the type and location of the equipment used. The current Container Security Initiative (CSI) protocol relies on transporting containers to centrally-managed customs facility where the contents are subjected to highly sensitive high-energy x-ray. While the percentage of containers targeted for inspection may be small, the process tends to be time-consuming and disruptive. In contrast, the industry-centric inspection scheme performs a rapid initial scan of 100 percent of inbound traffic as a part of the flow into or within the marine terminal. This is immediately followed, when required, by a secondary inspection using more time-sensitive equipment. The initial and secondary scan can be done using a new passive-detection technology call muon tomography that was originally developed by Los Alamos National Laboratory. Muon tomography can be used to rapidly create three-dimensional images of the objects within cargo containers by using naturally occurring subatomic particles.[8]

The value of routinely obtaining an image of a container's contents as they move through the world's marine terminals is that it can help to immediate validate a low-risk shipment is indeed low-risk. It can also speed up the inspection process associated with shipments that are targeted for examination because they have been determined to be high-risk. Because these images would be available immediate after a container arrives at a marine terminal, concerns can be resolved well before the container is scheduled for loading aboard a container ship. Further, in the event of a security breach, these images can serve as an invaluable forensic tool that will support the rapid isolation of risk. Finally, the these images can support the rapid recovery of the intermodal transportation system in the event of a major security incident, by providing the means to quickly restore trust that in-transit shipments can be double-checked for their safety. In this way cargo can be safely off-loaded at the arrival port.

V. The Broader Case for Building Infrastructure Resilience

Americans know that natural disasters like earthquakes, hurricanes, and tornadoes cannot be prevented. In the nearly ten years that have passed since the attacks on the World Trade Center and the Pentagon, they have also begun to make an uneasy accommodation to the ongoing threat of terrorism as well. The May 1, 2011 killing of Osama bin Laden will not put an end to attacks on innocent civilians and critical infrastructure on U.S. soil.

Even though the risk of terrorism is now a permanent future of 21st century life, U.S. policy makers and elected officials have generally overlooked the extent to which decisions about infrastructure investment, design, and regulation can play a role in elevating or dampening that risk. As a consequence, they are missing out on both an opportunity to provide a compelling rationale for investing in infrastructure and insuring that when new investments are made, those investments incorporate measures that will mitigate the risk and consequence of attempts to target them.

The case for building more resilient infrastructure should be a compelling one even in the absence of the threat of man-made and natural disasters. Nearly everyday there are media reports that make clear the consequences of deferred maintenance and repair of old and overstressed infrastructure. From bridges collapsing, congested highways, seaports, and airports, to a passenger rail system that is decades behind the rest of the developed world, there is no shortage of evidence that the United States is neglecting a national transportation system that was once the envy of the world. Add to that a power grid that often cannot handle seasonal rises in temperature, and old pipelines that fail under residential homes and the picture is one of reckless neglect of the essential underpinnings of an advanced society. Modern Americans are acting like grandchildren who are heirs to a mansion that they refuse to maintain. From the street it still looks like a nice house. But as the wiring and plumbing start to fail, the house becomes increasingly unlivable.

Taking infrastructure for granted is not something the United States can afford to do. A new emphasis on building resilience can help change the public's lack of enthusiasm for stepped-up investments in the critical foundations of an advance society. The twin realities that resilience can provide safety and security as well as bolster competitiveness translate into a ripe opportunity for broadening the political base for tackling this important agenda. There is historical precedence for successfully making this kind of case. In creating the interstate highway system, President Dwight Eisenhower made sure to highlight the national defense value that the system could provide by supporting rapid mobilization and urban evacuation.

While emphasizing the role that infrastructure plays in assuring the nation's resilience can strengthen the case for investing in infrastructure, the process of embedding resilience into infrastructure requires specific measures and actions. For the most part, the expertise for developing and the capacity for carrying out those measures and actions do not lie within the federal government. It is the owners and operators of our country's infrastructure who are best able to identify and mitigate vulnerabilities to the systems they run. Yet the information and intelligence about threats to infrastructure lie almost exclusively within the federal government that is reluctant to share what it knows out of a concern that this knowledge will end up in the wrong hands. The result is that important information and perspectives are not shared, compromising the goal of advancing infrastructure resilience.

The federal government is aware that it needs to better cooperate with the private sector. In 2010, the Department of Homeland Security's Office of Infrastructure Protection announced the creation of the "Engagement Working Group" (EWG). The purpose of the EWG is to share classified information with representatives of the private sector in order to better develop strategies to counter threats to infrastructure. While this is a commendable effort, arguably there is a serious flaw with the program. Federal officials will provide security information only to vetted company security officers, who in turn are typically barred from relaying such information to executives and managers who do not hold active security clearances. As a result, investment and operational decisions are often made with little if any attention paid to the potential security stakes—especially for companies where security officers are not a part of the C-suite or where their recommendations are seen as damaging to the bottom-line. Furthermore, without well-tended relationships with decision makers beyond the corporate security office, federal officials will continue to miss out on critically needed insight and perspective of much of the financial and operational expertise of corporate America.

The federal agencies responsible for protecting this country, and their state and local counterparts, still need to do much more work to integrate, fully, the expertise of owners and operators of critical infrastructure and systems. Countering both natural and man-made threats most effectively and efficiently requires both a more open dialogue between federal officials and infrastructure experts and the implementation of truly cooperative, public-private, practitioner-guided programs that build infrastructure resilience.

One promising model for advancing a cooperative, practitioner-guided infrastructure resilience process is the Port Authority of New York and New Jersey's Applied Center of Excellence for Infrastructure Resilience (ACEIR). When the Department of Homeland Security was formed in 2003, it chartered twelve academic Centers of Excellence with the goal of fostering multidisciplinary research in security technologies and processes and providing thought leadership on security policy. This was a good start, but an important next step is to properly test and validate solutions that can function in a demanding operational environment. The White House National Security Strategy released in 2010 recognizes this imperative and calls for employing innovative technology and processes through new, strong and flexible public-private partnerships in order to create next generation, resilient infrastructure. ACEIR is an innovative approach to forging that kind of partnership. The Port Authority, as the nation's largest infrastructure owner and operator, should be applauded for taking the initiative to create an entity dedicated to bridging theory with practical application.

Metropolitan New York offers the ideal environment for developing and testing infrastructure resilience measures. The Port Authority's facilities support the movement of people and goods for one of the world's most densely populated and commercially active regions. The diversity of facilities which include the World Trade Center site and multi-modal transportation systems (tunnels, bridges, bus terminals, airports, maritime facilities, mass transit rail), that cross state borders can test concepts in the environment where they need to be most effective—at the intersection of critical infrastructure interdependencies. And, without addressing the vulnerabilities of critical infrastructure interdependencies, the end game of a more secure society will never be achieved.

As a test-bed, the Port Authority can subject promising technologies and processes to very demanding operational volume and velocity challenges. Those that hold up under the kind of enormous operational stress to which systems in New York are subjected, are likely to fare quite well if adopted nationwide. Infrastructure operators would know that there is little risk that these tools and practices would fail in their urban areas.

In the summer of 2010, the Port Authority stood up ACEIR to facilitate the provision of a real world test-platform for technological applications and processes. Its purpose is to ensure that research projects are vetted at the outset by frontline operators, engineers, and managers. Over time, ACEIR can also provide a venue for providing industry input into the federal research and development projects. Rather than simply evaluating projects developed by federal agencies, ACEIR could be an excellent source for identifying new research needs. Though still in its formative stage, ACEIR can and should be replicated for other infrastructure sectors.

Efforts to advance infrastructure resilience must have as a strategic priority ensuring that any new investments made in extending the lifespan of current infrastructure systems, integrate measures that will assure their continuity in the face of disruptive risk. The time for doing so is now. In 2008, the American Society of Civil Engineers evaluated the nation's inventory of infrastructure and gave it a grade of "D." They identified an investment gap of more than $2 trillion to repair U.S. roads, bridges, ports and other critical facilities and systems. That tab cannot be put off indefinitely. When the nation finally begins to attend to its ailing foundations, it will have a historic opportunity to incorporate measures that assure its resilience in the face of man-made and natural disturbances.

The United States is still in the formative stages of crafting the means to secure infrastructure and build resilient infrastructure systems. The most serious challenge to address is the interdependencies among infrastructure sectors. The inescapable reality is that no system operates in isolation. Because these interdependencies are so vast and complicated, the best place to try and understand them is not at the national level, but within regions and communities. This means that developing resilient infrastructure systems must necessarily be from the bottom up as opposed to the top down. But, advancing resilience at the community level requires that the civic and business leaders of those communities have the tools to do so, that they have a way to measure their progress, and that there be clear benefits for reaching a recognized standard.

One way to tangibly reward communities is to provide them with better bond ratings and lower insurance premiums if they are able to demonstrate that they have adopted measures that both drive down the risk of damages and improve the speed of recovery. But making insurance an ally in dealing with the risk of catastrophic events is challenging for three reasons. First, insurers tend to steer away from things that may involve ruinous losses and insolvency. Second, insurers want to have as broad a pool of policyholders as they can to diversify the risk. Therefore they need to be confident that enough people will elect to buy their insurance product to allow for this diversification. Third, private insurance companies need to be confident that the measures they would be subsidizing by way of reduced premiums do in fact mitigate risk and that their clients are actually adopting these measures.

Federal and state governments can help lower or eliminate each of these barriers for insurers. For instance, government could cap the risk that insurance companies face by effectively becoming a reinsurer. That is, the government can establish a ceiling on the amount of losses a private insurance company would have to pay, and agree to make up the difference to the policyholder if the losses exceed the cap. The government can also help assure an adequate pool of customers for the insurance companies by providing a tax break to the insurers who write new policies or by providing grants to communities to subsidize the initial premiums. Finally, the government can establish and reinforce the standards against which the insurance incentive is set.

A very promising model for deepening private-public cooperation and aligning financial incentives for building and maintaining preparedness at the local level is the "Community Resilience System Initiative" that has been developed by the Community and Regional Resilience Institute (CARRI) as a project initially based out of Oakridge National Laboratory. CARRI has led an effort to define the parameters of resilience, modeled on the creation of the fire and building codes over a century ago. Drawing on a two-year prototype effort undertaken in Charleston, South Carolina, Gulfport, Mississippi, and Memphis, Tennessee, the initiative set out to identify the policies, practices and capabilities that can increase the ability of communities to maintain essential functions with little disruption or, when disrupted, to recover those functions rapidly and with minimal loss of economic and social value. To accomplish this, the initiative sought to help community stakeholders: (1) understand what characterizes resilience; (2) how to assess resilience; (3) how to prioritize options for improving their resilience; (4) how to objectively measure the impact of the improvements; and (5) how they can be rewarded for their investments.

After two years of field research, CARRI spent an additional eighteen months convening a network of former governors and former and current mayors, emergency planners, finance and insurance executives, representatives from various government agencies and academics to develop detailed guidelines and comprehensive supporting resources that will allow communities to devise resilience plans. These insights have been embedded into web-enabled tool, that can be quickly modified and upgraded as new lessons are learned. This tool is being tested in eight communities across the United States.

The community resilience system has been designed to provide community leaders the ability to assess their resilience, plan how to make their communities more resilient, implement and sustain those plans, and also evaluate and revise planning as needed. The system includes an emphasis on infrastructure, thereby infusing it with the kind of local knowledge and expertise that will improve the prospects for it to be replicated and quickly adopted by other communities nationwide.

VI. A Unifying Imperative

One final benefit of making resilience a national imperative is that it reinforces what unites a society as opposed to what divides it. Quite simply, it is not possible to build resilience without substantial collaboration and cooperation at all levels within a society. Individuals must develop the means to withstand, rapidly recover from, and adapt to the risks they face at a personal and family level. Companies and communities must look within and beyond themselves to ensure that they are prepared to handle what may come their way as a result of internally and externally generated risks. Finally, at the national, level, the emphasis on resilience highlights the necessity for forging relationships and developing protocols for dealing with shared risks.

In short, a determination to confront ongoing exposure to catastrophic man-made and natural disasters is not an act of pessimism or paranoia. Nor is it something that is inherently a cost center. Resilience is essential for building and maintaining the elements necessary for a productive and competitive economy. It is a mature recognition that things go wrong from time to time, and that in preparing for such times, one is reminded not to take important and critical things for granted.

Critical Thinking Questions

1. In the absence of a catastrophic disaster, how can we assess a community's resilience?
2. Can resilience be manufactured by local, state, and federal leaders, or is it something that needs to develop organically among a community's members?
3. What is the role of the private sector in building or nurturing community resilience?

Notes

1. Stephen Flynn, "American The Vulnerable," *Foreign Affairs* LXXXI: 1 (Jan-Feb. 2002): 60–74.

2. Joint Testimony of David Heyman, Paul Zukunft, and Kevin McAleenan before the Subcommittee on Border and Maritime Security, Committee on Homeland Security, on "Balancing Maritime Security and Trade Facilitation: Protecting Our Ports, Increasing Commerce and Securing the Supply Chain," on Feb 7, 2012; p. 10.
3. "Estimating the Operational Impact of Container Inspections at International Ports." Nitin Bakshi, Stephen Flynn, Noah Gans, *Management Science,* 57:1 (Jan 2011): 1–20.
4. Stephen Flynn, "Overcoming the Flaws in the U.S. Government Efforts to Improve Container, Cargo, and Supply Chain Security." Hearing on "Container, Cargo and Supply Chain Security—Challenges and Opportunities" before the Homeland Security Appropriations Subcommittee, Committee on Appropriations, U.S. House of Representatives (April 2, 2008).
5. "Strategy to Enhance Global Supply Chain Security, U.S. Department of Homeland Security (July 2007).
6. http://www.dhs.gov/xlibraiv/assets/plcy-internationalsupplychainsecuritystrategy.pdf "National Strategy for Global Supply Chain Security," The White House (Jan 2012). http://www.whitehouse.gov/sites/default/files/national_strategy_for_global_supply_chain_security.pdf
7. "Countering the threat of nuclear terrorism," Nitin Bakshi, Stephen Flynn, Noah Gans, The Wharton School, University of Pennsylvania, Issue Brief (January 2012) http://opim.wharton.upenn.edu/risk/library/WRCib2012a_Port-Security.pdf
8. Muon tomography scanners are under development by Decision Sciences International Corp. In the interest of disclosure, the principle investigator for this report, Dr. Stephen Flynn, serves on Decision Sciences' advisory council. http://www.decisionsciencescorp.com/solutions_template.aspx?id=34

Building Population Resilience to Terror Attacks

Unlearned Lessons from Military and Civilian Experience

Michael T. Kindt

I. Introduction

On September 11, 2001, terrorists attacked the United States in a coordinated attack on our air transportation system and U.S. public symbols, causing the greatest single loss of civilian life in the history of our nation due to terrorism. The attacks in Washington D.C., New York, and Pennsylvania rocked the entire nation, awakening all Americans to the dangers of terrorism that had been known for years by other nations.

The response by America was dramatic as the nation hunkered down in an effort to ensure no more attacks. All air traffic was grounded for three days, security was increased throughout the nation, the list of targets perceived to be at-risk increased, and travel, particularly by air, plummeted. It took months for Americans to return to the air in the same numbers as before these horrific attacks, and many Americans still fear airline travel. The caution of our leaders in shutting down the system and the public reluctance to travel by air, while understandable, multiplied the negative impact of the terror attacks on the U.S. economy, furthering the aims of our attackers.

On July 8, 2005, terrorists attacked the United Kingdom, killing 58 and injuring hundreds in a coordinated attack on the London mass transit system. Despite the shock of these attacks, London mass transit resumed some routes the same afternoon and opened all routes as soon as they were repaired. Londoners returned to these systems the next day in apparent defiance of the risks posed by terrorists. Is this dramatically different response seen in these two nations that share so much in common, a uniquely British characteristic?

This ability to maintain normal operations is not the sole property of the British. Large groups of Americans respond in heroic fashion to tragedies every day. These Americans represent our armed forces and our emergency first responders. How then, do some seem to maintain business as usual or bounce back quickly while others struggle following a tragedy? The answer is resilience.

Resilience, according to psychological literature, is the ability to cope with a negative or traumatic event and return quickly to a healthy level of functioning. Traumatic events which can test the resilience of a nation or community include not only terror attacks, but also natural disasters and accidents. Clearly the British population was more resilient to a traumatic terror event than the American population. Although it is impossible to determine precisely why the British were able to return to normal functioning more quickly than the Americans, an understanding of resilience suggests some very likely explanations.

Resilience to trauma is increased by a number of factors, which include preparation for the trauma, perceived ability to cope with trauma, and, perhaps most important, experience of successful recovery to past trauma. Clearly, London has had more experience dealing with the effects of bombing than the United States. Beginning with attacks on civilian targets by the Germans in WWII and continuing through attacks by the Irish

Republic Army over the past few decades, the United Kingdom has had to learn to live with terror to a much greater extent than America.

Has our nation learned from our recent experiences and those of the United Kingdom? A review of current programs and initiatives reveals that while there are both historical and current models of resilience, our population is not prepared to cope effectively with another significant attack or disaster. The model of resilience provided by the United States military has not been modified to benefit the nation, past national programs to build resilience have not been revitalized, and current efforts build resilience are inadequate or ignored. These shortcomings leave the people of the United States unprepared for attack.

This paper will examine in detail the concept of resilience and techniques to enhance the resilience of the public. It will examine the model of resilience preparation provided by the military, explore past national efforts to prepare for attack, and examine initiatives related to this area that have not yet borne fruit in terms of their ability to enhance our resilience. Finally, recommendations will be made to improve the overall resilience of the United States to terror attacks and disasters.

II. Resilience

The Concept of Resilience

According to the American Psychological Association, resilience "is the process of adapting well in the face of adversity, trauma, tragedy, or even significant sources of stress."[1] Sir Michael Rutter defined it as facing ". . . stress at a time and in a way that allows self-confidence and social competence to increase through mastery and appropriate responsibility."[2] Resilience then has several components. It involves facing a stress or a threat in a way that builds confidence in the individual's ability to master future threats. It also involves somehow having personal responsibility for the successful response to that threat. That is, resilience cannot grow from having someone else manage a crisis or threat. A lack of personal responsibility for the successful response to a threat cannot build resilience or confidence.

Thus, one key to the development of resilience is having had the experience of being faced with responsibility in a threat or crisis and successfully managing that crisis. Resilience does not guarantee that an event will not have an impact on an individual or that person will never experience distress or difficulty coping. Rather, resilience is the characteristic that allows one to resume functioning with minimal disruption.

Further, resilience is not an all-or-nothing characteristic. Everyone has a degree of resilience, and some may be more resilient to one type of stress than to another.[3] For example, some people may manage the stress induced by time pressure at work much better than they handle relationship stresses at home. More relevant to the preparation for terror attacks, individuals and communities on America's Gulf Coast may have developed a significant amount of resilience to the effects of hurricanes, based on past experience of successfully preparing for, surviving and recovering from them. While this resilience to hurricanes may enable confidence in coping with future hurricanes, it may not translate well to the response to a chemical or biological terrorist attack. The degree to which resilience translates from one event to another may depend on the extent to which an individual is familiar with a threat or feels a sense of control in the response to it.[4]

While different individuals may manifest resilience in different situations, there are a number of characteristics common to resilient individuals. The characteristics can be grouped into three general categories. These categories are individual characteristics, social ties, and coping strategies.

The first category of resilience factors is individual characteristics. This category includes *optimism,* the ability to see hope for the future even in difficult circumstances. Another individual feature is *self-efficacy,* or a sense that the individual can utilize available resources to manage the event or task at hand effectively. Self-efficacy is related to *mastery,* which is the ability to take control of the situation one is placed in, and break a large problem down into smaller pieces and begin with these small steps to work to resolve the problem. Resilient people also demonstrate a sense of *coherence,* which represents a belief that the events that happen in life make sense, and allows them to place even traumatic events in a bigger picture of life.[5]

While the definitions are informative, they do not directly illustrate how these individual characteristics relate to better coping during a terrorist attack. In preparation or response to a bombing or chemical or biological attack, a resilient person would demonstrate optimism by believing that he or she, their community, and the nation would be able to cope with the crisis and recover to see better days. Self-efficacy would enable the individual to believe that by accessing and making use of available information and resources they can work to protect themselves and begin to recover. Mastery would allow them to use available information and personal resources to take steps to evacuate or prepare shelter, or identify personal plans for safety. A sense of coherence would allow the person to see the attack as part of a larger war on terror (rather than an unforeseen bolt from the blue) and part of a larger life that, although negatively affected by the attack, can still go on.

These resilient features allow an individual to respond well and be maximally effective in the event of a crisis. An individual without one or all of these individual characteristics is more likely to be overwhelmed by the stress of crisis and be more reliant on the support of others, creating drain on the rescue and healthcare systems.

In addition to these individual characteristics, the social ties that bind people together also contribute to resilience. People who are able to ask for and receive support from social groups such as family, friends, church, or community are more resilient to stress than those who either cannot seek support or have none available. While it seems obvious that receiving support would help an individual cope well with stress, there is also evidence that providing support for others in times of crisis is helpful for the person providing the support. This may explain why one in three Americans contributed to the recovery after 9/11 by contributing either time, money, or blood.[6]

The final set of factors contributing to resilience is related to coping strategies. Even with the individual characteristics identified above, a person must still utilize coping strategies to respond effectively to an attack. These strategies include stepping back to see the big picture before rushing to solve a problem, breaking large and potentially overwhelming problems into more achievable tasks, and taking breaks from the crisis to rest or refocus energy.[7]

High resilience to stress is the combination of a positive individual perspective, strong social connectedness, and effective problem solving skills all of which allow an individual to cope positively with even traumatic events such as a terror attack. Although some individuals are by nature or experience more resilient than others, resilience is a trait that can be improved.[8]

Building Resilience

The American Psychological Association (APA) has produced a series of brochures reviewing information to enhance resilience. These are posted on their website for public access. The APA identifies several factors toward building resilience that may not only be utilized by individuals, but could also be enhanced by federal, state, and local policy. The APA recommends that individuals build connections with others, including social and civic groups, to help develop avenues for social support in the event of a crisis. Creation or support of local organizations with abilities to bring individuals together to create support networks is one method of helping the population to build resilience.

Another technique for increasing resilience is taking decisive action. This is a way of reducing the anxiety of indecision. By taking action, individuals can focus on the action at hand, rather than feeling stuck in uncertainty. Government agencies could facilitate this aspect of resilience by providing clear guidance of actions that should be taken in preparation for the general risk of disasters and terror attacks. Additionally, direct guidance should be provided for coping with specific threats as risk increases or immediately following an attack.

Keeping things in perspective is another method of enhancing resilience. As individuals improve their ability to look at the big picture of events they can better direct their actions and moderate emotional reactions. Larger efforts to communicate clearly about the risk of terror attacks, particularly in comparison to the other threats inherent in modern life, can help reduce anxiety associated with terror attacks. For example, despite the emphasis placed on securing our nation from terrorism, the relative risk to Americans is rather low, with more people in the United States killed by lightning over the last 40 years than killed by terrorist attacks.[9] Providing accurate data to allow the population to place the threat of terror attacks in the proper perspective would be one method of enhancing resilience.

A final technique for increasing resilience is to avoid seeing crises as too large to be managed, and by beginning to break down a crisis into more manageable pieces. Authorities could greatly enhance resilience in this area by providing pre-attack information, directing small steps that the population could take to improve their security from attacks. Thus, it appears clear that with the proper motivation and allocation of resources, the nation could embark on a program to mobilize the population to be confident in its own ability to respond to a significant threat. In fact, such a program has been utilized by the United States in past.

This understanding of resilience and how it can be enhanced is particularly important in light of current knowledge regarding human behavior in the face of threat or disaster. Recent work by Anthony Mawson highlights the marked disparity between how people are presumed to behave during disasters and their actual behavior. He finds that in contrast to the prevailing belief that in the face of disaster there will be mass panic and/or violence as people recklessly flee to safety, there is little evidence to support this belief.

Mawson finds that rather than panicking and fleeing, research suggests that people are much more likely to engage in activities that are supportive of others or involve seeking familiar people or places. He cites four mistaken assumptions that contribute to the belief that panic is likely in disaster situation. First, that the drive for self-preservation will result in fleeing the scene or fighting others. Second, individuals will choose to move toward a safe location. Third, physical dangers will create more panic than other types of stress. Fourth, panic is only prevented by strict social discipline and leadership.[10] These mistaken assumptions can lead those in positions of responsibility and authority to attempt to avert such panic by not releasing information about a potential disaster or attack. This behavior could potentially make panic more likely when a disaster does occur.[11]

Mawson goes on to outline four corollaries to these mistaken assumptions that reflect research on human behavior in times of crisis or disaster. First, more than the drive to flee to safety, people are motivated by a desire to be with familiar people (family, friends, etc.) and in familiar places, even if this means moving toward the danger. Second, people tend to move not toward an objectively safe place but toward people and places they perceive to be safe. Third, separation from these familiar people or places during a disaster may be more disturbing than the actual physical threat. Fourth, the key to avoiding panic may not be firm social control or discipline but the presence of familiar people.[12]

These findings by Mawson mesh well with the basic concepts of resilience reviewed earlier. One of the key factors in resilience was the ability to reach out to provide support to and receive support from others in times of stress. This ability to affiliate with others during crisis or stress then appears to not only help individuals cope with a crisis, but on a large scale enables groups to avoid panic behavior. This drive for the familiar has both advantages and disadvantages for emergency planners.

On the positive side, based on Mawson's research, mass panic is a much less likely outcome of disaster than may often be feared. On the negative side however, the tendency to seek out familiar people and places may lead many to ignore early warnings to evacuate or seek shelter leaving them at greater risk when danger occurs.[13] This potential appears to have been clearly demonstrated by the behavior of tens of thousands of citizens of New Orleans who opted to remain in their homes and with their families despite warnings before Hurricane Katrina to seek higher ground. This unwillingness or inability to heed warnings and seek shelter resulted in an overwhelmed emergency response system. The challenge for those seeking to build population resilience to attack will be to build on this desire to be with familiar others and support each other while enabling people to follow evacuation warnings and other directions.

In the devastation of the Gulf Coast left by Hurricane Katrina, the nation turned to the one organization in America that exemplifies facing stress in a way that builds self confidence and mastery, the United States military.

U.S. Military as a Model of Resilience

By virtue of its mission to protect the nation, members of the military must be prepared at all times to respond to and perform in a wide range of life threatening circumstances around the world. Despite the risk of chemical, biological, radiological, nuclear, and conventional attack, thousands volunteer to accept these risks each year and perform exceptionally around the world. Thus, while not discussing it directly, military training and organization has long recognized the importance of building the ability to master intense threat and stress in a productive and unified manner.

Research and commentary from as early as the 1940s speak of the preparation of combat troops and their reactions on the battlefield in terms very similar to those used today to talk about resilience. S.L.A Marshall, in his classic, *Men Against Fire,* addresses many of the challenges of preparing men for and leading men into the intense danger that is combat. Marshall wrote of the need to prepare soldiers for the type of situations they would encounter on the battlefield so they would feel more prepared when encountering that danger. Such preparation requires realistic training, including live fire exercises, that will allow soldiers to approximate the fear they may feel in battle and prepares them to have the confidence to cope effectively.[14]

Marshall writes at length of the factors that enable men to face the fear and danger of the battlefield noting, "I hold it to be one of the simplest truths of war that the thing that enables an infantry soldier to go on with his weapons is the near presence or presumed presence of a comrade . . . he would rather be unarmed with comrades around him than altogether alone, though possessing the most perfect of quick firing weapons."[15] Even 60 years ago, while not described as resilience, then the concepts of efficacy and perceived social support were recognized as key features in preparing soldiers to cope well with crisis.

Marshall goes on to address the factors that prevent panic and uncontrolled fleeing of troops in combat. Marshall notes that it is intelligence and training that allow soldiers to overcome their fear and desire to huddle together for safety and continue with their mission. He also notes the importance of leaders providing clear instructions in order to ensure continued focus on the mission. In fact, Marshall asserts that it is only when this communication breaks down that soldiers are likely to panic on the battlefield.

Based on his investigation of seven incidents of panic among troops in combat, he determined that none were caused by a "spontaneous movement of a body of men."[16] Rather these incidents of panic grew out of deliberate acts of a few that were misunderstood by others and led to the panic of many. In each case, the deliberate withdrawal of as few as one soldier, when not explained to others, led to mass disorderly panic. Marshall concludes then that in the chaos and danger of combat it is of primary importance to communicate clearly so that individuals will know what is happening and what is expected of them.[17]

Marshall's personal conclusions about the importance of the social bond in combat and the need to prepare soldiers adequately for battle were echoed in a large scale study of attitudes of soldiers in WWII. This study, authored by Samuel Stouffer and first published in 1949, found that soldiers responded less to worries about self-preservation and more to concerns about finishing the task at hand and preserving the unity of the unit in the face of attack. This environment placed a priority then on developing connections to others in the unit and the ability to make friends with and rely on others quickly. This report also emphasized the importance of training to simulate battle and create fear. This experience of fear would help men to learn to acknowledge fear and see their ability to continue to perform despite it.[18]

Although these historical accounts do speak directly of resilience, it is clear that they address many significant resiliency components that are vital to coping with acute stressors, including self-efficacy, mastery, the value of supporting and being supported by others. These same factors are still addressed by the U.S. military today and many military programs are designed to create a sense of resilience in members of the military. While all branches of the service have generally comparable programs, this analysis will focus on the programs of the United States Air Force that directly or indirectly contribute to the resilience of its members.

Returning to the definition of resilience as "the process of adapting well in the face of adversity, trauma, tragedy, or even significant sources of stress,"[19] we can see its parallels in modern military training. Most aspects of military training throughout history have been designed to create a sense of confidence that soldiers, sailors, or airmen can face threats of danger and overcome them.

Today, this process starts in basic training. Basic military training is designed to teach the critical importance of discipline, teamwork, and foundational knowledge needed to succeed as an airman. It also prepares recruits physically as warriors in the profession of arms.[20] These concepts of discipline and teamwork combine to create the sense that the individual is no longer alone and they can accomplish more by working together as team.

These concepts, along with the knowledge of how to respond to a wide range of threats and the trust that following the commands of leadership will lead to success, create some of the initial facets of resilience. Specifically, basic training starts to build the sense of social connectedness, that the recruit can support others and will be supported by others (emphasized in the work of Mawson and Stouffer), while simultaneously increasing self confidence and self efficacy.

This concept of connectedness is enhanced in the Air Force on mastery of wartime skills during Warrior Week, when a recruit is first recognized as an Airman and presented with an Airman's coin as a symbol of the bond with other airmen. In addition to these aspects of resilience, Airmen also learn the specific skills necessary to protect themselves and their fellow airmen. Some of these specific skills include how to wear the chemical protection suit and how to perform self-aid and buddy care in the event of an injury. These specific training programs build the sense of mastery that the airman can respond appropriately in the event of a crisis. These initial facets of resilience learned in basic training are reinforced throughout the military experience.

The entire military environment of on-base housing areas, commissaries, exchanges, and chapels continues to build a strong sense of community that strengthens the connectedness encouraging resilience. Each unit further works to create a sense of camaraderie and esprit de corps that fosters not only a feeling of being part of the Air Force but also as being part of a smaller unit family. Airmen are taught that First Sergeants are available to help them with their problems, and First Sergeants work to identify the needs of the members of the unit and ensure that personnel are referred to the agencies on base that are able to provide assistance.

Base communities provide a wide range of support services that strengthen the bonds of community connectedness and facilitate members of the base community in helping others to be successful. Programs such as Life Skills, Family Advocacy, Family Support Centers, and Chapels provide services designed to address personal, financial, and spiritual needs at all stages of a military career. These services are not only designed to support individuals, but also to ensure that the stresses of military life are being taken care of so that military members can focus, when necessary, on deployment and crisis, confident that they and their families are prepared. Together these military culture and community-based programs create a firm foundation of the basic facets of resilience. Military members are trained and supported to feel connected and capable of responding to any situation they may encounter.

Other Air Force programs are specifically designed and implemented to help build resilience, the capability to perform when called upon, and the ability to adapt to extreme circumstances when necessary. The Family Care Program requires all military members to have a plan for the care of their families in the event of deployment or recall. Airmen who are married to other military members, single parents, and members with special needs family members must document a workable plan to ensure families are cared for should the airman be deployed or recalled for a crisis. These plans must be periodically reviewed to ensure they can be activated at any time.[21] This plan helps to ensure that a call to duty will not overly stress a member with difficult family circumstances.

Another program designed to build resilience is the Suicide and Violence Prevention Education and Training program. This program, while not focused on the threat of terrorism or attack, serves to educate all personnel regarding the risk factors for suicide and workplace violence, with the goal of reducing suicides and incidents of violence. The program emphasizes the role of supervisors and co-workers being involved in the lives of those around them and recognizing the signs of difficulties in coping. The program specifically addresses a number of resilience factors addressed earlier in this article including self-efficacy, optimism, personal control, and social support as critical factors in preventing suicide and violence. The program reviews local procedures for seeking help from the range of base helping agencies and ensures members are aware of the support available to help with stress. This training is required for all Air Force members every 15 months in conjunction with the Air Expeditionary Force cycle.[22]

A final program that warrants specific consideration in terms of the resilience of the Air Force population is the Traumatic Stress Response Program. The goal of this program is to increase resilience in those who may be, or have been, exposed to a traumatic event, through education, training and referrals. This training, then, is one military program that works directly to building resilience in the face of trauma. The program requires trained multi-disciplinary Traumatic Stress Response Teams to be maintained at each base. These teams, with representatives from key helping agencies, may be augmented by peer members who assume a special role of helping those assigned to their specific functional unit. The policy states the goal of providing preventive critical incident stress management services to Air Force members whenever possible.[23]

These preventive programs focus on educating members about the stress they may encounter during a particular deployment or as part of a traumatic duty such as body recovery following an accident. Prevention training provides insight into the normal reactions during trauma so individuals are prepared not just for the stressful events, but also for their own reactions. Individuals are specifically trained in coping techniques to use in response to any stress reactions to ensure they maintain the highest level of functioning possible. Since many stressors and traumatic events cannot be predicted, debriefings are also conducted for those who have been exposed to a traumatic event. This debriefing also normalizes the reaction to stress and works to facilitate a sense of mastery over the reaction and the expectation for a return to normal functioning.

While it is clearly impossible to send all Americans through Air Force Basic Training to improve their ability to respond in the event of a terrorist attack, the programs produced by the Air Force and other military services demonstrate that individuals and groups can be made more resilient through focused preparation efforts. These efforts, however, have not been adopted on a national level and represent a missed opportunity in our national preparedness efforts. Despite the failure to learn lessons from the military regarding resilience, the federal government has in the past pushed the population toward greater resilience and has made some new (if not yet successful) efforts in that direction since 9/11.

III. Federal Efforts to Build Resilience

Historical Precedent

The threat of terrorism in the aftermath of the 9/11 attacks on New York and Washington D.C. was not the first grave danger that has threatened the American citizenry. The United States as a nation actually has experience in building national preparedness for attack. In the late 1940s the United States faced a significant threat-atomic attack by the Soviet Union. In evaluating how to prepare Americans to respond to such a threat, the Federal Civil Defense Act was passed in 1950 creating the Federal Civil Defense Agency (FCDA).[24]

In her book, *Civil Defense Begins at Home,* Laura McEnaney outlines some of the practical and political motivations of the government's decision to place preparedness in the hands of the population rather than establishing the federal government as the primary protector of Americans against attack. She notes that civil defense had been a grass roots organization since WWI, and had been continued successfully during WWII.

McEnaney observes that precedence was not the only motivation for placing preparation in the hands of the communities. Planners at the time had also observed in cities that had been subjected to aerial bombing, most lives had been saved by local defense teams and these efforts had been a great success in coping with WWII bombings in Great Britain.

Yet other factors were also involved. The government wanted to avoid the expectation that it could protect everyone, a task that would have been impossible following an atomic attack. Additionally, there was concern that if the population came to expect the government to protect them they would not practice effective civil defense. Thus, McEnaney concludes the proposal for reliance on self-help "was advantageous because it released the government from complete responsibility for citizen protection while giving people a tangible role to play in the defense of their own country."[25]

Despite the catastrophic level of risk to the population posed by atomic weapons (compared to the threat faced in WWII) the government embarked on an extensive program in the 1950s and 1960s to put homeland response to an attack firmly in the hands of the population. McEnaney details the efforts during this period to create an elaborate program to educate the public regarding preparation for an atomic attack. This effort reflected the primary view and approach taken in the face of nuclear war. A 1947 War Department study recommended "the fundamental principle of civil defense is self-help . . . it is incumbent upon each individual to protect himself, his home and his family to the maximum before calling for aid. To implement the self-help principle, the populace should be organized into small groups under leaders and trained . . . Calls for aid should not be made until the situation is beyond the control of the group."[26]

The efforts of the government, enhanced by cooperation from all sectors of society, including the mass media, generated a tremendous amount of response from the public. The Federal Civil Defense Agency, created in 1950, reported that by 1953, 4.5 million people had enlisted in the United States Civil Defense Corps, and by 1956 the Warden Service, comprised of those who led neighborhood efforts, numbered 800,000.[27]

Although resilience as a concept was not studied at the time, these efforts in the face of nuclear war reflect many of the principles outlined in the earlier discussion of resilience. When faced with the potentially overwhelming threat of a nuclear attack, the government made systematic efforts to put the focus of survival on the individual Americans. They provided education and training on responding to a nuclear attack and empowered individuals to believe that by taking small manageable actions, they could increase their ability to survive an attack. This empowerment and direction likely enhanced the resilience of the nation at the time.

Despite this recent historical example of a massive campaign to involve the population of the nation in a primary role in enhancing their own security, this has not been the primary focus in securing the nation against terrorism. Although there is much more an individual can do to adequately prepare for or even prevent a terrorist attack (compared to person's ability to prepare for or prevent a nuclear attack), the focus since 9/11 has been heavily on government responsibility for security.[28] The focus at the federal level has been on aviation security, improved intelligence gathering and coordination, and direct military action against terrorist threats. Despite this focus, there have been some federal initiatives that have the potential to address the need to increase population resilience.

Current Efforts Toward Resilience

Although resilience is not mentioned specifically, the National Strategy for Homeland Security clearly addresses the idea that securing the nation requires not only the reliance on public resources but also the focused effort of the American people.[29] There are two major initiatives that address issues relevant to psychological resilience. Both, though well-intentioned, have failed to meet the mark in enhancing the ability of American citizens to respond effectively in the event of a major attack or catastrophe. These initiatives are the Homeland Security Advisory System (HSAS) and the Citizen Corps.

The Homeland Security Advisory System was unveiled by then Assistant to the President for Homeland Security Tom Ridge (he was later named the first Secretary for Homeland Security) on March 12, 2002. The system was established by Homeland Security Presidential Directive-3 to provide "a comprehensive and effective means to disseminate information regarding the risk of terrorist acts to Federal, State, and local authorities and to the American people."[30] The Homeland Security Advisory System appears to have never experienced very wide-ranging support from either the public or government agencies. From its inception, the Homeland Security Advisory System has faced criticism from the public, including jokes from comedians and cartoonists, and more serious critiques from journalists and security experts.[31] Despite this ridicule and criticism, the system did initially appear to have some effectiveness in capturing the attention of the American people and altering their behavior in regard to the terrorist threat.

The pinnacle of public respect for and confidence in the Homeland Security Advisory System may have been demonstrated in February 2003. On February 7, 2003, Attorney General Ashcroft, Secretary Ridge, and FBI Director Mueller made a joint announcement of an increase in the Homeland Security Advisory System level from Yellow to Orange. This increase was accompanied by clear statements indicating that there were specific threats against "apartment buildings, hotels, and other soft or lightly guarded targets."[32] In this same announcement, the Attorney General mentioned a specific chemical, biological, or radiological threat with ricin having recently been connected to an Al Qaeda group in England.

Secretary Ridge made some of his first statements advising Americans on actions they could take to prepare themselves for attack, including developing family emergency plans and putting together an emergency supply kit. The combination of identification of a more specific threat and concrete recommendations for public action addressed the features for improving resilience noted earlier by providing concrete, small steps the public could take to counter the threat, and a dramatic public response followed.

The days following the Homeland Security Advisory System increase to the Orange level saw Americans rush to stores to purchase duct tape and plastic sheets, among other emergency supplies. One writer described the public reaction as a "zero-to-60 mobilization" of the American public in the war on terrorism.[33] Despite the success of the Homeland Security Advisory System in mobilizing the population in this situation, the overall trend is one of decreasing confidence in the system as accusations were leveled proposing that the system was being manipulated for political purposes.[34]

Confidence in the Homeland Security Advisory System was further eroded in May 2005 by statements made by former DHS Secretary Ridge. He stated there were often significant disagreements within the administration about whether or not to raise the threat levels. According to former Secretary Ridge, he often argued the threat level should not be raised because of poor intelligence or because the country did not need to be put on alert. He further stated that in some cases where he disagreed with raising the threat level he was over-ruled by other members of the Homeland Security Advisory Council.

The new Secretary for Homeland Security, Michael Chertoff, has also acknowledged the system is under review and that it requires improvements.[35] Without specific, credible threats that can be trusted by the American public, the Homeland Security Advisory System will not be an effective tool for encouraging the population to prepare for and effectively cope with a terror attack. Thus, the Homeland Security Advisory System must be considered a failure relative to its potential to build resilience.

The second major federal initiative relevant to psychological resilience is the Citizen Corps. Launched by President Bush in his 2002 State of the Union address, the mission of the Citizen Corps is "to harness the power of every individual through education, training, and volunteer service to make communities safer, stronger, and better prepared to respond to the threats of terrorism, crime, public health issues and disasters of all kinds."[36] Although not mentioning the concept of resilience directly, the mission statement of the Citizen Corps clearly echoes both the themes of resilience in making people better able to respond as well as the techniques of increasing resilience through preparedness and building support through community ties. The Citizen Corps (part of the larger Freedom Corps) included 5 major programs.

- The Community Emergency Response Team program which trains members in basic disaster response skills; these skills enable individuals to assist their communities and workplaces to become more prepared for attack or disaster.
- The Fire Corps advocates the use of trained civilian volunteers to provide support to local fire and rescue teams thereby increasing their capabilities.
- An expansion of the Neighborhood Watch Program to build on existing community focus on crime prevention and enable these groups to also focus on terrorism awareness.
- The Medical Reserve Corps which organizes volunteers to increase the capacity of local medical teams to respond in the event of a tragedy.
- The Volunteers in Police program which encourages individuals to support the local police departments to increase outreach capacity particularly in times of emergency.[37]

These programs together create a wide range of activities that can benefit both the individuals participating and the community at large by increasing preparedness and disaster capability. The guide for community leaders states that having citizens who are better prepared to care for themselves will enable the emergency personnel to focus on the most serious local problems, and that building of the Citizen Corps will build community pride and cohesion.[38]

The Citizen Corps webpage suggests that these programs are meeting with great success throughout the country, reporting that there are 2,117 Citizen Corps councils serving 210,000,000 people or 73% of the United States population.[39] While these numbers appear to suggest an impressive level of public involvement in these valuable programs, other data suggests that this may not be the case. Despite a call for all communities to establish a Citizen Corps program and a report of 69% coverage of the nation, the National League of Cities reports that there are 19,429 municipal governments in the United States.[40] This indicates that fewer than 11% of municipal governments have established a Citizen Corps council. The difference in the number of communities with councils and the reported percentage of the population served by the Citizen Corps may be due to a disproportional creation of councils by large cities.

There is also significant disparity in the number of people who are reportedly served by Citizen Corps Councils (210 million) and the number of people who even know the Citizen Corps exists. According to a survey conducted in June and July of 2003, by OCR Macro for the Department of Homeland Security, only 8% of the population was even aware the Citizen Corps existed. They also reported that of the 8% who had heard of the Citizen Corps, many could not give an accurate description of what the program was.[41] This general lack of awareness seems to be supported by the numbers of individuals actually being trained and taking part in Citizen Corps programs.

The 2004 Citizen Corps Annual Report (no further reports has been released as of this publication date) indicates that relatively few individuals were actually taking part in training volunteer programs being offered the by Corps through the end of 2004. The report cites that 58,756 individuals had completed Community Emergency Response training since the program became part of the Citizen Corps. The report also cited total numbers participating in the Volunteers in Police Service program at 73,000 and the number in Medical Service Corps at 30,000. Only 1,194 people had taken part in the Fire Corps by the end of the reporting period.[42] Combining these figures provides a total involvement of approximately 165,000 people participating in the Citizen Corps programs. With an estimated United States population of approximately 295,000,000 this equates to only .05% of the population being engaged in these programs. This compares very unfavorably to the 4.5 million who enrolled in the Civil Defense Corps in the first three years of its existence.[43]

There has been some significant criticism of these programs which helps explain the differences in the numbers reported served by the Citizen Corps and the number aware of the program and participating in it. These criticisms suggest that many of the Citizen Corps Councils are merely preexisting programs such as Neighborhood Watch that have been renamed Citizen Corps programs, or some of the Councils may exist on paper only without actual citizen involvement.[44] Recent studies appear to confirm this assessment. The quarterly review of citizen preparedness released in the fall of 2006 revealed that despite the increased media attention and impact of Hurricane Katrina, "Americans today are no better prepared for a natural disaster or terrorist attack than they were in 2003 ."[45]

Regardless of the cause of low involvement, it is clear that federal government efforts to inspire civilian involvement in homeland security have failed to achieve the level of involvement prompted by the civil defense movement of the 1950s. These programs have also apparently failed to increase the overall preparedness of the population. Thus, the Citizen Corps must also be considered a failure relative to the development of resilience in the American citizenry.

Today's programs appear to have great potential to increase the resilience of the individuals who participate in them, but figures indicate that this promise is being wasted. While some people are benefiting, and some councils may be working effectively to build resilience in the community, the overall program does not appear to be effective. If utilized effectively to reach out to and engage Americans in working toward their security and the security of their communities, personal and community resilience could be greatly enhanced. The current program metrics of tracking percentage of population covered by a council seems to be a dramatic misrepresentation of the Citizen Corps ability to meet the mission to "harness the power of every individual."[46]

Efforts to Address Deficits

There has been some recognition within the government of the need to increase the focus on improving the psychological preparedness of the population to terror attacks. The Department of Homeland Security (DHS) has identified the need for additional research on behavioral health issues related to resilience and sponsored one initiative to address this need. During 2005, the Department of Homeland Security created a number of Centers of Excellence at universities to increase understanding of different factors relating to domestic preparedness for terror attacks.

In January of 2005, the Department of Homeland Security announced the creation of a Center of Excellence for Behavioral and Social Research on Terrorism and Counter-Terrorism. In addition to research on the questions related to the causes of terrorism and strategies to counter it, this center will "examine the psychological impact of terrorism on society and strengthening the population's resilience in the face of terrorism."[47]

Headquartered at the University of Maryland with support of universities across the country, the center, renamed the National Consortium for the Study of Terrorism and Responses to Terrorism (START), has already created several working groups including one focusing on societal responses to terrorist threats and attacks. This working group, chaired by some of the leading researchers in social resilience, has already started projects investigating best practices for preparing communities, school-based preparedness programs, and community resilience to terrorist threat.[48] If the funding for such programs continues, the START program could identify valuable tools and programs for enhancing individual and community resilience.

Another initiative to improve the focus on population resilience began in Congress. Prompted by a desire to increase the national focus on the development of resilience to terror attacks, Congressmen Kennedy, Weldon, Turner, Smith, Frost, and Thompson introduced, on February 5, 2003, to the House of Representatives a bill "to improve homeland security by providing for national resilience in preparation for and in the event of a terrorist attack."[49] This bill, entitled the *National Resilience Development Act* cites recommendations by the National Academy of Sciences to ensure the public health infrastructure is prepared to cope with the psychological as well as physical consequences of any attack. The bill also encourages use of techniques developed in Israel to enhance resilience of individuals and decrease the effects of terror attacks.

The overall goal of the Act is to "identify effective strategies to respond to the behavioral, cognitive and emotional impacts of terrorism; to coordinate efforts in researching, developing and implementing programs to increase the psychological resilience and mitigate distress reactions and maladaptive behaviors of the of the American public."[50] The *National Resilience Development Act,* which has been endorsed by former New Jersey Governor and 9/11 Commission Chairman Thomas Kean,[51] would also establish an Interagency Task Force including the Director of the Centers for Disease Control, Director of the National Institute of Mental Health, the Surgeon General of the Public Health Service, the Director of the Office of Public Health Preparedness, and several other agencies, to track progress toward achieving community resilience goals. Despite the important issues raised in this bipartisan bill, the Act has been referred to the Committee on Energy and Commerce, Committee on Transportation and Infrastructure, and the Judiciary Committee for review. The Act was reintroduced in 2004 and again referred to committees and no action has yet been taken on the bill.[52]

The initiatives being taken in Congress and by the DHS confirm that there is interest (if little measurable accomplishment) in addressing America's need for increased resilience to attack. However, interest alone is not enough to prepare our nation for terror attacks and disasters. Concrete programs, based on the past successes of the government and military, combined with efforts to measure effectiveness, must be initiated to better prepare the population.

IV. Recommendations

Before recommendations for improving the resilience of the American population can be effectively considered, it is important to address a prerequisite for all resilience initiatives—establish national level leadership to make resilience an important national goal. The political dialogue on the Global War on Terror, to the extent that it has involved the American people at all, has been to recommend that they "go about their business." Homeland Security Advisory System levels change with no indication of how the public should prepare. The general public has been encouraged to believe that the best defense against terror is a military offensive against terrorists and those who harbor them. Americans' involvement in this military offensive has been limited to placing "I support our troops" stickers on their vehicles, with little personal sacrifice or effort required.

Although the strategy of pre-emption and taking the fight to the terrorists in Iraq has its merits, it does not eliminate the threat of attacks here at home. In fact, this general theme of "don't worry, we have it covered" serves to decrease resilience as individuals feel there is nothing they can or should do to prepare, decreasing their sense of efficacy and control. Without a clear emphasis at the national level on the vital role individuals can and should play in preparing themselves and their communities for attack, no other recommendations will bear fruit.

The establishment of a positive, consistent, national message which says, "We as American people are all vital parts of a team, each with our own critical roles, working together to prepare to ultimately defeat terrorism," would begin to create at a national level the sense of mission, purpose, and teamwork developed in a military basic training program. It would empower individuals to accept a role and try to fulfill it. This message would also give life to the mission of programs such as the Citizen Corps "to harness the power of every citizen" toward preparing our nation. With this emphasis on resilience established, other recommendations can be considered.

First, the Homeland Security Advisory System should be significantly revised or abandoned. The most constructive revision to the HSAS would be the elimination of general nationwide threat level changes in favor of more specific alerts targeted at specific regions or industries. These alerts should always be accompanied by specific recommendations for public action in response to that threat. The alerts should be followed by targeted surveys of affected individuals and organizations to assess the extent to which recommendations were followed. This would provide some structured feedback on the effectiveness of the warning system, and help to identify constraints on individual preparedness.

This system would then better mirror the Force Protection levels established by the military to secure bases. Under this system, changes can be made base, command, or DoD-wide and are accompanied by specific changes in procedures for all to follow. Moves toward greater specificity of warning and increased guidance as to how these warnings should be addressed by the public, would appear to be well received by the population, increase confidence in the system, and enhance resilience as people learn not just to be more afraid, but rather how they can be more prepared.

Second, existing programs in the Citizen Corps must be maximized to capitalize on their potential for success. As outlined earlier, many of the Citizen Corps programs that have been established have tremendous potential to increase individual and community resilience, but have underachieved. These programs should be re-energized and proper metrics established to track their progress and success. Resilience programs in the Air Force are not measured by how many Suicide Prevention programs or Traumatic Stress Response teams exist, but by what percentage of their population is trained and ready to go. Similarly, the metric for success of the Citizen Corps program should not be the percentage of people living in a community that has a Citizen Corps Council, but how many people in that community have been trained or engaged by that Council. Such metrics would allow for more accountability of the money being spent on Citizen Corps programs now, and be used to provide justification for additional spending. This would also allow benchmarking of the techniques used by the most successful Councils so these techniques can be distributed to all Councils.

Additionally, the Department of Homeland Security, along with other national leaders, should work to communicate more directly to the population regarding why and how they should be prepared. There is currently a great deal of valuable, practical information on the *Ready.gov* website that can help an individual or family prepare for attack or disaster. The help in preparing emergency plans found on this website and the confidence preparedness brings can be a key step in building resilience. However, this information is only accessible if people become curious enough to look for it, or call the Department of Homeland Security phone line to request it. Without guidance that important information is available, few will likely take this initiative.

Increased national emphasis on resilience could include media campaigns or direct mailings, advising Americans of the specific risks and precautions that can be taken in their region to make them safer. Partnerships could be developed with retailers to pre-package readiness kits along with flyers advising buyers on how to use them. In the same way that the Air Force recognizes the completion of training with an Airman's coin, the Department of Homeland Security could provide stickers or flags that Americans could use to identity their homes and workplaces as "Ready."

Perhaps the most successful program that falls under the Citizen Corps is the Neighborhood Watch program, with over 11,000 neighborhood groups nationwide.[53] These programs, which have already expanded beyond crime prevention to terrorism watch, could be encouraged to expand further to help identify neighbor residents who may not be able to care for themselves in a time of emergency, or those without transportation during evacuation situations. The disabled or shut-in could also be identified through this program and information shared with the local police departments who sponsor the watches. This would build a greater sense of connectedness in the community and reduce the reliance on emergency personnel to respond in a crisis.

Two key factors in resilience are optimism and confidence in ability to respond to a threat. Consequently, training opportunities to build preparedness skills should be expanded. One training program that is very valuable both to individuals and communities is provided by Community Emergency Response Training. Although the full training requires 20 hours to complete, the program launched a web-based training program open to all Americans to familiarize them with the concepts of emergency response.

Created in 2003, this web-based program was completed by only 5,320 people in 2004. Clearly more emphasis needs to be placed marketing and engaging individuals to complete the training. The military, of course, does not have to worry about marketing training programs in order to increase attendance; it simply makes things mandatory. Although it is not practical to make preparedness training mandatory for all Americans, partnerships that have been used in the past could be revitalized to increase Americans resilience.

Perhaps the easiest partnership for training and educating Americans, and one used heavily in the 1950s and 60s, is through the nation's schools. Many remember "duck and cover" drills and science films regarding the effects of atomic bombs. Although "duck and cover" drills are clearly outdated, a partnership between the Department of Homeland Security and the Department of Education could work to include preparedness and resilience topics in public school curriculum. While it may not be necessary for all Americans to complete Community Emergency Response Team training, self aid and buddy care skills or cardio-pulmonary resuscitation (CPR) could be added to health curricula. Israel has already taken steps in this area, developing resilience building programs for high school students, and is working to establish this nationwide.[54]

Finally, new efforts that have been initiated, such as the National Resilience Development Act and the new Study of Terrorism and Responses to Terrorism program, should be supported so that new tools and techniques for enhancing resilience can be developed and disseminated to ensure that all Americans can maximize their ability to respond to a disaster.

V. Conclusion

Based on this review, it can be concluded that resilience is a key attribute in being prepared to deal with crisis and adversity whether it comes in the form of an attack, a disaster, or a combat situation, and to recover in its aftermath. Resilience is a skill that can be improved both for individuals and communities, through building confidence, efficacy, problem solving skills, and social connectedness.

The United States has knowledge and experience in building such resilience in populations and groups dating back to the 1940s and 50s, when not only were troops prepared for battle, but the nation as a whole was prepared for a devastating attack. This knowledge continues to be utilized in the U.S. military to prepare troops for a wide range of traumatic experiences. Unfortunately, this knowledge and experience has not been more widely utilized to prepare the population for attack following 9/11. This lack of preparation on the part of individuals, families, and communities was clearly demonstrated in the aftermath of Hurricane Katrina. The ineffectiveness of warnings systems were highlighted in that even with days of advance warning, these systems did not create the desired behavior in the population. Thousands of people had difficulty coping with the storm.

The Homeland Security Advisory System was designed to help alert the population to the danger of an attack, but has been ineffective in advising people how to prepare for attacks and has subsequently failed in changing behavior. The Department of Homeland Security Citizen Corps programs show some potential for preparing people to better respond and recover in the face of attack but these efforts have reached far too few people to have any real impact on population resilience. Based on the review of these programs and the evidence provided by the response to Hurricane Katrina, the nation has not learned the lessons provided by the Cold War and the military, and the resilience of the American people to attack remains dangerously low. Although not addressed by the 9/11 Commission, utilizing the graded rating scale the commission used to evaluate progress toward implementing their recommendations, the effectiveness of national efforts at building resilience in the population would be graded no better than a C-.[55] Clearly much remains to be done.

While there are many things the government can do to prevent an attack from happening, no amount of pre-emption, intelligence, or security can eliminate the possibility of attack. As long as the threat exists, efforts must be made to enable the general population to respond as well as possible when an attack occurs. Without greater emphasis on increasing the resilience of the population, thousands or millions could be at greater risk if or when another significant attack occurs. For any of the techniques or recommendations to enhance resilience to be effective on a large scale, it will take significant and sustained leadership at the national level.

Although our military is strong and our security sound, our nation could be significantly stronger if we were truly able to, "harness the power of every individual"[56] toward making our nation as strong as it could be. All Americans must be included and encouraged to build the confidence to do their part and to have the optimism that, by doing their part, they make themselves, their families, their communities, and our nation as safe as it can be from those who would do us harm.

Critical Thinking Questions

1. What key obstacles or challenges have constrained previous efforts to enhance national or community resilience, and how can these be overcome?
2. Assuming that there are indeed effective tools and techniques that leaders can use to build or nurture community resilience, have these been a priority for homeland security policy and strategy? Why or why not?
3. Who in your community is best positioned to lead an effort to build or improve community resilience?

Notes

1. "The Road to Resilience," *American Psychological Association*, On-line, Internet, available from http://apahelpcenter.org/featuredtopics/feature.php?id=6&ch=2.
2. Michael Rutter, "Family and School Influences on Cognitive Development," *Journal of Child Psychology and Psychiatry*, 1985, vol. 26, 683–704.
3. "Promoting Resilience," New York State Office of Mental Health; *OMH Quarterly*, March 2003, On-line, Internet, available from http://omh.state.ny.us/omhweb/omhq/q0303/Resiliance.htm.
4. Ibid.
5. "Fostering Resilience in Response to Terrorism: A Fact Sheet for Psychologists Working with Adults," *American Psychological Association*, On-line, Internet, available from http://www.apa.org/psychologists/pdfs/adults.pdf.
6. Ibid.
7. Ibid.
8. Ibid.
9. John Mueller, "Simplicity and the Spook," reprinted from *International Studies Perspectives*, vol. 6, No 2, May 2005, AWC Terrorism Elective Reader.
10. Anthony Mawson, "Understanding Mass Panic and Other Collective Responses to Threat and Disaster" *Psychiatry*, 68, Summer 2005.
11. Ann E. Norwood, "Commentary on 'Understanding Mass Panic and Other Collective Responses to Threat and Disaster:' Debunking the Myth of Panic," *Psychiatry*, 68, Summer 2005.
12. Anthony Mawson, "Understanding Mass Panic and Other Collective Responses to Threat and Disaster," *Psychiatry*, 68, Summer 2005.
13. Ibid.
14. S.L.A. Marshall, *Men Against Fire: The Problem of Battle Command*; (1947; repr., Norman, OK: University of Oklahoma Press, 2000).
15. Ibid., 42–43.
16. Ibid., 145.
17. Ibid.
18. Samuel A. Stouffer et al., *The American Soldier: Combat and its Aftermath, Volume II;* (Princeton, NJ: Princeton University Press, 1949).
19. "The Road to Resilience," *American Psychological Association.*
20. United States Air Force, Basic Military Training, "About Basic Military Training," On-line, Internet, available from http://www.lackland.af.mil/737web/bmt.htm.
21. Air Force Instruction (AFI) 36-2908, *Family Care Plans,* 1 October 2000.
22. Air Force Instruction (AFI) 44-154, *Suicide and Violence Prevention Education and Training Program,* 3 January 2003.
23. Air Force Instruction (AFI) 44-153, Traumatic Stress Response, 1 May 2006.
24. "From Civil Defense to Emergency Management," On-line, Internet, available from http://fcgov.com/oem/civildefense.php.
25. Laura McEnaney, *Civil Defense Begins at Home;* (Princeton, NJ: Princeton University Press, 2000), 24.
26. Report to the War Department Civil Defense Board, February 1947. In McEnaney, *Civil Defense Begins at Home,* 24.
27. McEnaney, *Civil Defense Begins at Home.*

28. David Hunt, *They Just Don't Get It: How Washington is Still Compromising Your Safety and What You Can Do About It;* (New York: Crown Forum, 2005).
29. Office of Homeland Security, *National Strategy for Homeland Security,* (Washington, DC, July 2002), On-line, Internet, available from http://www.dhs.gov/interweb/assetlibrary/nat_stra_hls.pdf.
30. Homeland Security Presidential Directive-3, Homeland Security Advisory System, 12 March 2002, On-line, Internet, available from http://www.whitehouse.gov/news/releases/2002/03/20020312-5.html.
31. Wikipedia, "Homeland Security Advisory System," On-line, Internet, available from http://en.wikipedia.org/wiki/Homeland_Security_Advisory_System.
32. Remarks by Secretary Ridge, Attorney General Ashcroft, and Director Mueller, (Washington, DC: U.S. Department of Homeland Security, Office of the Press Secretary, 7 February 2003), On-line, Internet, available from http://www.dhs.gov/dhspublic/display?content=451.
33. Linda Feldman, "Terror Alerts Create a Run on Duct Tape," *Christian Science Monitor,* 13 February 2003, On-line, Internet, available from http://www.csmonitor.com/2003/0213/p01s02-ussc.html.
34. Mimi Hall and Kevin Johnson, "Ridge on Defensive after Terror Alert," *USA Today,* 3 August 2004, On-line, Internet, available from http://www.usatoday.com/news/washington/2004-08-03-terror-analysis_x.htm.
35. Mimi Hall, "Ridge Reveals Clashes on Alerts," *USA Today,* 10 May 2005.
36. Department of Homeland Security, *Citizen Corps Annual Report 2004,* (Washington, DC 2005, 1), On-line, Internet, available from http://www.citizencorps.gov/pdf/news/CC_AR2004_SFS.pdf.
37. Department of Homeland Security, "Citizen Corps Programs and Partners," On-line, Internet, available from http://www.citizencorps.gov/programs/.
38. Department of Homeland Security, "Citizen Corps: A Guide for Local Officials," On-line, Internet, available from http://www.citizencorps.gov/pdf/council.pdf.
39. Department of Homeland Security, "Council Profiles and Resources," On-line, Internet, available from http://www.citizencorps.gov/councils/.
40. National League of Cities; "About Cities," On-line, Internet, available from http://www.nlc.org/about_cities/cities_101/138.cfin.
41. OCR Macro, "2003 Citizen Corps Survey of U.S. Households," (11785 Beltsville Drive, Calverton, MD 20705), On-line, Internet, available from www.citizencorps.gov/ppt/citizen_corps_2003_survey_results.ppt.
42. Department of Homeland Security, *Citizen Corps Annual Report 2004.*
43. McEnaney, *Civil Defense Begins at Home.*
44. Natasha Chin, "Inspiring Preparedness in a Complacent America; Homeland First Response," On-line, Internet, available from http://www.jems.com/homelandfirstresponse/CitizenResponder.HTML.
45. OCR Macro, "Fall 2006 Citizen Preparedness Review: A Quarterly Review of Citizen Preparedness Research" (11785 Beltsville Drive, Calverton, MD 20705) On-line, Internet, available from http://www.citizencorps.gov/pdf/cp_surveysdbase_112006.pdf.
46. Department of Homeland Security, *Citizen Corps Annual Report 2004.*
47. Department of Homeland Security, "Homeland Security Centers of Excellence," On-line, Internet, available from http://www.dhs.gov/dhspublic/display?theme=27&content=3856.

48. START "Areas and Projects," On-line, Internet, available from http://www.start.umd.edu/research/areas/index.asp.
49. HR 3774 IH National Resilience Development Act 4, Feb 2004, On-line, Internet, available from http://thomas.loc.gov/cgi-bin/query/z?c108:H.R.3774.IH.
50. Ibid.
51. Comments by Governor Tom Kean at Bill Drop of "The National Resilience Development Act of 2003," On-line, Internet, available from http://www.healthtogether.org/healthtogether/resources/news_kennedy_bill_drop.html
52. HR 3774.
53. Department of Homeland Security, *Citizen Corps Annual Report 2004.*
54. "Immunizing the Public Against Terrorism: The ICT Educational Project," On-line, Internet, available from http://www.ict.org.il/institute/Projectdet.cfm?ProjectID=l.
55. Thomas H. Kean et al., *Final Report on 9/11 Commission Recommendations,* (Washington, DC: 9/11 Public Discourse Project, December 2005).
56. Department of Homeland Security, *Citizen Corps Annual Report 2004.*

A Social Infrastructure for Hometown Security

Advancing the Homeland Security Paradigm

Robert Bach and David Kaufman

The United States, through a concerted national effort that galvanizes the strengths and capabilities of Federal, State, local, and Tribal governments; the private and non-profit sectors; and regions, communities, and individual citizens—along with our partners in the international community—will work to achieve a secure Homeland that sustains our way of life as a free, prosperous, and welcoming America.

—Vision Statement, 2007 National Strategy for Homeland Security[1]

The nation's homeland security strategy calls on federal, state, and local governments, businesses, communities, and individuals across the country to work together to achieve a shared vision of a secure way of life. Yet for over seven years, through attacks, threats, and disasters, the core ingredient in efforts to achieve that goal remains elusive.[2] The American public has been left out and is largely missing in action.

This elusiveness persists because of a misdiagnosis of the way the American people experience homeland security practices, inappropriate application of border screening and verification techniques to domestic public life, and an incomplete strategic preparedness framework that relies excessively on top-down federal management. This article argues for a new approach that engages the American people in ways that invites their participation in understanding, assessing, and mitigating risk. New community-oriented techniques are needed that draw heavily on community policing models and public health philosophies; the federal government needs to invert its strategic planning and funding processes, seize the moment and leverage the restructuring of the Federal Emergency Management Agency (FEMA) and other priorities as opportunities to put communities first. The new administration has issued a national call to service. This call offers an opportunity to invest in a social infrastructure for homeland security that will bring the American people fully into strengthening their own preparedness.

Elusive Public Engagement

The nation's leaders often acknowledge a critical role for the American public in homeland security, but how to achieve it has proven elusive. Just two months after the 9/11 attacks, for instance, President Bush called on Americans "to serve by bettering our communities and, thereby, defy and defeat the terrorists."[3] A few years later, Homeland Security Secretary Tom Ridge, reiterated the call: "President Bush has said, 'The true strength of the country lies in the hearts and souls of our citizens.' He is absolutely right. The federal government cannot micro-manage the protection of America. Instead, homeland security must become a priority in every city, every neighborhood, every home, and with every citizen."[4]

<table>
<tr><td colspan="4">Report Documentation Page</td><td colspan="2">Form Approved
OMB No. 0704-0188</td></tr>
<tr><td colspan="6">Public reporting burden for the collection of information is estimated to average 1 hour per response, including the time for reviewing instructions, searching existing data sources, gathering and maintaining the data needed, and completing and reviewing the collection of information. Send comments regarding this burden estimate or any other aspect of this collection of information, including suggestions for reducing this burden, to Washington Headquarters Services, Directorate for Information Operations and Reports, 1215 Jefferson Davis Highway, Suite 1204, Arlington VA 22202-4302. Respondents should be aware that notwithstanding any other provision of law, no person shall be subject to a penalty for failing to comply with a collection of information if it does not display a currently valid OMB control number.</td></tr>
<tr><td colspan="2">1. REPORT DATE
MAY 2009</td><td colspan="2">2. REPORT TYPE</td><td colspan="2">3. DATES COVERED
00-00-2009 to 00-00-2009</td></tr>
<tr><td colspan="4" rowspan="3">4. TITLE AND SUBTITLE
A Social Infrastructure for Hometown Security: Advancing the Homeland Security Paradigm</td><td colspan="2">5a. CONTRACT NUMBER</td></tr>
<tr><td colspan="2">5b. GRANT NUMBER</td></tr>
<tr><td colspan="2">5c. PROGRAM ELEMENT NUMBER</td></tr>
<tr><td colspan="4" rowspan="3">6. AUTHOR(S)</td><td colspan="2">5d. PROJECT NUMBER</td></tr>
<tr><td colspan="2">5e. TASK NUMBER</td></tr>
<tr><td colspan="2">5f. WORK UNIT NUMBER</td></tr>
<tr><td colspan="4">7. PERFORMING ORGANIZATION NAME(S) AND ADDRESS(ES)
Naval Postgraduate School,Center for Homeland Defense & Security,Monterey,CA,93943</td><td colspan="2">8. PERFORMING ORGANIZATION REPORT NUMBER</td></tr>
<tr><td colspan="4" rowspan="2">9. SPONSORING/MONITORING AGENCY NAME(S) AND ADDRESS(ES)</td><td colspan="2">10. SPONSOR/MONITOR'S ACRONYM(S)</td></tr>
<tr><td colspan="2">11. SPONSOR/MONITOR'S REPORT NUMBER(S)</td></tr>
<tr><td colspan="6">12. DISTRIBUTION/AVAILABILITY STATEMENT
Approved for public release; distribution unlimited</td></tr>
<tr><td colspan="6">13. SUPPLEMENTARY NOTES</td></tr>
<tr><td colspan="6">14. ABSTRACT</td></tr>
<tr><td colspan="6">15. SUBJECT TERMS</td></tr>
<tr><td colspan="3">16. SECURITY CLASSIFICATION OF:</td><td rowspan="2">17. LIMITATION OF ABSTRACT
Same as Report (SAR)</td><td rowspan="2">18. NUMBER OF PAGES
13</td><td rowspan="2">19a. NAME OF RESPONSIBLE PERSON</td></tr>
<tr><td>a. REPORT
unclassified</td><td>b. ABSTRACT
unclassified</td><td>c. THIS PAGE
unclassified</td></tr>
</table>

Standard Form 298 (Rev. 8-98)
Prescribed by ANSI Std Z39-18

Yet after Hurricane Katrina it became clear that many Americans were unprepared and uninvolved. The White House's own after action report pointedly advised that "[w]e as a Nation—Federal, State, and local governments; the private sector; as well as communities and individual citizens—have not developed a shared vision of or commitment to *preparedness*. . . . Without a shared vision . . . we will not achieve a truly transformational *national* state of preparedness."[5]

The urgency to overcome this missing link is clear. Yet misdiagnosis of the problem obstructs urgent action. The problem is not, as many emergency managers and security officials lament, the emergence of a "nanny society" that thrives on a general atmosphere of dependence on government aid that has eliminated individuals' abilities and willingness to seek opportunities and accept responsibilities. Forced into a nanny role, the argument goes, federal and state officials must repeatedly remind local residents that they are "on their own" for seventy-two to ninety-six hours before the government can reach them and provide assistance.

Rather, government officials and the public fundamentally misunderstand and mistrust each other. The American public, for instance, is much more interested in preparing for emergencies than government officials believe. Recent polling shows that a large majority of Americans nationwide have paid attention and gained information about terrorist threats.[6] The problem is that they do not fully trust the government to inform them correctly or to deliver on its promises. They also do not know what to do to prepare effectively, having been told simply to live their normal lives[7] and prepare individual ready kits;[8] advice that provides little confidence of protection in the face of large and uncertain risks. Most importantly, though, research suggests that the reasons why people do not behave the way government plans expect them to is that local residents and communities do not hold the views and expectations that government planners believe they do. In short, government planners are out of touch with local residents. They are ill-informed about the very public they lament does not care or listen to their instructions.[9]

Lack of trust, perceived misplaced investments, repeated alerts to risks that are not explained, and bungled emergency responses have created a deep division between federal government strategies and the willingness of the American public to embrace them. Even federal emergency officials accept this condition. Former FEMA Administrator Paulison, for instance, blamed the agency's response to Katrina for a current lack of public confidence and admits that it will be difficult to earn the public's trust. "I don't know if people are going to believe what I tell them," he says, "and maybe they shouldn't."[10]

As candidate for president, then Senator Obama pushed hard for the need to overcome this division, issuing a call for the American public "to step into the strong current of history"[11] He chastised previous efforts that failed to mobilize communities across the land. Referring to Americans' readiness to serve after the 9/11 attacks, he said, "We were ready . . . to answer a new call for our country, but the call never came." "Instead of a call to service, we were asked to go shopping."[12]

By most accounts, the likely security challenges in the next few years will demand much greater involvement of the public, not only to sustain public support for large-scale funding, but more importantly, because the public will be crucial to greater effectiveness in preventing and responding to these threats. The treacherous currents ahead include homegrown terrorism and domestic radicalization; and as a recent bipartisan congressional report on future threats emphasized, pandemic illness, whether natural or manmade, poses an almost certain threat in the next few years.[13] Difficult crosscurrents ahead will also require emergency response and recovery strategies that do not depend on large-scale federal deployments ahead of every threatening storm. Effectiveness in each situation will fall as much (if not more) on the capacities of local communities, neighbors, and families, than on federal response teams and billions of dollars of new equipment. The challenge is to understand how to engage the public *collectively and on a large scale* across the nation to build this capacity.

Transforming the Mission

A first step in transforming homeland security strategy is to recognize that current efforts undermine preparedness every bit as much as they support it. Paradoxically, the successes of government initiatives in the last few years—and there have been many—have also made more evident and urgent the need to reach well beyond top-down governmental approaches. Progress in developing a "national management system," emanating from the Department of Homeland Security (DHS), has also decreased the participation of a broad range of joint decision-makers in communities across the country. Community engagement has been left to become a 'nice thing to do;' rather than to take its proper place as the cornerstone of effective security.[14]

After 9/11, the nation's homeland security strategy focused heavily on governmental initiatives, primarily at the federal level, to improve information and intelligence sharing, screen persons and cargos entering the United States, harden critical assets, and improve government response capabilities. As is often noted, these initiatives launched the largest growth in the federal bureaucracy since World War II, founding entirely new mammoth agencies such as the Transportation Security Administration, DHS, U.S. Northern Command, and the Office of the Director for National Intelligence. All were designed to ensure the internal security of the U.S. homeland and to prosecute a "global war on terror" abroad. But they also involved top-down management systems and military-style command and control strategies in planning and implementation, often focusing on a doctrine of offense and preemption. As President Bush stated in his September 20, 2001 address to a joint session of Congress, "We will take defensive measures against terrorism to protect Americans. . . . These measures are essential. But the only way to defeat terrorism as a threat to our way of life is to stop it, eliminate it, and destroy it where it grows."[15]

Misapplied Border Security Strategies

These largely impressive efforts to stand-up a new federal bureaucracy, however, have created a vast divide between a homeland security enterprise, with all the power and wealth of large government and corporate engagement, and the experiences of the American public. Nowhere is this more apparent than in the way security measures have been implemented at our nation's borders and within the United States. The current homeland security paradigm's offensive and defensive strategies converge at the nation's borders in a layered system-of-systems approach to screening and verification of all things deemed a potential risk. The strategy and its tools promote early detection of potential threats, allowing time to analyze them and respond before reaching U.S. shores, and providing repeated opportunities to catch threats that successfully avoid an earlier screen. This strategy works well at the border where—starting with forward deployment overseas—the layered system of surveillance, screening, and analysis monitors and approves shipping, cargo, and people attempting to breach the nation's perimeter. Under the circumstances, the strategy also optimizes efficiencies; as former Deputy Secretary of Homeland Security Admiral James Loy has described it, the approach does not "look for a needle in a haystack, but lifts the hay from the needle."[16]

However, as it has been applied to the American public—individuals and communities *inside* the United States—this screening, verification, and approval approach is in conflict with a core value and faith of American democracy: the presumption of innocence. Subjecting Americans to numerous screening activities, as has become normal behavior at airports, is not necessarily the problem. Nor is increased use of new intrusive technology, much of which could be made more compatible with civil liberties and privacy protections. Rather, discarding the presumption of innocence, even if unintentionally, is what does damage to public trust and engagement in homeland security. Walking through a public airport, for instance, does not in itself evoke particular privacy rights. But an individual does have a strong expectation that, in behaving normally, he or she is not considered a risk and therefore presumed guilty until screened.

Applying border strategies to the interior of the United States, as currently practiced, undermines the willingness of Americans to work with a government that has *de facto* raised questions about their trustworthiness. These strategies focus on passivity, not engagement, on technical expertise rather than public understanding, and on classified information rather than on transparency. This approach makes Americans more dependent on governmental protection, ceding their own personal security to bureaucratic skillfulness. In a real sense, the current homeland security strategy creates the very dependence on government and the feelings of powerlessness that officials then misdiagnose as complacency, apathy, and denial. Feeling at risk in everyday, normal behavior runs counter to the commonsense vision of what Americans believe is a secure homeland. And, as administration officials observed after Hurricane Katrina, without such a vision the nation will not be prepared.

Engaging the Citizenry

The way around this conundrum is not to abandon all screening, but to have citizens fully aware and engaged in why and how the screening and surveillance occurs. This calls for new approaches—not borrowed from border screening and surveillance, but ones that turn to community involvement and civic engagement for the skills needed to secure the homeland. Unfortunately, all that Americans have been offered is generalized information and abstract advice through web sites and marketing campaigns (e.g., www.Ready.gov) and an underfunded suite of programs aimed at increasing volunteer action that have reached, at best, one percent of local residents. Americans have not been engaged in the kind of joint decision-making and cooperative planning for homeland security that fully engages local communities.

Top-down national management initiatives and frameworks weaken the nation's preparedness and communities' safety because they do not generate action among those who must perform well for the security effort to succeed. Fortunately, we can learn from other experiences in the nation's history. As a nation, for instance, we have rethought our approach to public safety to meet similar challenges. Over a twenty year period, community-oriented policing transformed a top-down enforcement strategy into an engagement-based model for public safety. The field of public health offers similar guidance. A vision of good health is not simply limited to highly skilled professionals responding to disease and does not only depend on the capabilities of government agencies employing the most advanced technology and techniques, although these are advantageous; public health relies on the willingness and success of healthy Americans to prevent illness through changed behaviors, greater knowledge, and acceptance of what is required of them. The Institute of Medicine embodies this approach in its very definition of public health: "what we, as a society, do collectively to assure the conditions for people to be healthy."[17]

The homeland security challenge for the new administration is to find ways to transform a government-defined mission into a societal norm. Achieving this norm, and a greater level of resiliency as a nation, calls for more than recognition of the problem and certainly more than rhetorical references to citizen and community preparedness. Taking a cue from public health and other disciplines more engaged with the American public, we must mobilize and focus on what we, as a society, can do collectively to ensure our safety and security.

A New Homeland Security Paradigm

A new strategy for securing the nation begins with engaging the American people in their local communities. Recent nationwide polling confirms that most Americans continue to think poorly of their government overall: when asked to assess government performance, only one in four rates the federal government positively.[18] Yet when the public comes into direct contact with federal employees doing their jobs, the approval rate increases sharply.[19]

Homeland security planners, professionals, and officials need to get out of their operations centers and office buildings and onto the street to work with Americans in ensuring our collective security. Priority initiatives need to focus on collective and connected activities in local communities. A new vision needs to be generated from and shared among local residents, businesses, and the various levels of government. It needs to be a vision that is defined by what we can do collectively to provide a desirable level of well-being, including safety, security, and peace. The American public must have the chance to ponder the tough choices, not just be the passive recipients of bad ones.

Such a community-oriented approach to public security will generate an array of new initiatives and redirect and strengthen existing programs. The following examples offer strategies to engage local communities fully in both planning and decision-making, and to build institutional partnerships that embrace and promote those new relationships.

A New, Joint Decision-Making Process

Perhaps the most critical first step is to find ways to overcome Americans' doubt and suspicion about the nature of the security challenge, including a realistic assessment of threats. Dependence and passivity result from continuously asking the American public to have faith in institutions that they have learned to suspect and which they believe have failed them.

- ***Dialog with the public about the risks we face and the actions we can take.*** The *National Strategy for Homeland Security* calls for the application of a risk-based framework across all homeland security efforts to identify and assess potential hazards, determine levels of acceptable relative risk, and prioritize and allocate resources among homeland security partners. Despite widespread recognition of the value of such an effort, no inclusive, easily accessible, and repeatable process exists for evaluating risks and for using that information to shape decision-making. Communicating risk information also needs to encourage local decision-making rather than merely shaping grant applications for federal funds. Sharing national risk assessments in an appropriate form with businesses and the public should encourage and enable organizations, individuals, and communities to engage in providing for their own security.

The United Kingdom conducts and shares a risk assessment annually, combining national, regional, and local results. It publishes a *National Risk Register* designed to "encourage public debate on security and help organisations, individuals, families and communities, who want to do so, to prepare for emergencies."[20] The conduct of such assessments nationally and at state and local levels, and the sharing of information on identified risks through public discourse and in town hall and community meetings by public officials, is a critical first step to engaging the public in the homeland security mission.

- ***Include local communities as joint decision-makers.*** Although the new administration's agenda clearly calls for renewed collaboration between the federal government and state governors, even a reinvigorated liaison function will not transform the nature of decision-making. Across a range of issues, from investments to setting priorities, local communities should be real partners in making security-related decisions. The Urban Areas Security Initiative and, in general, the federal grants process, offers a framework for financial assistance to be reorganized to include joint decision-making that involves local communities. For example, priority could be given to local alliances (including government agencies) that establish direct connections among various sectors and groups in local areas.

  In other areas of social policy a variety of planning and funding mechanisms have emerged that combine federal, state, and local needs and interests. In workforce training, for instance, Workforce Investment Boards bring together private employers, job training providers, and local governments to set priorities and distribute funds. For certain needs, the federal government or state governments could directly fund common-purpose projects, providing local communities with resources through mechanisms similar to the long-standing Community Development Block Grants.

  Focusing on local involvement in joint decision-making could also mobilize and leverage the resources of local residents who routinely contribute to projects through community foundations. Few of these foundations currently focus on preparedness projects, though some offer disaster relief assistance. Safety and security-oriented projects that more closely connect with the involvement of local residents could significantly enhance participation and spread it among all subgroups in the local population.

- ***Seize on FEMA regionalization plans to recalibrate and reorganize the relationship between DHS and local communities.*** Current efforts to bolster FEMA regions as intermediaries between the federal, state, tribal, and local governments respond in part to the need to engage in new forms of joint decision-making. An opportunity exists to transform these regional activities from "federal monitors" and hierarchical intermediaries to catalysts for a broad network of multi-sector community partners. *DHS should restart and invert its annual preparedness strategic planning process.* Federal initiatives need to seek out and understand local and state risks and priorities, and clearly identify and distinguish truly national needs that require federal action from the vast array of capacities and authorities that rest in the hands of state and local governments and communities. Drawing on new forms of inter-sector collaboration that emphasize horizontal, shared interests, and authorities, FEMA regional efforts could lead this effort, becoming promoters of community-oriented security initiatives rather than federal outreach managers who enhance programs designed and controlled by the Department of Homeland Security.[21]

- ***Establish a National Institute of Preparedness.*** The new administration's agenda promises to take a research-based approach to good public policymaking. Although the DHS Science and Technology Directorate has led the way in testing new technologies and techniques, a broader independent agency is needed to promote a science of preparedness, especially in terms of the complexities of community involvement. This initiative could resemble the National Institute of Justice, housed within the Department of Justice, or could be established as a new independent agency similar to the National Institute of Health. Each of these entities is known for its independent research and evaluation of long-term issues of social and health policy and for putting rigorous scientific debate and demonstration ahead of short-term policy imperatives.

  The goal would be to develop, test, and support initiatives among clusters of local and regional public, private and non-governmental groups aimed at increasing the effectiveness of preparedness activities. Establishing a National Institute of Preparedness would create a vibrant national research program aimed at finding good strategies and truly assessing the extent to which the nation's residents are prepared to prevent and protect against, respond to, and recover from terrorist attacks, natural disasters, and other emergencies.

Leading from the Front

A clear weakness resulting from the federal government-led homeland security strategy has been its failure to appreciate and capitalize on local law enforcement agencies in support of the homeland security mission. In its report, *Leading from the Front*, the International Association of Chiefs of Police reminded the federal administration that the foundation of policing in America, whether dealing with crime or terrorism, is deeply rooted in local law enforcement agencies, where the trust of the American people has had to be direct and sustained.[22]

Unfortunately, the nation currently faces a potential schism between federal homeland security initiatives and local law enforcement communities over both funding and purpose. As Los Angeles Police Chief William Bratton has described,[23] many local communities perceive that terrorist threats may be overblown, creating more fear than safety. Local police may also be using limited resources unnecessarily and inappropriately to monitor law-abiding citizens. At the same time, traditional crime continues to rise, transnational drug cartels and gangs are consolidating their presence in both rural and urban communities, and, ironically, the potential for these criminal activities and groups to help support terrorism is increasing.

The new administration needs to act aggressively and quickly to prevent a counterproductive schism from further undermining public support for homeland security initiatives. While senior police officials have expressed concerns about the crime-fighting blind spots that domestic security efforts may have created, the nation's homeland security leaders have cautioned against using domestic security programs to help pay for day-to-day policing needs. "I don't think we want to take a program designed for one purpose and slowly massage it into another purpose," former DHS Secretary Chertoff has said. "If you are pursuing street crime, I don't think all the organs of national security should be involved in that."[24]

The problem is that this schism will weaken the nation's capacity to identify and prevent domestic terrorism and radicalization, two of the most important threats facing the country in the next few years. Simultaneously, it will also weaken the advances that local police departments have made in working with communities to counter other public insecurities. A federal-local schism is unnecessary. As various observers have argued, the purpose, advantages, and benefits of a community-policing approach to local law enforcement are well suited to preventing and responding to terrorist activity.[25] Local law enforcement officers are far more likely to come into contact with those who may be directly or indirectly involved in terrorist activities than any federal official, and most certainly will be among the first responders to any future attack. For example, in 2005, in Torrance, California, local police arrested two men for robbing a gas station—and wound up uncovering a militant plot to attack Los Angeles-area synagogues and military installations. Good police work is good counterterrorism.[26]

The community-policing approach employed by local law enforcement agencies offers several specific advantages in overcoming the deep divide between the federal homeland security strategy and public support and engagement.

- ***Improved information sharing.*** Community policing offers a different approach to information sharing and surveillance than the top-down, federal-led efforts to screen and monitor local activities and verify the innocence of everyday American citizens. Although counterterrorism activities differ in some crucial ways from crime prevention, the philosophy of community policing encourages innovation in engaging local communities, defining problems, and sustaining connections between police and local residents that may be helpful to homeland security strategies. In particular, a community-led approach could provide a clear alternative to a top-down, federal strategy that has created disturbing tensions between policing, preparedness, and civil liberties. Community-policing officers could serve as trusted intermediaries to encourage the necessary dialogue between security authorities and local residents on the nature of the risks that a community faces.
- ***Preventing homegrown radicalization***. Radicalization is a social process that over time transforms otherwise well-established residents into disenfranchised militants willing to lash out with violence against people and property. The New York City Police Department, for instance, describes radicalized youths as otherwise "unremarkable" local residents who conceptualize and plan attacks against their country of residence inspired or ideologically driven by al Qaeda teachings.[27] Preventing this transformation from unremarkable to threat-laden requires a level of community engagement that is simply impossible to achieve through federal initiatives. Most importantly, it requires awareness and willingness on the part of local residents to cooperate with local police authorities. That awareness and willingness comes from experience

working with or at least knowing about successful—and publicly accepted—police activities. The local officer who works in the same geographical area for several years and has helped with traffic, school, and family problems, or worked with community groups to shut down drug houses and other safety risks, is far more likely to observe radicalizing behaviors before they reach the point of violent action than any federal network of information-sharing agencies. He or she is also a much better user of federally-produced intelligence information and more likely to observe the initial, nuanced acts of a terrorist plot that are typically obscured by links to other criminal threats such as a gangs, gun-running, drug trafficking, and recently released prisoners who may have been radicalized while incarcerated.

- ***Reducing Americans' fear of uncertainty and risk***. If the goal of terrorism is to create fear far beyond the immediate harm, community policing offers a model for directly combating that objective through engagement and cooperation. Local law enforcement agencies have a strong self-interest in understanding fear in their communities if they hope to be effective. As recent debates over issues related to racial profiling and hate crimes have shown, local police agencies' abilities to prevent terrorism may turn on how well they are able to understand their communities and work to solve everyday crime in those same communities.[28]

Applying the lessons from a community-policing approach to community-oriented terrorism prevention could open a new line of thinking about the role of DHS regional offices and officers. As noted previously, FEMA regionalization offers an opportunity to begin to change the relationship between federal, state, tribal, and local agencies. Beyond becoming a catalyst for inter-sector coordination, however, a community oriented philosophy will require FEMA and its sister DHS components and agencies to reorient some of their operating approaches. Community-policing agencies are more "flat" than most organizations—that is, they are decentralized, network-oriented organizations in which officers working with neighborhood groups have more authority than usual to make decisions. This structure allows and even encourages officers to work as partners in joint decision-making, not having to always withhold judgment while they check with geographically distant and organizationally remote authorities.

Community-oriented agencies are also more focused on smaller geographical areas that have organic rather than jurisdictional connections. This focus and flexibility allows more effective alignment of problem solving with the diverse partners needed to make necessary changes in programs and funding. A major challenge for DHS and FEMA regional efforts will be to create and maintain a cross-jurisdictional focus that is not so broad that the relationships become merely consultative rather than oriented toward joint problem-solving and decision-making.

A Call to Service

"Through service, I found a community that embraced me, citizenship that was meaningful."

—Barack Obama

Throughout the most recent presidential campaign, nearly all candidates embraced a call to service, urging the American public to do more in their communities to improve the quality of life. The new administration's plan calls for a significant investment in expanding the volunteer corps, including AmeriCorps, Peace Corps, Energy Corps, and Environmental Corps. Joining others, the plan calls for tax breaks, summer jobs, internships and college tuition in exchange for some form of public service.

Obviously, homeland security and emergency management should take their place in this roll call of valued public services. The problem is that, under current strategies, there is little room for this type of public service in homeland security. The current citizen corps programs offer only limited opportunities for engagement. Community Emergency Response Team (CERT) training, which has been useful, is limited to specific training activities and, by itself, does not generate continuous activities in a community;[29] and Citizen Corps Councils have generated far less activity than expected or needed.[30]

At a local and regional level, the mobilization of residents to become educated, trained and involved in homeland security needs to take on a more sustainable effort. For this to happen, it needs to be integrated into the community's routine activities, its local governance, work life, recreation, and shopping. The rich diversity of the nation's communities means that no one type of program or set of initiatives will work everywhere. Yet every community could become involved. A national campaign is needed that focuses on community preparedness, starting perhaps with public health.

Numerous creative ways to stimulate this community engagement exist. We need to find and expand the moments in which Americans routinely defy the allegations of complacency and denial and where they value the connectivity to their community which homeland security and emergency management strategies have ignored. A block grant challenge—a Community Preparedness Block Grant (CPBG), modeled perhaps after the success of infrastructure repair and historical preservation funds—could be a useful example. A preparedness corps of diverse local residents could organize neighborhood campaigns to, among other activities, canvas and teach the elderly how to turn off their natural gas in an emergency and link them to neighbors to whom they can turn if an incident occurs. These and many other ideas already exist in local communities across the country. They can be heard anecdotally at conferences, or read in local newspapers and researchers' stories, but they await more widespread mobilization, support, and leadership.

The challenge is not simply to acknowledge the need for such community activities, but to find a proper place for such activities within our homeland security strategy and execute their role effectively.[31] Currently, efforts to engage local communities are primarily considered ways to get the government's message across and perhaps add helpers to the professional response cadre during an incident. A community-oriented homeland security strategy, in contrast, would value the ideas and the people engaged in the community because they are the fulcrum of effectiveness. In the same way that the nation relies on the professional expertise of its intelligence officers, border screeners, and critical infrastructure protectors, it must rely on the ability of local residents to be effective public citizens.

Toward a Social Infrastructure for Homeland Security

From a shared vision of a way of life to everyday interactions with neighbors, an effective homeland security strategy requires the full participation of the American public. The full array of these social activities, programs, and relationships constitutes an essential foundation, what can easily be called a "social infrastructure for homeland security." Like other infrastructures, it needs priority attention and support. And like other infrastructures, it has fallen into disrepair.

During the Cold War, the American public had a social compact with the federal government to lend its political and financial support for distant, not-well-understood actions overseas against a communist threat. The public came to expect protection from these overseas risks and, in exchange, wanted to go about its business of working hard, raising families, and enjoying the prosperity that lasted nearly half a century.

Today's asymmetric threats have changed the way we think about the world and the compact between the federal government and the public. The initial round of homeland security strategies has not yet caught up with this global and internal transformation. While the nation fights overseas, a new social compact at home is needed that redefines opportunities and responsibilities just as much as world events are changing the risks and challenges to the American way of life.[32]

Ask any homeland security or emergency management professional what makes them most successful in their activities and most will say that it is the trust that they developed in their coworkers and colleagues *well before* an incident or operation. Trust is also the glue that makes communities work. At a time when trust in government, trust in public health institutions, and trust in the financial system are weakening, it is unlikely that efforts to mobilize the public to be prepared for emergencies will work. The first step in the long transition to a new social compact, then, may be the most direct—to repair and build the trust that makes our most critical activities succeed. Social trust may be the meaning we can all find in community service, and strengthening it may be the way to navigate through the deep currents of our future.

Critical Thinking Questions

1. Do national leaders overestimate or underestimate the ability of citizens to understand, assess and mitigate risk? Explain.
2. Are there examples of other countries that have made the kinds of "social infrastructure" investments recommended in this article?
3. What risks are inherent in the community-oriented policy recommendations offered here?

Notes

1. Homeland Security Council, *National Strategy for Homeland Security* (Washington, DC: Government Printing Office, 2007), 13.
2. Amanda J. Dory, "American Civil Security: The U.S. Public and Homeland Security," *The Washington Quarterly* 27, no. 1 (2003): 37–52.
3. President George W. Bush, November 8, 2001. Quoted in *NCPC* (Washington, DC: National Crime Prevention Council, January 2002), 1.
4. "Homeland Security Secretary Ridge Speaks About the Patriot Act," Prepared Remarks of Homeland Security Secretary Tom Ridge at the Allegheny County Emergency Operations Center, July 15, 2004.

5. *The Federal Response to Hurricane Katrina: Lessons Learned*, 66.
6. Megumi Kano, Michele M. Wood, Dennis S. Mileti, and Linda B. Bourque, *Public Response to Terrorism. Findings from the National Survey of Disaster Experiences and Preparedness* (Berkeley, CA: Regents of the University of California, November 12, 2008).
7. An example is President Bush's statement: ". . . Get on board. Do your business around the country. Fly and enjoy America's great destination spots. Get down to Disney World in Florida. Take your families and enjoy life, the way we want it to be enjoyed." Remarks by President Bush at O'Hare International Airport, September 27, 2001.
8. Department of Homeland Security Press Release launching a Citizen Preparedness Campaign urging all Americans to "make a kit, make a plan, and be informed," February 19, 2003.
9. Roz D. Lasker, "Redefining Readiness: Terrorism Planning Through the Eyes of the Public" (New York: Center for the Advancement of Collaborative Strategies in Health, New York Academy of Medicine, September 14, 2004).
10. Brad Heath, "Deeply set disturbance within American communities and the American faith in its government and core institutions," *USA TODAY*, May 9, 2007, http://www.usatoday.com/news/nation/2007-05-09-emergencies_N.htm.
11. Jonathan Weisman, "Obama Calls for National Service Democrat Visiting GOP Strongholds," *Washington Post*, July 3, 2008.
12. Ibid.
13. Commission on the Prevention of WMD Proliferation and Terrorism, *World at Risk: The Report of the Commission on the Prevention of WMD Proliferation and Terrorism* (New York: Random House, December 2008).
14. A study conducted after World War II shows that local organizational preparedness during peacetime was the most effective strategy for saving lives from conventional attacks, Matthew Dallek, "Civic Security. Why FDR's bottom-up brand of civic defense should inspire progressive plans for homeland security today," *Democracyjournal.org* (Winter 2008): 16.
15. Address by President George W. Bush to Joint Session of Congress, September 20, 2001.
16. See Admiral Loy's testimony before the National Commission on Terrorist Attacks Upon the United States, January 27, 2004, Hart Senate Office Building, Washington, DC.
17. Institute of Medicine, ed., *The Future of Public Health* (Washington, DC: National Academies Press, 1988), 19.
18. *In the Public We Trust. Renewing the Connection between the Federal Government and the Public* (Partnership for Public Service and Gallup Consulting, November 2008), 2.
19. Ibid, 3.
20. Cabinet Office, *National Risk Register* (2008), 3.
21. See for example, Center for Homeland Defense and Security, *Multi-Jurisdictional, Network Alliances and Emergency Preparedness* (Monterey, CA: Naval Postgraduate School, December 2008.
22. International Association of Chiefs of Police, "Leading from the Front: Law Enforcement's Role in Combating And Preparing for Domestic Terrorism." *The International Association of Chiefs of Police's Response to the Attacks on the United States of America on September 11, 2001* (Alexandria, VA, n.d.)

23. William Bratton, George Kelling, and R.P. Eddy, "The blue front line. For cops, fighting crime and terror go hand in hand,"*city-journal.org,* September 20, 2007, www.city-journal.org/html/eon2007-09-20.html
24. David Johnston, "A City's Police Force Now Doubts Terror Focus," *NYTIMES.COM*, July 24, 2008.
25. Matthew C. Scheider and Robert Chapman, "Community Policing and Terrorism," April 2003, http://www.homelandsecurity.org/journal/Articles/Scheider-Chapman.html.
26. Bratton and others, "The blue front line."
27. Mitchell D. Silber and Arvin Bhatt, "Radicalization in the West: The Homegrown Threat" (New York: New York City Police Department, 2007).
28. Scheider and Chapman, "Community Policing and Terrorism."
29. CERT programs have, however, been used as the catalyst for community-wide initiatives in some locations.
30. David Heyman and James Jay Carafano, *Homeland Security 3.0: Building a National Enterprise to Keep America Safe, Free, and Prosperous* (Washington, DC: The Heritage Foundation, Heritage Special Report, SR-23, September 18, 2008).
31. See Dory, "American Civil Security," for an earlier attempt to define such a role.
32. Rahm Emanuel and Bruce Reed, *The Plan. Big Ideas for America* (New York: Public Affairs, 2006).

Unit Three

Public Security and Civil Liberties

UNIT THREE provides a diverse collection of perspectives on the legal and ethical controversies surrounding contemporary efforts to secure the homeland. Amid the flurry of activity meant to protect America from future terrorist attacks, we face an additional challenge of maintaining a balance between freedom and security. Clearly, in reacting to global terrorism, we cannot allow our freedoms to be diminished. As Benjamin Franklin so aptly put it, "They that can give up essential liberty to obtain a little temporary safety deserve neither liberty nor safety." In the first reading, Erik Dahl of the Naval Postgraduate School reviews the debate over whether a domestic intelligence agency was needed after 9/11. He then describes the current system of homeland security intelligence within the United States, including the growth of new intelligence organizations at the state and local level, and argues that this constitutes a *de facto* domestic intelligence organization. He then demonstrates that the development of this domestic intelligence structure has moved the balance between security and liberty quite firmly in the direction of more security, but less liberty. He concludes his essay by arguing that even though these developments might very well be acceptable to the American people, there is an urgent need for a better-informed national discussion about domestic intelligence.

Next, Torin Monahan of Vanderbilt University examines the unique challenges of the homeland security intelligence mission. In her view, fusion centers (most of which are located within state and local police departments) illustrate the ways in which "surveillance" pervades all aspects of social life—imperatives to collect, share, analyze, and act on data increasingly shape the activities of public institutions, private companies, and individuals. She then describes several instances where fusion centers provided information that led to law enforcement personnel erroneously impinging on the civil liberties of individuals and concludes that fusion centers require more sophisticated legal constraints and public oversight.

In the following reading, University of Pittsburgh Professor David Harris explores the controversies surrounding illegal immigration and its intersections with national security and law enforcement. In particular, he describes how the rebranding of the immigration problem as a national security issue began a process that culminated in laws at the state level, such as Arizona's S.B. 1070. While the Arizona law was not intended as a national security measure, it represents exactly what the anti-immigration advocates have longed for—a way to force state and local law enforcement agencies into the immigration fight. However, he argues, this statute actually harms national security, and almost guarantees that local law enforcement will cause damage to the most important weapon we have for fighting terrorism: the gathering of intelligence. This is one reason why so many police leaders and police departments have strongly opposed rebranding efforts that would press them into the realm of immigration enforcement. They see the effort to do this as diametrically opposed to promoting public safety. Without the community on their side, they cannot get the help and information they need to do their jobs well.

The last section of UNIT THREE offers three compelling and diverse—yet complementary—perspectives on the USA PATRIOT Act, passed by Congress on October 24, 2001, and signed into law by President Bush two days later. Because the Act provided broad new powers to various agencies of the federal government—particularly in the area of gathering information about communications, financial transactions, and other activities—it has become a focal point in the struggle to maintain civil liberties while increasing the nation's security. In the first of these readings, Nancy Chang (formerly the senior litigation attorney at the Center for Constitutional Rights in New York) calls it an attack on the Bill of Rights. On the opposite side of the debate, three other attorneys—Brian Hook, Margaret Peterlin, and Peter Walsh—contend in the next reading that intelligence and information sharing among governmental agencies will not occur without many of the provisions in the Act. And in the final reading, Roger Golden (a senior civilian at Maxwell Air Force Base) takes a nuanced approach in the middle of these two opposing viewpoints, emphasizing the need to ensure a healthy balance between freedom and security. He notes that for now, we have witnessed a shift toward security with the potential loss of a degree of the freedom, but American history suggests that a shift in the other direction is likely once the threat to security is perceived as sufficiently reduced.

This collection of readings highlights just a few of the most important dimensions of the debate over how to effectively maintain a balance between freedom and security. From the surveillance of Internet communications to restrictions on what the media can report in the global war on terrorism, few public debates have been more central to American values than maintaining this balance. How we eventually resolve this debate will certainly have lasting implications for the long-term health of the entire republic.

Learning Objectives

After studying the materials in UNIT THREE, students will have an ability to articulate many of the most important dimensions of the debate over how to effectively maintain a balance between freedom and security. Students will also develop a solid understanding of key homeland security topics including domestic intelligence, surveillance, information sharing, and immigration.

Recommended Resources

Docobo, Jose. "Protecting America's Communities: A Law Enforcement Perspective," in James Forest (ed.), *Homeland Security: Protecting America's Targets* (Westport, CT: Praeger, 2006).

Foreign Intelligence Surveillance Act, Public Law 112–90 (October 1978). Online at: http://uscode.house.gov/download/pls/50C36.txt

Homeland Security Act (HSA) of 2002, Public Law 107–296 (November 2002). Online at: http://www.dhs.gov/xlibrary/assets/hr_5005_enr.pdf

Jenkins, Brian Michael "The NDAA Makes It Harder to Fight Terrorism," *RAND Corporation* (February 1, 2012—Original appeared on ForeignAffairs.com). Available at http://www.rand.org/commentary/2012/02/01/FA.html

Jenkins, Brian Michael. "A Final Word on the NDAA," *RAND Corporation* (May 6, 2012—Original appeared on ForeignAffairs.com). Available at http://www.rand.org/commentary/2012/05/06/FA.html

Levin, Carl "Senator Levin Sets the Record Straight on the NDAA: What the Law Does and Doesn't Do on Detention," *Foreign Affairs* (March 15, 2012). Available at http://www.foreignaffairs.com/articles/137335/carl-levin/senator-levin-sets-the-record-straight-on-the-ndaa

Lewis, Jeffrey. "The Role of Technology in Protecting America's Gathering Places," in James Forest (ed.), *Homeland Security: Protecting America's Targets* (Westport, CT: Praeger, 2006).

Strickland, Lee. "Without Civil Liberties Homeland Security Will Fail," *University of Maryland* (December 23, 2005). Available at http://www.newsdesk.umd.edu/archive/release.cfm?year=2005&ArticleID=1197

Thornburgh, Dick "Balancing Civil Liberties and Homeland Security: Does the USA PATRIOT Act Avoid Justice Robert H. Jackson's 'Suicide Pact'?" *Albany Law Review* (June 28, 2005). Online at http://www.albanylawreview.org/articles/Thornburgh%28final%29.pdf

USA PATRIOT Act, Public Law 107-56 (October 2001). Online at: http://www.justice.gov/oig/special/s0708/final.pdf

Section 3.1

Legal and Ethical Controversies in Securing the Homeland

Domestic Intelligence Today

More Security but Less Liberty?

Erik J. Dahl

One of the most important questions about intelligence reform after the 9/11 attacks was whether the United States should establish a new domestic intelligence agency—an American equivalent of the British MI-5, some suggested. Supporters of the idea argued that only a completely new organization would be able to provide the fresh thinking and strength of focus that was needed, and they pointed out that the US was the only Western country without such an organization. Critics said the Federal Bureau of Investigation (FBI) was already well on its way to reinventing itself as just the sort of intelligence-driven agency the country needed and that establishing a new domestic intelligence agency would require the creation of a costly new bureaucracy to duplicate capabilities that already existed.

That debate was eventually settled in the negative. Although a number of major reforms were made to American intelligence—including, most notably, the establishment of the position of the Director of National Intelligence (DNI)—no central domestic intelligence agency has been created. Instead, the intelligence functions of the FBI have been beefed up and several new organizations have been created, including the National Counterterrorism Center (NCTC). Although occasionally the argument is still heard that the US needs a domestic intelligence service,[1] in general most intelligence professionals and outside observers appear to agree that no new domestic intelligence organization is necessary.

But this essay argues that even though we as a nation decided not to establish a domestic intelligence organization, we have in recent years done just that: we have created a vast domestic intelligence establishment, one which few Americans understand and which does not receive the oversight and scrutiny it deserves. There is good news here: this domestic intelligence system appears to have been successful in increasing security within the US, as demonstrated by numerous foiled terrorist plots and the lack of another major successful attack on American soil since 9/11. But there is also bad news: these gains are coming at the cost of increasing domestic surveillance and at the risk of civil liberties.

This essay begins by reviewing the debate over whether a domestic intelligence agency was needed after 9/11. It then describes the current system of homeland security intelligence within the US, including the growth of new intelligence organizations at the state and local level, and argues that this constitutes a de facto domestic intelligence organization. Next it demonstrates that the development of this domestic intelligence structure has moved the balance between security and liberty quite firmly in the direction of more security, but less liberty. The essay concludes by arguing that even though these developments might very well be acceptable to the American people, we cannot know whether they are acceptable or not without a better-informed national discussion about domestic intelligence.[2]

The Debate over a Domestic Intelligence Agency

One aspect of the debate over intelligence reform following the 9/11 attacks was the question of whether the United States should establish a new domestic intelligence agency.

Although the question was often framed in terms of whether the US should create an organization modeled on the British MI-5, several options were widely discussed.

The change supported by many experts was to form an independent intelligence service within the FBI. The FBI already had the lead on most domestic intelligence issues and since 9/11 had been increasing its focus on intelligence, so forming such an organization within the FBI appeared to be the simplest option, involving few changes to the rest of the intelligence community. A group of six experienced intelligence and national security experts, writing in *The Economist*, argued for this approach.[3] The *WMD Commission Report* also supported such a change, proposing that the counter-terrorism, counter-intelligence, and intelligence services of the FBI be combined to create a new National Security Service.[4]

Critics, however, argued either that such a change was unnecessary because the FBI was already transforming itself into an intelligence-driven agency, or that it would be a dangerous move because the FBI was likely to remain primarily a law enforcement organization, unsuited to the intelligence mission and inclined to use its increasing intelligence and surveillance powers at the risk of civil liberties.

Another idea was to create a new intelligence agency under the newly created Department of Homeland Security (DHS). Federal Judge Richard Posner, for example, argued for such an organization, to be called the Security Intelligence Service, with the head of this agency to be dual-hatted as the DNI's deputy for domestic intelligence.[5]

The idea that was most often talked about was to create a wholly new, independent organization, possibly modeled on the British MI-5 (which is officially known as the Security Service). Supporters of the idea noted that most Western countries have some sort of domestic intelligence agency. In Britain MI-5 collects and analyzes domestic intelligence, but it has no police power or arrest authority; foreign intelligence in the British system is handled by MI-6, the Secret Intelligence Service.[6] Critics argued that the MI-5 model was unlikely to be applicable to the US because Britain is a much smaller, more centralized country with fewer local police forces and a powerful Home Office, while the US is much larger and decentralized, with thousands of independent local police and sheriff's departments.

Experts also examined domestic intelligence models from other countries, including Australia, India, France, and Germany.[7] Other than MI-5, the model most often pointed to as appropriate for the US was the Canadian Security Intelligence Service (CSIS). The CSIS was established relatively recently (1984), after the Canadian national police force (the Royal Canadian Mounted Police) was found to have broken the law and violated civil liberties in dealing with Quebec separatist groups and other internal threats.[8]

Support for a new domestic intelligence agency was never as strong as it had been for other major reforms such as the establishment of a Director of National Intelligence. The 9/11 Commission recommended against creating such a new agency, and although discussion continues about whether or not the nation's domestic intelligence structure is adequately organized, there seems to be little impetus for setting up a US version of MI-5.[9]

The most extensive study of the question was conducted by RAND, at the request of the Department of Homeland Security, and resulted in three volumes of reports.[10] RAND was specifically not asked by DHS to offer recommendations, but these reports can hardly be seen as ringing endorsements for the idea of a new domestic agency. When the RAND researchers surveyed a group of experts, most expressed the view that the current organization for domestic intelligence wasn't very good; but they also said they did not think that any reorganization was likely to improve the situation.[11] Gregory Treverton summed up the study this way: "Caution and deliberations are the watchwords for this study's conclusions."[12]

Current Domestic Intelligence Organization

In its analysis for DHS, RAND outlined what it called the "domestic intelligence enterprise."[13] This enterprise encompasses a complex system that includes counterterrorism organizations led by the NCTC; other federal-level organizations and efforts, including those within the FBI, DHS, and Department of Defense; and state, local, and private sector activities. Some of the experts consulted by RAND saw this domestic intelligence enterprise as problematic because it was uncoordinated and thus potentially ineffective; one described domestic intelligence as "a pickup ballgame without a real structure, leadership, management, or output."[14] But even though our domestic intelligence system may not have a centralized structure, it is more coordinated and also more effective than most Americans realize, and constitutes a de facto—but little understood—domestic intelligence system.

It is difficult, if not impossible, for the American public to accurately gauge the size of the country's domestic intelligence effort. Much of that effort is deservedly kept secret, as is the overall scope of America's intelligence activities at home and abroad. The size of the national intelligence community is not precisely known, but in 2009 then-Director of National Intelligence Dennis Blair described it as a 200,000-person, $75 billion per year enterprise.[15] By the next year the intelligence budget had grown to $80.1 billion. That number is believed to be twice what it was in 2001, and it is considerably more than the $53 billion spent on the Department of Homeland Security in 2010.[16]

An investigation into the country's intelligence and counterterrorism structure by *The Washington Post* described what it called "a Top Secret America hidden from public view and lacking in thorough oversight."[17] The *Post* found that some 854,000 people hold top secret security clearances, and that at least 263 government agencies and organizations had been created or reorganized as a response to 9/11.

The office of the DNI is itself a large entity, with some 1,800 employees as of 2010, and has come to be considered one of the seventeen top-level agencies of the intelligence community.[18] Within the Department of Homeland Security there are at least nine separate intelligence elements, including the Office of Intelligence and Analysis and intelligence organizations of six separate DHS components: Customs and Border Protection, Immigration and Customs Enforcement, Citizenship and Immigration Services, Transportation Security Administration, the Coast Guard, and the Secret Service.[19]

Since 9/11 the FBI has greatly increased the priority it gives to intelligence and counter-terrorism, setting up a new National Security Branch, increasing the number and status of its intelligence analysts, and establishing Field Intelligence Groups in each of its fifty-six field offices. The FBI has also been busy developing new networks of informants within the United States: its 2008 budget request said that it "recruits new CHS [confidential human sources] every day," and needed more money to do it, with apparently 15,000 sources needing to be validated.[20]

Some elements of national and military intelligence have become more involved in domestic surveillance since 9/11. The National Security Agency (NSA), for example, which was revealed in 2005 to have been involved in what was called the Terrorist Surveillance Program, reportedly continues to conduct a significant amount of domestic intelligence collection.[21] As an indication of the growth in the NSA's business—although presumably much of the growth is in foreign intelligence—the agency is building a new data storage center in Utah that will reportedly cost $1.7 billion and occupy as much as one million square feet of space, larger than the US Capitol building.

Some domestic counterintelligence activities of the Department of Defense have drawn criticism since 9/11, in particular the now-defunct Counterintelligence Field Activity (CIFA). But in general, military and other national security intelligence capabilities have not been utilized domestically to any great degree, because of civil liberties concerns as well as Posse Comitatus restrictions on the use of military personnel for law enforcement. For example, an effort to establish a National Applications Office (NAO) to coordinate the domestic use of reconnaissance satellites failed after members of Congress opposed it.[22] And the US Northern Command, established after the 9/11 attacks to coordinate US military support for homeland defense and security, has been careful to focus most of its intelligence efforts toward homeland defense—focusing on threats from outside the US—and takes a very limited role in domestic intelligence and surveillance (such as helping to coordinate reconnaissance assets when needed to support state and federal authorities following emergencies such as the Gulf oil spill and Hurricane Katrina).

Another area where military capabilities have not seen widespread domestic use is with unmanned aerial vehicles, or UAV. Although UAV have become a mainstay of US military operations overseas, they are little used within the US, even by civilian authorities. United States Customs and Border Protection does operate small numbers of UAV along the country's northern and southern borders, and a few local law enforcement agencies have experimented with the technology, but they remain an underutilized capability.[23]

A growth area for intelligence since 9/11 has been in the development of national intelligence centers, combining and coordinating efforts of a wide variety of organizations on specific problems. In some cases these centers are new, such as the National Counterterrorism Center and the National Counterproliferation Center. In other cases already existing intelligence organizations have been redesignated as national centers, such as the National Maritime Intelligence Center at Suitland, Maryland, and the National Center for Medical Intelligence at Fort Detrick, Maryland.

There are a number of other new or growing federal intelligence agencies and organizations, including the El Paso Intelligence Center (EPIC), a multi-agency counter drug center run jointly by the DEA and DHS, and the interagency National Gang Intelligence Center. There are also operational organizations that are significant users of intelligence, including the 106 FBI-led Joint Terrorism Task Forces that are critical tools in combating domestic terrorism, and High Intensity Drug Trafficking Area (HIDTA) Intelligence and Investigative Support Centers, which are counter-drug efforts sponsored by the Office of National Drug Control Policy.[24] There are also two Joint Interagency Task Forces (JIATFs), one in Hawaii and the other in Key West, Florida, which are interagency counter-drug organizations nominally under Department of Defense control.

At the next level down from the federal level of intelligence is a network of seventy-two state and local intelligence fusion centers. These centers receive DHS funding and support, and many of them have a DHS intelligence liaison officer assigned to them full time, providing analytical support and reach-back capability to DHS headquarters. These fusion centers are not widely known, but they have had some notable successes in helping to prevent terrorist attacks and assisting law enforcement agencies in capturing criminals.[25]

These fusion centers, however, have also generated controversy.[26] The American Civil Liberties Union argues that:

> The federal government's increasing efforts to formalize, standardize, and network these state, local, and regional intelligence centers—and plug them directly into the intelligence community's Information Sharing Environment—are the functional equivalent of creating a new national domestic intelligence agency that deputizes a broad range of personnel from all levels of government, the private sector, and the military to spy on their fellow Americans.[27]

Bruce Fein, a lawyer and former federal official who is a frequent government critic, testified before the House Homeland Security Committee that the US "should abandon fusion centers that engage 800,000 state and local law enforcement officers in the business of gathering and sharing allegedly domestic or international terrorism intelligence."[28]

The best known of these state and local organizations is actually not part of the national fusion center network: the New York Police Department's intelligence division.[29] The NYPD intelligence effort includes liaison officers in some eleven countries overseas, analysts who reportedly speak more languages than can be found in the New York office of the FBI, and even a program that takes police recruits out of the police academy and places them in undercover positions, in some cases conducting investigations inside mosques in the New York City area.[30]

Balancing Security and Liberty

The 9/11 Commission argued that we should not have to trade security for liberty, calling the choice between the two a "false choice."[31] But it seems that the balance and the tradeoff are very real today. There is nothing new in this: as a RAND study notes, "Throughout US history, in times of national security crisis, civil liberties have been curtailed in exchange for perceived greater security, the balance between liberties and security generally being restored after each crisis."[32] What is new today, ten years after the 9/11 attacks, is that the balance has not yet been restored, and in some ways the balance continues to shift toward greater governmental power.

In some cases, this increased government authority is obvious: more intrusive screening at airports, for example, continues the tilt toward greater security at the expense of liberty (and occasionally, dignity). In other cases, the greater powers of government are less evident. As an example, there is a great deal of attention paid today to the previously little-known Foreign Intelligence Surveillance Court (FISC), which is empowered to issue warrants for domestic searches and surveillance under the Foreign Intelligence and Surveillance Act (FISA). But while fewer than fifty FISA orders were issued in 2006, during that same year the FBI issued more than 28,000 of what are called National Security Letters (NSLs), which can authorize search or surveillance of US persons but do not require review by a court or judge.[33] In 2010 the FBI made 24,287 NSL requests pertaining to US persons, but only 1,579 applications to the FISC for surveillance and search authority.[34]

The FBI is expanding its domestic intelligence and surveillance operations in other ways, as well. It is changing its own internal rules to give its agents more leeway to conduct investigations and surveillance, such as by searching databases or sorting through a person's trash.[35] And it appears to be making greater use of undercover informants in intelligence investigations, leading in some cases to successful arrests and prosecutions, but in others to controversy.[36]

One of the most controversial aspects of domestic intelligence after 9/11 was the Patriot Act, which significantly expanded the ability of government authorities to collect information within the US and lowered the "wall" separating criminal investigation from foreign intelligence gathering. In the years since it was first passed several of the Patriot Act's provisions have been renewed, adding tighter controls of government activity. But in general the government has retained its increased authorities. Several of these provisions, which had been scheduled to "sunset," or expire, were renewed in May 2011, with the renewal receiving as much attention for the way it happened—President Obama, who was in Europe, authorized the use of an autopen machine to sign the bill into law—as for the fact that it occurred at all.[37]

Because so much of intelligence work—including domestic intelligence—needs to be hidden from view, a considerable amount of secrecy might be acceptable as long as the American public could be confident that its legislators or others were watching out for the public. As Gregory Treverton writes, "The public doesn't need to know the details of what is being done in its name. It does need to know that some body independent of an administration does know and does approve."[38] The problem is that Congressional oversight of intelligence matters is widely regarded as weak, and much of the day-to-day supervision of intelligence agencies is conducted by organizations such as the National Security Council, the Office of Management and Budget, and agency inspectors general. Such oversight is often useful, but it still means the Executive Branch is supervising itself.

Concerns over oversight of the national intelligence community are heightened when the focus shifts to state and local intelligence efforts. Although most local fusion centers receive federal funds and receive operating guidelines from DHS and the Department of Justice, they are under state or local control and as such are not subject to any strong, centralized oversight. And programs such as the Nationwide Suspicious Activity Reporting Initiative, which is being implemented in cities and states around the country, show great potential for helping to prevent terrorist attacks and detect other criminal activity, but they also raise questions about civil liberties.[39]

Critics argue that in the past ten years the balance between security and liberty his shifted far too much toward security, leading to a great increase in government power. In the words of Laura Murphy of the ACLU, "It feels as though scissors have cut out whole portions of our liberties in the name of fighting the war on terrorism."[40] This may be an overstatement, but it does seem clear that the development of a vast domestic intelligence structure since 9/11 has moved the balance quite firmly in the direction of more security, and less liberty.

Conclusion: Where to From Here?

By its very nature, domestic and homeland security intelligence is intrusive and risks infringing on civil liberties. As then-Secretary of Homeland Security Michael Chertoff put it:

> Intelligence, as you know, is not only about spies and satellites. Intelligence is about the thousands and thousands of routine, everyday observations and activities. Surveillances, interactions—each of which may be taken in isolation

> as not a particularly meaningful piece of information, but when fused together, gives us a sense of the patterns and the flow that really is at the core of what intelligence analysis is really about.[41]

These thousands and thousands of observations are largely observations about people and events in America, and in the years since 9/11 America has created a domestic intelligence system to collect them. In some cases the people are terrorists or other types of criminals, and the intelligence collected has helped to prevent bad events from happening. But in many cases these observations, this intelligence, is about routine activities undertaken by ordinary Americans and others who do not intend to cause harm.

Unless the threat situation changes dramatically, we are not likely to see a new American domestic intelligence agency anytime soon. In the place of an "American MI-5," however, a huge and expensive domestic intelligence system has been constructed. This system has thus far succeeded in keeping America safer than most experts would have predicted ten years ago, but it has also reduced civil liberties in ways that many Americans fail to understand. Precisely because it was unplanned and is decentralized, this domestic intelligence system has not received the oversight it deserves. In the long run, American liberty as well as security will gain from a fuller discussion of the benefits and risks of homeland security intelligence.

Critical Thinking Questions

1. Is our nation's current domestic intelligence apparatus sufficient and effective, or do you agree with those who argue that the United States should create a domestic security service like the British MI-5? Why or why not?
2. Who's in charge of domestic intelligence, and how are they held accountable?
3. Who in the United States is best positioned to lead the kind of "national discussion about domestic intelligence" the author suggests?

Notes

1. See for example James Burch, "Intelligence and Homeland Security," in Loch K. Johnson and James J. Wirtz, eds., *Intelligence: The Secret World of Spies, An Anthology*, 3rd ed. (NY: Oxford University Press, 2011), 499–516.
2. Although this essay focuses on domestic intelligence, the debate over the balance between security and liberty touches on many other issues including the proper handling and treatment of terrorism suspects, enhanced interrogation and torture, and overseas military operations such as targeted killings. For discussion of some of these broader issues, see the hearing on "Civil Liberties and National Security" before the House Judiciary Committee Subcommittee on the Constitution, Civil Rights, and Civil Liberties, December 9, 2010, http://judiciary.house.gov/hearings/hear_101209.html.
3. "America Needs More Spies," *The Economist*, July 12, 2003.
4. Commission on the Intelligence Capabilities of the United States Regarding Weapons of Mass Destruction (the Silberman-Robb Commission), *Report to the President of the United States* (March 31, 2005), 465, http://www.fas.org/irp/offdocs/wmd_chapter10.pdf.
5. Posner is a prolific writer on intelligence (and other topics). See for example his "Remaking Domestic Intelligence," American Enterprise Institute working paper #111, June 20, 2005, http://www.aei.org/docLib/20050621_DomesticIntelligence3.pdf.

6. For background on MI-5 see Todd Masse, *Domestic Intelligence in the United Kingdom: Applicability of the MI-5 Model to the United States* (Washington, DC: Congressional Research Service, May 19, 2003).
7. Burch, "Intelligence and Homeland Security"; Brian A. Jackson, ed., *Considering the Creation of a Domestic Intelligence Agency in the United States: Lessons from the Experiences of Australia, Canada, France, Germany, and the United Kingdom* (Santa Monica, CA: RAND, 2009).
8. Gregory F. Treverton, *Intelligence for an Age of Terror* (NY: Cambridge University Press, 2009), 127. Richard Posner also sees value in the CSIS model; see his "Remaking Domestic Intelligence," cited above.
9. An example of the continuing discussion about domestic intelligence is Eric Rosenbach and Aki Peritz, "Domestic Intelligence," Belfer Center for Science and International Affairs Memorandum, Harvard Kennedy School, July 2009, at http://belfercenter.ksg.harvard.edu/publication/19152/domestic_intelligence.html.
10. Brian A. Jackson, ed., *The Challenge of Domestic Intelligence in a Free Society* (Santa Monica, CA: RAND, 2009); Jackson, *Considering the Creation of a Domestic Intelligence Agency in the United States*; and Gregory F. Treverton, *Reorganizing U.S. Domestic Intelligence: Assessing the Options* (Santa Monica, CA: RAND, 2008).
11. Treverton, *Reorganizing U.S. Domestic Intelligence*, chap. 5.
12. Treverton, *Reorganizing U.S. Domestic Intelligence*, 101.
13. Jackson, *The Challenge of Domestic Intelligence*, Figure 3.1, p. 52.
14. Ibid., note 14, p. 72.
15. Siobhan Gorman, "Spy Chief Says U.S. Hunting al Qaeda More Effectively," *The Wall Street Journal*, September 17, 2009.
16. Ken Dilanian, "U.S. Reveals Skyrocketing Cost of Intelligence Gathering Since 9/11 Attacks," *Los Angeles Times*, October 28, 2010.
17. Dana Priest and William M. Arkin, "A Hidden World, Growing Beyond Control," *The Washington Post*, July 19, 2010.
18. The personnel figures were noted in a speech by David R. Shedd, the Deputy Director of National Intelligence for Policy, Plans, and Requirements, in April 2010: http://www.dni.gov/speeches/20100406_2_speech.pdf. It should be noted that the current DNI, James Clapper, has said he intends to streamline the office.
19. Mark A. Randol, "The Department of Homeland Security Intelligence Enterprise: Operational Overview and Oversight Challenges for Congress," Congressional Research Service, March 19, 2010.
20. Federal Bureau of Investigation, *FY 2008 Authorization and Budget Request to Congress*, 4–23 and 4–24, at http://www.justice.gov/jmd/2008justification/pdf/33_fbi_se.pdf. See also the Federation of American Scientists Secrecy News Blog, "The FBI as an Intelligence Organization," August 27, 2007, http://www.fas.org/blog/secrecy/2007/08/the_fbi_as_an_intelligence_org.html.
21. Siobhan Gorman, "NSA's Domestic Spying Grows as Agency Sweeps Up Data," *Wall Street Journal*, March 10, 2008.
22. Jeffrey T. Richelson, "The Office That Never Was: The Failed Creation of the National Applications Office," *International Journal of Intelligence and Counterintelligence* 24, no. 1 (2011): 68–118.

23. Chad C. Haddal and Jeremiah Gertler, *Homeland Security: Unmanned Aerial Vehicles and Border Surveillance* (Washington, DC; Congressional Research Service, July 8, 2010); Peter Finn, "Domestic Use of Aerial Drones by Law Enforcement Likely to Prompt Privacy Debate," *The Washington Post*, January 23, 2011.
24. The HIDTA program is a combined effort of federal, state, and local law enforcement authorities covering at least part of forty-five states. As of 2010, there were thirty-two Intelligence and Investigative Support Centers in the program. See Office of National Drug Control Policy, *High Intensity Drug Trafficking Areas Program Report to Congress* (June 2010), http://www.whitehousedrugpolicy.gov/pdf/hidta_2010.pdf.
25. The Colorado Information and Analysis Center (CIAC), for example, was recognized as the Fusion Center of the Year in February 2010 for its support to the Najibullah Zazi terrorism investigation, and more recently it provided information that helped lead to the arrest of a bombing suspect; see "Fusion Centers: Empowering State and Local Partners to Address Homeland Security Issues," DHS blog July 18, 2011, http://blog.dhs.gov/2011/07/fusion-centers-empowering-state-and.html.
26. Ken Dilanian, "Fusion Centers Gather Terrorism Intelligence—and Much More," *Los Angeles Times*, November 15, 2010.
27. Mike German and Jay Stanley, "Fusion Center Update," American Civil Liberties Union, July 2008, http://www.aclu.org/pdfs/privacy/fusion_update_20080729.pdf.
28. Bruce Fein, statement before the Subcommittee on Intelligence Sharing and Terrorism Risk Assessment, House Committee on Homeland Security, hearing on "The Future of Fusion Centers: Potential Promise and Dangers," April 1, 2009, http://hsc-democrats.house.gov/hearings/index.asp?ID=186.
29. Alan Feuer, "The Terror Translators," *New York Times*, September 17, 2010.
30. Tom Hays, "FBI No-show in NYC Terror Probe Raises Questions," Associated Press, May 14, 2011.
31. The National Commission on Terrorist Attacks Upon the United States, *The 9/11 Commission Report, authorized ed.* (New York: Norton, 2004), 395.
32. Genevieve Lester, "Societal Acceptability of Domestic Intelligence," in *The Challenge of Domestic Intelligence in a Free Society*, Brian A. Jackson, ed., (Santa Monica, CA: RAND, 2009), 90.
33. U.S. Department of Justice Office of the Inspector General, *A Review of the FBI's Use of National Security Letters: Assessment of Corrective Actions and Examinations of NSL Usage in 2006*, 108, http://www.justice.gov/oig/special/s0803b/final.pdf). See also Edward C. Liu, *Amendments to the Foreign Intelligence Surveillance Act (FISA) Extended Until June 1, 2015* (Washington, DC; Congressional Research Service, June 16, 2011).
34. See "Domestic Intelligence Surveillance Grew in 2010," entry in the Federation of American Scientists Secrecy News blog, http://www.fas.org/blog/secrecy/2011/05/2010_fisa.html.
35. Charlie Savage, "F.B.I. Agents Get Leeway to Push Privacy Bounds," *New York Times*, June 13, 2011.
36. Jerry Markon, "Tension Grows Between Calif. Muslims, FBI after Informant Infiltrates Mosque," *Washington Post*, December 5, 2010.
37. The three provisions were technically amendments to the Foreign Intelligence Surveillance Act (FISA); two had been originally enacted as part of the Patriot Act, and

one had been included in the Intelligence Reform and Terrorism Prevention Act of 2004. For background see Liu, *Amendments to the Foreign Intelligence Surveillance Act*.

38. Gregory Treverton, "Intelligence Test," *Democracy* 11 (Winter 2009): 65, http://www.democracyjournal.org/11/6667.php.
39. John Farmer, Jr., "How to Spot a Terrorist," *New York Times*, September 28, 2010.
40. Laura W. Murphy, "Stopping the Flow of Power to the Executive Branch," testimony before the Subcommittee on the Constitutions, Civil Rights and Civil Liberties, Committee on the Judiciary, U.S. House of Representatives, December 9, 2010.
41. "Remarks by the Secretary of Homeland Security Michael Chertoff," Bureau of Justice Assistance, March 14, 2006, at http://www.dhs.gov/xnews/speeches/speech_0273.shtm.

The Future of Security? Surveillance Operations at Homeland Security Fusion Centers

Torin Monahan

The U.S. "War On Terror" has fueled remarkable developments in state surveillance. In the aftermath of the terrorist attacks of September 11, 2001, the country witnessed a rise in domestic spying programs, including warrantless wiretaps of the communications of citizens, investigations into the borrowing habits of library patrons, infiltration of peace-activist groups by government agents, and the establishment of tip hotlines to encourage people to report suspicious others (Monahan, 2010). Rather than interpret these and similar developments as originating with the "war on terror," scholars in the field of surveillance studies have correctly noted that the events of September 11 provided an impetus for a surge in many preexisting, but perhaps dormant, forms of state surveillance (Wood, Konvitz, and Ball, 2003). Similarly, such domestic surveillance practices neither began nor ended with the George W. Bush administration; instead, state surveillance has grown and mutated in response to changing perceptions of the nature of terrorist threats and the predilections of the Obama administration.

In particular, the Department of Homeland Security (DHS) has renewed its commitment to creating a robust, nationwide network of "fusion centers" to share and analyze data on citizens and others. As of 2010, at least 72 fusion centers existed at the state and regional levels throughout the United States, with many of them listed as "intelligence centers" or "information analysis centers." Officially, such centers prioritize counterterrorism activities, such as conducting "threat assessments" for events and linking "suspicious activities reports" to other data to create profiles of individuals or groups that might present terrorist risks. In this capacity, fusion centers engage in a form of "intelligence-led policing" that targets individuals who match certain profiles and singles them out for further monitoring or preemptive intervention (Ratcliffe, 2003; Wilson and Weber, 2008).

Most fusion centers are located within state and local police departments. Police, FBI, and DHS analysts, whose salaries are usually funded by their respective organizations, typically staff the centers. A common exception is when police representatives are funded in part or completely by DHS grants for the centers. In addition to conducting threat assessments and compiling suspicious-activities reports, fusion center analysts routinely respond to requests for information from state and local police, other fusion centers, or government agencies and organizations such as the FBI, DHS, the Secret Service, or the Department of Defense. When seen as pertinent, fusion centers also share information with private companies, such as those operating public utilities or managing other critical infrastructures (Electronic Privacy Information Center, 2008; Monahan, 2009).

Although the Los Angeles County Terrorism Early Warning Center, established in 1996, is often credited as being the first fusion center (German and Stanley, 2008), most were formed after the release of the September 11 Commission Report in 2004. The early fusion centers built upon and often incorporated the Federal Bureau of Investigation's "Joint Terrorism Task Force" (JTTF) program, thereby hardwiring FBI connections into fusion centers, but allowing for greater information sharing than JTTFs afforded (German and Stanley, 2007). Since their inception, the orientation of many fusion centers has expanded to include "all hazards" and "all threats," such as responding to environmental catastrophes or investigating non-terrorist criminal gangs (Rollins, 2008). One likely reason for this expansion is that the police departments housing fusion centers are trying to translate DHS priorities and apply DHS funds to address local needs (Monahan and Palmer, 2009).

Fusion centers are rapidly becoming a hallmark of the Obama administration's domestic security apparatus. Since 2009, 14 more fusion centers have come on line and the DHS and the Department of Justice have pledged more funding support for fusion centers (Burdeau, 2010; Geiger, 2009). On the surface, the increase in financial and political support for fusion centers should not be that surprising since DHS Secretary Janet Napolitano was a vocal advocate of the well-regarded Arizona-based fusion center, which she helped to create when she was governor of that state (Hylton, 2009). As DHS Secretary, Napolitano (2009) has reaffirmed this support: "I believe that Fusion Centers will be the centerpiece of state, local, federal intelligence-sharing for the future and that the Department of Homeland Security will be working and aiming its programs to underlie Fusion Centers." Attorney General Eric Holder (2010) has also affirmed fusion centers as vital to the ongoing "war on terror": "We are at war. This is the reality in which we live. And our fusion centers are on the frontlines of America's best, and most effective, efforts to fight back."

On a deeper level, fusion centers are probably aligned better with the politics of the Obama administration because its surveillance practices *appear* to be passive, disembodied, and objective. For instance, it has profoundly increased the use of unmanned aerial vehicles (UAVs) internationally and domestically (Wall and Monahan, 2011; Waiters and Weber, 2010). Barring instances of obvious abuse, the fusion and analysis of abstract forms of disparate data do not, in themselves, seem particularly egregious. Indeed, the stated purposes of fusion centers, at least in principle, sound innocuous and rational: "The [fusion] centers' goals are to blend law enforcement and intelligence information, and coordinate security measures to reduce threats in local communities" (U.S. Department of Homeland Security, 2008). Analysts at fusion centers could be thought of as engaging in types of "soft surveillance" (Marx,2006) that are minimally invasive, at least for most people, and therefore are not nearly as objectionable to the general public as the more invasive articulations of police or state surveillance, such as physical searches, mandatory DNA collection, or telecommunication wiretaps.

Although fusion centers were formed under the Bush administration, largely in response to criticism from the September 11 Commission over intelligence failures leading up to the September 11 attacks, politically speaking this finding of failure was a sore point for President Bush and the relevant security agencies, such as the Federal Bureau of Investigation, the Central Intelligence Agency, and the National Security Agency. Moreover, whereas DHS was established rapidly in 2002, DHS-sponsored fusion centers did not substantially take off until 2005. A case could be made that the supposedly objective, intelligence-led orientation of fusion centers was actually in tension with the general timbre of aggressive, masculinist intervention that characterized many aspects of the "war on terror" under the Bush administration. In contradistinction, the patient police work done by analysts in fusion centers could be viewed as being much smarter and more reflective, and therefore somewhat feminized compared to other modalities of the "war on terror." DHS officials have explicitly referred to fusion centers as engaging in "thoughtful analysis" (Riegle, 2009) and have implemented workshops and classes to teach fusion center analysts "critical thinking, analytic tools, techniques, and writing" (U.S. Department of Homeland Security, 2008: 16). These articulations are a far cry from the action-oriented counterterrorism myths circulated by entertainment shows like *24*, which were embraced by former White House deputy chief of staff Karl Rove and former DHS Secretary Michael Chertoff, among others (Monahan, 2010). In this light, the operations and concept of fusion centers resonate better with the crafted image of President Obama as a thoughtful, measured, and intelligent leader.

Surveillance of abstract data—or "dataveillance" (Clarke, 2001)—may be perceived as being less intrusive and less threatening than are video cameras, wiretaps, or other technologies that are traditionally associated with surveillance (Ericson and Haggerty, 1997; Marx, 2006). Provided that the data do not involve information considered sensitive, such as pharmacy or bank records, people definitely do not find dataveillance to be as intrusive as physical searches of individuals or individual property (Slobogin, 2008). Nonetheless, these viewpoints neglect the extent to which personal data are constantly being generated, captured, and circulated by the many information systems and technologies with which people come in contact (e.g., cell phones, credit cards, the Internet). When "fused," whether by a marketing firm or a state entity, these data can paint a disturbingly fine-grained representation of individuals, their associations, preferences, and risks. Anyone who has access to such "data doubles" (Haggerty and Ericson, 2006) is in a position to know and act on a great deal of information that might otherwise be considered personal and private. It is perhaps much more personal and private than that which could be gleaned from more traditional surveillance techniques. Even more disconcerting for individuals is the fact that although the data generated by our many information systems are always partial and sometimes grossly inaccurate, they can still negatively affect one's life experiences and chances (e.g., through one's credit score or one's terrorist-risk score).

Therefore, the phenomenon of fusion centers must be situated within the context of surveillance societies. Broadly speaking, surveillance societies operate upon imperatives of data gathering and data monitoring, often through technological systems, for purposes of governance and control (Lyon, 2001; Monahan, 2010; Murakami Wood et al., 2006). These particular logics of surveillance were not invented by U.S. national security agencies in response to the September 11 attacks. Instead, fusion centers and other surveillance-oriented security organizations draw upon existing practices of voracious data collection and fluid information exchange, as exemplified by social networking sites such as Facebook or private-sector data aggregators such as Entersect, a company that actively partners with fusion centers to share its purported "12 billion records on about 98 per cent of Americans" (O'Harrow, Jr., 2008).

Thus, there is also a neoliberal dimension to fusion centers, in that they purchase data from the private sector, sometimes hire private data analysts, and share information with industry partners (Monahan, 2009). By forming information-sharing partnerships, analysts at fusion centers seek to "connect the dots" to prevent future terrorist attacks. Meanwhile, government officials are very interested in figuring out ways in which DHS in general and fusion centers in particular can assist the private sector, presumably by enabling and protecting the ability of companies to profit financially (Monahan, 2010). As DHS Under Secretary Caryn Wagner stated in her 2010 testimony before the House Subcommittee on Homeland Security:

> I&A [DHS's Office of Intelligence and Analysis] will continue to advocate for sustained funding for the fusion centers as the linchpin of the evolving homeland security enterprise. While I&A's support to state, local and tribal partners is steadily improving, there is still work to be done in *how best to support the private sector*. We intend to explore ways to extend our efforts in this area beyond the established relationships with the critical infrastructure sectors (Wagner, 2010; emphasis added).

In some respects, fusion centers suffer from a mandate that is too open-ended and from guidelines that are too ambiguous. The task of fusing data to produce "intelligence" that can be used to prevent terrorist acts or respond to "all crimes" or "all hazards" amounts to an invitation for individuals at these centers to engage in almost any surveillance practices that make sense to them. As noted, this flexibility could have the redeeming value of allowing police departments to use DHS and other resources for needs that are perceived as being meaningful for particular jurisdictions (Monahan and Palmer, 2009). However, evidence suggests that people at some fusion centers are also exploiting the significant leeway granted to them to engage in racial profiling, political profiling, illegal data mining, and illegal data collection. The surveillance capabilities of fusion centers enable and invite "mission creep" or "function creep," whereby analysts draw upon the resources at their disposal to exceed the policies and laws that are intended to govern their activities (*Ibid.*). Moreover, the guidelines for fusion centers are quite ambiguous and there is a general absence of oversight regarding their activities (German and Stanley, 2007). In the following sections, I will review in detail a few cases of abuse by fusion centers and discuss the issues raised by such examples.

Fusion Center Abuses

Given the secretive nature of fusion centers, including their resistance to freedom of information requests (German and Stanley, 2008; Stokes, 2008), the primary way in which the public has learned about their activities is through leaked or unintentionally disseminated documents. For instance, a "terrorism threat assessment" produced by Virginia's fusion center surfaced in 2009 and sparked outrage because it identified students at colleges and universities—especially at historically black universities—as posing a potential terrorist threat (Sizemore, 2009). In the report, universities were targeted because of their diversity, which is seen as threatening because it might inspire "radicalization." The report says: "Richmond's history as the capital city of the Confederacy, combined with the city's current demographic concentration of African-American residents, contributes to the continued presence of race-based extremist groups . . . [and student groups] are recognized as a radicalization node for almost every type of extremist group" (Virginia Fusion Center, 2009: 9). Although the American Civil Liberties Union (ACLU) and others have rightly decried the racial-profiling implications of such biased claims being codified in an official document, the report itself supports the interpretation that minority students will be and probably have been targeted for surveillance. The report argues: "In order to detect and deter terrorist attacks, it is essential that information regarding suspected terrorists and suspicious activity in Virginia be closely monitored and reported in a timely manner" (*Ibid*: 4). Other groups identified as potential threats by the Virginia fusion center were environmentalists, militia members, and students at Regent University, the Christian university founded by evangelical preacher Pat Robertson (Sizemore, 2009).

Another threat-assessment report, compiled by the Missouri Information Analysis Center (MIAC), found "the modern militia movement" to be worthy of focused investigation. The 2009 report predicted a resurgence in right-wing militia activities because of high levels of unemployment and anger at the election of the nation's first black president, Barack Obama, who many right-wing militia members might view as illegitimate and/or in favor of stronger gun-control laws (Missouri Information Analysis Center, 2009). The greatest stir caused by the report was its claim that "militia members most commonly associate with 3rd party political groups. . . . These members are usually supporters of former Presidential Candidate: Ron Paul, Chuck Baldwin, and Bob Barr" (*Ibid*.: 7). When the report circulated, many libertarians and "Tea Party" members took great offense, thinking the document argued that supporters of third-party political groups were more likely to be dangerous militia members or terrorists. In response, libertarian activists formed a national network called "Operation Defuse," which is devoted to uncovering and criticizing the activities of fusion centers and is actively filing open-records requests and attempting to conduct tours of fusion centers. Operation Defuse could be construed as a "counter-surveillance" group (Monahan, 2006) that arose largely because of outrage over the probability of political profiling by state-surveillance agents.

Fusion centers have also been implicated in scandals involving covert infiltrations of nonviolent groups, including peace-activist groups, anti-death penalty groups, animal-fights groups, Green Party groups, and others. The most astonishing of the known cases involved the Maryland Coordination and Analysis Center (MCAC). In response to an ACLU freedom of information lawsuit, it came to light in 2008 that the Maryland State Police had conducted covert investigations of at least 53 peace activists and anti-death penalty activists for a period of 14 months. The investigation proceeded despite admissions by the covert agent that she saw no indication of violent activities or violent intentions on the part of group members (Newkirk, 2010). Nonetheless, in the federal database used by the police and accessed by MCAC, activists were listed as being suspected of the "primary crime" of "Terrorism—anti-government" (German and Stanley, 2008: 8). Although it is unclear exactly what role the fusion center played in these activities, they were most likely involved in and aware of the investigation. After all, as Mike German and Jay Stanley (2008: 8) explain:

> Fusion centers are clearly *intended* to be the central focal point for sharing terrorism-related information. If the MCAC was not aware of the information the state police collected over the 14 months of this supposed terrorism investigation, this fact would call into question whether the MCAC is accomplishing its mission.

Police spying of this sort, besides being illegal absent "reasonable suspicion" of wrongdoing, could have a "chilling effect" on free speech and freedom of association. The fact that individuals were wrongly labeled as terrorists in these systems and may still be identified as such could also have negative ramifications for them far into the future.

Another dimension of troubling partnerships between fusion centers and law enforcement was revealed with the 2007 arrest of Kenneth Krayeske, a Green Party member in Connecticut. On January 3, 2007, Krayeske was taking photographs of Connecticut Governor M. Jodi Rell at her inaugural parade. He was not engaged in protest at the time. While serving as the manager of the Green Party's gubernatorial candidate, he had publicly challenged Governor Rell over the issue of why she would not debate his candidate (Levine, 2007). At the parade, police promptly arrested Krayeske (after he took 23 photographs) and later charged him with "B reach of Peace" and "Interfering with Police" (*Ibid.*). Connecticut's fusion center, the Connecticut Intelligence Center (CTIC), had conducted a threat assessment for the event and had circulated photographs of Krayeske and others to police in advance (Krayeske, 2007). The police report reads: "The Connecticut Intelligence Center and the Connecticut State Police Central Intelligence Unit had briefed us [the police] on possible threats to Governor Rell by political activist [*sic*], to include photographs of the individuals. One of the photographs was of the accused Kenneth Krayeske" (quoted in Levine, 2007). Evidently, part of the reason Krayeske was targeted was that intelligence analysts, most likely at the fusion center, were monitoring blog posts on the Internet and interpreted one of them as threatening: "Who is going to protest the inaugural ball with me?... No need to make nice" (*CNN.com*, 2009). According to a CNN report on the arrest, after finding that blog post, "police began digging for information, mining public and commercial data bases. They learned Krayeske had been a Green Party campaign director, had protested the gubernatorial debate and had once been convicted for civil disobedience. He had no history of violence" (*Ibid.*). The person who read Krayeske his Miranda rights and attempted to interview him in custody was Andrew Weaver, a sergeant for the City of Hartford Police Department who also works in the CTIC fusion center (Department of Emergency Management and Homeland Security, 2008).

These few examples demonstrate some of the dangers and problems with fusion centers. Fusion center threat assessments lend themselves to profiling along lines of race, religion, and political affiliation. Their products are not impartial assessments of terrorist threats, but rather betray biases against individuals or groups who deviate from—or challenge—the status quo. According to a *Washington Times* commentary that became a focal point for a congressional hearing on fusion centers, as long as terrorism is defined as coercive or intimidating acts that are intended to shape government policy, "any dissidence or political dissident is suspect to fusion centers" (Fein, 2009). Evidence from the Maryland and Connecticut fusion center cases suggests that their representatives are either involved in data-gathering and investigative work, or are at least complicit in such activities, including illegal spying operations (German and Stanley, 2008). The Connecticut case further shows that individuals working at fusion centers are actively monitoring online sources and interviewing suspects, a departure from the official Fusion Center Guidelines that stress "exchange" and "analysis" of data, not data acquisition through investigations (U.S. Department of Justice, 2006).

One important issue here is that fusion centers occupy ambiguous organizational positions. Many of them are located in police departments or are combined with FBI Joint Terrorism Task Forces, but their activities are supposed to be separate and different from the routine activities of the police or the FBI. A related complication is that fusion center employees often occupy multiple organizational roles (e.g., police officers or National Guard members *and* fusion center analysts), which can lead to an understandable, but nonetheless problematic, blurring of professional identities, rules of conduct, and systems of accountability. Whereas in 2010 DHS and the Department of Justice responded to concerns about profiling by implementing a civil liberties certification requirement for fusion centers, public oversight and accountability of fusion centers are becoming even more difficult and unlikely because of a concerted effort to exempt fusion centers from freedom of information requests. For example, according to a police official, Virginia legislators were coerced into passing a 2008 law that exempted its fusion center from the Freedom of Information Act; in this instance, federal officials threatened to withhold classified intelligence from the state's fusion center and police if they did not pass such a law (German and Stanley, 2008). Another tactic used by fusion center representatives to thwart open-records requests is to claim that there is no "material product" for them to turn over because they only "access," rather than "retain," information (Hylton, 2009).

Although it may be tempting to view these cases of fusion center missteps and infractions as isolated examples, they are probably just the tip of the iceberg. A handful of other cases has surfaced recently in which fusion centers in California, Colorado, Texas, Pennsylvania, and Georgia have recommended peace activists, Muslim-rights groups, and/or environmentalists be profiled (German, 2009; Wolfe, 2009). The Texas example reveals the ways in which the flexibility of fusion centers affords the incorporation of xenophobic and racist beliefs. In 2009, the North Central Texas Fusion System produced a report that argued that the United States is especially vulnerable to terrorist infiltration because the country is too tolerant and accommodating of religious difference, especially of Islam. Through several indicators, the report lists supposed signs that the country is gradually being invaded and transformed: "Muslim cab drivers in Minneapolis refuse to carry passengers who have alcohol in their possession; the Indianapolis airport in 2007 installed footbaths to accommodate Muslim prayer; public schools schedule prayer breaks to accommodate Muslim students; pork is banned in the workplace; etc." (North Central Texas Fusion System, 2009: 4). Because "the threats to Texas are significant," the fusion center advises keeping an eye out for Muslim civil liberties groups and sympathetic individuals, organizations, or media that might carry their message: hip-hop bands, social networking sites, online chat forums, blogs, and even the U.S. Department of Treasury (*Ibid.*).

Recent infiltration of peace groups seems to reproduce some of the sordid history of political surveillance of U.S. citizens, such as the FBI and CIA's COINTELPRO program, which targeted civil rights leaders and those peacefully protesting against the Vietnam War, among others (Churchill and Vander Wall, 2002). A contemporary case involves a U.S. Army agent who infiltrated a nonviolent, anti-war protest group in Olympia, Washington, in 2007. A military agent spying on civilians likely violated the Posse Comitatus Act. Moreover, this agent actively shared intelligence with the Washington State Fusion Center, which shared it more broadly (Anderson, 2010). According to released documents, intelligence representatives from as far away as New Jersey were kept apprised of the spying:

> In a 2008 e-mail to an Olympia police officer, Thomas Glapion, Chief of Investigations and Intelligence at New Jersey's McGuire Air Force Base,

> wrote: "You are now part of my Intel network. I'm still looking at possible protests by the PMR SDS MDS and other left wing antiwar groups so any Intel you have would be appreciated. . . . In return if you need anything from the Armed Forces I will try to help you as well" (*Ibid*.: 4).

Given that political surveillance under COINTELPRO is widely considered to be a dark period in U.S. intelligence history, the fact that fusion centers may be contributing to similar practices today makes it all the more important to subject them to public scrutiny and oversight.

Transgressive Data Collection

By now it should be apparent that fusion center personnel are neither objectively assessing terrorist threats nor passively analyzing preexisting data. Fusion centers may appear to be more impartial and rational than previous forms of state surveillance. Yet they have incorporated previous surveillance modalities, including their prejudicial beliefs and invasive techniques, and merged them with dataveillance capabilities that amplify the potential for civil liberties violations and personal harm. Even if fusion center activities were restricted to passive data analysis, which they are not, they could still transgress existing laws that are intended to protect people from unreasonable searches. Specifically, Title 28, Part 23 of the Code of Federal Regulations states that law enforcement agencies "shall collect and maintain criminal intelligence information concerning an individual only if there is reasonable suspicion that the individual is involved in criminal conduct or activity and the information is relevant to that criminal conduct or activity" (in German and Stanley, 2008: 2). When fusion center analysts create profiles of risky individuals and then engage in data mining to identify people who match those profiles, they are effectively bypassing the "reasonable suspicion" requirement for intelligence operations.

Aside from the known cases of abuse, in their official capacity fusion centers are apparently exploiting a technicality in terms of what constitutes "collecting" and "maintaining" criminal intelligence information. The implied reasoning is this: provided that fusion centers merely analyze data stored in databases housed elsewhere, they are not violating the "reasonable suspicion" stipulation even if they are conducting "dragnet" or "fishing expedition" searches that would have been illegal with previous generations of computing technology that did not depend entirely on networks. This rationalization is especially specious when analysts can access police records that are located in the same buildings as the fusion centers. Nonetheless, DHS and Department of Justice guidelines explicitly encourage fusion centers to access as much data as possible, extending "beyond criminal intelligence, to include federal intelligence as well as public and private-sector data" (quoted in German and Stanley, 2007: 7). In an unusually candid statement, Sheriff Kevin Rambosk, who is associated with the Florida fusion center, justifies widespread data sharing as a way to compete with criminals who similarly move across jurisdictional lines:

> We know as law enforcement professionals that there are no jurisdictional boundaries for criminals. . . . And we historically and intuitively know that the more information that we can share with one another, the more cases can be solved, the more crimes can be prevented, and the more information each of

> our agencies will have to continue to make Collier County one of the safest places in Florida to live (Mills, 2010).

The implication of this assertion is that there should not be any jurisdictional or legal boundaries for law enforcement to collect and share data either, including data from the private sector, which fusion centers in Florida access through a system called "Florida Integrated Network for Data Exchange and Retrieval" or "FINDER" (*Ibid.*).

Conclusion: Surveillance Iterations

Although criminals or terrorists may be crossing jurisdictional boundaries and breaking the law, state agencies and agents do more harm than good when they ignore existing legal constraints or seek out exemptions from public oversight. The few problematic cases reviewed in this article illustrate that without due respect for the "reasonable suspicion" provision on police intelligence-gathering activities, fusion center personnel engage in or endorse racial, political, and religious profiling; they perceive challenges to the status quo as threatening and possibly "terrorist"; they support the investigation and arrest of law-abiding individuals, marking them as "terrorists" in official databases, perhaps in perpetuity; and they exert a chilling effect on free speech in that activists and others are more likely to temper their activities to avoid similar kinds of harmful scrutiny.

It is important to note that the politics of those being targeted by fusion centers spans the spectrum from right-wing militia members to left-wing anti-war activists. Some may be surprised that individuals supporting progressive causes would be seen as threats during a Democratic presidency. Yet these cases underscore that the politics of many environmentalists, anti-war activists, and other progressives are still radical vis-á-vis the mainstream politics of contemporary Washington. Moreover, law enforcement cultures are typically quite conservative (Greene, 2007; Reiner, 2010) and, similar to other organizations, slow to change (Zhao, He, and Lovrich, 1998). Thus, the outcomes of national elections are unlikely to produce discernable near-term changes in the cultures of these organizations.

If today's surveillance state were to fully embody Barack Obama's campaign rhetoric of respect for "the rule of law," fusion centers would differ markedly. The blurring or suspending of the law are supposedly practices that characterized the "war on terror" under the Bush administration. Impatience with bureaucratic constraints upon counterterrorism efforts or frustration with the burden of protecting civil liberties are similarly more readily associated with the masculinist orientation of the previous administration. Fusion centers could strictly follow stipulations on intelligence gathering; they could erect barriers between public and private databases; they could embrace transparency and accountability by complying with, rather than avoiding, freedom of information requests.

Instead of romanticizing the ideals that could have been achieved, or might yet be achieved, I prefer to conclude by highlighting what can be learned from the example of fusion centers. First, fusion centers show the ways in which the logics of "surveillance societies" pervade all aspects of social life, including the operations of government organizations. Imperatives to collect, share, analyze, and act on data increasingly shape the activities of public institutions, private companies, and individuals. The capabilities of new media technologies simply augment this particular drive, which is unchecked or under-regulated in most domains, and the realm of national security is no different. If governments are reluctant to impose serious restrictions on data sharing more generally, except perhaps for particularly sensitive data such as those contained in medical records, one should not be surprised that government agencies would avail themselves of similar data-sharing functions (Regan, 2004). Second, the unstandardized composition and mission of fusion centers may afford them ample flexibility, but it also allows particularistic biases to shape their activities. When made public, such biases may embarrass fusion center officials, but they are undoubtedly more damaging to the targets of unwarranted surveillance and intervention. The latter must contend with legal battles and fees, emotional stress, and perhaps even physical abuse associated with being marked as terrorist suspects (Guzik, 2009). For surveillance states to be more democratic, their police apparatuses should possess and follow clear guidelines that respect the law, and subject their activities to routine public scrutiny. To do otherwise is a recipe for abuse.

Acknowledgment: This material is based upon a research project being conducted by the author and Priscilla Regan. The work is supported by the National Science Foundation under grant number SES 0957283.

Critical Thinking Questions

1. Some observers have argued that "if you have nothing to hide, scrutiny and domestic surveillance shouldn't worry you." Do you agree? Why or why not?
2. Could something like COINTELPRO ever happen again? Why or why not?
3. What kinds of constraints or reforms would you recommend, if any, be implemented at local fusion centers?

References

Anderson, Rick 2010 "Watching the Protesters." *Seattle Weekly News* (June 9). At *www.seattleweekly.com/2010-06-09/news/watching-the-protesters/1.*

Burdeau, Cain 2010 "Holder: Intelligence-Sharing Centers Vital." *Associated Press* (February 23). At *www.washingtonexaminer.com/local/ap/holder-intelligence-sharing-centers-vital-85071812.html.*

Churchill, Ward and Jim Vander Wall 2002 *The COINTELPRO Papers: Documents from the FBI's Secret Wars Against Dissent in the United States.* Cambridge, MA: South End Press.

Clarke, Roger 2001 *While You Were Sleeping . . . Surveillance Technologies Arrived.* At *www.anu.edu.au/people/Roger.Clarke/DV/AQ2001.html.*

CNN.com 2009 "Are You on the List?" (September 30). At *www.cnn.com/video/?/video/crime/2009109130/willis.fusion.centers.cnn.*

Department of Emergency Management and Homeland Security 2008 Department of Emergency Management and Homeland Security Coordinating Council Meeting Minutes. Hartford, CT. At *www.ct.gov/demhs/lib/demhs/docsuploaded/ cood_council_minutes/cc_mins_9_18_08.pdf.*

Electronic Privacy Information Center 2008 "Information Fusion Centers and Privacy." At *http://epic.org/privacy/fusion/.*

Ericson, Richard V. and Kevin D. Haggerty 1997 *Policing the Risk Society.* Toronto: University of Toronto Press.

Fein, Bruce 2009 "Surveilling for Clues of Evil Intent." *WashingtonTimes.com* (April 1). At *www.washingtontimes.com/news/2009/apr/01/surveilling-for-clues-of-evil-intent/*.

Geiger, Harley 2009 "Fusion Centers Get New Privacy Orders Via DHS Grants. December 15." At *www.cdt.org/blogs/harley-geiger/fusion-centers-get-new-privacy-orders-dhs-grants*.

German, Michael 2009 Testimony in Support of Senate Bill 931 Before the Joint Committee on Public Safety and Homeland Security. Boston. At *www.scribd.com/doc/24658143/MikeGerman-Former-FBI-testimony-sb93IMA-Fusion-Center-2009*.

German, Michael and Jay Stanley 2008 ACLU Fusion Center Update. July. At *www.aclu.org/pdfs/privacy/fusion_update_20080729.pdf*.

2007 "What's Wrong with Fusion Centers?" (December). At *www.aclu.org/files/pdfs/privacy/fusioncenter_20071212.pdf*.

Greene, Jack R. 2007 "Human Rights and Police Discretion: Justice Service or Denied?" *Sociology of Crime Law and Deviance* 9: 147–169.

Guzik, Keith 2009 "Discrimination by Design: Predictive Data Mining as Security Practice in the United States' 'War on Terrorism.'" *Surveillance & Society* 7, 1: 1–17.

Haggerty, Kevin D. and Richard V. Ericson 2006 "The New Politics of Surveillance and Visibility." K.D. Haggerty and R.V. Ericson (eds.), *The New Politics of Surveillance and Visibility*. Toronto: University of Toronto Press: 3–25.

Holder, Eric 2010 "Attorney General Eric Holder Speaks at the Fourth Annual National Fusion Center Conference." New Orleans, LA: Department of Homeland Security. At *www.justice.gov/ag/speeches/2010/ag-speech-100223.html*.

Hylton, Hilary 2009 "Fusion Centers: Giving Cops Too Much Information?" *Time.com*. At *www.time.com/time/nation/article/0,8599,1883101,00.html*.

Krayeske, Ken 2007 "And Justice for All . . ." At *www.the40yearplan.com/article_052507_And_Justice_For_All.php*.

Levine, Dan 2007 "Arresting Development." Cal Law (January 12): 5. At *www.the40yearplan.com/pdf/annotation.pdf*.

Lyon, David 2001 *Surveillance Society: Monitoring Everyday Life*. Buckingham, England; Philadelphia: Open University.

Marx, Gary T. 2006 "Soft Surveillance: The Growth of Mandatory Volunteerism in Collecting Personal Information—'Hey Buddy Can You Spare a DNA?'" T. Monahan (ed.), *Surveillance and Security: Technological Politics and Power in Everyday Life*. New York: Routledge: 37–56.

Mills, Ryan 2010 "Fla. Police Agencies to Start Using Data-Sharing Tools." *Naples Daily News* (February 12). At *www.policeone.com/police-products/communications/articles/2003592-Fla-police-agencies-to-start-using_data_sharing_tools/*.

Missouri Information Analysis Center 2009 MIAC Strategic Report, 02/20/09. "The Modern Militia Movement." Jefferson City, MO. At *www.scribd.com/doc/13232178/MIAC-Strategic-Report-The-Modern-Militia-Movement*.

Monahan, Torin 2010 *Surveillance in the Time of Insecurity*. New Brunswick: Rutgers University Press.

2009 "The Murky World of 'Fusion Centers.'" *Criminal Justice Matters* 75, 1: 20-21.

2007 "'War Rooms' of the Street: Surveillance Practices in Transportation Control Centers." *The Communication Review* 10, 4: 367–389.

2006 "Counter-Surveillance as Political Intervention?" *Social Semiotics* 16, 4: 515-534.

Monahan, Torin and Neal A. Palmer 2009 "The Emerging Politics of DHS Fusion Centers." *Security Dialogue* 40, 6: 617–636.

Murakami Wood, David (ed.), Kirstie Ball, David Lyon, Clive Norris, and Charles Raab 2006 *A Report on the Surveillance Society*. Wilmslow: Office of the Information Commissioner.

Napolitano, Janet 2009 "Remarks by Homeland Security Secretary Janet Napolitano to the National Fusion Center Conference in Kansas City, Mo., on March 11,2009." Kansas City, MO: Department of Homeland Security. At *www.dhs.gov/ynews/speeches/sp_1236975404263.shtm.*

Newkirk, Anthony B. 2010 "The Rise of the Fusion-Intelligence Complex: A Critique of Political Surveillance after 91/11." *Surveillance & Society* 8, 1 : 43–60.

North Central Texas Fusion System 2009 *Prevention Awareness Bulletin*. At *www.privacylives.com/wp-content/uploads/2009/03/texasfusion_021909.pdf.*

O'Harrow, Jr., Robert 2008 "Centers Tap into Personal Databases." *Washington Post* (April 2). At *www.washingtonpost.com/wp-dyn/content/article/2008/04/01/ AR2008040103049.html.*

Ratcliffe, Jerry H. 2003 "Intelligence-led Policing." *Trends and Issues in Crime and Criminal Justice* 248: 1–6.

Regan, Priscilla M. 2004 "Old Issues, New Context: Privacy, Information Collection and Homeland Security." *Government Information Quarterly* 21, 4:481–497.

Reiner, Robert 2010 *The Politics of the Police*. New York: Oxford University Press.

Riegle, Robert 2009 Testimony of Director Robert Riegle, State and Local Program Office, Office of Intelligence and Analysis, before the Committee on Homeland Security, Subcommittee on Intelligence, Information Sharing, and Terrorism Risk Assessment, "The Future of Fusion Centers: Potential Promise and Dangers." Washington, D.C. At *www.dhs.gov/ynews/testimony/testimony_1238597287040.shtm.*

Rollins, John 2008 *Fusion Centers: Issues and Options for Congress*. Washington, D.C.: Congressional Research Service. At *wwwfas.org/sgp/crs/intel/RL34070.pdf.*

Sizemore, Bill 2009 "Report: Region May Be a Hotbed for Terrorist Recruiting." *The Virginian-Pilot* (April 26). At *http://hamptonroads.com/2009/ 04/report-region-may-be-hotbed-terrorist-recruiting.*

Slobogin, Christopher 2008 "Government Data Mining and the Fourth Amendment." *The University of Chicago Law Review* 75, 1 : 317–341.

Stokes, Jon 2008 "Fusion Center Meltdown: Feds Stifling Open Government in VA?" *Ars Technica* (March 24). At *http://arstechnica.com/security/news/ 2008/03/fusion-centermeltdown-feds-stifling-open-government-in-va.ars.*

U.S. Department of Homeland Security 2008 "DHS' Role in State and Local Fusion Centers Is Evolving." Washington, D.C.: U.S. Department of Homeland Security. At *www.dhs.gov/xoig/assets/mgmtrpts/OIG_09-12_Dec08.pdf.*

U.S. Department of Justice 2006 "Fusion Center Guidelines: Developing and Sharing Information and Intelligence in a New Era." Washington, D.C.: U.S. Department of Justice. At *www.iir .com/global/products/fusion_center_guidelines_law_enforcement.pdf.*

Virginia Fusion Center 2009 *Virginia Terrorism Threat Assessment*. Richmond, VA: Department of State Police. At *www.rawstory.com/images/other/vafusioncenterterrorassessment.pdf.*

Wagner, Caryn 2010 Testimony of Under Secretary Caryn Wagner before the House Subcommittee on Homeland Security on the President's Fiscal Year 2011 Budget Request for the Department's Office of Intelligence and Analysis. Washington, D.C.: Department of Homeland Security. At *www.dhs.gov/ynews/testimony/testimony_1267716038879.shtm.*

Wall, Tyler and Torin Monahan 2011 "Surveillance and Violence from Afar: The Politics of Drones and Liminal Security-Scapes." *Theoretical Criminology* 15, 3: 239–254.

Walters, William and Jutta Weber 2010 "UCAV Surveillance, High-Tech Masculinities and Oriental Others." *A Global Surveillance Society?* Conference at City University London.

Wilson, Dean and Leanne Weber 2008 "Surveillance, Risk and Preemption on the Australian Border." *Surveillance & Society* 5, 2: 124–141.

Wolfe, Gavi 2009 "What We Know about Recent Surveillance of Lawful First Amendment Activity." Massachusetts: American Civil Liberties Union of Massachusetts. At *http://aclum.org/sos/aclu_domestic_surveillance_what_we_know.pdf.*

Wood, David, Eli Konvitz, and Kirstie Ball 2003 "The Constant State of Emergency? Surveillance after 9/11." K. Ball and F. Webster (eds.), *The Intensification of Surveillance: Crime, Terrorism and Warfare in the Information Age*. London: Pluto Press: 137–150.

Zhao, Jihong, Ni He, and Nicholas P. Lovrich 1998 "Individual Value Preferences among American Police Officers: The Rokeach Theory of Human Values Revisited." *Policing: An International Journal of Police Strategies & Management* 21, 1: 22–37.

Immigration And National Security

The Illusion of Safety through Local Law Enforcement Action

David A. Harris

I. Introduction

Illegal immigration has long been a subject of controversy in the United States. Just surveying recent decades, illegal immigration became a hot topic in the 1980s, provoking action in the Congress. The legislation that resulted,[1] signed by President Ronald Reagan in 1986, promised to stem the tide of illegal immigration while simultaneously providing a path toward citizenship for those already in the U.S.[2] This compromise held for more than a decade, but in the 1990s, under the weight of an increasing illegal immigrant population, mostly from Mexico and countries in Central America, tension again began to rise over the issue. Most of the arguments had to do with economics and labor: illegal workers were taking the jobs that Americans should have, argued critics; they suppressed wages and made it easy for employers to fire deserving citizens in favor of exploitable foreigners eager and willing to work for peanuts under any conditions, anti-immigration advocates claimed.[3] In addition, some argued that the large number of Latinos coming into the U.S. constituted a great burden on American taxpayers, as they overloaded schools, hospitals, and other social services.[4] Yet others complained that these immigrants were swamping American culture, with their refusals to learn English and their stubborn adherence to their own ways of doing things.[5] Governor Pete Wilson of California said that it seemed "impossible" for immigrants in his state "to assimilate with our own people or to make any change in their habits," leading Californians to see "great danger that . . . the state will be overrun by them unless prompt action is taken to restrict their immigration."[6]

Yet few of these arguments proved to have much traction with the public outside of the core group of anti-immigration advocates and their most ardent supporters. Government at all levels simply ignored the issue, and the federal government, whose job it has always been to enforce immigration law, seemed uninterested. Anti-immigration advocates called for action, and in at least one instance in the 1990s, Congress bestirred itself. It enacted an immigration reform law in 1996.[7] The law included a provision that allowed for voluntary agreements between the Immigration and Naturalization Service (INS) and any state or local police department, under which a group of officers in the department would receive limited training in immigration law and procedure and become "cross deputized," with a degree of authority to enforce immigration law.[8] This law, known colloquially as "Section 287(g)," attracted little notice, despite the fact that those clamoring for stronger immigration enforcement desired the involvement of state and local police. By early 2001, none of the nation's approximately 17,000 police agencies had decided to enter into a voluntary Section 287(g) agreement.[9]

But, as with so much of American life and policy making, the terrorist attacks of September 11, 2001, brought significant changes. And, over the next several years following the attacks, advocates for stricter immigration enforcement began an effort to bring lawmakers and others around to their side. They did this by "rebranding" their argument, changing their characterization of the issue from one centering on economics and labor, or the changing of American culture, to national security. The borders and their openness risk our security in our post-September 11th world, they cried; with terrorists so clearly out to get us, we can not risk continuing our same old approach, they said; we have to regard the ease with which undocumented people crossed the Southwestern border as a grave risk to our safety.

This article will argue that the rebranding of the immigration problem as a national security issue began a process that culminated in laws at the state level, such as Arizona's S.B. 1070.[10] While the Arizona law was not intended as a national security measure, it represents exactly what the anti-immigration advocates have longed for—a way to force state and local law enforcement agencies into the immigration fight. Ironically, S.B. 1070 shows us that, if we wanted to *harm* our national security, we could hardly think of anything more likely to accomplish this than a law that does what S.B. 1070 mandates. It almost guarantees that local law enforcement will cause damage to the most important weapon we have for fighting terrorism: the gathering of intelligence.

II. The Rebranding of Immigration

Until the mid-2000s, advocates of utilizing local law enforcement to strengthen immigration controls gained little traction. Before September 11, 2001, no state or local police agency had signed a Memorandum of Understanding under Section 287(g) to involve itself in immigration enforcement. In the immediate aftermath of the attacks, only one police agency, the Florida State Police, entered into a 287(g) agreement,[11] and even this agreement covered only a very small number of that agency's sworn personnel.[12] No other police department had come forward. A few others eventually joined, such as the Alabama State Police, and a few California law enforcement agencies including the Costa Mesa Police Department, the Orange County Sheriff's Department, the San Bernardino Sheriff's Department, and a small unit of Los Angeles County Sheriff's Deputies working at the Los Angeles County jail, but not many.[13] Those opposed to immigration, including many who wanted to supplement the resources of the federal border patrol and customs agencies with local law enforcement efforts, were not getting what they wanted. Thus the rebranding began.

Advocates for organizations that had long been in the forefront of the immigration debate, calling for stronger border enforcement, began to fashion their arguments to include national security concerns. Indeed, they began to lead with it. The point, they said, was obvious: our porous borders with Mexico[14] could allow penetration by members of al Qaida. If thousands of poor Mexican and Central American peasants could make it into America in search of work day after day, so could a determined terrorist. And while they could cite little or no evidence to support this point, they did not let the (lack of) facts stand in the way of a rhetorically effective argument.

Mark Krikorian, then the executive director of the Center for Immigration Studies, advanced this idea in an article he wrote for the *National Interest*. "In a very real sense, the primary weapons of our enemies are not inanimate objects at all, but rather the terrorists themselves—especially in the case of suicide attackers. Thus keeping the terrorists out or apprehending them after they get in" is the key to prevailing against them.[15] "[C]ontrolling the Mexican border, apart from the other benefits it would produce, is an important security objective; at least two major rings have been uncovered which smuggled Middle Easterners into the United States via Mexico, with help from corrupt Mexican government employees."[16] Krikorian cited just one example of terrorist danger flowing from the U.S.—Mexican border to support his argument. He said that Mahmoud Kourani, the brother of Hizbollah's security chief, allegedly entered the country using this method.[17] Kourani was, in fact, arrested in Dearborn, Michigan, but his arrest stimulated more talk about terrorism than the actual facts of the case could support. The authorities chose to prosecute him only for harboring an illegal immigrant, and charged him with no terrorism-related offenses of any kind.[18] He served only a few months in jail—hardly what one would expect had he actually posed the typed of danger Krikorian seemed to fear.[19]

Others followed the same path as Krikorian. Conservative political commentator Tony Blankley, who formerly served as a top aide to then U.S. House Speaker Newt Gingrich after a stint as the editorial page editor of *The Washington Times*, also emphasized the danger to national security posed by illegal immigration from Mexico. In his 2005 book *The West's Last Chance: Will We Win the Clash of Civilizations?*, Blankley wrote that the Mexican border with the U.S. represented an important threat to our national security.[20] For support, Blankley relied on the Congressional testimony of James Loy, then Deputy Secretary of Homeland Security and the former Commandant of the U.S. Coast Guard. Blankley argued that the porous nature of the Mexican border posed a significant risk of terrorist infiltration,[21] quoting Loy as testifying that "[r]ecent information from ongoing investigations, detentions and emerging threat streams strongly suggests that al Qaida has considered using the Southwest border to infiltrate the United States. Several al Qaida leaders believe operatives can pay their way into the country through Mexico and also believe that illegal entry is more advantageous than legal entry for operational security reasons."[22] This statement would seem to support Blankley, Krikorian, and others who argued that illegal Mexican immigration posed a national security threat—until one reads the next sentence of Deputy Secretary Loy's testimony, omitted by Blankley: "However, there is currently no conclusive evidence that indicates al Qaida operatives have made successful penetrations into the United States via this method."[23]

Other government officials, not mentioned by Krikorian, Blankley, or other advocates for tighter immigration enforcement along the Mexican border on national security grounds, said that the facts presented a far different picture. For example, in 2003, debate flared in the U.S. over the use of Mexican consular identification documents—called *matricula consular* cards—by Mexicans in the U.S. Banks in the U.S. had begun to accept these cards as sufficient identification for opening bank accounts, and an increasing number of undocumented immigrants began opening accounts with the cards in order to deposit their earnings, so that they would not have to carry large sums of cash with them all the time.[24] Carrying thousands of dollars on their persons had made many Mexicans the targets of robberies and violence, by predators who knew that the victims would hesitate to report these crimes to police for fear of deportation. The *matricula consular* cards thus became a way to lessen the risk of these robberies, through conventional banking.[25] Opponents of immigration decried the use of these cards, saying that terrorists could use them to facilitate their actions and launch attacks from across the Mexican border. But David Aufhauser, a former Treasury Department official in the George W. Bush administration, could not hide his incredulity at these assertions. Noting that those making these statements, like those engaged in rebranding immigration, supplied no supporting evidence, Aufhauser called the idea of a connection between use of the *matricula consular* cards by illegal immigrants from Mexico and terrorism "comic."[26]

But, as stated above, those who wished to have stricter enforcement along the U.S.—Mexican border were not to be deterred by a minor inconvenience like a lack of facts backing up what they had decided to say. They forged ahead, making the argument over and over, insisting that only by enlisting local and state law enforcement in the immigration fight could we make the nation safe from terrorist attacks.

III. The Reaction of State and Local Law Enforcement to the Rebranding of Immigration as a National Security Issue

Leaders of state and local law enforcement agencies heard the call of these advocates, but they did not heed it. In fact, in contrast to their full-throated embrace of other announced national priorities, such as the "War on Drugs," non-federal police agencies seemed to want no part of the action against immigration law violators, even if this constituted (as anti-immigration advocates argued) a danger to our national security. As I have shown elsewhere, the answer of state and local police officials to the call for involvement of their agencies in immigration enforcement was a near unanimous refusal.[27]

For some in local law enforcement, the issue was the proper balance of federal and state relations. These officials said that, for them, the enforcement of immigration law remained a federal responsibility, and state and local agencies simply should not have a role in this effort.[28] For others, the additional burdens of enforcing immigration law would impose a fiscal burden that states and localities could not carry.[29] In times of ever-leaner budgets for states and cities, this could not help but concern leaders. For yet other agencies, they already found themselves swamped, not just with growing traditional police department duties, but with new responsibilities for homeland security issues, such as seeing to the safety of vulnerable municipal buildings or industrial installations or large public gatherings, a responsibility which had fallen to them since September 11, 2001.[30]

But one reason for not wishing to get involved predominated in nearly every discussion of whether state and local police should get involved in immigration enforcement: doing so would constitute bad law enforcement policy. It would degrade the ability of departments to accomplish their core mission: providing public safety. Local police involvement in immigration enforcement, they said, was incompatible with what police officers attempted to accomplish day after day.[31]

The reasons for this begin with community policing. Almost any law enforcement agency anywhere in the country will say today that it practices community policing. These words have different meanings in different places; in some police departments community policing is a pervasive philosophy, practiced at every level of the department; in others, it is an add-on program, seen as mere public relations and not "real policing."[32] But anywhere that it is done in a meaningful way, it has proven itself effective in creating long-term gains in public safety.

Though it takes myriad forms and can be seen in many types of police departments—urban and suburban, rural towns and big cities—serious, real efforts at community policing have a common core. It begins with the idea of partnership. The police must realize that they cannot fix public safety problems alone. They must have the help, support, and above all else, the information that only the community they serve can provide.[33] Information concerning what is happening on the streets when the police are not there, on which people in the community represent genuine threats, or on who did what and when in terms of a particular crime all must come from the people who live and work in a community.[34] The police cannot be everywhere at once, and only the dumbest criminals commit their crimes in front of the police. For its part, the community must realize that, like the police, they cannot make their neighborhoods safe, livable and thriving places through only their own efforts. They must have the help and support of the police if they are to have stable neighborhoods secure from crime and disorder. Said differently, both the police and the community must understand that they cannot crack the public safety nut unless they work together, as partners, giving each other what is necessary to make their efforts work. Only by working in such a partnership can any city or town create real public safety gains that are sustainable over the long term.

Any true partnership must rest, in fact *can only* rest, on a relationship of trust.[35] Police and community must work to make this happen, because this kind of trust cannot simply be requested or pledged or handed over freely; it must be earned, especially when the parties come to the relationship against a background of distrust, built up over many years. Of course, this is often the situation faced by police and communities attempting to build a working relationship, especially (though not only) in urban settings. But, when real community policing takes hold, both sides recognize that there is no alternative to a real partnership, and no other way to create it than to build a strong relationship over time in which both partners prove to each other that they can trust one another.

Despite the difficulties of accomplishing this, police departments nationwide do it today, because they have seen the results: community policing works. It helps them to understand the communities in which they work, to get more cooperation and information from them, and to know what the law enforcement priorities of the people actually are. And few things sell as well in law enforcement as proven success. Some observers may mistake community meetings between police and the citizens in the communities they serve as political correctness or simple occasions for venting. But this disregards the real self-interests at stake for everyone involved, especially the police themselves. Better, more solid connections with the community, built on a foundation of real trust, produce results. With more public confidence and information, police can do a better job. So the effort, when under taken fully and in good faith, proves worthwhile.

For example, police in Austin, Texas noted a spike in violent robberies in which victims were murdered. Most of the victims were Latino immigrants from Mexico and Central America. Because these people did not have access to traditional banks, it was well known that they had to carry large amounts of cash on their persons, making them inviting targets for robbery.[36] Despite this, their illegal immigration status made them hesitant to get involved with the police, even to report their own victimization—a vicious cycle making them all the more attractive to predators. Taking all of this into consideration, Austin police theorized that reported robbery/murders were the tip of the iceberg, and many more people were being robbed than they knew about. They decided that they had to solve this problem by working with the community, regardless of immigration status, to help victims overcome the fear of police and to make similarly situated individuals less attractive as targets. Austin police officers began to deliver a new message to immigrant communities, using community meetings and an advertising campaign utilizing Spanish-language media: in Austin, police won't question victims about their immigration status. The police were only interested in making the public safe from criminals, so people could come forward without fear of deportation. Police also created arrangements with local banks to accept Mexican identification cards so that migrants could safely put their money away and not have to carry it around on their person. This resulted in a dramatic change: the immigrant community began to come forward with information about crimes, allowing the police to fight the robbers and killers who had been preying on Austin's poor. The strategy, incidentally, also brought crime down across the city.[37]

Building this type of relationship with the average constituency of native-born citizens can be difficult. Think how much harder it is to accomplish these things in immigrant communities, as the Austin police did, where a substantial percentage of people in affected neighborhoods speak a language other than English, creating barriers to basic communication. Residents may also be from a culture considerably different than mainstream America, another barrier that must be surmounted and which could cause gross misunderstandings. And some immigrants may come to the U.S. from countries in which police were nearly always corrupt, violent, or predatory.[38] A knock on the door from the police in these countries is always bad news—immigrants from these countries always begin with considerable mistrust and fear of police authority. Add to this the fact that, in most immigrant communities, especially those from Latin America, there may be considerable numbers of people in the U.S. illegally, mixed with a population of those who have become citizens. Some may be American citizens living with parents who do not have legal status. Other households in these communities feature a mixture of immigration statuses: one adult may be legal, while the others are not; children may be natural born American citizens, but their parents may lack legal status.[39] As of 2005, 3.2 million people in the U.S. live in such "mixed status" households.[40] This will naturally make people in these immigrant communities reluctant to interact with the police; even those who are legally in the country may hesitate to call the police if they think this would put other members of their household in jeopardy.[41]

All of this means that, if police officers want the kinds of partnerships built on trust with immigrant communities that are necessary for community policing to succeed, they must work especially hard to make it happen. And many have done this, realizing that it is just as important to reach out to immigrant communities as any other. This is true not only for large police departments in the traditional immigration gateway cities like New York, Chicago, and Los Angeles, but also for smaller police departments in many rural areas and small towns, which have seen the fastest recent growth in immigrant populations.[42]

With a keen understanding of both the importance of building relationships with these immigrant communities and the difficulty of this task, local police recognized immediately that getting involved in the enforcement of immigration could only hurt them. If these communities saw them as assisting in anti-immigration "sweeps" or enforcement operations, they reasoned, it would destroy any trust that police had managed to build with these communities. Trust would be replaced by fear—fear of the state and its police, fear of investigation, and most of all fear of deportation. Fear would keep people from communicating with the police; many would be hesitant to contact the police for any reason, even when they or their family members became victims of serious crimes, for fear that deportation would lead to the destruction of their families and households. This fear would mean, in blunt terms, less information for police in their pursuit of criminals and predators in these communities, leaving such people on the street, free to victimize others.[43]

This explains why so many police leaders and police departments strongly opposed rebranding efforts that would press them into the realm of immigration enforcement. They saw the effort to do this as diametrically opposed their interest in promoting public safety. "It's very difficult in the immigration communities to get information," Hans Marticiuc, President of the Houston Police Officers Unions said, "and if there's fear of being reported . . . because of illegal status, then it just makes our job that much more difficult and it makes the city have that much more criminal activity."[44] The "Major City Chiefs," a national organization of police chiefs from the largest cities in the U.S., took the same position. Enforcement of immigration law by local police departments would, in their opinion, "undermine the level of trust and cooperation between local police and immigrant communities," resulting in "increased crime against immigrants and in the broader community."[45] Without the community on their side, they could not get the help and information they needed to do their jobs well. And that was a sacrifice, one they saw as profoundly unwise, they did not want to make.

IV. The Likely Effect on National Security of Forcing Local Police into Immigration Enforcement

We now come to the present. In 2010, the advocates for tougher border enforcement, and particularly for the use of local police in immigration enforcement, finally got their wish. The State of Arizona enacted a law that requires all of its police officers, "if practical," to inquire into immigration status whenever a police officer has a "reasonable suspicion" that someone they legally encounter or stop may be an illegal immigrant.[46] No law enforcement agency can opt out.[47] The law, S.B. 1070, is the first piece of state-wide legislation anywhere in the country to require police to investigate immigration status. And, while not a national law, it does accomplish (if only in one state) what anti-immigration advocates have long wanted—local police in Arizona now must serve as part of the immigration enforcement apparatus. At this writing, a federal district court has enjoined this part of the law along with some others; other portions of the statute were upheld.[48] The U.S. Court of Appeals for the Ninth Circuit upheld the judge's decision on appeal.[49] Advocates for the law immediately stated they would appeal to the U.S. Supreme Court, where they expect to win.[50]

This gives us a chance to ask an important question. Suppose that the provision mandating local police inquiry into immigration status ultimately goes into effect . . . how would this effect national security? Arizona is, of course, a state that borders Mexico, and by all accounts it is among the most frequent crossing points into the U.S. for undocumented workers.[51] Thus we can engage in a thought experiment. Would the involvement of state and local police in immigration enforcement make us safer from terrorist threats to our national security? It is important to note that the advocates for S.B. 1070 appeared not to have considered national security as the reason for enacting the law; in fact, there is no evidence that concerns about national security impacted the debate over the law in the state.[52] But the question remains legitimate: whether intended or not, how would S.B. 1070 impact national security along the Mexico–Arizona border? Would it, as advocates for local law enforcement involvement in immigration law argued previously, make the country more secure from terrorism?

To find an answer, we should look not to advocates for either stronger immigration enforcement through local police, or to their opposites in the debate. Rather, let us look to people who know something about national security and how it may be achieved. And the public record gives us the opportunity to do just that.

First, we would do well to listen to two individuals with long experience in these matters: Harry "Skip" Brandon and Vincent Cannistraro.[53] Brandon served in the FBI for twenty-three years. During that time he was the Bureau's deputy assistant director for counterterrorism and counterintelligence. He had worldwide responsibility for the Bureau's anti-terrorism and national security efforts, and worked in coordination with all of the intelligence communities of the government.[54] Cannistraro was the former chief of operations and analysis in the CIA's Counterterrorism Center. He also served as special assistant for intelligence in the Office of the Secretary of Defense. For a number of years, he worked as a clandestine CIA operative in the Middle East, Africa, and Europe.[55] These two men possess an unmatched combination of experience and insight into fighting terrorism.

In the aftermath of the attacks on September 11, 2001, there was an unprecedented focus on what law enforcement and intelligence agencies should do vis-à-vis our communities of Muslim immigrants. What would make us safer and help secure our country against terrorism? Both Brandon and Cannistraro participated in this debate, and on matters of how to handle and work with immigrant communities amidst a terrorist threat, they found common ground. The arguments they have made about working with Muslim communities apply with equal force to working with other groups of immigrants. Brandon says that the only way a terrorist attack such as the one on September 11, 2001, might have been prevented would have been for the nation to have a better developed, more precise intelligence gathering capability, especially in the U.S.[56] Cannistraro emphatically agrees. "I have always said that the problem of [preventing] terrorism is the one of getting intelligence," he says. "If we do not have good intelligence, we do not have good anti-terror measure[s] because . . . intelligence is supposed to give us early warning."[57] Cannistraro explains that only one source exists to get this kind of intelligence when some small number of immigrants may be involved in terrorist activity: the intelligence can only come from immigrant communities themselves. Members of these communities are the ones on the ground who will see potentially suspicious behavior, notice those who do not fit in, and spot people who differ from the norm in specific ways.[58]

If al Qaida operatives attempted to come into the U.S. via the same routes and methods used by Mexican and Central American immigrants seeking work, virtually the only ones who might see this and notice something amiss would be those same Mexicans and Central American immigrants. Thus, the ability to work with immigrant communities, and to get information from them, is vital. If al Qaida operatives hide in our Muslim communities in the U.S., law enforcement *must* be able to work with those communities to unearth this information. If al Qaida operatives cross the border among Mexican and Central American migrants, the same principle applies. Law enforcement at every level "needs to be able to collect intelligence on imminent threats in the United States," Cannistraro says. "To do that, it needs to work with immigrant communities."[59] Treating whole communities with suspicion—in the Arizona context, seeing anyone who "looks Mexican" as "reasonably suspicious" and therefore deserving of an immigration inquiry—will destroy any chance to obtain information, because it will cause mistrust and fear. If we are serious about national security at the border, we simply cannot afford to have this happen, "because we need to have the trust and cooperation of people in those communities," Cannistraro says.[60]

The other authorities worth listening to on the subject of fighting terrorist attacks are members of the U.S. military, particularly in the context of the recent struggles in Iraq. In 2006, Iraq seemed to be sliding towards chaos and civil war. Sectarian violence was rife, with suicide bombings occurring in many densely populated neighborhoods.[61] The military fought a constant struggle against terrorists using improvised explosive devices to attack military vehicles and personnel.[62] At roughly this point, President Bush put General David Petraeus in command.[63] Petraeus, himself a Princeton Ph.D., convened a council of "warrior scholars" to help him rewrite the Army's counterinsurgency protocols, in order to fight the terrorists they were facing more effectively.[64] The resulting strategies changed the course of the war. For example, in a document entitled "Headquarters, Multinational Force Iraq's Counterinsurgency Guidance," dated September 16, 2008, the following appears under the heading *How We Think*:

> The environment in which we operate is complex and demands that we employ every weapon in our arsenal, kinetic and non-kinetic. To fully utilize all approaches we must understand the local culture and history. Learn about the tribes, formal and informal leaders . . . understand how the society functions.[65]

Studies of successful military efforts in Iraq revealed that this was exactly how the units that had done the best had operated. "Overwhelmingly, the units that seemed to be winning the fight had made significant inroads with local leaders, had found proactive ways to understand and respect local cultural norms, and had addressed specific community needs."[66] By understanding these needs, successful commanders and their units were able to build relationships and, over time, create trust with those in charge of neighborhoods and villages.[67] Trust, it turned out, not greater firepower or more soldiers, was what led to the most successful efforts.

These stories lead one inexorably to two observations. First, it is easy to see that counterterrorism intelligence gathering, and military success against insurgents who use terrorism as a primary weapon, both look a lot like something local law enforcement agents in the U.S. understand well: community policing. All of these efforts come down to the use of knowledge and intelligence gained on the ground, requiring the cooperation of the local population. Whether that population lives in an American city or an Iraqi village does not turn out to make a significant difference; what counts in both settings is building relationships based on trust. Second, those relationships lead to support and intelligence, and intelligence is the lifeblood of success, whether the struggle is for domestic public safety, the unearthing of al Qaida sleeper cells, or the winning of the battle against insurgents in Iraq.

It follows that anything that would interfere with this method of operation, any strategy or policy that would hurt the ability of law enforcement or counterintelligence personnel to make these connections must be seen as, at best, a net loss. And it is difficult to see S.B. 1070, and its requirement that Arizona's police make immigration inquiries, as anything but an effort that would damage whatever trust might exist between police and immigrant communities. With the police required to focus on immigrants, required to question them about their immigration status and required to get proof of citizenship, it seems inevitable that the immigrant communities of Arizona will become fearful of interaction with the police. The curtailment of communication in such a situation is inevitable.

V. Conclusion

To be sure, those who supported the passage of Arizona's S.B. 1070 do not seem to have wanted the measure to become law in order to address issues of national security. But the existence of the law gives us a chance to consider what might happen to our national security as a result of S.B. 1070's central operating principle: local police should enforce immigration law. Given what experts tell us about fighting terrorism—that the collection and use of intelligence is all important to our success, and that terrorist-defeating intelligence can only come from those living in close physical, cultural, and linguistic proximity to potential terrorists—there is every reason to think that the getting local police into the fight against illegal immigration represents exactly the wrong strategy. Let us hope that the advocates who "rebranded" immigration enforcement as national security in order to press local police into the effort do not ultimately triumph in the debate. If they do, they'll get just the opposite of what they've advertised: less safety and less security for all of us.

Critical Thinking Questions

1. Do you support efforts to have local law enforcement engaged in identifying and arresting illegal immigrants, as seen in Arizona? Why or why not?
2. Do you agree with the author that these efforts create challenges for law enforcement in areas of community policing and counterterrorism? Explain.
3. What strategies would you recommend to address the problem of illegal immigration without detracting from the effectiveness of homeland security efforts?

Notes

1. Immigration Reform and Control Act of 1986 (IRCA), Pub. L. No. 99–603, 100 Stat. 3359.
2. *See, e.g.*, Steven S. Mukamal, *Viewpoints: Our Hounded Immigrants*, Newsday, March 6, 1987 (describing IRCA as providing amnesty for settled illegal immigrants while upping penalties on employers); Antonio H. Rodriguez, *Amnesty Proves Insufficient; Gaps In Management and Law Immigration Reform,* L.A. Times, August 2, 1987 (describing amnesty provisions). It is interesting indeed to look back at the passage of the 1986 bill and recall that the path to citizenship for long-settled immigrants was called an amnesty, even by President Reagan himself. *See, e.g.*, Edwin Meese, III, *An Amnesty By Any Other Name . . . , N.Y. Times, May 24, 2006.*
3. *See, e.g.*, Herbert A. Sample, *Do Illegal Migrants Take Minority Jobs? New Research Adds Fuel to Fierce Debate*, Sacramento Bee, August 29, 1993 ("When Reps. Elton Gallegly and Duncan Hunter talk about stemming illegal immigration, they frequently claim that undocumented workers snare job opportunities from American minorities"); Terry Anderson, *Overrunning America*, San Jose Mercury News, June 12, 1996

(arguing that jobs that used to go to black Americans now go to recent immigrants); Mae M. Cheng, *Queens Residents Give a Mixed View*, Newsday, November 8, 1998 ("Residents of Queens, one of the nation's most diverse counties, applaud immigrants' contributions to the local economy but also believe these newest New Yorkers have taken jobs from native-born Americans and depressed salaries"); Art Silverstein, *Job Market a Flash Point for Natives, Newcomers,* L.A. Times, November 15, 1993 (quoting an American worker as saying that, when foreigners compete for jobs with Americans, "somebody gets hurt. Somebody gets left out in the cold, and I don't want it to be me. I was born and raised in this country. . . . If Americans want those jobs, they should be able to get those jobs."); Joseph P. Ritz, *Businesses Aiding Invasion of Illegal Aliens,* Buffalo News, July 25, 1993 (immigrants, particularly illegal ones, "blamed for enabling employers to perpetuate low-skilled, low-paying industries while ignoring the desires of poor Americans—especially blacks—to gain higher-skill, higher paying jobs"); Michael Gormley, *As the U.S. Economy Falls, Resentment of Immigrants Rises*, Albany Times Union, September 7, 1993 (describing "a backlash whipped by fear that newcomers are taking jobs, deflating wages . . ."); Mukamal, *supra* note 2 ("With unemployment as high as 10.4 percent that year, the impulse to protect American workers from competition by aliens spread through Congress").

4. *See, e.g., Immigration: Newcomers Are Burdening U.S. Taxpayers*, Dallas Morning News, October 17, 1993 ("In America today, jobs are the principal magnet for immigration. Increasingly, however, taxpayers and government officials are identifying a second magnet: taxpayer-funded social services . . . Can taxpayers afford to spend billions of social service dollars on people who are present illegally on U.S. soil?"); William Claiborne, *California Faces New Welfare Reality: Counties With Large Immigrant Population Fear Financial Hit*, Washington Post, August 2, 1996 (public official, faced with having to provide medical care for illegal immigrants, says "It's just devastating. These people will be at the doorsteps of our hospitals with communicable diseases, and we'll have to take care of them. It's an awful situation, because we just don't have the money"); Diane Rado, *Study: State Pays $884-million for Illegal Aliens*, ST. Petersburg Times, March 13, 1994 ("Taxpayers [in Florida] are spending $2.53-billion a year to provide services to a steady stream of immigrants. And an estimated $884-million of that goes to care for people who shouldn't even be here—illegal aliens"); Robert L. Jackson, *New Study on Immigration Cites High Costs*, L.A. Times, September 23, 1994 (study comparing taxes paid by immigrants to education and social services provided to them resulted in large net expense to states); Debra Beachy, *Immigrants Cost Texas Government 4.68 Billion in 1992, Study Finds*, Houston Chronicle, March 3, 1994 ("A new study by a Rice University economist . . . says immigrants—both legal and illegal—cost Texas $4.68 billion more in 1992 than they paid in taxes").
5. *See, e.g.*, Reena Shah Stamets, *Immigration Crusade Is Personal War*, ST. Petersburg Times, August 14, 1995 (quoting American citizen, himself a child of immigrants, as saying that he "saw America becoming this strange country . . . [Opponents of immigration are] not evil, mean people. We're just afraid, concerned about our home").
6. Jeff Jacoby, *We Can't Let Facts, Logic Get in the Way of a Good Snit at Immigrants*, Sun-Sentinel, November 26, 1994;
7. Illegal Immigration Reform and Immigrant Responsibility Act (IIRAIRA), Pub. L. No. 104–208, 110 Stat. 3009–546 (1996).
8. 8 U.S.C. §1357(g).

9. *See infra* note 12.
10. S.B. 1070, 2010 Ariz. Sess. Laws 0113, amended by 2010 Ariz. Sess. Laws 0211 (H.B. 2162, 49th Leg., 2d Sess. (Ariz. 2010)) (*hereinafter* S.B. 1070).
11. James Jay Carafano, *No Need for the CLEAR Act: Building Capacity for Immigration Counterterrorism Investigations*, Executive Memorandum No. 925, The Heritage Foundation (April 21, 2004), *available at* http://www.heritage.org/Research/HomelandDefense/em925.cfm (accessed April 6, 2011).
12. *See, e.g.*, Michael Ramage, General Counsel, Florida Dept. of Law Enforcement, Presentation to the International Association of Chiefs of Police Legal Officers Section: Emerging Immigration Issues for Local Law Enforcement (Sept. 25, 2005) (on file with author) (discussing Florida's 287(g) Memorandum of Understanding, which included approximately 70 officers who "Are NOT involved in general immigration enforcement efforts" (emphasis in original); *Southeast Asks Sheriff to Consider Immigration Enforcement*, Journal News (Westchester, N.Y.), Feb. 24, 2007 ("The Florida Department of Law Enforcement was the first to take part in the federal program in 2002. Some 62 agents and state and local officers have been trained. The agency has limited its authority to domestic security concerns, in places such as airports and seaports . . .").
13. Miriam Jordan, *The New Immigration Cops: Cities and States Take on Difficult Duty of Handling Undocumented Workers,* Wall ST. J., Feb. 2, 2006.
14. Rarely, if ever, was Canada and its vast border with the U.S. a subject of concern, though it clearly could have been. *See, e.g.,* U.S. Gov't Accountability Office, GAO-09-93, Northern Border Security: DHS'S Report Could Better Inform Congress by Identifying Actions, Resources, and Time Frames Needed to Address Vulnerabilities (2008) (Dept. of Homeland Security reported its northern border vulnerabilities, such as terrorism, drug trafficking, and illegal immigration to Congress); *see also* U.S. Gov't Accountability Office, GAO-11-97, Enhanced DHS Oversight and Assessment of Interagency Coordination is Needed for the Northern Border (2010) (calling for "DHS-level oversight and attention to enforcing accountability of established agreements" to meet ongoing challenges with coordination and lack of resources).
15. Mark Krikorian, *Keeping Terror Out*, 75 Nat'l Int. 77, 78 (2004).
16. *Id.* at 82.
17. *Id.* at 83.
18. David Shepardson, *FBI Links Two Terror Cases,* Detroit News, April 18, 2004.
19. *Id.*
20. Tony Blankley, The West's Last Chance: Will We Win the Clash of Civilizations? 172 (2005).
21. *Id.*
22. *Id.*, quoting *Current and Projected National Security Threats to the United States: Hearing Before the S. Select Comm. on Intelligence,* 109th Cong., 41 (2005) (prepared statement of Admiral James Loy, Deputy Secretary, U.S. Dept. of Homeland Security).
23. *Current and Projected National Security Threats to the United States: Hearing Before the S. Select Comm. on Intelligence,* 109th Cong., 41 (2005) (prepared statement of Admiral James Loy, Deputy Secretary, U.S. Dept. of Homeland Security).
24. For a fuller picture of these facts and the debate surrounding the *matricula consular* cards, *see* David A. Harris, Good Cops: The Case for Preventive Policing 190–92 (2005) [*hereinafter* Harris, Good Cops]; *and see* pages 13–14 *infra*.
25. *Id.*

26. *Morning Edition: Popularity of Consular ID Cards Among Illegal Latino Immigrants* (NPR Broadcast Nov. 25, 2003).
27. David A. Harris, *The War on Terror, Local Police, and Immigration Enforcement: A Curious Tale of Police Power in Post-9/11 America,* 38 Rutgers L. J. 1, 33-44 (2006) [*hereinafter* Harris, *The War on Terror*].
28. *Id.* at 35 ("In other police departments, the refusal to get involved in immigration enforcement stemmed from strong beliefs about the proper responsibility of the federal government to secure the nation's borders . . .[enforcement of immigration law by local police puts those officers], untrained in the law's unending nuances, at a great disadvantage").
29. *Id.* ("[L]ack of resources simply would not allow [local police] officers to take on immigration responsibilities . . . [and] the contemporaneous collapse of the economy in many areas of the country" has made this problem even worse").
30. *Id.* (Local police forces are especially reluctant to get involved in immigration enforcement "in light of the overwhelming number of new homeland security tasks they now must undertake" in the post 9/11 era).
31. *Id.* at 37-44.
32. *See* Harris, Good Cops, at 23-24.
33. *See, e.g.*, Robert Trojanowicz & Bonnie Bucqueroux, Community Policing: A Contemporary Perspective 11, 12 (1990).
34. *Id.* at 11 (calling information from the community "the lifeblood of policing. Without the facts, police officers cannot solve problems," and this type of information must come from "law abiding people, through both formal and informal contacts").
35. Harris, Good Cops at 37 (noting that with the growing mainstream popularity of community policing in the U.S. over the past two decades, "more and more American police departments and their communities" have created "partnerships based on collaboration and trust").
36. *See* discussion of *matricula cards* at note 24 *supra* and accompanying text.
37. Harris, Good Cops at 191-193.
38. Harris, *The War on Terror*, at 40 and n. 13.
39. *Id.* at 39-40.
40. Jeffrey S. Passel, Pew Hispanic Center, *Unauthorized Migrants: Numbers and Characteristics* (June 14, 2005), *available at* http://pewhispanic.org/reports/report.php?ReportID=46 (3.2 million people live in mixed status households in which some persons do not have legal status).
41. Harris, *The War on Terror*, at 40-41 ("[F]or local police, immigrants' fear of contact with law enforcement emerges as a major obstacle in the constant fight to make the streets safe").
42. *Id.* at 37-38 (noting that many cities and towns in every region of the country, not just traditional large immigrant destination cities, have burgeoning immigrant populations, and have made strong efforts to work with these populations).
43. *Id.* at 40-42.
44. Peggy O'Hare, *HPD Policy on Aliens is Hands-Off*, Houston Chron., Mar. 3, 2003 (internal citations omitted).
45. Major City Chiefs, Immigration Committee Recommendations for Enforcement of Immigration laws by Local Police Agencies 6 (2006), *available at* http://judiciary.house.gov/media/pdfs/wiles081706.pdf.

46. S.B. 1070, *supra* note 10, at §11-1051B (" . . .where reasonable suspicion exists that the person [who police encounter] is an alien who is unlawfully present in the United States, a reasonable attempt shall be made, when practicable, to determine the immigration status of the person").
47. *Id., supra* note 10, at §11-1051A ("[N]o official or agency of this state or a county, city, town or other political subdivision of this state may adopt a policy that limits or restricts the enforcement of federal immigration laws to less than the full extent permitted by federal law").
48. Order, *U.S. v. State of Arizona*, No. CV 10-1413-PHX-SRB, U.S. Dist. Ct., D. Ariz., July 28, 2010 (enjoining key parts of the statute, while allowing other aspects to go into effect).
49. *U.S. v. State of Arizona*, No. 10-16645, D.C. No. 2:10-cv-01413-SRB, United States Court of Appeals for the Ninth Circuit, *decided* April 11, 2011 (upholding district court's decision).
50. Marc Lacey, *Appeals Court Rules Against Arizona Law*, N.Y. Times, April 11, 2011 (main sponsor of bill in state legislature calling the fight over S.B. 1070 "a battle of epic proportions" that would ultimately be settled in the Supreme Court; state attorney general predicting that the Supreme Court would uphold the law).
51. *See* Donald L. Bartlett, et al., *Illegal Aliens: Who Left the Door Open?*, TIME, March 30, 2006; John Lantigua, *Vigilantes Sweep Desert for "Chickens,"* Palm Beach Post, Dec. 8, 2003 ("Local church and legal authorities estimate that during the peak winter and spring seasons, more than 2,000 undocumented migrants per day cross the eastern Arizona border"); Daniel Gonzalez, *Bush Policy Turns Mesa Airport Into Deportation Hub,* Arizona Republic, Mar. 4, 2007 (". . . Arizona is the country's main crossing point for undocumented immigrants along the southern border . . ."); *Time to Breathe*, Timesdaily.Com, AUGUST 1, 2010, *accessed* April 22, 2011 *at* http://www.timesdaily.com/section/news10 (characterizing Arizona as "the primary crossing point for many undocumented workers"); *Photographer Recounts Crossing U.S. Border With Mexican Illegal Immigrants*, National Geographic News, October 28, 2010, *available at* http://news.nationalgeographic.com/news/2003/01/0123_030123_border.html (calling a 261-mile-long stretch of the Sonoran Desert in Southern Arizona "[t]he busiest gateway for illegal immigrants crossing the U.S.-Mexico border for the past five years").
52. In fact, the proponents of S.B. 1070 made their motives clear in the bill itself. While S.B. 1070 made use of the criminal law and law enforcement, its purpose was not to fight crime, or to enhance national security. It was simpler: to use "attrition" to rid the state of illegal immigrants. As the "Intent" section of the law states, "The legislature declares that the intent of this act is to make attrition through enforcement the public policy of all state and local government agencies in Arizona. The provisions of this act are intended to work together to discourage and deter the unlawful entry and presence of aliens and economic activity by persons unlawfully present in the United States." S.B. 1070, §2.
53. Remarks of Harry "Skip" Brandon and Vincent Cannistraro, 26th National Legal Conference on Immigration & Refugee Policy, Session I: National Security and Immigrant Rights, April 2, 2003, Washington, D.C., *collected in* In Defense of the Alien: Volume XXVI, Proceedings of the 2003 Annual National Legal Conference on Immigration and Refugee Policy (2003, Center for Migration Studies, Joseph Fugolo, ed.) (*hereinafter* Remarks of Brandon and Cannistraro).

54. Harris, Good Cops at 219.
55. *Id.*
56. Remarks of Brandon and Cannistraro, *supra* note 53, at 25.
57. *Id.* at 11, 13.
58. *Id.* at 12.
59. *Id.* at 11.
60. *Id.* at 12.
61. *See, e.g.*, Alissa J. Rubin & Damien Cave, *In a Force for Iraqi Calm, Seeds of Conflict*, N.Y. Times, Dec. 23, 2007 (describing the organization of "Awakening" groups as a possible prelude to yet more conflict and even civil war); Robin Wright & Peter Baker, *Iraqi Shiite Leader Speaks Bluntly in Washington*, Washington Post, Dec. 5, 2006, (describing "the danger of a civil war" and "escalating sectarian strife" in Iraq); Jeffrey Fleishman & Qaisar Ahmed, *The Conflict in Iraq: Possible Cabinet Shake-Up; Growing Diaspora*, L.A. TIMES, Dec. 14, 2006 (describing Iraq as "tumbl[ing] into civil war" amidst "a numbing diary of suicide bombings, sectarian militia attacks and dusk-to-dawn bloodshed").
62. *See, e.g.*, Nancy Trejos, *5 U.S. Troops Added To Death Toll in Iraq*, Washington Post, Dec. 29, 2006 (in December 2006, when approximately 100 U.S. troops died in Iraq, "most were killed by roadside bombs"); Solomon Moore, *Monthly U.S. Toll At 2-Year High*, L..A. Times, December 30, 2006 ("More than half the fatalities in December occurred during attacks involving improvised explosive devices"); *Iraq Digest*, Chicago Tribune, Dec. 29, 2006 ("Roadside bombs and exploding vehicles accounted for 408 of the 807 fatalities suffered by U.S. forces in Iraq this year—or 51 percent of the year's fatalities as of Thursday").
63. Michael R. Gordon & Thom Shanker, *Bush to Name a New General to Oversee Iraq,* N.Y. Times, Jan. 5, 2007 (reporting that President Bush would name Petraeus commander in Iraq); Mark Tran, *Bush Poised to Name New Iraq Commander,* The Guardian, Jan. 5, 2007 (reporting Bush's imminent announcement naming Petraeus as new commander in Iraq).
64. James Joyner, *Petraeus' Princeton PhD Posse,* Outside the Beltway, Feb. 2, 2007, *available at* http://www.outsidethebeltway.com/archives/petraeus_princeton_phd_posse_/ (*accessed* Dec. 13, 2008). For a brief account of this series of actions, *see* Jack L. Cowell & Charles "Chip" Huth, Unleashing the Power of Unconditional Respect: Transforming Law Enforcement and Police Training 103-105 (2010). I encountered the sources cited here regarding the military's new counterinsurgency materials in Cowell and Huth's very insightful book, and I thank them for bringing this information to my attention.
65. Headquarters, Multinational Force Iraq's Counterinsurgency Guidance (Sept 16, 2008), *available at* http://www.mnf-iraq.com/images/CGs_Messages/odierno_coin_guidance .pdf (last visited Sept. 5, 2009).
66. Lt. Col. Jack Marr, Maj. John Cushing, Maj. Brandon Garner, & Capt. Richard Thompson, *Human Terrain Mapping: A Critical First Step to Winning the COIN Fight*, Military Review, March-April 2008.
67. *Id.*

Section 3.2

Competing Perspectives on the USA PATRIOT Act

The USA PATRIOT Act

What's So Patriotic about Trampling on the Bill of Rights?[1]

Nancy Chang

Just six weeks after the September 11 terrorist attacks on the World Trade Center and the Pentagon, a jittery Congress—exiled from its anthrax-contaminated offices and confronted with warnings that more terrorist assaults were soon to come—capitulated to the Bush Administration's demands for a new arsenal of anti-terrorism weapons. Over vigorous objections from civil liberties organizations on both ends of the political spectrum, Congress overwhelmingly approved the Uniting and Strengthening America by Providing Appropriate Tools Required to Intercept and Obstruct Terrorism Act, better known by its acronym, the USA PATRIOT Act.[2] The House vote was 356-to-66, and the Senate vote was 98-to-1. Along the way, the Republican House leadership, in a raw display of force, jettisoned an anti-terrorism bill that the House Judiciary Committee had unanimously approved and that would have addressed a number of civil liberties concerns.[3] The hastily drafted, complex, and far-reaching legislation spans 342 pages. Yet it was passed with virtually no public hearing or debate, and it was accompanied by neither a conference nor a committee report. On October 26, the Act was signed into law by a triumphant President George W. Bush.[4]

The USA Patriot Act Confers Vast and Unchecked Powers to the Executive Branch

Although a number of its provisions are not controversial, the USA PATRIOT Act nevertheless stands out as radical in its design. To an unprecedented degree, the Act sacrifices our political freedoms in the name of national security and upsets the democratic values that define our nation by consolidating vast new powers in the executive branch of government. The Act enhances the executive's ability to conduct surveillance and gather intelligence, places an array of new tools at the disposal of the prosecution, including new crimes, enhanced penalties, and longer statutes of limitations, and grants the Immigration and Naturalization Service (INS) the authority to detain immigrants suspected of terrorism for lengthy, and in some cases indefinite, periods of time. And at the same time that the Act inflates the powers of the executive, it insulates the exercise of these powers from meaningful judicial and Congressional oversight.

It remains to be seen how the executive will wield its new authority. However, if the two months that have elapsed since September 11 serve as a guide, we should brace ourselves for a flagrant disregard of the rule of law by those charged with its enforcement. Already, the Department of Justice (DOJ) has admitted to detaining more than 1,100 immigrants, not one of whom has been charged with committing a terrorist act and only a handful of whom are being held as material witnesses to the September 11 hijackings.[5] Many in this group appear to have been held for extended time periods under an extraordinary interim regulation announced by Attorney General John Ashcroft on September 17 and published in Federal Register on September 20.[6] This regulation sets aside the strictures of due process by permitting the INS to detain aliens without charge for 48 hours or an uncapped "additional reasonable period of time" in the event of an "emergency or other extraordinary circumstance." Also, many in this group are being held without bond under the pretext of unrelated criminal charges or minor immigration violations, in a modern-day form of preventive detention. Chillingly, the Attorney General's response to the passage of the USA PATRIOT Act was not a pledge to use his new powers responsibly and guard against their abuse, but instead was a vow to step up his detention efforts. Conflating immigrant status with terrorist status, he declared: "Let the terrorists among us be warned, if you overstay your visas even by one day, we will arrest you."[7]

Furthermore, the Administration has made no secret of its hope that the judiciary will accede to its broad reading of the USA PATRIOT Act just as pliantly as Congress acceded to its broad legislative agenda. In a letter sent to key Senators while Congress was considering this legislation, Assistant Attorney General Daniel J. Bryant, of DOJ's Office of Legislative Affairs, openly advocated for a suspension of the Fourth Amendment's warrant requirement in the government's investigation of foreign national security threats.[8] The Bryant letter brazenly declares:

> As Commander-in-Chief, *the President must be able to use whatever means necessary to prevent attacks upon the United States;* this power, by implication, includes the authority to collect information necessary to its effective exercise. . . . The government's interest has changed from merely conducting foreign intelligence surveillance to counter intelligence operations by other nations, to one of preventing terrorist attacks against American citizens and property within the continental United States itself. The courts have observed that even the use of deadly force is reasonable under the Fourth Amendment if used in self-defense or to protect others. . . . Here, for Fourth Amendment purposes, the right to self-defense is not that of an individual, but that of the nation and its citizens. . . . *If the government's heightened interest in self-defense justifies the use of deadly force, then it certainly would also justify warrantless searches.*[9]

Suspension of Civil Liberties

The Administration's blatant power grab, coupled with the wide array of anti-terrorism tools that the USA PATRIOT Act puts at its disposal, portends a wholesale suspension of civil liberties that will reach far beyond those who are involved in terrorist activities. First, the Act places our First Amendment rights to freedom of speech and political association in jeopardy by creating a broad new crime of "domestic terrorism," and by denying entry to non-citizens on the basis of ideology. Second, the Act will reduce our already lowered expectations of privacy under the Fourth Amendment by granting the government enhanced surveillance powers. Third, non-citizens will see a further erosion of their due process rights as they are placed in mandatory detention and removed from the United States under the Act. Political activists who are critical of our government or who maintain ties with international political movements, in addition to immigrants, are likely to bear the brunt of these attacks on our civil liberties.

Silencing Political Dissent

Section 802 of the USA PATRIOT Act defines for the first time a federal crime of "domestic terrorism" that broadly extends to "acts dangerous to human life that are a violation of the criminal laws" if they "appear to be intended . . . to influence the policy of a government by intimidation or coercion," and if they "occur primarily within the territorial jurisdiction of the United States."[10] Because this definition is couched in such vague and expansive terms, it may well be read by federal law enforcement agencies as licensing the investigation and surveillance of political activists and organizations based on their opposition to government policies. It also may be read by prosecutors as licensing the criminalization of legitimate political dissent. Vigorous protest activities, by their very nature, could be construed as acts that "appear to be intended . . . to influence the policy of a government by intimidation or coercion." Further, clashes between demonstrators and police officers and acts of civil disobedience—even those that do not result in injuries and are entirely non-violent—could be construed as "dangerous to human life" and in "violation of the criminal laws." Environmental activists, anti-globalization activists, and anti-abortion activists who use direct action to further their political agendas are particularly vulnerable to prosecution as "domestic terrorists."

In addition, political activists and the organizations with which they associate may unwittingly find themselves the subject of unwanted government attention in the form of surveillance and other intelligence-gathering operations. The manner in which the government implements the Act must be carefully monitored to ascertain whether activists and organizations are being targeted selectively for surveillance and prosecution based on their opposition to government policies. The First Amendment does not tolerate viewpoint-based discrimination.[11]

Furthermore, Section 411 of the Act poses an ideological test for entry into the United States that takes into consideration core political speech. Representatives of a political or social group "whose public endorsement of acts of terrorist activity the Secretary of State has determined undermines United States efforts to reduce or eliminate terrorist activities" can no longer gain entry into the United States.[12] Entry is also barred to non-citizens who have used their "position of prominence within any country to endorse or espouse terrorist activity," if the Secretary of State determines that their speech "undermines United States efforts to reduce or eliminate terrorist activities."[13]

Tolling the Death-Knell on Privacy

The USA PATRIOT Act[14] launches a three-pronged assault on our privacy. First, the Act grants the executive branch unprecedented, and largely unchecked, surveillance powers, including the enhanced ability to track email and Internet usage, conduct sneak-and-peek searches, obtain sensitive personal records, monitor financial transactions, and conduct nationwide roving wiretaps. Second, the Act permits law enforcement agencies to circumvent the Fourth Amendment's requirement of probable cause when conducting wiretaps and searches that have, as "a significant purpose," the gathering of foreign intelligence. Third, the Act allows for the sharing of information between criminal and intelligence operations and thereby opens the door to a resurgence of domestic spying by the Central Intelligence Agency.

1). Enhanced Surveillance Powers. By and large, Congress granted the Administration its longstanding wish list of enhanced surveillance tools, coupled with the ability to use these tools with only minimal judicial and Congressional oversight. In its rush to pass an anti-terrorism bill, Congress failed to exact in exchange a showing that these highly intrusive new tools are actually needed to combat terrorism and that the Administration can be trusted not to abuse them.

The recent decision in *Kyllo v. United States*[15] serves as a pointed reminder that once a Fourth Amendment protection has been eroded, the resulting loss to our privacy is likely to be permanent. In *Kyllo*, the Supreme Court concluded that the use of an advanced thermal detection device that allowed the police to detect heat emanating from marijuana plants growing inside the defendant's home constituted a "search" for the purposes of the Fourth Amendment and was presumptively unreasonable without a warrant. The Court placed great weight on the fact that the device was new, "not in general public use," and had been used to "explore details of a private home that would previously have been unknowable without physical intrusion."[16] Implicit in the Court's holding is the principle that once a technology is in general public use and its capabilities are known, a reasonable expectation of privacy under the Fourth Amendment may no longer attach. Several of the Act's enhanced surveillance tools, and the civil liberties concerns they raise, are examined below.

Sneak and Peek Searches: Section 213 of the Act authorizes federal agents to conduct "sneak and peek searches," or covert searches of a person's home or office that are conducted without notifying the person of the execution of the search warrant until after the search has been completed. Section 213 authorizes delayed notice of the execution of a search warrant upon a showing of "reasonable cause to believe that providing immediate notification . . . may have an adverse result."[17] Section 213 also authorizes the delay of notice of the execution of a warrant to conduct a seizure of items where the court finds a "reasonable necessity" for the seizure.

Section 213 contravenes the "common law 'knock and announce' principle," which forms an essential part of the Fourth Amendment's reasonableness inquiry.[18] When notice of a search is delayed, one is foreclosed from pointing out deficiencies in the warrant to the officer executing it, and from monitoring whether the search is being conducted in accordance with the warrant. In addition, Section 213, by authorizing delayed notice of the execution of a warrant to conduct a seizure of items, contravenes Rule 41(d) of the Federal Rules of Criminal Procedure, which requires that, "The officer taking property under the warrant shall give to the person from whom or from whose premises the property was taken a copy of the warrant and a receipt for the property taken or shall leave the copy and receipt at the place from which the property was taken."

Under Section 213, notice may be delayed for a "reasonable period." Already, DOJ has staked out its position that a "reasonable period" can be considerably longer than the seven days authorized by the Second Circuit Court of Appeals in *United States v. Villegas*,[19] and by the Ninth Circuit Court of Appeals in *United States v. Freitas*.[20] DOJ states in its *Field Guidance on New Authorities (Redacted) Enacted in the 2001 Anti-Terrorism Legislation*[21] that "[a]nalogy to other statutes suggest [*sic*] that the period of delay could be substantial if circumstances warrant," and cites in support of this proposition a case that found a 90-day delay in providing notice of a wiretap warrant to constitute "a reasonable time." Notably, Section 213 is not limited to terrorism investigations, but extends to all criminal investigations, and is not scheduled to expire.

Access to Records in International Investigations: Section 215[22] is one of several provisions in the USA PATRIOT Act that relaxes the requirements, and extends the reach, of the Foreign Intelligence Surveillance Act of 1978 (FISA).[23] Under Section 215, the Director of the FBI or a designee as low in rank as an Assistant Special Agent in Charge may apply for a court order requiring the production of "any tangible things (including books, records, papers, documents, and other items)" upon his written statement that these items are being sought for an investigation "to protect against international terrorism or clandestine intelligence activities."[24] A judge presented with an application under Section 215 is required to enter an order if he "finds that the application meets the requirements of this section."[25]

Notably absent from Section 215 is the restriction in the FISA provision it amends that had required the government to specify in its application for a court order that "there are specific and articulable facts giving reason to believe that the person to whom the records pertain is a foreign power or an agent of a foreign power."[26] Now, under Section 215, the FBI may obtain sensitive personal records by simply certifying that they are sought for an investigation "to protect against international terrorism or clandestine intelligence activities." The FBI need not suspect the person whose records are being sought of any wrongdoing. Furthermore, the class of persons whose records are obtainable under Section 215 is no longer limited to foreign powers and their agents, but may include United States citizens and lawful permanent residents, or "United States persons" in the parlance of the FISA.[27] While Section 215 bars investigations of United States persons "solely upon the basis of activities protected by the first amendment to the Constitution," it does nothing to bar investigations based on other activities that tie them, no matter how loosely, to an international terrorism investigation.[28]

The FISA provision that was amended by Section 215 had been limited in scope to "records" in the possession of "a common carrier, public accommodation facility, physical storage facility, or vehicle rental facility."[29] Section 215 extends beyond "records" to "tangible things" and is no longer limited in terms of the entities from whom the production of tangible things can be required.[30] A Congressional oversight provision will require the Attorney General to submit semi-annual reports on its activities under Section 215.[31] Section 215 is scheduled to expire on December 31, 2005.

Tracking Internet Usage: Under Section 216 of the Act, courts are required to order the installation of a pen register and a trap and trace device[32] to track both telephone and Internet "dialing, routing, addressing and signaling information"[33] anywhere within the United States when a government attorney has certified that the information to be obtained is "*relevant* to an ongoing criminal investigation."[34] Section 216 states that orders issued under its authority cannot permit the tracking of the "contents of any wire or electronic communications." However, in the case of email messages and Internet usage, the Act does not address the complex question of where the line should be drawn between "dialing, routing, addressing and signaling information" and "content." Unlike telephone communications, where the provision of dialing information does not run the risk of revealing content,[35] email messages move together in packets that include both address and content information. Also, the question of whether a list of web sites and web pages that have been visited constitutes "dialing, routing, addressing and signaling information" or "content" has yet to be resolved.

By providing no guidance on this question, Section 216 gives the government wide latitude to decide what constitutes "content." Of special concern is the fact that Section 216 authorizes the government to install its new Carnivore or DCS1000 system, a formidable tracking device that is capable of intercepting all forms of Internet activity, including email messages, web page activity, and Internet telephone communications.[36] Once installed on an Internet Service Provider (ISP), Carnivore devours *all* of the communications flowing through the ISP's network—not just those of the target of surveillance but those of all users—and not just tracking information but content as well. The FBI claims that through the use of filters, Carnivore "limits the messages viewable by human eyes to those which are strictly included within the court order."[37] However, neither the accuracy of Carnivore's filtering system, nor the infallibility of its human programmers, has been demonstrated. While Section 216 requires the government to maintain a record when it utilizes Carnivore, this record need not be provided to the court until 30 days after the termination of the order, including any extensions of time.[38] Section 216 is not scheduled to expire.

2). Allowing Law Enforcement Agencies to Evade the Fourth Amendment's Probable Cause Requirement. Perhaps the most radical provision of the USA PATRIOT Act is Section 218, which amends FISA's wiretap and physical search provisions. Under FISA, court orders permitting the executive to conduct surreptitious foreign intelligence wiretaps and physical searches may be obtained without the showing of probable cause required for wiretaps and physical searches in criminal investigations. Until the enactment of the Act, orders issued under FISA's lax standards were restricted to situations where the gathering of foreign intelligence information was "*the* purpose" of the surveillance.[39]

Under Section 218, however, orders may be issued under FISA's lax standards where the primary purpose of the surveillance is criminal investigation, and the gathering of foreign intelligence information constitutes only "a *significant* purpose"of the surveillance.[40] As a result, Section 218 allows law enforcement agencies conducting a criminal investigation to circumvent the Fourth Amendment whenever they are able to claim that the gathering of foreign intelligence constitutes "a significant purpose." In doing so, Section 218 gives the FBI a green light to resume domestic spying on government "enemies"—a program that reached an ugly apex under J. Edgar Hoover's directorship.

In the seminal case of *United States v. United States District Court for the Eastern District of Michigan (Keith),*[41] the Supreme Court rejected President Richard Nixon's ambitious bid for the unchecked executive power to conduct warrantless wiretaps when investigating national security threats posed by *domestic* groups with no foreign ties. The Court recognized that national security cases reflect "a convergence of First and Fourth Amendment values not present in cases of 'ordinary' crime."[42] With respect to the First Amendment, the Court wisely observed that "[o]fficial surveillance, whether its purpose be criminal investigation or ongoing intelligence gathering, risks infringement of constitutionally protected privacy of speech" because of "the inherent vagueness of the domestic security concept . . . and the temptation to utilize such surveillances to oversee political dissent."[43]

With respect to the Fourth Amendment, the Court acknowledged the constitutional basis for the President's domestic security role, but refused to exempt the President from the Fourth Amendment's warrant requirement.[44] The Court explained that the oversight function assumed by the judiciary in its review of applications for warrants "accords with our basic constitutional doctrine that individual freedoms will best be preserved through a separation of powers and division of functions among the different branches and levels of Government."[45]

Notably, the *Keith* Court declined to examine "the scope of the President's surveillance power with respect to the activities of *foreign* powers, within or without this country."[46] To fill the vacuum left in the wake of the *Keith* decision, in 1978 Congress enacted FISA, which is premised on the assumption that Fourth Amendment safeguards are not as critical in foreign intelligence investigations as they are in criminal investigations. The Supreme Court has yet to rule on FISA's constitutionality. However, both the Fourth and Ninth Circuits have cautioned that applying FISA's lax standards to criminal investigations raises serious Fourth Amendment concerns. In *United States v. Truong Dinh Hung*, the Fourth Circuit held that "the executive should be excused from securing a warrant only when the surveillance is conducted '*primarily*' *for foreign intelligence reasons*," because "once surveillance becomes *primarily a criminal investigation*, the courts are entirely competent to make the usual probable cause determination, and because, importantly, individual privacy interests come to the fore and government foreign policy concerns recede when the government is primarily attempting to form the basis for a criminal prosecution."[47] In a similar vein, the Ninth Circuit held in *United States v. Johnson* that "the investigation of criminal activity cannot be the primary purpose of [FISA] surveillance" and that "[FISA] is not to be used as an end-run around the Fourth Amendment's prohibition of warrantless searches."[48]

The constitutionality of Section 218 is in considerable doubt. The extremist position staked out by DOJ in the Bryant Letter, which argues that "[i]f the government's heightened interest in self-defense justifies the use of deadly force, then it certainly would also justify warrantless searches," would undermine the separation of powers doctrine.[49] Until the Supreme Court weighs in on this matter, the government will find itself in a quandary each time it seeks to prosecute a criminal defendant based on evidence that, although properly obtained under the lesser showing required by Section 218, does not meet the probable cause showing required by the Fourth Amendment. Should the government decide to base prosecutions on such evidence, it will run the risk that the evidence will be suppressed under the Fourth Amendment exclusionary rule.[50] Section 218 is scheduled to expire on December 31, 2005.

3). Sharing of Sensitive Criminal and Foreign Intelligence Information. Section 203 of the USA PATRIOT Act authorizes the disclosure, without judicial supervision, of certain criminal and foreign intelligence information to officials of the FBI, CIA, and INS, as well as other federal agencies, where receipt of the information will "assist the official . . . in the performance of his official duties."[51] Section 203(a) permits the disclosure of matters occurring before a grand jury—a category that is as boundless in scope as the powers of a grand jury to subpoena records and witnesses.[52] Section 203(b) permits the disclosure of recordings of intercepted telephone and Internet conversations.[53] And Section 203(d) permits the disclosure of foreign intelligence obtained as part of a criminal investigation.[54]

While some additional sharing of information between agencies is undoubtedly appropriate given the nature of the terrorist threats we face, the Act fails to protect us from the dangers posed to our political freedoms and our privacy when sensitive personal information is widely shared without court supervision. A cautionary tale can be found in the 1976 report of the Senate's Church Committee, which revealed that the FBI and CIA had spied on thousands of law-abiding citizens, from civil rights workers to anti-Vietnam War protestors, who had been targeted solely because they were believed to harbor politically dissident views.[55] Section 203(a) is not scheduled to expire. Subsections (b) and (d) of Section 203, however, are scheduled to expire.

Stripping Immigrants of Constitutional Protections

The USA PATRIOT Act deprives immigrants of their due process and First Amendment rights through two mechanisms that operate in tandem. First, Section 411 vastly expands the class of immigrants who are subject to removal on terrorism grounds through its broad definitions of the terms "terrorist activity," "engage in terrorist activity," and "terrorist organization." Second, Section 412 vastly expands the authority of the Attorney General to place immigrants he suspects are engaged in terrorist activities in detention while their removal proceedings are pending.

1). Expanding the Class of Immigrants Subject to Removal. Section 411 vastly expands the class of immigrants that can be removed on terrorism grounds.[56] The term "terrorist activity" is commonly understood to be limited to pre-meditated and politically-motivated violence targeted against a civilian population.[57] Section 411, however, stretches the term beyond recognition to encompass any crime that involves the use of a "weapon or dangerous device (other than for mere personal monetary gain)."[58] Under this broad definition, an immigrant who grabs a knife or makeshift weapon in the midst of a heat-of-the-moment altercation or in committing a crime of passion may be subject to removal as a "terrorist."

The term "engage in terrorist activity" has also been expanded to include soliciting funds for, soliciting membership for, and providing material support to, a "terrorist organization," even when that organization has legitimate political and humanitarian ends and the non-citizen seeks only to support these lawful ends.[59] In such situations, Section 411 would permit guilt to be imposed solely on the basis of political associations protected by the First Amendment.[60]

To complicate matters further, the term "terrorist organization" is no longer limited to organizations that have been officially designated as terrorist and that therefore have had their designations published in the Federal Register for all to see.[61] Instead, Section 411 now includes as "terrorist organizations" groups that have never been designated as terrorist if they fall under the loose criterion of "two or more individuals, whether organized or not," which engage in specified terrorist activities.[62] In situations where a non-citizen has solicited funds for, solicited membership for, or provided material support to, an undesignated "terrorist organization," Section 411 saddles him with the difficult, if not impossible, burden of "demonstrat[ing] that he did not know, and should not reasonably have known, that the act would further the organization's terrorist activity."[63] Furthermore, while Section 411 prohibits the removal of a non-citizen on the grounds that he solicited funds for, solicited membership for, or provided material support to, a designated "terrorist organization" at a time when the organization was not designated as a "terrorist organization," Section 411 does *not* prohibit the removal of a non-citizen on the grounds that he solicited funds for, solicited membership for, or provided material support to, an undesignated "terrorist organization" *prior* to the enactment of the Act.[64]

2). Detention at the Attorney General's Decree. At the same time that Section 411 vastly expands the class of immigrants who are removable on terrorist grounds, Section 412 vastly inflates the Attorney General's power to detain immigrants who are suspected of falling into that class.[65] Upon no more than the Attorney General's unreviewed certification that he has "reasonable grounds to believe" that a non-citizen is engaged in terrorist activities or other activities that threaten the national security, a non-citizen can be detained for as long as seven days without being charged with either a criminal or immigration violation.[66] This low level of suspicion falls far short of a finding of probable cause, and appears even to fall short of the "reasonable and articulable suspicion" that supports a brief investigatory stop under the Fourth Amendment.[67]

If the non-citizen is charged with an immigration violation, he is subject to mandatory detention and is ineligible for release until he is removed, or until the Attorney General determines that he should no longer be certified as a terrorist.[68] While the immigration proceedings are pending, the Attorney General is required to review his certification once every six months.[69] However, Section 412 does not direct the Attorney General either to inform the non-citizen of the evidence on which the certification is based, or to provide the non-citizen with an opportunity to contest that evidence at an Immigration Judge hearing or other administrative review procedure. Instead, Section 412 limits the non-citizen's ability to seek review of the certification to a habeas corpus proceeding filed in federal district court, appeals from which must be filed in the Court of Appeals for the District of Columbia.[70] Since habeas proceedings are civil rather than criminal in nature, the government has no obligation under the Sixth Amendment to provide non-citizens with free counsel in such proceedings.[71]

Even where a non-citizen who is found removable is deemed eligible for asylum or other relief from removal, Section 412 does not permit his release.[72] Further, in the event that the non-citizen is found removable, but removal is "unlikely in the reasonably foreseeable future"—most likely because no other country will accept him—he may be detained for additional periods of six months "if the release of the alien will threaten the national security of the United States or the safety of the community or any person."[73] Only habeas review of such a determination is available under Section 412.[74]

The Due Process Clause "applies to all 'persons' within the United States, including aliens, whether their presence is lawful, unlawful, temporary, or permanent."[75] Yet, Section 412 exposes immigrants to extended, and, in some cases, indefinite, detention on the sole authority of the Attorney General's untested certification that he has "reasonable grounds to believe" that a non-citizen is engaged in terrorist activities. It remains to be seen what evidentiary safeguards, if any, the Attorney General will build into his regulations implementing Section 412. It also remains to be seen how rigorous federal court habeas reviews of such certifications will be and to what extent the courts will demand that the Attorney General base his certification on objective evidence. Nevertheless, it is hard to avoid the conclusion that the Act will deprive non-citizens of their liberty without due process of law.[76]

3). The Political Implications of the USA PATRIOT Act for Immigrants. In short, immigrants who engage in political activities in connection with any organization that has ever violated the law risk being certified as terrorists, placed in mandatory detention, and removed, whether on a technical immigration violation or on terrorism grounds. Immigrants cannot protect themselves from such risks by simply avoiding association with organizations that have been designated as "terrorist organizations" because the Act broadens that term to include undesignated groups. Nor can immigrants protect themselves from such risks by limiting themselves to activities that are protected by the First Amendment, such as soliciting membership for, soliciting funds for, and providing material support to, a "terrorist organization" towards the goal of furthering the organization's lawful ends, because the Act broadens the term "engage in terrorist activity" to include these activities. Ironically, in the post-USA PATRIOT Act world, immigrants who are intent on avoiding such risks should refrain from any associations with organizations that could potentially be deemed terrorist, even if their association is strictly confined to activities that further the humanitarian and peace-oriented goals of the organization, such as training members of such a organization on how to present international human rights claims to the United Nations, representing such an organization in peace negotiations, and donating humanitarian aid to such an organization.

Will the Judiciary Rein in the Executive and Uphold the Bill of Rights?

Our commitment to the Bill of Rights and to the democratic values that define this nation has been put to the test by the events of September 11. Already, Congress and the Administration have demonstrated their eagerness to sacrifice civil liberties in hopes of gaining an added measure of security. The task of upholding the Bill of Rights—or acquiescing in its surrender—will soon fall to the judiciary, as lawsuits testing the constitutionality of the USA PATRIOT Act wind their way through the courts.

In what we have come to regard as some of the most shameful episodes in our history, the judiciary has consistently bowed to the wishes of the political branches of government in times of crisis by finding the state interest in national security to be paramount to all competing interests. During World War I, the Supreme Court upheld the conviction of socialist Eugene Debs for expressing his opposition to World War I, refusing to recognize his non-violent, anti-war advocacy as speech protected by the First Amendment.[77] More recently, following the bombing of Pearl Harbor during World War II, the Supreme Court upheld an Executive Order mandating the internment of more than 100,000 Japanese-Americans and Japanese immigrants based solely on their ancestry, refusing to recognize their preventive detention as a violation of the Equal Protection Clause.[78]

The extent to which the judiciary will defer to the Administration's views on the troubling First and Fourth Amendment issues presented by the USA PATRIOT Act, will tolerate ethnic and ideological profiling by the Administration as it implements the Act, and will allow the due process rights of immigrants in detention to be eroded remains to be seen. Certainly, the more anxious the times become, the more likely the judiciary will be to side with the Administration—at least where judges are convinced that the measures are vital to the national security, are not motivated by discriminatory intent, and tread as lightly as possible upon civil liberties. The recent words of Supreme Court Justice Sandra Day O'Connor, who so often figures as the swing vote on pivotal decisions, do not hold out hope for a vigorous defense of our political freedoms by the judiciary. Following a visit to Ground Zero, where the World Trade Centers once stood, the Justice bleakly predicted, "We're likely to experience more restrictions on personal freedom than has ever been the case in this country."[79]

Critical Thinking Questions

1. Have the author's criticisms of the USA PATRIOT Act been justified by the way this legislation has been implemented over the last decade? Why or why not?
2. Why are so many U.S. citizens suspicious of their government's efforts to ensure security?
3. Do you agree with the author's central point that the executive branch has amassed new powers that are insulated from "meaningful judicial and Congressional oversight"? Why or why not?

Notes

1. Nancy Chang is the Senior Litigation Attorney at the Center for Constitutional Rights, a progressive non-profit legal and educational organization in New York City. This article is an excerpt from her book, *Silencing Political Dissent: How Post-September 11 Antiterrorism Measures Threaten Our Civil Liberties* (Seven Stories Press 2002).
2. Uniting and Strengthening America by Providing Appropriate Tools Required to Intercept and Obstruct Terrorism Act of 2001, Pub. L. No. 107-56.
3. Adam Clymer, "Antiterrorism Bill Passes; U.S. Gets Expanded Powers," *The New York Times*, Oct. 26, 2001, at A1; Robin Toner and Neil A. Lewis, "House Passes Terrorism Bill Much Like Senate's, but With 5-Year Limit," *The New York Times*, Oct. 13, 2001, at B6; Jonathan Krim, "Anti-Terror Push Stirs Fears for Liberties; Rights Groups Unite To Seek Safeguards," *The Washington Post*, Sept. 18, 2001, at A17; Mary Leonard, "Civil Liberties," *The Boston Globe*, Sept. 21, 2001, at A13.
4. Adam Clymer, "Bush Quickly Signs Measure Aiding Antiterrorism Effort," *The New York Times*, Oct. 27, 2001, at B5.
5. Amy Goldstein, et al., "A Deliberate Strategy of Disruption," *Washington Post*, Nov. 4, 2001, at A1.
6. See 66 Federal Register 48334-35 (Sept. 20, 2001). Congress denied the Attorney General's request for the codification of this interim regulation in the USA PATRIOT Act and limited to seven days the time aliens suspected of terrorist activity can be detained without charge. Although the interim regulation would appear to be in tension with the Act, it has not yet been rescinded.

   This interim regulation appears to have been drafted with the holding of *County of Riverside v. McLaughlin*, 500 U.S. 44 (1991), in mind. In *County of Riverside*, the Supreme Court considered the Fourth Amendment rights of individuals who had been arrested without a warrant and placed in detention. The Court ruled that after such an arrestee has been held in detention for 48 hours, the burden shifts to the government to show a bona fide emergency or an extraordinary circumstance for failing to provide the arrestee with a judicial probable cause determination. In marked contrast to the arrestees in *County of Riverside*, all of whom were arrested based on a probable cause finding by the arresting officer, the interim regulation has been drafted to support the detention of any non-citizen in this country, even when a basis for suspecting him of a criminal or immigration violation is entirely lacking.
7. Dan Eggen, "Tough Anti-Terror Campaign Pledged," *Washington Post*, Oct. 26, 2001, at A1.
8. This undated letter was sent to Senators Bob Graham, Orrin Hatch, Patrick Leahy, and Richard Shelby. A copy of this letter is on file with the author.
9. Bryant Letter at p. 9 (emphasis added).
10. USA PATRIOT Act § 802, amending 18 U.S.C. §2331.
11. See *R.A.V. v. City of St. Paul*, 505 U.S. 377 (1992).
12. USA PATRIOT Act § 411(a), amending 8 U.S.C. §1182(a)(3)(B)(i)(IV)(bb).
13. USA PATRIOT Act § 411(a), amending 8 U.S.C. §1182(a)(3)(B)(i)(VI).
14. Out of concern for the dangers that the USA PATRIOT Act's enhanced surveillance procedures pose to our privacy, and over the strong objections of the Administration, Congress has scheduled some—though not all—of these procedures to sunset, or expire, on December 31, 2005. See USA PATRIOT Act § 224(a). However, Congress

has exempted from the operation of any sunset clause: (1) foreign intelligence investigations that began before the sunset date, and (2) offenses that began or occurred before the sunset date. See USA PATRIOT Act § 224(b).

15. 121 S. Ct. 2038, 2046 (2001).
16. *Ibid.*
17. USA PATRIOT Act § 213, amending 18 U.S.C. §3103a. The definition of the term "adverse result" in Section 213 is borrowed from a statute establishing the standards under which the government may provide delayed notice when it searches stored email and other wire and electronic communications—searches that are not nearly as intrusive as physical searches of one's home or office. The term is defined in 18 U.S.C. §2705(a)(2) as: "(A) endangering the life or physical safety of an individual; (B) flight from prosecution; (C) destruction of or tampering with evidence; (D) intimidation of potential witnesses; or (E) otherwise seriously jeopardizing an investigation or unduly delaying a trial."
18. *Wilson v. Arkansas*, 514 U.S. 927, 929 (1995).
19. 899 F.2d 1324, 1337 (2d Cir. 1990).
20. 800 F.2d 1451, 1456 (9th Cir. 1986).
21. *See* http://www.cdt.org/security/011030doj.
22. USA PATRIOT Act § 215, amending 50 U.S.C. §§ 1862 and 1863.
23. 50 U.S.C. §1801 *et seq.*
24. USA PATRIOT Act § 215, amending 50 U.S.C. 1862(a)(1).
25. USA PATRIOT Act § 215, amending 50 U.S.C. §1862(c)(1).
26. *See* 18 U.S.C. §1862(b)(2)(B), prior to its amendment by USA PATRIOT Act § 215.
27. FISA defines the term "United States persons" to include United States citizens and lawful permanent residents. *See* 50 U.S.C. §1801(i).
28. USA PATRIOT Act § 215, amending 50 U.S.C. §1862(a)(1).
29. *See* U.S.C. §1862(a), prior to its amendment by USA PATRIOT Act § 215.
30. USA PATRIOT Act § 215, amending 50 U.S.C. §1862.
31. USA PATRIOT Act § 215, amending 50 U.S.C. §1863.
32. Pen registers record telephone numbers of outgoing calls. *See* 18 U.S.C. §3127(3). Trap and trace devices record telephone numbers from which incoming calls originate. *See* 18 U.S.C. §3127(4).
33. USA PATRIOT Act § 216(c)(3) amending 18 U.S.C. §3127(4) (emphasis added).
34. USA PATRIOT Act § 216(b) amending 18 U.S.C. §3123(a).
35. In the case of orders for pen registers and trap and trace devices, the Electronic Communications Privacy Act of 1986 demands only "a certification by the applicant that the information likely to be obtained is relevant to an ongoing criminal investigation." 18 U.S.C. §§ 3122(b)(2). *See also Smith v. Maryland*, 442 U.S. 735 (1979). However, providing telephone dialing information does not reveal the contents of telephone communications.
36. USA PATRIOT Act §216 (b) amending 18 U.S.C. §3123(a)(3)(A).
37. *Internet and Data Interception Capabilities Developed by the FBI*, Statement of Dr. Donald M. Kerr, Assistant Director, Laboratory Division, July 24, 2000.
38. USA PATRIOT Act § 216(b) amending 18 U.S.C. §3123(b)(3).
39. 50 U.S.C. §§ 1804(a)(7)(B) and 1823(a)(7)(B) (emphasis added).
40. USA PATRIOT Act § 218, amending 50 U.S.C. §§ 1804(a)(7)(B) and 1823(a)(7)(B) (emphasis added).

41. 407 U.S. 297 (1972).
42. 407 U.S. at 313.
43. 407 U.S. at 320.
44. *Ibid.*
45. 407 U.S. at 317.
46. 407 U.S. at 309 (emphasis added).
47. *United States v. Truong Dinh Hung*, 629 F.2d 908, 915 (4th Cir. 1980) (emphasis added).
48. *United States v. Johnson*, 952 F.2d 565, 572 (9th Cir. 1992).
49. *See supra* Note 8 and the accompanying text.
50. The exclusionary rule is a judicially created rule that bars prosecutors from using incriminating evidence obtained in violation of the Fourth Amendment to prove guilt. See, e.g., *Mapp v. Ohio*, 367 U.S. 643, 655 (1961).
51. USA PATRIOT Act § 203(a), (b), and (d). The information that may be shared must involve either "foreign intelligence or counterintelligence," as that term is defined in the National Security Act of 1947, at 50 U.S.C. §401a, or "foreign intelligence information," as that term is defined in Section 203(a)(1), (b)(2)(C), and (d)(2).
52. USA PATRIOT Act § 203(a), amending Rule 6(e)(3)(C) of the Federal Rules of Criminal Procedure.
53. USA PATRIOT Act § 203(b), amending 18 U.S.C. §2517(6).
54. USA PATRIOT Act §§ 203(d) and 905(a).
55. Select Committee to Study Governmental Operations with Respect to Intelligence Activities, *Intelligence Activities and the Rights of Americans, Final Report of the Senate Select Committee to Study Governmental Operations with Respect to Intelligence Activities,* 94th Cong., 2nd Sess. (1976).
56. Under the Immigration and Nationality Act (INA), non-citizens who have or are engaged in "terrorist activities" or activities that threaten the national security are subject to removal from the United States. *See* 8 U.S.C. §1227(a)(4)(A) and (B).
57. Since 1983, the United States government has defined the term "terrorism," "for statistical and analytical purposes," as the "premeditated, politically motivated violence perpetrated against noncombatant targets by subnational groups or clandestine agents, usually intended to influence an audience." *See Patterns of Global Terrorism 2000,* United States Department of State, Introduction (April 2001).
58. USA PATRIOT Act § 411(a), amending 8 U.S.C. §1182(a)(3)(B)(iii)(V)(b).
59. USA PATRIOT Act § 411(a), amending 8 U.S.C. §1182(a)(3)(B)(iv)(IV)(bb) and (cc), (V)(bb) and (cc), and (VI)(cc) and (dd).
60. The Supreme Court has described guilt by association as "alien to the traditions of a free society and the First Amendment itself." *NAACP v. Claiborne Hardware Co.,* 458 U.S. 886, 932 (1982). *See also Healy v. James,* 408 U.S. 169, 186 (1972).
61. USA PATRIOT Act § 411(a) amended 8 U.S.C. §1182(a)(3)(B)(vi)(I) to include as a "terrorist organization" any foreign organization so designated by the Secretary of State under 8 U.S.C. §1189, a provision that was introduced in the Antiterrorism and Effective Death Penalty Act of 1996. As of October 5, 2001, 26 organizations had been designated as foreign terrorist organizations under 8 U.S.C. §1189. *See* 66 Federal Register 51088-90 (Oct. 5, 2001). In order to qualify as a designated "foreign terrorist organization" under 8 U.S.C. §1182(a)(3)(B)(vi)(I), the Secretary of State must find that "(A) the organization is a foreign organization; (B) the organization engages in

terrorist activity; and (C) the terrorist activity of the organization threatens the security of United States nationals or the national security of the United States." *See* 8 U.S.C. §1189(a)(1)(A)-(C).

In addition, USA PATRIOT Act § 411(a) amended 8 U.S.C. §1182(a)(3)(B)(vi)(II) to include as a "terrorist organization" any domestic or foreign organization so designated by the Secretary of State in consultation with or upon the request of the Attorney General under Section 411. On December 5, 2001, the Secretary of State, in consultation with the Attorney General, designated 39 groups as Terrorist Exclusion List organizations under this provision. *See* 66 Federal Register 63619-63620 (Dec. 7, 2001). In order to qualify as a designated "terrorist organization" under 8 U.S.C. §1182(a)(3)(B)(vi)(II), a "finding" must be made that the organization engages in one or more of the "terrorist activities" described in 8 U.S.C. §1182(a)(3)(B)(iv)(I)-(III). These activities consist of: (1) "commit[ting] or incit[ing] to commit, under circumstances indicating an intention to cause death or serious bodily injury, a terrorist activity;" (2) "prepar[ing] or plan[ning] a terrorist activity;" and (3) "gather[ing] information on potential targets for terrorist activity." *See* 8 U.S.C. §1182(a)(3)(B)(iv)(I)-(III).

62. USA PATRIOT Act § 411(a), amending 8 U.S.C. §1182(a)(3)(B)(vi)(III). In order to qualify as an undesignated "terrorist organization" under 8 U.S.C. §1182(a)(3)(B)(vi)(III), "a group of two or more individuals, whether organized or not," must engage in one or more of the "terrorist activities" described in 8 U.S.C. §1182(a)(3)(B)(iv)(I)-(III). *See supra* Note 59.
63. USA PATRIOT Act § 411(a), amending 8 U.S.C. §1182(a)(3)(B)(iv)(IV)(cc), (V)(cc), and (VI)(dd).
64. USA PATRIOT Act § 411(c)(3)(A) and (B).
65. USA PATRIOT Act § 412(a), adding 8 U.S.C. §1226A(a).
66. USA PATRIOT Act § 412(a), adding 8 U.S.C. §1226A(a)(3) and (5).
67. *See, e.g., Terry v. Ohio,* 392 U.S. 1, 20–22 (1968).
68. USA PATRIOT Act § 412(a), adding 8 U.S.C. §1226A(a)(2).
69. USA PATRIOT Act § 412(a), adding 8 U.S.C. §1226A(a)(7).
70. USA PATRIOT Act § 412(a), adding 8 U.S.C. §1226A(b)(1) and (2)(A)(iii) and (iv).
71. *See INS v. Lopez-Mendoza,* 468 U.S. 1032 (1984).
72. USA PATRIOT Act § 412(a), adding 8 U.S.C. §1226A(a)(2).
73. USA PATRIOT Act § 412(a), adding 8 U.S.C. §1226A(a)(6).
74. USA PATRIOT Act § 412(a), adding 8 U.S.C. §1226A(b)(1).
75. See *Zadvydas v. Davis,* 121 S.Ct. 2491, 2500 (2001).
76. While the USA PATRIOT Act does not explicitly authorize the use of secret evidence in immigration proceedings, its provisions are certain to encourage its use. Since 1996, the INA has explicitly provided for the use of such evidence in removal proceedings before the Alien Terrorist Removal Court. *See* 8 U.S.C. §1531 *et seq.* In addition, the INS has long taken the position that it is authorized to use secret evidence in bond proceedings. *See, e.g., Al Najjar v. Reno,* 97 F.Supp.2d 1329 (S.D.Fl. 2000); *Kiareldeen v. Reno,*71 F.Supp.2d 402 (D.N.J. 1999).
77. *See Debs. v. United States,* 249 U.S. 211 (1919).
78. *See Korematsu v. United States,* 323 U.S. 214 (1944).
79. Linda Greenhouse, "In New York Visit, O'Connor Foresees Limits on Freedom," *The New York Times*, Sept. 29, 2001, at B5.

The USA PATRIOT Act and Information Sharing between the Intelligence and Law Enforcement Communities

Brian H. Hook, Margaret J. A. Peterlin, and Peter L. Welsh

The nature of the threat to United States national security and, especially, the nature of the threat posed by terrorist operations has changed fundamentally in the past decade. Shortly after the September 11 attacks, Ambassador Paul Bremer, who headed the National Commission on Terrorism, observed that "[t]he threat of terrorism is changing dramatically. It is becoming more deadly and it is striking us here at home."[1] Contemporary terrorism traces its roots to the acts of political violence, such as the murder of eleven Israeli athletes at the Munich Olympics in 1972, committed in Western Europe during the late 1960s and 1970s. However, as Ambassador Bremer argues, today's terrorists have little in common with the pragmatic terrorists of the Cold War era.[2]

Much of the terrorist activity during the 1960s and 70s was inspired by Marxist-Leninist ideology, and the terrorists who acted in furtherance of that ideology did so principally to draw attention to their cause and gain certain worldly political concessions. These groups also were motivated by secular rather than apocalyptic ends. For example, they sought to drive the United States out of Western Europe, to compel Britain to withdrawn from Northern Ireland or to undermine NATO.[3] By gaining attention through terrorist acts, the old school of terrorists believed that they could increase support among the general public in the West for their ideology. Moreover, these groups were quick to claim responsibility for a terrorist attack and would often release a document seeking political concessions consistent with Marxist ideology. By proceeding with the purpose of persuading the public in the West of the rightness of their cause and commending its widespread adoption, these early terrorist groups were necessarily constrained in the level of terror they could inflict. By inflicting human casualties, earlier terrorist groups ran the risk of alienating people from their cause. They, therefore, adopted certain limitations on the destruction they were prepared to inflict.[4] As Ambassador Bremer has noted, "[t]here was a self-constraint built into the terrorists" acts and the number of casualties they were willing to inflict."[5]

The predominate terrorist threat today comes from militant Islam. Of the 19 Foreign Terrorist Organizations published by the State Department, 10 are Islamic organizations.[6] The groups that have launched the terrorist campaign against America are driven by a profound hatred of Western religion and Western civilization. These terrorists are not, moreover, motivated principally by pragmatic political goals. In the words of Ambassador Bremer, "[t]hese men do not seek a seat at the table; they want to overturn the table and kill everybody at it."[7] As such, they are not amenable to calculated or deterrent measures. Islamic terrorists have defined a mode of total war in which their military inferiority to the West is overcome by an indirect confrontation with the West. This strategy was detailed in *The Quranic Concept of War*, published in 1979 by S.K. Malik, a militant Pakistani brigadier.[8] Arguing in favor of terror as a strategy for war, Malik writes, "terror struck into the hearts of the enemies is not only a means, it is the end in itself. Once a condition of terror into the opponent's heart is obtained hardly anything left is to be achieved. It is the point where the means and ends meet and merge. Terror is not a means of imposing decision upon the enemy; it is the decision we wish to impose upon him."[9] Today's terrorists are opposed to Western liberalism, as such, and seek the destabilization or destruction of pro-Western governments.[10]

The threat from escalating terrorist attacks is also an imminent one. As Yossef Bodansky argues in his biography, *Bin Laden*, Islamic extremists are "determined to ensure that [the] malaise that had already destroyed Christendom did not penetrate and similarly corrupt and destroy the modern world. All means, including the use of violence and terrorism, were justified to prevent such corruption."[11] Given the eagerness with which certain Islamic terrorists are seeking weapons of mass destruction, moreover, there evidently is not sufficient time for liberal democratic mores to counteract extremist Islam.[12] The current circumstances, by and large, rule out proceeding by political or diplomatic half-measures.

Combating such a network presents entirely new challenges to Western governments and to the intelligence and law enforcement communities in the West. Because of the need to defend on all fronts against a terrorist attack, homeland security has an unusually great need for highly efficient and sophisticated intelligence and law enforcement operations. Ambassador Bremer explains,

> The terrorists take advantage of two important asymmetries. First, in the fight against terrorism, defenders have to protect all of their points of vulnerability around the world; the terrorist has only to attack the weakest point. This lesson was brought home to the U.S. government when Al-Qaeda attacked the American embassies in Nairobi and Dar es-Salaam in August, 1998, two embassies thought to be in little danger and, thus, ill-protected. Secondly, the costs of launching a terrorist attack are a fraction of the costs required to defend against it. To shoot up an airport, a terrorist needs only an AK-47 assault rifle; defending that same airport costs millions of dollars. The September 11 attacks probably cost less than $2 million and caused over $100 billion in damage and business disruption. Thus, the new terrorism reverses the conventional wisdom that, in military operations, the offense must be three times as strong as the defense. How, then, are we to fight this new and increasingly dangerous threat? The proper objective of a counter-terrorist policy is to prevent attacks before they happen. So, more than in any other field of foreign and national security affairs, success in the fight against terrorism depends on having good intelligence.[13]

Gaining and making effective use of "good intelligence" against this new threat, moreover, requires a change in the operational structure of intelligence and law enforcement agencies as well as more effective modes of cooperation between the agencies.

Many have argued—even before the events of September 11—that the intelligence and law enforcement communities are not institutionally capable of meeting the new terrorist threat. Just one month before the World Trade Center bombing, for example, a CIA veteran who spent nine years in the Directorate of Operations for the Middle East wrote in the *Atlantic Monthly* that "Westerners cannot visit the cinder-block, mud-brick side of the Muslim world—whence bin Laden's foot soldiers mostly come—without announcing who they are. No case officer stationed in Pakistan can penetrate either the Afghan communities in Peshawar or the Northwest Frontier's numerous religious schools, which feed manpower and ideas to bin Laden and the Taliban, and seriously expect to gather useful information about radical Islamic terrorism—let alone recruit foreign agents."[14] Another CIA veteran pointedly identified a related problem: "the CIA probably doesn't have a single truly qualified Arabic-speaking officer of Middle Eastern background who can play a believable Muslim fundamentalist who would volunteer to spend years of his life with shitty food and no women in the mountains of Afghanistan. For Christ's sake, most case officers live in the suburbs of Virginia. We don't do that kind of thing."[15]

Information sharing between the law enforcement and intelligence communities is especially critical in the new fight against terrorism.[16] Considerable emphasis has recently been placed on the fact that the war on terrorism is precisely that, a war.[17] As Ambassador Bremer argues, intelligence is crucial to winning this war on terrorism. But so, too, is law enforcement. Indeed, the on-the-ground fight against terrorism has much in common with a criminal investigation. In fighting this war, the U.S., by and large, is not engaging an enemy that is massed on a battlefield and that may be defeated by conventional forces utilizing standard wartime intelligence capabilities. It is not sufficient to destroy and/or confiscate the enemy's battlefield capabilities and disperse its troops. Rather, rooting out the secretive, diffuse cells of today's terrorists—particularly, those that may remain in the United States—requires tactics that are similar to those employed in certain criminal investigations. The neutralization of the threat posed to those cells may involve the arrest of the individuals involved. The intelligence and law enforcement communities must, therefore, work together with a level of coordination not previously achieved in the history of the two communities.

Brief History of Interagency Information Sharing

The USA PATRIOT Act promotes greater cooperation and information sharing between the intelligence and law enforcement communities. In doing so, the PATRIOT Act does not overturn the *status quo ante* with respect to coordination between intelligence and law enforcement. Although restricted in certain particular respects (such as grand jury secrecy, for example) and often plagued by political infighting and bureaucratic inefficiencies, there is nevertheless a long history in America of cooperation and information sharing between the CIA and the FBI.[18] The PATRIOT Act, moreover, does not change qualitatively the law or policy with regard to cooperation or information sharing between the law enforcement and intelligence communities. The relevant provisions of the PATRIOT Act are consistent with pre-existing law. Indeed, most of the provisions of the PATRIOT Act have generally been in effect by executive order for at least twenty years.[19] What the PATRIOT Act principally seeks to correct is the bureaucratic friction that has too often existed between these two agencies.[20]

Origins of the Separation of Law Enforcement and Intelligence

The law enforcement and intelligence functions of the United States have, for the most part, been allocated between the Federal Bureau of Investigation, on the one hand, and the

Central Intelligence Agency, National Security Agency, and military intelligence organizations, on the other hand. The separation between the law enforcement and intelligence communities was established partly out of a concern for protecting civil liberties but significantly as a result of bureaucratic compromises.

Originally called simply the Bureau of Investigations, the Federal Bureau of Investigation was established in 1908 by Attorney General Charles Joseph Bonaparte. The Bureau of Investigations came into its own during the First World War when it coordinated attempts to infiltrate and suppress radical organizations, such as the International Workers of the World movement.[21] The FBI's formal intelligence-gathering efforts were, moreover, started shortly thereafter in the immediate wake of several terrorist acts committed by certain of these same radical groups in the summer of 1919.[22] In response to those attacks, the Bureau of Investigations started the General Intelligence Division which was formally organized on August 1, 1919 and headed from the outset by the young J. Edgar Hoover.[23] In the ensuing years, the General Intelligence Division developed into extensive and sophisticated counter-intelligence operation.[24] By the end of the Second World War, the FBI was engaged in significant efforts to combat foreign espionage both at home as well as abroad.[25] The FBI's counterintelligence efforts, while conducted mostly by means of law-enforcement tactics, were nevertheless far-reaching in scope.[26] One of the FBI's main counterintelligence functions during the post- Second World War era, for example, was the "surveillance of hostile foreign diplomats and their premises."[27] Given the breadth of the FBI's post-war counter-espionage efforts, moreover, conflicts with the other intelligence agencies—especially, the newly-formed National Intelligence Authority (precursor to the NSA) and Central Intelligence Group (precursor to the CIA),—were inevitable.[28] In 1946, J. Edgar Hoover attempted to persuade President Truman to place the nascent Central Intelligence Group under the direct control of Hoover and the FBI.[29] Truman, however, refused.[30] The President explained to others, at the time, that he did not want to place one man (particularly, J. Edgar Hoover) in charge of law enforcement and domestic and foreign intelligence.[31]

Although concerns about placing the main federal law enforcement and intelligence powers in the hands of one person account, in part, for the modern day division of authority between the FBI and the CIA, those concerns do not suggest that information sharing or coordination between the FBI and the CIA pose any threat to civil liberties. As Angelo Codevilla has argued, "[i]n realty and contrary to conventional wisdom, the CIA has *no* weapons with which to threaten civil liberties. The FBI, not the CIA, has the power of arrest. The FBI, not the CIA, can work with federal and state prosecutors. Nevertheless, the myth that the division of responsibility for [counterintelligence] has something to do with safeguarding civil liberties is an enduring one."[32] Rather than serving a legitimate concern for the protection of civil liberties, Codevilla has suggested that the separation of the intelligence and law enforcement communities was, in some significant part, the result of "a series of bureaucratic compromises" and that the stakes in the ensuing struggles "were simply pieces of bureaucratic turf."[33]

The allocation of the pieces of bureaucratic turf between the law enforcement and intelligence communities has occurred in several stages during the post-war era. There are at least three stages to this process: (1) the establishment of the Central Intelligence Agency and the National Security Agency in 1947; (2) the Church Committee; and (3) the Reagan administration.

The Post-war Era—The National Security Act of 1947

The CIA and NSA were established as separate government agencies with passage of the National Security Act of 1947. The Act, moreover, includes the original mandate granted to the Director of Central Intelligence.[34] Notably, Section 103-3 of the National Security Act, specifying the "Responsibilities of Director of Central Intelligence," provides, in relevant part, that the Director of Central Intelligence shall, "collect intelligence through human sources and by other appropriate means, except that the Agency shall have no police, subpoena, or law enforcement powers or internal security functions."[35] The term "internal security functions" has no clear meaning under the Act and the term has been used liberally by critics of the CIA to attempt to limit the agency's powers.[36] At least one source has stated that "[t]he statutory language regarding the authorities and functions of the new Central Intelligence Agency was left intentionally vague. In part this reflected the bureaucratic sensitivities involved in specifying in the law the DCI's roles and missions in regard to other agencies, and, in part, the desire to avoid wording that other governments might find offensive."[37]

The Turmoil of the 1970s—The Rockefeller Commission and Church Committee

Certain high profile cases involving domestic intelligence gathering, and subsequent political scrutiny of those cases, have further defined the post-war allocation of power between the CIA and FBI. In June of 1975, the Commission on CIA Activities Within the United States, also known as the Rockefeller Commission, released its final Report to the President. Shortly thereafter, the Senate Select Committee to Study Governmental Operations With Respect to Intelligence Activities, known as the Church Committee (after its Chairman, Senator Frank Church) released its report on the CIA.[38] The Rockefeller Commission and Church Committee reports detailed a number of activities which both reports characterized as abuses of the CIA's statutory authority. For example, the Rockefeller Commission found that, between 1952 and 1973, the CIA conducted a mail intercept program which involved the U.S. government opening thousands of letters sent to and from persons living within the United States.[39] The Commission also found that the CIA established a Special Operations Group to conduct surveillance of American dissident groups.[40] The efforts of the Special Operations Group, dubbed Operation CHAOS, resulted in the collection of significant information and materials on domestic dissident groups.[41] Cold War partisans seized on such abuses of intelligence collection techniques to demonize the CIA. These attacks on the CIA, however, had at least as much to do with the role that the CIA played in its foreign intelligence operations, and how those operations fit within the Cold War political *gestalt*, than with domestic intelligence activities, as such.[42]

More importantly, the Rockefeller Commission and the Church Committee did not rule out information sharing between the law enforcement and intelligence communities and, indeed, recommended *greater* coordination between the CIA and the FBI. Although both the Rockefeller Commission and Church Committee relied on a somewhat simplistic or anachronistic conceptual framework which contemplates that the CIA's activities could be strictly limited to what the Commission frequently refers to as "foreign intelligence matters,"[43] both bodies also acknowledged the need for some significant measure of coordination between the law enforcement and intelligence communities. Indeed, the Church

Committee observed that there has been a long history of coordination between the CIA and FBI and recommended still closer coordination between the agencies, especially in their counterintelligence efforts:[44]

> *Coordination between CIA and FBI counterintelligence units is especially critical.* The history of CIA-FBI liaison has been turbulent, though a strong undercurrent of cooperation has usually existed at the staff level since 1952 when the Bureau began sending a liaison person to the CIA on a regular basis. The sources of friction between the CIA and FBI in the early days revolved around such matters as the frequent unwillingness of the Bureau to collect positive intelligence for the CIA within the United States or to help recruit foreign officials in this country. In 1970 an essentially minor incident resulted in an order from FBI Director Hoover to discontinue FBI liaison with the Central Intelligence Agency. Although informal communications between CIA and FBI staff personnel continued, it was not until the post-Hoover era that formal liaison relations were reestablished. *Today, there is still a need for closer coordination of FBI and CIA counterintelligence efforts.*[45]

The Rockefeller Commission's Report, moreover, observed that the National Security Act, "was intended to promote coordination, not compartmentation [sic] of intelligence between government departments."[46] In addition, the Commission's report states that "legitimate domestic CIA activities occasionally cross the path of FBI investigations. Daily liaison is therefore necessary between the two agencies."[47] The Commission also recommends that, "[t]he Director of Central Intelligence and the Director of the FBI should prepare and submit for approval by the National Security Council a detailed agreement setting forth the jurisdiction of each agency and providing for effective liaison with respect to all matters of mutual concern."[48]

The Reagan Era

Much of the information sharing policy embodied in the USA PATRIOT Act has been in effect for at least twenty years pursuant to an Executive Order issued by President Reagan. In December of 1981, President Reagan issued Executive Order 12333 on "United States Intelligence Activities." Executive Order 12333 was intended to clarify the relationship among the various intelligence agencies of the United States Government. The Order includes as one of its goals "to the greatest extent possible consistent with applicable United States law and this Order, and with full consideration of the rights of United States persons, all agencies and departments should seek to ensure full and free exchange of information in order to derive maximum benefit from the United States intelligence effort."[49] The Order contains many of the same policies embodied in the PATRIOT Act. For example, the Order provides that the Director of Central Intelligence shall, "coordinate foreign intelligence and counterintelligence relationships between agencies of the Intelligence Community and the intelligence or internal security services of foreign governments, . . . "[50] The Order further provides that the collection by the CIA of "foreign intelligence or counterintelligence within the United States shall be coordinated with the FBI . . ." and that the CIA shall, "without assuming or performing any internal security functions, conduct counterintelligence activities within the United States in coordination with the FBI.[51] The Order defines both "counterintelligence" and "foreign intelligence" to include gathering information on "international terrorist activities."[52] The Order also provides that the FBI shall, "[c]onduct counterintelligence activities outside of the United States in coordination with the CIA" and that the FBI shall, "[c]onduct within the United States, when requested by officials of the Intelligence Community designated by the President, activities undertaken to collect foreign intelligence or support foreign intelligence collection requirements of other agencies within the Intelligence Community . . ."[53]

Information Sharing and the USA PATRIOT Act

The following section provides a brief overview of the provisions of the PATRIOT Act that relate to information-sharing between the intelligence and law enforcement communities.

Section 203—Section 203 of the PATRIOT Act amends Rule 6 of the Federal Rules of Criminal Procedure, governing grand jury secrecy, to permit disclosure of certain information presented before a grand jury. Prior to the PATRIOT Act, law enforcement officials were generally restricted by Rule 6 of the Rules of Criminal Procedure from sharing information provided to a grand jury with members of the intelligence community. While it is important to prevent evidence presented to a grand jury from leaking to the general public, there is little reason to prevent intelligence officials from gaining access to such information on a confidential basis.[54] Section 203 of the PATRIOT Act now permits disclosure of "matters involving foreign intelligence or counterintelligence" occurring before a grand jury to "any Federal law enforcement, intelligence, protective, immigration, national defense or national security official in order to assist the official receiving that information in the performance of his official duties." The information disclosed may only be used, moreover, "as necessary in the conduct of that person's official duties subject to any limitations on the unauthorized disclosure of such information." Section 203 also permits law enforcement to disclose the contents of any wire, oral or electronic communication, or evidence derived therefrom, to any other Federal law enforcement, intelligence, protective, immigration, national defense or national security official.

Section 901—Amends section 103 the National Security Act of 1947, which sets forth the DCI's role as head of intelligence, to provide that the Director of Central Intelligence shall provide assistance to the Attorney General to ensure that information derived from electronic surveillance or physical searches under the Foreign Intelligence Surveillance Act [FISA] is "disseminated so it may be used efficiently and effectively for foreign intelligence purposes."[55] Section 901 clarifies, however, that the DCI shall have "no authority to direct, manage, or undertake electronic surveillance or physical search operations pursuant to [FISA] unless otherwise authorized by statute or executive order."

Section 902—Clarifies that the definition of the term "foreign intelligence," under the National Security Act shall also include "international terrorist activities." The term "counterintelligence" under the Act already included "international terrorist activities" within its definition.[56]

Section 903—States the sense of Congress that "officers and employees of the intelligence community of the Federal Government, acting within the course of their official duties, should be encouraged, and should make every effort, to establish and maintain intelligence relationships with any person, entity or group for the purpose of engaging in lawful intelligence activities. . . ."

Section 905—Amends the National Security Act of 1947 to add a new section, titled "Disclosure of Foreign Intelligence Acquired in Criminal Investigations; Notice of Criminal Investigations of Foreign Intelligence Sources." This new section provides, *inter alia*, that "the Attorney General, or the head of any other department or agency of the Federal Government with law enforcement responsibilities shall expeditiously disclose to the Director of Central Intelligence . . . foreign intelligence acquired by an element of the Department of Justice or an element of such department or agency, as the case may be in the course of a criminal investigation."

Section 906—This section requires that, not later than February 1, 2002, the Attorney General, the DCI and the Secretary of the Treasury jointly submit to Congress a report on the feasibility and desirability of reconfiguring the Foreign Terrorist Asset Tracking Center and the Office of Foreign Assets Control of the Department of Treasury to provide for the "effective and efficient analysis and dissemination of foreign intelligence relating to the financial capabilities and resources of international terrorist organizations."

Section 907—Requires that no later than February 1, 2002, the Director of Central Intelligence, in consultation with the Director of the FBI, submit to the appropriate committees of Congress a report on the establishment and maintenance within the intelligence community of an element for purposes of producing timely and accurate translations of foreign intelligence to be shared with all other elements of the intelligence community.

Section 908—Requires the Attorney General, in consultation with the DCI, to develop a program to provide training to certain officials in the Federal, State and Local governments who are not ordinarily engaged in the collection, dissemination, and use of foreign intelligence. Such training would seek to assist these officials in "identifying foreign intelligence information in the course of their duties, and utilizing foreign intelligence information in the course of their duties, to the extent that the utilization of such information is appropriate for such duties."

These sections represent the main provisions of the Act that allow for increased information sharing. They do not define the limits of the Act's impact on the relationship between the law enforcement and intelligence communities, however. In addition to providing for greater information sharing, for example, the PATRIOT Act also expands many of the FBI's surveillance powers.[57] Any analysis of information sharing must consider the scope and quantity of information shared. Limited sharing presents a different, and perhaps less challenging, question than more-expansive sharing.

Intelligence Collection as Distinguished from Information Sharing

Central to the issue of information sharing between the intelligence and law enforcement communities is how, rather than whether, these communities should share information. Furthermore, of paramount importance is how the information is collected in the first instance, and this shifts the inquiry to one of tracking the use of information and the mechanics and methods of surveillance.[58] As section II demonstrates, the history of intelligence collection has included episodes of overreaching.[59] Even were that not the case, a call for oversight is not inherently an accusation. Rather, it is the civic obligation of both Congress and the citizenry. In our view, the notion that a rule of law is preferred over rule by man properly includes the corollary that scrutinizing that law is not the same as scrutinizing the man.

A wide variety of oversight methods exist to vet intelligence collection, and the Act employs these methods to different degrees and in different contexts. Over time the question will become whether the combination of power granted to the intelligence and law enforcement communities and the oversight applied have resulted in the proper balance between liberty and security in that same area. This section considers, among the possibilities, three oversight tools as well as a discussion of how those oversight tools were or were not applied to a particular provision of the act.[60] This section also considers how the oversight tools may affect the manner and extent of cooperation between the intelligence and law enforcement communities. The three oversight tools discussed immediately below are judicial involvement, congressional oversight, and sunset provisions.

Since these tools are broadly equivalent, two general considerations are raised. First, each oversight option includes a different accompanying cost. For law enforcement this normally means that the employed option slows the process in some more or less acceptable way.[61] If the process is not slowed, then already strained resources are reprogrammed in order to meet the oversight requirement. These potential drawbacks can be conveniently reduced to two phrases: mission compromise and manpower drain. A third potential drawback is the overdissemination of sensitive information and the risk of compromising the usefulness of that information.[62] In order to "smoke them out of their holes," we must first discover the location of the hole and then strike when we know they are there.[63] That cannot be done, however, if the terrorists know what we know.[64] These three shape the adaptability of a particular oversight tool to reducing the risk associated with a specific collection technique.

Second, some of the oversight options present standard controversies. For instance, it tends to be the uncommon prosecutor that believes the exclusionary rule does anything more useful than complicate an already unfortunate situation. Another common concern is that congressional oversight rarely occurs.[65] This chapter does not address such controversies. Instead, the focus is on the appropriateness of the pairing of the power granted and the oversight tool selected.

Judicial Involvement

The Act's provisions task the judiciary repeatedly. Few of these tasks are new, however. Most of them are mere extensions of a common task to a new item. Some are reductions of the judiciary's role. One example is the involvement of the judiciary in section 209. This section removed stored communications (or yet unopened voicemails) from the definition of "wire communication," as found in 18 U.S.C. section 2510(1). Previously, law enforcement needed a wiretap order to access stored, unopened email. To some, section 209 rationalizes the treatment of stored voice and non-voice communications. To others, rationality demanded that access to such communications require a wiretap order. If wiretap orders unduly slow the pursuit of information that can be too easily deleted by a potential defendant, then one must look to another of the tools to resolve a lingering concern. Of the remaining options, congressional oversight hearings, FOIA requests, and media coverage are the only practical options. Those with concerns should, moreover, focus their efforts in one of these three areas.

Section 216 authorizes courts to grant pen register and trap and trace orders that are valid nationwide. The controversy surrounding (and nearly consuming) this "Carnivore" provision abated only after a requirement that a complete recording of the information extracted, to include the agents involved, and the configuration of the device during its use would be provided to the relevant judge 30 days after termination of the order. Advocates of the report hope it serves as a bulwark against the improper capture of content under an order that allows only for the capture of addressing information, in the same manner that a trap and trace order for telephones allows only for the capture of dialing information. This report, occurring *ex parte*, does not endanger any classified information and therefore it does not threaten to compromise the mission.

Opponents of the reporting requirement may contend that it is a manpower drain, despite the fact that it appears that the FBI generates the report already and is simply required to provide a copy to the judge. Still, the balance may not yet be ideal. Depending on the duration of the initial trap and trace order a report submitted 30 days after termination may not be sufficient. A more cautious approach would link the interval of the order and the reporting interval. For example, if an initial order is for one year, the reporting requirement could be every three months during the order, with the final report due 30 days after termination. When an initial order is for one month, the final report may be sufficient as the only report. Again, it is impossible to predict whether such an adjustment will be necessary, though it is an option that could improve oversight while remaining sensitive to the mission concerns.

One concern with judicial involvement as an oversight tool relates to the need to contain information. In order to engage clandestine organizations, it is often necessary to have meaningful limits on the use and dissemination of information.[66] The Act sought to correct a too-strict approach. A too-loose approach would lead to an equally ineffectual effort. The first of two possible responses is to limit dissemination by limiting judicial involvement in the process. The second is to limit dissemination through the use of tight controls within the judiciary. A first moderate step may be to require the use of sealed documents before adopting outright limitations on the role of the judiciary.

Congressional Oversight

The Act may rejuvenate the art of congressional oversight. Among the options, congressional hearings may compromise the mission the least. This is because most hearings occur *ex post*. Missions either would be accomplished or abandoned by the time testimony began. That hearings occur after-the-fact also tends to negate the over-dissemination concern. When methods of intelligence gathering are under review, classified hearings are certainly available. Those who malign congressional oversight as ineffectual should consider redirecting their energies to sharpening this tool. The unalterable need for greater information sharing means that the U.S. no longer has the luxury of simply separating law enforcement and intelligence agencies. Separation is a security risk.

Lack of oversight is a potential liberty risk, however. One obstacle to even classified oversight hearings is that they are not costless. While they may not generate the costs associated with mission compromise or over-dissemination, they will be a manpower drain. For those with concerns, this inconvenience is likely to be seen as the exchange for increases in surveillance powers. Members might express impatience when agents or appointees claim unavailability for hearings. This security/liberty pairing means that these agencies must do more on both fronts. The complete obligation to the American people means that the agencies will be responsive to congressional requests and inquiries.

Sunset Provisions

The sunset provision applies to many, but not all, of the surveillance provisions of the bill. Interestingly, it does not apply to the controversial section 216, discussed *supra*. The sunset provisions evoked heated negotiations. Having a sunset may mean that law enforcement and intelligence agencies are less likely to realign their bureaucracies as necessary to maximize their information-sharing potential. New operating procedures need to be written, disseminated, and translated into behaviors for the Act to have its intended beneficial result. If agents believe the basis for such efforts will disappear in a short span of time, they may approach the task with an inadequate amount of zeal. Or, more realistically, they may have to rush the process so as to benefit from the provision. Rushed procedures may not be the most secure.

A sunset provision can serve several purposes. First, it has the potential to encourage the good habit of congressional engagement on both sides. Congress has an incentive to discover whether it wants to renew the powers and agencies have an incentive to win renewal. Second, a sunset can be an encouragement for agencies to take additional care in crafting their initial operating procedures. During this period, these careful procedures can become rooted practices. Once rooted, the practices are less likely to change even if the provisions are later made permanent. Ending with the result that additional sunsets are not needed because a sunset was first used. Third, the sunset can be an absolute backstop to any concerns. Legislative inertia works against passage. If the powers prove to be inherently problematic they will most likely expire. Of course, this point loops back to one of the disadvantages of sunsets: inherently helpful powers can also expire.

In comparing these two viewpoints the internal conflict of using a sunset in this circumstance becomes apparent. Several large bureaucracies need to dramatically and quickly alter operational methods while at the same time ensuring that they do so in a careful fashion so as both to accomplish and demonstrate that they remain institutionally sensitive to liberty concerns.

Other Oversight Tools

Beyond the three oversight tools of judicial involvement, congressional oversight, and sunset provisions, there are other options. Lawmakers can apply the exclusionary rule to evidence obtained in a manner that violates the law.[67] This puts the impetus for oversight in the hands of defense attorneys. As mentioned previously, some debate the value of the exclusionary rule. *Mens rea* requirements increase the quality of proof necessary to receive a search warrant or wiretap order. Overreaching is not just less likely, it is less possible, when a judge must be presented with probable cause that a person *knowingly* contributed money to a terrorist organization.

The next three oversight tools rely on action by the citizenry to be effective. The first creates a civil cause of action for willful disclosures of information that extend beyond what the statute allows.[68] Freedom of Information Act (FOIA)[69] requests provide another opportunity for citizens to educate themselves as to how the agencies are operating. Amendments to FOIA that overreach the legitimate need to restrict access to government records should be resisted. To date, it appears that the Department is evaluating FOIA in light of the present security environment. On October 12, 2001, Secretary Ashcroft released a new FOIA memorandum in which he announced a change in the legal standard the department would use to determine whether it will defend an agency's decision on a particular FOIA request.[70] The last tool needs no greater explanation than simply identifying it: press coverage.

In sum, the mere fact that law enforcement and intelligence agencies are sharing information does not raise concerns. Increased cooperation is necessary to restore security. Hand-in-hand, however, comes the realization that we do not have the luxury of structural separation as an alternative to vigorous oversight. Each relevant group—Congress, the agencies (to include the new Office of Homeland Security[71]), and the citizenry—must become more involved in security and more involved in oversight.

Conclusion

The coordination and information sharing contemplated by the USA PATRIOT Act between elements of the intelligence community, including the CIA and the FBI, is consistent with existing law governing the activities of law enforcement and the intelligence community. America's history includes periods of cooperation and information sharing between the CIA and the FBI. In addition, although the method by which government officials conduct surveillance and gather information has significant implications on civil liberties, the simple sharing of information between two elements of the intelligence community, or between the intelligence community and the law enforcement community, does not implicate necessarily civil liberties. Information can be shared in a manner consistent with the protection of civil liberties. It is the nature and techniques of the surveillance that matters. Who performs the surveillance may also matter, but the conditions of the performance are of the most critical importance.[72] Moreover, it is also possible that the participation of multiple government agencies in the same intelligence operation, far from threatening civil liberties, might serve instead to check potential overreaching by individuals within one of the agencies.[73] In the end, the focus of attention should be principally on the techniques by which intelligence is gathered domestically and not on whether other members of the intelligence community are permitted to view the intelligence gathered as a result of those operations.

Critical Thinking Questions

1. Over the past decade, has the USA PATRIOT Act resulted in the kind of intelligence and information sharing among government agencies that was sorely lacking before 9/11? Explain.
2. In both this chapter and the previous one, the authors suggest that Congressional oversight of domestic intelligence efforts rarely occurs. Do you agree? Why or why not?
3. Based on the past decade of experience, are there lessons we should draw that should be incorporated into a major revision of the USA PATRIOT Act?

Notes

1. L. Paul Bremer III, *Testimony Before the Senate Select Committee on Intelligence* (June 8, 2000).
2. *Ibid.*

3. The Baader-Meinhoff group in Germany, *Action Directe* in France, the Red Brigades in Italy, the Irish Republican Army, and the Palestine Liberation Organization were all animated by such practical agendas.
4. It also bears emphasizing that these terrorist groups only threatened Americans when they were outside the country.
5. L. Paul Bremer III, *Speech to the Heritage Society* (July 12, 2000).
6. Abu Sayyaf Group; Armed Islamic Group; Hamas; Harakat ul-Mujahidin; Hizballah; Islamic Group; Islamic Movement of Uzbekistan; Al-Jihad; Palestinian Islamic Jihad; and Al-Qaeda. State Department Publication, Foreign Terrorist Organizations, released 2001.
7. L. Paul Bremer III, "A New Strategy for the New Face of Terrorism," *National Interest*, No. 65-S, p. 24 (Thanksgiving 2001)
8. S.K. Malik, *The Quranic Concept of War* (Quoted in Yossef Bodansky, *Bin Laden*, p. XV (Roosevelt, CA: Prima Publishing 1999)).
9. *Ibid.*
10. *See e.g.* Norman Podhoretz, "Israel Isn't the Issue," *Wall Street Journal*, September 20, 2001.
11. The Ayatollah Kohmeini popularized the view in the Muslim world that America is oriented principally around money-making and that such an orientation, according to Khomeini, makes "prostitution [the] community's way of life." One follower of Khomeini's described America as "a collection of casinos, supermarkets, and whore-houses linked together by endless highways passing through nowhere." *Quoted in* Bodansky, *Bin Laden* at XIII. Accordingly, Islamic fundamentalists have long sought an end to what they consider unjust occupation of Muslim lands by those who they view as corrupt Westerners.
12. *See e.g.* Paul A. Rahe, *Republics: Ancient and Modern*, Vol. 2, pp. 85–104 (Chapel Hill: University of North Carolina Press 1994).
13. Bremer, "A New Strategy for the New Face of Terrorism," *supra* note 7 at 25.
14. Reuel Marc Gerecht, "the Counterterrorist Myth," *The Atlantic Monthly*, July/August 2001.
15. *Ibid.*
16. Bremer, "A New Strategy for the New Face of Terrorism," *supra* note 7 at 25.
17. *See e.g.* "Getting Serious," *Wall Street Journal*, September 13, 2001; Douglas W. Kmiec, "War Crimes Are Different," *Wall Street Journal*, November 15, 2001.
18. *See e.g.* Edward Jay Epstein, *The Assassination Chronicles: Inquest, Counterplot and Legend* (New York: Carrol & Graf 1992); Curt Gentry, *J. Edgar Hoover: The Man and His Secrets*, p. 418 (New York: Plume 1991); *Final Report of the Select Committee to Study* Governmental Operations with Respect to Intelligence Activities, Vol. 1, p. 440 (Washington DC: GPO 1976)(herein the "Report of the Church Committee").
19. *See* "United States Intelligence Activities," Executive Order 12333 (December 3, 1981).
20. *See* Gentry, *supra* note 17, at 410*ff.*; *see also* Stewart Baker, "Dangerous Secrets," *Wall Street Journal*, October 5, 2001 ("[T]he grand jury rules have the effect putting Justice in a position of primacy among the agencies. [Prior to passage of the PATRIOT Act] the Justice Department [could] make exceptions to the no-sharing rule, but only for CIA analysts who agree to work as prosecutors" assistants, and so long as prosecutorial goals take precedence over intelligence ones.")

21. Gentry, *supra* note 17, at 70 *ff.*
22. *Ibid.*
23. *Ibid.*
24. Angelo Codevilla, *Informing Statecraft: Intelligence for a New Century*, pp.134*ff.* (New York: The Free Press 1992).
25. *Ibid.*
26. *Preparing for the 21st Century: An Appraisal of U.S. Intelligence*, Report of the Committee on the Role and Capabilities of U.S. Intelligence, Appendix, p. A-4 (Washington DC: GPO March 1, 1996); *see also* Codevilla, *supra* note 23, at 136.
27. *Ibid.*
28. Gentry, *supra* note 17, at 326-7.
29. *Ibid.*
30. *Ibid.*
31. *Id.*; *cf. Report to the President by the Commission on CIA Activities within the United States*, p. 11 (Washington D.C.: GPO 1975) (herein the "Report of the Rockefeller Commission").
32. Codevilla, *supra* note 23, at 136.
33. *Ibid.*
34. *See* 50 U.S.C. 403 *et seq.*
35. 18 U.S.C. "403-3.
36. *See e.g. Report of the Rockefeller Commission*, *supra* note 30, at 10-11.
37. *Preparing for the 21st Century*, *supra* note 25, at p. A-4.
38. The House Select Intelligence Committee, known as the Pike Committee, conducted a parallel investigation, as well.
39. *Report of the Rockefeller Commission*, *supra* note 30, at 20-21.
40. *Ibid.* at 23-4.
41. *Ibid*; *see also Report of the Church Committee*, *supra* note 17, at 436.
42. *See e.g.* "Unspooking Spooks," *Wall Street Journal*, September 18, 2001; Tom Clancy, "How We Got Here" *Wall Street Journal*, September 18, 2001.
43. Notably, the Report of the Rockefeller Commission recommends that Section 403 of the National Security Act be amended to "[m]ake explicit that the CIA's activities must be related to *foreign* intelligence." *Report of the Rockefeller Commission*, *supra* note 30 at 12. In so recommending, the Commission lost sight of the fact, that the CIA has an important role to play in domestic *counterintelligence*.
44. The focus of counterintelligence is on developing capabilities to thwart clandestine threats to national security. *See* Abraham N. Shulsky and Gary J. Schmitt, *Silent Warfare: Understanding the World of Intelligence*, 2d ed. (Washington DC: Brassey's 1993). Counterterrorism is closely analogous to, and arguably, subsumed within counterintelligence. *See* Executive Order 12333, *supra* note 18 at "3.4(a).
45. *Report of the Church Committee*, *supra* note 17 at 440 (emphasis added).
46. *Report of the Rockefeller Commission*, *supra* note 30 at 22.
47. *Ibid.* at 38
48. *Ibid.* at 39.
49. EO 12333, *supra* note 18 at '1.1.
50. *Ibid.* at '1.5. The "Intelligence Community is defined by the Order to include both the CIA and the intelligence elements of the FBI. *See* EO12333, *supra* note 18, at "3.4(f).

51 . *Ibid.* at '1.8(a) and (d).
52. *Ibid.* at '3.4(a) and (d).
53. *Ibid.* at '1.14.
54. *See e.g.* Stewart Baker, "Dangerous Secrets," *Wall Street Journal*, October 5, 2001.
55. For more detailed discussion of FISA and changes to FISA effected by the PATRIOT Act, *see* Tom Gede, Montgomery N. Kosma and Arun Chandra, "Developing Necessary and Constitutional Tools for Law Enforcement," Federalist Society White Paper on Anti-Terrorism Legislation: Surveillance and Wiretap Laws, pp.6 *ff.* (November 2001), available at www.fedsoc.org.
56. 50 U.S.C. 401a(3); *Cf.* Executive Order 12333, *supra* note 18, at "3.4(a).
57. *See* Gede, Kosma and Chandra, "Developing Necessary and Constitutional Tools for Law Enforcement," *supra* note 62.
58. *See Ibid.*
59. *Report of the Rockefeller Commission, supra* note 30, at 23-4.
60. The last two options, available to the at-large citizenry, were not aspects of particular provisions.
61. This concern was raised throughout the Conference Committee negotiations.
62. This concern was raised throughout the Conference Committee negotiations.
63. President Bush in an interview as reported by CNN. This quote can be viewed at www .cnn.com/2001/us/09/15/bush/terrorism.
64. This point has been emphasized as recently at December 1, 2001 by Israeli Prime Minister Sharon in an interview with Chris Matthews following another act of war by a group of terrorists, this time the victims were inhabitants and visitors to Zion Square in Jerusalem.
65. Donald R. Wolfensberger, Dir., The Congress Project Woodrow Wilson Center, *Congressional Oversight: Rules of the Road Less Traveled*, presented before the Oversight Workshop United States Congress on Monday, June 28, 1999 (characterizing Congressional oversight as "the road less traveled" and explaining the political disincentives that keeps it that way).
66. *Countering the Changing Threat of International Terrorism*, Report of the National Commission on Terrorism (Washington DC: GPO June, 2000).
67. In determining whether to exclude, courts "evaluate the circumstances of [a] case in the light of the policy served by the exclusionary rule . . ." *Brown v. Illinois*, 422 U.S. 590, 604 (1975). "the rule is calculated to prevent, not repair. Its purpose is to deter—to compel respect for the constitutional guaranty in the only effectively available way—by removing the incentive to disregard it . . . [D]espite its broad deterrent purpose, the exclusionary rule has never been interpreted to proscribe the use of illegally seized evidence in all proceedings or against all persons." " *Id.* at 599–600 (citations omitted). The exclusionary rule has its limitations . . . as a tool of judicial control . . . [In] some contexts the rule is ineffective as a deterrent . . . Proper adjudication of cases in which the exclusionary rule is invoked demands a constant awareness of these limitations . . . [A] rigid and unthinking application of the . . . rule . . . may exact a high toll in human injury and frustration of efforts to prevent crime. *Terry v. Ohio*, 392 U.S. 1, 13-15 (1968). Three exceptions to the exclusionary rule have emerged: the independent source exception, the attenuation exception, and the inevitable discovery exception. *People v. LoCicero (After Remand)*, 453 Mich. 496, 508–509 (1996) (citations

omitted). In *Nix v. Williams*, 467 U.S. 431, 442-43 (1984), the United States Supreme Court explained the deterrent purpose of the exclusionary rule, the Court stated: The core rationale consistently advanced by this Court for extending the exclusionary rule to evidence that is the fruit of unlawful police conduct has been that this admittedly drastic and socially costly course is needed to deter police from violations of constitutional and statutory protections. This Court has accepted the argument that the way to ensure such protections is to exclude evidence seized as a result of such violations notwithstanding the high social cost of letting persons obviously guilty go unpunished for their crimes. On this rationale, the prosecution is not to be put in a better position than it would have been in if no illegality had transpired. By contrast, the derivative evidence analysis ensures that the prosecution is not put in a worse position simply because of some earlier police error or misconduct.

68. *See* section 223 of the Act.
69. 5 U.S.C. section 552.
70. FOIA Post, "*New Attorney General FOIA Memorandum Issued,*" available at www.usdoj.gov/oip/foiapost/2001foaipost19.htm. Under the new standard—sound legal basis—the releasing department's decision will be defended if it is based on a sound legal and factual footing. The previous standard was a "foreseeable harm" standard. These standards should be compared to determine the net effect on the amount of information that is released. Whether a more or less open government is preferred is a normative question for each citizen to answer for himself.
71. This office should consider including an oversight role as it establishes its procedures. As the central information clearinghouse, based on a flow chart created by the administration, this office may be in a good position to monitor the monitors. Additionally, the executive branch may consider altering the executive order that modeled the office after the National Security Council; Thomas Ridge, serving in the same capacity as National Security Adviser Condoleezza Rice, is not a Cabinet secretary and is not required to appear before Congress. *See* Preston, Mark "*Ridge Rebuffs Hill Requests,*" Roll Call, November 5, 2001.
72. If the CIA were to conduct domestic operations, or begin to task the FBI, then alarm we consider overly cautious here might be demanded. Just as restrictions on military assistance to domestic authorities has continuing validity (and contains reasonable exceptions) so may restrictions on the domestic operation of the CIA. *See* 18 U.S.C. 1385, commonly called the *Posse Comitatus* Act.
73. The goals of Executive Order 12333, which provides guidelines for coordination among the different elements of the United States Intelligence community, include "fostering analytical competition among appropriate elements of the Intelligence Community" and "ensuring that appropriate mechanisms for competitive analysis are developed so that diverse points of view are considered fully and differences of judgment within the Intelligence Community are brought to the attention of national policymakers." Executive Order 12333, *supra* note 18, at '1.1(a), 1.5(k).

What Price Security?

The USA PATRIOT Act and America's Balance Between Freedom and Security

Roger Dean Golden

It is a melancholy reflection that liberty should be equally exposed to danger whether the government have too much power or too little.
—James Madison in a letter to Thomas Jefferson, October 17, 1788.[1]

On September 11, 2001, terrorists crashed jetliners into the two World Trade Center towers in New York City and the Pentagon in Washington, DC. These attacks were successful in many ways. Of course, there was the immediate devastation of some 3,000 people killed, with thousands more wounded. Billions of dollars in property damage also resulted from the attacks. In the weeks that followed, more effects were evident. Americans truly were terrorized and traumatized, realizing that they were not safe in their own homeland. While the lives of those closest to the tragedies were changed radically, virtually all Americans felt some emotional effect from the attacks. In addition, the American economy, already beginning to falter, was dealt a severe blow. Certainly, if the terrorists' goal was to punish America, their success was significant.

However, the terrorists may have accomplished an even greater long-term victory, with implications for the future of all Americans. As a reaction to the September 11th attacks, Congress rapidly passed the USA PATRIOT Act on October 24, 2001, and President Bush signed it into law two days later.[2] This Act provided broad new powers to various agencies of the federal government, particularly in the area of gathering information which might lead to the arrest of terrorists or prevent future terrorist acts. Among other issues, the USA PATRIOT Act addresses intelligence gathering related to communications, funding, and other activities of possible terrorists.

The weighty question is, to what degree does this new Act infringe upon the freedoms of American citizens? Does this Act allow the federal government to intrude in an unacceptable manner into the private lives of Americans? Does it diminish the civil liberties that Americans hold dear? Does it represent a shift toward increasing security while taking away freedom? If this Act has resulted in a loss of freedom and reduced civil liberties for Americans, then have not the terrorists accomplished an even greater long-term victory as a result of their attacks? Have we conceded a portion of victory to the terrorists by sacrificing freedom to increase security?

The Balance Between Security and Freedom

They that can give up essential liberty to obtain a little temporary safety deserve neither liberty nor safety.

—Benjamin Franklin

Freedom and security may be viewed on a continuum, with the assumption that as one is increased, the other may decrease. A nation that has total freedom may be characterized by anarchy, with minimum security for individuals in the state. Every person is free to do as he pleases, with no restrictions by the state. In such a nation, one person may use his freedom to the detriment of other people, resulting in anarchy. On the opposite end of the spectrum, a state may best be able to ensure maximum security only by severely limiting the freedoms of individuals. The state may seek to protect its citizens by controlling their lives. Such a state may ultimately constitute a dictatorship. This totalitarian state is the type of state pictured in George Orwell's novel *1984*. A model of this continuum for a nation reflecting a healthy balance between security and freedom would be as follows:

However, as freedom is increased, security is decreased and the nation moves toward anarchy. Conversely, as security is increased, freedom is decreased, and the nation moves toward dictatorship. Thus, one might argue that America has historically found a healthy balance between freedom and security. However, due to reactions to the recent crisis of terrorism, the fulcrum in America has moved toward security. Consequently, as security has increased, freedom has decreased, and America may be moving toward an unhealthy balance. The model would be adjusted to reflect this movement as follows:

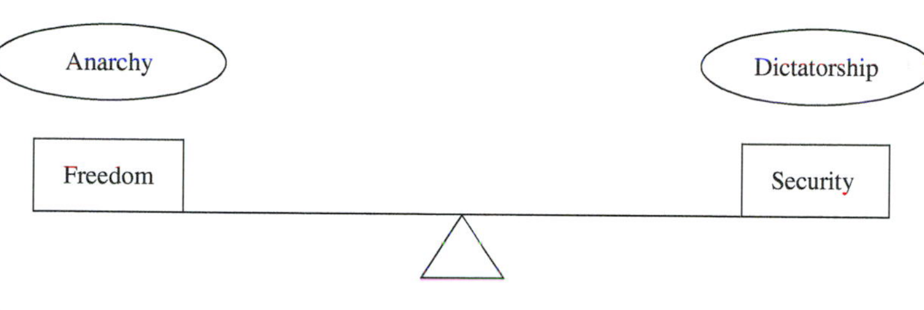

FIGURE 1

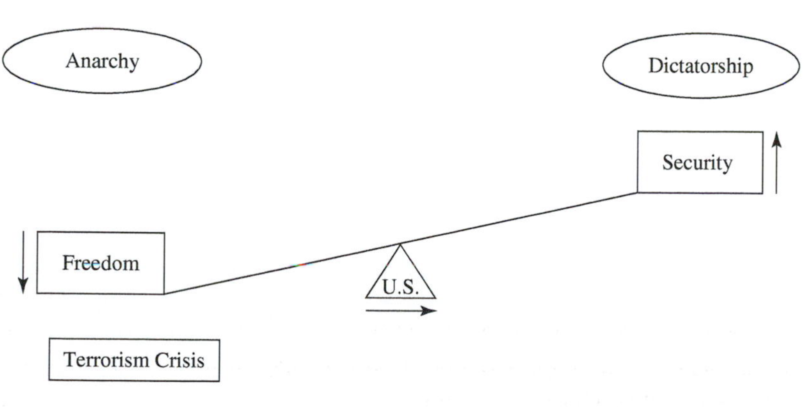

FIGURE 2

Has America experienced an unhealthy shift in the balance between freedom and security as a result of the reactions to the terrorism of September 11, 2001? Champions of civil liberty argue that such a shift has taken place and that America is moving toward dictatorship. An examination of the USA PATRIOT Act from an American historical perspective may prove useful in determining whether this fear is plausible.

The Origins of Freedom

> *Is life so dear, or peace so sweet, as to be purchased at the price of chains and slavery? Forbid it, Almighty God! I know not what course others may take; but as for me, give me liberty or give me death!*
>
> —Patrick Henry, March 23, 1775

In 1776, America's founding fathers wrote in the *Declaration of Independence* that "we hold these truths to be self-evident, that all men are created equal, that they are endowed by their Creator with certain unalienable rights, that among these are life, liberty and the pursuit of happiness . . ." With this statement, the founding fathers expressed the heritage that was to be American—a heritage of liberty bestowed by the Creator himself. Infringement of this liberty was the reason given for the thirteen colonies revolting against the King of England and declaring their independence as the United States of America. The *Declaration of Independence* was enacted on July 4, 1776, and signed by representatives of the thirteen states, who pledged their lives, their fortunes, and their sacred honor to support this document and the liberty it proclaimed.

This principle of preeminent liberty was codified by the founding fathers in the governing document which they wrote to establish the basic law for America, *The United States Constitution*. The *Constitution* was completed on September 17, 1787. The preamble to the *Constitution* states:

> We the People of the United States, in Order to form a more perfect Union, establish Justice, insure domestic Tranquility, provide for the common defence, promote the general Welfare, and *secure the Blessings of Liberty to ourselves and our Posterity*, do ordain and establish this Constitution for the United States of America. (*Emphasis added*).

The objective of the *Constitution* was to establish the overall system of government that would defend the security of the people and provide domestic peace and welfare. However, the greater goal of the *Constitution* was the securing of liberty. The purpose of the law was so that liberty might be protected. Thus, a healthy balance was established between security and liberty in the *Constitution*.

In order to clarify the liberties which the founding fathers believed to be the unalienable rights of all Americans, the U.S. Congress added the first ten amendments to the *Constitution*, ratified on December 15, 1791 (just four years after the signing of the *Constitution*). The *Bill of Rights*, as these ten amendments have commonly been called, provides for specific rights and freedoms to be guaranteed to Americans. The first amendment rights include freedom of religion, freedom of speech, freedom of the press, freedom to assemble peacefully, and freedom to petition the government for redress of grievances. The second amendment provides the right to bear arms. The fourth amendment provides

"The right of the people to be secure in their persons, houses, papers, and effects, against unreasonable searches and seizures." The fifth amendment provides that no person shall be "deprived of life, liberty, or property, without due process of law." Amendment nine recognizes that there are rights which even the *Constitution* may not enumerate. This amendment states: "The enumeration in the Constitution, of certain rights, shall not be construed to deny or disparage others retained by the people." Thus, the forefathers established the importance of civil liberties, with the principle that the *Constitution* and the body of law were there for the protection of the rights of the citizens.

Over the course of America's history, the body of law established by the U.S. Congress and interpreted by the courts has sought to maintain a proper balance between security and liberty. If security is threatened by a crisis, Congress may enact a law which represents a shift toward security at the cost of reduced freedom. This shift toward security may also be effectuated by a Presidential Executive order or other actions of the executive branch. However, if a law is too intrusive on liberty, it is likely that the Supreme Court will invalidate the law, moving the fulcrum back toward freedom, even at the cost of a potential reduction in security. Congress may also pass laws expanding or guaranteeing freedom, moving the balance toward freedom with possible reductions in security. Certainly, the fulcrum has shifted from time to time in one direction or the other. Historians might disagree as to the degree the fulcrum has shifted toward freedom or toward security, but examples of movement in both directions can be cited.

In 1928, writing the majority decision in *Olmstead v. U.S.*, Justice Louis Brandeis introduced the "right to privacy," which had not been specifically listed in the *Constitution*. Brandeis wrote, "To protect that right, every unjustifiable intrusion by the government upon the privacy of the individual, whatever the means employed, must be deemed a violation of the Fourth Amendment." Brandeis considered the right to privacy as "the right to be left alone—the most comprehensive of rights, and the right most valued by civilized men."[3] With this Supreme Court decision, the fulcrum moved toward increased freedom. Yet, the decision made it more difficult for the federal government to gather information that might ensure security. The right to privacy has subsequently been regarded to be as fundamental as the other civil liberties specifically enumerated in the *Bill of Rights*.

There are also examples of the fulcrum moving toward security at the cost of freedom. One of the most glaring examples was the treatment of Japanese-American citizens during World War II. After the Japanese attacked Pearl Harbor on December 7, 1941, the U. S. experienced great fear, particularly in the west, where citizens thought Japan would attack next. On February 14, 1942, President Roosevelt issued Executive Order 9066, which ordered Japanese residents to be taken from their homes and placed in camps supervised by the War Relocation Authority. Over 120,000 Japanese were placed in austere conditions in these camps, even though two-thirds of these Japanese people were American citizens. There was no evidence of a threat, or even disloyalty, by any of these Japanese people. Yet the Executive Order was not canceled until 1944, and the camps were not completely closed until March 1946.[4] The U.S. Supreme Court upheld these incarcerations. The fulcrum had shifted toward supposed security for Americans in general, but had resulted in a total loss of freedom for thousands of Japanese-Americans.

In January 2001, Tampa, Florida, used face-recognition cameras to scan the crowds at the Super Bowl. Faces were to be matched by computer with faces of known criminals, hopefully leading to arrest of those criminals. After the Super Bowl, the cameras were moved to the Ybor City region of Tampa, where police continued to try to identify criminals.[5] Civil libertarians protested this technique as an invasion of privacy, but the cameras were only removed after they proved ineffective in leading to the apprehension of criminals. Consideration is being given to use of similar face-recognition technology in airports and seaports to try to identify terrorists attempting entry into the U.S. Opponents argue that this technology deprives Americans of the right to privacy, moving the fulcrum toward security at the cost of freedom.

American history includes many other examples of movement in one direction or the other. U.S. Representative Jerrold Nadler said that the U.S. has often limited civil rights during war time, including the 1798 Alien Sedition Act, the 1917 Espionage Act and Palmer raids, COINTEL during the Vietnam War, and McCarthyism during the Cold War. He also noted that America has had to apologize for each of these cases.[6] Over time, America has continued to seek a healthy balance between freedom and security. Crisis has usually been the impetus for any moves toward security. Such is the case with the USA PATRIOT Act and other federal government actions following the September 11, 2001, terrorist attacks.

The USA PATRIOT Act

We're likely to experience more restrictions on personal freedom than has ever been the case in this country.

—Supreme Court Justice Sandra Day O'Connor, after a visit to Ground Zero, the site of the terrorist attacks on the World Trade Center in New York.[7]

The USA PATRIOT Act is actually 167 pages of documents, which primarily modify existing laws on a variety of subjects. The title is an acronym for "*Uniting and Strengthening America by Providing Appropriate Tools Required to Intercept and Obstruct Terrorism.*" The Act's primary focus is to grant the federal government increased powers for surveillance and intelligence gathering on individuals residing in the United States. These individuals may include both citizens and noncitizens. Other provisions of the Act cover a variety of issues related to the war on terrorism.

With the anthrax scare in full swing and many lawmakers shut out of their offices, the Act passed Congress with virtually no debate. According to Senator Russell Feingold, the only senator voting against the bill, most senators were very unaware of the details of the Act.[8] U.S. Representative Jerrold Nadler said that the version of the bill approved by the House Judiciary Committee had been thrown out, with House Republican leaders and Attorney General John Ashcroft crafting a new version. Although only two copies of the lengthy new bill were printed at 10:00 a.m., the bill passed the House three hours later by an overwhelming majority vote of 356 to 66.[9] In fact, the bill could only be understood by comparing it to the several other laws it amended. Critics of the bill contend that the federal executive department used this opportunity to railroad through many intrusive practices Congress had refused to allow in the past. Senator Feingold said, "There is no doubt that if we lived in a police state it would be easier to catch terrorists. That would not be America."[10]

The Act addresses a number of different areas in order to provide tools for the government to combat terrorism within the United States. Title I discusses antiterrorism funding and philosophical issues. Title I, Sec 102 (b) states: "It is the sense of Congress that the civil rights and civil liberties of all Americans, including Arab Americans, Muslim

Americans, and Americans from South Asia, must be protected, and that every effort must be taken to preserve their safety."[11] Thus, Congress stated their intention to maintain the balance between security and freedom. However, critics of the Act argue that, in spite of those stated intentions, the Act severely infringes on civil liberties of all Americans.

Title II of the Act provides for enhanced surveillance procedures. Authority to intercept wire, oral, and electronic communications is expanded if these communications may be related to terrorism or computer fraud and abuse. This title includes 25 separate sections, providing significant new authority for the government to monitor all forms of communication, including postal mail, e-mail, voice mail, telephone, and computer communications. Search warrants will be easier to obtain, more powerful, broader in scope, and will provide for warrants to be valid for longer periods of time. Typical language of this title indicates that the Federal Bureau of Investigation " . . . may make an application for an order requiring the production of any tangible things (including books, records, papers, documents, and other items) for an investigation to protect against international terrorism or clandestine intelligence activities."[12]

One statute revised by the USA PATRIOT Act is the Foreign Intelligence Surveillance Act (FISA) of 1978. Congress passed FISA after learning that the Federal Bureau of Investigation (FBI) had performed extensive surveillance on American citizens during the previous two decades. FISA severely restricted domestic surveillance, establishing guidelines for when and how wiretaps could be performed on American citizens. FISA was an example of Congress moving the fulcrum toward liberty at the possible cost of security. The USA PATRIOT Act significantly loosens some of the restrictions of FISA, moving the fulcrum back toward security at the potential cost of freedom.

For example, the USA PATRIOT Act allows "roving" wiretaps that can follow a person wherever he goes, including a neighbor's computer, a library computer, his home or office computer, or any phone he may use. Critics argue that the new provision may violate the Fourth Amendment to the *Constitution*, which prohibits unreasonable searches and requires that warrants "particularly describ[e] the place to be searched, and the persons or things to be seized." Under the USA PATRIOT Act, national search warrants may be requested, whereas previously, separate warrants had to be obtained for every jurisdiction. The USA PATRIOT Act also changed the Electronic Communications Privacy Act (18 U.S.C. sec 2703) so that nationwide search warrants can be issued for voice mail and e-mail. The only probable cause that is required is a reasonable suspicion that a person may be acting for a foreign power. Search warrants are powerful, and can be enforced immediately, even against resistance.[13]

Wiretapping authority is also broadened by the USA PATRIOT Act. FISA allowed wiretaps only if a federal judge determined that the target individual had probably committed a serious crime, with those crimes specifically listed. The USA PATRIOT Act added a number of crimes related to terrorism and cyber-crime to the list justifying wiretapping. In addition, an internet service provider may be required to gather information such as web sites visited or e-mail headers.[14] Critics argue that, once such broad access is allowed to an individual's communications, there is no way to ensure that the agency only gathers information relevant to an investigation, or that information will not be used to harm individuals who are not involved in terrorism. Therefore, the right to privacy may have been significantly diminished by the USA PATRIOT Act.

Title III of the USA PATRIOT Act addresses "International Money Laundering Abatement and Anti-Terrorist Financing." The Act contends that money laundering totaling over $600 billion annually permits funding of terrorism and international crime. This portion of the Act is designed to "increase the strength of . . . measures to prevent, detect, and prosecute international money laundering and the financing of terrorism."[15] The Act includes new authority to gather information, seize funds, and levy heavy criminal penalties, including fines and prison time, for money laundering. Areas of concern for civil liberty activists include new requirements for financial institutions such as banks to gather additional information and report more information to government agencies. Securities brokers and dealers are required to report activities that they judge to be "suspicious."[16] Many of the new provisions represent changes to the "Bank Secrecy Act," removing some of the privacy Americans have historically had in their financial transactions and arrangements.

Title IV of the USA PATRIOT Act provides measures to protect the borders of the United States. The State Department and the Immigration and Naturalization Service (INS) are provided more access to the criminal records of persons attempting to enter the United States. The U.S. Attorney General is given two million dollars for an "integrated automated fingerprint identification system for ports of entry and overseas consular posts." The Act includes an extensive definition of terrorism and provides for mandatory detention of any suspected terrorist. The criteria for detention is "reasonable grounds" to believe that the person "is engaged in any . . . activity that endangers the national security of the United States."[17]

Title V aims to remove obstacles to investigating terrorism. Section 504 provides for more coordination and sharing of information between intelligence and law enforcement officials. Section 505 provides broader authority to obtain telephone bills and records and financial records. Sections 507 and 508 give authority to collect educational records. In each case, information previously considered private can be more readily obtained by federal agencies.[18]

Title VI provides financial benefits for victims of terrorism, public safety officers, and their families and does not appear to contain any civil liberty issues. Title VII expands information sharing between federal, state, and local law enforcement agencies. The Act provides $150 million to the Bureau of Justice Assistance to establish and operate "secure information sharing systems to enhance the investigation and prosecution abilities of participating enforcement agencies in addressing multi-jurisdictional terrorist conspiracies and activities." Critics fear a "big brother"-type government gathering all kinds of information on its citizens and using this information for wrong purposes.[19]

Title VIII strengthens criminal laws against terrorism. Statutes of limitation are removed for certain terrorism offenses. Maximum penalties are increased. Domestic terrorism, cyberterrorism, bio-terrorism, terrorism conspiracies, and terrorism as racketeering are addressed. Even harboring of terrorists and providing material support for terrorists are discussed, with new penalties including fines and up to ten years in prison.[20]

Title IX discusses improved intelligence against terrorism, amending the National Security Act of 1947 to make clear the responsibilities and authorities for various federal agencies in dealing with terrorism. The Director of Central Intelligence is given broader authority to gather intelligence that possibly relates to terrorist activities. Requirements for reporting to Congress on intelligence gathering activities are softened.[21]

Title X includes a number of miscellaneous provisions, including efforts to provide some protections for civil liberties. Section 1001 says that the "Inspector General of the Department of Justice shall designate one official who shall review information and receive complaints alleging abuses of civil rights and civil liberties by employees and officials of the Department of Justice."[22] Section 1002 expresses the sense of Congress that "in the quest to identify, locate, and bring to justice the perpetrators and sponsors of the terrorist attacks . . . the civil rights and civil liberties of all Americans, including Sikh-Americans, should be protected."[23]

Reactions to the USA PATRIOT Act

> *I don't think the American public has even begun to grasp the kind of sacrifices we've been called to make in civil liberties in this war on terrorism.*
>
> —Vermont Law School Professor Stephen Dycus[24]

Since the USA PATRIOT Act became law, many voices have been raised in criticism of the Act, alleging that Americans have suffered serious loss of civil liberties. A statement by Nancy Chang, senior litigation attorney at the Center for Constitutional Rights in New York, is representative of the level of concern. Ms. Chang said:

> To an unprecedented degree, the Act sacrifices our political freedoms in the name of national security and upsets the democratic values that define our nation by consolidating vast new powers in the executive branch of government. The Act enhances the executive's ability to conduct surveillance and gather intelligence, places an array of new tools at the disposal of the prosecution, including new crimes, enhanced penalties, and longer statutes of limitations, and grants the Immigration and Naturalization Service (INS) the authority to detain immigrants suspected of terrorism for lengthy, and in some cases indefinite, periods of time. And at the same time that the Act inflates the powers of the executive, it insulates the exercise of these powers from meaningful judicial and Congressional oversight.[25]

Ms. Chang believes that the Act gives the federal government "unchecked surveillance powers" related to e-mail, Internet, and personal and financial records. She sees the Act as violating both First and Fourth Amendment rights, as well as virtually dismantling the right to privacy.[26]

The Electronic Frontier Foundation (EFF) expresses similar concerns, saying, "The civil liberties of ordinary Americans have taken a tremendous blow with this law, especially the right to privacy in our online communications and activities." EFF says that many of the provisions are aimed at nonviolent cybercrimes that do not involve terrorism at all. Specific concerns include increased surveillance, overly broad provisions, and "spying" on Americans by the CIA and the FBI. EFF is also concerned about the lack of accountability to Congress, which may lead to misuse of the new powers.[27]

On November 18, 2002, a three judge federal panel upheld provisions of the USA PATRIOT Act allowing expanded wiretap and other information collecting and sharing by the Justice Department and U.S. Intelligence Agencies. This decision by the panel stopped efforts of the Foreign Intelligence Surveillance Court to restrict surveillances by the FBI and the Justice Department. After the latest decision, Attorney General John Ashcroft quickly increased surveillance on terrorist suspects. Civil liberties advocates assailed the decision as allowing the government to eavesdrop on telephone conversations, read private e-mail, and search private property, even if there is no evidence of wrongdoing by the targeted individual.[28] The American Civil Liberties Union (ACLU) argued that the ruling violates rights to free speech and due process and said that the ruling would give the government free reign for "intrusive surveillance warrants."[29]

The ACLU has joined with the American Bookseller's Foundation for Free Expression, the Electronic Privacy Information Center, and the American Library Association's Freedom to Read Foundation to file suit against the Department of Justice (DOJ). These organizations allege that the DOJ refuses to release information concerning what actions it has taken under provisions of the USA PATRIOT Act. Of particular concern is the seizing of records from bookstores and libraries even when no criminal activity has been demonstrated. DOJ says it cannot release the information due to possible detriment of national security. The plaintiffs want to build a case that information is being gathered unnecessarily and used improperly.[30]

Attorney General Ashcroft has said, "I don't have the power to erode the Constitution. I wouldn't do it if I could." However, Ashcroft also said, "We don't need any leads or preliminary investigations" to send undercover agents into public meetings or public places, including churches or mosques "under the same terms and conditions of any member of the public."[31] The government only needs a "reasonable indication," rather than the previous standard of probable cause.[32] The chairman of the House Judiciary Committee, James Sensenbrenner disagreed, stating, "We can have security without throwing respect for civil liberties into the trash heap. We don't have to go back to the bad old days when the FBI was spying on people like Martin Luther King." Roger Pilon of the Cato Institute went further, stating, "This is now an executive branch that thinks it's a law unto itself."[33]

Some Congressmen are not satisfied with the Executive Branch's actions under the USA PATRIOT Act. Senator Richard Durbin said the bill represented a "leap of faith, born of fear. This administration, this Department of Justice, has abused that faith." Senator Patrick Leahy, chairman of the Senate Judiciary Committee, has threatened subpoenas if the Justice Department does not give the requested information. House Judiciary Committee Chairman James Sensenbrenner has echoed the threat of subpoenas.[34]

Supporters of the USA PATRIOT Act contend that the expanded authorities are needed to protect the security of Americans. They are not opposed to civil liberties but, "Dead people have no civil liberties at all."[35] *The Village Voice* has quoted Attorney General Ashcroft as saying, "To those who scare peace-loving people with phantoms of lost liberty, my message is this: Your tactics only aid terrorists, for they erode our national unity and diminish our resolve. They give ammunition to America's enemies."[36] Associate Deputy Attorney General David Kris told the Senate Judiciary Committee, "What is at stake is nothing less than our ability to protect this country from foreign spies and terrorists."[37]

Supporters of the Act point out that we are at war, and the old standards no longer apply. With the crisis surrounding U.S. security, reasonable suspicion is a more realistic standard than the probable cause standard, which refers to mere criminal activity, not terrorism. Supporters cite the case of one terrorist, Zacarias Moussaoui. The government was actually arguing over whether to search Moussaoui's computer, even though he was not even in the country legally and could certainly not be considered a U.S. person.[38]

Writing in *The American Criminal Law Review*, Jennifer M. Collins notes that the events of September 11 changed reality. Ms. Collins notes that there has been a strong separation between law enforcement and the foreign intelligence community for the fifty years of the CIA's existence. Now, however, Ms. Collins cautiously argues that the ongoing danger of terrorism justifies "lowering the wall of separation between the grand jury and other agencies of the government to improve coordination and the sharing of national security information—with the goal of safeguarding the nation's security and its citizens."[39]

One recurring theme of supporters of increased government authority is that without adequate power, the government cannot protect the very liberty Americans hold dear. Laurence Tribe, of the Harvard Law School, noted that "civil liberties are not only about protecting us from our government. They are also about protecting our lives from terrorism." Supporters also cite the example of President Abraham Lincoln's emergency actions during the Civil War. When Lincoln suspended the writ of *habeas corpus*, he justified the action with the statement, "Must a government, of necessity, be too strong for the liberties of its own people, or too weak to maintain its own existence?"[40] Supporters argue that, without the additional authorities given to government by the USA PATRIOT Act, the government will not have the tools of power to defend the lives—much less the freedom—of Americans.

Conclusion

> *For rulers are not a terror to good works, but to the evil. Wilt thou then not be afraid of the power? Do that which is good, and thou shalt have praise of the same: For he is the minister of God to thee for good. But if thou do that which is evil, be afraid; for he beareth not the sword in vain: for he is the minister of God, a revenger to execute wrath upon him that doeth evil.*
>
> —The Holy Bible, King James Version, Romans 13:3-4

The USA PATRIOT Act certainly represents a shift toward security even at the cost of potential loss of freedom. However, the majority of Americans appear willing to accept this shift. In a February 2002 Greenberg poll, sixty-two percent of those responding agreed, "Americans will have to accept new restrictions on their civil liberties if we are to win the war on terrorism." In late September 2001, a NBC/Wall Street Journal poll found seventy-eight percent of respondents approving surveillance of internet communications. Sixty-three percent of respondents to a Harris poll approved camera surveillance on streets and public places. In 1998, Chief Justice William Rehnquist recognized that a national crisis can shift the balance between freedom and security toward security, "in favor of the government's ability to deal with the conditions that threaten the national well-being."[41]

However, as time passes and the events of September 11, 2001, begin to diminish, the minds of the American people may change. A November 2001 Investor's Business Daily poll found fifty-eight percent of respondents worried about losing "certain civil liberties in light of recently passed antiterrorism laws." By March 2002, a Time/CNN poll found sixty-two percent of respondents concerned that "the U.S. Government might go too far in restricting civil liberties."[42] Americans in general may be willing to accept some loss of freedom so long as the government uses the new powers to consistently target the "evil doers" of terrorism. However, if Americans believe their own personal civil liberties have been unnecessarily or overly limited, active opposition is likely to increase.

Does America still have a healthy balance between freedom and security? At this point, the fulcrum has shifted toward security with the potential loss of a degree of the freedom previously enjoyed by Americans. Whether this shift toward security will have significant permanent effect obviously remains to be seen. If America follows historical patterns, the people will force the fulcrum back toward freedom once the threat to security is perceived as sufficiently reduced. In the meantime, to the extent that any degree of freedom is lost for Americans, the terrorists will have achieved some measure of victory.

Critical Thinking Questions

1. Do face recognition systems or other technologies used by law enforcement in recent years diminish our freedoms and "right to privacy"? Explain.
2. Of the various components of the USA PATRIOT Act, which do you feel is the most controversial, and why?
3. Will the threat to homeland security ever be perceived as sufficiently reduced to a point where the surveillance and intelligence gathering powers of the USA PATRIOT Act may be significantly changed?

Notes

1. "The Question of a Bill of Rights," Letter to Thomas Jefferson, October 17, 1788, from James Madison. On-line. Internet, 2 December 2002. Available from http://www.constitution.org/jm/17881017_bor.htm.
2. Mary Minow, "The USA PATRIOT Act," *Library Journal*, vol. 127, October 1, 2002, 52–55.
3. "Your Right to Privacy." On-line. Internet, 25 November 2002. Available from http://www.rightoprivacy.com/.
4. Roy Webb, archivist, "Japanese-American Internment Camps During World War II." On-line. Internet, 25 November 2002. Available from http://www.lib.utah.edu/spc/photo/9066/9066.htm.
5. "Face Recognition," Electronic Privacy Information Center. On-line. Internet, 25 November 2002. Available from http://www.epic.org/privacy/facerecognition.
6. Jane Adas, "New York Congressman Nadler Calls USA PATRIOT Act Extreme Danger to Civil Rights," *The Washington Report on Middle East Affairs*, vol. 21, August, 2002, 57–58.
7. Nick Gillespie, "What Price Safety?: Freedom for Safety," *Reason*, vol. 34, October, 2002, 24–26.
8. Minow, 52–55.
9. Adas, 57–58.
10. Alisa Solomon, "Things We Lost in the Fire," *The Village Voice,* vol. 47, September 11-September 17, 2002, 32–36.
11. *USA PATRIOT Act*, H.R. 3162, October 24, 2001, 10.
12. Ibid., 25.
13. Minow, 52–55.
14. Ibid., 52–55.
15. *USA PATRIOT Act*, 37.
16. Ibid., 71.
17. Ibid., 103–106.
18. Ibid., 119–126.

19. Ibid., 132.
20. Ibid., 132–149.
21. Ibid., 150–154.
22. Ibid., 154.
23. Ibid., 155.
24. Gina Holland, "Government Surveillance Powers Scrutinized," *The Montgomery Advertiser,* November 20, 2002, 5A.
25. Nancy Chang, "The USA PATRIOT Act: What's So Patriotic About Trampling on the Bill of Rights?" (Selection 3.2.1)
26. Chang, The USA PATRIOT Act
27. "EFF Analysis of the Provisions of the USA PATRIOT Act," Electronic Frontier Foundation. On-line. Internet, 26 November 2002. Available from http://www.eff.org/Privacy/Surveillance/Terrorism_militias/20011031_eff_usa_patriot_analysis.html.
28. Holland, 5A.
29. Curt Anderson, "Ruling Expands Wiretap Powers," *The Montgomery Advertiser*, November 19, 2002, 6A.
30. Steven Zeitchik, "Groups Sue over Patriot Act," *Publishers Weekly,* vol. 249, October 28, 2002, 16.
31. Nat Hentoff, "Citizens Resist War on the Bill of Rights," *Free Inquiry,* vol. 22, Fall 2002, 13–14.
32. Joe Feuerherd, "September 11: A Year Later—Congress Questions Patriot Act Policies," *National Catholic Reporter*, vol. 38, September 6, 2002, 7.
33. Hentoff, "Citizens Resist War on the Bill of Rights," 13–14.
34. Jess Bravin, "Leahy Warns Justice Department on New Powers," *The Wall Street Journal*, September 11, 2002, A4.
35. Minow, 52–55.
36. Nat Hentoff, "The Sons and Daughters of Liberty," *The Village Voice*, vol. 47, July 2, 2002, 34. *(Note that this quote is reported by The Village Voice, which may be a biased source. The context of the alleged quote is not provided in The Village Voice article.)*
37. Bravin, A4.
38. Richard Lowry, "A Better Bureau," *National Review*, vol. 54, July 1, 2002, 28-30.
39. Jennifer M. Collins, "And the Walls Came Tumbling Down: Sharing Grand Jury Information with the Intelligence Community under the USA PATRIOT Act," *The American Criminal Law Review*, vol. 39, Summer, 2002, 1261–1286.
40. Mackubin Thomas Owens, "Liberty & Security: A Prudential Balance," *National Review On-line.* On-line. Internet, 01 December 2002. Available from http://www.nationalreview.com/comment/comment-owens120401.shtml.
41. Jon B. Gould, "Playing With Fire: The Civil Liberties Implications of September 11th," *Public Administration Review*, vol. 62, September, 2002, 74–79.
42. Gould, 74–79.

Unit Four

Alternatives to Explore

This final section of the book offers a diverse set of opinions and assessments about the present and future prospects of homeland security. In the first reading, Gene Dodaro, the Comptroller General of the United States, reviews the status of progress made in implementing homeland security measures since 9/11 and identifies a number of areas where considerable work is necessary, particularly in border security, aviation security, emergency preparedness and response, and confronting the threat of weapons of mass destruction. He also identifies several key foundational challenges facing the Department of Homeland Security (DHS). First, DHS needs to forge effective partnerships and strengthen the sharing and utilization of information. Second, a variety of managerial challenges have contributed to schedule delays, cost increases, and performance problems in a number of programs aimed at delivering important mission capabilities, such as container security technologies. DHS does not yet have enough skilled personnel to carry out activities in various areas, such as acquisition management. DHS has also not yet developed an integrated financial management system, impacting its ability to have ready access to reliable information for informed decision making. Finally, limited strategic and program planning by DHS and limited assessment to inform approaches and investment decisions have contributed to programs not meeting strategic needs in an efficient manner. He concludes that DHS has made significant strides in protecting the nation, but has yet to reach its full potential.

Next, David Rittgers of the Cato Institute provides a provocative essay in which he argues that the Department of Homeland Security should be abolished and its components reorganized into more practical groupings. The agencies tasked with immigration, border security, and customs enforcement belong under the same oversight agency, which could appropriately be called the Border Security Administration. The Transportation Security Administration and Federal Air Marshals Service should be abolished, and the federal government should end support for fusion centers. The remaining DHS organizations should return to their former parent agencies. His underlying rationale for these recommendations is that the creation of the DHS as an umbrella organization that would oversee 22 preexisting federal agencies has led to wasteful spending, management and oversight complications, and far too many opportunities for politicians to disguise pork barrel spending as defense and security-related. Further, intelligence and security has become overly politicized and ideological, with negative impacts on law enforcement investigations and civil liberties. He concludes that DHS has proven to be an unnecessary and costly reorganization of government, thus abolishing it can save billions annually and alleviate the mounting pressure on civil liberties that we have experienced under an ever-expanding homeland security bureaucracy.

Professor Nadav Morag of the Naval Postgraduate School then describes how "homeland security" is a uniquely American concept. In particular, the legal and institutional tools with which the United States is able to deal with threats outside its borders (in the context of what is referred to as "national security") differ markedly from those it is able to employ inside its borders. Meanwhile, countries such as Australia, Canada, Germany, France, the UK, Israel, Japan, Italy, the Netherlands, and others had never really viewed domestic threats as qualitatively different from overseas threats and were able to use tools—such as the military—both externally and internally. However, in contrast to Rittgers' viewpoint, Morag argues that U.S. security objectives could be strengthened if other countries adopt the same logic and view their disparate homeland security efforts as part of the same set of objectives requiring a joint policy, doctrinal, and organizational framework. If and when this does occur, it will make it considerably easier for the United States to improve its ability to safeguard homeland security because it, and its global partners, will be viewing the problem in the same way and integrating their respective resources and strategies accordingly.

And finally, Susan Sim, a vice president of The Soufan Group in Singapore, offers a comparative homeland security perspective based on Singapore's "Home Team" concept. Ms. Sim, a former police officer and consultant to the Singapore government on homeland security issues, describes in detail Singapore's inclusive approach to protecting the homeland, particularly how the Ministry of Home Affairs in Singapore educates its security professionals to achieve smooth interagency cooperation and operations during times of stress. Singapore's success in inculcating a spirit of cooperation among disparate security organizations is rooted in the "Home Team" concept, which educates members of eight different security organizations together at Singapore's Home Team Academy. Learning to work together in an academic environment prepares security professionals to operate together in an interagency environment when it counts: during times of crisis. Ms. Sim's article gives us pause to consider the possibility of a U.S. Homeland Security Academy that might achieve similar results.

Collectively, these readings are intended to promote lively discussions in classes and seminars on the challenges of homeland security. Instructors and students will also find that these readings provoke thoughtful questions for research papers and final exam questions.

Learning Objectives

The chapters in UNIT FOUR will help students develop a diversity of perspectives on U.S. homeland security, including the pros and cons of our current strategic and organizational approach. Students will also develop an ability to articulate various points of debate about alternative models to consider.

Recommended Resources

Belton, Patrick. "Lessons to be Learned from the British Experience in Critical Infrastructure Protection," in James Forest (ed.), *Homeland Security: Protecting America's Targets* (Westport, CT: Praeger, 2006).

Booz, Allen, Hamilton. (2010). *Risk and crisis communications: Best practices for government agencies and non-profit organizations.* Online at: http://www.boozallen.com/media/file/Risk-and-Crisis-Communications-Guide.pdf

Bradley, James M. and Richard L. Lyman, "The Public Safety Model: A Homeland Security Alternative," *The Police Chief* (Vol. 73, No. 3), March 2006. Available at http://www.policechiefmagazine.org/magazine/index.cfm?fuseaction=display_arch&article_id=837&issue_id=32006

Cardew, Paul and Chris Boucek. "Terrorism and Mass Transit: A UK Viewpoint," in James Forest (ed.), *Homeland Security: Protecting America's Targets* (Westport, CT: Praeger, 2006).

Department of Homeland Security (2010), DHS Report to Congress: Quadrennial Homeland Security Review. Online at: http://www.dhs.gov/quadrennial-homeland-security-review-qhsr

Department of Homeland Security, *Implementing 9/11 Commission's Recommendations* (2011). Online at: http://www.dhs.gov/implementing-911-commission-recommendations

Freese, Kevin. "Cross-Border Issues in Protecting Critical Infrastructure from Terrorism," in James Forest (ed.), *Homeland Security: Protecting America's Targets* (Westport, CT: Praeger, 2006).

Government Accountability Office, *Department of Homeland Security: Progress Made and Work Remaining in Implementing Homeland Security Missions 10 Years after 9/11* (September 2011). Online at: http://www.dhs.gov/xlibrary/assets/mgmt/cfo_apr_fy2011_appb.pdf

Homeland Security Act (HSA) of 2002, Public Law 107-296 (November 2002). Online at: http://www.dhs.gov/xlibrary/assets/hr_5005_enr.pdf

Kemp, Roger L. *Homeland Security: Best Practices for Local Government*, ICMA Publications (2010).

Rudolph, Chris. "International Migration and Homeland Security: Coordination and Collaboration in North America," in James Forest (ed.), *Homeland Security: Protecting America's Targets* (Westport, CT: Praeger, 2006).

Section 4.1

Progress Made and Work Remaining in Implementing Homeland Security Missions 10 Years after 9/11

Gene L. Dodaro

What GAO Found

Since it began operations in 2003, DHS has implemented key homeland security operations and achieved important goals and milestones in many areas to create and strengthen a foundation to reach its potential. As it continues to mature, however, more work remains for DHS to address gaps and weaknesses in its current operational and implementation efforts, and to strengthen the efficiency and effectiveness of those efforts to achieve its full potential. DHS's accomplishments include developing strategic and operational plans; deploying workforces; and establishing new, or expanding existing, offices and programs. For example, DHS

- issued plans to guide its efforts, such as the Quadrennial Homeland Security Review, which provides a framework for homeland security, and the *National Response Framework,* which outlines disaster response guiding principles;
- successfully hired, trained, and deployed workforces, such as a federal screening workforce to assume security screening responsibilities at airports nationwide; and
- created new programs and offices to implement its homeland security responsibilities, such as establishing the U.S. Computer Emergency Readiness Team to help coordinate efforts to address cybersecurity threats.

Such accomplishments are noteworthy given that DHS has had to work to transform itself into a fully functioning department while implementing its missions—a difficult undertaking that can take years to achieve. While DHS has made progress, its transformation remains high risk due to its management challenges. Examples of progress made and work remaining include:

> **Border security.** DHS implemented the U.S. Visitor and Immigrant Status Indicator Technology program to verify the identities of foreign visitors entering and exiting the country by processing biometric and biographic information. However, DHS has not yet determined how to implement a biometric exit capability and has taken action to address a small portion of the estimated overstay population in the United States (individuals who legally entered the country but then overstayed their authorized periods of admission). DHS also deployed infrastructure to secure the border between ports of entry, including

Why GAO Did This Study

The terrorist attacks of September 11, 2001, led to profound changes in government agendas, policies and structures to confront homeland security threats facing the nation. Most notably, the Department of Homeland Security (DHS) began operations in 2003 with key missions that included preventing terrorist attacks from occurring in the United States, reducing the country's vulnerability to terrorism, and minimizing the damages from any attacks that may occur. DHS is now the third-largest federal department, with more than 200,000 employees and an annual budget of more than $50 billion. Since 2003, GAO has issued over 1,000 products on DHS's operations in such areas as transportation security and emergency management, among others. As requested, this testimony addresses DHS's progress and challenges in implementing its homeland security missions since it began operations, and issues affecting implementation efforts. This testimony is based on a report GAO issued in September 2011, which assessed DHS's progress in implementing its homeland security functions and work remaining.

What GAO Recommends

While this testimony contains no new recommendations, GAO previously made about 1,500 recommendations to DHS. The department has addressed about half of them, has efforts underway to address others, and has taken additional action to strengthen its operations. In commenting on GAO's report upon which this testimony is based, DHS stated that the report did not address all of DHS's activities. The report was based on prior work, which GAO reflected throughout the report.

more than 600 miles of fencing. However, DHS experienced schedule delays and performance problems with the Secure Border Initiative Network, which led to the cancellation of this information technology program.

Aviation security. DHS developed and implemented Secure Flight, a program for screening airline passengers against terrorist watchlist records. DHS also developed new programs and technologies to screen passengers, checked baggage, and air cargo. However, DHS does not yet have a plan for deploying checked baggage screening technologies to meet recently enhanced explosive detection requirements, a mechanism to verify the accuracy of data to help ensure that air cargo screening is being conducted at reported levels, or approved technology to screen cargo once it is loaded onto a pallet or container.

Emergency preparedness and response. DHS issued the National Preparedness Guidelines that describe a national framework for capabilities-based preparedness, and a Target Capabilities List to provide a national-level generic model of capabilities defining all-hazards preparedness. DHS is also finalizing a National Disaster Recovery Framework. However, DHS needs to strengthen its efforts to assess capabilities for all-hazards preparedness, and develop a long-term recovery structure to better align timing and involvement with state and local governments' capacity. DHS should also improve the efficacy of the grant application process by mitigating duplication or redundancy within the various preparedness grant programs.

Chemical, Biological, Radiological and Nuclear (CBRN) Threats

DHS assessed risks posed by CBRN threats and deployed capabilities to detect CBRN threats. However, DHS should work to improve its coordination of CBRN risk assessments, and identify monitoring mechanisms for determining progress made in implementing the global nuclear detection strategy.

GAO's work identified three themes at the foundation of DHS's challenges.

Leading and coordinating the homeland security enterprise. DHS has made important strides in providing leadership and coordinating efforts among its stakeholders. However, DHS needs to take additional action to forge effective partnerships and strengthen the sharing and utilization of information, which has affected its ability to effectively satisfy its missions. For example, the expectations of private sector stakeholders have not been met by DHS and its federal partners in areas related to sharing information about cyber-based threats to critical infrastructure. In 2005, GAO designated information sharing for homeland security as high risk because the federal government faced challenges in analyzing and sharing information in a timely, accurate, and useful way.

Implementing and integrating management functions for results. DHS has enhanced its management functions, and has plans in place to further strengthen the management of the department for results. However, DHS has not always effectively executed or integrated these functions. In 2003, GAO designated the transformation of DHS as high risk because DHS had to transform 22 agencies into one department. DHS has demonstrated strong leadership commitment and begun to implement a strategy to address its management challenges. However, these challenges have contributed to schedule delays, cost increases, and performance problems in a number of programs aimed at delivering important mission capabilities, such as container security technologies. DHS also faced difficulties in deploying some technologies that meet defined requirements. Further, DHS does not yet have enough skilled personnel to carry out activities in various areas, such as acquisition management; and has not yet developed an integrated financial management system, impacting its ability to have ready access to reliable information for informed decision making.

Strategically managing risks and assessing homeland security efforts. Forming a new department while working to implement statutorily mandated and department-initiated programs and responding to evolving threats, was, and is, a significant challenge facing DHS. Key threats have impacted DHS's approaches and investments. It is understandable that these threats had to be addressed immediately as they arose. However, limited strategic and program planning by DHS and limited assessment to inform approaches and investment decisions have contributed to programs not meeting strategic needs in an efficient manner.

Given DHS's leadership responsibilities in homeland security, it is critical that its programs are operating as efficiently and effectively as possible, are sustainable, and continue to mature to address pressing security needs. Eight years after its creation and 10 years after September 11, 2001, DHS has indeed made significant strides in protecting the nation, but has yet to reach its full potential.

Chairman King, Ranking Member Thompson, and Members of the Committee:

I am pleased to be here today to discuss our work on progress made by the Department of Homeland Security (DHS) and work remaining in implementing its homeland security missions since it began operations in March 2003. The nation is about to pass the 10-year anniversary of the September 11, 2001, terrorist attacks. The events of that day led to profound changes in government agendas, policies, and structures to confront homeland security threats facing the nation. This milestone provides an opportunity to reflect on the progress DHS has made since its establishment and challenges it has faced in implementing its missions, as well as to identify issues that will be important for the department to address as it moves forward, based on work we have completed on DHS programs and operations in key areas.

DHS was established with key missions that include preventing terrorist attacks from occurring within the United States, reducing U.S. vulnerability to terrorism, minimizing resulting damages, and helping the nation recover from any attacks that may occur. DHS is now the third-largest federal department, with more than 200,000 employees and an annual budget of more than $50 billion. We have evaluated numerous departmental programs since DHS began its operations, and issued more than 1,000 reports and congressional testimonies in areas such as border security and immigration, transportation security, and emergency management, among others.

We have made approximately 1,500 recommendations to DHS designed to strengthen its operations, such as to improve performance measurement efforts, strengthen management processes, enhance coordination and information sharing, and increase the use of risk information in planning and resource allocation decisions, as well as to address gaps and challenges in its mission operations that have affected DHS's implementation efforts. DHS has implemented about half of these recommendations, has actions underway to address others, and has taken additional steps to strengthen its mission activities.

However, we reported that the department has more to do to ensure that it conducts its missions efficiently and effectively, while simultaneously preparing to address future challenges that face the department and the nation. Addressing these issues will likely become increasingly complex as domestic and world events unfold, and will be particularly challenging in light of the current fiscal environment and constrained budgets.

In 2003, we designated the implementation and transformation of DHS as high risk because it represented an enormous undertaking that would require time to achieve in an effective and efficient manner.[1] Additionally, the components that merged to form DHS already faced a wide array of existing challenges, and any DHS failure to effectively carry out its mission could expose the nation to potentially serious consequences. The area has remained on our high-risk list since 2003.[2] Our prior work on mergers and organizational transformations, undertaken before the creation of DHS, found that successful transformations of large organizations, even those faced with less strenuous reorganizations than DHS, can take years to achieve.[3]

In 2007, we reported on progress made by DHS in implementing its mission and management functions by assessing actions DHS took to achieve performance expectations within each function.[4] We reported that DHS made progress in implementing all of its mission and management functions since it began operations, but progress among the areas varied significantly. For example, we reported that DHS made more progress in implementing its mission functions than its management functions. We also reported that DHS generally had not established quantitative goals and measures for assessing its performance and, as a result, we could not assess where along a spectrum of progress DHS stood in achieving its missions. Subsequent to the issuance of this report, DHS continued to take action to strengthen its operations and the management of the department, including enhancing its performance measurement efforts. At the request of this Committee, following the issuance of our report, we provided DHS with feedback on the department's performance goals and measures as DHS worked to better position itself to assess its results. Based on its internal review efforts and our feedback, DHS took action to develop and revise its performance goals and measures in an effort to strengthen its ability to assess its outcomes and progress in key mission areas. For fiscal year 2011, DHS identified 85 strategic measures for assessing its progress in achieving its Quadrennial Homeland Security Review (QHSR) missions and goals.[5] The department plans to report on its results in meeting established targets for these new measures at the end of the fiscal year.

In February 2010, DHS issued its first QHSR report, outlining a strategic framework for homeland security to guide the activities of the department and its homeland security partners, including federal, state, local, and tribal government agencies; the private sector; and nongovernmental organizations. The report identified five homeland security missions—Preventing Terrorism and Enhancing Security, Securing and Managing Our Borders, Enforcing and Administering Our Immigration Laws, Safeguarding and Securing Cyberspace, and Ensuring Resilience to Disasters—and goals and objectives to be achieved within each mission. In addition, in July 2010 DHS issued a report on the results of its Bottom-Up Review (BUR), a departmentwide assessment to align DHS's programmatic activities, such as investigating drug smuggling and inspecting cargo at ports of entry, and its organizational structure to the missions and goals identified in the QHSR.[6]

My statement is based on a report we issued in September 2011 assessing DHS's programs and operations.[7] As requested, the report and my statement address the progress made by DHS in implementing its homeland security missions since it began operations, remaining work, and crosscutting and management issues that have affected DHS's implementation efforts.

The report is based on our work on DHS since it began operations, supplemented with work completed by the DHS Office of Inspector General (IG), with an emphasis on work completed since 2008 to reflect recent work, and updated information and documentation provided by the department in July and August 2011. It is also based on our ongoing work on some DHS programs for various congressional committees, as noted throughout the report. For this ongoing work, as well as updated information provided by DHS, we examined program documentation and interviewed agency officials, among other things. This statement highlights key, recent work at DHS, but does not address all products we and DHS IG issued related to the department, nor does it address all of DHS's homeland security-related activities and efforts. To determine what progress DHS has made in implementing its mission functions and what work, if any, remains, we identified 10 DHS functional areas, which we define as categories or areas of DHS's homeland security responsibilities. These functional areas are based on those areas we identified for DHS in our August 2007 report on DHS's progress in implementing its mission and management functions, and our analysis of DHS's QHSR and budget documents, such as its congressional budget justifications.[8] These areas include: (1) aviation security; (2) chemical, biological, radiological, and nuclear (CBRN) threats; (3) critical infrastructure protection—physical assets; (4) surface transportation security; (5) border security; (6) maritime security; (7) immigration enforcement; (8) immigration services; (9); critical infrastructure protection—cyber assets; and (10) emergency preparedness and response.[9] To identify sub-areas within these functional areas, we identified performance expectations, which we define as composites of the responsibilities or functions that the department is to achieve or satisfy based on our analysis of requirements, responsibilities, and goals set for the department by Congress, the administration, and DHS itself and its components. In particular, we used expectations identified in our August 2007 report as a baseline, and updated, or added to, these expectations by analyzing requirements and plans set forth in homeland security-related laws, presidential directives and executive orders, national strategies, and DHS's and components' strategic plans and documents. We then aligned our functional areas to the five QHSR missions based on our review of the QHSR and BUR reports and DHS's fiscal year 2012 budget documents.

To identify key areas of progress and work that remains in each functional area, as well as crosscutting issues that have affected DHS's implementation efforts, we examined our and the DHS IG's past reports. We selected key work that we and the DHS IG have completed related to the functional areas, sub-areas, and crosscutting issues. We examined the methodologies used by the DHS IG in its reports, including reviewing the scope, methodological steps, and limitations. We determined that the DHS IG reports were sufficiently reliable for the purposes of our report to provide examples of, and to supplement our work on, DHS's progress and work remaining. We identified crosscutting issues based on analysis of our work in each functional mission area to determine common themes that have affected DHS's implementation efforts across the various mission areas. We conducted this performance audit from April 2011 through September 2011, in accordance with generally accepted government auditing standards. Those standards require that we plan and perform the audit to obtain sufficient, appropriate evidence to provide a reasonable basis for our findings and conclusions based on our audit objectives. We believe that the evidence obtained provides a reasonable basis for our findings and conclusions based on our audit objectives.

In commenting on our September 2011 report, DHS acknowledged our work to assess the progress the department has made in enhancing the nation's security and the challenges that still exist. The department discussed its views of its accomplishments since 2001, such as the creation and management of the Visa Security Program; the establishment of fusion centers to serve as focal points for the analysis and sharing on threat and vulnerability-related information; and passenger screening and prescreening programs, among other things. We recognize the department's progress in these and other areas in the report, as well as identify existing challenges that will be important for DHS to address moving forward. DHS further noted that the report did not address all of DHS's homeland security-related activities and efforts. DHS also stated that the report's assessments of progress in each homeland security mission area were not comprehensive because we and the DHS IG completed varying degrees of work for each area. We reflect in the report that it was primarily based on work we completed since DHS began operations, supplemented with the work of the DHS IG, with an emphasis on work completed since 2008 and updated information provided by DHS in July and August 2011. As such, the report identified that our work and that of the DHS IG did not cover all of DHS's homeland security-related programs and activities, and that the report was not intended to do so. Further, we noted in the report that because we and the DHS IG have completed varying degrees of work (in terms of the amount and scope of reviews completed) for each functional area, and because different DHS components and offices provided us with different amounts and types of information, the report's assessments of DHS's progress in each area reflected the information available for our review and analysis and were not necessarily equally comprehensive across all 10 areas.

DHS Continues to Implement and Strengthen Its Mission Functions, but Key Operational and Management Challenges Remain

Since DHS began operations in March 2003, it has developed and implemented key policies, programs, and activities for implementing its homeland security missions and functions that have created and strengthened a foundation for achieving its potential as it continues to mature. However, the department's efforts have been hindered by challenges faced in leading and coordinating the homeland security enterprise; implementing and integrating its management functions for results; and strategically managing risk and assessing, and adjusting as necessary, its homeland security efforts.[10] DHS has made progress in these three areas, but needs to take additional action, moving forward, to help it achieve its full potential.

DHS Has Made Progress in Implementing its Mission Functions, but Program Weaknesses and Management Issues Have Hindered Implementation Efforts

DHS has made important progress in implementing and strengthening its mission functions over the past 8 years, including implementing key homeland security operations and achieving important goals and milestones in many areas. The department's accomplishments include developing strategic and operational plans across its range of missions; hiring, deploying and training workforces; establishing new, or expanding existing, offices and programs; and developing and issuing policies, procedures, and regulations to govern its homeland security operations. For example:

- DHS issued the QHSR, which provides a strategic framework for homeland security, and the *National Response Framework,* which outlines guiding principles for disaster response.

- DHS successfully hired, trained, and deployed workforces, such as a federal screening workforce which assumed security screening responsibilities at airports nationwide, and the department has about 20,000 agents to patrol U.S. land borders.
- DHS created new programs and offices, or expanded existing ones, to implement key homeland security responsibilities, such as establishing the United States Computer Emergency Readiness Team to, among other things, coordinate the nation's efforts to prepare for, prevent, and respond to cyber threats to systems and communications networks. DHS also expanded programs for identifying and removing aliens subject to removal from the United States and for preventing unauthorized aliens from entering the country.
- DHS issued policies and procedures addressing, among other things, the screening of passengers at airport checkpoints, inspecting travelers seeking entry into the United States, and assessing immigration benefit applications and processes for detecting possible fraud.

Establishing these elements and others are important accomplishments and have been critical for the department to position and equip itself for fulfilling its homeland security missions and functions.

However, more work remains for DHS to address gaps and weaknesses in its current operational and implementation efforts, and to strengthen the efficiency and effectiveness of those efforts to achieve its full potential. For example, we have reported that many DHS programs and investments have experienced cost overruns, schedule delays, and performance problems, including, for instance, DHS's recently cancelled technology program for securing U.S. borders, known as the Secure Border Initiative Network, and some technologies for screening passengers at airport checkpoints. Further, with respect to the cargo advanced automated radiography system to detect certain nuclear materials in vehicles and containers at ports DHS pursued the acquisition and deployment of the system without fully understanding that it would not fit within existing inspection lanes at ports of entry. DHS subsequently canceled the program. DHS also has not yet fully implemented its roles and responsibilities for developing and implementing key homeland security programs and initiatives. For example, DHS has not yet developed a set of target capabilities for disaster preparedness or established metrics for assessing those capabilities to provide a framework for evaluating preparedness, as required by the Post-Katrina Emergency Management Reform Act.[11] Our work has shown that DHS should take additional action to improve the efficiency and effectiveness of a number of its programs and activities by, for example, improving program management and oversight, and better assessing homeland security requirements, needs, costs, and benefits, such as those for key acquisition and technology programs. Table 1 provides examples of key progress and work remaining in DHS's functional mission areas, with an emphasis on work we completed since 2008.

Impacting the department's ability to efficiently and effectively satisfy its missions are: (1) the need to integrate and strengthen its management functions; (2) the need for increased utilization of performance assessments; (3) the need for an enhanced use of risk information to inform planning, programming, and investment decision-making; (4) limitations in effective sharing and use of terrorism-related information; (5) partnerships that are not sustained or fully leveraged; and (6) limitations in developing and deploying

TABLE 1 Examples of Key Progress and Work Remaining in DHS's Efforts to Implement Its Homeland Security Missions on Which We and the DHS IG Have Reported

QHSR mission	Functional area	Summary of key progress and work remaining
Mission 1: Preventing Terrorism and Enhancing Security	Aviation security	**Key progress:** DHS enhanced aviation security in key areas related to passenger prescreening, passenger checkpoint screening, checked baggage screening, and air cargo security. For example, DHS developed and implemented Secure Flight as a passenger prescreening program to match airline passenger information against terrorist watchlist records. DHS also deployed technology to screen passengers and checked baggage at airports. For example, in response to the December 25, 2009, attempted attack on Northwest flight 253, DHS revised the advanced imaging technology procurement and deployment strategy, increasing the planned deployment of advanced imaging technology from 878 to between 1,350 and 1,800 units.[a] Further, DHS is screening passengers using staff trained in behavior detection principles and deployed about 3,000 Behavior Detection Officers to 161 airports as part of its Screening of Passengers by Observation Techniques program. Moreover, DHS reported, as of August 2010, that it had established a system to screen 100 percent of domestic air cargo (cargo transported within and outbound from the United States) transported on passenger aircraft by, among other things, creating a voluntary program to facilitate screening throughout the air cargo supply chain and taking steps to test technologies for screening air cargo. **What remains to be done:** DHS should take additional action to strengthen its aviation security efforts. For example, a risk-based strategy and a cost-benefit analysis of airport checkpoint technologies would improve passenger checkpoint screening. TSA's strategic plan to guide research, development, and deployment of passenger checkpoint screening technologies was not risk-based and did not reflect some of the key risk management principles, such as conducting a risk assessment based on the three elements of risk—threat, vulnerability, and consequence—and did not include a cost-benefit analysis and performance measures. Further, in March 2010, we reported that it was unclear whether the advanced imaging technology would have detected the weapon used in the December 25, 2009 attempted terrorist attack based on the preliminary testing information we received. DHS also had not validated the science supporting its Screening of Passengers by Observation Techniques program, or determined if behavior detection techniques could be successfully used across the aviation system to detect threats before deploying the program. DHS completed a program validation study in April 2011 which found that the program was more effective than random screening, but that more work was needed to determine whether the science could be used for counterterrorism purposes in the aviation environment. Moreover, DHS does not yet have a plan and schedule for deploying checked baggage screening technologies to meet recently enhanced explosive detection requirements. In addition, DHS does not yet have a mechanism to verify the accuracy of domestic and inbound air cargo screening data to help ensure that screening is being conducted at reported levels, and DHS does not yet have approved technology to screen cargo once it is loaded onto a pallet or container—both of which are common means of transporting air cargo on passenger aircraft, thus requiring that screening occur before incorporation into pallets and containers.

(*Continued*)

QHSR mission	Functional area	Summary of key progress and work remaining
	CBRN threats	**Key progress:** DHS made progress in assessing risks posed by CBRN threats, developing CBRN detection capabilities, and planning for nuclear detection. For example, DHS develops risk assessments of CBRN threats and has issued seven classified CBRN risk assessments since 2006. DHS also assessed the threat posed by specific CBRN agents in order to determine which of those agents pose a material threat to the United States, known as material threat assessments. With regard to CBRN detection capabilities, DHS implemented the BioWatch program in more than 30 metropolitan areas to detect specific airborne biological threat agents. Further, DHS established the National Biosurveillance Integration Center to enhance the federal government's capability to identify and track biological events of national concern. In addition, DHS coordinated the development of a strategic plan for the global nuclear detection architecture—a multidepartment effort to protect against terrorist attacks using nuclear and radiological materials through coordinated activities—and has deployed radiation detection equipment. **What remains to be done:** More work remains for DHS to strengthen its CBRN assessment, detection, and mitigation capabilities. For example, DHS should better coordinate with the Department of Health and Human Services in conducting CBRN risk assessments by developing written policies and procedures governing development of the assessments. Moreover, the National Biosurveillance Integration Center lacks resources necessary for operations, such as data and personnel from its partner agencies. Additionally, work remains for DHS in its implementation of the global nuclear detection architecture. Specifically, the strategic plan for the architecture did not include some key components, such as funding needed to achieve the strategic plan's objectives, or monitoring mechanisms for determining programmatic progress and identifying needed improvements. DHS officials told us that they will address these missing elements in an implementation plan, which they plan to issue by the end of 2011.
	Critical infrastructure protection—physical assets	**Key progress:** DHS expanded its efforts to conduct risk assessment and planning, provide for protection and resiliency, and implement partnerships and coordination mechanisms for physical critical assets. For example, DHS updated the *National Infrastructure Protection Plan* to include an emphasis on resiliency (the capacity to resist, absorb, or successfully adapt, respond to, or recover from disasters), and enhanced discussion about DHS risk management. Moreover, DHS components with responsibility for critical infrastructure sectors, such as transportation security, have begun to use risk-based assessments in their critical infrastructure related planning and protection efforts. Further, DHS has various voluntary programs in place to conduct vulnerability assessments and security surveys at and across facilities from the 18 critical infrastructure sectors, and uses these assessments to develop and disseminate information on steps asset owners and operators can take to protect their facilities. In addition, DHS coordinated with critical infrastructure stakeholders, including other federal regulatory authorities to identify overlaps and gaps in critical infrastructure security activities. **What remains to be done:** Additional actions are needed for DHS to strengthen its critical infrastructure protection programs and efforts. For example, DHS has not fully implemented an approach to measure its effectiveness in working with critical asset owners and operators in their efforts to adopt measures to mitigate

QHSR mission	Functional area	Summary of key progress and work remaining
		resiliency gaps identified during various vulnerability assessments. Moreover, DHS components have faced difficulties in incorporating risk-based assessments in critical infrastructure planning and protection efforts, such as in planning for security in surface transportation modes like highway infrastructure. Further, DHS should determine the feasibility of developing an approach to disseminating information on resiliency practices to its critical infrastructure partners to better position itself to help asset owners and operators consider and adopt resiliency strategies, and provide them with information on potential security investments.
	Surface transportation security	**Key progress:** DHS expanded its efforts in key surface transportation security areas, such as risk assessments and strategic planning; the surface transportation inspector workforce; and information sharing. For example, DHS conducted risk assessments of surface transportation modes and developed a transportation sector security risk assessment that assessed risk within and across the various modes. Further, DHS more than doubled its surface transportation inspector workforce and, as of July 2011, reported that its surface inspectors had conducted over 1,300 site visits to mass transit and passenger rail stations to complete station profiles, among other things. Moreover, DHS allocates transit grant funding based on risk assessments and has taken steps to measure performance of its Transit Security Grant Program, which provides funds to owners and operators of mass transit and passenger rail systems. In addition, DHS expanded its sharing of surface transportation security information by establishing information networks. **What remains to be done:** DHS should take further action to strengthen its surface transportation security programs and operations. For example, DHS's efforts to improve elements of risk assessments of surface transportation modes are in the early stages of implementation. Moreover, DHS noted limitations in its transportation sector security risk assessment—such as the exclusion of threats from "lone wolf" operators—that could limit its usefulness in guiding investment decisions across the transportation sector as a whole. Further, DHS has not yet completed a long-term workforce plan that identifies future needs for its surface transportation inspector workforce. It also has not yet issued regulations for a training program for mass transit, rail, and bus employees, as required by the Implementing Recommendations of the 9/11 Commission Act of 2007.[b] Additionally, DHS's information sharing efforts would benefit from improved streamlining, coordination, and assessment of the effectiveness of information sharing mechanisms.
Mission 2: Securing and Managing Our Borders	Border security	**Key progress:** DHS expanded its efforts in key border security areas, such as inspection of travelers and cargo at ports of entry, security of the border between ports of entry, visa adjudication security, and collaboration with stakeholders. Specifically, DHS has undertaken efforts to keep terrorists and other dangerous people from entering the country. For example, DHS implemented the U.S. Visitor and Immigrant Status Indicator Technology (US-VISIT) program to verify the identities of foreign visitors entering and exiting the United States by storing and processing biometric and biographic information. DHS established plans for, and had begun to interact with and involve stakeholders in, developing an exit capability. DHS deployed technologies and other infrastructure to secure the border between ports of entry, including more than 600 miles of tactical infrastructure, such as fencing, along

(*Continued*)

QHSR mission	Functional area	Summary of key progress and work remaining
		the border. DHS also deployed the Visa Security Program, in which DHS personnel review visa applications to help prevent individuals who pose a threat from entering the United States, to 19 posts in 15 countries, and developed a 5-year expansion plan for the program. In addition, DHS improved collaboration with federal, state, local, tribal, and international partners on northern border security efforts through, among other things, the establishment of interagency forums. **What remains to be done:** More work remains for DHS to strengthen its border security programs and operations. For example, although it has developed a plan, DHS has not yet adopted an integrated approach to scheduling, executing, and tracking the work needed to be accomplished to deliver a comprehensive biometric exit solution as part of the US-VISIT program. Further, DHS experienced schedule delays and performance problems with its information technology program for securing the border between ports of entry—the Secure Border Initiative Network—which led to its cancellation. Because of the program's decreased scope, uncertain timing, unclear costs, and limited life cycle management, it was unclear whether DHS's pursuit of the program was cost-effective. DHS is transitioning to a new approach for border technology, which we are assessing. With regard to the Visa Security Program, DHS did not fully follow or update its 5-year expansion plan. For instance, it did not establish 9 posts identified for expansion in 2009 and 2010, and had not taken steps to address visa risk at posts that did not have a Visa Security Program presence. Additionally, DHS should strengthen its oversight of interagency forums operating along the northern border.
	Maritime security	**Key progress:** DHS expanded its efforts in key maritime security areas, such as port facility and vessel security, maritime security domain awareness and information sharing, and international supply chain security. For example, DHS strengthened risk management through the development of a risk assessment model, and addressed risks to port facilities through annual inspections in which DHS identified and corrected deficiencies, such as facilities failing to follow security plans for access control. Further, DHS took action to address risks posed by foreign seafarers entering U.S. seaports by, for example, conducting advance-screening before the arrival of vessels at U.S. ports, inspections, and enforcement operations. DHS developed the Transportation Worker Identification Credential program to manage the access of unescorted maritime workers to secure areas of regulated maritime facilities. DHS also implemented measures to help secure passenger vessels including cruise ships, ferries, and energy commodity vessels such as tankers, such as assessing risks to these types of vessels. Moreover, for tracking vessels at sea, the Coast Guard uses a long-range identification and tracking system, and a commercially provided long-range automatic identification system. For tracking vessels in U.S. coastal areas, inland waterways, and ports, the Coast Guard operates a land-based automatic identification system, and also either operates, or has access to, radar and cameras in some ports. DHS also developed a layered security strategy for cargo container security, including deploying screening technologies and partnering with foreign governments. **What remains to be done:** DHS should take additional action to strengthen its maritime security efforts. For example, because of a lack of technology capability, DHS did not electronically verify identity and immigration status of foreign

QHSR mission	Functional area	Summary of key progress and work remaining
		seafarers, as part of its onboard admissibility inspections of cargo vessels, thus limiting the assurance that fraud could be identified among documents presented by them. In addition, the Transportation Worker Identification Credential program's controls were not designed to provide reasonable assurance that only qualified applicants acquire credentials. For example, during covert tests of the Transportation Worker Identification Credential at several selected ports, our investigators were successful in accessing ports using counterfeit credentials and authentic credentials acquired through fraudulent means. Moreover, DHS has not assessed the costs and benefits of requiring cruise lines to provide passenger reservation data for screening, which could help improve identification and targeting of potential terrorists. Further, the vessel tracking systems used in U.S. coastal areas, inland waterways, and ports had more difficulty tracking smaller and noncommercial vessels because these vessels were not generally required to carry automatic identification system equipment, and because of the technical limitations of radar and cameras. In addition, DHS has made limited progress in scanning containers at the initial ports participating in the Secure Freight Initiative, a program at selected ports with the intent of scanning 100 percent of U.S.-bound container cargo for nuclear and radiological materials overseas, leaving the feasibility of 100 percent scanning largely unproven. CBP has not yet developed a plan for full implementation of a statutory requirement that 100 percent of U.S.-bound container cargo be scanned by 2012.[c]
Mission 3: Enforcing and Administering Our Immigration Laws	Immigration enforcement	**Key progress:** DHS expanded its immigration and customs enforcement programs and activities in key areas such as overstay enforcement, compliance with workplace immigration laws, alien smuggling, and firearms trafficking. For example, DHS increased its resources for investigating overstays (unauthorized immigrants who entered the United States legally on a temporary basis then overstayed their authorized periods of admission) and alien smuggling operations, and deployed border enforcement task forces to investigate illicit smuggling of people and goods, including firearms. In addition, DHS took action to improve the E-Verify program, which provides employers a voluntary tool for verifying an employee's authorization to work in the United States, by, for example, increasing the program's accuracy by expanding the number of databases it can query. Further, DHS expanded its programs and activities to identify and remove criminal aliens in federal, state, and local custody who are eligible for removal from the United States by, for example, entering into agreements with state and local law enforcement agencies to train officers to assist in identifying those individuals who are in the United States illegally. **What remains to be done:** Key weaknesses remain in DHS's immigration and customs enforcement efforts. For example, DHS took action to address a small portion of the estimated overstay population in the United States, and lacks measures for assessing its progress in addressing overstays. In particular, DHS field offices had closed about 34,700 overstay investigations assigned to them from fiscal year 2004 through 2010, as of October 2010; these cases resulted in approximately 8,100 arrests, relative to a total estimated overstay population of 4 million to 5.5 million.[d] Additionally, we reported that since fiscal year 2006, U.S. Immigration and Customs

(*Continued*)

QHSR mission	Functional area	Summary of key progress and work remaining
		Enforcement within DHS allocated about 3 percent of its investigative work hours to overstay investigations Moreover, DHS should better leverage opportunities to strengthen its alien smuggling enforcement efforts by assessing the possible use of various investigative techniques, such as those to follow cash transactions flowing through money transmitters that serve as the primary method of payment to those individuals responsible for smuggling aliens. Further, weaknesses with the E-Verify program, including challenges in accurately estimating E-Verify costs, put DHS at an increased risk of not making informed investment decisions.
	Immigration services	**Key progress:** DHS improved the quality and efficiency of the immigration benefit administration process, and expanded its efforts to detect and deter immigration fraud. For example, DHS initiated efforts to modernize its immigration benefit administration infrastructure; improve the efficiency and timeliness of its application intake process; and ensure quality in its benefit adjudication processes. Further, DHS designed training programs and quality reviews to help ensure the integrity of asylum adjudications. Moreover, in 2004 DHS established the Office of Fraud Detection and National Security, now a directorate, to lead immigration fraud detection and deterrence efforts, and this directorate has since developed and implemented strategies for this purpose. **What remains to be done:** More work remains in DHS's efforts to improve its administration of immigration benefits. For example, DHS's program for transforming its immigration benefit processing infrastructure and business practices from paper-based to digital systems missed its planned milestones by more than 2 years, and has been hampered by management challenges, such as insufficient planning and not adhering to DHS acquisition guidance before selecting a contractor to assist with implementation of the transformation program. Additionally, while the Fraud Detection and National Security Directorate put in place strategies for detecting and deterring immigration fraud, DHS should take additional action to address vulnerabilities identified in its assessments intended to determine the extent and nature of fraud in certain applications. Further, despite mechanisms DHS had designed to help asylum officers assess the authenticity of asylum claims, such as identity and security checks and fraud prevention teams, asylum officers we surveyed cited challenges in identifying fraud as a key factor affecting their adjudications. For example, 73 percent of asylum officer survey respondents reported it was moderately or very difficult to identify document fraud.
Mission 4: Safeguarding and Securing Cyberspace	Critical infrastructure protection—cyber assets	**Key progress:** DHS expanded its efforts to conduct cyber security risk assessments and planning, provide for the protection and resilience of cyber assets, and implement cyber security partnerships and coordination mechanisms. For example, DHS developed the first National Cyber Incident Response Plan in September 2010 to coordinate the response of multiple federal agencies, state and local governments, and hundreds of private firms, to incidents at all levels. DHS also took steps to secure external network connections in use by the federal government by establishing the National Cybersecurity Protection System, operationally known as Einstein, to analyze computer network traffic information to and from agencies. In 2008, DHS developed Einstein 2, which incorporated network intrusion detection technology into the capabilities of the initial version of the system. Additionally, the

QHSR mission	Functional area	Summary of key progress and work remaining
		department made progress in enhancing its cyber analysis and incident warning capabilities through the establishment of the U.S. Computer Emergency Readiness Team, which, among other things, coordinates the nation's efforts to prepare for, prevent, and respond to cyber threats to systems and communications networks. Moreover, since conducting a major cyber attack exercise, called Cyber Storm, DHS demonstrated progress in addressing lessons it had learned from this exercise to strengthen public and private incident response capabilities. **What remains to be done:** Key challenges remain in DHS's cyber security efforts. For example, to expand its protection and resiliency efforts, DHS needs to lead a concerted effort to consolidate and better secure Internet connections at federal agencies. Further, DHS faced challenges regarding deploying Einstein 2, including understanding the extent to which its objective was being met because the department lacked performance measures that addressed whether agencies report whether the alerts represent actual incidents. DHS also faces challenges in fully establishing a comprehensive national cyber analysis and warning capability. For example, the U.S. Computer Emergency Readiness Team did not fully address 15 key attributes of cyber analysis and warning capabilities. These attributes are related to (1) monitoring network activity to detect anomalies, (2) analyzing information and investigating anomalies to determine whether they are threats, (3) warning appropriate officials with timely and actionable threat and mitigation information, and (4) responding to the threat. For example, the U.S. Computer Emergency Readiness Team provided warnings by developing and distributing a wide array of notifications; however, these notifications were not consistently actionable or timely. Additionally, expectations of private sector stakeholders are not being met by their federal partners in areas related to sharing information about cyber-based threats to critical infrastructure.
Mission 5: Ensuring Resilience to Disasters	Emergency preparedness and response	**Key progress:** DHS expanded its efforts to improve national emergency preparedness and response planning; improved its emergency assistance services; and enhanced emergency communications. For example, DHS developed various plans for disaster preparedness and response. In particular, in 2004 DHS issued the *National Response Plan* and subsequently made revisions to it, culminating in the issuance of the *National Response Framework* in January 2008, which outlines the guiding principles and major roles and responsibilities of government, nongovernmental organizations, and private sector entities for response to disasters of all sizes and causes. Further, DHS issued the National Preparedness Guidelines that describe a national framework for capabilities-based preparedness, and a Target Capabilities List, designed to provide a national-level generic model of capabilities defining all-hazards preparedness. DHS also assisted local communities with developing long-term disaster recovery plans as part of its post-disaster assistance. For example, DHS assisted Iowa City's recovery from major floods in 2008 by, among other things, identifying possible federal funding sources for specific projects in the city's recovery plan, and advising the city on how to prepare effective project proposals. DHS is also finalizing a National Disaster Recovery Framework, intended to provide a model to identify and address challenges that arise during the disaster recovery process. Moreover, DHS issued the National Emergency Communications Plan—the first strategic document for improving emergency communications nationwide.

(*Continued*)

QHSR mission	Functional area	Summary of key progress and work remaining
		What remains to be done: More work remains in DHS's efforts to assess capabilities for all-hazards preparedness and provide long-term disaster recovery assistance. For example, DHS has not yet developed national preparedness capability requirements based on established metrics to provide a framework for assessing preparedness. Further, the data DHS collected to measure national preparedness were limited by reliability and measurement issues related to the lack of standardization. Until a framework for assessing preparedness is in place, DHS will not have a basis on which to operationalize and implement its conceptual approach for assessing local, state, and federal preparedness capabilities against capability requirements and identify capability gaps for prioritizing investments in national preparedness. Moreover, with regard to long-term disaster recovery assistance, DHS's criteria for when to provide the assistance were vague, and, in some cases, DHS provided assistance before state and local governments had the capacity to work effectively with DHS. Additionally, DHS should improve the efficacy of the grant application and review process by mitigating duplication or redundancy within the various preparedness grant programs. Until DHS evaluates grant applications across grant programs, DHS cannot ascertain whether or to what extent multiple funding requests are being submitted for similar purposes.

Source: GAO analysis based on the areas included in our September 2011 report.

[a] Advanced imaging technology units produce an image of a passenger's body that DHS personnel use to look for anomalies, such as explosives or other prohibited items.

[b] The Implementing Recommendations of the 9/11 Commission Act requires TSA to issue regulations for a training program to prepare mass transit, rail, and over-the-road bus employees for potential security threats and conditions. 6 U.S.C. §§ 1137, 1167, 1184.

[c] See Pub. L. No. 110-53, § 1701(a), 121 Stat. 266, 489-490 (2007) (amending 6 U.S.C. § 982(b)).

[d] According to our April 2011 report, the most recent estimates from the Pew Hispanic Center approximated that, in 2006, out of an unauthorized resident alien population of 11.5 million to 12 million in the United States, about 4 million to 5.5 million were overstays. Pew Hispanic Center, *Modes of Entry for the Unauthorized Migrant Population* (Washington, D.C.: May 22, 2006).

technologies to meet mission needs. DHS made progress in addressing these areas, but more work is needed, going forward, to further mitigate these challenges and their impact on DHS's mission implementation.

For instance, DHS strengthened its performance measures in recent years and linked its measures to the QHSR's missions and goals. However, DHS and its components have not yet developed measures for assessing the effectiveness of key homeland security programs, such as programs for securing the border and preparing the nation for emergency incidents. For example, with regard to checkpoints DHS operates on U.S. roads to screen vehicles for unauthorized aliens and contraband, DHS established three performance measures to report the results of checkpoint operations. However, the measures did not indicate if checkpoints were operating efficiently and effectively and data reporting and collection challenges hindered the use of results to inform Congress and the public on checkpoint performance. Moreover, DHS has not yet established performance measures to assess the effectiveness of its programs for investigating alien smuggling operations and foreign nationals who overstay their authorized periods of admission to the United States, making it difficult for these agencies to determine progress made in these areas and evaluate possible improvements.

Further, DHS and its component agencies developed strategies and tools for conducting risk assessments. For example, DHS has conducted risk assessments of various surface transportation modes, such as freight rail, passenger rail, and pipelines. However, the department needs to strengthen its use of risk information to inform its planning and investment decision-making. For example, DHS could better use risk information to plan and prioritize security measures and investments within and across its mission areas, as the department cannot secure the nation against every conceivable threat.

In addition, DHS took action to develop and deploy new technologies to help meet its homeland security missions. However, in a number of instances DHS pursued acquisitions without ensuring that the technologies met defined requirements, conducting and documenting appropriate testing and evaluation, and performing cost-benefit analyses, resulting in important technology programs not meeting performance expectations. For example, in 2006, we recommended that DHS's decision to deploy next-generation radiation-detection equipment, or advanced spectroscopic portals, used to detect smuggled nuclear or radiological materials, be based on an analysis of both the benefits and costs and a determination of whether any additional detection capability provided by the portals was worth their additional cost. DHS subsequently issued a cost-benefit analysis, but we reported that this analysis did not provide a sound analytical basis for DHS's decision to deploy the portals. In June 2009, we also reported that an updated cost-benefit analysis might show that DHS's plan to replace existing equipment with advanced spectroscopic portals was not justified, particularly given the marginal improvement in detection of certain nuclear materials required of advanced spectroscopic portals and the potential to improve the current-generation portal monitors' sensitivity to nuclear materials, most likely at a lower cost. In July 2011, DHS announced that it would end the advanced spectroscopic portal project as originally conceived given the challenges the program faced.

As we have previously reported, while it is important that DHS continue to work to strengthen each of its functional areas, it is equally important that these areas be addressed from a comprehensive, departmentwide perspective to help mitigate longstanding issues that have impacted the department's progress.

Key Themes Have Impacted DHS's Progress in Implementing Its Mission Functions

Our work at DHS has identified several key themes—leading and coordinating the homeland security enterprise, implementing and integrating management functions for results, and strategically managing risks and assessing homeland security efforts—that have impacted the department's progress since it began operations. These themes provide insights that can inform DHS's efforts, moving forward, as it works to implement its missions within a dynamic and evolving homeland security environment. DHS made progress and has had successes in all of these areas, but our work found that these themes have been at the foundation of DHS's implementation challenges, and need to be addressed from a departmentwide perspective to position DHS for the future and enable it to satisfy the expectations set for it by the Congress, the administration, and the country.

Leading and coordinating the homeland security enterprise. While DHS is one of a number of entities with a role in securing the homeland, it has significant leadership and coordination responsibilities for managing efforts across the homeland security enterprise. To satisfy these responsibilities, it is critically important that DHS develop, maintain and leverage effective partnerships with its stakeholders, while at the same time addressing DHS-specific responsibilities in satisfying its missions. Before DHS began operations, we reported that the quality and continuity of the new department's leadership would be critical to building and sustaining the long-term effectiveness of DHS and achieving homeland security goals and objectives. We further reported that to secure the nation, DHS must form effective and sustained partnerships between components and also with a range of other entities, including federal agencies, state and local governments, the private and nonprofit sectors, and international partners.

DHS has made important strides in providing leadership and coordinating efforts. For example, it has improved coordination and clarified roles with state and local governments for emergency management. DHS also strengthened its partnerships and collaboration with foreign governments to coordinate and standardize security practices for aviation security. However, DHS needs to take additional action to forge effective partnerships and strengthen the sharing and utilization of information, which has affected its ability to effectively satisfy its missions. For example, we reported that the expectations of private sector stakeholders have not been met by DHS and its federal partners in areas related to sharing information about cyber-based threats to critical infrastructure. Without improvements in meeting private and public sector expectations for sharing cyber threat information, private-public partnerships will remain less than optimal, and there is a risk that owners of critical infrastructure will not have the information and mechanisms needed to thwart sophisticated cyber attacks that could have catastrophic effects on our nation's cyber-reliant critical infrastructure. Moreover, we reported that DHS needs to continue to streamline its mechanisms for sharing information with public transit agencies to reduce the volume of similar information these agencies receive from DHS, making it easier for them to discern relevant information and take appropriate actions to enhance security.

In 2005, we designated information sharing for homeland security as high risk because the federal government faced serious challenges in analyzing information and sharing it among partners in a timely, accurate, and useful way. Gaps in sharing, such as agencies' failure to link information about the individual who attempted to conduct the December 25, 2009, airline bombing, prevented the individual from being included on the federal government's consolidated terrorist watchlist, a tool used by DHS to screen for persons who pose a security risk. The federal government and DHS have made progress, but more work remains for DHS to streamline its information sharing mechanisms and better meet partners' needs. Moving forward, it will be important that DHS continue to enhance its focus and efforts to strengthen and leverage the broader homeland security enterprise, and build off the important progress that it has made thus far. In addressing ever-changing and complex threats, and with the vast array of partners with which DHS must coordinate, continued leadership and stewardship will be critical in achieving this end.

Implementing and integrating management functions for results. Following its establishment, the department focused its efforts primarily on implementing its various missions to meet pressing homeland security needs and threats, and less on creating and integrating a fully and effectively functioning department from 22 disparate agencies. This initial focus on mission implementation was understandable given the critical homeland security needs facing the nation after the department's establishment, and the enormous challenge posed by creating, integrating, and transforming a department as large and complex as DHS. As the department matured, it has put into place management policies and processes and made a range of other enhancements to its management functions—acquisition, information technology, financial, and human capital management. However, DHS has not always effectively executed or integrated these functions. In 2003, we designated the transformation and integration of DHS as high risk because DHS had to transform 22 agencies into one department, and failure to effectively address DHS's management and mission risks could have serious consequences for U.S. national and economic security. Eight years later, DHS remains on our high-risk list. DHS has demonstrated strong leadership commitment to addressing its management challenges and has begun to implement a strategy to do so. Further, DHS developed various management policies, directives, and governance structures, such as acquisition and information technology management policies and controls, to provide enhanced guidance on investment decision making. DHS also reduced its financial management material weaknesses in internal control over financial reporting and developed strategies to strengthen human capital management, such as its *Workforce Strategy for Fiscal Years 2011–2016.*

However, DHS needs to continue to demonstrate sustainable progress in addressing its challenges, as these issues have contributed to schedule delays, cost increases, and performance problems in major programs aimed at delivering important mission capabilities. For example, in September 2010, we reported that the Science and Technology Directorate's master plans for conducting operational testing of container security technologies did not reflect all of the operational scenarios that U.S. Customs and Border Protection was considering for implementation. In addition, when it developed the US-VISIT program, DHS did not sufficiently define what capabilities and benefits would be delivered, by when, and at what cost, and the department has not yet determined how to deploy a biometric exit capability under the program. Moreover, DHS does not yet have enough skilled personnel to carry out activities in various areas, such as acquisition management; and has not yet implemented an integrated financial management system, impacting its ability to have ready access to reliable, useful, and timely information for informed decision making. Moving forward, addressing these management challenges will be critical for DHS's success, as will be the integration of these functions across the department to achieve efficiencies and effectiveness.

Strategically managing risks and assessing homeland security efforts. Forming a new department while working to implement statutorily mandated and department-initiated programs and responding to evolving threats, was, and is, a significant challenge facing DHS. Key threats, such as attempted attacks against the aviation sector, have impacted and altered DHS's approaches and investments, such as changes DHS made to its processes and technology investments for screening passengers and baggage at airports. It is understandable that these threats had to be addressed immediately as they arose. However, limited strategic and program planning by DHS and limited assessment to inform approaches and investment decisions have contributed to programs not meeting strategic needs or not doing so in an efficient manner. For example, as we reported in July 2011, the Coast Guard's planned acquisitions through its Deepwater Program, which began before DHS's creation and includes efforts to build or modernize ships and aircraft and supporting capabilities that are critical to meeting the Coast Guard's core missions in the future, is unachievable due to cost growth, schedule delays and affordability issues. In addition, because FEMA has not yet developed a set of target disaster preparedness capabilities and a systematic means of assessing those capabilities, as required by the Post-Katrina Emergency Management Reform Act and Presidential Policy Directive 8, it cannot effectively evaluate and identify key capability gaps and target limited resources to fill those gaps.

Further, DHS has made important progress in analyzing risk across sectors, but it has more work to do in using this information to inform planning and resource allocation decisions. Risk management has been widely supported by Congress and DHS as a management approach for homeland security, enhancing the department's ability to make informed decisions and prioritize resource investments. Since DHS does not have unlimited resources and cannot protect the nation from every conceivable threat, it must make risk-informed decisions regarding its homeland security approaches and strategies.

Moreover, we have reported on the need for enhanced performance assessment, that is, evaluating existing programs and operations to determine whether they are operating as intended or are in need of change, across DHS's missions. Information on the performance of programs is critical for helping the department, Congress, and other stakeholders more systematically assess strengths and weaknesses and inform decision making. In recent years, DHS has placed an increased emphasis on strengthening its mechanisms for assessing the performance and effectiveness of its homeland security programs. For example, DHS established new performance measures, and modified existing ones, to better assess many of its programs and efforts.

However, our work has found that DHS continues to miss opportunities to optimize performance across its missions because of a lack of reliable performance information or assessment of existing information; evaluation among feasible alternatives; and, as appropriate, adjustment of programs or operations that are not meeting mission needs. For example, DHS's program for research, development, and deployment of passenger checkpoint screening technologies lacked a risk-based plan and performance measures to assess the extent to which checkpoint screening technologies were achieving the program's security goals, and thereby reducing or mitigating the risk of terrorist attacks. As a result, DHS had limited assurance that its strategy targeted the most critical risks and that it was investing in the most cost-effective new technologies or other protective measures. As the department further matures and seeks to optimize its operations, DHS will need to look beyond immediate requirements; assess programs' sustainability across the long term, particularly in light of constrained budgets; and evaluate tradeoffs within and among programs across the homeland security enterprise. Doing so should better equip DHS to adapt and respond to new threats in a sustainable manner as it works to address existing ones.

Concluding Observations

Given DHS's role and leadership responsibilities in securing the homeland, it is critical that the department's programs and activities are operating as efficiently and effectively as possible, are sustainable, and continue to mature, evolve and adapt to address pressing security needs. DHS has made significant progress throughout its missions since its creation, but more work is needed to further transform the department into a more integrated and effective organization. DHS has also made important progress in strengthening partnerships with stakeholders, improving its management processes and sharing of information, and enhancing its risk management and performance measurement efforts. These accomplishments are especially noteworthy given that the department has had to work to transform itself into a fully functioning cabinet department while implementing its missions—a difficult undertaking for any organization and one that can take years to achieve even under less daunting circumstances.

Impacting the department's efforts have been a variety of factors and events, such as attempted terrorist attacks and natural disasters, as well as new responsibilities and authorities provided by Congress and the administration. These events collectively have forced DHS to continually reassess its priorities and reallocate resources as needed, and have impacted its continued integration and transformation. Given the nature of DHS's mission, the need to remain nimble and adaptable to respond to evolving threats, as well as to work to anticipate new ones, will not change and may become even more complex and challenging as domestic and world events unfold, particularly in light of reduced budgets and constrained resources. To better position itself to address these challenges, our work has shown that DHS should place an increased emphasis and take additional action in supporting and leveraging the homeland security enterprise, managing its operations to achieve needed results, and strategically planning for the future while assessing and adjusting, as needed, what exists today. Addressing these issues will be critically important for the department to strengthen its homeland security programs and operations. Eight years after its establishment and 10 years after the September 11, 2001, terrorist attacks, DHS has indeed made significant strides in protecting the nation, but has yet to reach its full potential.

Chairman King, Ranking Member Thompson, and Members of the Committee, this concludes my prepared statement. I would be pleased to respond to any questions you may have at this time.

Critical Thinking Questions

1. Does the U.S. homeland security effort overall receive an adequate level of funding? If so, are the challenges identified in this article more an issue of re-prioritizing that funding?
2. What are the most positive results of homeland security efforts since 9/11?
3. What are the most difficult homeland security challenges we will have to confront over the next ten years?

Notes

1. GAO, *High-Risk Series: An Update,* GAO-03-119 (Washington, D.C.: January 2003). In addition to this high-risk area, DHS has responsibility for other areas we have designated as high risk. Specifically, in 2005 we designated information sharing for homeland security as high risk, involving a number of federal departments including DHS, and in 2006, we identified the National Flood Insurance Program as high risk. Further, in 2003 we expanded the scope of the high-risk area involving federal information security, which was initially designated as high-risk in 1997, to include the protection of the nation's computer-reliant critical infrastructure.
2. GAO, *Major Management Challenges and Program Risks: Department of Homeland Security,* GAO-03-102 (Washington, D.C.: January 2003).
3. See GAO, *Highlights of a GAO Forum: Mergers and Transformations: Lessons Learned for a Department of Homeland Security and Other Federal Agencies,* GAO-03-293SP (Washington, D.C.: Nov. 14, 2002), and *Results-Oriented Cultures: Implementation Steps to Assist Mergers and Organizational Transformations,* GAO-03-669 (Washington, D.C.: July 2, 2003).
4. GAO, *Department of Homeland Security: Progress Report on Implementation of Mission and Management Functions,* GAO-07-454 (Washington, D.C.: Aug. 17, 2007). We defined performance expectations as a composite of the responsibilities or functions—derived from legislation, homeland security presidential directives and executive orders, DHS planning documents, and other sources—that the department was to achieve or satisfy in implementing efforts in its mission and management areas. The performance expectations were not intended to represent performance goals or measures for the department.
5. DHS, *Quadrennial Homeland Security Review Report: A Strategic Framework for a Secure Homeland* (Washington, D.C.: February 2010). The Implementing Recommendations of the 9/11 Commission Act required that beginning in 2009, and every 4 years thereafter, DHS conduct a quadrennial review that provides a comprehensive examination of the homeland security strategy of the United States. Pub. L. No. 110-53, § 2401(a), 121 Stat. 266, 543-45 (2007) (codified at 6 U.S.C. § 347).
6. DHS, *Bottom-Up Review Report* (Washington, D.C.: July 2010). As a result of the BUR, DHS acknowledged that it had complementary department responsibilities and

capabilities, which it subsequently formalized in a sixth mission published in the fiscal year 2010-2012 Annual Performance Report—"Providing Essential Support to National and Economic Security"—to fully capture the scope of DHS's missions.

7. GAO, *Department of Homeland Security: Progress Made and Work Remaining in Implementing Homeland Security Missions 10 Years after 9/11,* GAO-11-881 (Washington, D.C.: Sept. 7, 2011).
8. GAO-07-454.
9. We focused these mission areas primarily on DHS's homeland security-related functions. We did not consider the Secret Service, domestic counterterrorism or intelligence activities because (1) we and the DHS IG have completed limited work in these areas; (2) there are few, if any, requirements identified for the Secret Service's mission and for DHS's role in domestic counterterrorism and intelligence (the Department of Justice serves as the lead agency for most counterterrorism initiatives); and (3) we address DHS actions that could be considered part of domestic counterterrorism and intelligence in other areas, such as aviation security, critical infrastructure protection, and border security.
10. DHS defines the homeland security enterprise as the federal, state, local, tribal, territorial, nongovernmental, and private-sector entities, as well as individuals, families, and communities, who share a common national interest in the safety and security of the United States and its population.
11. See 6 U.S.C. § 749.

Section 4.2

Disasters, Catastrophes, and Policy Failure in the Homeland Security Era[1]

Thomas A. Birkland

Abstract

The September 11 attacks triggered federal policy changes designed to influence emergency management in the United States, even though these attacks did not suggest a need for a wholesale restructuring of federal policy in emergency management. Instead, for several reasons, federal policy's emphasis on terrorism and emergency management significantly degraded the nation's ability to address natural disasters. The federal government sought to create a top-down, command and control model of emergency management that never fully accounted for, positively or normatively, the way local emergency management works in practice. The Obama administration will have to address the questions raised by the reorganization of federal emergency management responsibilities. While the context in which these changes have occurred is unique to the U.S. federal system, there are interesting implications for emergency management in nonfederal systems.

KEY WORDS: disaster and risk management, homeland security, national governance, policy change, policy failure

Introduction

Our ability to predict precisely when and where the next natural disaster, industrial accident, or terrorist attack will strike is limited. It is primarily constrained by the limits of natural and physical science, so we can only trade in probabilities.[2] Similarly, we trade in probabilities when dealing with other risks, but can make some educated "guesses" that improve predictability, albeit slightly. We strongly suspect, for example, based on existing terrorist-group behavior, that cities like New York, Washington, and Los Angeles are more prone to terrorism than are, say, Boise or Des Moines. We also know that hurricanes strike the U.S. East and Gulf coasts primarily during "hurricane season," June 1 to December 1 of each year.

Beyond these limited predictions, we can make very few claims, except to note with certainty that there will be more disasters, catastrophes, and crises in the very near future.[3] The trends are clear: the monetary toll of natural disasters continues to grow worldwide, as human populations continue to expand into vulnerable areas and as urbanization creates and exacerbates vulnerability (Comfort et al., 1999; Jacobs, 2005). Furthermore, the threat of terrorism became substantially more *visible* because of the September 11 attacks, although the risk of significant terrorist attacks on the United States, from either foreign or domestic sources, had been considered for some time before September 11 (Rimington,

2002; Rubin, 2000; Rubin, Cumming, & Tanali, 2002). The September 11 attacks, by themselves, did not provide a great deal of additional risk information. The attacks on Washington and New York did serve as a major focusing event that generated unprecedented interest in terrorism as a problem within U.S. national borders, and significantly changed the mass public's perception of the risk of terrorism. Of course, one can argue that attention to the terrorist hazard was "too low" before the September 11 attacks, particularly among the public (Birkland, 2006, chapter 2).

Mass casualty attacks and disasters generate domestic political pressure to "do something," and Hurricane Katrina gained worldwide attention to the apparent inability of the most advanced industrialized nation in the world to respond to natural disaster of this scope after having remade much of its emergency management after September 11 (Cooper & Block, 2006). And while most large "focusing events" can reveal a range of policy failures and prospects for learning (Birkland, 1998; May, 1992), it is important to consider whether and to what extent the "correct" lessons were learned. Two "lessons" that policy makers derived from the September 11 attacks were the putative need to create what became the Department of Homeland Security, or DHS, and, once such an idea gained acceptance, the "need" for the Federal Emergency Management Agency (FEMA) to be a part of that agency.

In the years after September 11, the controversy over the formation of DHS has largely been forgotten. The fundamental question of that controversy was "do we need a department of homeland security?" The Bush administration was reluctant to create such an agency, and did so only in the face of political pressure. We do know that, nearly six years after the DHS was born, that it remains, to many critics, a bureaucratic morass (Glasser & Grunwald, 2005) and a "problem" that the new administration and its DHS secretary would have to address (Bender, 2008).

While these problems have greatly influenced FEMA, they are not the focus of this article; rather, I argue that, from an emergency-management perspective, there was little about the September 11 attacks that suggested major problems with emergency management in the United States that would require, *inter alia*, the inclusion of FEMA into DHS.

Emergency response in both New York City and, especially, at the Pentagon (where the Arlington County Fire Department was the incident commander), given the scale of the event, was reasonably well organized. Officials in New York were able to adapt and respond to the event in spite of failures of communications systems (Haddow, Bullock, & Coppola, 2007, p. 313) and in spite of the New York Police Department's (NYPD) and the Fire Department's (FDNY's) long-standing practice of not sharing a single incident command system (Hauer, 2004; Slepicka, 2008). They were also able to, under extreme duress, relocate the city's Emergency Operations Center first from 7 WTC to the Police Academy, and then to Pier 92. The City of New York's size and capacity allowed for a functional computing and communications network to be established very quickly (Dawes et al., 2004). In the end, the ability to respond to such events is both a function of planning and of improvisation (Harrald, 2006; Mendonca & Wallace, 2004; Rodriguez, Trainor, & Quarantelli, 2006; Wachtendorf & Kendra, 2005), because, as the now well-worn saying goes, "no war plan survives contact with the enemy."

Given this generally good performance, and given other, equally sound "reasons" for the nation's failure to detect or prevent the September 11 attacks, (e.g., poor intelligence gathering; poor national security, military planning, and doctrine; poor immigration controls), why was FEMA moved into DHS? While on its face such a move might seem logical on something like "civil defense" grounds, FEMA had already been badly damaged by the Bush Administration's failure to understand the field of emergency management and the reality of federal intervention in a system that generally works from the bottom-up, with help, when needed, from the federal government.

September 11, Katrina, and Emergency Management in the United States

The United States is a federal system, in which power is divided between federal and state governments. States, in turn, create local governments to allow for a measure of local "home rule" and to carry out state functions. The division between federal and state responsibilities is defined in the U.S. Constitution, as shaped by over 200 years of practice and changes in government philosophy. Emergency management remains the responsibility of local and state governments, with the federal government serving as a source of support for local effort. The federal government, through FEMA, also became a source of considerable encouragement for the broad adoption of programs like hazard mitigation, which are often not undertaken without some sort of incentive. Such a system differs from unitary systems, such as those in most of the European Union and Asia, in that policy making is not confined to the national government.

Hurricane Katrina revealed that this "shared governance" system (Birkland & Waterman, 2008; Gomez & Wilson, 2008; Kweit & Kweit, 2006; May & Williams, 1986; Scavo, Kearney, & Kilroy, 2008; Schneider, 1990) for disaster management was strained. Local governments and the State of Louisiana were overwhelmed (Mississippi somewhat less so), and it appeared that federal aid was not quickly forthcoming, despite Governor Blanco's request for an emergency declaration on Monday, August 27. Indeed, defenders of the administration's response to Katrina tend to blame Governor Blanco's supposed failure to seek a presidential disaster declaration instead of lower-level presidential declaration of emergency. Governor Blanco's choice appeared to stem from a belief that a disaster declaration would federalize the state's National Guard units, something the governor did not want to do. On August 27, Blanco also wrote to the president seeking a federal disaster declaration, which was made on August 29. Indeed, even Homeland Security Secretary Michael Chertoff eventually indicated that most response problems were in FEMA, not at the state or local level (Curtius, 2005). This may be too critical of FEMA however, as New Orleans Mayor Ray Nagin and his staff failed to execute the existing emergency plan, and New Orleans' response capacity fell far short of the needs during the storm (Cooper & Block, 2006).

Katrina may well have overwhelmed any response authority: the state, the city, county and parish governments,[4] and even the "better" Clinton-era FEMA. This is the very argument made by the Bush Administration in its review of the overall response to Hurricane Katrina (United States Executive Office of the President, Assistant to the President for Homeland Security and Counterterrorism, 2006). Others argue that the response system broke much more thoroughly and rapidly than it would have under the "old" FEMA (Clarke, 2005; Perrow, 2005; Tierney, 2005). Under President Clinton, FEMA Administrator James Lee Witt—a former state emergency manager in Arkansas—took the helm of an adrift and dispirited FEMA in 1993 (Haddow et al., 2007; Murray,

2001a, 2001b). Witt steered FEMA away from its former civil defense orientation, and stressed intergovernmental cooperation, ideas that were successfully tested during the Midwest floods of 1993. After the floods, Witt sought to promote mitigation in concert with state and local agencies. The culmination of these efforts was Project Impact, which promoted public-private partnerships at the community level to promote hazard mitigation (Freitag, 2001). None of this was to say that Witt's administration was perfect, but Witt was much more progressive than his predecessors, or his successors, and the Witt years marked the high point of FEMA's prestige and morale (Haddow et al., 2007; Kamen, 2008; Murray, 2001a,b; Roberts, 2006).

While this discussion of what happened in Hurricane Katrina is illustrative, one does not need the storm to advance my central argument: that FEMA was an agency in decline as attention shifted from natural hazards to terrorism, and from mitigation to response. Indeed, the decay of FEMA's reputation and authority had begun before September 11, as I show next.

The Bush Administration and the Decline of FEMA

The Bush administration eliminated Project Impact. When Michael Brown spoke to the 2001 Natural Hazards Workshop in Boulder, Colorado, in his role as FEMA general counsel, he stated that Project Impact was dropped because the administration saw little value in funding what they believed to be frivolous community-building activities. Such a position was plausible because there was scant evaluation data proving the effectiveness of Project Impact. However, the value of the *idea* of mitigation was also devalued. While the Administration continued mitigation funding under the Disaster Mitigation Act of 2000 (Haddow et al., 2007), Congress appropriated less money and made these grants competitive rather providing funding based on recent disaster experience. Local financial contributions were also raised (Association of State Flood Plain Managers, 2006), making it more difficult for local governments to support mitigation efforts. FEMA leaders were not effective advocates for improvements in the mitigation program or for increases in mitigation funding, possibly because of its leaders' failure to understand the substantive value of mitigation, Indeed, as Tierney (2005) notes, "within DHS, the concept of mitigation has all but disappeared—except, of course, with respect to prevention and deterrence of terrorist attacks." And, of course, prevention is not really the same as mitigation.

Bush administration attitudes toward scientifically and technically sound mitigation were demonstrated well before September 11 by then-director Joseph Albaugh's castigation of Davenport, Iowa, officials for failing to build a floodwall. The city chose not to build a floodwall because it took an environmentally friendlier approach, of the sort promoted by Witt and others in the 1990s: to remove buildings from floodplains and use the land as open space (Birkland et al., 2003; Environmental Defense, 2001). The wisdom of such a decision may, in same ways, have been vindicated by the extensive failure of levees and floodwalls in New Orleans during Hurricane Katrina (Seed et al., 2006).

By mid-2001, it appeared that progress in promoting natural disaster mitigation was declining. FEMA became more concerned with emergency response rather than with comprehensive emergency management, including natural hazard mitigation based on all-hazards concepts (Department of Homeland Security, Office of the Inspector General, 2006, 135 ff). The September 11 attacks reinforced the response orientation, consonant with extensive media and policy maker attention to the efforts of firefighters, police,

EMTs, and other "first responders." However, this emphasis on "response" following September 11 was not balanced by increasing attention to mitigation. FEMA was conceived largely as a response-supporting organization when its preparedness functions were removed from FEMA under the Homeland Security Act and placed in a separate organization in DHS. The Post-Katrina Reform Act of 2006 returned these functions to FEMA.

This does not deny the need for improvement in response methods and capacities, both in New York and nationally, after September 11 (National Commission on Terrorist Attacks upon the United States, 2004; New York City Fire Department, 2005). But response was not, and is not, the only aspect of the disaster cycle worthy of attention, particularly considering how well the response worked in New York and the Pentagon under very trying conditions—and FEMA did sound work in NGO coordination and volunteer management. The post-September 11 focus on response was accompanied—perhaps not purposefully—by a decrease in attention to natural hazards in general, and to all hazard mitigation specifically (Department of Homeland Security, Office of the Inspector General, 2006).

The Focus on "Prevention"

The idea of "prevention" of terrorism is clearly desirable, but confusing this term with "mitigation," and therefore making a parallel to natural disasters, is hard to draw, particularly because FEMA and most local emergency managers have neither the power nor the expertise to *prevent* terrorist attacks. These functions reside in national law enforcement and intelligence agencies, such as the Central Intelligence Agency (CIA) and the Federal Bureau of Investigation (FBI). In natural hazards policy, "mitigation" encompasses efforts such as building codes and land use planning to limit the extent of damage in a disaster. Such tools, such as construction codes for blast damage or for improved ventilation in the face of biological and chemical threats, are appropriate in the terrorist case. And to be fair, one cannot rely solely on mitigation because events will still occur, and response to such events is necessary: mitigation does not eliminate damage; it simply attenuates it to a greater or lesser extent. In a similar vein, we cannot *prevent* all terrorist attacks. Even with sound counterterrorism programs, a few attacks will inevitably succeed.

The very agencies that may have the greatest influence on *preventing* an attack, rather than on intercepting it, are those agencies that were *not* folded into the Department of Homeland Security, including the FBI, CIA, and important parts of the Department of Defense (Harris, 2003). By contrast with these agencies, FEMA and other organizations were politically weaker and less able to mobilize their constituencies to help prevent their absorption into DHS. Today, DHS remains a sprawling, and ineffective agency (Bender, 2008) and its development into a more effective organization will challenge President Obama and Janet Napolitano, his nominee to head the agency.

Explaining the Change in Tone and Emphasis in Emergency Management

The civil-defense and quasimilitary tone of post 9/11 emergency management discourse was dominated by rhetoric and behaviors similar to those of the Cold War-era military-industrial complex (Monahan & Beaumont, 2006).[5] One can draw a direct line from the end of the Cold War, to the emergence of terrorism as a threat before 2001, to the recasting of many defense and security contractors' missions as "homeland security," differing little from the national security state that preceded it (Tierney, 2005). Building on the untested belief that these consultants and firms were competent in dealing with terrorist threats,[6] and unconstrained by government's apparent ignorance of or disdain for the decades of social science knowledge amassed on disasters, crises, and "extreme events," a new system of homeland security was created that contains, within it, (i) the assumption that September 11 revealed shortcomings in local and regional responses to disasters that required federal (i.e., top-down) policy intervention and direction; and (ii) the assumption that better planning would necessarily yield better responses. Certainly, planning for disasters is an important feature of local government and of public security, and many observers have expressed dissatisfaction with the level and pace of careful local planning for natural disasters (Berke & Campanella, 2006; Burby, 2006; McConnell & Drennan, 2006; Olshansky, 2006; Tierney, 2005). The so-called "all hazards" approach suggests that planning for disasters not be so specific that plans cannot accommodate a range of hazards, from meteorological or geophysical to accidental to intentional (Department of Homeland Security, Office of the Inspector General, 2006).

The second assumption is characterized by, first, a top-down system in which decisions are made in Washington, DC, and subordinates' compliance is expected and is gained through either coercion (the threat of taking money away) or inducements (the possibility of gaining resources, even if those resources are not quite what the community needs). We know that this top-down approach runs counter to the collaborative design of a national emergency management system more broadly and to emerging notions of networked governance as a more empirically accurate description of how public programs are really managed (Choi & Kim, 2007; Lagadec & Rosenthal, 2003; Mandell, 2001; Wachtendorf & Kendra, 2005). While no one would claim that the pre-September 11 system was perfect, it worked reasonably well on many levels, even when "ideal type" systems, such as "incident command" had not been created (Drabek, 1985; Schneider, 1992; Tierney, 2005). Through the promulgation of the National Response Plan (NRP) (which was only months old when Katrina struck), NRP's replacement, the National Response Framework (NRF), and the National Incident Management System (NIMS), the federal government sought to assert greater influence over local disaster preparedness and response.

September 11 provided the rationale for such intervention under neither the old notions of cooperative or coercive federalism. Rather, as Birkland and Waterman (2008) found, changes might well be explained under the rubric of "opportunistic federalism," which Conlan (2006, p. 667) defines as

> a system that allows—and often encourages—actors in the system to pursue their immediate interests with little regard for the institutional or collective consequences. For example, federal mandates, policy preemptions, and highly prescriptive federal grant programs tend to be driven by opportunistic policy makers who seek to achieve their own policy and political goals regardless of traditional norms of behavior or boundaries of institutional responsibility.

This idea of opportunistic federalism is entirely consistent with the "opportunistic" and episodic nature of nearly all disaster policy, since change in disaster and crisis policy is often event-driven. In creating DHS, Congress, with the president's assent, moved FEMA into the new agency without regard for its existing organizational and intergovernmental relationships, many of which were developed based on hazards experience. Furthermore, homeland security "experts" made policy without consulting the vast amounts of knowledge accumulated by social scientists and practitioners on how people and organizations actually behave in disasters (Tierney, 2005).

After Hurricane Katrina, the administration decided that the National Response Plan unwieldy, and decided to create a new National Response Framework (NRF). The federal government attempted to write the NRF with almost no input from state and local emergency managers who already had experience working under the NRP and who were beginning to gain an appreciation for its strengths and weaknesses (Hsu, 2007; International Association of Emergency Managers, 2007). The NRF process is a clear example of, again, the federal tendency to look at emergency management failures as evidence for the need for more centralized planning from the top down, rather than looking at such failures as opportunities to improve coordination and collaboration throughout the network of responsible agencies.

The legal and political authority for disaster management rests within state and local government (Waugh & Streib, 2006, p. 136).We know from extensive research in natural disasters that actual response is not hierarchical; rather, a seemingly chaotic response system emerges that ultimately reveals its logic as actors improvise to provide the goods and services—ranging from rescue to bottled water—needed in a disaster (Kendra & Wachtendorf, 2003, 2006; Mendonca & Wallace, 2004; Wachtendorf & Kendra, 2005).

The new emergency management system unduly relied on new and often unproven hardware, computing technology, systems of intelligence gathering, and the like, to predict, prevent, or mitigate future homeland security threats. The Office of Domestic Preparedness (ODP) enables localities to purchase equipment to prepare for terrorist events by providing funds for state and local governments to purchase specialized equipment for first responders in preparation for chemical, biological, radiological, and nuclear terrorist attacks (Haddow et al., 2007, p. 204). This focus on hardware and on so-called "technology" has meant that equipment was first distributed to local agencies based on a form of distributive "equity." Political debates over how funds have been or should be distributed to state and local governments for disaster preparedness had become an important part of post-September 11 preparedness, where smaller cities are flush with preparedness funds while Washington and New York are left wanting. Some of this funding has certainly been valuable, but much money has been spent on politically distributive spending, or, as known in American politics "pork-barrel spending." In 2006, the funding formula required awarding an equal amount of funds to states (Eggen, 2006). To its credit, DHS changed its practices, and

> has adopted a process of continuing improvement in its methods for assessing risk and measuring grant applicants' effective use of resources. SHSP [State Homeland Security Program] and UASI [Urban Area Security Initiative] grant allocations continue to be based on a three-step process: (i) risk assessments to determine areas eligible to apply for grants, (ii) effectiveness assessments of the grant applicants' investment justifications, and (iii) final grant allocations . . . Generally, we found that DHS has constructed a reasonable methodology to assess risk and allocate funds (Government Accountability Office, 2008).

Thus, while redistributive politics played a role, at least in the funding arena, DHS gained a greater appreciation for risk, driven in large part by complaints from areas that believed themselves to be at greatest risk, which resulted in the legislative requirement that risk be accounted, as enacted in the Consolidated Security, Disaster Assistance and Continuing Appropriations Act, P.L. 110–329.

The federal government replaced an "all-hazards" framework with a homeland security framework that would then be applied, somehow, to all hazards. This is a subtle but important distinction, which helps to explain the scenario-driven basis of the National Response Framework, the National Incident Management System, the Homeland Security strategy, and other documents that place vague homeland security threats higher on the agenda than preparation for regular, but catastrophic, natural disasters. While many disaster professionals sought to promote the all hazards approach after September 11, for fear that terrorism concerns would overwhelm existing systems (and would ignore existing knowledge) in emergency management, it now seems clear that revisiting the all-hazards approach is necessary if for no other reason than to afford emergency managers the opportunity to calibrate their preparation and approaches to their communities' most important hazards.

This sort of flexibility is contemplated in the new, less formulaic NRF, but, given the outcry the new framework elicited from professional emergency managers, it is difficult to see if this framework will be any less top-down than the National Response Plan it replaces. Following Hurricane Katrina, the NRF was heralded because DHS developed it in consultation with state and local emergency management officials, something that was not associated with the adoption of the NRP (Hsu, 2008a). Perhaps its *implementation*, if nothing else, will be open to greater flexibility and local initiative than was the implementation of the NRP.

The predicted results of these errors in thinking and planning were the damage, loss of life, and confused response to Hurricane Katrina (Cooper & Block, 2006). The poor response to this event did not serve anyone well because it suggested that, even when the threat is known—its time, place, manner, and warning period—the nation still could not rouse itself to prepare for and respond to the threat.

Prospects for the Future

The Obama administration will have the opportunity to reconsider its organization of federal support for emergency management as an overlapping, but not congruent, aspect of homeland security. President Obama has nominated Janet Napolitano to serve as Secretary of Homeland Security, although as of this writing there is little information about her stance toward FEMA and emergency management generally. There are, therefore, not yet any options that have been denied to the administration, and there are at least three possible directions that the Obama administration could take to reform and, presumably, strengthen emergency management.

In scenario 1, the new president could continue to make homeland security the primary federal concern in emergency management. In other words, emergency management, and FEMA, would continue to serve the civil defense function it filled during the 1950s through mid-1980s; the 1990s would be a historical oddity in FEMA's history, and federal response to natural disasters would likely suffer, because terrorism would still be the prime motivator for the NRF. This scenario seems unlikely, given FEMA's continued efforts throughout the hazard and disaster cycle, but FEMA's emphasis would likely refocus on natural disasters if another major event like Katrina recurs, which is rather more likely than a catastrophic terrorist attack.

Scenario 2 would see a return to something like the way FEMA existed before it was moved into DHS. In this scenario, FEMA would be removed from DHS. It would certainly have to network with DHS, but there is no particular need to keep FEMA in DHS; indeed, there was no particular need to create DHS at all, and its components still have not gelled into a single agency, if they ever will. Even if we assume that FEMA has key homeland security functions, we also know that not all homeland security functions are contained within DHS; indeed, many of the most important are left outside DHS, such as the major intelligence services that were found so wanting after the September 11 attacks.

In scenario 3, an enlightened administration could move FEMA beyond the vision that James Lee Witt laid out for it by returning hazard mitigation to a primary goal of national policy. Innovative tools for promoting mitigation, such as fully funding the pre- and post-mitigation grant programs, encouraging something like Project Impact, and working as a *partner* with local emergency managers would characterize the new agency. The agency would support efforts to build community *resilience* and to reduce vulnerability through some form of sustainable development or "smarter growth" practices (leaving aside for now the problems of defining "sustainability"). FEMA could continue to offer technical support to state and local government through units such as the U.S. Fire Administration, but it would emphasize partnership and assistance, not command and control.

In the first scenario, current trends that promote vulnerability will continue unabated. There will be more catastrophic natural disasters because of increased population growth in vulnerable areas of the nation. Better responses will be a function of better state and local preparedness and mitigation efforts, such as those in California, Florida, and North Carolina, states with substantial disaster experience (Birkland, 2006). In other states, disasters and catastrophes will exist and may worsen because few attempts have been made by the federal government to encourage states and localities to recognize their vulnerabilities, assess hazards, and take disaster mitigation steps. With no incentives to mitigate—and plenty not to, such as the relentless pressure to develop real estate (Burby, 2006)—communities will become more vulnerable. The federal executive branch will continue to use copious amounts of disaster relief as a political and economic palliative, while states and local governments follow local political and near-term economic incentives to rebuild as quickly as possible in the same vulnerable ways and places. Economic activity and tax revenue return to the status quo ante, but vulnerability exists or even increases.

Scenario 1 describes what happened on the Gulf Coast after Katrina. In Biloxi, for example, victims have sold their damaged properties (sometimes for handsome sums) to growing, larger Gulf Coast casinos or high-rise luxury condominium developers. While these new buildings are somewhat more robust than the ones they replaced, vulnerability will increase as higher population densities are placed near hurricane zones; at the same time, tourists, a challenging population, must be encouraged to be vigilant and to evacuate in a timely manner.

In the second scenario, a new FEMA administrator, reporting to and supported by the president and separate from DHS and its inexpert top leadership would return FEMA to the prestige and competence it enjoyed in the 1990s. Incompetent political appointees would be replaced by competent emergency managers, not just at the Administrator's level, but throughout the agency. FEMA would return to its pre-2001 role as the main federal *coordinator* of efforts to prepare for, mitigate, respond to, and recover from all manner of disasters, but would seek to work more cooperatively with local and state governments based on *their* assessment of their needs. While separate from DHS, FEMA would work closely, under the NRF, with other federal agencies to assist state and local government in disaster response. FEMA's primary responsibility would be in predisaster mitigation, preparedness, and postdisaster consequence management. To the extent that a terrorist attack leaves evidence, FEMA would yield to law enforcement and intelligence agencies, but it would be well-understood that, in the immediate aftermath of a disaster, protecting human life is of paramount importance, and that state and local emergency response agencies, aided and supported by FEMA, would be the principal parties at the scene.

The third scenario would yield improvements far beyond the state of the art. In this scenario, not only would FEMA be separate from DHS and have the president's ear, but FEMA and the president would support initiatives that explicitly seek to improve community disaster resilience through efforts to reduce vulnerability. A key way to do this would be to embrace, as a national policy goal, efforts to induce communities to plan land use and economic development in a sustainable manner. As Dennis Mileti (1999) argues:

> Natural hazard mitigation will not be successful at reducing losses and disruption in the long term until it is integrated into the considerations of the daily activities of everyone who has an influence on disaster losses. This, in turn, will not be possible until hazards mitigation is housed within a redesigned national culture that favors sustainable development and people are reorganized to support that cultural shift.

Of course, the very meaning of "sustainable" is open to question, and as an organizing principle, this term has gained very little traction among disaster planners and emergency managers. But the essential argument is correct: long-term losses will increase unless everyone with a role to play in increasing or decreasing vulnerability incorporates disaster resilience as a part of what they do. FEMA, along with other national level agencies—the Environmental Protection Agency, the Geological Survey, the Forest Service, the National Oceanic and Atmospheric Administration, among others—could partner in providing the sort of assistance that communities can use to plan better for disaster *resilience*, not just response.

Critics of the scenarios offered here would rightly ask "what about homeland security?" Homeland security is clearly important; no one in New York, London, Madrid, or Washington would deny the importance of counterterrorism. But regardless of how much time, money, and effort we spend, some terrorist attacks will still occur, which is why preparedness and response are also important. This was as much as admitted in the administration's 2002 Homeland Security strategy (Office of Homeland Security, 2002), even as presidential candidate John Kerry earned ridicule for saying the same thing (Bai, 2004; CNN, 2004). Catastrophic terrorism is certainly possible, and its catastrophic force may be a function of technological changes that have improved terror groups' access to weapons of mass destruction, coupled perhaps with the shift to mass casualty terrorism as a particular goal of terrorist attacks. The logic is that the larger, more spectacular, and more fatal the event, and the bigger the impact of the attack, the greater its intimidation value, which, in turn, leads to the sociopolitical changes sought by the attackers.

However, many of the things that make terrorist attacks more catastrophic, such as tightly connected, but not resilient, infrastructure—are also the same factors that have made communities more vulnerable to natural disasters, including vulnerable and unsustainable urban forms that rely on outmoded methods of transport, communication, and the provision of public utilities (Aguirre, 2006; Buckle, 2005; Coaffee & Rogers, 2008; Rose, 2007; Vale & Campanella, 2005). The *consequences* of natural disasters are therefore similar to the consequences of terrorist attacks. And the predisaster planning for these events—training for "first responders," structural and nonstructural mitigation efforts, intergovernmental planning, establishment of communication and warning systems, and so on—are not so different that they cannot be addressed, with minor changes in doctrine and tactics, by emergency managers who are already familiar with a broad range of hazards (Perry & Lindell, 2003). Resilient communities that seriously adopt the all-hazards approach will therefore be able to respond to and bounce back from terrorism as well as from natural disasters.

Since September 11, 2001, however, emergency management expertise has been turned on its head. The real experts, the state and local officials who are first to the scene of natural disasters, and from whom we have a great deal to learn, have been subordinated to the "expertise" of federal law enforcement officials, military officers, and, often, civilian contractors, many of which have little to no experience in any sort of disaster or emergency management. Federal policies have focused more on distributive spending—that is, pork (de Rugy, 2005; Roberts, 2005)—turf battles and on contractor relationships in the new "homeland security complex"[7] than on efforts to improve response and resilience.

Because the second and third scenarios are currently unlikely to happen, we can be reasonably certain that future disasters will become more common, and catastrophic disasters are more likely to occur, as more places become more vulnerable to major disasters. In the United States, the most likely catastrophic natural disasters are hurricanes and earthquakes. Terrorism may pose catastrophic risks, but the risk of terrorism is not yet well understood. While catastrophic terrorist events will remain rare, their possibility distorts federal decision making out of proportion to the relative risk of any community from a terrorist attack compared with the risk of major natural disasters.

Future disasters and catastrophes will be more damaging and will yield longer recovery times because the federal government has provided confusing mandates and poor planning direction for state and local governments. Federal funding priorities further distort local planning efforts, causing more attention to be paid to less likely terrorist incidents than to more likely natural disasters.

The outcomes of disasters and catastrophes will be variable; some states have undertaken their own efforts to prepare for, mitigate, and respond to disasters, while other states still lag behind.

Past research suggests that these trends toward greater vulnerability will continue unabated, because disaster-relief programs are very popular among politicians, the general public does not give much thought to disaster policies until disasters happen, and many communities lack the political will or legal powers to shape development and planning in ways that would reduce overall community vulnerability. In this environment, the putative public interest will always be subordinate to narrower interests, like builders and real estate agents, who are motivated by short-term profit rather than community resilience.

These are sobering trends, but failing to recognize them and correct problems now will yield worse disasters later. The "window of opportunity" for major policy change in the wake of the apparent post-Katrina failures has closed. Over three years have elapsed, and the national agenda has been, and is likely to be, dominated by news of major economic dislocations and of the continued anti-insurgency efforts in Iraq and Afghanistan. It is unlikely that the new administration will make more than a marginal difference in the actual management of the emergency management system, regardless of the location of FEMA or other agencies in the greater DHS system.

Critical Thinking Questions

1. Do you agree with the author's contention that a focus on terrorism has degraded our nation's ability to deal effectively with natural disasters? Why or why not?
2. Compare this chapter to the essay by Gov. Keating in Unit Two of this book. What similarities and differences do you see?
3. Have our nation's homeland security efforts weakened, instead of strengthened, community resilience overall? Why or why not?

Notes

1. This is an expanded article first presented at the 2008 conference on "Surviving Future Disasters: Identifying critical challenges and effective strategies for transboundary disaster management," at the Stephenson Disaster Management Institute, Louisiana State University, Baton Rouge, April 2008. The opinions expressed herein are solely those of the author. I thank Kristin O'Donovan for research assistance, and Arjen Boin and two reviewers for their comments.
2. Interestingly, the initial enactment of the National Earthquake Hazard Reduction Act (NEHRA, PL 108-360, 1977) included a program for advancing earthquake prediction, but such prediction is beyond our reach scientifically, and, even if we had probabilistic earthquake forecasting available in the same way that weather forecasting is available, the response to such forecasts would likely be very disruptive to local communities and the economy (Lomnitz & Gibowicz, 1995; National Research Council, Committee on Socioeconomic Effects of Earthquake, 1978). Hurricanes can be forecast to hit within a certain area (the "cone of probability") within a certain period, but these forecasts are available hours, not weeks or more, in advance.
3. There is a qualitative difference between a disaster which affects a relatively small area and affects, but does not overwhelm, regional capacity to respond, and a catastrophe, which is so large that even regional resources must be augmented by outside help (Perry & Quarantelli, 2005). Hurricane Katrina was, by this standard, a catastrophe (Quarantelli, 2005).
4. Every state in the United States, with the exception of Alaska and Louisiana, is organized into counties. The equivalent unit in Louisiana is the parish. Orleans Parish and the City of New Orleans are essentially the same jurisdiction.
5. To confirm this claim one need only review DHS's list of prime contractors at http://www.dhs.gov/ xlibrary/assets/opnbiz/OSDBU-DHS_Prime_Contractors_List.pdf
6. An assumption tested by, for example, Boeing's failure to deliver a "high tech" virtual fence between the United States and Mexico (Hsu, 2008b).

7. A term used by critics to point out the similarities between the new system and the Cold War "military industrial complex," but also adopted by DHS as a less critical term for the broader community of scholars, contractors, decision makers, and the like in the homeland security field. See "Department of Homeland Security Broad Agency Announcement: Initial University-Based Center of Excellence" at http://www.dhs.gov/xnews/releases/press_release_0220.shtm/

References

Aguirre, B. E. (2006). *On the concept of resilience*. Newark: University of Delaware, Disaster Research Center.

Association of State Flood Plain Managers. (2006). Improving the pre-disaster mitigation program. Retrieved November 1, 2008, from http://www.floods.org/PDF/ASFPM_PDM_White_Paper_0306.pdf

Bai, M. (2004, October 10). Kerry's undeclared war. *New York Times Magazine*. Retrieved October 6, 2008, from http://www.nytimes.com/2004/10/10/magazine/10KERRY.html?pagewanted=all

Bender, B. (2008, December 1). Homeland Security Department in total disarray. *Boston Globe*. Retrieved December 26, 2008, from http://www.boston.com/news/nation/washington/articles/2008/11/30/ homeland_security_in_disarray_officials_warn/

Berke, P. R., & Campanella, T. J. (2006). Planning for postdisaster resiliency. *Annals of the American Academy of Social and Political Science*, *604*(1), 192–207.

Birkland, T. A. (1998). Focusing events, mobilization, and agenda setting. *Journal of Public Policy*, *18*(3), 53–74.

Birkland, T. A. (2006). *Lessons of disaster*. Washington, DC: Georgetown University Press.

Birkland, T. A., & Waterman, S. (2008). Is federalism the reason for policy failure in hurricane Katrina? *Publius*, *38*(4), 692–714.

Birkland, T. A., Burby, R. J., Conrad, D., Cortner, H., & Michener, W. K. (2003). River ecology and flood hazard mitigation. *Natural Hazards Review*, *4*(1), 46–54.

Buckle, I. (2005). Protecting critical infrastructure systems. Paper read at CAE Resilient Infrastructure Conference, at Rotorura, New Zealand. Retrieved October 2, 2008, from http://www.caenz.com/info/ 2005Conf/pres/Buckle.pdf

Burby, R. J. (2006). Hurricane Katrina and the paradoxes of government disaster policy: Bringing about wise governmental decisions for hazardous areas. *The Annals of the American Academy of Political and Social Science*, *604*(1), 171–191.

Choi, S. O., & Kim, B-T. (2007). Power and cognitive accuracy in local emergency management networks. *Public Administration Review*, *67*(s1), 198–209.

Clarke, L. (2005). Worst case Katrina. Social Science Research Council 2005. Retrieved November 22, 2005, from http://understandingkatrina.ssrc.org/Clarke/

CNN. (2004). Bush campaign to babcerf_txse ad on Kerry terror quote. Retrieved October 2, 2008, from http://www.cnn.com/2004/ALLPOLITICS/10/10/bush.kerry.terror/

Coaffee, J., & Rogers, P. (2008). Rebordering the city for new security challenges: From counter-terrorism to community resilience. *Space & Polity*, *12*(1), 101–118.

Comfort, L., Wisner, B., Cutter, S., Pulwarty, R., Hewitt, K., Oliver-Smith, A., et al. (1999). Reframing disaster policy: The global evolution of vulnerable communities. *Global Environmental Change Part B: Environmental Hazards*, *1*(1), 39–44.

Conlan, T. (2006). From cooperative to opportunistic federalism: Reflections on the half-century anniversary of the Commission on Intergovernmental Relations. *Public Administration Review*, *66*(5), 663–676.

Cooper, C., & Block, R. (2006). *Disaster: Hurricane Katrina and the failure of homeland security.* New York: Times Books.

Curtius, M. (2005, October 20). Chertoff puts the onus on FEMA: The Homeland Security secretary tells a House panel that local and state officials were not at fault for government lapses in addressing Katrina. *Los Angeles Times*, A14.

Dawes, S. S., Birkland, T. A., Tayi, G. K., & Schneider, C. A. (2004). *Information technology and coordination: Lessons from the World Trade Center response*. Albany: Center for Technology in Government, University at Albany, State University of New York.

Department of Homeland Security, Office of the Inspector General. (2006). *A performance review of FEMA's disaster management activities in response to Hurricane Katrina*. Washington, DC: Department of Homeland Security. Retrieved December 27, 2008, from http://www.dhs.gov/xoig/assets/mgmtrpts/OIG_06-32_ Mar06.pdf

de Rugy, V. (2005). *What does Homeland Security spending buy?* Washington, DC: American Enterprise Institute. Retrieved October 2, 2008, from http://www.ciaonet.org/wps/aei001/aei001.pdf

Drabek, T. E. (1985). Managing the emergency response. *Public Administration Review*, *45*(Special Issue, January), 85–92.

Eggen, D. (2006, January 4). DC may benefit as DHS bases grants on risk. *Washington Post*, A1.

Environmental Defense. (2001). *Davenport close to model for river cities, says Environmental Defense*. Retrieved November 20, 2005, from http://www.environmentaldefense.org/pressrelease.cfm?ContentID=113

Freitag, R. (2001). The impact of Project Impact on the Nisqually Earthquake. *Natural Hazards Observer*, *25*(5). Retrieved May 14, 2009, from http://www.colorado.edu/hazards/o/archives/2001/may01/may01a.html# nisqually

Glasser, S. B., & Grunwald, M. (2005, December 22). Department's mission was undermined from start. *Washington Post*, A1. Retrieved May 14, 2009, from http://www.washingtonpost.com/wp-dyn/content/ article/2005/12/21/AR2005122102327_pf.html

Gomez, B. T., & Wilson, M. (2008). Political sophistication and attributions of blame in the wake of Hurricane Katrina. *Publius: The Journal of Federalism Forthcoming*, *38*(4), 633–650.

Government Accountability Office. (2008). Homeland Security grant program risk-based distribution methods: Presentation to Congressional Committees—November 14, 2008 and December 15. Retrieved December 26, 2008, from http://www.gao.gov/new.items/d09168r.pdf

Haddow, G. D., Bullock, J. A., & Coppola, D. P. (2007). *Introduction to emergency management.* Boston: Elsevier.

Harrald, J. R. (2006). Agility and discipline: Critical success factors for disaster response. *The Annals of the American Academy of Political and Social Science*, *604*(1), 256–272.

Harris, S. (2003). Homeland Security cedes intelligence role. *Government Executive*, February 26. Retrieved December 27, 2008, from http://www.govexec.com/story_page_pf.cfm?articleid=24997&printer friendlyvers=1

Hauer, J. M. (2004). Testimony of Jerome M. Hauer before the National Commission on Terrorist Attacks upon the United States. Retrieved December 26, 2008, from http://www.9-11commission.gov/hearings/ hearing11/hauer_statement.pdf

Hsu, S. S. (2007). States feel left out of disaster planning. *Washington Post*, August 8, A1. Retrieved December 27, 2008, from http://www.washingtonpost.com/wp-dyn/content/article/2007/08/07/ AR2007080702115.html

Hsu, S. S. (2008a). DHS to unveil new disaster response plan; FEMA will regain power; State, local input included. *Washington Post*, January 19, A3.

Hsu, S. S. (2008b, February 28). Virtual fence along border to be delayed; U.S. retooling high-tech barrier after 28-mile pilot project fails. *Washington Post*, A1.

International Association of Emergency Managers. (2007). News release: National Response Framework is not a good replacement for the NRP. November 9. Retrieved December 27, 2008, from http://www.iaem.com/pressroom/documents/IAEMnewsreleaseNRP080907.pdf

Jacobs, B. (2005). Urban vulnerability: Public management in a changing world. *Journal of Contingencies and Crisis Management*, *13*(2), 39–43.

Kamen, A. (2008, November 25). Disasters, recoveries and FEMA. *Washington Post*, A13. Retrieved December 27, 2008, from http://www.washingtonpost.com/wp-dyn/content/article/2008/11/24/AR2008112402461.html?hpid=news-col-blogs

Kendra, J. M., & Wachtendorf, T. (2003). *Creativity in emergency response after the World Trade Center attack. Beyond September 11th: An account of post-disaster research*. Boulder: Natural Hazards Research and Applications Information Center, University of Colorado.

Kendra, J. M., & Wachtendorf, T. (2006). Community innovation and disasters. In H. Rodrìguez, E. L. Quarantelli, & R. R. Dynes (Eds), *Handbook of disaster research* (pp. 316–334). New York: Springer.

Kweit, M. G., & Kweit, R. W. (2006). A tale of two disasters. *Publius*, 36(3), 375–392.

Lagadec, P., & Rosenthal, U. (2003). Critical networks and chaos prevention in highly turbulent times. *Journal of Contingencies and Crisis Management*, *11*(3), 97–98.

Lomnitz, C., & Gibowicz, S. J. (1995). Fundamentals of earthquake prediction. *Pure and applied geophysics*, *145*(2), 363.

Mandell, M. P., (Ed.) (2001). *Getting results through collaboration: Networks and network structures for public policy and management*. Westport: Quorum Books.

May, P. J. (1992). Policy learning and failure. *Journal of Public Policy*, *12*(4), 331–354.

May, P. J., & Williams, W. (1986). *Disaster policy implementation: Managing programs under shared governance*. New York: Plenum Press.

McConnell, A., & Drennan, L. (2006). Mission impossible? Planning and preparing for crisis. *Journal of Contingencies and Crisis Management*, *14*(2), 59–70.

Mendonca, D., & Wallace, W. A. (2004). Studying organizationally-situated improvisation in response to extreme events. *International Journal of Mass Emergencies and Disasters*, *22*(2), 5–29.

Mileti, D. S. (1999). *Disasters by design: A reassessment of natural hazards in the United States*. Washington, DC: Joseph Henry Press.

Monahan, R., & Beaumont, E. H. (2006). Big time security. *Forbes.com*, August 3. Retrieved October 4, 2008, from http://www.forbes.com/business/2006/08/ 02/homeland-security-contracts-cx_rm_0803homeland.html

Murray, M. (2001a). A tough act to follow at FEMA. *National Journal*, *33*(22), 1664–1665.

Murray, M. (2001b). Lessons from a master of disaster. *National Journal*, *33*(2), 133–135.

National Commission on Terrorist Attacks upon the United States. (2004). *The 9/11 Commission Report: Final report of the National Commission on Terrorist Attacks upon the United States*. New York: Norton.

National Research Council, Committee on Socioeconomic Effects of Earthquake. (1978). *A program of studies on the socioeconomic effects of earthquake predictions*. Washington, DC: National Research Council.

New York City Fire Department. (2005). McKinsey Report: Increasing FDNY's Preparedness. Retrieved May 14, 2009, from http://www.nyc.gov/html/fdny/html/mck_report/toc.html

Olshansky, R. B. (2006). Planning after Hurricane Katrina. *Journal of the American Planning Association*, *72*(2), 147–153.

Perrow, C. (2005). *Using organizations: The case of FEMA*. Social Science Research Council 2005. Retrieved November 22, 2005, from http://understandingkatrina.ssrc.org/Perrow/

Perry, R. W., & Lindell, M. K. (2003). Preparedness for emergency response: Guidelines for the emergency planning process. *Disasters*, *27*(4), 336–350.

Perry, R. W., & Quarantelli, E. L. (Eds). (2005). *What is a disaster? New answers to old questions*. Philadelphia: Xlibris.

Quarantelli, E. L. (2005). *Catastrophes are different from disasters: Some implications for crisis planning and managing drawn from Katrina*. Social Science Research Council 2005. Retrieved October 21, 2005, from http://understandingkatrina.ssrc.org/Quarantelli

Rimington, S. (2002). Terrorism did not begin on September 11. *The Guardian*, September 4. Retrieved September 23, 2003, from http://www.guardian.co.uk/print/0,3858,4493943-110340,00.html

Roberts, P. S. (2005). Shifting priorities: Congressional incentives and the Homeland Security granting process. *Review of Policy Research*, *22*(4), 437–449.

Roberts, P. S. (2006). FEMA and the prospects for reputation-based autonomy. *Studies in American Political Development*, *20*(1), 57–87.

Rodriguez, H., Trainor, J., & Quarantelli, E. L. (2006). Rising to the challenges of a catastrophe: The emergent and prosocial behavior following Hurricane Katrina. *Annals of the American Academy of Political and Social Science*, *604*(1), 82–101.

Rose, A. (2007). Economic resilience to natural and manmade disasters: Multidisciplinary origins and contextual dimensions. *Environmental Hazards*, *7*(4), 383–398.

Rubin, C. B. (2000). *Emergency management in the 21st century: Coping with Bill Gates, Osama bin-Laden, and Hurricane Mitch*. Natural Hazards Research Working Paper #104. Boulder: Natural Hazards Research and Applications Information Center, Institute of Behavioral Science, University of Colorado. Retrieved May 14, 2009, from http://www.colorado.edu/hazards/publications/wp/wp104/wp104.html

Rubin, C. B., Cumming, W. B., & Tanali, I. R. (2002). *Terrorism timeline: Major milestone events and their U.S. outcomes (1988–2001)*. Arlington: Claire B. Rubin and Associates.

Scavo, C., Kearney, R. C., & Kilroy, R. J. Jr. (2008). Challenges to federalism: Homeland Security and disaster response. *Publius*, *38*(1), 81–110.

Schneider, S. K. (1990). FEMA, federalism and "Frisco." *Publius*, *20*(3), 97–115.

Schneider, S. K. (1992). Governmental response to disasters: The conflict between bureaucratic procedures and emergent norms. *Public Administration Review*, *52*(March/April), 135–145.

Seed, R. B., Bea, R. G., Abdelmalak, R. I., Athanasopoulos, A. G., Boutwell, G. P., Bray, J. D., et al. (2006). *Investigation of the performance of the New Orleans flood protection systems in Hurricane Katrina on August 29, 2005*. Berkeley: Independent Levee Investigation Team, University of California, Berkeley. Retrieved January 25, 2008, from http://www.ce.berkeley.edu/~new_orleans/report/intro&summary. pdf

Slepicka, L. (2008). FDNY chief says incident command belongs to fire departments. Retrieved December 27, 2008, from http://cms.firehouse.com/web/online/News/ FDNY-Chief-Says-Incident-Command-Belongs-toFire-Departments/46$48995

Tierney, K. J. (2005). *The red pill.* Social Science Research Council. Retrieved November 12, 2006, from http://understandingkatrina.ssrc.org/Tierney/

United States Executive Office of the President, Assistant to the President for Homeland Security and Counterterrorism. (2006). *The federal response to Hurricane Katrina: Lessons learned.* Washington, DC: Executive Office of the President.

United States Office of Homeland Security. (2002). *National strategy for Homeland Security.* Washington, DC: Office of Homeland Security.

Vale, L. J., & Campanella, T. J. (Eds). (2005). *The resilient city: How modern cities recover from disaster.* New York: Oxford University Press.

Wachtendorf, T., & Kendra, J. M. (2005). Improvising disaster in the city of jazz: Organizational response to Hurricane Katrina. Social Science Research Council 2005. Retrieved November 25, 2005, from http://understandingkatrina.ssrc.org/Tierney/

Waugh, W. L., & Streib, G. (2006). Collaboration and leadership for effective emergency management. *Public Administration Review*, *66*(Special Issue, December), 131–140.

Section 4.3

Abolish the Department of Homeland Security

David Rittgers

Executive Summary

After the terrorist attacks of September 11, 2001, Congress created the Department of Homeland Security (DHS), an umbrella organization that would oversee 22 preexisting federal agencies. The idea was to improve the coordination of the federal government's counterterrorism effort, but the result has been an ever-expanding bureaucracy.

DHS has too many subdivisions in too many disparate fields to operate effectively. Agencies with responsibilities for counterfeiting investigations, border security, disaster preparedness, federal law enforcement training, biological warfare defense, and computer incident response find themselves under the same cabinet official. This arrangement has not enhanced the government's competence. Americans are not safer because the head of DHS is simultaneously responsible for airport security and governmental efforts to counter potential flu epidemics.

National defense is a key governmental responsibility, but focusing too many resources on trying to defend every potential terrorist target is a recipe for wasteful spending. Our limited resources are better spent on investigating and arresting aspiring terrorists. DHS responsibilities for aviation security, domestic surveillance, and port security have made it too easy for politicians to disguise pork barrel spending in red, white, and blue. Politicians want to bring money home to their districts, and as a result, DHS appropriations too often differ from what ought to be DHS priorities.

The Department of Homeland Security should be abolished and its components reorganized into more practical groupings. The agencies tasked with immigration, border security, and customs enforcement belong under the same oversight agency, which could appropriately be called the Border Security Administration. The Transportation Security Administration and Federal Air Marshals Service should be abolished, and the federal government should end support for fusion centers. The remaining DHS organizations should return to their former parent agencies.

Terrorism remains a serious problem, but policymakers ought to be more candid with the American public. Instead of pandering to fear and overreacting to every potential threat, policymakers should keep the risk of terrorist attacks in perspective and focus public resources on cost-effective measures.

Introduction

The terrorist attacks on September 11, 2001, prompted numerous changes in American national security policy, including the creation of a Department of Homeland Security (DHS). The rationale for the new cabinet agency was that it would improve the federal government's counterterrorism efforts. Now that several years have passed since its creation, we have an adequate record to assess how the agency has done in that regard. This paper will begin with a brief review of the birth of DHS, and then summarize its structure and organization. The post-9/11 reorganization has failed for several reasons. First, DHS has too many subdivisions in too many disparate fields to operate effectively. Second, DHS spends millions on pork barrel programs that are disguised as counterterrorism measures. Third, DHS duplicates the work of other police agencies and assumes aviation and airport security responsibilities that ought to be handled by the airline industry. Congress should acknowledge its mistake and abolish the Department of Homeland Security.

Creation of the Department of Homeland Security

The idea of a Department of Homeland Security had been proposed even before the September 11 attacks. In early 2001 the U.S. Commission on National Security/21st Century, chaired by former senators Warren Rudman (R-NH) and Gary Hart (D-CO), recommended the creation of a "National Homeland Security Agency" that would bring together the Federal Emergency Management Agency (FEMA), Customs Service, Coast Guard, and Border Patrol in order to prevent and respond to national security threats.[1] The report was one of several competing proposals to reorganize domestic counterterrorism and disaster response capabilities under a single independent agency or a coordinator within either the Executive Office of the President or the Department of justice.[2]

The first step toward what is now known as DHS came about when President Bush formed the Office of Homeland Security following 9/11, an executive branch office intended to facilitate intergovernmental communication to respond to terrorist threats.[3] President Bush appointed former governor Tom Ridge (R-PA) as the first director of homeland security. The same executive order created the Homeland Security Council, a domestic-focused body that would parallel the foreign-oriented National Security Council, with membership to include the president; vice president; attorney general; secretaries of the Treasury, Defense, Health and Human Services, and Transportation; directors of FEMA, the Federal Bureau of Investigation (FBI), and the Central Intelligence Agency (CIA); and the assistant to the president for Homeland Security.

The Homeland Security Council was an unnecessary creation; the National Security Council already had the capability and responsibility to coordinate all of the tasks that have since been delegated to the Homeland Security Council and DHS.[4] The Obama administration's consolidation of the support staff for the National and Homeland Security Councils is a tacit admission of this duplication of effort.[5]

Nevertheless, some members of Congress, led by Sen. Joseph Lieberman (D-CT), believed that the Homeland Security Council provided insufficient government oversight of homeland security and argued for a new cabinet-level position that coordinated and controlled the budget of a number of agencies with terrorism prevention and response capabilities.[6] Though initially resistant to the creation of a new federal agency, President Bush eventually embraced the plan. By mid-2002, White House staffers were meeting to redesign the federal government in what they would later describe as a "rushed and almost random" series of deliberations.[7] In a nod to conservative principles, Bush promised to keep the reorganization revenue-neutral, a proposition that seems laughable in retrospect.[8]

Even as DHS was being proposed, policy experts and White House staffers predicted a painful growth in bureaucracy. The proposal that would eventually determine the department's scope was the fourth of four options proposed to Secretary Ridge by RAND

Corporation expert Michael A. Wermuth.[9] When Ridge chose that option, "Wermuth warned Ridge it was a horrible idea. He spoke of 'train wrecks coming, a clash of cultures . . . you're going to strangle yourself in bureaucracy for years.' "[10]

Harvard security expert Richard Falkenrath played a key role in creating the new bureaucratic structure. He "thought it would be nice to give the new department a research lab" and called a friend to ask which of the three Department of Energy labs would fit the bill. Based on the friend's brief response, the Lawrence Livermore National Laboratory was added to the list, Falkenrath not realizing "that he had just decided to give the new department a thermonuclear weapon simulator."[11] Falkenrath also moved the enforcement duties of the Immigration and Naturalization Service from the Department of Justice to DHS without moving over the immigration judges who presided over deportation hearings, because he did not know there were immigration judges.[12]

Congressional Debate

The congressional hearings that examined the scope of DHS provided indications that lawmakers were moving hastily. Rep. Dan Burton (R-IN), chairman of the House Government Reform Committee, started a hearing by suggesting that DHS would be "a Defense Department for the United States, if you will," seemingly oblivious to the fact that the Department of Defense is the "Defense Department for the United States."[13] While proponents of DHS made claims that the consolidation of agencies would be more efficient and could save money in the long run, Rep. John Duncan (R-TN) said that past predictions of savings and simplification by adding new layers of bureaucracy had not come true. Duncan cited past governmental reorganizations that produced ever-greater spending by the federal government, yet "those departments were created with words saying that they were going to increase efficiency and do away with overlapping and duplication of services and so forth . . . the same things we're hearing now."[14]

Rep. Henry Waxman (D-CA) expressed concerns to then-Homeland Security director Tom Ridge about the size of the proposed organization. "The bill you have proposed includes 21 deputy, under, and assistant secretaries. This is more than double the number of deputy and assistant secretaries at Health and Human Services, which administers a budget that is three times bigger than the budget we expect for this agency. If the objective is not to grow government, why does the new department need so many deputy and assistant secretaries?"[15]

Paul C. Light of the Brookings Institution raised the prospect that DHS would simply be too big a ship to steer. Light focused on the largely unconnected tasks that DHS agencies would perform and highlighted the "50 percent rule," the principle that organizations should only be put under the same umbrella of management if at least 50 percent of their responsibilities overlap.[16] The structure of DHS obviously fails to conform with this principle.

Rep. David Obey (D-WI) questioned the wisdom of having two sets of infectious disease researchers on the government payroll—one at DHS and one at the Department of Health and Human Services: it's "as if you set up two fire departments in the same town and assigned one to handle arson and another fires caused by accident."[17]

In spite of the opposition of a few members of Congress, the Homeland Security Act of 2002 passed by large margins, 299–121 in the House and 90–9 in the Senate.[18]

TABLE 1 Current Structure of the Department of Homeland Security (legacy/parent agency in parentheses)

Original Agency (Department)	Current Agency/Office
The U.S. Customs Service (Treasury)	U.S. Customs and Border Protection (CBP)—inspection, border and ports of entry responsibilities
	U.S. Immigration and Customs Enforcement (ICE)—customs law enforcement responsibilities
The Immigration and Naturalization Service (Justice)	CBP—inspection functions and the U.S. Border Patrol
	ICE—immigration law enforcement: detention and removal, intelligence, and investigations
	U.S. Citizenship and Immigration Services—adjudications and benefits programs
The Federal Protective Service (General Service Administration)	ICE
The Transportation Security Administration (Transportation)	Transportation Security Administration
Federal Law Enforcement Training Center (Treasury)	Federal Law Enforcement Training Center
The Federal Emergency Management Agency (FEMA)	FEMA
Office for Domestic Preparedness (Justice)	Responsibilities distributed within FEMA
Strategic National Stockpile and the National Disaster Medical System (HHS)	Returned to Health and Human Services, July, 2004
Nuclear Incident Response Team (Energy)	Responsibilities distributed within FEMA
Domestic Emergency Support Teams (Justice)	Responsibilities distributed within FEMA
National Domestic Preparedness Office (FBI)	Responsibilities distributed within FEMA
Chemical, Biological, Radiological, Nuclear Countermeasures Programs (Energy)	Science & Technology Directorate
Environmental Measurements Laboratory (Energy)	Science & Technology Directorate
National Biological Warfare Defense Analysis Center (Defense)	Science & Technology Directorate
Plum Island Animal Disease Center (Agriculture)	Science & Technology Directorate
Federal Computer Incident Response Center (GSA)	US-CERT, Office of Cybersecurity and Communications in the National Programs and Preparedness Directorate
National Communications System (Defense)	Office of Cybersecurity and Communications in the National Programs and Preparedness Directorate
National Infrastructure Protection Center (FBI)	Dispersed throughout the department, including Office of Operations Coordination and Office of Infrastructure Protection
Energy Security and Assurance Program (Energy)	Integrated into the Office of Infrastructure Protection
U.S. Coast Guard (Transportation)	U.S. Coast Guard
U.S. Secret Service (Treasury)	U.S. Secret Service

Source: Department of Homeland Security, "Who Became a Part of the Department?" http://www.dhs.gov/xabout/history/editorial_0133.shtm.

Structure of the Department of Homeland Security

Congress transferred a number of federal agencies that had previously been organized under the Departments of Justice, Treasury, Transportation, Agriculture, and Defense to a new umbrella agency, the Department of Homeland Security. Table 1 shows how DHS is currently structured (legacy/parent agency in parentheses).[19]

Consolidating so many agencies and responsibilities creates its own set of problems. As will be discussed below, congressional predictions of unnecessary bureaucracy, duplication of effort, and wasteful spending have come to pass.

A Morass of Inefficiency and Waste

Congress made a dreadful mistake by consolidating unconnected national security responsibilities under DHS. National security is a whole-of-government responsibility that can only be addressed with a subset of the cabinet and the heads of relevant agencies, such as the National Security Council. Indeed, the failings within the federal government leading up to the 9/11 terrorist attacks lay primarily with the CIA and FBI neither of which became a part of DHS.

Creating DHS resulted in an unwieldy organization with too many components. To solve the management issues created by the DHS structure, the federal government is now building a new headquarters to house the capital region components of DHS. And yet DHS headquarters components are too big to fit in the largest D.C.-area government construction project since the Pentagon.

Creating a New Bureaucracy to Fix Problems in Existing Ones

Among the governmental mistakes leading up to the 9/11 attacks was the poor coordination between the FBI and CIA. The *9-11 Commission Report* notes that the CIA missed multiple "operational opportunities" that might have prevented the attacks. The CIA monitored an al Qaeda planning meeting in Kuala Lumpur, Malaysia, in January 2000 but lost track of several attendees who flew to Bangkok.[20] Two of those terrorists, Nawaf al Hamzi and Khalid al Midhar, later flew to Los Angeles. The mishaps in tracking those terrorists—who would later fly American Airlines Flight 77 into the Pentagon—highlights several shortcomings in the intelligence effort against al Qaeda. First, the CIA did not develop a transnational plan for tracking the al Qaeda members at the Kuala Lumpur meeting. Neither did the CIA put either of the two men on a watch list, notify the FBI when the CIA learned that they possessed valid U.S. visas, nor did the CIA notify any other agency when it discovered that al Hamzi had flown to Los Angeles.

The FBI also suffered from internal agency failures: field agents identified many threats, yet FBI supervisors did not act on those warnings. An agent in Phoenix, Arizona, identified the tool that al Qaeda would use on 9/11—hijacked airliners. He sent a memorandum to the New York Field Office warning of the "possibility of a coordinated effort by Usama Bin Ladin" to send students to civil aviation schools in the United States.[21] The agent based his warning on the "inordinate number of individuals of investigative interest" attending local flight schools. FBI agents in the Minneapolis Field Office believed that Zacharias Moussaoui, the convicted "20th hijacker," was an "Islamic extremist preparing for some future act in furtherance of radical fundamentalist goals," and that his plan might involve hijacking a plane. The FBI National Security Law Unit disapproved the Minneapolis Field Office's request for a Foreign Intelligence Surveillance Act (FISA) warrant to search Moussaoui's laptop prior to the 9/11 attacks.

Spending tens of billions of dollars creating the Department of Homeland Security had nothing to do with fixing those errors, but instead created more bureaucracy.

Span of Control

The structure of DHS creates waste and inefficiency. The problem stems from a span of control that is too large and spread across too many disciplines. "Span of control" is a term of art from management theory; it refers to the number of subordinates reporting to a supervisor. Traditional models hold that one manager can effectively lead five or six subordinates, but adding subordinates (or subordinate agencies, in the case of DHS) can lead to reduced performance and morale in the organization. "Spans may be limited by where people are and by the problems of control and communication over distance. Also, a supervisor can exercise more effective control over a broader span in a stable situation than under dynamic conditions."[22] While stable bureaucratic conditions allow for a broader span of control than crisis management, there is a limit to how many organizations can fit under one umbrella and still be effectively managed.

DHS is no stranger to the concept of span of control. Disaster response experts stress that idea when operating the Incident Command System (ICS), a recommended set of emergency management practices:

> The general rule is five subordinate units per supervisory position, although allowance is made to vary this ratio under special circumstances. If tasks are relatively simple or routine, taking place in a small area, communications are good, and the incident character is reasonably stable, then one supervisor may oversee up to eight subordinate units. Conversely, if the tasks are demanding, taking place over a large area, and incident character is changing, then the span of control might be reduced to one supervisor per two or three subordinates.[23]

Somewhat ironically, FEMA, a DHS subordinate administration, teaches this theory in its Emergency Management Institute.[24]

The difficulties of management are compounded by the wide variety of tasks that DHS is expected to perform: disaster response, border security, maritime rescue, biological weapons research, and domestic intelligence analysis, just to name a few. Given the wide geographic distribution of DHS offices and the dynamic nature of its mission, it should come as no surprise that the agency is often criticized as being mismanaged, or that DHS consistently ranks near the bottom of employee surveys on satisfaction with management.[25]

If consolidation of unrelated agencies were an effective way to run government, the cabinet would have just one member responsible for all agencies—the secretary of Government—and be done with it. As George Washington University law professor Jeffrey Rosen points out, the unwieldy amalgamation of nearly two dozen legacy agencies into DHS makes little sense in terms of effective government. "Both [political] parties seem incapable of acknowledging an uncomfortable but increasingly obvious truth: that the Department of Homeland Security was a bureaucratic and philosophical mistake."[26]

The department's 22 federal agencies operate out of 70 buildings at 40 locations in Washington, D.C., and at the time of Rosen's observation in 2008, reported to 88 congressional oversight committees. The situation has worsened. There are now 108 congressional committees, subcommittees, and panels claiming jurisdiction over DHS operations.[27]

DHS is now building a consolidated headquarters in an effort to compensate for the difficulties in managing a large number of agencies at different locations across the national capital region. The $3.4 billion dollar complex in southwest Washington, D.C., will relocate DHS employees to 176 acres at the former grounds of the St. Elizabeth's hospital, including a new $435 million, 1.8-million-square-foot headquarters for the Coast Guard.[28]

Remarkably, DHS has so many components that this gigantic new facility—the largest government construction project since the Pentagon—will still be inadequate. The consolidation would reduce the number of DHS locations in the capital region from the current 46 to a range of 7 to 10, but the multibillion dollar project will only house 14,000 of the 35,000 DHS employees in the D.C. area and is projected to save only $400 million in management expenses over the next 30 years.[29] It seems unlikely that these savings can be projected 30 years out with such certitude.

Costly congressional oversight, employee dissatisfaction, and a new headquarters complex that cannot house all DHS headquarters personnel are not problems that can be addressed with better management or a more efficient staff. The structure of DHS *is* the problem. Congress should not give DHS a massive portfolio of responsibility and then complain about the resulting oversight nightmare. Congress should instead divide the responsibilities of DHS into more manageable groupings. Keeping border security in DHS's successor agency and parceling out preparedness tasks to other cabinet heads (an arrangement that will resemble pre-DHS federal organization) would be a more sensible and workable organization.

Waste in DHS Grant Programs

DHS's creation spurred a growth in spending as well as an increase in bureaucracy. Federal spending on homeland security has increased from $19.5 billion in 2002 to $44.1 billion in 2010.[30] Much of that money was wasted; a recent study by Professors John Mueller and Mark Stewart found that in order to survive a cost-benefit analysis, increased homeland security expenditures "would have to deter, prevent, foil, or protect against 1,667 otherwise successful [attempted Times Square car bomb] type attacks per year, or more than four per day."[31]

Congress has used homeland security as a way to legitimize pork barrel spending, most evidently in the $34 billion in DHS grants to states and localities over the last nine years.[32] These grant programs exhibit the pathologies common to other grant programs, such as extravagant overspending, encouraging state and local officials to devote their time lobbying (or hiring grant management personnel to get more grants) instead of solving problems, and unfair redistribution of taxpayer money among states.[33] The amorphous threat of terrorism and aggregation of so many responsibilities under DHS encourages wasteful spending. Economist Veronique de Rugy describes this as "the political effect of the phrase *homeland security,* which tends to short-circuit skepticism. Even DHS activities unrelated to homeland security are apt to see their funding increase, on the assumption that they have something to do with the function indicated by the department's name."[34]

DHS grants are structured so that members of Congress from both urban and rural areas end up with pots of money to allocate to certain constituents. The two main grant programs, the Urban Areas Security Initiative (UASI) and the State Homeland Security Program (SHSP), benefiting urban and rural areas respectively, guarantee a handout to every state.[35] Current statutory language requires a minimum of one quarter of UASI and SHSP funds be devoted to counterterrorism efforts. SHSP funding is doled out regardless of population, giving rural and less populous states higher per-capita expenditures. Budgeting without regard for population density, critical infrastructure, or other potential risk assessment metrics guarantees wasteful spending. After all, al Qaeda has focused its attacks almost exclusively in urban areas.[36]

In the first year of DHS grant funding, SHSP programs took the lion's share of the funds, netting $2 billion, while UASI funds amounted to almost $600 million.[37] The SHSP provision of equal funds to all of the states, regardless of population or anticipated threats, proved an easy sell for rural representatives and senators.

Here are some examples of the reckless spending:

- Knox County, Ohio (population 54,500), used over $100,000 in homeland security grant funds to purchase a hazardous materials trailer and a truck to tow it. The equipment sat unused and was later sold because of high maintenance costs. "I think it was a total waste of taxpayer dollars from the federal government on down," County Commissioner Tom McLarnan said. "A total waste."[38]
- A California urban area acquired 55 large-screen digital televisions costing $74,394 as part of a new training system for its fusion center. Inspectors discovered that the state had purchased the televisions but not the associated training software. "On the day [the inspectors] visited, all of the televisions were being used to monitor the same television station."[39]
- Bennington, New Hampshire (population 1,273), received $6,500 for chemical weapons suits.[40]
- Rear Admiral Harvey Johnson, commander of Coast Guard's District Seven in Miami, decided his official residence wasn't stylish enough, opting for a "6,200-square-foot, four-bedroom, four-bath home that costs taxpayers $111,600 per year in lease payments. Utilities, maintenance, and other upkeep (such as the cleaning service for the backyard swimming pool) are extra."[41]
- Grand Forks, North Dakota (population 52,838), has more biochemical suits and gas masks than police officers to wear them. Mason County, Washington (population 60,699), purchased a $63,000 hazardous materials decontamination unit, even though it has no hazmat team.[42]
- Members of Congress inserted a $15 million earmark for a border checkpoint upgrade in the tiny village of Whitetail, Montana (population 71).[43] The border checkpoint in Westhope, North Dakota, which serves an average of 73 people a day, also received $15 million for an upgrade.[44] The border checkpoints at Laredo, Texas, serving 55,000 travelers and 4,200 trucks daily, and processing $116 billion in goods annually, were rated the government's highest priority but received no additional money.[45]

Aware of the gold-rush pathology in DHS grant programs, Congress has reduced the amount of state-directed SHSP funding[46] and changed formulas mandating spending ratios to the states.[47]

Congress can do more. If SHSP grants were eliminated, taxpayers would save over $500 million a year at current funding levels.[48] The case for doing this is strong; the lack of a risk assessment and uniform treatment of all jurisdictions make this program an unequivocal handout to the states. At a minimum, SHSP grants should be restructured in one of two ways: (1) rural terrorism targets should apply for funds and compete based on neutral risk assessments as urban jurisdictions are required to do; or (2) grants should be reduced to a level of funding that would force states to prioritize public monies toward anti-terrorism efforts that survive a cost-benefit analysis. As an initial benchmark, members of Congress could eliminate all SHSP funding except for the levels required to meet the current law enforcement terrorism prevention activities minimum, which by law must compose a quarter of SHSP funds. Doing so would reduce the federal budget by $394 million, and lawmakers would be able to defend their fiscal restraint with the honest statement that they had not reduced funds devoted to state and local counterterrorism efforts by a penny.[49]

But even though Congress reduced handouts to the states under SHSP several years after the program's inception, they increased the funding of the urban-oriented UASI program and loosened restrictions on "urban" spending, allowing more areas to qualify for those funds. UASI began in 2003 by providing funds for seven large cities that make obvious terrorism targets but then quickly expanded to provide funds for 23 more urban areas. By FY 2010, the number was up to 64 urban areas and $832 million. Smaller cities such as Bakersfield, California (population 347,483), qualified for money under UASI, a far cry from the original intent of the program.[50]

The rapid expansion of UASI grants pushed funds to unlikely terrorism targets. A June 2008 Government Accountability Office (GAO) report found that while the Tier I UASI grants (obvious targets such as Los Angeles; New York; and Washington, D.C.) were based on reasonable findings of risk, the Tier II UASI grants (the remaining 50+ cities) were not. "Rather, DHS considered all states and urban areas equally vulnerable to a successful attack and assigned every state and urban area a vulnerability score of 1.0 in the risk analysis model, which does not take into account any geographic differences."[51] A subsequent GAO report in 2009 found that DHS provided few useful metrics to justify the money spent. "FEMA's assessments do not provide a means to measure the effect UASI regions' projects have on building regional preparedness capabilities—the goal of the UASI program."[52]

Congress has begun to move UASI spending in the right direction. The FY 2011 budget, passed halfway through the fiscal year, reduced funding to $663 million: $540 million for the 11 Tier I cities and $121 million for 20 Tier II cities.[53] This spending reduction is long overdue, but Congress can do better. Proposed grant budgets for FY2012 provide for $1 billion in total grants, a two-thirds reduction from historical levels, but the cuts face heavy opposition.[54]

If the al-Qaeda network can be defeated by giving federal funds to localities for unused biological warfare equipment, armored vehicles, and extravagant checkpoints at barely-used border crossings, then the United States can declare victory now. Of course al Qaeda can't be defeated this way, and leaders in Congress should stop using homeland security grants as a way to direct money into their home districts. Homeland security grant programs can be significantly reduced without endangering public safety.

Flying the Unfriendly Skies

DHS expenditures in aviation security deserve particular scrutiny. Most aviation security funds are spent on static defensive measures that are susceptible to waste, questionable in their potential for success, or may be more effectively delivered by the private sector than the government. Moreover, the controversial Advanced Imaging Technology (AIT) units, or "body scanners," fail a cost-benefit analysis. Congress should privatize airport screeners and pass the financial burden of passenger aviation security from the taxpayer to the flying public.

Prior to 9/11, airports and airlines were responsible for airport screening. In the wake of the terrorist attacks, Congress enacted the Aviation and Transportation Security Act, which (1) created the Transportation Security Administration (TSA), (2) federalized airline passenger screening, (3) expanded the Federal Air Marshal Service, and (4) mandated the installation of hardened cockpit doors.[55] Since the TSA took over, the number of airport screeners on the federal payroll has grown from 20,000 to 48,000.[56]

Aviation security in the United States is on the wrong track because it is viewed by policymakers as a public good when it is in fact a private good. Aviation security measures continue to escalate in intrusiveness and cost without regard for cost-effectiveness because the American taxpayer is always footing the bill. Once privatized, only cost-effective security programs will be retained, and the flying public will have the level of security that it is willing to pay for.

From Shoe Checks to Body Scanners

When terrorist plots directed at commercial aviation became more inventive, aviation security authorities adopted reactive pre-screening procedures. For example, after Richard Reid's attempted detonation of a "shoe bomb," the TSA announced new rules requiring airline passengers to remove their shoes for explosive screening or x-ray analysis. And after authorities discovered a plot to bring liquid explosives onto airliners in 2006, the TSA placed restrictions on the quantity of liquids in passengers' carry-on luggage.

The latest trend in airport security is the use of "body scanner" machines that can see beneath the traveler's clothing.[57] Current policy allows for the screening of all passengers by either (1) body scanner machines or (2) magnetometer screening supplemented with a "pat-down" search. Advocates of body scanners argue that explosives hidden under clothing, such as the bomb carried by Farouk Abdulmutallab in the attempted Christmas Day bombing in 2009, require expanded use of body scanners.[58]

Yet the case for body scanners has been overstated. In a recent study, academics Mark G. Stewart and John Mueller assumed that body scanner technology had a 50 percent chance of successfully accomplishing each of the following three tasks: (1) preventing a suicide bomber from boarding an aircraft; (2) preventing detonation of an explosive device because the use of the AIT prevented bomb construction with detectable and reliable materials; and (3) preventing a suicide bomber from getting a bomb past security that was large enough to down an aircraft.[59] The study concluded that to be cost-effective, body scanner machines "every two years would have to disrupt more than one attack effort with body-borne explosives that otherwise would have been successful despite other security measures, terrorist incompetence and amateurishness, and the technical difficulties in setting off a bomb sufficiently destructive to down an airliner."[60]

The GAO's review of body scanners found that "it remains unclear whether the [body scanner technology] would have been able to detect the weapon Abdulmutallab used in his attempted attack."[61] Body scanners are effective in detecting high-density objects (such as guns, knives), and hard explosives (such as C-4), but less so with low-density materials like thin plastics, gels, powders, and liquids. Airplane bombing plots have already focused on liquid explosives.[62] An undercover TSA agent recently snuck a firearm through AIT machines at the Dallas/Fort Worth International Airport several times, showing a weak point of the system—the attentiveness of the officers monitoring the machine, a weakness not shared by the traditional metal detector system.[63]

Another weakness of body scanner technology is that it can be easily defeated by terrorists who are willing to place explosives *inside* their bodies. As one commenter notes, "all males have a body cavity. Females have two body cavities. In prisons, these body cavities are habitually used to smuggle drugs and improvised weapons past body searches, including strip searches."[64]

Terrorists have already employed explosives hidden in a body cavity, but not yet on an airplane. On August 28, 2009, Prince Mohammed bin Nayef, the Saudi deputy Interior minister and leader of that nation's counterterrorism efforts, survived an attempted assassination.[65] Abdullah Hassan Taleh al-Asiri, a member of al Qaeda in the Arabia Peninsula, the same organization that sponsored failed Christmas Day bomber Abdulmutallab,[66] detonated a bomb hidden inside his anal cavity while meeting with Prince Mohammed to discuss the terms of Asiri's "surrender" to the Saudi kingdom and entry into an amnesty program. While the attack only injured Prince Mohammed, terrorists might use the same method to smuggle explosives aboard a plane, remove them in the plane's restroom, and place them against the hull of the aircraft.

For all of the above reasons, spending large amounts of money on body scanners is a wasteful use of counterterrorism dollars. Canceling a broader implementation of body scanners will result in some savings: the TSA has installed almost 500 scanners, and hopes to install up to 1,000 by the end of 2011, at a cost of $150,000 to $180,000 per unit.[67] The real savings are in personnel costs, where taxpayers can save $340 million annually by simply not hiring the additional employees that are needed to operate body scanner machines.[68]

Taxpayers should also stop footing the bill for more body scanner machines because they may be paying for another form of the technology within a few years. DHS revealed in July 2011 that al Qaeda in the Arabian Peninsula was interested in surgically implanting bombs in the human body, sparking discussion of the next generation of scanner technology, one that will see *through* the human body.[69] If unsuccessful terrorist attempts to acquire and employ sophisticated technology such as weapons of mass destruction are any indicator, this threat is hyped beyond terrorists' ability to actually deliver such a weapon.[70] In any event, surgically implanted bombs may not prove effective in bringing down an airplane; as the attempted Saudi assassination demonstrates, the bearer of the bomb absorbs a significant amount of the bomb's force. The decision to purchase the next generation of body scanners should be borne by the aviation industry and the flying public, where it will face more intense scrutiny than in Congress.

Constitutional Questions and Mission Creep

TSA checkpoints were established to thwart terrorists, but that objective does not make all TSA actions proper. Current screening practices—AIT machines or full body pat-downs—push at the boundaries of constitutional principles governing searches and seizures. In some instances, screeners have expanded their searches to discover evidence of *any* crime or wrongdoing, an unconstitutional practice beyond the TSA's limited aviation security authority.

The Constitution bars government authorities from engaging in unreasonable searches and seizures. While the Supreme Court has upheld brief, suspicionless seizures at highway checkpoints to deter drunk driving[71] and to intercept illegal immigrants,[72] checkpoints may not be employed to pursue general crime control.[73] Airport searches, however, are administrative in nature and individuals entering certain areas of an airport have a reduced expectation of privacy.[74] Taking the special needs of aviation security into consideration, federal courts have held that suspicionless searches of all passengers prior to boarding are constitutionally permissible.[75]

AIT scanners were designed as a secondary screening device, but their use as a primary means of passenger screening fails the legal tests set forth by federal courts. Courts have consistently upheld blanket application of a magnetometer—a "metal detector"—as a means of primary screening, with use of a metal detection wand or pat-down for those who set off the magnetometer.[76] As law professor Jeffrey Rosen points out, the language of the decisions upholding the pre-AIT screening regime may lead a court to conclude that the newer (and more intrusive) screening regime is unconstitutional.[77] One federal appellate court held in 2007 that "a particular airport screening search is constitutionally reasonable provided that it 'is no more extensive nor intensive than necessary, in light of the current technology, to detect the presence of weapons or explosives.'"[78] In 2006 then-judge (now Supreme Court justice) Samuel Alito likewise ruled that a magnetometer (primary) and wand (secondary) screening regime was "minimally intrusive" and "well-tailored to protect personal privacy."[79]

The Electronic Privacy Information Center (EPIC) filed suit against DHS on the basis of the primary-secondary screening issue, claiming that "the TSA body scanner rule subjects all travelers to the most invasive search available as primary screening, without any escalation."[80] While the D.C. Circuit rejected this argument and constitutional objections, it did order the TSA to go through a notice-and-comment rulemaking procedure, which will force that agency to respond to public complaints about the invasiveness and effectiveness of screening procedures.[81]

Ultimately, this controversy may be settled by technology, not a federal court. Software is available that renders a stick-figure image of a person passing through an AIT machine, and a red dot on the image highlights potential threats for secondary screening.[82] This modification greatly reduces privacy concerns for passengers, and implementation of this software may blunt criticism of AIT scanners.

The fact that the federal government is the primary provider of airport screening creates concerns other than revealing body scanner images, particularly when TSA screeners unlawfully detain travelers or look for evidence of crimes outside of the aviation security field.

A consistent body of checkpoint case law bars TSA screeners from looking for evidence of crimes beyond plots against aviation security, a reminder that persons do not surrender all liberties or expectations of privacy while traveling.[83] Courts will exclude evidence obtained by checkpoint searches that exceed the scope of TSA's aviation security mission.[84]

Checkpoint mission creep prompted a policy change after agents harassed Steven Bierfeldt, a staffer for Campaign for Liberty, a nonprofit libertarian political organization. Bierfeldt had just left a convention in Missouri and was flying out of Lambert-St. Louis International Airport when he was subjected to an unlawful detention by TSA screeners.[85] Bierfeldt was carrying $4,700 in a lockbox from the sale of tickets, apparel, and paraphernalia associated with Campaign for Liberty. TSA screeners considered that amount of cash suspicious, and took Bierfeldt to a private screening room to interrogate him, threatening him with arrest and prosecution unless he revealed the source and purpose of the money. Bierfeldt was eventually released, but he surreptitiously recorded the detention and questioning with his cell phone.

The American Civil Liberties Union (ACLU) filed suit on Bierfeldt's behalf, alleging that "TSA agents are instructed as a matter of standard operating procedure to search for 'contraband' beyond weapons and explosives," a practice that exceeds TSA's statutory authority.[86] In response to the lawsuit, the TSA revised its screening guidelines in the fall of 2009.[87] The new directives tell TSA employees that "screening may not be conducted to detect evidence of crimes unrelated to transportation security."[88]

Yet there is reason to suspect that the revision of screening policies has not deterred TSA employees from fishing for contraband or evidence of crimes beyond the agency's aviation security mandate. TSA screeners scrutinized Kathy Parker, a business manager, in apparent violation of the new guidelines while she was departing from Philadelphia International Airport.[89] Parker was carrying an envelope with a deposit slip and $8,000 worth of checks made out to her and her husband. As Philadelphia police officers joined the TSA screeners, Parker was told that they suspected her of embezzling the money and leaving town in a "divorce situation" because the checks were "almost sequential." Only after police tried unsuccessfully to contact her husband by phone did they decide to release Parker and allow her to leave the security checkpoint. Clearly this detention had nothing to do with aviation security.

Some experts advocate an adoption of Israeli-style interrogations in lieu of body scanners or other technological approaches, an invitation to more TSA mission creep.[90] This methodology could not be scaled up from the relatively small Israeli aviation market and applied in the United States without at least quintupling (probably more) the TSA's annual budget.[91] In spite of this, the TSA has recently started a pilot program at Logan International Airport in Boston that uses brief interrogations to identify potential threats.[92] This expansion of the preexisting Screening of Passengers by Observation Techniques (SPOT) program seems unlikely to ferret out any terrorists. SPOT has helped arrest 2,000 criminals since 2003, but none have been charged with terrorism.[93] Encouraging behavioral screening may produce more nonterrorism arrests, but it will also produce false positives that burden the flying public with the prospect of detention and law enforcement investigation, all based on the hunch of a TSA screener. And as the Bierfeldt and Parker cases demonstrate, these hunches may be based on poor judgment and exceed the TSA's limited aviation security mission.

TSA mission creep is not limited to airports, as trains, buses, boats, and subways may soon have airport-style security.[94] Placing checkpoints on these other forms of mass transit also represents a costly reversal of policy. Former secretary of Homeland Security Michael Chertoff opposed expansion of airport procedures to bus and train terminals after the London commuter bombings because of the insurmountable cost of defending an enormous number of transit targets.[95] The trial deployment of a joint DHS team to a Tampa bus station gave a preview of what expanded TSA jurisdiction would look like.[96] Officers from TSA checked passengers for bombs, Customs and Border Protection (CBP) agents checked the immigration status of travelers, and Immigration and Customs Enforcement (ICE) agents looked for drugs and large amounts of cash. Although those activities are conducted separately on a routine basis, the synergistic effect of surrendering privacy on multiple fronts presents exactly the kind of general law enforcement checkpoint that the Constitution was written to prevent.

Privatize Aviation Security

The clearest way to reduce spending on airport screening and prevent TSA mission creep is to re-privatize airport security. That would save $3 billion and place financial responsibility for security where it belongs—with the passengers, airlines, and airports, not the taxpayer.[97]

Using private passenger screeners in lieu of TSA employees will provide savings for the taxpayer without reducing aviation security. Contract screeners are already employed at over a dozen airports under the Screening Partnership Program (SPP).[98] BearingPoint, a management and consulting contractor, conducted a study of the SPP airports and found that those screeners performed consistent with or better than TSA screeners, while screening costs were marginally reduced in most cases.[99] TSA has consistently argued that private sector screeners would be more expensive, but the GAO questioned the TSA's methodology in comparing airport screening costs.[100]

Allowing airports the latitude to organize and manage their own security will further increase performance. The GAO response to the TSA pilot program assessment found that while "TSA officials said they had not granted contract officials more flexibility because they wanted to ensure that procedures were standardized, well coordinated, and consistently implemented throughout all airports to achieve consistent security," the airports employed practices that "enabled the private screening contractors to achieve efficiencies that are not currently available at airports with federal screeners."[101]

Private passenger screening will also reduce costs because of the two-tier security in place; while TSA employees conduct the bulk of passenger screening, cargo screening and other aviation security duties remain the responsibilities of airports. Removing this artificial separation of responsibility would allow airports to reduce costs further.

Unionization Will Not Improve Aviation Security

Unfortunately, the TSA is limiting the Screening Partnership Program to the 16 airports currently involved,[102] and TSA screeners are unionizing.[103] Unionization of airport security will put a flawed set of incentives in place: if employees know that they can be fired for ineffectiveness in screening, they are more likely to remain alert. The same cannot be said for federal employees, who are notoriously hard to fire.[104] Indeed, a recent analysis by *USA Today* found that some workers are more likely to die of natural causes than get laid off or fired.[105]

Just as it has harmed Customs and Border Protection (CBP), unionization will weaken aviation security. The Federal Labor Relations Authority (FLRA), the appellate authority for collective bargaining arbitrations, has gone overboard in upholding CBP employee grievances on basic issues of performance and discipline. For example, the FLRA upheld an arbitrator's decision to overturn a three-day suspension for falling asleep on the job.[106] The FLRA also upheld an employee grievance against changing the number of hours of remedial firearms training when a Border Patrol agent is deficient in firearms qualification.[107]

CBP is also required to negotiate with union representatives on the reassignment of employees, a problematic requirement in the aviation security context.[108] Air carriers already move faster than the TSA when changing schedules and volume on routes, creating a local surplus or deficit of screeners until the TSA can shift employees.[109] A recent congressional study highlighted the use of the National Deployment Force, a pool of TSA screeners that deploy to offset seasonal demand and other labor shortages at non-SPP airports, at significant additional cost to cover travel expenses.[110] Allowing TSA screeners to engage in collective bargaining will further hamper the ability of that bureaucracy to adapt to changing circumstances. Congress should privatize airport screening rather than see it burdened by collective bargaining.

Real Privatization

Real privatization would not, however, merely consist of expanding the Screening Partnership Program. In SPP airports, TSA picks the contractor that will provide screening services, pays the contractor, and ensures that the contracted screeners apply TSA screening protocols.[111] Real privatization would allow airports and airlines to decide who will provide passenger screening and pay for security with private, not public, funds.

The biggest obstacle to re-privatization of airport security is that private aviation stakeholders—airlines, airports, and screening contractors—do not want to bear legal responsibility for a terrorist attack. With regard to liability, there are two options facing policymakers. If aviation security liability must be limited in order to move toward a free market model, Congress has already created a path for doing so. Airports and security contracting firms can apply for certification under the Support Anti-Terrorism by Fostering Effective Technologies (SAFETY) Act, a federal law that limits their liability.[112]

The better answer is that airport and airline liability should not be capped. Limiting liability handicaps the market incentives that provide for effective security. The insurance industry and businesses in general have adapted to terrorism. A recent insurance study found that 27 percent of businesses purchased terrorism insurance in 2003, whereas 61 percent purchase it now.[113] Terrorism insurance rates have dropped consistently since the 2001 attacks, and firms can now insure a $303 million property for $9,541 per year, a small fraction of total insurance costs.[114] The commercial aviation industry can—and should—provide its own security.

Air Marshals versus Flight Deck Officers: A Cost-Benefit Analysis of Deterrence

Aviation security funding is often misspent. The federal government allocates funds for armed personnel on passenger flights through two programs: (1) the Federal Air Marshal

Service (FAMS), and (2) the Federal Flight Deck Officer (FFDO) program, which arms pilots to repel hijackers.[115] The idea of having an air marshal present to deal with any terrorist attack on passenger aviation is attractive. Unfortunately, the reality is that air marshals cost too much to protect even a small fraction of aviation traffic, and terrorist attacks on aviation have largely moved away from hijacking to bombing. Federal counter-hijacking efforts should focus on arming pilots and abolishing FAMS.

The number of air marshals increased from 33 in 2001 to an undisclosed number in the thousands over the last nine years (the actual number of air marshals is classified). The Federal Air Marshal Service has produced little on such a large investment, and the service can be cut without negatively affecting aviation security. The service averages 4.2 arrests each year, and current appropriations are $860 million, meaning that each arrest costs an average of $215 million.[116]

To be sure, arrests are not the only metric that matters; the *potential* of having a police agent trained in rapid close-quarters marksmanship is itself a deterrent to hijacking. But the deterrent achieved must be weighed against the cost. With air marshals covering no more than 10 percent of the passenger flights in the United States, policymakers must consider whether $860 million is worth (at best) a one-in-ten chance of having an air marshal present to counter any particular terrorist plot.[117] Post-9/11 proposals to place, as Israel has, air marshals on all flights, would prove exorbitantly ex-pensive.[118] Assuming that costs remain proportional, moving from 10 percent coverage to placing air marshals on all flights would cost $8.6 billion annually—more than is currently spent on the whole of the TSA.

One study, which assumed air marshal presence on 10 percent of all flights, still found that the cost per life saved was $180 million, far more than the $1 million to $10 million that the Office of Management and Budget recommends. Hardened cockpit doors proved more cost-effective, with an estimated $800,000 spent per life saved.[119]

Arming pilots is a cost-effective alternative to air marshals. Commercial pilots have volunteered in significant numbers for the FFDO program, only to face repeated bureaucratic obstacles.[120] Seventy percent of commercial pilots have military experience with firearms.[121] And while the training requirements for FFDO status are lower than those for an air marshal, the FFDO role is different; he or she is merely trying to prevent terrorist access to the cockpit, a much simpler task than the arrest of hijackers in the passenger compartment. Economist John Lott notes that "terrorists can only enter the cockpit through one narrow entrance, and armed pilots have some time to prepare themselves as hijackers penetrate the strengthened cockpit doors."[122] The firearm storage policy imposed on FFDOs, which requires them to put a padlock through the trigger guard of the handgun while it is in its holster, creates the foreseeable risk of pressing the trigger against the lock and has already caused one accidental discharge in the cockpit of an airliner.[123] This requirement should be removed and the FFDO program expanded (or the certification for arming pilots simply left to the airlines) to provide additional deterrence to would-be hijackers at significantly reduced expense. TSA spends $25 million each year on FFDO and crew training and $860 million on air marshals.[124] Congress should abolish the Federal Air Marshals Service. If airlines believe that this program is worth funding, they should be free to replicate it on their flights, passing the cost on to their passengers—and not the taxpayers.

Arming counter-hijacking personnel is only a small part of the security picture. As security expert Bruce Schneier notes, "only two effective countermeasures were taken in the wake of 9/11: strengthening cockpit doors and passengers learning they need to fight back."[125] Airline passengers have taken an active part in thwarting terrorist attackers, such as "shoebomber" Richard Reid in 2001, and Farouk Abdulmutallab in 2009. In both instances, passengers quickly tackled the would-be bombers when foul play was suspected. Airline passengers' heightened alertness post-9/11 is also evident in the many instances where they have subdued unruly or intoxicated fellow travelers.[126] While TSA director John Pistole has called TSA screeners the "last line of defense,"[127] the TSA website actually bestows that honor on the passengers, listing them as the last of 21 layers of aviation security.[128] Airlines recently asked that air marshals be moved out of first-class seats, a tacit recognition that the nature of the terrorist threat to aviation has changed from hijacking to in-flight explosives.[129] Policymakers should go further and simply abolish the Federal Air Marshal Service.

Reforming Domestic Counterterrorism

The post-9/11 increase in funding for counterterrorism intelligence has not necessarily resulted in a proportional increase in security gains. There are two problems. First, the growth of the intelligence community has created considerable overlap in intelligence responsibilities, and that overlap has impeded the identification of national security threats. Second, agencies with new domestic counterterrorism responsibilities have an incentive to over-report potential threats in order to justify their continued existence.

Using Constitutional Filters to Focus on Viable Leads

When police investigative methods are used within our constitutional framework, they can be effective against terrorists in the United States. Individuals engaging in terrorist acts will invariably violate criminal laws. In that sense, domestic counterterrorism is domestic law enforcement.

The Code of Federal Regulations provides a definition for "terrorism" with two components: an act, "the unlawful use of force and violence against persons or property," united with an intent, "to intimidate or coerce a government, the civilian population, or any segment thereof, in furtherance of political or social objectives."[130] The simple expression of political views, however bizarre or vile, does not fall within the parameters of the terrorism statute. The law does not require a successful terrorist attack before an arrest can be made; conspiracies to commit a crime of violence are also unlawful, and can be investigated in order to prevent attacks from occurring in the first place.

The Constitution provides a filter for identifying worthwhile leads. That filter is probable cause.[131] The probable cause requirement is a help, not a hindrance, to effective law enforcement and domestic counter-terrorism. As former undercover FBI agent Mike German puts it, "requiring the police to present evidence of probable cause to a neutral arbitrator before a search or arrest simply ensures the police will not waste time searching for nonexistent evidence and bothering innocent people."[132]

Each terrorist attack is followed by a predictable lament that intelligence officials were unable to "connect the dots." The problem may be increasingly one not of internal hurdles that prevent officials from talking to each other to connect the dots, but an obsession on collecting as many dots as possible, making effective analysis impossible. Collecting the dots is a necessary part of police work and counterterrorism, but without a filter to determine which dots add up to an indication of terrorist intent, collecting more dots will be counterproductive.

Many investigations begin with the gathering of information on otherwise lawful activity that, when aggregated and analyzed, seems to give an indication of criminal intent or action. Buying a ski mask or a gun is lawful, but government surveillance of all of those with guns or ski masks would be an absurd way to try to identify potential bank robbers. Millions of false positives would be produced. So too with purchases of box cutters and airplane tickets. The 9/11 hijackers were more readily identifiable by an indicator more closely connected with an intent to do harm—an interest in flight schools.

The FBI organizes domestic counterterrorism efforts under Joint Terrorism Task Forces (JTTFs), which are partnerships between local, state, and federal law enforcement agencies. DHS subordinate agencies, such as the Secret Service and Immigrations and Customs Enforcement, provide agents to JTTFs.

Good police work has produced hundreds of terrorism convictions since 2001.[133] Police officers have successfully infiltrated or conducted surveillance of suspicious groups to prevent attacks, and investigated attacks after they have happened in order to prosecute terrorists. Domestic counterterrorism is a law enforcement function, and keeping government within the bounds dictated by the Constitution is both more likely to apprehend real terrorists and avoid labeling large portions of the American public as threats to national security.

Adding More Hay to the Haystack Does Not Help the Government Identify Terrorists

The growth in intelligence spending since 2001 has resulted in such a massive amount of intelligence reporting that no one in government can make serious use of it.[134] Intelligence officials readily admit that the amount of information gathered is unwieldy. As one senior official has said, "I'm not going to live long enough to be briefed on everything."[135]

The attempted Christmas Day bombing of an international flight by Farouk Abdulmutallab in 2009 demonstrated how a massive collection of intelligence can actually be counterproductive. Before the attack took place, President Obama ordered a secret military task force to Yemen to track down leaders of al Qaeda in the Arabian Peninsula. The task force began to collect information about the terrorist organization for analysis, hoping to pinpoint the threat and then preempt it. As the *Washington Post* reported, "that was the system as it was intended. But when the information reached the National Counterterrorism Center (NCTC) in Washington for analysis, it came buried within the 5,000 pieces of general terrorist-related data that are reviewed each day. Analysts had to switch from database to database, from hard drive to hard drive, from screen to screen, just to locate information that might warrant further study."[136]

As terrorist activity increased, "the flood of information into the NCTC became a torrent." Vague clues about a "Nigerian radical who had gone to Yemen" and the "report of a father in Nigeria worried about a son who had become interested in radical teachings and had disappeared inside Yemen" were lost in the deluge of information. Abdulmutallab left Yemen, boarded a plane in Amsterdam bound for Detroit, and was fortuitously tackled by a passenger as he tried to detonate explosives hidden within his pants. In this case, as in many others, the last line of defense—airline passengers—succeeded where government had failed.

Case Study: The Rise of Fusion Centers

Fusion centers are state, local, and regional information- and intelligence-sharing institutions that were created to improve the flow of information between law enforcement agencies. Federal guidelines published by the departments of Justice and Homeland Security define them as "a collaborative effort of two or more agencies that provide resources, expertise, and information to the center with the goal of maximizing their ability to detect, prevent, investigate, and respond to criminal and terrorist activity."[137]

Local officials created fusion centers in order to work around the problem of FBI policies that precluded sharing information with local and state agencies. Local officers working in a JTTF are barred from sharing information with their parent organization. Fusion centers, formed initially as partnerships between state and local entities, do not have these information-sharing restrictions, and so they grew in number and scope as a result.

Traditional law enforcement standards of investigation, intended to comply with constitutional requirements, filter out bad information and narrow investigations down to productive leads. Fusion centers, however, exemplify the trend in overspending and duplication of effort in counterterrorism intelligence.

Fusion center supporters have difficulty demonstrating the need for continued funding for their operations. When asked by the *Washington Post* for some examples of fusion center successes, one state official cited the arrest and detention of a Muslim man for videotaping the Chesapeake Bay Bridge.[138] The man, an American citizen, was ultimately released and was not charged with a crime.

Another case frequently cited as a fusion center success did not even require fusion center involvement.[139] In 2005 four men were arrested for a plot to bomb buildings in the Los Angeles area. Los Angeles police officers tracked a cell phone left behind at an armed robbery, then arrested the man and an accomplice after the pair conducted another stickup. The search of the primary suspect's apartment revealed knives, bulletproof vests, jihadist propaganda, and documents outlining a plan for a terrorist attack. A phone call to federal counterterrorism authorities led to two additional arrests. In this instance, the advertised "benefit" of fusion centers was really the ability of a local police officer (who was not working in a fusion center) to *call the FBI*. Repeating that sort of success does not require an additional layer of bureaucracy—all that is needed is the training of local and state police officers as to what may constitute evidence of a terrorist plot.

Although local and state authorities play a key role in preventing and responding to terrorist threats, the FBI already has a "no terrorism lead goes unaddressed" policy that makes fusion centers a bureaucratic redundancy.[140] The burden should be on DHS to show why claimed fusion center successes are a result of their unique duplication of FBI effort, and why coordination of counterterrorism information should not be centered in JTTFs or FBI Field Intelligence Groups instead.[141]

In 2007 the ACLU published a report that highlighted several bureaucratic realities underlying the creation of fusion centers.[142] First, it would be expensive for police officers who do not work for the federal government to get and maintain security clearances.[143] Second, state and local agencies correctly surmised that they have a role in preventing terrorist attacks and created fusion centers to share information and fill this role. Third, it also seems likely that DHS officials felt a need to create a domestic intelligence capability in order to be taken seriously by the Department of Justice and FBI on counterterrorism matters.

A good example of this duplication of effort is the Los Angeles fusion center, the Joint Regional Intelligence Center (JRIC). The JRIC maintains a squad known as CT-6, which vets all but the obviously worthless tips. Since the FBI Joint Terrorism Task Forces have an identical procedure, it seems wasteful to have a JTTF and the JRIC in the same city, possibly pursuing the same leads. If the two entities coordinate which of them will pursue individual tips, something that seems likely with the presence of FBI agents in the JRIC, then this undermines the argument for creating fusion centers in the first place. One fusion center expert likens a lack of FBI-fusion center coordination to a reinstatement of the bureaucratic barriers that left America vulnerable to al Qaeda's attack: "Without [an FBI-fusion center] loop, we're operating the way things were before 9/11, where we uncovered the dots, but don't connect them in time."[144] Eliminating fusion centers would route terrorism information into one pipeline instead of two.

The use of local officers affiliated with a JTTF to screen tips is a sensible employment of resources; if the FBI were to modify some of its classification policies so that local agencies would have the benefit of information from such squads within the JTTF, then it seems unlikely that fusion centers would be able to justify their continued existence. Many fusion centers advertise the fact that they are co-located with JTTFs to demonstrate their information-sharing utility. However, that is not a reason to maintain fusion centers—it is instead a reason to merge their responsibilities into the JTTF itself.

As the ACLU report points out, the gap that the fusion centers sought to fill was not big enough to justify their existence. As a result, fusion centers have expanded their workload to "all-crimes, all-hazards" in order to qualify for a broader range of grant monies. "This expansion of the articulated mission of fusion centers reflects an evolving search for purpose, bounded on one side by the need not to duplicate the mission of existing institutions such as federal agencies and state Emergency Operations Centers, and on the other by the desire to do something that is actually useful."[145]

Perhaps the most controversial things associated with fusion centers are the threat reports that they produce. Many reports make blanket assertions that do little to identify real threats. Some amount to counterterrorism by demographics. For example, the police-run Virginia Fusion Center (VFC) described the commonwealth's universities as potential hotbeds for terrorist recruiting, taking special note of historically African American post-secondary schools and student groups: "While the majority of individuals associated with educational institutions do not engage in activities of interest to the VFC, it is important to note that University-based student groups are recognized as a radicalization node for almost every type of extremist group."[146] Citizens cannot obtain information about the VFC; the Virginia General Assembly enacted a law in 2008 exempting the center from transparency laws.[147]

The North Central Texas Fusion System produced a report in February 2009 suggesting that state law enforcement agents should monitor the lawful lobbying activities of Islamic groups.[148] That report singles out communities that have made accommodations for Muslim residents, such as the installation of footbaths in the Indianapolis airport, then notes, somewhat ominously, that "tolerance is growing in more formal areas" when discussing the expansion of Islamic finance.[149] "Given the stated objectives of these lobbying groups and the secretive activities of radical Islamic organizations, it is imperative for law enforcement officers to report these types of activities to identify potential underlying trends emerging in the North Central Texas region."[150] This report seems tailor-made to encourage surveillance and reporting that has more to do with left-right culture wars than aiding the police in identifying activities that produce a reasonable suspicion that crime is afoot.

The Missouri Information Analysis Center, another fusion center, produced a report that labeled anyone with minority-party political paraphernalia as a potential terrorist. "Political Paraphernalia: Militia members most commonly associate with 3rd party political groups. It is not uncommon for militia members to display Constitutional Party, Campaign for Liberty, or Libertarian material. These members are usually supporters of former presidential candidates Ron Paul, Chuck Baldwin, and Bob Barr."[151]

Fusion centers represent an unfortunate return to treating lawful dissent as a threat to society. The FBI's Counter Intelligence Program (COINTELPRO) and "red squads" of urban police departments that infiltrated innocuous student groups and peace activists during the Cold War have their heirs in today's fusion centers. In the 1960s the decision to spy on communists, anti-war protesters, and the civil rights activists was a conscious one. In contrast, fusion centers' search for purpose and the "all-crimes, all-hazards" approach stems from a make-work incentive. There are not enough terrorists to go around; the police and the FBI already identify and prosecute potential terrorists whenever possible, so fusion centers seem to be treating mere political dissent as a threat without any indication of violent intent in order to justify their continued existence.

Instead of limiting investigation and prosecution to real threats, police surveillance of lawful political activity is evident across the nation. At its Spy Files website, the ACLU has compiled dozens of accounts of political surveillance by local, state, and federal law enforcement officials, military organizations, and private corporations over the last decade.[152] Most recently, the Pennsylvania State Homeland Security Office suspended funding for a contractor after it came to light that the contractor had conducted surveillance on and reported the activities of a broad swath of peaceful protest groups.[153] One of the contractor's reports is long on beliefs but short on threats to public safety: it provides dates and information about upcoming local rallies or planned protests associated with anarchist, Irish, Muslim, antiwar, anti-gas drilling, anti-nuclear power, anti-Muslim, Tea Party, anti-Tea Party, environmental, anti-rodeo, and anti-deportation organizations—yet only reports one prior instance of civil disobedience associated with any of those groups.[154]

DHS Supervision of Fusion Centers Will Compound Their Problems

Because of the remarkable growth of fusion centers nationwide, DHS has created a unit to oversee them, the Joint Fusion Center Program Management Office (JFC-PMO).[155] The aggregation of fusion center reporting and the creation of a national network will only amplify the faults that fusion centers have. Fusion centers looking for larger data pools may now have access to other states' information, making it easier to publish overblown and unfounded conclusions.

Interstate information-sharing agreements may also make it easier for fusion centers to race to the bottom with respect to oversight and transparency laws, storing data in jurisdictions where it is least likely to face scrutiny. DHS seems an unlikely agency to provide more accountability for civil liberties in fusion center practices: in July 2010 an internal DHS e-mail obtained by the Associated Press revealed that political appointees at DHS deflected Freedom of Information Act (FOIA) requests by seeking information about requesters above and beyond what is required by law, such as finding out the individuals' political affiliations and leanings in order to assess potential political blowback from the release of documents.[156]

DHS officials have repeatedly made the case that federal oversight will help fusion centers "respect and protect the privacy, civil rights, and civil liberties of American citizens."[157] Indeed, the DHS privacy office issued a report finding potential problems with fusion center mission creep and a "lack of guidance on privacy while sharing or storing information."[158]

Past DHS treatment of dissent as a standalone indicator of terrorist threat ought to concern people across the political spectrum. In a May 2003 advisory, DHS warned local law enforcement agencies that terrorists may include those who "expressed dislike of attitudes and decisions of the U.S. government."[159] More recently, a DHS official assigned to the Wisconsin Statewide Information Center, issued a "threat assessment" warning about both pro-life and pro-choice groups present at a February 2009 rally. An internal review found that the report had violated intelligence-gathering guidelines.[160]

In 2009 DHS released its most publicly criticized threat assessment, *Rightwing Extremism: Current Economic and Political Climate Fueling Resurgence in Radicalization and Recruitment,* which labeled millions of innocent Americans potential terrorists.[161] The report detailed how "rightwing extremists" could be motivated by political issues such as "immigration and citizenship, the expansion of social programs to minorities, and restrictions on firearms ownership and use."[162]

The report adopted a sweeping definition for "extremism": "Rightwing extremism in the United States can be broadly divided into those groups, movements, and adherents that are primarily hate-oriented (based on hatred of particular religious, racial or ethnic groups), and those that are mainly anti-government, rejecting federal authority in favor of state or local authority, or rejecting government authority entirely. It may include groups and individuals that are dedicated to a single issue, such as opposition to abortion or immigration."[163] The report further defined veterans returning from Iraq and Afghanistan as potential threats, and warned that "rightwing extremists will attempt to recruit and radicalize returning veterans in order to exploit their skills and knowledge derived from military training and combat."[164] Mainstream political advocacy groups were rightly offended at being labeled potential terrorists or "rightwing extremists." For example, the head of the American Legion, a prominent veterans and civic organization, sent a letter of protest to Secretary of Homeland Security Janet Napolitano, prompting a personal visit and apology.[165] House Homeland Security Committee chairman Rep. Bennie Thompson (D-MS) was critical as well, "Unfortunately, this report appears to have blurred the line between violent belief, which is constitutionally protected, and violent action, which is not."[166]

Politicized Threat Reporting Does Not Identify Terrorists

Demand for terrorism intelligence creates bureaucratic incentives in fusion centers and other police agencies to label certain political groups as threats to national security. When intelligence analysts come to perceive their own political opposites as potential terrorists, or substitute the judgment of nongovernmental political organizations for that of the intelligence agency they work for, terrorism investigations go awry.

The trend of politicized threat reporting nowhere clearer than in the DHS *Rightwing Extremism* and North Texas Fusion System reports, providing left- and right-wing spin respectively. As revealed by a FOIA request filed by Americans for Limited Government,[167] the DHS *Rightwing Extremism* report largely outsourced its "analysis" to a nonprofit organization that cited only five specific instances of violence over a span of 15 years as the basis for its broad claims about potential terrorism threats.[168] DHS provided a list of the sources supporting the report.[169] Nearly a quarter of the cited sources came from the Southern Poverty Law Center (SPLC) website. While the SPLC may be held in high regard by its donors, the government agency ostensibly responsible for domestic counterterrorism should never cede its analysis of potential threats to a private nonprofit organization that may have an agenda that would be inappropriate for the federal government.[170] The SPLC has separately labeled the Family Research Council, a socially conservative nonprofit organization, a "hate group" for its opposition to homosexuality, and placed it in the same category as skinhead gangs and Ku Klux Klan franchises.[171] Political commentary should not be the basis for allocating scarce police resources.

The North Texas Fusion System report provides a mirror image of threat reporting from a combination of pro-Israel and conservative viewpoints. The report cites the Anti-Defamation League website, as well as those of Christian Broadcasting Network, *Human Events,* and *Front Page Magazine.*[172] These sources may provide interesting reading for their members and adherents, but their agendas should not become the basis for domestic counterterrorism. Using the political left-right divide as an organizing principle for domestic surveillance and the identification of potential threats is both ineffective as an investigative technique and damaging to political discourse in the United States.

Conclusion

The Department of Homeland Security has proven to be an unnecessary and costly reorganization of government. DHS's structure complicates management, frustrates oversight, and encourages wasteful spending. DHS grant programs also distort state and local spending priorities. If America could be made safer by wasteful spending on unused decontamination gear, Congress could declare victory now.

The Department of Homeland Security should be abolished and its components reorganized into more practical groupings. The agencies tasked with immigration, border security, and customs enforcement belong under the same oversight agency, which could appropriately be called the Border Security Administration. The Transportation Security Administration and Federal Air Marshal Service should be abolished.

DHS should also get out of the domestic intelligence business. The FBI and local police agencies already handle every other domestic criminal threat, and terrorism should be no exception. Federal and state legislators should end funding to fusion centers and move whatever legitimate tip-screening and information sharing functions they provide to FBI Joint Terrorism Task Forces. Political dissent should never become a key indicator of terrorist intent.

Abolishing DHS and reorganizing its components can save billions annually and alleviate the mounting pressure on civil liberties that we have experienced under ever-expanding homeland security bureaucracy. Terrorism remains a serious problem, but a sprawling Department of Homeland Security is not the proper way to address that threat.

Critical Thinking Questions

1. What do you think of the author's suggestion to reorganize DHS components into sector-specific agencies, like "Border Security Administration"?
2. Do you agree with the assertion that creating a centralized DHS has created too many opportunities for politicians to disguise pork barrel spending as defense and security-related? If so, what examples can you draw from to illustrate this?
3. Compare this reading to the Trybula-Whitley piece in Unit Two. What are the similarities and differences?

Notes

1. U.S. Commission on National Security/21st Century, "Road Map for National Security: Imperative for Change," January 31, 2001, p. 15, http://www.cfr.org/pdf/Hart-Rudman3.pdf.
2. See Raymond J. Decker, director, Defense Capabilities and Management, "Combating Terrorism: Observations on Options to Improve the Federal Response," Testimony before the Subcommittee on Economic Development, Public Buildings, and Emergency Management of the House Committee on Transportation and Infrastructure, and the Subcommittee on National Security, Veterans Affairs, and International Relations, Committee on Government Reform, 107th Cong., 1st sess., April 24, 2001, http://www.investigativeproject.org/documents/testimony/123.pdf.
3. Executive Order 13228, "Establishing the Office of Homeland Security and the Homeland Security Council," October 8, 2001.
4. "The roles of the homeland security adviser and the Homeland Security Council appear to be redundant with those of the national security adviser and the NSC. For 55 years, the NSC existed to provide for the national security, but as soon as the nation was attacked at home, a new security bureaucracy was thought to be needed. By creating a new cabinet department, U.S. policymakers appear to subscribe to the strange notion that the NSC should provide for security only overseas." See "Homeland Security," *Cato Handbook for Congress: Policy Recommendations for the 108th Congress* (Washington: Cato Institute, 2003), p. 66.
5. See Helene Cooper, "In Security Shuffle, White House Merges Staffs," *New York Times,* May 27, 2009. This was originally recommended by the 9/11 Commission. See *The 9/11 Commission Report: Final Report of the National Commission on Terrorist Attacks upon the United States* [hereinafter *"9/11 Commission Report"*] (New York: Norton, 2004), p. 406.
6. I use the term "homeland security" only because of its commonality in policy circles. James Fallows accurately describes the term as "abhorrently un-American, odiously Teutono/Soviet." James Fallows, "Year End Pensees: More on Security," *Atlantic,* January 15, 2009, http://www.theatlantic.com/science/archive/2009/01/year-end-pensees-more-on-security/9354/. The concept of "homeland security" is at the root of many of the ills plaguing DHS, since its invocation justifies additional bureaucracy, clothes pork-barrel spending in a patina of patriotism, and sacrifices civil liberties in the name of over-hyped terrorist threats.
7. Jeffrey Rosen, "Man-Made Disaster," *New Republic,* December 24, 2008, http://www.tnr.com/article/man-made-disaster.

8. Some have argued that DHS's structure is the product of: (1) efforts by Congress to preserve committee jurisdiction in spite of changed governmental structure, cutting against the stated goals of centralization and coordination; (2) President Bush's desire to reduce resources devoted to DHS agencies' legacy regulatory mandates; and (3) a fearful American public that favored bold action in the wake of the September 11 terrorist attacks. President Bush intended to swing the focus of the DHS agencies away from their regulatory duties and toward security duties, in essence moving the pendulum of government in the direction his party favored. See Dara Kay Cohen, Mariano-Florentino Cuéllar, and Barry R Weingast, "Crisis Bureaucracy: Homeland Security and the Political Design of Legal Mandates," *Stanford Law Review* 59 (2006): 714–32. Subsequent Congresses and budgets have moved DHS' focus back toward these regulatory duties and maintained elevated levels of security spending, producing a rachet effect instead of a pendulum swing.
9. Susan B. Glasser and Michael Grunwald, "Department's Mission Was Undermined from Start," *Washington Post,* December 22, 2005, http://www.washingtonpost.com/wp-dyn/content/article/2005/12/21/AR2005122102327.html.
10. Quoted in ibid.
11. Ibid.
12. Ibid.
13. Quoted in Hearing before the House Committee on Government Reform, 107th Cong., 2nd sess., p. 2, June 20, 2002, http://frwebgate.access.gpo.gov/cgi-bin/getdoc.cgi?dbname=107_house_hearings&docid=f:81325.pdf. Mark Souder (R-IN) wanted to move the Drug Enforcement Administration (DEA) to DHS on the basis that "more than 4,000 Americans die each year from illegal drug use—at least the equivalent of a terrorist attack." The DEA managed to avoid that move after Director Ridge promised close coordination between the two agencies.
14. Quoted in ibid., p. 79.
15. Quoted in ibid., p. 103.
16. "My inclination, and it is just that, an inclination, would be to focus the department more directly on border security, information analysis and infrastructure protection. That would mean, for example, that FEMA would remain exactly where it is, that there would be no chemical, biological, radiological, and nuclear counter-measures directorate, meaning that [the Animal and Plant Health Inspection Service] would also stay where it is. Although Congress could always remove the Coast Guard, FEMA, APHIS, and the other units should the reorganization prove overly broad, my preference is to start with the most logical combinations, then add as needed. In a similar vein, no pun intended, Congress can always decide later to split the national pharmaceutical stockpile from the Public Health Service." Paul C. Light, nonresident senior fellow, Brookings Institution, *Assessing the Proposed Department of Homeland Security,* Testimony before the Subcommittee on Civil Service, Census and Agency Organization of the House Committee on Government Reform, 107th Cong., 2nd sess., June 26, 2002, http://www.brookings.edu/testimony/2002/0626homelandsecurity_light.aspx.
17. Quoted in Guy Gugliotta, "Unintended Tasks Face New Security Agency," *Washington Post,* June 10, 2002.

18. See House Vote on H.R. 5710 (Homeland Security Act of 2002), November 14, 2002: Library of Congress, Roll Call Vote # 477, http://clerk.house.gov/evs/2002/roll477.xml. See Senate Vote on H.R. 5005 (Homeland Security Act of 2002), November 14, 2002, United States Senate website, http://www.senate.gov/legislative/LIS/roll_call_lists/roll_call_vote_cfm.cfm?congress=107&session=2&vote=00249.
19. Department of Homeland Security, "Who Became a Part of the Department?" http://www.dhs.gov/xabout/history/editorial_0133.shtm.
20. *9/11 Commission Report,* p. 181.
21. Ibid., p. 272.
22. George P. Hattrup and Brian H. Kleiner, "How to Establish the Proper Span of Control for Managers," *Industrial Management,* November 1, 1993, p. 28.
23. Erik Auf der Heide, "The Incident Command System (ICS)," in *Disaster Response: Principles of Preparation and Coordination* (AMC, Hawaii: Center of Excellence in Disaster Humanitarian Assistance, 1989), http://orgmail2.coe-dmha.org/dr/DisasterResponse.nsf/section/07?opendocument&home=html.
24. FEMA Emergency Management Institute IS-200 Lesson Plan, http://training.fema.gov/emiweb/downloads/IS200%20Lesson%20Summary.pdf.
25. The 2006 Federal Human Capital Survey ranked 36 federal agencies with employee surveys. DHS ranked 36th in job satisfaction, 36th in results-oriented performance culture, 35th in leadership and 33rd in talent management, consistent with the 2004 survey results. DHS deputy secretary Michael Jackson issued a memorandum to all employees promising improvement. "These results deliver a clear and jolting message from managers and line employees alike. I am writing to assure you that, starting at the top, the leadership team across DHS is committed to address the underlying reasons for DHS employee dissatisfaction." Karen Rutzick, "Loud and Clear," *Government Executive,* April 1, 2007, http://www.govexec.com/features/0407-01/0407-01na4.htm.
26. Rosen, "Man-Made Disaster."
27. "Inside Washington: For Homeland Security Department, Too Much of a Good Thing?" Associated Press, May 17, 2011, http://www.wash ingtonpost.com/politics/inside-washington-for-homeland-security-department-too-much-of-a-good-thing/2011/05/17/AFoPjV5G_story. html; NPR, "Who Oversees Homeland Security? Um, Who Doesn't?" July 20, 2010, NPR, http://www.npr.org/templates/story/story.php?storyId=128642876.
28. Mike M. Ahlers, "Ground Broken on $3.4 Billion Homeland Security Complex," CNN, September 9, 2009, http://www.cnn.com/2009/POLITICS/09/09/homeland.security.headquarters/ index.html.
29. Tim Kauffman, "GSA, DHS Detail Plans for Consolidating Leased Office Space," *Federal Times,* March 25, 2010, http://www.federaltimes.com/article/20100325/DEPARTMENTS03/3250306/.
30. President George W. Bush, *Securing the Homeland, Strengthening the Nation,* Washington, February 2002, p. 8, http://www.dhs.gov/xlibrary/assets/homeland_security_book.pdf. "The President signed the DHS Appropriations Act 2010, (P.L. 111–83) into law on October 28, 2009. The Act provides gross budget authority of $51.9 billion for DHS for FY2010. The Act provides $44.1 billion in net budget authority for DHS for FY2010." Jennifer E. Lake and Chad C. Haddal, "Homeland Security Department: FY2010 Appropriations," Congressional Research Service, December 14, 2009, p. 1, http://www.fas.org/sgp/crs/homesec/R40642.pdf. Though Congress passed the FY2011

budget, it did so halfway into the fiscal year. This paper will use FY2010 and FY2011 budgeting as appropriate.

31. John Mueller and Mark G. Stewart, "Terror, Security, and Money: Balancing the Risks, Benefits, and Costs of Homeland Security," presented at the panel, "Terror and the Economy: Which Institutions Help Mitigate the Damage?" at the Annual Convention of the Midwest Political Science Association, Chicago, April 1, 2011, p. 17, http://polisci .osu.edu/faculty/jmueller/MID11TSM.PDF.
32. "Since FY2002, Congress has appropriated over $34 billion for homeland security assistance to states, specified urban areas and critical infrastructures (such as ports and rail systems), the District of Columbia, and U.S. insular areas." Shawn Reese, "Department of Homeland Security Assistance to States and Localities: A Summary and Issues for the 111th Congress," Congressional Research Service, April 30, 2010.
33. The five key pathologies of grant programs are: (1) a gold-rush response that produces extravagant overspending; (2) unfair redistributions of taxpayer money between states; (3) reduction of state government flexibility and innovation; (4) costly federal, state, and local bureaucracies to administer the grants; and (5) the time and information "overload" they create for citizens and federal politicians. Chris Edwards, *Downsizing Government* (Washington: Cato Institute, 2005), pp. 110–16.
34. Veronique de Rugy, "Are We Ready for the Next 9/11?" *Reason,* March 1, 2006, http:// reason.com/archives/2006/03/01/are-we-ready-for-the-next-9–11.
35. A comprehensive discussion of all DHS grants is beyond the scope of this paper. Congress should review all DHS grant programs with an eye toward fiscal federalism, risk assessment, and deficit reduction.
36. "[A] review of terrorist attacks conducted by or attributed to al-Qaeda reveals that other than five attacks, every al-Qaeda attack outside of Iraq occurred in an urban area with a population of over 510,000 people. Of the five exceptions, two were in Saudi Arabia (Dhahran and Khobar), one was in Pakistan (Marden), one was on the Tunisian island of Djerba, and the last was the nightclub attack on the Indonesian island of Bali." Matt A. Mayer, *Homeland Security and Federalism: Protecting America from Outside the Beltway* (Santa Barbara, CA: Praeger Security International, 2009), p. 64.
37. See FY07 Homeland Security Grant Program, http://www.dhs.gov/xlibrary/assets/ grants_st-local_fy07.pdf.
38. Quoted in Melissa Raines, "Hazmat Trailer, Truck to Be Sold," *Mount Vernon News* (Ohio), August 26, 2008, http://www.mountvernonnews.com/local/08/06/24/hazmat_sale.php4.
39. Department of Homeland Security, *The State of California's Management of Urban Areas Security Initiative Grants Awarded During Fiscal Years 2006 through 2008,* OIG-11–46, February 2011, p. 13.
40. Jordan Carleo-Evengelist, "No Town Left Behind in Terror Funding Flow," Boston University Washington Journalism Center, Fall 2003, http://www.bu.edu/washjocenter/ Fall-2003/Fall_2003Stories/Carleo-Evangelist_Jordan/ Dhsfund.htm.
41. David Villano, "The High Cost of Homeland Defense," *Miami New Times,* October 9, 2003, http://www.miaminewtimes.com/2003-10-09/news/the-high-cost-of-homeland-defense/.
42. Kevin Diaz, "Pork-Barrel Security," *Star Tribune* (Minneapolis, MN), September 11, 2004.
43. Travis Kavulla, "Checkpoint to Nowhere: A Stimulus Boondoggle in Big Sky Country," *National Review,* September 2, 2009.

44. "Editorial: Checkpoint Follies," *Las Vegas Review-Journal,* August 28, 2009, http://www.lvrj.com/opinion/55668737.html.
45. Several watchdog groups have provided detailed accounting of wasteful spending: Citizens against Government Waste; the *Texas Tribune* (which keeps a tally of homeland security funds broken down by Texas county); and the Center for Investigative Reporting, which has a complete database of homeland security spending since DHS's creation. See Citizens against Government Waste, http://www.cagw.org/; "Per-Capita Homeland Security Spending in Texas," *Texas Tribune,* http://www.texastribune.org/library/data/texas-homeland-security-grants/; and "Price of Peril," Center for Investigative Reporting, http://www.centerforinvestigativereporting.org/files/homelandsecurity/priceofperil.html.
46. SHSP funding peaked at $2,066,295,000 in FY03 and was $842,000,000 in FY10. See "FY07 Homeland Security Grant Program," http://www.dhs.gov/xlibrary/assets/grants_st-local_fy07.pdf, and "FY10 Homeland Security Grant Frequently Asked Questions," http://www.fema.gov/pdf/government/grant/2010/fy10_hsgp_faq.pdf. The FY11 budget, though passed halfway into the fiscal year, further cut SHSP spending to $526 million. See Department of Homeland Security, "DHS Announces Grant Guidance for Fiscal Year (FY) 2011 Preparedness Grants," news release, May 19, 2011, http://www.dhs.gov/ynews/releases/pr_1305812474325.shtm.
47. Formulas from the USA PATRIOT Act required 0.75 percent of grant money to go to each state, regardless of population. See P.L. 107–206, Sec. 1014(c)(3), 116 Stat. 820. This was amended by the 9/11 Act of 2007 with a declining scale of mandated spending for each state—0.375 percent in FY08 moving to 0.35 percent by FY12. See P.L. 110–53, Sec. 204(c)(3)(e), 121 Stat. 278.
48. Department of Homeland Security, "DHS Announces Grant Guidance for Fiscal Year (FY) 2011 Preparedness Grants," news release, May 19, 2011, http://www.dhs.gov/ynews/releases/pr_1305812474325.shtm.
49. This is not to say that waste would be eliminated. DHS grants for "terrorism prevention" purposes support excessive spending at the local level. A Memphis Police official justified his city's use of terrorism funds to fight local gang crime thusly: "We have our own terrorists, and they are taking lives every day. . . . No, we don't have suicide bombers—not yet. But you need to remain vigilant and realize how vulnerable you can be if you let up." Quoted in Dana Priest and William M. Arkin, "Monitoring America," *Washington Post,* December 20, 2010, http://projects.washington post.com/top-secret-america/articles/monitoring-america/.
50. Jeff Goodman, "Region Secures $1 Million for Emergency Preparedness," Bakersfield.com, July 21, 2010, http://www.bakersfield.com/news/local/x1974424854/Region-secures-1-million-for-emergency-preparedness.
51. See General Accountability Office, "Homeland Security: DHS Risk-Based Grant Methodology Is Reasonable, But Current Version's Measure of Vulnerability Is Limited," June 2008, GAO-08-852, http://gao.gov/cgi-bin/getrpt?GAO-08-852.
52. See General Accountability Office, "Urban Area Security Initiative: FEMA Lacks Measures to Assess How Regional Collaboration Efforts Build Preparedness Capabilities," July 2009, GAO-09-651, http://www.gao.gov/new.items/d09651.pdf.
53. Department of Homeland Security, "DHS Announces Grant Guidance for Fiscal Year (FY) 2011 Preparedness Grants," news release, May 19, 2011, http://www.dhs.gov/ynews/releases/pr_1305812474325.shtm.

54. Mickey McCarter, "House Democrats Fight Proposed Cuts to DHS Grant Programs," *Homeland Security Today,* May 25, 2011, http://www.hstoday.us/industry-news/general/single-article/house-democrats-fight-proposed-cuts-to-dhs-grant-programs/d52057cfe87d8bfa3f4304c5e67d6f16.html.
55. P.L. 107–71.
56. Transportation Security Administration, "Our Workforce," http://www.tsa.gov/who_we_are/workforce/index.shtm.
57. "TSA uses two types of imaging technology: millimeter wave and backscatter. Currently, there are 488 imaging technology units at 78 airports. In March 2010, TSA began deploying 450 advanced imaging technology units, which were purchased with American Recovery and Reinvestment Act (ARRA) funds." Transportation Security Administration: Advanced Imaging Technology (AIT), http://www.tsa.gov/approach/tech/ait/index.shtm.
58. Gale Rossides, acting transportation security administrator, "Advanced Imaging Technology—Yes, It's Worth It," TSA Blog, March 31, 2010, http://blog.tsa.gov/2010/03/advanced-imaging-technology-yes-its.html; Michael Chertoff, "Former Homeland Security Chief Argues for Whole-body Imaging," *Washington Post,* January 1, 2010, http://www.washingtonpost.com/wp-dyn/content/article/2009/12/31/AR2009123101746.html.
59. Mark G. Stewart and John Mueller, "Risk and Cost-Benefit Analysis of Advanced Imaging Technology Full Body Scanners for Airline Passenger Security Screening," Centre for Infrastructure Performance and Reliability (CIPAR), University of Newcastle, UK, January 2011, p. 18, http://hdl.handle.net/1959.13/805595.
60. Ibid., p. 13.
61. See Steve Lord, director, Homeland Security and Justice Issues, Government Accountability Office, "Aviation Security: TSA Is Increasing Procurement and Deployment of the Advanced Imaging Technology, but Challenges to This Effort and Other Areas of Aviation Security Remain," Testimony before the Subcommittee on Transportation Security and Infrastructure Protection of the House Committee on Homeland Security, 111th Cong., 2nd sess., March 17, 2010, p. 9, www.gao.gov/new.items/d10484t.pdf.
62. "The plotters had planned to use liquids in drink bottles, smuggled in hand baggage, to combine into explosive cocktails aboard flights high over the Atlantic, British and American officials said." Alan Cowell and Dexter Filkins, "British Authorities Say Plot to Blow Up Airliners Was Foiled," *New York Times,* August 10, 2006, http://www.nytimes.com/2006/08/10/world/europe/11terrorcnd.html.
63. Grant Stinchfield, "TSA Source: Armed Agent Slips Past DFW Body Scanner," NBC Dallas Forth-Worth, February 18, 2011, http://www.nbcdfw.com/news/local/TSA-Agent-Slips-Through-DFW-Body-Scanner-With-a-Gun-116497568.html.
64. Edward N. Luttwak, "The Body Scanner Scam," *Wall Street Journal,* January 18, 2010, http://online.wsj.com/article/SB10001424052748704541004575010962154452900.html.
65. Scott Stewart, "AQAP: Paradigm Shifts and Lessons Learned," *STRATFOR,* September 2, 2009, http://www.stratfor.com/weekly/20090902_aqap_paradigm_shifts_and_lessons_learned.
66. Al Qaeda in the Arabia Peninsula "proudly proclaimed that 'the mujahedeen brothers in the manufacturing department' had supplied the explosives, 'though a technical

error' led to the 'incomplete detonation."' Mark Hosenball, "The Radicalization of Umar Farouk Abdulmutallab," *Newsweek,* January 2, 2010.

67. Brian Bennett, "Less Invasive Body Scanner Software Tested at Airports," *Los Angeles Times,* February 2, 2011, http://articles.latimes.com/2011/feb/02/nation/la-na-tsa-scanners-20110202; Aaron Smith, "Stimulus to Bring Body Scanners to Airports," *CNN Money,* January 5, 2010, http://money.cnn.com/2010/01/05/technology/full_body_scanner/.
68. See Lord.
69. William Saletan, "Sew-In Bombers," *Slate,* July 7, 2011, http://www.slate.com/id/2298657/.
70. See John Mueller, "The Atomic Terrorist?" in *Terrorizing Ourselves: Why U.S. Counterterrorism Policy Is Failing and How to Fix It,* ed. Benjamin Friedman, Jim Harper, and Christopher Preble (Washington: Cato Institute, 2009), p. 139.
71. *Michigan Department of State Police v. Sitz,* 496 U.S. 444 (1990).
72. *United States v. Martinez-Fuerte,* 428 U.S. 543 (1976).
73. *City of Indianapolis v. Edmond,* 531 U.S. 32, 43 (2000).
74. "Our holding also does not affect the validity of border searches or searches at places like airports and government buildings, where the need for such measures to ensure public safety can be particularly acute." Ibid., pp. 47–48.
75. *United States v. Davis,* 482 F.2d 893, 908 (1973) (Holding that airline searches are constitutionally permissible because they are "conducted as part of a general regulatory scheme in furtherance of an administrative purpose, namely, to prevent the carrying of weapons or explosives aboard aircraft, and thereby to prevent hijackings."); *United States v. Hartwell,* 436 F.3d 174, 178 (2006), *cert. denied,* 127 S. Ct. 111 (2006); *United States v. Aukai,* 497 F.3d 955, 960 (2007).
76. See *Hartwell,* 436 F. 3d 174, 179–80 (2006); *Aukai,* 497 F.3d 955, 962 (2007).
77. Jeffrey Rosen, "Why the TSA Pat-Downs and Body Scans Are Unconstitutional," *Washington Post,* November 28, 2010, http://www.washingtonpost.com/wp-dyn/content/article/2010/11/24/AR2010112404510.html.
78. *Aukai,* p. 962, *citing United States v. Davis,* p. 913.
79. *Hartwell,* p. 180.
80. Brief of Petitioner, *Electronic Privacy Information Center v. Napolitano,* no. 10-1157 (D.C. Cir. Nov. 1, 2010), p. 32, http://epic.org/EPIC_Body_Scanner_OB.pdf.
81. *Electronic Privacy Information Center v. United States Department of Homeland Security,* no. 10-1157, 2011 U.S. App. LEXIS 14503 (D.C. Cir. July 15, 2011).
82. Bennett.
83. The Supreme Court has held that checkpoint searches may not become limitless searches motivated by a desire to uncover "evidence of ordinary criminal wrongdoing." See *City of Indianapolis v. Edmond,* pp. 37-42. Lower federal courts have addressed this in greater depth and specificity in the aviation security context. See *United States v. Marquez,* 410 F.3d 612, 617 (2005) (approving airport screening where "nothing in the record indicat[ed] that [the searching agent] was looking for drugs or criminal evidence."); *United States v. $124,570 U.S. Currency,* 873 F.2d 1240, 1243 (1989) ("While narrowly defined searches for guns and explosives are constitutional as justified by the need for air traffic safety, a generalized law enforcement search of all passengers as a condition for boarding a commercial aircraft would plainly be unconstitutional.") (citing *United States v. Davis,* p. 910).

84. See *United States v. Fofana,* 620 F. Supp. 2d 857 (2009) (suppressing evidence discovered when a TSA screener manipulated an envelope full of paper in an attempt to find razor blades, and, having felt nothing as rigid as a blade, opened the envelope and discovered fake passports); *United States v. McCarty,* 672 F. Supp. 2d 1085 (2009) (suppressing evidence discovered in checked baggage where a TSA screener investigated the nature of pictures that fell out of a computer bag based on a child protection motive, not an aviation security one); But see *Higerd v. Florida, Florida Law Weekly* 35 (2011): 2874 (admitting evidence through the good faith exception where TSA policy required a screener to "thumb through" a stack of papers, discovering child pornography).
85. Scott McCartney, "Is Tougher Airport Screening Going Too Far?" *Wall Street Journal,* July 16, 2009, http://online.wsj.com/article/SB10001424052970204556804574261940842372518.html.
86. Brief of Petitioner, *Bierfeldt v. Napolitano,* no. 09-01117 (D.C. Dist. June 18, 2009), p. 9, http://www.aclu.org/files/pdfs/safefree/bierfeldtvnapolitano_complaint.pdf
87. Stephen Dinan, "Airport Rules Changed after Ron Paul Aide Detained," *Washington Times,* November 11, 2009, http://www.washington times.com/news/2009/nov/11/rules-changed-after-paul-aide-detained-at-airport/?page=1.
88. Transportation Security Administration, TSA Management Directive no. 100.4: Transportation Security Searches, September 1, 2009, p. 6.
89. Daniel Rubin, "An Infuriating Search at Philadelphia International Airport," *Philadelphia Inquirer,* August 18, 2010.
90. See "How the Israelis Do Airport Security," CNN, January 10, 2010, http://edition.cnn.com/2010/OPINION/01/11/yeffet.air.security.israel/ (interview with the former head of security for El Al Airlines).
91. While no exact calculation of a transition to Israeli-style procedures is available, there is no question that security spending would dramatically increase. *Washington Post* columnist Dana Milbank writes that security spending by the relatively small Israeli aviation industry could not be replicated in the U.S. market. "El Al, Israel's national carrier, reported spending $107,828,000 on security in 2009 for the 1.9 million passengers it carried. That works out to about $56.75 per passenger. The United States, by contrast, spent $5.33 billion on aviation security in fiscal 2010, and the air travel system handled 769.6 million passengers in 2009 (a low year), according to the Bureau of Transportation Statistics. That amounts to $6.93 per passenger. The analogy isn't perfect, because security is largely handled by the airline in Israel and by the government here. (In both countries, the government pays just under two-thirds of the security costs.) But this rough comparison indicates that Israel spends more than eight times as much on security per passenger. To duplicate that, the United States would need to spend an extra $38 billion a year." Dana Milbank, "Why the Israeli Security Model Can't Work for the U.S.," *Washington Post,* November 25, 2010. *Bloomberg* writer Peter Robison found that Israeli spending per passenger dwarfs that in the U.S.: "[El Al Chairman Israel] Borovich estimated El Al's security bill at $100 million a year, which amounts to $76.92 per trip by its 1.3 million passengers. Half is paid by the Israeli government. By contrast, the TSA spent $4.58 billion on aviation security, or just $6.21 per trip by 737 million passengers, in fiscal 2005." Peter Robison, "Israeli-Style Air Security, Costly and Intrusive, May Head West," *Bloomberg,* August 24, 2006, http://www.bloomberg.com/apps/news?pid=newsarchive&sid=aFyfihM1e3G4&refer=politics. *Foreign*

Policy writer Annie Lowrey calculates that a transition to Israeli-style security would require a workforce of 3 million TSA screeners and cost $150 billion a year. Annie Lowrey, "What Would It Cost for the U.S. to Get Israel-Level Airport Security?" *Foreign Policy,* January 7, 2010, http://blog.foreignpolicy.com/posts/2010/01/07/would_you_pay_25_for_71_seconds_of_scrutiny_in_an_airport.

92. Andrew Seidman, "TSA Launching Behavior-Detection Program at Boston Airport," *Los Angeles Times,* August 17, 2011, http://www.latimes.com/news/nationworld/nation/la-na-tsa-logan-20110818,0,59862.story.
93. Ibid.
94. Jordy Yager, "Next Step for Tight Security Could Be Trains, Boats, Metro," *The Hill,* November 23, 2010, http://thehill.com/homenews/administration/130549-next-step-for-body-scanners-could-be-trains-boats-and-the-metro-.
95. Chertoff told editors of the Associated Press: "The truth of the matter is that a fully loaded airplane with jet fuel, a commercial airliner, has the capacity to kill 3,000 people. A bomb in a subway car may kill 30 people. When you start to think about your priorities, you're going to think about not having a catastrophic event first." Nicole Gaouette and Mary Curtius, "$31.8-Billion Homeland Security Bill Passes," *Los Angeles Times,* July 15, 2005.
96. "Homeland Security Targets Bus Traffic in Tampa," *ABC Action News,* February 16, 2010, http://www2.abcactionnews.com/dpp/news/region_west_hillsborough/Homeland-Security-targets-bus-traffic-in-Tampa.
97. The FY2010 budget allocated $2,759,000,000 for passenger and baggage screening, $150 million for the Screening Partnership Program, and $129 million for checkpoint support. See Lake and Haddal, Table 11, p. 43.
98. Transportation Security Administration, "Screening Partnership Program," http://www.tsa.gov/what_we_do/optout/spp_news.shtm.
99. See Transportation Security Administration, "Private Screening Operations Performance Evaluation Report," April 16, 2004, www.tsa.gov/assets/pdf/Summary_Report.pdf.
100. The TSA has estimated in the past that SPP airports cost approximately 17.4 percent more to operate than non-SPP airports, and separately hired a contractor that found SPP airports cost 9 to 17 percent more than non-SPP airports. Government Accountability Office, "Aviation Security: TSA's Cost and Performance Study of Private-Sector Airport Screening," GAO-09-27R, January 9, 2009. The TSA made GAO-recommended changes to its methodology to control for the additional cost of overlapping contract and government administrative personnel and the long-term costs of public employee retirement. In January 2011 the TSA revised its numbers and found that SPP airport screeners would cost 3 percent more than federal screeners, but the GAO responded that its recommendations had only been partially implemented. Government Accountability Office, "Aviation Security: TSA's Revised Cost Comparison Provides a More Reasonable Basis for Comparing the Costs of Private-Sector and TSA Screeners," GAO-11-375R, March 4, 2011. A House Transportation and Infrastructure Committee report likewise found significant savings from using SPP screeners instead of TSA screeners. United States House of Representatives, Committee on Transportation and Infrastructure, Oversight and Investigations, "TSA Ignores More Cost-Effective Screening Model," June 3, 2011.
101. See Government Accountability Office, "Aviation Security: Private Screening Contractors Have Little Flexibility to Implement Innovative Approaches," Statement

of Norman J. Rabkin, managing director, Homeland Security and Justice, Testimony before the Subcommittee on Aviation, Committee on Transportation and Infrastructure, House of Representatives, April 22, 2004, www.gao.gov/new.items/d04505t.pdf.

102. Stephen Losey, "TSA Halts Expansion of Privatized Airport Screening," *Federal Times,* January 31, 2011, http://www.federaltimes.com/article/20110131/DEPARTMENTS03/101310303/.
103. Joe Davidson, "TSA Employees Can Vote on Union Representation, Labor Board Rules," *Washington Post,* November 12, 2010, http://voices.washingtonpost.com/federal-eye/2010/11/tsa_employ ees_can_vote_on_unio.html?wprss=federal-eye.
104. Denise Kirsten Wills, "You're Fired," *Government Executive,* March 1, 2006, http://www.govexec.com/features/0306-01/0306-01s3.htm.
105. Dennis Cauchon, "Some Federal Workers More Likely to Die than Lose Jobs," *USA Today,* July 19, 2011.
106. United States Department of Homeland Security, Customs, and Border Protection, 63 FLRA 495 (2009).
107. United States Department of Homeland Security, Border and Transportation Security Directorate, Bureau of Customs and Border Protection, Washington, 63 FLRA 600 (2009).
108. United States Department of Homeland Security, Customs, and Border Protection, Washington, 63 FLRA 434 (2009).
109. For a more detailed analysis of this subject, see Robert Poole, *Airport Security: Time for a New Model,* Reason Foundation Policy Study no. 340 (2006), pp. 4–5.
110. United States House of Representatives, Committee on Transportation and Infrastructure, Oversight and Investigations, pp.17; 21–22.
111. The controversial pat-down of an eight-month-old child at Kansas City International was performed not by TSA screeners, but by contract screeners acting under TSA screening guidelines. See Robert A. Cronkleton, "Photo of Pat-Down of Baby at KCI Goes Worldwide," *Kansas City Star,* May 20, 2011, http://www.kansascity.com/2011/05/10/2865800/photo-of-pat-down-of-baby-at-airport.html.
112. See 49 U.S.C. § 44920 (2005).
113. Marsh Inc., "The Marsh Report: Terrorism Risk Insurance 2010," p. 10, http://insurance marketreport.com/Default.aspx?alias=insurance marketreport.com/terrorism2010.
114. Ibid., p. 16.
115. Potential hijackers also face resistance from armed agents who are not employed by the Air Marshal Service. Federal, state, and local law enforcement officers can fly armed on commercial flights (federal law enforcement officers are generally authorized to carry a firearm on a commercial flight on or off duty, but state and local officers can carry arms only when they are on duty). These personnel would not be affected by any adjustment in FAMS and FFDO policy changes.
116. Statement of Congressman John J. Duncan, Jr., June 19, 2009, http://duncan.house.gov/2009/06/22062009.shtml. The FY 2011 budget increased funding for FAMS to $929,802,000. See P.L. 112–10, Sec. 1620. The substance of the arrests matters as well; air marshals have not countered any 9/11-style hijacking attempts and their arrests stem from the same sorts of incidents that prompt airline passengers to subdue unruly or intoxicated fellow travelers. See Anahad O'Connor, "Air Marshals Intervene in Incident on Plane," *New York Times,* April 7, 2010; Transportation Security Administration, "Federal Air Marshals Make Arrest on International Flight," news release,

June 26, 2008, http://www.tsa.gov/press/happenings/federal_arrest_international_flight.shtm; see also fn. 131 (listing passenger interventions). The rapid increase in the number of air marshals also resulted in loose hiring standards and significant criminality within air marshal ranks. See Michael Grabell, "Air Marshals: Undercover and Under Arrest," ProPublica.org, November 13, 2008, http://www.propublica.org/article/federal-air-marshals-and-the-law.

117. A CNN Investigation found that fewer than 1 percent of all domestic flights have air marshals on board. See Drew Griffin, Kathleen Johnston and Todd Schwarzschild, "Sources: Air Marshals Missing from Almost All Flights," CNN, March 25, 2008, http://www.cnn.com/2008/TRAVEL/03/25/siu.air.marshals/. The TSA website countered that a higher number of flights had air marshal coverage, but the number remains classified and no figure higher than 5 percent is publicly cited. See Transportation Security Administration, "Federal Air Marshal Shortage?" http://www.tsa.gov/approach/mythbusters/fams_shortage.shtm.
118. See Ethan Rider, "Handguns and Air Marshals," Airliners.net, November 15, 2003, http: //www.airliners.net/aviation-articles/read.main?id=64.
119. See Mark G. Stewart and John Mueller, "Assessing the Risks, Costs and Benefits of United States Aviation Security Measures," Centre for Infrastructure Performance and Reliability, University of Newcastle, Research Report no. 267.04.08, (2008), http://polisci.osu.edu/faculty/jmueller/stewarr2.pdf.
120. "TSA officials told the 50 people who provide the training that the program would be moved from the Federal Law Enforcement Training Center in Glynco, G.A. [sic], to a facility in Artesia, N.M., in a remote southeast section of the state. . . . Rep. Peter DeFazio, D-Ore. [sic], the ranking Democrat on the aviation committee, complained that the changes came as a surprise to Congress. . . . 'It's just another attempt by the administration to disrupt the program at the behest of the airlines who have always opposed arming pilots."' Fred Bayles, "Pilots Say TSA Disrupting Gun Training," *USA Today,* June 6, 2003.
121. John R. Lott, Jr., "Pilots Still Unarmed," *New York Post,* January 6, 2004.
122. Ibid.
123. Mike M. Ahlers, "Report: Pilots' Holsters Make Guns Vulnerable to Accidental Discharge," CNN, December 2, 2008, http://www.cnn.com/2008/TRAVEL/12/02/tsa.holster/index.html.
124. Lake and Haddal, Table 11, p. 43.
125. Bruce Schneier, *Beyond Fear: Thinking Sensibly About Security in an Uncertain World* (New York: Springer, 2006), pp. 247–48.
126. "A woman having an apparent panic attack over turbulence on a JetBlue flight bound for Newark was tackled by several passengers as she rose from her seat and banged into an emergency exit door while complaining to the flight crew, an FBI spokesman said." Jonathan Dienst, "Turbulence Leads to Turbulence on JetBlue Flight," NBC New York, September 9, 2010, http://www.nbcnewyork.com/news/local-beat/Turbulence-Leads-to-Turbulence-On-JetBlue-Flight-102566229.html; "Phil Orlandella, a spokesman for the Massachusetts Port Authority, says the 22-year-old Israeli man ran toward the cockpit and pounded on the door. He says passengers and crew helped to subdue the man." "Mid-Air Drama: Passenger Tackled after Banging on Cockpit Door," NBC New York, April 25, 2009, http://www.nbcnewyork.com/news/local-beat/Flight-Diverted-To-Boston.html; "A man who claimed to have a bomb aboard a Los Angeles-bound

airliner and lunged for a door as it landed was tackled by other passengers and held for questioning Wednesday, authorities said." "Fellow Passengers Tackle Man as Plane Lands at LAX," NBC Los Angeles, January 7, 2009, http://www.nbclosangeles.com/news/local-beat/Fellow-Passengers-Tackle-Man-as-Plane-Lands-at-LAX.html.

127. Quoted in Joshua Norman, "Senators and TSA Defend 'Love Pats' at Airports," CBS News. com, November 17, 2010, http://www.cbsnews.com/stories/2010/11/17/national/main7063414.shtml.
128. Transportation Security Administration, "What We Do: Layers of Security," http://www.tsa.gov/what_we_do/layers/index.shtm.
129. Alan Levin, "Airlines Seek to Move Air Marshals from First Class," *USA Today,* October 18, 2010.
130. 28 C.F.R. 0.85(l).
131. See Fourth Amendment, U.S. Constitution. "[N]o Warrants shall issue, but upon *probable cause.*" (Emphasis added.)
132. Mike German, *Thinking Like a Terrorist* (Washington: Potomac Books, 2007), p. 194.
133. The Justice Department's Executive Office for United States Attorneys reported "bringing 3,094 anti-terrorism cases against 3,925 defendants during fiscal years 2002 through 2006, and concluding 2,609 cases against 3,098 defendants during the same time frame," while the Administrative Office of the United States Courts reports a total of 99 terrorism cases filed against 153 defendants during the same period, but the Department of Justice's Counterterrorism Section "counted 527 defendants charged in international terrorism and terrorism-related cases between September 11, 2001, and November 15, 2007." Numbers vary greatly depending on whether the focus is on "terrorism" or "terrorism-related" prosecutions. See Richard B. Zabel and James J. Benjamin, Jr., "In Pursuit of Justice: Prosecuting Terrorism Cases in the Federal Courts," Human Rights First, May 2008, p. 21, http://www.humanrightsfirst.org/pdf/080521-USLS-pursuit-justice.pdf. Zabel and Benjamin chose to focus on 107 cases with 257 defendants for analysis of the criminal justice system's effectiveness in prosecuting terror suspects. Ibid., p. 23.
134. Dana Priest and William M. Arkin, "A Hidden World, Growing Beyond Control," *Washington Post,* July 19, 2010.
135. Quoted in ibid.
136. Ibid.
137. See Bureau of Justice Assistance, Office of Justice Programs, U.S. Department of Justice, "Fusion Center Guidelines: Developing and Sharing Information and Intelligence in a New Era," August 2006, p. 2, www.it.ojp.gov/documents/fusion_center_guidelines_law_enforcement.pdf.
138. Mary Beth Sheridan and Spencer Hsu, "Localities Operate Intelligence Centers to Pool Terror Data," *Washington Post,* December 31, 2006, http://www.washingtonpost.com/wp-dyn/content/article/2006/12/30/AR2006123000238.html.
139. See Shane Harris, "L.A.'s Anti-Terrorism Hub Serves as a Model," *National Journal,* May 2, 2007; John Rollins and Timothy Connors, "State Fusion Center Processes and Procedures: Best Practices and Recommendations," Manhattan Institute Policing Terrorism Report no. 2, September 2007, http://www.manhattan-institute.org/html/ptr_02.htm.
140. See National Commission on Terrorist Attacks upon the United States: Tenth Public Hearing (April 14, 2004), Statement of Robert S. Mueller, III, director, FBI, before the

National Commission on Terrorist Attacks upon the United States, http://www.fbi.gov/congress/congress04/mueller041404.htm.

141. Department of Homeland Security, "Fusion Center Success Stories," http://www.dhs.gov/files/programs/gc_1296488620700.shtm. The Congressional Research Service gave a variation of this proposal in a report outlining Congress' options for defining federal participation in fusion centers, placing fusion centers under the supervision of the FBI's Field Intelligence Groups. John Rollins, "Fusion Centers: Issues and Options for Congress," Congressional Research Service, January 18, 2008, pp. 74–75.
142. Michael German and Jay Stanley, "What's Wrong with Fusion Centers?" American Civil Liberties Union, December 2007, http://www.aclu.org/files/pdfs/privacy/fusioncenter_20071212.pdf. Mike German and Jay Stanley, "Fusion Center Update," American Civil Liberties Union, July 2008, www.aclu.org/pdfs/privacy/fusion_update_20080729.pdf.
143. As retired police officer and fusion center advocate Stephen Serrao notes, this focus on security clearances ironically hampers the work of fusion centers today: "Many fusion centers that will never have to deal with top secret information have been built to this standard, and now employees and processes must meet the top secret standard. Unfortunately, many of the staff assigned to work there don't have top secret clearance, so they are literally sitting in the hall outside the facility without access to many informational systems. Meanwhile, most centers are dealing with top secret data less than five percent of the time. We are overbuilding and over-securing these centers at significant cost, and it is causing great inefficiency. For example, entering a door at some fusion centers can take up to five minutes because of the complex, locking mechanisms on the door to meet the top secret standard; yet, when you get inside, there is no top secret information being handled at that facility. The data is usually unclassified and, in some cases, is open source. Over-securing the facility hampers access, thereby hindering investigations." Stephen Serrao, "Fusion Centers: Defining Success," HSToday.us, October 13, 2009, http://www.hstoday.us/blogs/best-practices/blog/fusion-centers-defining-success/d2adf8a8025faecbe0268d81fe1d3c54.html.
144. Quoted in ibid.
145. German and Stanley, "What's Wrong with Fusion Centers?" pp. 6–7.
146. Commonwealth of Virginia Department of State Police Virginia Fusion Center, "2009 Virginia Terrorism Threat Assessment," March 2009 (on file with author).
147. See Va. Code Ann. §§ 52–48, 52–49 (2010). A lawsuit filed by the Electronic Privacy Information Center (EPIC) uncovered a Memorandum of Understanding between the VFC and the FBI where the VFC agreed to submit any requests for information under state freedom of information laws to the FBI before information would be released, giving credibility to fears that the law was reportedly passed at the behest of the federal government. See Memorandum of Understanding between the Federal Bureau of Investigation and the Virginia Fusion Center, http://epic.org/privacy/virginia_fusion/MOU.pdf; Electronic Privacy Information Center, "Letter to Virginia Senate RE: HB 1007: Open Government and the Virginia Fusion Center," February 26, 2008, http://epic.org/privacy/fusion/Letter_to_Senate_02_25_08.pdf.
148. North Texas Fusion System, *Prevention Awareness Bulletin,* February 19, 2009 (on file with author).
149. Ibid., p. 4.
150. Ibid., p. 5.

151. Missouri Information Analysis Center, MIAC Strategic Report: The Modern Militia Movement, February 20, 2009, http://epic.org/miac-militia-2009.pdf.
152. http://www.aclu.org/spy-files.
153. Mark Scolforo, "Pa. State Police Says Bulletins Caused Headaches," Associated Press, September 27, 2010, http://news.yahoo.com/s/ap/us_homeland_security_bulletin; Angela Couloumbis, "Pa. Acting as Security Agent for Energy Interests?" *Philadelphia Inquirer,* September 14, 2010, http://www.philly.com/philly/news/breaking/20100914_Pa__acting_as_security_agent_for_energy_interests_.html; Angela Couloumbis, "Pa. Senate Hearing Learns Officials Raised Red Flags Over Intelligence Contractor, *Philadelphia Inquirer,* September 28, 2010. http://www.philly.com/inquirer/front_page/20100928_Pa__Senate_hearing_learns_officials_raised_red_flags_over_intelligence_contractor.html.
154. Pennsylvania Office of Homeland Security, *Pennsylvania Intelligence Bulletin* no. 131, August 30, 2010 (on file with author).
155. Matthew Harwood, "DHS to Create New Office to Support Intelligence Fusion Centers," *Security Management,* October 1, 2009, www.securitymanagement.com/news/dhs-create-new-office-support-intelligence-fusion-centers-006287.
156. Kim Zetter, "Report: Political Appointees Vetted DHS Public Records Requests," *Wired,* July 22, 2010, http://www.wired.com/threatlevel/2010/07/foia-filtered; Jennifer Epstein and MJ Lee, "DHS Called FOIA Vetting 'Bananas,'" *Politico,* March 28, 2011, http://www.politico.com/news/stories/0311/52033.html.
157. See Robert Riegle, director, State and Local Program Office, Office of Intelligence and Analysis, Testimony before the Committee on Homeland Security, Subcommittee on Intelligence, Information Sharing, and Terrorism Risk Assessment, "The Future of Fusion Centers: Potential Promise and Dangers," April 1, 2009; see also Caryn Wagner, under secretary and chief intelligence officer and principal deputy under secretary Bart R. Johnson, Testimony before the House Committee on Homeland Security, on the Office of Intelligence and Analysis' Vision and Goals, May 12, 2010; Janet Napolitano, secretary of the Department of Homeland Security, Testimony before the Senate Committee on Homeland Security and Governmental Affairs, "Eight Years after 9/11: Confronting the Terrorist Threat to the Homeland," September 30, 2009; Bart R. Johnson, acting under secretary for intelligence and analysis, Testimony before the Subcommittee on Intelligence, Information Sharing, and Terrorism Risk Assessment, "I&A Reconceived: Defining a Homeland Security Intelligence Role," September 24, 2009.
158. See Department of Homeland Security Privacy Office, "Privacy Impact Assessment for the Department of Homeland Security State, Local, and Regional Fusion Center Initiative," December 11, 2008, pp. 26, 30, www.dhs.gov/xlibrary/assets/privacy/privacy_pia_ia_slrfci.pdf.
159. Jack Douglas, Jr., "U.S. Security Memos Warn of Little Things," *Fort Worth Star-Telegram,* May 25, 2003.
160. "Feds Admit Wrongly Tracking Wisconsin Abortion Groups," *Chicago Daily Herald,* February 9, 2010.
161. Department of Homeland Security, "Rightwing Extremism: Current Economic and Political Climate Fueling Resurgence in Radicalization and Recruitment," April 7, 2009, http://www.fas.org/irp/eprint/rightwing.pdf.
162. Ibid., pp. 3–4.
163. Ibid., p. 2, fn.
164. Ibid., p. 7.

165. See "DHS Apologizes for Language in Report," http://ourvoice.legion.org/story/1543/dhs-apologizes-language-report; "DHS Secretary to Legion: 'I'm Sorry,'" http://ourvoice.legion.org/story/1629/dhs-secretary-legion-im-sorry; "Homeland Security Chief Apologizes to Veteran Groups," http://www.cnn.com/2009/POLITICS/04/16/napolitano.apology/.
166. Bennie G. Thompson, Letter to Homeland Security Secretary Napolitano, April 14, 2009, http://www.fas.org/irp/congress/2009_cr/hsc041409.pdf.
167. Freedom of Information Request from Bill Wilson, President, Americans for Limited Government to Catherine M. Papoi, Deputy Chief FOIA Officer, Privacy Office, U.S. Department of Homeland Security (April 17, 2009) (on file with author).
168. The five examples were the following: (1) Timothy McVeigh and the 1995 Oklahoma City bombing, pp. 2, 7, 8; (2) shooting deaths of three Pittsburgh police officers on April 4, 2009, p. 3; (3) arrest of six militia members in April 2007 for weapons and explosives violations, p. 5; (4) arrest of militia member in Wyoming in February 2007 for plans to kill illegal immigrants at the Mexican border, p. 5; (5) arrest of three militia members in Michigan for possession of pipe bombs, automatic weapons, and ordnance with intent to attack federal facilities, pp. 6–7.
169. Letter from Vama T. Locket, associate director, Disclosure & FOIA Operations, Privacy Office, U.S. Department of Homeland Security, to Nathan Mehrens, Americans for Limited Government (August 5, 2009) (on file with author).
170. The Southern Poverty Law Center (SPLC) has long been criticized for inflating threats from conservative groups for financial gain and notoriety. "Cofounded in 1971 by civil rights lawyer cum direct-marketing millionaire Morris Dees . . . the SPLC spent much of its early years defending prisoners who faced the death penalty and suing to desegregate all-white institutions like Alabama's highway patrol. That was then. Today, the SPLC spends most of its time—and money—on a relentless fund-raising campaign, peddling memberships in the church of tolerance with all the zeal of a circuit rider passing the collection plate . . . The center earned $44 million last year alone—$27 million from fund-raising and $17 million from stocks and other investments—but spent only $13 million on civil rights programs, making it one of the most profitable charities in the country." Ken Silverstein, "The Church of Morris Dees: How the Southern Poverty Law Center Profits from Intolerance," *Harper's Magazine,* November 2000, pp. 54–57. See also David Kopel, "The Militias Are Coming," *Reason,* August/September 1996, http://reason.com/archives/1996/08/01/the-militias-are-coming.
171. Southern Poverty Law Center, "Groups," http://www.splcenter.org/get-informed/intelligence-files/groups; See also Sean Lengell, "Family Research Council Labeled a 'Hate Group,'" *Washington Times,* November 24, 2010, http://www.washingtontimes.com/news/2010/nov/24/frc-labeled-a-hate-group/.
172. The North Texas Fusion System's sources are, in their entirety: a posting on the Anti-Defamation League website; an article by terror pundit Robert Spencer at *Human Events,* a posting on the Family Security Matters website citing Robert Spencer; a book review of Robert Spencer's *Stealth Jihad: How Radical Islam Is Subverting America without Guns or Bombs* at the *Front Page Magazine* website; an article entitled *Stealth Jihad* citing Robert Spencer and his book at the Christian Broadcasting Network website; an op-ed by Frank Gaffney on Muslim finance; a post at the *Counterterrorism Blog* on a Muslim financial conference; and a report by the Jamestown Foundation on a radical Islamic group. See North Texas Fusion System, p. 5.

Section 4.4

Does Homeland Security Exist Outside the United States?

Nadav Morag

Homeland security is a uniquely American concept. It is a product of American geographic isolation and the strong tendency throughout American history to believe that there was a clear divide between events, issues, and problems outside US borders and those inside US borders. Among other things, the legal and institutional tools with which the United States is able to deal with threats outside its borders (in the context of what is referred to as "national security") differ markedly from those it is able to employ inside its borders. In the aftermath of the terrorist attacks on September 11, 2001, American leaders realized that they would need new tools to deal with large-scale terrorist threats and yet they were constrained by the Constitution, legislation, and federalism. Consequently, they largely could not apply tried and tested national security tools and methodologies to the domestic arena. Homeland security policies, institutions, and methodologies thus developed to fill this void between what the US could do overseas and what it was unable to do domestically. The subsequent inability to deal with large-scale disasters, such as that produced by Hurricane Katrina in late August of 2005, led to a broadening of the definition of homeland security to include large significant disasters, major public health emergencies, and other large-scale events that had the potential to endanger the citizenry, economy, rule of law, and the general functioning of government and society.[1]

America's sister democracies around the world did not undergo the dual shocks of 9/11 and Katrina; thus, these countries did not face situations of significant social or economic chaos resulting from such a wide range of threats. Some of them, like Israel and the United Kingdom, had to cope with significant terrorist threats while others, such as Japan, had to cope with significant natural disasters, but none had to cope with massive and unprecedented terrorist events and natural disasters in the space of only a few years. Moreover, countries such as Australia, Canada, Germany, France, the UK, Israel, Japan, Italy, the Netherlands, and others had never really viewed domestic threats as qualitatively different from overseas threats and were able to use tools—such as the military—both externally and internally (though, of course, not in precisely the same way). Given the above, it is not surprising that the concept of homeland security, as an integrative idea that brings together domestic preparedness, response, and recovery efforts with respect to threats ranging from large-scale terrorism to natural disasters to pandemics (to name a few) was largely alien to these countries. It is not that other democracies did not prepare for, attempt to mitigate, respond to, and recover from terrorism, natural disasters, public health emergencies, threats to critical infrastructure, and the like; it is just that they did not view all of these activities as interlinked and part of a common effort designed to head off and, failing that, cope with and recover from events that could produce massive social and economic disruption.

With the creation, in the United States, of homeland security as a policy framework and practitioner and academic discipline during the course of the first decade of the twenty-first century, other democracies took notice and some began to use the terminology of homeland security without, necessarily, understanding its scope or *raison d'être*. Most countries have still not truly come around to the idea that counter-terrorism, emergency management, critical infrastructure protection, public health, combating large-scale crime, etc. are part and parcel of the same overall problem: that of maintaining social and economic stability and governmental functioning in the face of events that threaten to overwhelm the capacity of government and society to cope.

A case in point is the United Kingdom. The UK is one of the most, if not the most, prolific producer of national and local governmental strategies. It has an elaborate and well-thought-out counterterrorism strategy known as CONTEST with four elements: Prevent, Pursue, Protect and Prepare.[2] Counterterrorism, as used in the UK, is a broad policy area that also includes maritime, aviation and border security, critical infrastructure protection, and resilience but it is not entirely equivalent to homeland security both because it does not address as broad a range of functions and because it is focused on preventing, preparing for, responding to, and coping with, terrorism. London and other local jurisdictions have also developed emergency management plans based on a three-tier incident management system (the tiers are referred to as gold, silver, and bronze) that separate the strategic functions from the tactical and operational ones.[3] These response systems will kick in during major terrorist incidents as well as disasters (the UK suffers from flooding on occasion), but they are not necessarily seen as integrally related to the counterterrorism effort.

From an organizational standpoint, a significant segment of the homeland security enterprise is housed in the Home Office, which is the national-level department that overseas aspects of the law enforcement mission. Although the UK's regional and national police forces are administratively independent, the Home Office does have oversight and funding influence over them. Moreover, the country's premier investigatory agency, the Serious and Organized Crime Agency (SOCA) is under the direct purview of the Home Office. The domestic intelligence mission, carried out by the British Security Service (MI5), is also under the authority of the Home Secretary. Finally, border security (the UK Border Agency operates under the auspices of the Home Office) and immigration are also within the Home Office's remit.[4] Nevertheless, functions such as those carried out by the Federal Emergency Management Agency (FEMA) and housed within the US Department of Homeland Security are not within the scope of Home Office operations. Moreover, at the state level, most homeland security agencies in the United States have a large emergency management component and many also include a public health component (though public health is primarily a local governmental function in the United States) and all of these do not exist in any one institution in the UK. In short, in terms of doctrine, policy, and organization, the UK does not view counterterrorism and emergency management (not to mention other elements of the homeland security enterprise) as part of a common operational sphere.

At the other end of the spectrum lies Canada, influenced as it is by its proximity and historic relationship to the United States. Canada has moved closer to the US model of a homeland security enterprise. Canada's national security policy (the reader will note this is national security more broadly, as opposed to just homeland security) incorporates the disciplines of law enforcement, intelligence, emergency management, public health, and transportation and border security, but it also includes aspects of international security that take it outside the sphere of the homeland security enterprise.[5] Organizationally Canada takes somewhat of a middle ground approach between the UK and the US in that, while it does not incorporate security and emergency management under the same organizational framework, it does view these disciplines as part of the overall public safety mission. The premier federal security department in the country is Public Safety Canada, which is responsible for federal law enforcement (via the Royal Canadian Mounted Police, RCMP, which also contracts to provincial and municipal governments to provide policing services) and intelligence (via the Canadian Security Intelligence Service, CSIS). While Public Safety Canada does not have direct organizational responsibility for emergency management in the way that DHS does via FEMA, it will play a coordinating role with federal ministries responsible for health and critical infrastructures, as well as with provincial and municipal authorities and the private sector.[6]

Israel arguably lies at the center of the spectrum. Though it does not possess an articulated national security strategy, let alone a homeland security one (Israeli prime ministers do not like to be penned in by formal strategies), it has, in practice, adopted elements of a homeland security doctrine that tie together the police, fire, EMS, the health system, and the military. Despite fighting major wars at least once a decade since independence, the country's civilian sector was largely exempted from military attack (though not terrorism). However, the current presence of long range/high payload surface-to-surface missiles, as well as short-range/low payload rockets, has made Israel's civilian population highly vulnerable. In the wake of the SCUD attacks on Israel in the 1991 Gulf War, the Israel Defense Force (IDF) recognized that the civilian sector had come to be part of the battle space (if not, indeed, the primary battle space) and created a fourth regional command (in addition to the Northern, Central and Southern Commands): the Homefront Command (HFC). The HFC was created to improve interagency cooperation between the military, first responders, and government ministries, to free the three IDF regional commands to focus exclusively on the front lines, to provide military resources to the civilian sector (capabilities such as search and rescue, WMD detection and response, etc.), and to enable the centralization of response efforts.[7] In normal times, the HFC is responsible for establishing emergency procedures, supervising preparedness exercises, and monitoring the preparedness of the health system, municipalities, the transportation system, and critical infrastructures. During periods in which Israel is facing an active wartime scenario (or potentially, a WMD terrorist attack or other mass casualty event), the Cabinet can declare a "limited state of emergency" whereupon the HFC is given command and control over the other response agencies. The integrative Israeli approach however, is focused primarily on the response piece of the homeland security mission. In terms of prevention and organizational structures, the police (Israel has a single national police force) coordinate with the domestic intelligence service, the Israel Security Agency (ISA, also known as the *Shin Bet* or *Shabak*) and the military (which has law enforcement powers in the West Bank), but each entity largely functions in its own operational sphere and according to its own operational doctrine.

Overall then, as the above examples have shown, homeland security is not really conceived of abroad as an "enterprise" and overarching discipline in the manner in which it is viewed in the United States. Whether or not it is entirely viewed in this manner in the United States is arguable since, at least from the organizational perspective, the homeland security mission is not even strictly confined to DHS at the federal level or to state or local homeland security offices at their respective levels of government. However, the homeland security enterprise is being actively developed as a discipline in the US and this is likely to continue to impact policies, strategies and institutions. Whether or not other countries will eventually adopt the same logic and view their disparate homeland security efforts as part of the same set of objectives requiring a joint policy, doctrinal, and organizational framework remains to be seen.

Notwithstanding the present absence overseas of homeland security as a coherent policy sphere, other countries are still engaging in homeland security-related policymaking and strategizing. Learning from other countries' experiences and approaches in this context is important not only because it makes sense for American decision makers to learn from the experiences of foreign governments (of which there are many) and thus avoid trying to "reinvent the wheel," but also because, in many cases, the threats are transnational and consequently safeguarding homeland security requires cooperation with other countries. Whether the threat emanates from radicalized Europeans accessing the United States under the visa waiver program in order to execute terrorist attacks, or aircraft passengers flying in to the US from an Asian city carrying the latest viral mutation with them, many homeland security threats emanate from abroad. Examples of such threats abound. In the terrorism sphere, in addition to the 9/11 attackers, Ahmed Resam (the "Millennium Bomber"), arrested in 1999, used Canada as a staging area for his plot to bomb the Los Angeles International Airport. Richard Reid (the "Shoe Bomber") boarded a Miami-bound flight in Paris in December 2001. The 2006 transatlantic liquid explosives plot (the "Overt Plot") was hatched and prepared in the UK and Umar Farouk Abdulmutallab (the "Underwear Bomber" or "Christmas Bomber") boarded his Detroit-bound flight in Amsterdam in December 2009. The potential and actual spillover of Mexican criminal violence into the US has also been an issue of concern for some time. In the pandemic sphere, the SARS outbreak in China led to the US public health system being put on alert in December 2003 and the outbreaks of avian influenza and swine flu in Southeast Asia and Mexico respectively led to pandemic concerns in the US. In short, there is no lack of examples of homeland security threats emanating from overseas. It therefore follows that addressing these threats will not only require international cooperation, but also an understanding of how other countries, particularly allied democratic nations, address these issues within their own borders before those issues reach US shores, and what their respective laws, institutions, and modes of operation allow those countries to do.

Ultimately then, as homeland security becomes more of a global enterprise, other countries may realize the logic of having objectives supersede tools and methodologies. In other words, they may come to adopt American logic that the ultimate objectives of ensuring social and economic stability and the continued rule of law in severe crisis situations means that operational spheres as seemingly disparate as counterterrorism, law enforcement in the face of massive criminal activity, securing transport systems, borders, and critical infrastructure, and coping with public health emergencies and the management of crisis situations are all essentially part of the same effort. If and when this does occur, it will make it considerably easier for the United States to improve its ability to safeguard homeland security because it, and its global partners, will be viewing the problem in the same way and integrating their respective resources and strategies accordingly.

Critical Thinking Questions

1. Why does the United States view security differently than other countries, in terms of dividing "national" and "homeland" into separate organizations and agencies?
2. Should the United States consider a wholesale governmental reform in which we adopt the security organizational model found in the countries mentioned in this article? What are the pros and cons of this?
3. Compare this chapter to the previous one. Would you lean more toward the views of Rittgers (abolish the DHS) or Morag (encourage other countries to adopt a DHS-like strategy and organization)? Explain.

Notes

1. See the differences in emphasis in the 2002 and 2005 versions of the *National Strategy for Homeland Security* as well as changing White House definitions of what falls within the Homeland Security mission space.
2. UK Government, *Countering International Terrorism: The United Kingdom's Strategy* (London: Stationery Office, 2006).
3. London Emergency Services Liaison Panel, *Major Incident Procedure Manual*, 7th (London: LESLP, 2007).
4. See the Home Office website: www.homeoffice.gov.uk
5. Canadian Privy Council Office, *Securing an Open Society: Canada's National Security Policy* (Ottawa: Canadian Government, 2004).
6. See http://www.publicsafety.gc.ca/prg/em/ci/index-eng.aspx.
7. See http://www.oref.org.il/82-en/PAKAR.aspx.

Section 4.5

Lessons from the Singapore Home Team Approach to Homefront Security

Susan Sim

In 1995, a catchy jingle with the tagline "The Home Team, Here to Make it Right" hit the airwaves in Singapore. It promised Singaporeans that the police, fire and emergency services; prisons, drug enforcement and immigration officials; and policy staff from the Ministry of Home Affairs were all united in keeping them safe. The best soccer players from these agencies even played together on a team—aptly named Home United—in Singapore's national soccer league.

But it was not until two years later, in 1997, that the Home Team was officially launched as "a completely different way of thinking, operating, managing and learning" for the law enforcement and security agencies grouped under the Ministry of Home Affairs (MHA Group).[1] The MHA Group, as then-minister in charge Wong Kan Seng put it, is the lead agency ensuring a safe and secure "best home" for Singapore, in line with the 1997 national vision of making Singapore a "country that offers her people a level of security and safety that is unrivalled anywhere else . . . where there is harmony and unity among people of many races, religions and cultures."[2]

Appointed Minister for Home Affairs in 1994, Wong felt that although the eight departments[3] reporting to him were highly competent and worked well together, they cooperated and coordinated as separate departments, each with its own mindset and interests deeply rooted in and conditioned by history. But Singapore, like the rest of the world, was on the threshold of rapid change. Email and the internet became more widely available in 1993, changing the way governments and society communicated. The information technology revolution and dot-com boom were fueling unprecedented economic growth and changing lifestyles as people became more connected across the world.

Wong wanted the MHA Group to be more proactive and strategic in developing solutions that integrated the various skill sets and capabilities of each department, so that the agency could be cohesive and better prepared to deal with emerging problems that might be beyond the functional competency of any single department. Carrying on as usual remained a viable option. But like his colleagues in the Singapore cabinet, Wong worried about external shocks and, in today's parlance, "black swan" events, and wanted his ministry to be ready to deal with anything.

The year 1995 had begun with an earthquake in Kobe, Japan that killed thousands, allegedly because the country's national and local emergency services were not better prepared.[4] In March, a Sarin gas attack on the Tokyo subway showed not only the ease with which terrorists can create weapons of mass destruction,[5] but also the vulnerability of mass transit systems to large casualty attacks. The Oklahoma City bombing a month later and the immediate scapegoating of Muslims amid the tragedy[6] offered a sobering lesson for multi-cultural Singapore: quick police work in identifying suspects is as crucial as saving lives. The indictment in New York that same month of Ramzi Ahmed Yousef for plotting to blow up flights in the Far East revealed he had planned to bomb a United

Airlines flight departing Singapore and another heading to Singapore.[7] Had Oplan Bojinka not been foiled by a fire in a Manila apartment in January, Singaporeans would surely have numbered among the 4,000 potential fatalities.

Wong decided that he needed a team nimble enough to deal with a fast-changing threat environment, one that thought and acted as a team. As he said in his farewell address to the Home Team 15 years later, he wanted "a team that was not so much of a relay but akin to a soccer team—fluid, adaptive and coordinated."[8] So in 1995, he conceived the idea of the Home Team, using the word "Home" from the Ministry of Home Affairs. In his words:

> Residing in this concept was a potentially powerful idea—the notion that if the synergistic potential of the Home Team can be harnessed and resources shared, it will be far greater than the sum of its individual departments. We implemented this idea in earnest, used it and publicized it at every opportunity, including re-branding the Police football club as Home United Football Club, to present the different facet of the Home Team.[9]

Wong—a seasoned politician who had begun his cabinet career[10] first running the Ministry for Community Development, then the Ministry of Foreign Affairs (and both portfolios concurrently for three years in the late 1980s)—enjoyed the confidence of then-Prime Minister Goh Chok Tong and a genuine friendship with his predecessor Shunmugam Jayakumar, with whom he swapped portfolios in 1994.

Wong's Home Team concept was not controversial politically and did not require legislative approval. As Minister for Home Affairs, Wong could restructure his departments as he saw fit. Parliament would, however, have to debate and approve legislative amendments to any change in enforcement powers vested in the uniformed and security services, as well as the ministry's budget. But with the ruling party enjoying an absolute majority in the unicameral Parliament, bills introduced by ministers were easily passed.

Yet Wong knew he could not mandate the Home Team by fiat. He had to convince his eight department heads that they lost nothing, but instead would be able to carry out their core missions more effectively by working with the other departments. He had to convey that the whole would indeed be larger than the sum of its parts.

Each department's staff had to be convinced, too, so Wong sent his most senior bureaucrat, the Permanent Secretary, on a "road show" to explain the concept. The officers on the ground were used to working only within their departments. The challenge was convincing them to think and operate beyond their usual silos, and to welcome other specialists on their turf to complement their own domain expertise.

To seed the idea of a Home Team identity, senior officers who were promoted in 1996 received their certificates from the minister at the first Home Team Senior Officer's Promotion ceremony. That ceremony continues to this day. Ministry staff also came up with the idea of the Home Team Achievement Award to recognize "pathfinders" and generate awareness of the importance of teamwork. Wong personally handed out the first awards at the Home Team Launching Workshop in 1997.

To prepare for the Home Team launch, hundreds of staff from all the departments spent a year working through and debating what the concept meant in practice. They created a vision statement: "We want to be world-class in serving our country, by delivering a safe and secure home for our people." While a shared vision and mission represented progress, they did not guarantee practical convergence. It remained to be seen whether standard operating procedures of different departments could be integrated to achieve faster and better results.

Implementing The Home Team Concept

It was fortuitous timing that the two largest departments in the MHA Group—the Singapore Police and the Civil Defense Force—were looking to upgrade their command, control and communications systems. Wong was able to tout the benefits of sharing infrastructure resources across the Home Team, and the natural progression to joint operations, at the 1997 HT Launch Workshop:

> Let me give you some concrete results. The first example actually marked the birth of the Home Team concept. The MHA Group struggled to design a state-of-the-art command, control and communications system. The project began in the Police. Civil Defense also wanted a C3 system. It was a struggle for the Police, even more so for Civil Defense. As the project developed, it became clear that we could not reap the real benefits unless the technology went further than just helping the Police or Civil Defense work well by itself. The C3 project now involves almost all our departments. Next, we learned that we could further maximize the benefits of the technology only if we revamped our operations across the departments. A multi-department, multi-discipline team is now rewriting our operating approaches and doctrines. If the MHA Group does not work seamlessly together and in fundamentally different ways, we will not be able to master new technology, and maximize the use of such a key resource.[11]

The next success story that tested the Home Team joint operations concept came with the opening of the Tuas Checkpoint in January 1998.

For an island state like Singapore, border security is a challenge—particularly the prevention of both illegal immigration and illicit drug and cigarette smuggling. Many of these illegal activities are attempted at the two land bridges linking Singapore to Malaysia. With the opening of a new causeway in the northwest of Singapore, a decision was made to bring all the different units—police, immigration, central narcotics and customs—together under one unified command: the Tuas Joint Operations Command.

By April 2003, immigration was slated to take on customs and excise duties at all the checkpoints. It was, says former Commissioner of the Immigration and Checkpoints Authority (ICA) Eric Tan, "a very important step because it allowed us to do more than just people clearance. We would now be able to do cargo clearance and also the clearance of conveyances and this helped to increase Singapore's border security."[12]

More interesting was his observation that the officers working at the checkpoints stopped seeing themselves as officers of individual departments. "Everybody is working together at the checkpoints with one sole purpose. That is to make our checkpoints as safe and secure as possible," Tan said.

Indeed, across the country, Home Team agencies were being grouped into four, and then five geographical sectors beginning early 2001. Within each sector, precinct officers from the different agencies conduct joint law enforcement operations as well as interact over sports and other recreational activity. In one such sectoral operation highlighted at the March 2001 Home Team Workshop, 90 officers from the police, immigration, civil defense, narcotics and prisons in the Southern Sector carried out a joint operation that netted 116 persons for immigration, vice, selling pirated movies on discs and drug-related offences. A number of entertainment outlets were also cited for breaching licensing and fire safety conditions.[13]

Current Commissioner of the Singapore Civil Defense Force (SCDF) Eric Yap was on his first posting in the ministry headquarters when the Home Team concept was being introduced. "I had the opportunity to see its conceptualization and over the years became involved in implementing what it represents at the ground in my various operational postings in SCDF. To my mind, it doesn't replace the rich heritage of each department but provides a common reference point to the objective we seek to achieve for Singapore—i.e., a safe and secure best home." He adds:

> In its simplest form, the HT concept brings new meaning and efficiency to joint ops. This can be in planning for contingency response for high security events, responding to daily emergencies, or conducting enforcement actions. This is possible as the many opportunities for inter-department interactions enable officers to be familiar with each other in and out of work.[14]

Today, sharing infrastructure and co-locating police stations and firehouses is the norm. As Yap notes, there are considerable cost savings when departments share infrastructure. One of his divisional headquarters and a fire station are co-located with a Neighborhood Police Centre (NPC). A new SCDF marine command will soon be located beside the Police Coast Guard's base. Singapore's new entertainment and business center, Marina Bay, will have a firehouse and police station standing side-by-side.[15]

For the smaller departments with a narrower focus, like the Central Narcotics Bureau (CNB), the ability to share not just infrastructure and common law enforcement capabilities like forensics, but also to leverage the human resources of the other departments—in particular the police force and the ICA—have allowed it to "do more for less," says CNB Director Ng Ser Song. He adds:

> CNB, with its strength of about 700 people and limited budget, will not be able to effectively enforce the Misuse of Drugs Act island-wide. We cannot afford a large patrolling force, so we find synergies by working with Police patrols. At the checkpoints, we leverage on ICA infrastructure, processes and officers to help us keep a tight lid on the inflow of drugs. On our own, there is no way we can do it.
>
> The boys are also conducting sector ops with their counterparts in Police, ICA, SCDF, Military Provost, going into an area with a big show of force and taking down all manner of crime. Sometimes we bring back more than 100 drug pushers/addicts, prostitutes, AWOL soldiers, and issue summons for safety/fire violations etc.
>
> As for intelligence sharing, it could not get better than now, where there are networks of trust at various levels of command.[16]

For instance, CNB surveillance units have been deployed for major security/public order operations to support the police, and the Police Intelligence Department provides covert coverage on the ground for CNB operations.

The networks of trust that CNB Director Ng cite are built from the working knowledge that Home Team departments and their key personnel gain through cross-postings during their careers. Ng, a police officer, had previously served in three other Home Team departments—Internal Security Department (ISD), the Immigration Department and the CNB—and held various command posts in the police, including the Airport Police and the Police Intelligence Department, before his current appointment as CNB director. He and the current Commissioner of Police, Ng Joo Hee, worked together in ISD early in their police careers. Police Commissioner Ng was previously Director of Prisons, and the current prisons director was formerly the Police Chief of Staff. SCDF Commissioner Eric Yap had served a few stints in the Ministry of Home Affairs Headquarters, including as Senior Director of the Homefront Security Division (HSD). The current Director of the Internal Security Department was Yap's predecessor at HSD. Until recently, ICA Commissioner Eric Tan was first a police, then an intelligence officer who had previously commanded CNB.

Such cross-postings of uniformed and civilian officers to different departments are not unusual within the Singapore public service, especially for those in the elite Administrative Service, whose members are recruited and groomed to assume the top posts in the civil service. But the Home Team uses postings not just for career development purposes, but also to nurture what it calls the "Home Team Plus" officer.

Wong, who was promoted to Deputy Prime Minister in 2005 while continuing to run the Home Affairs portfolio, stressed the importance of people, not just structures or processes, during his 17 years at the helm of the Home Team. In his farewell speech in 2010, he left two clear messages:

> Even as the Home Team concept evolves and takes root, two things must always be clear. Firstly, the Home Team identity is not meant to displace or erode our officers' identification with and pride in their parent service be it the Police, SCDF, ICA, Prisons or others. Instead, the Home Team identity enlarges the possibilities for growth for the officer in a larger family and enhances the potential for greater efficacy and creative solutions for individual departments in the Home Team by leveraging on the strengths of its collective diversity.
>
> Secondly, what lies at the heart of the Home Team is not just systems or technology or hardware but more importantly, its people. It is the officers at work, day in and day out, who determine what being a Home Team officer really means. Indeed as a community of professionals and practitioners dedicated to a common mission of keeping Singapore and Singaporeans safe and secure, a strong fellowship has grown over time.
>
> Indeed, in a crisis—and we have seen quite a few in the last 17 years—the most valuable asset is always the people and not systems or standard operating procedures. This is because a crisis is seldom a textbook occurrence.

It demands agility, resilience, team work and a high quality of situational awareness of officers in charge.

A Home Team career is therefore not a job for the faint-hearted—it is exacting and demanding and requires a readiness to make sacrifices and to persevere in the face of adversity. Some officers have even faced personal dangers, and in some instances, sacrificed their lives in the course of duty.[17]

The Home Team Gears Up to Fight Terrorism

The Home Team revised its mission statement after the September 11 attacks on the U.S. in 2001 and the discovery of a homegrown terrorist network in Singapore soon after.

Speaking to private sector volunteers[18] in October 2001, Wong observed:

September 11 has changed our way of life. It sharply reminds us of the key role that the Home Team agencies and partners, i.e. you in the committees and boards, have to play to help maintain the sense of security and alertness. It is all the more so now with terrorism. No longer is it only crime or drugs . . . With the change in the security landscape, we need to work with you, the committees, with the key leaders in the private sector, to be involved in preparedness. For example, to be more involved in civil defense preparedness, to be more in-tuned to security concerns, and to help others outside of the Home Team partnership to understand the overall picture. All of us have to play our part to maintain racial harmony which is so fragile.[19]

The new mission statement announced in July 2002—"We work as a team, in partnership with the community, to make Singapore our safe and secure Best Home"—reflects the emphasis on community engagement in Singapore's counterterrorism strategy following the uncovering of the Jemaah Islamiyah terrorist network in late 2001. This approach was in large part driven by the Internal Security Department, whose then-director, Benny Lim, advised Minister Wong Kan Seng and the political leadership that they had to embrace the Muslim community as a major stakeholder in fighting terrorism if Singapore's carefully balanced religious harmony were to hold.[20]

As Wong revealed a year after ISD announced the detention of 15 individuals for plotting terrorist attacks in Singapore:

I do not believe there has ever been an occasion where ISD officers visited and reached out to Muslim organizations and leaders even before the details of the operation were made public. Working closely with these leaders to establish understanding of sensitivities, to maintain calm and composure, ISD's concern was on the larger issues of ethnic harmony at stake in such an episode. ISD officers also openly briefed an audience of over 1,700 grassroots leaders' meeting with the PM, not once but twice. These collective efforts were worthwhile, as the outcome minimized the potential negative fall-out that the JI episode could have had on our society. This shows the sensitivity of ISD in handling security issues which can have serious implications on racial and religious harmony.[21]

FIGURE 1 The Home Team Mission Statement (www.mha.gov.sg)

ISD Director Lim felt that if Singapore, as it took action against terrorist groups, were to avoid falling into the trap of creating gulfs both between the state and the minority Muslim community and among the different ethnic and religious groups, the government had to openly acknowledge the existentialist threat the country faced from an ideology that purported to be about defending Islam and which appealed to extremists who considered themselves Muslims. Although Singapore is a secular state with a strict injunction against religious meddling in politics, he argued that Islamic scholars and community leaders had to play a crucial role in refuting the hijacking of their religion by violent extremists.

ISD was at one point monitoring almost 100 suspected members of the Jemaah Islamiyah (JI), a terrorist network based in Indonesia and spanning Malaysia, the Philippines and Singapore. Lim knew that even as ISD rounded them up under Singapore's preventive detention law—the Internal Security Act—it would have to plan for their eventual release, since the law is designed to neutralize threats to national security and detention orders are for a maximum of two years in the first instance. He took a gamble on inviting a group of civilians, including prominent religious clerics with personal reputations to protect, in the rehabilitation of the JI detainees. Now widely known and lauded as the Religious Rehabilitation Group, these clerics were originally wary of their involvement with ISD.

As Lim recounted in a 2012 interview, at the time these Muslim leaders stepped forward to work with ISD to craft the rehabilitation approach, "it was untested, uncharted territory and went against the grain of conventional views. It's a measure of their conviction and courage that they stepped out."[22] This community involvement was also crucial on a strategic level because it enabled Muslim Singaporeans to see themselves not as a community under siege, but as a crucial partner of the secular state in ensuring national security.[23]

This partnership between the community and the security authorities in Singapore was then and continues to be led from the highest levels of government. But it is largely possible because of the longstanding relationships of trust between ISD officers and key community leaders.

Given the Singapore state's definition of race and religious relations as being fragile, it is to be expected that its security service would discreetly monitor all the various ethnic and religious communities for potential subversive and extremist elements. What this has meant is that ISD field officers have a good feel for the ground. It is not a popular job and Muslim officers, for example, have had to face down critics who sought to ostracize them.

But Lim felt that as much as ISD could be conscientious and diligent, there was always an element of luck that led to the uncovering of the JI network. In January 2000, Singapore's stringent visa policy had led to Yemeni al-Qaeda operative Walid Muhammad

Salih bin Attash being denied entry to Singapore at Changi Airport and deported to Kuala Lumpur. The Osama bin Laden aide was supposed to meet Ibrahim Abu Nibras and Fahd al Quso in Singapore. The two Yemenis were bringing Walid, also known as Khallad, money from al Qaeda. Khallad was also carrying out orders from bin Laden to gather surveillance on flights in Southeast Asia for a parallel operation to fly planes into American targets in East Asia at the same time that planes hijacked in the United States were to be crashed or exploded.

All three Yemenis were denied entry to Singapore for no other reason than that they did not have valid visas. Khallad moved his meeting with Nibras and Quso to Bangkok. Two of the 9/11 conspirators who were in Kuala Lumpur en route to the U.S. went with Khallad to Bangkok because "they thought it would enhance their cover as tourists to have passport stamps from a popular tourist destination such as Thailand."[24] From Bangkok, Khallad reported the results of his surveillance mission to bin Laden in Afghanistan. Soon after, the al Qaeda leader cancelled the East Asia part of the planes operation.

Singapore's strict visa regime had begun during the Gulf War. ISD had then advised the Immigration Department to impose visa requirements on a number of countries deemed to pose significant security risks, including Yemen. There was pressure from the business community to lift them as soon as possible. But ISD believed the visa controls and tight border checks were a reason there was no terrorist activity in Singapore, unlike in Jakarta and Manila, and kept the controls in place despite arguments that they lessened Singapore's appeal as an investment destination for petrodollars.

However, even such stringent visa controls have their limitations. After the September 11 attacks, al Qaeda sent a Canadian passport holder, Mohd Mansour Jabarah, and an Indonesian bomb-maker with a Philippine passport, Fathur Rohman al-Ghozi, to enlist the help of the JI network for a series of terrorist attacks in Singapore. Their passports gave them visa-free entry and were not on any watch list, so the operatives were allowed to enter.

Fortunately, the JI network was by then under surveillance by ISD because of a tip-off. The version most Singaporeans know is that soon after the 9/11 attacks, a Singaporean Muslim informed ISD that Muhammad Aslam bin Yar Ali Khan, a Singaporean of Pakistani descent, boasted that he personally knew bin Laden. What has been left out of the narrative is that the informant knew the ISD officer he spoke to. He did not see his warning to ISD as a betrayal of a fellow Muslim or his community. He saw Aslam as a potential security threat to Singapore who needed to be checked out.

Uncovering Jemaah Islamiyah[25]

On 5 January 2002, Singaporeans were stunned to learn that ISD had uncovered a home-grown terrorist network that was on the verge of assembling several large bombs. In a few short paragraphs, the press release from MHA that day said 15 persons had been arrested between 9 and 24 December 2001, of which 13 were "cell members of a clandestine organization which calls itself Jemaah Islamiyah." Several of these persons had been to Afghanistan, where they underwent short periods of training in al Qaeda terrorist camps. They collected funds for terrorist groups and had targeted and conducted surveillance on establishments in Singapore to bomb. The group not only knew how to make bombs—they were attempting to procure large quantities of ammonium nitrate to make several bombs.

Some members of the network were believed to have fled the country. Key figures were linked to militant elements in Malaysia and Indonesia, including one Hambali (born Riduan Isamuddin, alias Encep Nurjaman), later determined to be an al Qaeda operative responsible for Southeast Asia operations.

More details were disclosed a week later, and following the arrest of another 21 persons in August, a white paper was presented to Parliament in January 2003.

600 hours, 65,000 Records and 988 Gigabytes Later

What has rarely been told is the enormous amount of legwork that went into uncovering JI, identifying its members and tracing their links throughout the region. More than 600 hours of surveillance were expended, over 65,000 data records of operational leads were generated and, at the height of the operation in November and December of 2001, dozens of teams of ISD investigators, researchers, engineers and field officers worked around the clock.

Not surprisingly for our modern, globalized world, the JI operatives were security conscious, tech-savvy and adept at hiding their records and plans in encrypted computer files. ISD's IT forensic teams accessed a total of 1,100 diskettes and 120 hard disks and processed 988 gigabytes of data in the first two phases of the security operations alone.

What really tipped the balance in Singapore's favor, however, were the years of discreet monitoring of potential subversive and extremist elements and of cultivating a feel for the ground, which succeeding generations of ISD field officers have honed.

Soon after the September 11 attacks, a Singaporean Muslim stepped forward and informed ISD that Muhammad Aslam bin Yar Ali Khan, a Singaporean of Pakistani descent, had links with al Qaeda. The informant was not afraid to go to ISD because he entrusted the officers to do the right thing.

Aslam was not unknown to ISD, which immediately put him and his associates under heightened surveillance. On October 4, Aslam left suddenly for Afghanistan, where he was subsequently detained by the Northern Alliance. When news of his arrest reached Singapore, ISD decided to arrest 15 of his associates before they could abscond. Interrogation and examination of their computer disks revealed they were JI members targeting U.S. assets in Singapore. Some 20 members escaped and fled, first to Malaysia and then to Indonesia.

After the arrests, a friendly intelligence agency gave the ISD a videotape found in the Afghanistan home of Muhammad Atef, bin Laden's second-in-command, who was reportedly killed in air strikes outside of Kabul. This videotape depicted Singapore's Yishun subway station and the shuttle buses that ferry U.S. military personnel to it, and included commentary in English by one of the plotters on how it could be bombed.

But perhaps the most significant discovery came in ISD's data-mining of immigration records combined with painstaking field investigation which identified the two foreign handlers of the Singapore JI cells: Mohd Mansor Jabarah and Fathur Rohman Al-Ghozi. The two men were the key figures behind the plot to stage a series of truck bomb attacks against several targets in Singapore. Jabarah had travelled to Singapore under his own name, as he had a clean Canadian passport. He stayed at a budget hotel in Singapore's Little India district, but registered the room under Al-Ghozi's false Filipino identity, "Alih Randy." Al-Ghozi himself stayed overnight at the office premises of one of the JI detainees in Geylang.

Timely Arrests

ISD shared these discoveries with friendly intelligence services, leading to the timely arrest of Al-Ghozi by Filipino authorities just as he was half way through procuring explosives to continue the operation against Singapore. At the time of his arrest, the bomb maker had in his possession more than a ton of TNT, hundreds of detonators and more than a mile of detonating cord. Jabarah's arrest in the Middle East exposed the al Qaeda connection not just to the specific terrorist plot against Singapore, but also to the JI organization and network in the region.

Yazid Sufaat, a Malaysian and another important al Qaeda-linked operative, had already obtained and stored four tons of ammonium nitrate in Muar, a Malaysian town 100 miles north of Singapore. Sufaat had housed two of the September 11 bombers in Kuala Lumpur when they were en route to the United States for the attacks. The Singaporean JI cell was to purchase another 17 tons of nitrate, to bring the total to 21 tons for six bombs—each bigger than the size of the bomb that brought down a federal building in Oklahoma City. When all was ready, the two foreign terrorists would assemble six truck bombs and direct where they were to be placed and detonated simultaneously.

With the ISD information, Malaysian police found the ammonium nitrate in an oil palm plantation in Johor. Just to be sure, ISD search teams also spent months conducting discreet checks over many suspected locations to verify that none of the explosives sought by JI had been slipped into and stashed away in Singapore.

Had JI succeeded in staging the attacks, more than 3,000 people would likely have died. Singapore would have had its own 9/11.

Disrupting JI's Regeneration

Continuing ISD security operations against JI in Singapore over the last decade, coupled with arrests of key leaders in Malaysia and Indonesia, have reduced JI's operational capabilities. But the group is re-positioning and rejuvenating itself. Much of the JI network and its infrastructure of radical schools continue to operate in the region; they know they are under watch and are consolidating their strength. Those JI terrorists who seek to mount operations are not using JI members but are leveraging on the support and resources of fraternal groups.

Perhaps most disturbing is that JI leaders prepared their succession plans years ago, sending their own children to Pakistan and Afghanistan in the late 1990s to be trained in terrorist tactics and groomed for leadership. Two young Singaporean men who had just turned 21 were arrested in 2003; one had fought with the Taliban in Afghanistan and the other trained with the Kashmiri militant group Laskhar e-Taiba.

The JI Plots

Singapore JI members are known to have at least six different plans to attack U.S. and other assets in Singapore. They include:

1. Use six truck bombs to mount simultaneous attacks against the Australian and British high commissions, the Israeli embassy, and U.S.-related targets like the U.S. embassy and naval vessels, as well as commercial buildings housing U.S. companies.

2. Launch a sea-borne suicide attack against U.S. naval vessels and personnel. A small vessel would collide with U.S. ships travelling eastward from Sembawang Wharf via Pulau Tekong.
3. Attack U.S. and Israeli businesses in Singapore not only to cause panic and chaos, but also to make American and Israeli investors lose confidence in Singapore.
4. Strike water pipelines, Changi Airport, Biggin Hill radar station, Mass Rapid Transit Operations Control Centre, Jurong Island, and the Ministry of Defence's Bukit Gombak Headquarters. JI would then implicate Malaysia and provoke a war, creating chaos that would allow JI to overthrow the Singapore and Malaysian governments.

The New Layered National Security Architecture

The al Qaeda and JI plots were thwarted by ISD, working independently of the rest of the Home Team. It was intelligence work that operated on a need-to-know basis. At the same time, in the immediate post-9/11 environment, the police and the other Home Team departments worked on "hardening" Singapore by tightening border security and ramping up security for key installations and high-value events. ISD was responsible for the risk assessments, with the police providing the operational plans and manpower; the ICA screened out potential terrorists and bomb-making materials, and the SCDF beefed up its hazmat response capabilities. Any suspicious indicators were referred to ISD for investigation.

ISD's success in uncovering and neutralizing the JI threat, which originated from outside Singapore, also led to a push, by the military policy establishment, to create "a suitable structure that will prevail over the traditional boundaries of the various policy, intelligence and operations agencies."[26]

Spurred further by the debate over intelligence and coordination failures in the United States that might have otherwise prevented 9/11, the post of Coordinating Minister for Security and Defense was created at Deputy Prime Minister (DPM) level in August 2003. Tony Tan, who was then DPM and Minister for Defense, relinquished his Defense portfolio and became the new Coordinating Minister and chairman of the Security Policy Review Committee, which comprises the ministers for Defense, Home Affairs and Foreign Affairs. The post of Permanent Secretary for National Security and Intelligence Coordination was also created to head the National Security Coordination Secretariat (NSCS), reporting directly to the Prime Minister through the Coordinating Minister. The NSCS in turn established a National Security Coordination Centre and a Joint Counter Terrorism Centre to support its policy and intelligence functions. Its staff was detailed from the intelligence services, the Home Team, the military and the Ministry of Information, Communications and the Arts.

The NSCS published "A National Security Strategy for Singapore" in 2004 to explain its *raison d'etre.* It declared that the "cornerstone of Singapore's strategy is a stronger and more robust inter-agency network," adding: "Given that transnational terrorism's center of gravity lies outside Singapore, a stove-piped approach to internal security and external defense will no longer work."[27]

The new National Security Architecture would have three pillars of policy, operations and capability development in an integrated national strategy of prevention, protection and response.[28]

Wisely, the architects decided to leave the operational coordination aspects to the Home Team, which has had an inter-agency crisis management structure called the Executive Group (EG)[29] since 1978. Tested rigorously by annual simulation exercises and other national crises such as the collapse of a hotel in 1986, the EG—led by the Permanent Secretary of the Ministry of Home Affairs—was called into action when four terrorists from Pakistan hijacked Singapore Airlines SQ 117 on a flight from Kuala Lumpur in 1991. The EG gave the order to military commandos to storm the plane after the hijackers pushed two flight stewards out of the plane and threatened to kill one passenger every ten minutes. All the terrorists were killed, and the hostages were rescued unharmed, leading the Singapore *Straits Times* to proudly declare: "Unlike some other countries, Singapore does not roll over and play dead when threatened by a gun. It can and will fight back, effectively, ruthlessly."[30]

But the NSCS' attempt at coordinating policy and intelligence assessments on terrorist threats through a layered, inter-agency approach led initially to fears that decisions on the conduct of operations could become politicized. ISD had no issue with sharing intelligence among partners within the national security community—it did not operate outside Singapore, but enjoyed effective working relationships with its external intelligence counterpart as well as many foreign intelligence services and law enforcement agencies. Traditionally, however, ISD has reported directly to the Minister for Home Affairs, not through the Permanent Secretary. The new architecture called for the creation of the Intelligence Coordination Committee, comprising the civilian leaders of the ministries of defense, home affairs and foreign affairs, to take charge of coordinating Singapore's counterterrorism intelligence activities. The "trio of wise men"—as the Intelligence Committee was privately dubbed—were powerful bureaucrats who could affect career prospects of every officer in the civil service. But they prudently focused on areas of convergence and gaps instead of peering over the shoulders of the director of ISD.

This implicit understanding crafted at the start was a function of personality, mutual respect, competency and pragmatism. In a small state like Singapore, where meritocracy is prized, political leaders have no powers of patronage within the civil service. Neither can top civil servants perpetuate personal fiefdoms. Under the Public Service Leadership scheme introduced in 2000, permanent secretaries must retire after a ten-year term even if they have not yet reached the official retirement age of 62. The idea is to allow for faster turnover so that younger officers of promise do not leave for the private sector in frustration. Permanent secretaries usually also rotate to other ministries at least once during their ten years at the top. For example, Benny Lim, Director of ISD during the JI arrests, was promoted to Permanent Secretary at the Ministry of Home Affairs in 2004, and since 2011, has been Permanent Secretary at the Ministry of National Development. He is concurrently Permanent Secretary in charge of National Security and Intelligence Coordination.

Confronting the Crime-Terror Nexus

In hindsight, perhaps the real value of Singapore's investment in the National Security Architecture post-9/11 was not so much "strategic convergence" or "policy coordination," but the greater sense of urgency and purpose it conveyed to the public. Publications like "The Fight Against Terror: Singapore's National Security Strategy" were designed to offer the public comfort that the Government was doing everything possible to protect them.

Certainly it gave non-Home Team agencies clearer roles to play in the protection of Singapore. Soldiers were empowered to join the police in joint patrols of key installations, a move the police welcomed to ease the strain on its resources. Similarly, the Air Force and Navy brought their considerable hardware and expertise to bear on Singapore's aviation and maritime security measures. The defense science organizations were encouraged to invest in innovation and development of new counter-terrorism related technologies even as the Ministry of Home Affairs expanded its Homefront Security Division to work with the design and construction industries to incorporate security features into buildings at the planning and design stage.

But perhaps indicative of the unity of purpose of the Home Team, there were no turf battles with the military or the external intelligence service. Additionally, it ramped up its community partnerships with industries and grassroots organizations. More than 100 Safety and Security Watch Group clusters have since sprung up to enhance security for industries and buildings, supported by the police with timely crime and security information, simple training and organization of joint patrols. The number of neighborhood watch groups has grown to 800 island-wide.[31] With assistance from the Home Affairs Ministry's Community Engagement Division, tens of thousands of citizens have created 26,000 Community Safety and Security Program (CSSP) projects[32] to address local safety or security issues. Some work with the Civil Defense Force on fire safety concerns and emergency preparedness, others with the police on specific crime issues or the CNB on preventive drug abuse education.

The overarching goal is to build community resilience from the ground up. Always concerned about how Singapore's social harmony will hold up in the event of a terrorist attack, the Singapore government started the Community Engagement Program (CEP) in 2005 to encourage bottom-up efforts to build networks of trust. Conscious of the paradox of top-down conception of bottom-up activity, the CEP Secretariat, which resides in the Ministry of Home Affairs, describes its job as "coordinating diversity."[33]

The nationwide annual emergency drills and simulation exercises that the Home Team has been organizing to test crisis response procedures for years also acquired a new urgency after 9/11—to prepare people to live with the threat of terrorism so that they remain resilient when bombs go off. Meanwhile, emergency preparedness exercises have the dual purpose of strengthening community bonds.

Within the Home Team, there was also a quiet evolution in the interpretation of its mission. The public mantra—"multiplicity of purpose but one shared mission"—worked well pre-2001 because the Home Team's "predominant focus was on law and order because this was the main focus of policing work," says Loh Ngai Seng, former Senior Director of the Homefront Security Division (HSD) in ministry headquarters. He adds:

> To implement the Home Team philosophy, you actually need to "swim against" the natural flow of things. Police by virtue of being the largest Department in the Home Team by some distance will overshadow every other Department unless the Police Commissioner of the day is motivated by the same desire to strengthen the Home Team identity.[34]

In 2005, with Benny Lim at the helm of the Ministry as Permanent Secretary, Loh oversaw the HSD's expansion, which resulted in a greater focus on terrorism across the Home Team's different areas of work. The main challenge was working with the Home

Team departments to strengthen the concept of a "crime-terror nexus," which suggests that, due to terrorist organizations' interactions with more traditional criminal groups and activities, departments should not view efforts to address the terrorist threat as distinct from their primary missions. For example, police patrols, CNB raids, ICA searches or SCDF checks might come across terrorist reconnaissance activity or a makeshift chemical lab during their normal course of work.

Loh believes that the mission shift was smooth because the then-director of the Police Intelligence Department, Ng Joo Hee (who is now Commissioner of Police), believed that the police units should adopt the crime-terror nexus outlook and held up the New York Police Department's approach as a model.

Minister Wong Kan Seng amplified this crime-terror nexus message when he spoke on "The Value of the Home Team Today" at the 2005 Home Team Senior Officers' Promotion Ceremony. He provided several scenarios:

> An ICA officer must not only be good at detecting a traveler trying to get in on a dubious passport, his mind must also be alert to the possibility that such a person may not be just an illegal immigrant. He could be a low-end digit of a larger chain or organized crime syndicate running an illegal passport business across many countries. Or he could be a terrorist who has exploited the services of such a criminal outfit to procure false documentation to travel and evade detection.
>
> Likewise, a traffic cop on encountering an illegally parked vehicle should not only issue a summons but should instinctively also ask himself the question whether this is more than just a traffic offender situation. Looking closely at the vehicle itself and where it is parked and making a judgment based on his experience, he may choose to make more checks. It may be a stolen car. It might even be a car bomb that he has stumbled onto.[35]

Training Together: The Home Team Academy

Training, Wong emphasized in that same speech, was the key to creating what he called the Home Team-plus officer.

A joint training facility had been planned since the mid-1990s. Originally known as the Law Enforcement Academy of Singapore, its first foundation stone was laid in November 2000. By the time the facility was ready in 2005, it had been renamed the Home Team Academy (HTA). The vision was "to take the HT concept to the next level by providing quality training to develop HT officers who possess cross-departmental competencies and can operate beyond their professional domains."[36]

HTA brings together all the training schools run by the individual Home Team departments. Each department, however, continues to be in charge of the training and development of its own officers in their core professional competencies.

HTA's role is to be "an incubator of human and organizational potential."[37] It defines its functions as:

- **A Joint Operations Training Academy,** allowing officers to acquire specialist skills in their respective services and imbuing them with a joint operations culture, encouraging them to work together seamlessly.

- **A Centre for Advanced Specialized Training,** working with different departments to develop officers who are competent in dealing with all aspects of the terrorist threat and relevant policing skills. The Behavioral Sciences Unit located at HTA has, for instance, conducted research into terrorist behavior to provide guidelines for frontline officers.[38]
- **A platform for engaging external partners,** playing a leading role in building and training a collaborative network of home-front security stakeholders in both the private and public sectors to keep up with potential threats.

To fulfill its multi-agency training mission, HTA runs mandatory foundation courses at basic and advanced levels for all Home Team officers, as well as a staff and command course for select senior personnel. These courses, which deliberately mix staff from different agencies, help to reinforce the Home Team identity by introducing officers to the work of each department and creating opportunities for interaction. Terrorism awareness is a key component of all the courses.

In its early years, HTA's key focus was homefront security and safety training. The subject is seen as knowledge development that straddles all the departments, ranging from border security to key installation protection, from the response of the front-liner or first officer at the scene in a hostile situation to a full-blown interagency management of a national crisis.

With counter-terrorism training now embedded in most training programs, whether run by individual departments or HTA, the academy is also being tasked to develop training programs in skill-sets applicable to all agencies.

More recently, Deputy Prime Minister and Minister for Home Affairs, Teo Chee Hean, announced that the Behavioral Sciences Unit was working with the Home Team departments to develop "a framework for Home Team Command Leadership, to help the Home Team identify, select and develop future leaders."[39] Once the developmental needs have been identified, command leadership will be a component of milestone programs such as the Home Team Senior Command and Staff Course.

The Challenge Ahead

A decade after 9/11, there is concern, says Loh Ngai Seng, that "the pendulum is now swinging back the other way" as public anxiety over terrorism ebbs. Will the Home Team philosophy face the same challenge, he wonders, as the U.S. has experienced in bringing together 22 different departments whose roles are quite disparate under a single agency, the Department of Homeland Security? Fighting terrorism can be a unifying mission, providing "a natural focal point at the operational level to pull together the efforts of different Home Team Departments, thereby strengthening the Home Team's actual level of collaboration." Dealing with potential chemical, biological and radiological threats or bombs on the subway has an immediacy of purpose that not only grips the imagination but also leaves no room for complacency. As Loh says, "I don't think that the tagline creating a 'safe and secure' Singapore has the same effect."[40]

Since he took over as commissioner of police in 2010, Ng Joo Hee has spoken often of mission clarity. The mission of the Singapore Police Force, Ng reminds his officers often, is "to prevent, detect and deter crime." It is not a reaction to concerns that the Home Team concept has diluted the police mission, he says, but a necessary way forward to face future challenges. It is how each police officer contributes to the Home Team vision of a safe and secure best home for Singapore:

> The HT idea, by acknowledging the differences in the roles of various departments, and therefore the importance of working together to deliver a greater good, actually encourages us to achieve shaper focus on our mission.
>
> I believe that an effective CEO (of any organization) has to do three things: (a) develop and communicate a clear mission and inspiring vision; (b) pick his team and (c) measure.[41]

Ng's three rules also explain why the Home Team concept has worked in Singapore thus far. As the conceptual mastermind Wong Kan Seng often reminded his staff, there was nothing accidental about the evolution of the Home Team:

> The concept of the Home Team is well known and familiar today. This did not just happen by itself. It is the result of effort and commitment over a decade by all the departments in the Ministry of Home Affairs. We persevered and continued with the Home Team initiative, making adjustments and evolving it to make it remain relevant to changes and new challenges. We persisted with the core idea and held steadfast to the confidence that it was the right direction to take. We need to sustain this effort. It requires the commitment of all in the Home Team—from the Minister and commanders down to the last officer on the ground.[42]

For the Home Team concept to continue to be relevant, Ng suggests that the default mode for Home Team officers be to constantly seek positive change, take quick action to effect these changes and make them a new reality. "Effective people," he says, "will not sit idly as they watch the world change around them, hoping that things will revert to status quo ante. Hope is not a good method. Fear, ignorance, inertia and perceived powerlessness are but states of mind."[43]

Critical Thinking Questions

1. What lessons can be drawn from the Singapore experience that might be useful for improving U.S. homeland security?
2. What are the most important factors that have contributed to the successful evolution of Singapore's "home team" approach?
3. Within the U.S. context, what are the primary legal, policy, and practical challenges to cross-posting uniformed officers and civilians to different agencies and departments?

Notes

1. Speech by Mr Wong Kan Seng, Minister for Home Affairs, at the Home Team Launching Workshop on 24 February 1997. Singapore: National Archives Library.
2. Ibid. Goh Chok Tong took over from Lee Kuan Yew as Prime Minister of Singapore in November 1990. By 1994, he had a relatively newer team in place. His Cabinet was faced with the twin challenge of growing Singapore's economic prosperity and the bonds between people and state; an independent survey by MasterCard had showed that

1 in 5 Singaporeans wished to emigrate, despite Singapore's economic success. The ensuing national soul-searching led to a "New Vision for a New Era". Goh announced the National Vision of "Singapore Our Best Home" in June 1997: "A Home where we feel comfortable with ourselves, where we look after one another, where everyone makes the country succeed. Our vision for Singapore is not houses of bricks and mortar, but homes with hearts and dreams. People who feel confident and secure. People who believe in Singapore and its future." (Source: Speech by Prime Minister Goh Chok Tong during the Debate on the President's Address in Parliament, "Singapore 21—A New Vision for a New Era", 5 June 1997.)

3. The eight departments in the MHA Group in 1997 were the Central Narcotics Bureau, Internal Security Department, National Registration Department, Prisons Department, Singapore Civil Defence Force, Singapore Immigration, Singapore Police Force and Ministry Headquarters. The National Registration Department was later folded into the Immigration Department, which evolved into the Immigration and Checkpoints Authority in 2003 with the addition of checkpoint enforcement work performed by the former Customs and Excise Department. The Home Team now comprises 10 agencies, with the establishment of the Home Team Academy and Casino Regulatory Authority in 2005 and 2008 respectively. The 10th member is the Singapore Corporation of Rehabilitative Enterprises (SCORE), which was established by statute in 1976 to run the Prisons Industries but not officially a member of the Home Team until recently.
4. "Kobe: Why did so few die?" *The Independent*, 19 January 1995.
5. "Terror in Tokyo: The Poison; Sarin Just One of Many Deadly Gases Terrorists Could Use", *New York Times*, March 22, 1995.
6. "Terror in Oklahoma: Islam In Oklahoma; Fear About Retaliation Among Muslim Groups", *New York Times*, April 21, 1995.
7. "Suspected Bombing Leader Indicted on Broader Charges", *New York Times*, April 14, 1995.
8. Speech by Deputy Prime Minister Wong Kan Seng at the Home Team Parade for Outgoing Minister for Home Affairs at the Home Team Academy, 30 October 2010.
9. Ibid.
10. The Singapore Parliament is modeled after the Westminster system of parliamentary democracy where Members of Parliament (MPs) are voted in at regular General Elections. Under the Singapore Constitution, the leader of the political party that secures the majority of seats in Parliament will be asked by the President, as Head of State, to become the Prime Minister (PM). The PM selects his Ministers from elected MPs to form the Cabinet, which is responsible for all Government policies and the day-to-day administration of the affairs of the state. It is responsible collectively to Parliament. (Source: www.parliament.gov.sg)
11. Wong Kan Seng, Home Team Launching Workshop, 24 February 1997.
12. Interview aired on the "Home Team 10 Video" (2005). The author thanks Kittybond Koo, Head of the Heritage Development Unit, Ministry of Home Affairs, for making the video available, and Jasminder Singh for transcribing the interviews.
13. Speech by Minister of Home Affairs Wong Kan Seng at the Home Team 2001 Flagship Workshop, 3 March 2001.
14. Email communication with author, August 12, 2012.
15. Ibid.

16. Interview with author, August 7, 2012.
17. Wong Kan Seng, Home Team Parade for Outgoing Minister for Home Affairs, 30 October 2010. Wong served six more months as Coordinating Minister for National Security before stepping down after the 2011 General Elections. He remains an elected Member of Parliament.
18. There are some 30 Boards, Councils and Committees that work with the Ministry of Home Affairs and the Home Team departments on safety and security issues, and counseling and helping exoffenders re-integrate into society. Their members are appointed from among community leaders, domain specialists and representatives of industry groupings, who volunteer their time, offering ideas and solutions. This author, for example, is a Member of the National Crime Prevention Council.
19. Speech by Minister for Home Affairs Wong Kan Seng at The Minister's Appreciation Dinner 2001, 19 October 2001.
20. Confidential discussions with senior ISD officials.
21. Speech by Minister for Home Affairs Wong Kan Seng at the ISD Intelligence Service Promotion Ceremony, 3 April 2003.
22. Wong Sher Main, "Life is More Complicated than Black and White", Challenge magazine, 13 March 2012. Retrieved at http://www.challenge.gov.sg/2012/03/life-is-more-complicated-than-black-andwhite/
23. Parts of this section are taken from an essay by the author, "How Singapore has kept terrorists at bay", published in The Straits Times (Singapore) on September 11, 2011.
24. The 9/11 Commission Report, New York: Norton, 2004.
25. This section is adapted from "The Story of the Home Team", written by the author for the launch of the Home Team Gallery at the Home Team Academy in 2008.
26. "The Fight Against Terror: Singapore's National Security Strategy", Singapore: National Security Coordination Centre, 2004, p. 8.
27. Ibid. p. 8.
28. Ibid. p. 38.
29. The EG was renamed Homefront Crisis Executive Group after the SARS crisis in 2003, to better reflect the range of contingencies it is set up to deal with. A Homefront Crisis Ministerial Committee chaired by the Minister for Home Affairs and comprising other Cabinet Ministers provides strategic and political guidance. (Source: Singapore's National Security Strategy, pp. 38–9.)
30. The Straits Times, 28 March 1991.
31. Ng Joo Hee, "Singapore's 30-year Experience with Community Policing", in Susan Sim (ed.), *Building Resilient Societies. Forging Global Partnerships*, Singapore: National Crime Prevention Council, 2012, pp. 119–120. The book can be downloaded from www.ncpc.gov.sg/pdf/ICPC_ebook_3_aug.pdf.
32. Susan Sim, *Making Singapore Safe: Thirty Years of the National Crime Prevention Council*, Singapore: Marshall Cavendish Editions, 2011, p. 162. The CSSP was first started in 1998.
33. Asad Latif, *Hearts of Resilience: Singapore's Community Engagement Programme*, Singapore: Institute of Southeast Asian Studies, 2011, p. 14.
34. Interview with author, August 8, 2012.
35. Speech by Minister for Home Affairs Wong Kan Seng at the Home Team Senior Officers' Promotion Ceremony, 1 June 2005.

36. Home Team Academy, *One in Body, Mind and Spirit*, Singapore, 2006, p. 10.
37. Benny Lim, cited in Home Team Academy, *One in Body, Mind and Spirit*, p. 49.
38. See for example, *Terrorist Footprints: Behavioural Clues of Terrorism, A Resource Guide Book for Home Team Officers*, Singapore: Behavioural Sciences Unit, 2010.
39. Speech by Deputy Prime Minister, Coordinating Minister for National Security and Minister For Home Affairs Teo Chee Hean at the Home Team Senior Officers Promotion Ceremony, 23 May 2011.
40. Interview with author, August 8, 2012.
41. Email communication with author, August 7, 2012.
42. Speech by Minister for Home Affairs Wong Kan Seng at the Launching Ceremony of the HomeTeamNS, 24 April 2005.
43. Opening Address by Commissioner of Police Ng Joo Hee to the Senior Police Officer Cadre at the Annual General Meetings of the Senior Police Officers Mess and the Singapore Senior Police Officers Association, 31 July 2012.

Credits

Section 1

From *Homeland Security Affairs*, Vol. IV, No. 2, June, 2008, pp. 1–30. Copyright © 2008 by Christopher Bellavita. Reprinted by permission of the author.

Congressional Research Service, 2012.

From *Dueling Delusions: Terrorism and Counterterrorism in the United States Since 9/11* (2011). Copyright © 2011 by John Mueller and Mark G. Stewart. Reprinted by permission of the authors.

From *Studies in Conflict & Terrorism*, Vol. 34, No. 2, 2011, pp. 65–101. Copyright © 2011 by Taylor & Francis Journals. Reprinted by permission via Rightslink.

An original essay written for this volume. Copyright © 2012 by Joshua Sinai. Used by permission of the author.

From *The Heritage Foundation Backgrounder*, No. 2219, December 10, 2008, pp. 1–7. Copyright © 2008 by The Heritage Foundation. Reprinted by permission.

From *Perspectives on Terrorism*, Vol. 5, No. 5–6, 2011, pp. 1–5. Copyright © 2011 by Terrorism Research Initiative. Reprinted by permission.

From *The Long Shadow of 911; America's Response to Terrorism.* Vol. 5, No. 5–6, 2011, pp. 1–5. Copyright © 2011 by Terrorism Research Initiative. Reprinted by permission.

From *Homeland Security: Protecting America's Targets*, 2006, pp. 37–50. Copyright © 2006 by Greenwood Press—ABC-CLIO, LLC. Reprinted by permission.

From *Homeland Security and Terrorism; Readings and Interpretations*, September 2005, pp. Entire Chapter. Copyright © 2005 by The McGraw-Hill Companies. Reprinted by permission.

An original essay written for this volume. Copyright © 2012 by John P. Sullivan. Used by permission of the author.

Section 2

From *Journal of Contingencies and Crisis Management*, Vol. 20 No. 2, June 2012, pp. 77–89. Copyright © 2012 by Wiley-Blackwell. Reprinted by permission via Rightslink.

An original essay written for this volume. Copyright © 2012 by Joanne Moore. Used by permission of the author.

From *The Long Shadow of 911; America's Response to Terrorism* (2011). Copyright © 2011 by Rand Corporation. Reprinted by permission.

From *Canadian Journal of Political Science,* 40:2, June, 2007, pp. 283–316. Copyright © 2007 by Canadian Political Science Association. Reprinted by permission.

An original essay written for this volume. Copyright © 2012 by David Trybula and John Whitley. Used by permission of the authors.

From *Homeland Security Affairs*, Vol. VI, No. 1, January 2010, pp. 1-19. Copyright © 2010 by Gary Cordner and Kathryn Scarborough. Reprinted by permission of the authors.

From *Journal of Homeland Security*, August 2001. Copyright © 2001 by Journal of Homeland Security. Reprinted by permission.

From *Homeland Security Affairs*, Supplement No. 2, 2008, pp. 1–6. Copyright © 2008 by Kevin Eack. Reprinted by permission of the author.

From *Center for National Policy*, March, 2012, pp. 1–39. Copyright © 2012 by Center for National Policy. Reprinted by permission.

From *The Counterproliferation Paper Series,* November, 2006, pp. 1–44. Copyright © 2006 by United States Air Force Counterproliferation. Reprinted by permission.

From *Homeland Security Affairs*, Vol. V, No. 2, May, 2009, pp. 1–14. Copyright © 2009 by Robert Bach and David J. Kaufman. Reprinted by permission of the authors.

Section 3

From *Homeland Security Affairs*, Vol. 7, The 911 Essays, September, 2011, pp. 1–9. Copyright © 2011 by Erik J. Dahl. Reprinted by permission of the author.

From *Social Justice*, vol. 37, no. 2–3, 2010–2011, pp. 84–98. Copyright © 2011 by Social Justice. Reprinted by permission.

From *Legal Studies Research Paper Series Working Paper No. 2011–27*, December, 2011, pp. 1–18. Copyright © 2011 by Arizonal Journal of International and Comparative Law. Reprinted by permission.

From *Homeland Security and Terrorism; 1 Edition*, 2006, pp. 369–383. Copyright © 2006 by The McGraw-Hill Companies. Reprinted by permission.

From *Homeland Security and Terrorism; 1 Edition*, 2006, pp. 384–399. Copyright © 2006 by The McGraw-Hill Companies. Reprinted by permission.

From *Homeland Security and Terrorism, 1 Edition*, 2006, pp. 400–412. Copyright © 2006 by The McGraw-Hill Companies. Reprinted by permission.

Section 4

Government Accountability Office, 2011.

From *Review of Policy Research,* Vol. 26, No. 4, 2009, pp. 423–438. Copyright © 2009 by Policy Studies Organization and American Political Science Association. Reprinted by permission of Wiley-Blackwell.

From *Policy Analysis*, 683, September 11, 2011, pp. 1–36. Copyright © 2011 by Cato Institute. Reprinted by permission via Copyright Clearance Center.

From *Homeland Security Affairs*, Vol. 7, The 9/11 Essay, June, September 2011, pp. 1–5. Copyright © 2011 by Nadav Morag. Reprinted by permission of the author.

An original essay written for this volume. Copyright © 2012 by Susan Sim. Used by permission of the author.

Contributors

Robert Bach, Ph.D., is currently on the faculty at the Center for Homeland Defense and Security at the Naval Postgraduate School and works with CNA's Institute for Public Research. Dr. Bach has served as a strategic consultant with the U.S. Department of Homeland Security on border and transportation security issues; his current research focuses on community participation in homeland security and emergency preparedness, and strategic planning.

Edwin Bakker is professor of (counter-) terrorism studies of the Institute of Public Administration of Leiden University. He heads the Centre of Terrorism (CTC) and Counterterrorism and is a Fellow of the International Centre for Counter-Terrorism (ICCT), both based in The Hague, The Netherlands.

Christopher Bellavita, Ph.D., teaches in the master's degree program at the Naval Postgraduate School in Monterey, California, and serves as the director of academic programs for the Center for Homeland Defense and Security.

Peter Bergen is Director of the National Security Studies Program at the New America Foundation and the author of four books, three of which were *New York Times* bestsellers.

Thomas A. Birkland, Ph.D., is the William T. Kretzer Professor of Public Policy at the School of Public and International Affairs, North Carolina State University. He is the author of several articles and books on disaster, including *After Disaster* and *Lessons of Disaster* (both Georgetown University Press).

Erik Brattberg is currently a Visiting Research Associate at the Center for Transatlantic Relations at the Paul H. Nitze School of Advanced International Studies at Johns Hopkins University. Concurrently, he is a Research Associate at the Swedish Institute of International Affairs, Stockholm.

Sean P. Burke is Associate Director of the George Kostas Research Institute for Homeland Security at Northeastern University. He has served as Vice President and Senior Fellow of the Center for National Policy and is a former U.S. Coast Guard officer.

James Jay Carafano, Ph.D., is Deputy Director of the Kathryn and Shelby Cullom Davis Institute for International Studies and Director of the Douglas and Sarah Allison Center for Foreign Policy Studies at the Heritage Foundation.

Nancy Chang is the manager for the Open Society National Security and Human Rights Campaign. At the time of this writing, she was the Senior Litigation Attorney at the Center for Constitutional Rights, a progressive nonprofit legal and educational organization in New York City.

Frank J. Cilluffo, Ph.D., is an Associate Vice President at The George Washington University and Director of the Homeland Security Policy Institute. He previously served as special assistant to the president for homeland security under George W. Bush.

Erik J. Dahl, Ph.D., is assistant professor of national security affairs at the Naval Postgraduate School in Monterey, California, and a faculty member of the Center for Homeland Defense and Security.

Beatrice de Graaf is Associate Professor at the Centre for Terrorism and Counterterrorism/Leiden University and Fellow of the International Centre for Counter Terrorism, The Hague.

Gene L. Dodaro is the Comptroller General of the United States. This chapter is drawn from his testimony before the U.S. House of Representatives, Committee on Homeland Security, on September 8, 2011.

Kevin Eack is chair of ASIS International's Council on Global Terrorism, Political Instability and International Crime. He is a former FBI Special Agent, former Illinois state prosecutor, and former member of the Illinois State Police.

Stephen E. Flynn, Ph.D., is Professor of Political Science and the Founding Co-Director of the George Kostas Research Institute for Homeland Security at Northeastern University. He has served as President of the Center for National Policy and as a Senior Fellow at the Council on Foreign Relations and is a former U.S. Coast Guard officer.

Roger Dean Golden, Ph.D., is Chief of the Matrixed Contract Support Division, HQ Standard Systems Group, Acquisitions Directorate, Maxwell Air Force Base.

David A. Harris, Ph.D., is Distinguished Faculty Scholar and Professor of Law, University of Pittsburgh. The author thanks Emily J. Boardman, University of Pittsburgh School of Law Class of 2012, for her assistance with research for this article.

Frank P. Harvey, Ph.D., is Professor of International Relations in the Department of Political Science at Dalhousie University in Halifax, Nova Scotia. In 2007 he was the J. William Fulbright Research Chair in Canadian Studies at the State University of New York Plattsburgh.

Bruce Hoffman, Ph.D., is Director of the Center for Peace and Security Studies and the Security Studies Program at Georgetown University.

Brian H. Hook is special counsel with LS2group and advises corporations and nonprofits on international strategy, political risk, and strategic planning. He previously served as Assistant Secretary of State for International Organizations. At the time of this writing, he was Advisor to the International Law and American Sovereignty Project, Department of Justice, Office of Legal Policy.

Brian Michael Jenkins is a senior adviser to the president of the RAND Corporation. He is the author of numerous books and reports on terrorism and national security.

David J. Kaufman is CNA's Director for Safety and Security and a member of the faculty at the Naval Postgraduate School's Center for Homeland Defense and Security. He is the former director for preparedness policy, planning and analysis in the Department of Homeland Security/FEMA's National Preparedness Directorate. Mr. Kaufman has more than 10 years' experience developing and implementing homeland security preparedness programs for states and local jurisdictions.

Frank Keating is the president and CEO of the American Bankers Association. He served two terms as Oklahoma's 25th governor and served Presidents Ronald Reagan and George H.W. Bush in the Treasury, Justice, and Housing departments. http://forms.aba .com/Press+Room/fkeating bio.htm

Lieutenant Colonel Michael Kindt, Ph.D., is currently the Deputy Director of the USAF Counterproliferation Center, and adjunct professor at the Air War College.

Mark Latonero, Ph.D., is Assistant Professor at the California State University Fullerton and Research Fellow at the USC Annenberg Center on Communication Leadership and Policy.

Torin Monahan is Associate Professor of Human and Organizational Development and Medicine at Vanderbilt University (e-mail: torin.monahan@vanderbilt.edu). He is a member of the International Surveillance Studies Network. Among his books are *Surveillance in the Time of Insecurity* (Rutgers University Press, 2010), *Schools under Surveillance: Cultures of Control in Public Education* (Rutgers University Press, 2010), *Surveillance and Security. Technological Politics and Power in Everyday Life* (Routledge, 2006), and *Globalization, Technological Change, and Public Education* (Routledge, 2005).

Nadav Morag, Ph.D., is a faculty member and deputy director for policy research at the Center for Homeland Security, Naval Postgraduate School. He is the author of *Comparative Homeland Security: Global Lessons* (Wiley & Sons, 2011) and is a former senior director at Israel's National Security Council.

John Mueller, Ph.D., is Woody Hayes Chair of National Security Studies in the Mershon Center and Professor of Political Science at the Ohio State University.

Paul Byron Pattak is a Fellow at the Potomac Institute for Policy Studies and CEO of Pi2 Strategies, LLC. He has served in various appointments and commissions for several presidential administrations.

Margaret J. A. Peterlin is an attorney in the private sector and has served as a legal advisor to several Congressional leaders. In 2007–2008 she was Deputy Undersecretary of Commerce for Intellectual Property and Deputy Director of the United States Patent and Trademark Office.

Shawn Reese is an analyst in Emergency Management and Homeland Security Policy for the Congressional Research Service.

Jack Riley is vice president and director of the RAND National Security Research Division. He previously served as associate director of RAND Infrastructure, Safety, and Environment and director of the RAND Homeland Security Center.

David Rittgers is a legal policy analyst with the Cato Institute. Previously, Mr. Rittgers served in the United States Army as an Infantry and Special Forces officer, including three tours in Afghanistan.

James S. Robbins, Ph.D., is Senior Editorial Writer for Foreign Affairs at the *Washington Times* and Senior Fellow in National Security Affairs at the American Foreign Policy Council.

Irina Shklovski, Ph.D., is Assistant Professor in the Digital Culture and Mobile Communication Research Group at the IT University of Copenhagen.

Susan Sim is a Vice-President for Asia of The Soufan Group. Currently an Adjunct Lecturer and consultant with the Home Team Academy of the Ministry of Home Affairs of Singapore, she is also Chairman of the Research Committee of the National Crime Prevention Council of Singapore. In 2009, she founded Strategic Nexus Consultancy, a research firm specializing in home front security and counterterrorism issues.

Joshua Sinai, Ph.D., is an Adjunct Associate Professor for Research, Virginia Tech Research Center—Arlington, specializing in terrorism and counterterrorism studies and education.

James E. Steiner, Ph.D., is Public Service Professor at the State University of New York at Albany's Rockefeller College where he teaches graduate-level courses in the craft of intelligence, with emphasis on intelligence analysis for homeland security. From 2006 until 2009 he was Intelligence Advisor to the Director of New York State's Office of Homeland Security and a consultant to the Chief Intelligence Officer in the Department of Homeland Security.

Mark G. Stewart, Ph.D., is Professor and Director of the Centre for Infrastructure Performance and Reliability at the University of Newcastle, Australia.

John P. Sullivan, Ph.D., is a career police officer. He currently serves as a lieutenant with the Los Angeles Sheriff's Department. He is also an Adjunct Researcher at the Vortex Foundation, Bogotá, Colombia; Senior Research Fellow at the Center for Advanced Studies on Terrorism (CAST); and Senior Fellow at Small Wars Journal-El Centro. He has published several books and is currently studying the impact of transnational organized crime on sovereignty in Mexico and other countries.

Katherine Tiedemann was at the time of this writing a research fellow in the National Security Studies Program at the New America Foundation.

Dave Trybula is one of the U.S. Army's senior uniformed economists and operations research systems analysts. He has held a variety of positions within the Army and Department of Defense and taught at the George Washington University and the United States Military Academy.

Bert B. Tussing is Director of the Homeland Defense and Security Issues Group and Elihu Root Chair of Military Studies in the Center for Strategic Leadership at the United States Army War College. He served 24 years in the U.S. Marine Corps, and several years at the Pentagon.

Peter L. Welsh is a partner in a Boston-area law firm and former political consultant.

John Whitley is an economist at the Institute for Defense Analyses (IDA) and an adjunct lecturer at George Washington University. Prior to joining IDA, he was the Director of Program Analysis and Evaluation (PA&E) at the Department of Homeland Security (DHS). John has also worked in the Department of Defense, the U.S. Senate, in academia, and served in the U.S. Army.

Index

T

U